ENCYCLOPEDIA OF EDUCATIONAL EVALUATION

*Concepts and Techniques
for Evaluating Education
and Training Programs*

Scarvia B. Anderson

Samuel Ball

Richard T. Murphy

& Associates

ENCYCLOPEDIA OF EDUCATIONAL EVALUATION

Jossey-Bass Publishers
San Francisco · Washington · London · 1976

ENCYCLOPEDIA OF EDUCATIONAL EVALUATION
Concepts and Techniques for Evaluating Education and Training Programs
by Scarvia B. Anderson, Samuel Ball, Richard T. Murphy,
and Associates

Copyright © 1973 and 1975 by: Jossey-Bass, Inc., Publishers
615 Montgomery Street
San Francisco, California 94111
&
Jossey-Bass Limited
3 Henrietta Street
London WC2E 8LU

Library of Congress Catalogue Card Number LC 74-6736

International Standard Book Number ISBN 0-87589-238-8

Manufactured in the United States of America

JACKET DESIGN BY WILLI BAUM

FIRST EDITION
First printing: November 1974
Second printing: February 1975
Third printing: May 1975
Fourth printing: November 1975

Code 7431

PREFACE

Only a few years ago, the educational paths that people might follow were fairly prescribed and predictable: elementary or grammar school, high school, and, for some, college. Education was "complete" when a student dropped out of school or graduated from high school or finished college. Training in business and industry was largely left to the goodwill of older workers; training in the military was largely a matter of testing endurance.

This pattern was comfortable for many and went relatively unchallenged until society began to experience dramatic changes in politics, economics, technology, and commitment to the welfare and productivity of all citizens. These changes in turn placed heavy demands on education, industry, and the military to re-examine their roles as teaching institutions; and new instructional programs burgeoned in the name of affirmative action, career education, compensatory education, competency-based training, curriculum reform, individualized instruction, life-long learning, and other "movements."

In the midst of all the excitement and activity, some program directors were taken aback when legislators, community groups, or boards of directors dared to ask for proof of the claims made for the programs. But increasingly those responsible for program development and implementation began to see the value in systematic evaluation, not only to demonstrate the worth of programs—their effectiveness and efficiency in meeting the needs they were designed to serve—but also to obtain information useful in program improvement. We hope that this *Encyclopedia of Educational Evaluation* will encourage that trend and provide specific aids to those interested in evaluation of education and training programs.

We recognize that *almost* everything there is to say about the evaluation of education and training programs has already been said—or written—somewhere. The problem is not so much to say more as to make some order out of the field and to bring its major concepts and techniques together in one place. That is what this *Encyclopedia* tries to do—and in terms that are generally comprehensible to program administrators, funding agents, and students coming new to the field, as well as to the social scientists and measurement specialists who have tended to dominate it. We do not claim to be entirely successful; some of the topics are highly technical and do not lend themselves to easy exposition.

Furthermore, we do not claim to be completely objective. Rather early in the development of the book we decided—quite deliberately—to let some of our values and viewpoints show. Thus, the reader will discern, among other things, that we prefer objective evidence over testimony; insist that measurement and evaluation, even though they are closely linked, are not the same thing; favor minimizing the jargon of evaluation and highlighting its conceptual underpinnings; respect good experimental and quasi-experimental designs for evaluation studies and believe that failure to use good designs is sometimes as much a matter of poor thinking as it is of practical pressures; place high value on the construct validity of measures; feel that a great deal needs to be done about improving the climate for and support of evaluation studies; want to substitute considered analyses for the mystiques that seem to be growing up around such concepts as accountability and criterion-referenced testing; and think that the common aspects of education and training should be emphasized rather than the distinctions.

Organization. Because of the alphabetical arrangement of articles in the *Encyclopedia of Educational Evaluation*, a school administrator interested in **Performance Contracting**, a training officer interested in **Job Analysis**, a funding agent concerned with writing a **Request for Proposal**, a university vice-president wanting to know more about **Institutional Evaluation**, an evaluator interested in the relationships between **Longitudinal** and **Cross-Sectional Studies**, and a student wondering about the meaning of **Attenuation** or **Goal-Free Evaluation** can usually enter the book directly at the topic of immediate interest. However, the book will not achieve its broad objective unless school and college administrators also consult entries in the statistical area, training officers read articles on experimental design, and students in the social sciences turn to entries dealing with the practical problems of field studies, for we hope that the book will help to open communication channels between the various parties to an evaluation effort. For example, the book should be an aid to program directors and sponsors when they arrange to include evaluation in their overall program plans, issue requests for proposals or award evaluation contracts, and read and interpret evaluation reports.

Most of the entries are brief, capturing the essence of the topic and then directing the reader interested in pursuing it in more depth to selected sources. However, when the major purpose is merely to define a term that may be encountered in the evaluation literature, entries are shorter than average (see, for example, **Cohort** and **Fade-Out**). And some rather long entries are included in order to treat a group of related concepts together (see, for example, **Achievement-Test Construction** and **Statistics**). A few entries are designed specifically as advance organizers or reader's guides to major sources; for example, the article on **Quasi-Experimental Design** is intended at least partly to ease the task of getting into the important Campbell-Stanley article in the *Handbook of Research on Teaching*.

Students and those reviewing the field of evaluation can also approach the *Encyclopedia* through the eleven major concept areas listed in the Classification of the Articles. Those who wish to read the articles under each category as a unit should note that the first articles listed are usually general and help to define the category. Later articles in a category may focus on increasingly specific applications and techniques. For example, the articles listed under the first heading, "Evaluation Models," move from such broad topics as the history of evaluation and the role of the evaluator to relatively narrow or specialized evaluation approaches.

Cross references. To keep the *Encyclopedia* from being too cumbersome, we usually do not repeat the same information under different headings. Thus, even though the notion that "students with different characteristics may profit more from one instructional strategy than another" goes by two names, trait-treatment interaction (TTI) and aptitude-treatment interaction (ATI), it is discussed only under **Trait-Treatment Interaction.** The reader who looks up ATI in the Index is referred to TTI. Furthermore, in some instances several major concepts are treated under one heading. Thus, the reader who looks up mean and the one who looks up standard deviation are both referred to **Statistics.** Throughout the articles, the appearance of a word or phrase in **This Kind of Type** indicates that the concept or technique is dealt with in detail under the designated heading.

Bibliographies. We have been parsimonious in listing bibliographic sources at the end of articles; the general rule was "no more than five" unless a longer list was explicitly justified. Therefore, in some instances we have omitted sources that others would judge as equally good or better. However, the reader can usually find ample additional reference lists in the sources themselves. If the reference source is a book, we provide a brief annotation or indicate the part of the book the reader should consult. We do not annotate most journal articles or book chapters since their titles are usually self-explanatory and their lengths less forbidding. Even though it sometimes meant leaving out attractive pieces, we gave preference to published and accessible sources. In addition, the Bibliography at the end of the *Encyclopedia* lists useful references.

Acknowledgments. This book was developed with funds provided largely by the Office of Naval Research (ONR) and with the encouragement of Victor Fields, Marshall J. Farr, and Joseph L. Young, Personnel and Training Research Programs, ONR. The immediate impetus for undertaking the work was a growing concern by the Navy about the adequacy of its present training efforts and the likely need to expand them in the future in the face of requirements to train an increasingly diverse population to perform increasingly diverse tasks. In considering innovations in training, the Navy was eager to have evaluation made an integral part of such programs. The research for the book was accomplished by Educational Testing Service; United States Office of Naval Research, Contract No. N 00014-72-C-0433, Contract Authority Identification No. NR 154-359.

We are also indebted to our distinguished advisory committee, Norman Frederiksen, Harry Harman, Frederic Lord, Albert P. Maslow, and Samuel Messick, who suggested materials for inclusion and criticized the results; to our colleagues who are listed under Contributors and whose initials appear at the ends of articles for which they were primary authors (they are not to be held completely responsible for the final versions, however, since it was necessary in many cases for us to rework materials in order to integrate content across articles); to Patricia Chmiel, Patricia Fisher, Eliza Kealy, Mary Kozma, Adele Lechowicz, Lucy Levitcher, JoAnne Luger, Climene Lubrano, and Linda Roggenburg, for valuable clerical support; to Elsa Rosenthal, who worked on many aspects of the ONR project in addition to writing several articles; to Roy Hardy, who suggested a number of improvements in the statistical articles; and especially to Gray Sidwell, who provided major editorial assistance.

Atlanta   Scarvia B. Anderson
September 1974   Samuel Ball
                                             Richard T. Murphy

CLASSIFICATION

OF THE ARTICLES

The first articles in each of the categories are usually general and help to define the category. Later articles may focus on increasingly specific applications and techniques.

EVALUATION MODELS

Evaluation history	140	Goal-free evaluation	178
Evaluation concepts	136	"Hard" and "soft"—shibboleths	
Scientific inquiry and		in evaluation	191
evaluation	348	Decision-making typology	117
Evaluator role	147	Discrepancy evaluation	127
Formative evaluation	175	Adversary model of evaluation	21
Summative evaluation	406	Transactional evaluation	450
Medical model of evaluation	245	Secondary evaluation	362

FUNCTIONS AND TARGETS OF EVALUATION

Training evaluation	439	Accreditation	4
Curriculum evaluation	109	Certification	53
Materials evaluation	241	Accountability	1
Institutional evaluation	202	Performance contracting	272
Needs assessment	254	Computer-assisted instruction	77
Staff evaluation	380	Competency-based	
Audit of evaluation	40	education/training	71

PROGRAM OBJECTIVES AND STANDARDS

Goals and objectives	179	Standards	386
Taxonomies of objectives	417	Mastery learning	236
Job analysis	222	Delphi technique	121

SOCIAL CONTEXT OF EVALUATION

Politics of evaluation	281	Field operations	169
Training of evaluators	442	Site selection	370
Compensatory education	68	Confidentiality of data	79
Request for proposal (RFP)	331	Fade-out	167
Bias in testing	43	Dissemination of evaluation	
Culture-fair test	107	results	130

PLANNING AND DESIGN

Planning and priorities	277	Matched sampling	238
Design of evaluation	122	Baseline measures	42
Experimental design	155	Pretest	289
Quasi-experimental design	301	Posttest	286
Ex post facto design	159	Survey methods	408
Cross-sectional study	104	Sampling	338
Longitudinal study	229	Item sampling	220
Cohort	65	Case-study method	46
Control group	85	Replication	330

SYSTEMS TECHNOLOGIES

Systems analysis	412	Program Evaluation and Review	
Planning-Programming-Budgeting		Technique (PERT)	290
System (PPBS)	279	Simulation	367
		Quality control	299

VARIABLES

Variables	465	Values measurement	462
Cognitive variables	63	Psychomotor variables	296
Intelligence measurement	205	Socioeconomic	
Grades	184	status (SES)	377
Cognitive styles	60	Treatment measurement	452
Affective variables	23	Criterion measurement	98
Attitudes	32	Side effects	364
Interest measurement	211	Cost considerations and	
Motivation	247	economic analysis	92

MEASUREMENT APPROACHES AND TYPES

Assessment	26	Situational tests	371
Data sources	114	Projective tests	293
Criterion-referenced		Content analysis	82
measurement	100	Interviews	214
Tests	425	Questionnaires	311
Standardized tests	383	Ratings	315
Test selection	428	Observation techniques	266
Achievement test		Unobtrusive measures	454
construction	8	Social indicators	374

TECHNICAL MEASUREMENT CONSIDERATIONS

Reliability	325	Expectancy tables	152
Validity	458	Composite variables	74
Score types	354	Component variables	73
Scales	345	Ipsative measures	217
Equivalent scores	133	Ceiling effect	51
Norms	263		

REACTIVE CONCERNS

Reactive effects of program		Practice effect	287
and evaluation	318	Response sets	334
Hawthorne effect	195	Test anxiety	423
John Henry effect	226	Test wiseness	434
Halo effect	189		

ANALYSIS AND INTERPRETATION

Data preparation	112	Statistical significance	397
Hypothesis testing	198	Interaction	208
Causality	48	Trait-treatment interaction	444
Change measurement	56	Lord's paradox	232
Statistics	400	Time-series analysis	436
Variance	469	Johnson-Neyman	
Regression	321	technique	228
Correlation	87	Multivariate analysis	250
Attenuation	29	Factor analysis	161
Independence	200	Commonality analysis	67
Statistical analysis	389	Path analysis	270
Statistical inference	395	Nonparametric statistics	257

CONTENTS

PREFACE   vii

CLASSIFICATION OF THE ARTICLES   xiii

CONTRIBUTORS   xxi

ARTICLES   1-472

Accountability   1   Affective Variables   23
Accreditation   4   Assessment   26
Achievement Test   Attenuation   29
    Construction   8   Attitudes   32
Adversary Model of   Audit of Evaluation   40
    Evaluation   21

Baseline Measures   42   Bias in Testing   43

Case-Study Method   46   Commonality Analysis   67
Causality   48   Compensatory Education   68
Ceiling Effect   51   Competency-Based
Certification   53   Education/Training   71
Change Measurement   56   Component Variables   73
Cognitive Styles   60   Composite Variables   74
Cognitive Variables   63   Computer-Assisted
Cohort   65   Instruction   77

Contents

Confidentiality of Data 79
Content Analysis 82
Control Group 85
Correlation 87
Cost Considerations and
  Economic Analysis 92

Criterion Measurement 98
Criterion-Referenced
  Measurement 100
Cross-Sectional Study 104
Culture-Fair Test 107
Curriculum Evaluation 109

Data Preparation 112
Data Sources 114
Decision-Making Typology 117
Delphi Technique 121

Design of Evaluation 122
Discrepancy Evaluation 127
Dissemination of
  Evaluation Results 130

Equivalent Scores 133
Evaluation Concepts 136
Evaluation History 140
Evaluator Role 147

Expectancy Tables 152
Experimental Design 155
Ex Post Facto Design 159

Factor Analysis 161
Fade-Out 167

Field Operations 169
Formative Evaluation 175

Goal-Free Evaluation 178
Goals and Objectives 179

Grades 184

Halo Effect 189
"Hard" and "Soft"—
  Shibboleths in
  Evaluation 191

Hawthorne Effect 195
Hypothesis Testing 198

Independence 200
Institutional Evaluation 202
Intelligence Measurement 205
Interaction 208

Interest Measurement 211
Interviews 214
Ipsative Measures 217
Item Sampling 220

Job Analysis 222
John Henry Effect 226

Johnson-Neyman
  Technique 228

Longitudinal Study 229

Lord's Paradox 232

Mastery Learning 236
Matched Sampling 238
Materials Evaluation 241

Medical Model of
  Evaluation 245
Motivation 247
Multivariate Analysis 250

Needs Assessment   254   Norms   263
Nonparametric Statistics   257

Observation Techniques   266

Path Analysis   270   Practice Effect   287
Performance Contracting   272   Pretest   289
Planning and Priorities   277   Program Evaluation and
Planning-Programming-   Review Technique
    Budgeting System   (PERT)   290
    (PPBS)   279   Projective Tests   293
Politics of Evaluation   281   Psychomotor Variables   296
Posttest   286

Quality Control   299   Questionnaires   311
Quasi-Experimental Design   301

Ratings   315   Reliability   325
Reactive Effects of   Replication   330
    Program and   Request for Proposal
    Evaluation   318   (RFP)   331
Regression   321   Response Sets   334

Sampling   338   Socioeconomic Status
Scales   345   (SES)   377
Scientific Inquiry and   Staff Evaluation   380
    Evaluation   348   Standardized Tests   383
Score Types   354   Standards   386
Secondary Evaluation   362   Statistical Analysis   389
Side Effects   364   Statistical Inference   395
Simulation   367   Statistical Significance   400
Site Selection   370   Statistics   400
Situational Tests   371   Summative Evaluation   406
Social Indicators   374   Survey Methods   408
                                       Systems Analysis   412

Taxonomies of Objectives   417   Training Evaluation   439
Test Anxiety   423   Training of Evaluators   442
Tests   425   Trait-Treatment
Test Selection   428   Interaction   444
Test Wiseness   434   Transactional Evaluation   450
Time-Series Analysis   436   Treatment Measurement   452

Unobtrusive Measures   454

Validity   458   Variables   465
Values Measurement   462   Variance   469

BIBLIOGRAPHY   473

NAME INDEX   499

SUBJECT INDEX   506

CONTRIBUTORS

Scarvia B. Anderson, *vice-president, Educational Testing Service (ETS), and director of Atlanta office*

William H. Angoff, *executive director, College Entrance Examination Board Programs Division, ETS*

Samuel Ball, *research psychologist, Educational Studies Division, ETS*

Albert E. Beaton, *director, Office of Data Analysis Research, ETS*

Marilynn Binkley, *statistical assistant, Division of Analytic Studies and Services, ETS*

Gerry Ann Bogatz, *associate program director, Elementary and Secondary School Programs, ETS*

Leonard S. Cahen, *research psychologist, Educational Studies Division, ETS*

F. Reid Creech, *research psychologist, Developmental Research Division, ETS*

Junius A. Davis, *director, Center for Educational Research and Evaluation, Research Triangle Institute, Durham, North Carolina*

Thomas F. Donlon, *senior research psychologist, Developmental Research Division, ETS*

Thomas W. Draper, *research assistant, Atlanta office, ETS*

Robert A. Feldmesser, *research sociologist, Educational Studies Division, ETS*

Ronald L. Flaugher, *senior research psychologist, Developmental Research Division, ETS*

Jim C. Fortune, *professor, Office of Educational Research and Evaluation, Virginia Polytechnic Institute and State University*

Norman Frederiksen, *director, Psychological Studies Division, ETS*

Jerilee Grandy, *research associate, Developmental Research Division, ETS*

Harry H. Harman, *director, Developmental Research Division, ETS*

Dean Jamison, *research economist, Educational Studies Division, ETS*

Robert L. Linn, *professor of educational psychology and psychology, University of Illinois, Urbana*

Frederic M. Lord, *senior research psychologist, Psychological Studies Division, ETS*

Gary L. Marco, *assistant area director, College Entrance Examination Board Analysis, ETS*

Albert P. Maslow, *director, Center for Occupational and Professional Assessment, ETS*

Samuel Messick, *vice-president for research, ETS*

Richard T. Murphy, *research psychologist, Educational Studies Division, ETS*

Marjorie E. Ragosta, *associate research psychologist, Educational Studies Division, ETS*

Michael Rosenfeld, *program director, Higher Education and Career Programs Division, ETS*

Elsa J. Rosenthal, *assistant to director for publications, Educational Studies Division, ETS*

Donald B. Rubin, *research statistician, Office of Data Analysis Research, ETS*

William B. Schrader, *senior research psychologist, Developmental Research Division, ETS*

Gray Sidwell, *assistant to director, Atlanta office, ETS*

Ann Z. Smith, *coordinator of internal communications, Publications and Information Administration, ETS*

Lawrence J. Stricker, *senior research psychologist, Psychological Studies Division, ETS*

Richard F. Thornton, *examiner, Higher Education and Career Programs Division, ETS*

Donald A. Trismen, *assistant director, Educational Studies Division, ETS*

Melvin M. Tumin, *professor of anthropology and sociology, Princeton University*

Wesley W. Walton, *executive associate to the vice-president, Elementary and Secondary School Programs, ETS*

Raymond G. Wasdyke, *associate examiner, Elementary and Secondary School Programs, ETS*

Amy H. Weber, *assistant editor, Publications and Information Administration, ETS*

Allen Yates, *research statistician, Office of Data Analysis Research, ETS*

ENCYCLOPEDIA OF EDUCATIONAL EVALUATION

Concepts and Techniques for Evaluating Education and Training Programs

ACCOUNTABILITY

Accountability is still a largely untested concept in the field of education. Defined variously as *responsibility, explicability,* and *answerability,* accountability has traditionally been used with reference to service in the public interest, where the stewardship of public funds requires obligatory accounting. Ambiguity occurs when the term is wrenched from its time-tested legal and financial context and applied specifically to education, where there is as yet no body of tradition to explain and support its application.

As used in recent years, accountability as an educational concept relates mainly to a concern for furthering the educational effectiveness of school systems. Two perennial themes in American education are involved in accountability and may sometimes conflict. On the one hand, it signifies a quest for efficiency, where efficiency implies a demand that public money not be wasted through fraudulence or incompetence. On the other hand, accountability implies an extension of the democratic quest for equality of educational opportunity. In this connection it has been interpreted by some to mean that the benefits of education must be shared equally by all; that is, not only the instrumentalities (inputs) of education but the achievements (outcomes) of a quality education are to be assured—in fact, guaranteed—as a right to all sectors of the population, regardless of students' origins or backgrounds or handicaps. The agonizing question, however, has been how to make the concept, in both its interpretations, operational.

A working definition of the term, which appears to accom-

1

modate the myriads of recently offered glosses, is that accountability represents acceptance of responsibility for consequences by
those to whom citizens have entrusted the public service of education. Such a definition applies, of course, not only to school systems but to any instructional program that happens to use public
funds. Accountability acknowledges the public's right to know
what actions have been taken in the schools it supports and how
effective these actions have been. Further, this definition of accountability suggests that the "redress" implicit in the concept is
more than the citizen's right to demand the imposition of penalties for failure in accomplishment. Rather, it suggests that educators should be required to *redesign* educational activity to achieve
educational effectiveness and efficiency.

If educators are to be held accountable for student performance, the desired performances must be clearly stated and
specified in advance (see **Goals and Objectives**), and the performance must be adequately measured (see **Reliability** and **Validity**).
It follows that evaluation, using **Tests** and other forms of measurement, is an intrinsic part of a properly conceived accountability system; indeed, accountability is unthinkable without proper
evaluation. Educational programs must be regularly monitored if
constituencies are to be kept informed about the status and progress of the schools, if legislatures are to make wise decisions about
funds for education, and if administrators and teachers are to
know how to plan their programs and accomplish their objectives.
That is, such information as the relationship of input to output,
the instructional treatments that show promise or success, and the
Variables that seem to have an effect on learning is clearly vital for
problem solving and decision making at every level.

The evaluation should also provide information on how
money has been spent and what return has been made on the investment. This information should be clearly presented to the public, together with information on alternative routes for efficiently
achieving goals within the time and budget provided to the school
system or to the individual program. The evaluator should compare those routes and the benefits accruing from each so as to help
in the design of intelligent and constructive policy. (See **Systems
Analysis**.)

Teachers have shown some reluctance to accept accountability systems, since they feel that the disclosures may distort their roles in and responsibilities for educational outcomes. It is, of course, the teacher who finally must translate objectives into student "behaviors," but teachers feel that it is not they alone who produce these outcomes, that hard-to-change conditions outside their control may equally explain why students learn or do not learn. If accountability depends solely on evaluating educational outcomes of instruction, there would appear to be some justice in teachers' fears that the buck would be made to stop with them—and that therefore all accountability systems are likely to become unduly negative and even punitive. (See **Politics of Evaluation.**)

But accountability can be a far more positive concept than this. Dyer has argued that the parties to the total system—teachers, principals, superintendent, board of education, and finally legislature—all have their roles in accountability systems. In his view, each level is responsible for making decisions and for the results of those decisions, and all elements in education systems are equally responsible for improving education within the constraints that society imposes. Administrators and legislators must authorize information systems and disseminate the data to teachers; and they are also to be held accountable for assisting teachers by providing in-service training, retraining, or any other corrective action that the evaluation has shown is necessary.

Accountability also implies the responsibility and obligation of the public to provide those supports, both financial and moral, necessary to the provision of effective education. In addition, according to some writers, accountability systems imply that the public should participate in important educational decisions, sharing the power to set the goals of systems and programs, to point out educational and training needs, and to suggest programs designed to satisfy those needs.

A number of "technologies" have been advanced as means toward making education and training programs accountable. In fact, some maintain that these technologies have made accountability systems appear to be finally feasible. Others argue, however, that the state of the art (or technology) does not yet permit pinning responsibility for outcomes on any particular sector or sectors of the educational community. (For a discussion of these aids to accountability systems, see the following entries: **Accredi-**

tation, Audit of Evaluation, Performance Contracting, Planning-Programming-Budgeting System, Program Evaluation and Review Technique, Taxonomies of Objectives.)—E. J. R.

Anderson, S. B. "Accountability: What, Who and Whither?" *School Management,* 1971, *15* (9), 28-29, 50.

Borich, G. D. (Issue Ed.) *Journal of Research and Development in Education,* 1971, *5*(1), 1-96. Special issue devoted to accountability; contains articles by R. T. Lennon, L. M. Lessinger, and B. Frieder (on motivation), and Borich (on the affective domain).

Browder, L. H. (Ed.) *Emerging Patterns of Administrative Accountability.* Berkeley, Calif.: McCutchan, 1971. Discusses the issues, economics, history, politics, and applications of accountability.

Dyer, H. S. "Toward Objective Criteria for Professional Accountability in the Schools of New York City." *Phi Delta Kappan,* 1970, *52,* 206-211.

Glass, G. V. "The Many Faces of Educational Accountability." *Phi Delta Kappan,* 1972, *53,* 636-639.

Lessinger, L. M. *Every Kid a Winner: Accountability in Education.* Palo Alto, Calif.: Science Research Associates, 1970. The author, considered the "father" of the contemporary accountability movement, discusses technologies that can make accountability possible.

———————— ACCREDITATION ————————

Accreditation is the process by which a program or institution is recognized as being in conformity with some agreed-upon standard. In the United States, although every state accredits schools and professional programs and publishes lists of "approved," "certified," "recognized," or "registered" institutions, the term *accreditation* more frequently refers to approval by voluntary associations and accrediting agencies rather than to state approval.

Early in the history of American education, a variety of institutions sprang up, some of which were of dubious quality. In 1870-71 the University of Michigan began sending faculty members to inspect secondary schools and certify their ability to prepare students for university admission—a practice that spread to other states. In 1905 the North Central Association of Colleges and Secondary Schools began regional accreditation of secondary schools, and in 1913 extended the practice to colleges and universities seeking membership. Subsequently, the influence of the National Conference Committee on Standards of Colleges and Secondary Schools led to wide acceptance of institutional accreditation of schools and colleges by the six regional associations: New England Association of Colleges and Secondary Schools, Middle States Association of Colleges and Secondary Schools, Southern Association of Colleges and Schools, North Central Association of Colleges and Secondary Schools, Northwest Association of Secondary and Higher Schools, and the Western Association of Schools and Colleges.

The early accrediting agencies concentrated on "policing" institutions and rejecting those that did not meet specific minimum standards. Today, however, accrediting agencies play a much more positive role. They try to help institutions assess their own strengths and weaknesses and improve their own programs, most often through a self-evaluation by the institution in light of its own goals. The third edition of the *Encyclopedia of Educational Research* (pp. 11-12) lists the following general aims of accrediting agencies at the college and university level:

> (a) to promote and maintain high standards of education in the arts and sciences, (b) to promote and maintain high standards of preparation for service in the professions, (c) to protect society against incompetent professional practitioners, (d) to inform the public concerning the quality of educational programs in higher institutions, (e) to facilitate the transfer of students from one institution to another, (f) to encourage experimentation and self-evaluation in

higher institutions, (g) to secure good scholars and teachers and adequate facilities for the field of higher education, (h) to protect colleges and universities from undue political interference, (i) to protect society against educational frauds.

A good example of the current approach to institutional evaluation appears in *Evaluative Criteria*. This handbook, developed jointly by the six regional accrediting associations, members of the Federation of Regional Accrediting Commissions of Higher Education (FRACHE), includes detailed forms for the collection and assessment of information on the secondary school and its community, the school's philosophy and objectives, curriculum, student-activities program, educational-media services, guidance services, facilities, administration, and faculty members. The handbook also describes the process by which a school carries out a self-evaluation and is visited by an outside committee. If the visiting committee approves the school, it is accredited by the regional association and ordinarily is not reevaluated for ten years.

The development and acceptance of accreditation procedures for schools and colleges were paralleled by similar activity by professional associations. Standards for professional programs were established, and approval was extended to institutions meeting those standards, first in medicine, then in law, and now in over forty fields ranging from architecture to veterinary medicine.

By 1949, so many professional accrediting agencies had been established at the higher-education level that several associations of higher institutions created the National Commission on Accrediting (NCA) to oversee these agencies, possibly restrict their number, and improve their standards and procedures of operation. The commission has not been successful in reducing the number of accrediting agencies; but, aided by the influence of the Accreditation and Institutional Eligibility Staff of the United States Office of Education, it has succeeded in modernizing professional accreditation in the direction pioneered by the regional associations.

In recent years, questions have been raised about the validity of the standards employed by accrediting agencies, and suggestions have been offered that the federal government should not rely heavily on accreditation as a requirement for institutional participation in federal programs. Accrediting agencies are currently attempting to assure the validity of their standards; but the fact that the third edition of the *Encyclopedia of Educational Research* contains a concise history of accreditation in the United States while the fourth edition contains no article on accreditation may indicate a decreasing emphasis on accreditation as a measure of quality.

This judgment may be premature, however, in view of plans for a new organization, the Council on Postsecondary Accreditation (COPA), as a result of the merging of the two existing national bodies, NCA and FRACHE. The governing board of COPA will be broadly representative, drawing its members from both the nonprofit and proprietary sectors, specialized and professional groups, trade and technical schools, the federal and state governments, college trustees, and private citizens. Activities will be limited to coordinating the work of other accrediting agencies in order to assure quality educational offerings; the council itself will not serve as an accrediting agency.

Within education, accreditation should be distinguished from Certification and licensure. Whereas accreditation applies to the recognition of institutions or programs of study, certification and licensure apply only to individuals. Licensure is the process by which states authorize individuals to practice an otherwise restricted profession; certification is the process by which states and professional bodies recognize the particular competence of individual practitioners.—R. T. M.

Commission on Elementary Schools. *A Guide to the Evaluation and Accreditation of Elementary Schools.* Atlanta: Southern Association of Colleges and Schools, 1971. The first effort by any of the six regional accrediting associations to evaluate elementary schools.

Harris, C. W. (Ed.) *Encyclopedia of Educational Research.* (3rd Ed.) New York: Macmillan, 1960. See the articles "Accreditation: Colleges and Universities," by Forbes and Burns, and "Accreditation: Secondary Schools," by Grizzell.

Mayor, J. R. *Accreditation in Teacher Education: Its Influence on Higher Education.* Washington, D.C.: National Commission on Accrediting, 1965. A judicious analysis of the topic. Appendices III and IV summarize basic information on the

six regional accrediting associations and twenty-nine professional accrediting agencies, including the National Council
for Accreditation of Teacher Education.

National Study of Secondary School Evaluation. *Evaluative Criteria.* (4th Ed.) Washington, D.C.: NSSSE, 1969.

Selden, W. K. *Accreditation: A Struggle over Standards in Higher
Education.* New York: Harper, 1960. The standard reference to accreditation at the higher-education level.

ACHIEVEMENT TEST CONSTRUCTION

It is not possible in this book to review all the techniques
for developing instruments to assess interests, values, attitudes,
aptitudes, and other important student characteristics that education and training programs are designed to enhance or change.
However, since most programs attempt to foster some knowledges
and skills that are amenable to assessment by well-developed techniques, and since instructors and evaluators frequently have to
make their own achievement tests for want of existing ones that
adequately reflect program objectives, we present here some general principles for constructing achievement tests and suggest some
sources of more detailed help. (See also the articles on **Attitudes,
Interest Measurement,** and **Values Measurement.**)

Construction of an achievement test begins with specification of the achievements the program is designed to stimulate; that
is, we must specify *what* we want students to know, understand,
and be able to do after a defined period of instruction (see **Goals
and Objectives**). After these specifications are made in some detail,
the test constructors can then select questions or item types that
are compatible with the achievements sought. There are two main
categories of test items: those where the student *recognizes* the
appropriate response, and those where the student *constructs* an
appropriate response. Items of the first kind lend themselves to a

wide variety of content and can, with ingenuity, be designed to assess understanding and thinking as well as knowledge of facts; furthermore, they are amenable to objective scoring, a great time and money saver. However, if a program goal is for students to be able to produce a product, there is no substitute for asking them to perform such a task during the course of the achievement assessment. Construction tasks generally do not permit objective scoring, and an integral part of the test-development process is the precise specification of the criteria by which the products will be rated. (See Tests.)

Recognition items. There are many variations on the theme of true-false, multiple-choice, and matching questions. The examples given here by no means exhaust them.

The true-false item has been in general ill repute in testing circles in recent years. Wesman questions whether the "game is worth the candle" because students have a 50-50 chance of answering items correctly. Ebel defends their use, however, when they are well constructed and when other item forms are inapplicable; for instance, when the ability of the student to detect the truth or falsity of propositions is the object of assessment. Here are two examples he provides (Ebel, p. 139):

> A receiver in bankruptcy acquires title to the bankrupt's property.   T   <u>F</u>

> More heat energy is required to warm a gallon of cool water from 50° F. to 80° F. than to heat a pint of the same cool water to boiling point.   <u>T</u>   F

Among the many pieces of advice handed out to those who write true-false items, the following seem most cogent: (1) The items should be based on significant propositions. (2) Experts should be able to agree on the truth or falsity of items. (3) Students who understand a proposition should not be sidetracked by irrelevancies, misleading wording, or the need to invoke unusual assumptions. (4) Students who do not understand a proposition should not be able to answer an item correctly through ordinary acquaintance with the way language is used or because the item writer has included specific determiners such as *all, always, never* (usually rendering the proposition false), or *sometimes, generally, may* (usually true). (5) When items are assembled into a test, there should be no discernible sequential pattern of correct answers (e.g., T F T F) or such a preponderance of Ts or Fs that students may be able to recognize the imbalance and profit from it. (See **Test Wiseness.**)

Ebel (pp. 127-130) provides an excellent discussion of items better suited to true-false than multiple-choice form, and vice versa. However, most writers agree that the multiple-choice form is the most generally useful objective item type. Some illustrations from an Educational Testing Service publication, *Multiple-Choice Questions: A Close Look,* illustrate the diversity of cognitive processes that these items can tap:

> The concept of the plasma membrane as a simple sieve-like structure is inadequate to explain the
> (A) passage of gases involved in respiration into and out of the cell
> (B) passage of simple organic molecules such as glucose into the cell
> (C) failure of protein molecules to pass through the membrane
> (D) inability of the cell to use starch without prior digestion
> (E) ability of the cell to admit selectively some inorganic ions while excluding others.

To answer this question correctly (correct answer E), the student must know that the *living* plasma membrane has properties in addition to those served by a piece of cellophane or similar material used in classical laboratory demonstrations of osmosis.

> *Directions:* Maintenant, vous allez entendre une conversation entre deux personnes. Attendez la deuxième réplique et ensuite choisissez la réponse qui convient le mieux.
> "Henriette, passe-moi cette petite robe légère qui se trouve dans mon armoire à glace."
> "Attends un moment; j'ai la bouche pleine de pâte dentifrice. J'aurai fini ma toilette dans un instant."
> (a) Ne te presse pas. Je la chercherai moi-même. (b) Je l'ai trouvée tout à l'heure. (c) Quand tu auras fini de te peigner. (d) Oui, je l'ai repassée hier soir.

The testing of a student's ability to understand a foreign language when spoken is a relatively recent development. Students listen to the recorded voices of native speakers in statements, short conversations, and short narrations. To select the right answer (a) to the question above, the student has to apply his knowledge of French grammar, vocabulary, and idiomatic expressions, and his understanding of the French sound system.

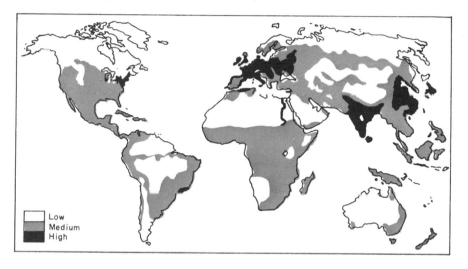

Low
Medium
High

Figure 1.

The shading on the map in Figure 1 is used to indicate (a) population density, (b) percentage of total labor force in agriculture, (c) per capita income, (d) death rate per thousand of population.

This question does not simply ask: What areas of the world have the highest population densities? Rather, it presents a novel situation in which the student must infer that, of the choices offered, only population density (a) provides a plausible explanation of the shadings on the map.

"In a flash it came upon me that *there* was the reason for advancing poverty with advancing wealth. With the growth of population, land grows in value, and the men who work it must pay more for the privilege. In allowing one man to own the land on which and from which other men live, we have made them his bondsmen in a degree which increases as material progress goes on. This is the subtle alchemy that in ways they do not realize is extracting from the masses in every civilized country the fruits of their weary toil."

The person most likely to have written these words is (a) John Jacob Astor, (b) William Jennings Bryan, (c) Thorstein Veblen, (d) Lincoln Steffens, (e) Henry George.

Note that in this item the student is *not* asked, or expected, to recognize the statement from memory. Instead, he is expected to read the excerpt carefully, to evaluate it in light of his knowledge and understanding of American intellectual history, and then to select from the five names listed the person to whom the statement might most reasonably be attributed. (The correct answer is e.)

The first multiple-choice item above is self-contained; i.e., except for the stem ("The concept of the plasma membrane as a simple sieve-like structure is inadequate to explain the . . .") and the choices (a-e), the student is not given any additional materials to refer to. The last three items, however, require the student to attend to a special stimulus (a recording, a map, or a printed text) in addition to the item itself. Test items can be based on many different kinds of materials, ranging from pictures and music to physical specimens and three-dimensional models. And there are many possible media of presentation: materials can be printed or typed, read aloud, or presented through recordings, slides, films, or displays.

Among other issues that arise in the development of multiple-choice items are these:

1. The number of choices. Most multiple-choice tests use four or five choices; recent multiple-choice tests for very young children use only three; and some tests have used seven or more. If reducing the student's opportunity to select the correct choice purely by chance were the only concern, then the test developer would always go for more, rather than fewer, choices. However, there are other considerations: testing time available (it takes longer to consider six choices than four), the content of the items (some material simply does not lend itself to the development of

three or more good distracters or incorrect choices), and the student population to be tested (three-choice items have proved practical with young children, who do not seem to have developed the guessing strategies frequently used by older students).

2. Correction for guessing. The traditional scoring formula designed to take account of essentially random marking when the test taker does not "know" the correct response is $R - [W/(n-1)]$, where R is the number of right answers on the test, W is the number of wrong answers, and n is the number of choices per item. However, as Thorndike (p. 59) points out, " 'Guessing' is a loose, general term for an array of behaviors that occur when an examinee . . . does not 'know' the answer." These behaviors include not only random guessing (perhaps the most unlikely behavior if the test is at all appropriate for the student) but also eliminating definitely wrong choices, using semantic or syntactic cues in the wording of the question, and responding to some element in one of the response choices even at a relatively low level of confidence. (Some of these test-taking strategies are not necessarily incompatible with important educational goals.) The situation is further complicated by the problem of individual **Response Sets** that may come into play. For example, some students are inclined to take risks while others are quite conservative, preferring not to mark any answer if they are not sure. The current trend in testing is away from the use of scoring formulas (partly, it must be admitted, for practical convenience) and toward encouraging all students to guess (to answer all items even if they are not sure). Increased attention is being given, too, to the development of items and test formats that either discourage guessing or take explicit account of it. Even so, individual proclivities to respond in particular ways when faced with uncertainty will probably always be with us.

3. The use of a "Don't know" choice. If the student is given a chance to mark "Don't know," will he do it? Or will he still try to beat the game by using whatever clues he can to get credit for the right answer, even when he doesn't know what it is? This issue is related to guessing, of course, and to personality-based response tendencies on the part of students; and measurement theorists and practitioners are divided about it. The "Don't know" option is being used in the National Assessment of Educational Progress,

even though investigators (for example, Finley and Berdie) have shown that low-ability students tend to avoid it. Mehrens and Lehmann recommend the inclusion of the "Don't know" option in tests used for instructional guidance but not for tests used in final evaluation. They would probably include **Formative Evaluation** efforts in the first category.

4. The development of plausible distracters. Distracters are usually derived by the test developer from his own experience with students and/or his predictions about the kinds of misconceptions or confusions they are likely to have in an area. He crosses his fingers that, when the test is tried out, the distracters will indeed distract and will be more distracting to low-achieving than to high-achieving students. Another approach to developing distracters—when time and resources are available—is to administer the questions to an appropriate sample of students in an open-ended format and ask them to supply the answers. Then the most frequent wrong answers can provide the basis for distracters when the test is recast into multiple-choice form. It is sometimes possible, too, to use more choices in a **Pretest** than are wanted for the final form of the test. Then the poorest distracters can be eliminated in the final form.

There are many published lists of suggestions for those who are attempting to write multiple-choice items. They include advice to state the problem clearly, invent plausible distracters that are similar in structure and content, avoid giving irrelevant cues to the right answer, avoid silly flaws in the correct option (e.g., a spelling error), avoid wrong scoring keys and multiple correct answers, avoid using "All of the above" as an option and use "None of the above" sparingly (Mehrens and Lehmann), avoid mixing "best answer" and "exception" answers in the same set (for example, in a series of questions requiring students to select correct grammatical forms, ask them suddenly to identify the form that is incorrect), and make sure that the correct answer falls in different positions across the items in a test. All of these seem to be good suggestions for producing a professional-looking test and one that students will have some confidence in. These are important enough objectives. However, as several authors (Dunn and Goldstein, McMorris et al.) have pointed out, although violations of so-called item-writing principles may result in easier or more difficult tests, we presently have little evidence to support the claim that such violations seriously threaten validity or reliability.

A third type of recognition-test item (in addition to true-false and multiple-choice items), the matching form, is one that many of us are familiar with from our school and college days. Here is an example adapted from a test Harold Gulliksen gave in Psychology 201:

> Before each of the statements below, write the number of the term from the following list which is exemplified by the statement:

> 1. Conversion   7. Oedipus complex
> 2. Depression   8. Overcompensation
> 3. Hallucination   9. Paranoia
> 4. Impulsivity   10. Projection
> 5. Introversion   11. Regression
> 6. Narcissism   12. Withdrawal

_____ I am the acme of things accomplished.

_____ How dear to my heart are the scenes of my childhood when fond recollection presents them to view.

_____ They go wild, simply wild, over me.

_____ The world is too much with us.

_____ I want a girl just like the girl that married dear old Dad.

_____ I'm drifting back to dreamland, for I know I'll find you there.

_____ I see blossoms and the trees are bare.

_____ I can resist everything except temptation.

_____ How all occasions do inform against me.

Note that the set above has the following characteristics that are generally recommended for test items of this type: the items within the response list are homogeneous in content, and the statements are similar; the list is short enough for the examinee to comprehend the range of choices; the number of items in the list is greater than the number of statements (so that a student can't get the last item right by elimination) and the basis for the match is clearly explained. A combination matching and multiple-choice exercise, called a _key-list exercise_, utilizes a very small number of responses and a large number of statements; students then use each response several times.

Construction items. The most frequently used kinds of tests where students construct their responses are the short-answer (or completion) test and the essay examination. Short-answer items look like this:

> The sum of scores divided by the number of scores is called the _____ .   [mean]

> What is the best way to ensure equivalence of the experimental and control groups?   [randomization]

Essay questions look like this (from Stalnaker, p. 519):

> Answer briefly each of the following questions. The essential points in each case can be covered in a few sentences. Be as definite and concise as possible.
> 1. What is meant by the statement that France, before 1789, was centralized but not unified?
> 2. Why did the Dreyfus affair become an issue of national significance?
> 3. Who said the following and to what end? "If happiness is present, we have everything, and when it is absent, we do everything with a view to possessing it."

These essay questions are superior in focus to many essay questions given in classrooms around the country ("Describe your summer vacation" or "Discuss the American Civil War"). However, even when questions are well constructed, scoring is not an easy task. The short-answer questions are easier to score; even in the examples given, however, some provisions have to be made for crediting alternative answers (e.g., "average" or "arithmetic mean" in the first example).

When tests are being used for program evaluation, it is not advisable to include an instruction such as "Answer four out of five of the following questions." Optional questions, as Stalnaker (p. 506) notes, "complicate measurement and introduce factors of judgment which are extraneous to the ability being measured." If the evaluator has more achievement items than can be given conveniently to each student, he should consider **Item Sampling**. This point is made here in connection with essay questions because it arises most frequently in connection with that item type. However, it applies generally across item types.

In the face of the scoring problems and burdens that essay and completion questions present, as well as the fact that fewer such questions than objective questions can usually be given in a specified period of time, the test developer needs to have a stronger case for using free-response questions than that they take less time to prepare. His strongest case comes, of course, from the objectives of the instructional program. The following course objectives, for example, *require* constructed responses in the achievement instruments:

Translate a passage from Cicero.

Make a scale drawing of a public building.

Speak extemporaneously on a popular topic for five minutes.

Write a letter of application for a job.

Prepare a soufflé.

Disassemble and assemble a rifle.

Write a proposal to evaluate an instructional program.

Analyze a blood sample.

Transpose a musical score to another key.

Edit a technical manuscript.

In some terminologies, tests to measure such behaviors are called *performance tests* (see also **Situational Tests**). The guidelines for constructing them have a lot in common with the guidelines for constructing good paper-and-pencil tests: (1) As part of the test-development process, specify the criteria for rating or scoring the performance or product. (2) State the problem so that the examinee is absolutely clear about what he is supposed to do. (3) If possible, tell the examinee the basis on which his performance will be judged. (4) Avoid any irrelevant difficulties in the testing content or procedures. (5) If possible, give the examinee an opportunity to perform the task more than once or to perform several task samples.

Technical characteristics. Whether the achievement test consists of recognition or construction items (or a combination), the developer will want to look into the following technical characteristics of the test: ·

1. Difficulty. Are the items generally at an appropriate level of difficulty for the student? If a significant number of scores on a multiple-choice test are in the "chance" range (for instance, below one fifth of the total score when there are five choices per item), the test is probably too difficult. Conversely, if the test is not a test of **Mastery Learning** and a disproportionate number of students earn nearly perfect scores, the test is probably too easy. The most usual index of difficulty for an item that can be scored right or wrong is percentage of students passing the item.

2. Speededness. Is the speededness of the test appropriate for the examinees and to the achievement being measured? If speed of performance is a course objective and thus a measurement objective (as in certain clerical and assembly tasks), the examinees should be asked to perform at acceptable levels of speed. However, if speed of performance is not at issue (as in certain critical-thinking or creative-thinking tasks), the test should be of a length that the majority of students can at least attempt every item. Typical indices of speededness are the percentage of examinees reaching a given point in the test, or the number of items reached by, say, 80 percent of the examinees.

3. Discrimination. When an external indicator of course performance (e.g., instructor's ratings) or the total score on the achievement test is used as the criterion for high- and low-achieving students, do items discriminate between students in the expected direction? Or do low students do well on some items that high students miss? Such items should be eliminated or inspected for possible flaws and revised. The usual index of item discrimination is the biserial **Correlation** of the item score with the criterion.

4. Homogeneity. Is student performance fairly consistent across the items of the test? The intercorrelations of scores for the items on the test provide information about the degree to which the items tend to measure similar attributes. In some cases, where the test constructor is attempting to obtain a precise estimate of an individual's location or position on a particular dimension of knowledge or skill, he wants these correlations to be high. In other cases, where he is deliberately attempting to cover diverse objectives in a single examination, the test constructor wants the correlations to be relatively low—or appropriately patterned (e.g., if there are five items for each of ten objectives, he wants the cor-

relations to be higher among the five items for each objective and lower between items for different objectives). **Factor Analysis** offers an additional means for documenting homogeneity and is particularly useful when large numbers of items are involved.

5. Reliability. Are the scores obtained from the test relatively stable indicators of knowledge and skill? If another set of items in the same areas had been used instead, would the students have been ordered in roughly the same way and have performed at approximately the same levels? If the test maker prepares two forms of the test, he can obtain answers to this question empirically. There are also techniques for estimating how students would have performed on a second test from comparison of their performance on different groups of items in the same test. (See **Reliability.**)

6. Validity. Do scores on the test relate to other indicators of student knowledge and skills? For example, do students with high test scores also display knowledge in classroom discussions? And do students with low test scores fail to display such knowledge in other situations? Correlations between test scores and such other indicators are the usual indices of validity. (See **Validity.**)

According to Richard Anderson, the most important obligations for the developer of an achievement test are (a) to document the rationale for selecting the items to be used and (b) to explicate fully the relationship between the items and the instructional program.—S. B. A.

Anderson, R. C. "How to Construct Achievement Tests to Assess Comprehension." *Review of Educational Research,* 1972, *42,* 145-170.

Anderson, S. B., and Melville, S. D. *Making Your Own Tests: Planning; Construction; Analysis.* A series of three filmstrips with sound. Princeton, N.J.: Educational Testing Service, 1963.

Dunn, T. F., and Goldstein, L. G. "Test Difficulty, Validity, and Reliability as Functions of Selected Multiple-Choice Item Construction Principles." *Educational and Psychological Measurement,* 1959, *19,* 171-179.

Ebel, R. L. *Measuring Educational Achievement.* Englewood Cliffs, N.J.: Prentice-Hall, 1965. See especially Chapter 3

("How to Plan a Classroom Test"), Chapter 4 ("The Characteristics and Uses of Essay Tests"), Chapter 5 ("How to Use True-False Tests"), Chapter 6 ("How to Write Multiple-Choice Test Items"), and Chapter 9 ("How to Judge the Quality of a Classroom Test").

Educational Testing Service. *Multiple-Choice Questions: A Close Look.* Princeton, N.J.: ETS, 1963.

Finley, C. J., and Berdie, F. S. *The National Assessment Approach to Exercise Development.* Denver: National Assessment of Educational Progress, 1970.

McMorris, R. F., Brown, J. A., Snyder, G. W., and Pruzek, R. M. "Effects of Violating Item Construction Principles." *Journal of Educational Measurement,* 1972, *9,* 287-295.

Mehrens, W. A., and Lehmann, I. J. *Measurement and Evaluation in Education and Psychology.* New York: Holt, 1973. See especially Chapter 8 ("The Essay Test: Preparing the Questions and Grading the Responses"), Chapter 9 ("Writing the Objective Item: Short-Answer, Matching, and True-False"), and Chapter 10 ("Writing Objective Test Items: The Multiple-Choice and Context-Dependent Items").

Siegel, A. I., Bergman, B. A., and Federman, P. *Some Techniques for the Evaluation of Technical Training Courses and Students.* Lowry Air Force Base, Colo.: Technical Training Division, 1972. See especially Chapter III, "Dependent Measures" (test construction, hierarchical and sequential testing, etc.).

Stalnaker, J. M. "The Essay Type of Examination." In E. F. Lindquist (Ed.), *Educational Measurement.* Washington, D.C.: American Council on Education, 1951. Pp. 495-530.

Thorndike, R. L. (Ed.) *Educational Measurement.* (2nd Ed.) Washington, D.C.: American Council on Education, 1971. See especially the articles by S. N. Tinkelman ("Planning the Objective Test," pp. 46-80), A. G. Wesman ("Writing the Test Item," pp. 81-129), S. Henrysson ("Gathering, Analyzing, and Using Data on Test Items," pp. 130-159), R. Fitzpatrick and E. J. Morrison ("Performance and Product Evaluation," pp. 237-270), and W. E. Coffman ("Essay Examinations," pp. 271-302).

———————— ADVERSARY MODEL OF EVALUATION ————————

Program evaluators, whatever the evaluation model they espouse, try to observe the tenets of scientific inquiry (see **Scientific Inquiry and Evaluation** and **Evaluation Concepts**). Each evaluator assumes that he is seeking the truth about a program and that finding the truth is dependent upon his efforts. Ideally, he gathers the best evidence he can, no matter what the implications (positive or negative) about the program. Then he presents the evidence as fairly and openly as possible. There are a number of variations within this structure (see **Evaluator Role**), but basically the evaluator is charged both with finding and presenting the evidence.

In recent years this conception of the evaluator within the framework of scientific research has been challenged. There are, of course, other approaches to reaching truth; and some challengers of our present framework have suggested that we try out instead the legal profession's approach. In the legal profession the evidence is assembled by law-enforcement agencies (or, in civil actions, by the parties involved). But the presenting of the evidence to the judge (decision maker, educational leader) is then assigned to two opposed groups—the prosecutor and the defender. The hope is that through their adversary positions, one presenting the evidence as negatively as possible and the other as positively as possible, truth will emerge.

As one might expect of this quite new approach to program evaluation, there is no established tradition, no agreement on what is specifically denoted by the term *adversary model,* and few examples of the use of the model in the practice of program evaluation.

Levine proposes that evaluations should include an adversary who will "cross-examine" all the evidence as it is collected in order to develop a rebuttal. Kourilsky argues for a setting which "guarantees the presentation of both sides of an issue at the decision-making phase." With an affirmative evaluator and a negative evaluator both making presentations, she argues, the evidence will be more thoroughly sifted, and unwitting biases and hidden assumptions will be exposed. Stake and Gjerde's evaluation of a program for talented youth is the best-known example of an adversary model in operation. That is, they first summarize the arguments most favorable to the program; and then, in an adversary section, they summarize the most damaging arguments. The reader is left to reconcile these two positions.

It is difficult for those of us outside the legal tradition to warm to the adversary model. Lawyers are trained to defend a client to the best of their ability no matter how heinous the crime or how clear the evidence that their client is responsible. Can this detachment from the evidence be part of an evaluator's characteristics? Can the evaluator of a mathematics program, who is assigned a positive advocacy role but who obtains strong evidence of negative effects, conscientiously argue for the continuation of the program? Does such an approach mean that good evidence is less important than the debating skills of the evaluator?

In spite of possible defects, the implementation of an adversary model could have the beneficial result of keeping evaluators "on their toes." If an evaluator knew that a critic from the other side of a case would be examining his side, he might make a special effort to tighten the evidence.—S. B.

Churchman, C. W. *Prediction and Optimal Decision.* Englewood Cliffs, N.J.: Prentice-Hall, 1961. Includes an examination of types of evidence and their effects on judgment.

Kourilsky, M. "An Adversary Model for Educational Evaluation." UCLA *Evaluation Comment,* 1973, *4* (2), 3-6.

Levine, M. "Scientific Method and the Adversary Model: Some Preliminary Suggestions." UCLA *Evaluation Comment,* 1973, *4* (2), 1-3.

Stake, R., and Gjerde, C. *An Evaluation of T City: The Twin City Institute for Talented Youth.* Urbana: Center for Instructional Research and Curriculum Evaluation, University of Illinois, 1971. An actual example of the use of the adversary model.

AFFECTIVE VARIABLES

Variables that refer to feelings or emotions are categorized as affective and are differentiated from **Cognitive Variables** (knowing and thinking) and **Psychomotor Variables** (movement). Consider, for example, a program to teach typing. If a test battery were constructed to assess the effects of that program, it might include a typing-speed test (psychomotor), a test to determine the trainee's knowledge of the proper format for memoranda and letters (cognitive), and a questionnaire to measure how the trainee feels about the program and about working as a typist (affective). These three categories of variables undoubtedly interact with each other in real life. We may feel good if we know an answer or can do something efficiently. Some variables are not simple to classify, and demarcation disputes are likely to occur when, for example, **Attitudes**, which have both affective and cognitive components, are involved. Thus, one's attitude toward Australians involves a feeling about them as well as knowledge about them.

Affective variables are usually assessed in terms of typical behavior. For example, we want to know what the student typically feels about himself or a situation. Cognitive and psychomotor variables, on the other hand, are frequently assessed in terms of maximal behavior. For example, we want to know how fast a person can type or how much knowledge about atomic weights a person has. A second distinction is that, with affective variables, there is little emphasis on the "correctness" of one response over some other response to a question. Thus, responses to the statement "I cry when I feel very happy" might range from "Always or almost always" to "Never or almost never." There is no generally right or wrong answer to such a statement; the "right" answer is only what is true for the individual (or useful to the interpreter). However, with items assessing cognitive variables, there is usually a correct response. Thus, different scores on a test assessing a cognitive variable indicate quantitative differences (student A knows more than student B), but different scores on a test assessing an affective variable are more likely to be interpreted as indicating qualitative differences (she is highly extroverted, and he is moderately introverted).

Krathwohl and his associates have attempted to classify affective variables in a fashion useful to evaluators (see **Taxonomies of Objectives**). However, affective variables, in contrast to cognitive variables, are less likely to be selected for use in an evaluation. There are two major reasons for this. The first is that affective variables are difficult to measure with **Validity** and **Reliability**. Suppose, for example, that an evaluator of a program to teach telegraphic processes wants to discover whether trainees are enjoying the program and whether they want a career involving the skills being taught. Suppose, further, that the evaluator decides to try to determine the trainees' feelings by asking them the questions directly. The trainees' responses would surely depend, in part at least, on who is asking the questions (the commanding officer or one of their buddies). And if a different method of assessment were used, such as observing the behavior of the trainees (number of absences, amount of reading on the topic area outside course time, etc.), the results might be difficult to interpret. Perhaps the trainees turn up at every session because they want to get the course over as quickly as possible and not because they enjoy it. Maybe they read related materials because they hate the course materials and consider them useless; thus, their extra reading would not necessarily indicate enthusiasm. There is little doubt that affective variables are more difficult to measure than cognitive variables.

A second major reason why affective variables are less likely to be selected for use in an evaluation applies mainly to training programs. These programs tend to emphasize intended cognitive or psychomotor outcomes (Docs the trainee know what the program tried to teach? Can the trainee perform the task properly?) over intended or unintended affective outcomes. In the short run, this probably makes sense. Certainly, if the training program does not achieve its stipulated cognitive or psychomotor outcomes, its value may be limited. In the long run, however, the affective variables may count most.

In more general educational programs (in contrast to training programs), affective goals are usually given greater emphasis.

Most of us can remember at least one high school course where the teacher made us learn the material quite well—but we disliked something about the course (perhaps the teacher) and did not subsequently develop our knowledge and skills in the subject as we might have if we had enjoyed the course. If a student's long-term development in a subject area is important, we should evaluate carefully how he feels toward his current program in that area. And, since usually the personal affective development of students (including such variables as feelings of self-worth) is also of consequence to educators, affective variables ought to be seriously considered in the selection of outcome variables for evaluation studies.

Possible affective changes may be of special interest to those evaluating college-level programs. While early studies did not obtain significant relationships between college experiences and affective changes in students, later studies using new techniques have shown that college environments and major fields of study can affect students' value systems (Feldman and Newcomb, Thistlethwaite).

To this point, we have discussed affective variables as dependent (outcome) variables and presented some reasons why affective variables are relatively neglected in evaluation research. Affective variables can also be used as independent (input) variables and as moderator (process) variables. (See **Variables.**) As an example of an affective *independent* variable, the students involved in a program evaluation might be divided into a motivated and an unmotivated group and the effects of the program looked at separately for these groups. As an example of an affective *moderator* variable, one might investigate the effects of a programmed lesson taught by teachers of differing levels of warmth and friendliness. These may, in fact, be very important kinds of questions. However, they are usually not the central questions for an evaluator. Usually the evaluator is asked to tell the program's sponsors whether the program has any overall effect. The evaluator is less likely to be asked additional questions such as "Is the effect present for different kinds of trainees?" and "Under what circumstances?" But it is in the process of answering these more sophisticated questions that affective variables are likely to be used. (See **Trait-Treatment Interaction.**)

It is true that affective variables are difficult to assess, less likely to be mentioned in specific training-program goals, and unlikely to be called for in simple evaluations, but it is also true that useful assessment procedures are available (e.g., see **Interest Measurement, Interviews, Observation Techniques, Questionnaires, Ratings**). And those who develop program goals and those who fund program evaluations should be better educated to the need to consider affective variables.—S. B.

Feldman, K. A., and Newcomb, T. M. *The Impact of College on Students.* San Francisco: Jossey-Bass, 1969.

Harrocks, J. E. *Assessment of Behavior.* Columbus, Ohio: Merrill, 1964. See Chapters 16-20 on personality and interest measures.

Jackson, D. N., and Messick, S. (Eds.) *Problems in Human Assessment.* New York: McGraw-Hill, 1967. See Parts 6-7 for discussions of methods and problems of assessing personality and attitudes.

Krathwohl, D. R., Bloom, B. S., and Masia, B. B. *Taxonomy of Educational Objectives. Handbook II: Affective Domain.* New York: McKay, 1956.

Thistlethwaite, D. L. "Accentuation of Differences in Values and Exposures to Major Fields of Study." *Journal of Educational Psychology,* 1973, *65,* 279-293.

Thornton, R. F., and Wasdyke, R. G. *A Taxonomy for the Development of Multidimensional Test Specifications.* Princeton, N.J.: Educational Testing Service, 1973. An interesting application of a complete taxonomy to the field of career development and testing.

ASSESSMENT

The term *assessment* is often used interchangeably with the terms *evaluation* and *measurement*. However, we believe that assessment, used precisely, has a narrower meaning than evaluation but a broader meaning than measurement. In its derivation, the word *assess* means "to sit beside" or "to assist the judge." It therefore seems appropriate in evaluation studies to limit the term *assessment* to the process of gathering the data and fashioning them into an interpretable form; judgments can then be made on the basis of this assessment.

Assessment, as opposed to simple one-dimensional measurement, is frequently described as multitrait-multimethod; that is, it focuses on a number of variables judged to be important and utilizes a number of techniques to assay them (**Tests, Questionnaires, Interviews, Ratings, Unobtrusive Measures,** etc.). Its techniques may also be multisource (data on the same variable may be collected from trainers, instructors, and course records; see **Data Sources**) and/or multijudge (ratings of the same trainee performance may be obtained from several assessors, whose judgments are then pooled or averaged). (See **Factor Analysis** for a discussion of the reduction of a large array of data to a smaller number of important dimensions.)

Two rather different examples of assessment are provided by the National Assessment of Educational Progress and the assessment centers organized and administered by many industrial and military organizations. The National Assessment of Educational Progress is a program that provides for the testing of American schoolchildren at the ages of nine, thirteen, and seventeen and of a sample of young adults. Tests are administered in reading, writing, science, and other academic areas. Based on the information provided by this National Assessment, educators, citizens, and political leaders then make judgments about the effectiveness of the educational system. In the industrial and military assessment centers employees are tested and observed by specially trained psychologists, sociologists, and other professional staff. These professional assessors then organize the information collected and prepare profiles on the individuals. The profiles provide the final materials on which the program directors will base their decisions about whether to promote, retain, or dismiss individuals. The process is intensive and complicated. A very thorough and readable description of such a center is given in the Office of Strategic Services report cited in the references.

Assessment, then, as we define it, precedes the final decision-making stage in evaluation; e.g., the decision to continue, modify, or terminate a training program. It is not, however, entire-ly divorced from decision making. In fact, the entire assessment process must be planned in light of possible and plausible alterna-tive decisions. Unfortunately, because of poor study design, the information collected in some evaluation studies may not allow the decision maker to distinguish between alternative decisions (see **Experimental Design**). To illustrate what we mean by alterna-tive decisions, the following examples are given: (1) The training program will be terminated if fewer than 50 percent of the train-ees perform satisfactorily on a battery of criterion tests upon com-pletion of the program. (2) The training program will be termi-nated if it costs more than a competing program that has achieved virtually the same results. (3) The training program will be con-tinued if the percentage of the trainees rated high by a team of assessors is significantly higher than the corresponding percentage rated high in a competing program. (4) The training program will be modified if trainee success is significantly related to some modi-fiable characteristic of the program (e.g., time spent on instruc-tion, frequency of classes, training of the instructor).

It is clear that such alternative decisions will constrain the assessment procedure and the experimental design. In some cases, more than one program must be involved for comparison pur-poses. In other cases, levels of significance and satisfactory scores on selected tests must be agreed upon and built into the assess-ment procedure.

Since, ordinarily, the decisions to be made will be based on a comprehensive description of a person, group, or situation, two general steps should be taken in designing a good assessment. First, the range of relevant behaviors and characteristics to be measured must be identified. For example, in a training program for pilots, the behaviors assessed should be the same as, or clearly predictive of, the behaviors needed by the pilot when actually flying. Iden-tifying such behaviors is often a difficult process. (See **Job Analy-sis**.) Second, reliable techniques for measuring these behaviors need to be selected and/or designed.—R. T. M.

Bray, D. W., and Grant, D. L. "The Assessment Center in the Mea-
      surement of Potential for Business Management." *Psycho-*
      logical Monographs, 1966, *80.*

Gadway, C. J. *Reading and Literature: General Information Year-book.* Denver: National Assessment of Educational Progress, 1972. A general introduction to the National Assessment program and an outline of the design of the project.

Jackson, D. N., and Messick, S. (Eds.) *Problems in Human Assessment.* New York: McGraw-Hill, 1967. Contains articles by recognized experts on almost every aspect of assessment. The first chapter, by Harold Gulliksen, presents a brief and simple introduction to factor analysis. See Chapter 6 for further explanation of the multitrait-multimethod technique in assessment.

McReynolds, P. (Ed.) *Advances in Psychological Assessment.* Palo Alto: Science and Behavioral Books, 1968, 1971. 2 vols. Chapters by some thirty authors on a broad range of assessment principles, techniques, and problems. Chapter V in Volume Two, "The Assessment of Managerial Talent," summarizes the approach used in industrial assessment programs.

Office of Strategic Services (OSS) Assessment Staff. *Assessment of Men.* New York: Holt, 1948. An interesting, readable, and thorough explanation of the assessment centers used in the OSS.

---------------------------------- ATTENUATION ----------------------------------

All measurement is subject to some error. As long as evaluators use certain statistical techniques to analyze their data, errors of measurement are not likely to jeopardize their conclusions. However, when they use other statistical techniques, their results may vary widely depending on whether they take errors of measurement into account—that is, whether they "correct for attenuation." This article addresses the need to correct for attenuation and discusses the highly technical issues involved in doing so.

Attenuation is defined as "the reduction in the **Correlation** between measures due to errors of measurement." In classical test theory, observed scores are conceptualized as the sum of a true score and an uncorrelated measurement error. Random errors of measurement cause the correlation between fallible measures to be less than it would have been if the measures were error free—i.e., perfectly reliable. Since the estimation of correlations among error-free measures frequently plays an important part in both theoretical formulations and practical applications, attenuation is a fundamental concept. (See also **Reliability**.)

Assuming that errors of measurement are uncorrelated with anything, we can obtain estimates of the reliabilities of the fallible measures. The reliabilities can be used to estimate what the correlation would be if the measures were free of measurement error. The resulting estimate of the disattenuated correlation is said to be "corrected" for attenuation.

While the importance of attenuation in theoretical work is generally recognized, it has frequently been ignored in applied work such as educational/training evaluation. Since the effect of random errors of measurement is always in the direction of lowering the correlation between two variables and since operational measures are always subject to error, many investigators see little to be gained from corrections for attenuation. As long as the analyses are limited to simple zero-order correlations, the failure to consider attenuation effects explicitly is generally not serious. In situations where conclusions are based on partial correlations, partial regression weights, an analysis of residual-gain scores, or an analysis of covariance, however, explicit consideration of attenuation effects becomes essential. Whereas the direction of the attenuation effect on the simple correlation is known without "correcting" the correlation, the direction of the effect on partial correlations, partial regression weights, or the outcome of an analysis of covariance is not generally known in advance. Thus, the conclusions of an evaluation study that uses one of the latter techniques might be radically altered after correcting for attenuation.

To illustrate the effects of attenuation, suppose that an evaluator wanted to assess the relationship between the number of hours that a student is exposed to special tutorial instruction and his achievement at the end of the instructional program. Since it is known that students with low **Pretest** scores receive more tutorial instruction than those with high pretest scores, he decides to partial the pretest out of the correlation between the number of hours of instruction and the **Posttest**. Given the correlations pretest with posttest = .6, pretest with hours of tutorial instruction = −.4, posttest with hours of tutorial instruction = −.3, the partial correlation of hours and posttest with pretest partialed out would be −.08. This result seems to indicate that there is little relationship between hours of tutorial instruction on posttest performance after pretest scores are "taken into account." In fact, if anything, there is a slight negative relationship, suggesting that more tutorial instruction may have a slight negative effect.

Suppose, however, that the posttest had a reliability of .81 but that the pretest was a shorter test with a reliability of only .49. If corrections for attenuation were made based on these reliabilities, the disattenuated partial correlation between hours of tutorial instruction and posttest score with pretest partialed out would be .84, and the conclusion would be that there is a very strong positive effect of tutorial instruction. This example is much more extreme than is apt to be encountered in practice. The extreme effect of the unreliability is due to the large difference between the reliability of the pretest and the reliability of the posttest. Nonetheless, this example may illustrate the fact that a disattenuated partial correlation can lead to quite different conclusions from those that would be made on the basis of an attenuated partial correlation.

As Lord (1962, p. 36) has noted, the need to correct partial correlations for attenuation "poses somewhat of a dilemma, since, first, it is often hard to obtain the particular kind of reliability coefficients that are required for making the appropriate correction, and, further, the partial correlation corrected for attenuation may be seriously affected by sampling errors. These obstacles can hardly justify the use of an uncorrected coefficient that may have a wrong sign, however." Similar comments could be made about partial regression weights and the analysis of covariance.

Attenuation problems also play an important part when simple change scores (i.e., posttest minus pretest) are used in evaluation studies. Difference scores are notorious for their low reliabilities. Thus, the search for correlates of change is limited by the attenuation of the correlations of change scores with other measures. (See **Change Measurement**.)—R. L. L.

Gulliksen, H. *Theory of Mental Tests*. New York: Wiley, 1950. Pp. 101-105.

Lord, F. M. "Elementary Models for Measuring Change." In C. W. Harris (Ed.), *Problems in Measuring Change*. Madison: University of Wisconsin Press, 1962. Pp. 21-38.

Lord, F. M. "Significance Tests for Partial Correlation Corrected for Attenuation." *Educational and Psychological Measurement*, 1974.

Lord, F. M., and Novick, M. R. *Statistical Theories of Mental Test Scores*. Reading, Mass.: Addison-Wesley, 1968. See pages 69, 137, 213, 344, 368, 465.

ATTITUDES

How we define the term *attitude* helps to determine the ways we measure it. There are many technical definitions of "attitudes," but most have features in common. By combining the common features, we find that an attitude is an implicit cue- and drive-producing response to socially salient characteristics and that it possesses evaluative properties. Each element of this definition needs further explanation.

The word *implicit* indicates that an attitude is within the individual. It cannot be seen, felt, touched, or observed in any direct fashion. It can be inferred from certain kinds of behavior but it must always remain an inference of the observer.

The phrase *cue- and drive-producing* means that an attitude held by a person will tend to cause that person to notice and do things selectively. If he has a positive attitude toward instructors, he may notice how helpful they are and may decide to stay after formal classes to continue a discussion. If, on the other hand, he has a negative attitude toward instructors, he may notice how often they get angry and may decide one day to exaggerate a slight cold so that he can stay away from his classes. By careful observation of the cues a person notices and the things he does thereafter, we can begin to infer his attitudes.

The notion that an attitude is a *response* suggests that behavior permitting a person's attitudes to be inferred can be elicited by providing appropriate stimuli. These stimuli can be verbal (as in a paper-and-pencil test) or nonverbal (as in observations of behavior under simulated conditions). In either case, the test maker can do something to provoke an attitudinal response.

The definition of an attitude also indicates that school and school-related activities are appropriate areas for assessment because they are *socially salient* in the life of the person being instructed. It is exceedingly rare to find children who have not developed attitudes toward school by the middle of their first year's experience in a classroom.

Finally, the definition reminds us that an attitude is, in a sense, a personal *evaluation.* It contains either a positive element (liking, wanting to be near) or a negative element (disliking, wanting to escape).

There are a number of techniques commonly used to assess attitudes. Almost all these techniques can be grouped under the headings "teacher ratings," "observer ratings," "ratings under simulated conditions," and "self-ratings." None of these techniques can be used with much confidence if the goal is precise assessment of the attitudes of a particular person. Too much error is likely to creep into individual assessments, thereby masking the true score. But, if the measurements are carefully made, groups can be assessed with relative accuracy. For example, we can show with some assurance that in general a particular program creates more positive attitudes toward the Navy as a career than some other program does. More than one assessment technique should be used if the evaluator wishes to increase confidence in his conclusions.

Teacher ratings. If we want to know whether a person has a positive attitude toward school, or whether, for example, he enjoys mathematics, a useful technique is to get the teacher or instructor to rate the person on these dimensions. The rationale is that the teacher has had sufficient experience with the student's behavior to be able to make correct inferences about the student's attitudes. A reasonable method is to give the teacher a five-point scale with the points carefully delineated. Here is an example of a descriptive-graphic rating scale:

> *Directions.* Make your ratings on each of the following attitudes by placing an X anywhere along the line. If you have insufficient knowledge of the person to make a particular rating, put a check mark in the margin and go on to the next rating.

Attitude Toward Reading Lessons

1	2	3	4	5
Acts bored, slow to take out materials, strongly prefers other activities.		Seems about as eager as other class members in reading lessons.		Asks teacher for reading activities, becomes happy and excited when reading lessons begin, often is seen reading.

People using the teacher-rating technique to assess the attitudes of students should be aware of certain persistent problems (see also **Ratings**): (1) Some teachers tend to use only one part of a scale for rating almost all students in their classes. The ratings may be oversevere, overcautious, or overgenerous. Whatever the reason for their using mainly one section of the scale, the result is that each student has about the same score. Thus, the assessments usually cannot be used for their intended purposes; e.g., to find the students who need special help or to see which programs elicit the most positive attitudes. Therefore, unless the class members are atypically uniform in their attitudes, a teacher should be encouraged to use all of the scale. (2) Most teachers tend to be influenced in their ratings by their overall impression of a student. If the teacher likes a student, he tends to rate the student high across all the desirable attitudes being assessed. This **Halo Effect** obscures the strengths and weaknesses of a student's attitude structure. It can be mitigated, though probably not eliminated, if teachers are warned about the tendency. (3) Sometimes ratings are invalid because the rater feels that his ratings of students or trainees will in some way be used to evaluate him, the rater. For example, suppose he hears that the school principal evaluates a teacher in part by the proportion of children in his class who have poor attitudes. Is the teacher now likely to rate his students generously? A rater is not likely to provide valid ratings if he imagines that there may be some consequences to him based on his ratings.

Observer ratings. To avoid the last problem, an independent observer might be introduced into the classroom to rate the student's attitudes. This procedure can involve a large commitment of time on the rater's part if all students in the class are to be rated. Even if only one student is to be rated, it might be some time before the situation offers an opportunity for the relevant behavior to occur so that the observer can make inferences about the student's attitudes. (See **Observation Techniques.**)

Ratings under simulated conditions. It is time consuming to follow a student around in a classroom for a long enough period to allow an independent observer to be able to infer his attitudes toward school and specific school-related activities. An observer with some training in clinical techniques could set up a room or corner of a room to simulate, say, a training environment. By setting up situations for the student in this simulated situation, directing conversations, and observing reactions, the observer can shorten the time required to make usefully accurate ratings of the student's attitudes. However, this is not a recommended means of assessing attitudes unless a skilled observer with special training is available. (See **Situational Tests.**)

Student self-report. An important and frequently used method of assessing attitudes is to elicit verbal behavior and then to make inferences about the attitudes that underlie that verbal behavior. At one extreme this might involve recording free conversations and then later carrying out a **Content Analysis.** At another extreme, the person whose attitudes are to be assessed is asked directly: "What do you think about this program?" "Do you like the teacher?" "Would you recommend this program to your friends?" Usually a paper-and-pencil test is employed to elicit verbal behavior. A method intelligible to students in the upper grades of elementary school and beyond is to provide a series of statements to which students respond "yes"-"no" (or "true"-"false"); for example:

> School is a very interesting place.
>
> I like to do extra work for my course at home in the evenings.
>
> I like to stay home from school.
>
> Each morning I look forward to coming to class.
>
> My teacher is often too busy when I need help.

It might be objected that items such as these are transparent; that is, the student will know what is being assessed and will react accordingly. Much depends on whether the person responding to the questions or statements sees the process as reflecting on him in some way. Anonymous self-report procedures are to be preferred whenever practicable.

Of the general problems that beset the self-report technique, one of the most worrisome is that the tester may intrude and to some degree affect the response being made. For example, female testers may affect males' responses, or the responses of a black may be affected by whether the tester is black or not.

If the evaluator wants to obtain an attitude score (rather than simply get answers to a few questions or responses to a few statements), there are a number of different ways by which self-report measures can be scaled (see **Scales**). The two most commonly used are those developed by Thurstone and by Likert. The Thurstone method involves scaling the predetermined attitudinal statements. A number of judges first rank these statements (say, from 1 to 10) from strongly negative to strongly positive. Each statement is then given a scale value (the mean of the judges' rankings). Here is an abridged example of a Thurstone-type scale on educational permissiveness:

	Scale Value
Students should work on whatever they want to in class.	9.3
Teachers and students should jointly reach consensus on a code of conduct.	6.1

> Students are given far too much freedom in to-
>   day's classroom.   2.4

The person whose attitude is to be measured is asked to agree or disagree with these statements. His score is found by ob- taining the mean value of the statements he agrees with.

In contrast, the Likert technique scales responses rather than statements. First, a number of attitudinal statements are col- lected, with neutral statements usually being avoided. The person whose attitude is to be measured responds to each statement by using, say, a five-point scale: 5, strongly agree; 4, agree; 3, not sure; 2, disagree; 1, strongly disagree. Each item is given a score from 5 to 1 corresponding to the scale, and the attitude score is obtained by summing over items. A Likert scale is easier to con- struct than a Thurstone scale and usually provides comparable data.

A third method of scaling attitudes through self-responses is the Semantic Differential developed by Osgood and his associates. The object toward which the attitude is directed (e.g., a place, a person, an idea) is seen as having three dimensions of meaning: evaluation (on a dimension from good to bad), potency (from strong to weak), and activity (from fast to slow). However, in most evaluations, these three dimensions are either ignored or else supplemented by others that seem logically to have greater rele- vance. Here is an example of the use of the Semantic Differential to assess attitudes toward countries.

> On each of the following pages there is a name
> of a country. It is followed by pairs of opposite
> words. Between each of the pairs of opposites are
> seven dashes. Put a check on the dash that indicates
> how you feel about that country. [An example would
> then be given.] What is wanted is your first impres-
> sion. There are no right or wrong answers. Make only
> one check for each pair of words. Do not skip any
> pairs of words or any countries.

AUSTRALIA

good	_ _ _ _ _ _ _	bad
passive	_ _ _ _ _ _ _	active
small	_ _ _ _ _ _ _	large

strong   — — — — — — —   weak
democratic   — — — — — — —   undemocratic
aggressive   — — — — — — —   peaceful
rich   — — — — — — —   poor
unified   — — — — — — —   divided
liberal   — — — — — — —   conservative
[Then the same pairs of adjectives would be used for other countries to enable comparisons to be made between countries.]

As other examples, students in a program could be asked to fill in a Semantic Differential on their teacher, the program itself, or themselves in the program. For any one of these, scores can be averaged across students in the program for each set of adjectives in order to obtain a global impression of the students' attitudes.

A fourth technique used to obtain scores from the self-reporting of attitudes is the *Q* sort originally developed by Stephenson. Here a person is given a set of cards, each containing an attitudinal statement. He then sorts these cards into piles—usually five. This technique and the more complex ones such as Guttman's scalogram, Lazarsfeld's latent structure analysis, and Coomb's unfolding technique cannot be given adequate treatment here. The references provided at the end of this entry should be consulted if more information is required.

Unobtrusive measures. Ideally, what a measure tells us about people's attitudes should *not* be a function of the presence of the tester or observer. One way of getting around this problem is to assess attitudes through records which are a normal part of an organization's routine data collection. Another technique is to look for simple pieces of physical evidence that indicate what people are doing—and then make inferences about attitudes accordingly. (See **Unobtrusive Measures.**)

Instrument selection. One question that an evaluator must face is whether to choose an already available attitude measure or to develop one himself, either by modifying available instruments or by starting from scratch. The availability of an appropriate instrument can be determined by a literature search (see **Test Selection**); but the vast majority of attitude measures will be inappropriate for any specific program evaluation. Constructing one's own attitude measure can be a complex task if it is to be done with technical sophistication. (The references provided with this article will provide guidelines.) One technique frequently used by evaluators is to take a measure already developed and modify it somewhat (e.g., by changing its vocabulary to make it relevant to the group to be assessed). Assuming copyright laws are not infringed, this kind of approach could provide a useful short cut.—S. B.

Ebel, R. L. *Essentials of Educational Measurement.* Englewood Cliffs, N.J.: Prentice-Hall, 1972. See especially Chapter 21 for a straightforward treatment of attitude scales.

Fishbein, M. (Ed.) *Readings in Attitude Theory and Measurement.* New York: Wiley, 1967. A relatively sophisticated presentation of virtually all aspects of attitude measurement.

Snider, J. G., and Osgood, C. E. *Semantic Differential Technique: A Sourcebook.* Chicago: Aldine, 1969. Includes discussions of the theory, methodology, and application of the technique.

Stanley, J. C., and Hopkins, K. D. *Educational and Psychological Measurement and Evaluation.* (5th Ed.) Englewood Cliffs, N.J.: Prentice-Hall, 1972. See especially Chapter 12, on assessment of the affective domain, for a clear and concise treatment of attitude measurement.

Stouffer, S. A., Guttman, L., Suchman, E. A., Lazarsfeld, P. F., Star, S. A., and Clausen, J. A. *Measurement and Prediction: Studies in Social Psychology—World War II.* Vol. 4. Princeton, N.J.: Princeton University Press, 1950. See pages 46-90 for a description of attitude scaling and problems of validity.

─────────────── AUDIT OF EVALUATION ───────────────

The idea of auditing evaluations came from the educational **Accountability** movement that developed in the 1960s. The accountability movement has been variously defined. Definitions include the vague and hopelessly general "to provide equality of educational opportunity at all levels of learning for all children," Lieberman's more specific and useful statement that accountability occurs when resources and efforts are related to results in ways that are useful for policy making and resource allocation, and Barro's even simpler and more direct statement that the basic idea of accountability is that the educators who run schools and school systems should be held responsible for educational outcomes—for what students learn.

If educators are to be held responsible, then it is necessary to develop measurement and evaluation systems that provide the data on which to make judgments. But the "accountants" who usually carry out the evaluation and who provide the data (e.g., assistant superintendents of school systems, principals, school psychologists, directors of testing programs) also work for, and are dependent on, those who run the system. So, by analogy with the financial world, it is thought necessary to bring in external, independent "auditors." These auditors will be more objective, and the evaluations they monitor more believable.

The role of evaluation auditor was given considerable status by regulations and practices surrounding Titles VII and VIII of the Elementary and Secondary Education Act (programs in bilingual education and programs to help dropouts and potential dropouts). Each program was required to provide an accountability (evaluation) plan and to retain an independent agency (e.g., university, research and development center, testing service) to audit the evaluation.

The actual work to be performed by the auditor varies somewhat, depending on the skills of those in the school system, funding arrangements, and program considerations. In general, the auditor looks over the evaluation plans, suggests changes if necessary, and, after amendments have been made, approves the plans. He monitors data collection; that is, he sees that the evaluation plans for measurement are being implemented. Later, he checks some of the analyses to ensure that they have been properly performed. Finally, he reads an early draft of the evaluation report, suggests changes, and approves the final version.

The use of an auditor of evaluations (sometimes called the EPA, educational program auditor; sometimes, the IEAA, independent educational accomplishment auditor) helps to ensure that evaluations are properly carried out. This is crucial if it is thought that vested interests in the system are improperly exerting their influence on the program evaluation, or if those carrying out the evaluation lack sufficient expertise. Note that the use of an auditor is usually less costly than "farming out" the total evaluation to an outside agency. It also helps build the evaluation skills of those in the system who are working under the auditor's general direction. Note, too, that the auditor may be a team of people rather than one person—an attractive idea because the work of an auditor demands many different skills.

The auditor (or team of auditors) works for those to whom the school system is accountable—not for the system itself. Thus, in federally funded programs the school is accountable to the federal government for the effective use of the government's funds—and the auditor's institutional authority therefore comes from the federal government. In the event of a dispute between the auditor and those being audited, this distinction is important.

The audit is similar to **Secondary Evaluation** except that the secondary evaluator works *after* the initial evaluation has been completed. Secondary evaluations occur more or less spontaneously in the world of evaluation, but the auditor role is a cultivated role dependent upon the accountability movement for its growth.

The future of evaluation auditing is not clear. It seems to be heavily dependent on the support of major program-funding agencies. If they lose interest in the role of the auditor, auditing probably will become one more outmoded profession—S. B.

Barro, S. M. "An Approach to Developing Accountability Measures for the Public Schools." *Phi Delta Kappan*, 1970, *52*, 196-205.

Kruger, W. S. "Program Auditor: New Breed on the Education Scene." *American Education*, 1970, *6*, 36.

Lessinger, L. "Engineering Accountability for Results in Public Education." *Phi Delta Kappan*, 1970, *52*, 217-225.

Lieberman, M. "An Overview of Accountability." *Phi Delta Kappan*, 1970, *52*, 194-195.

———————— BASELINE MEASURES ————————

The term *baseline measures* is used in medical research and evaluation to indicate physiological measures obtained before the onset of disease, accident, or new treatment. It is used similarly in educational evaluation to indicate levels of performance of trainees before program intervention. These levels may be purposefully assessed through a **Pretest,** or they may be assessed through the use of routinely collected records (see **Unobtrusive Measures**).

Evaluators need to obtain baseline measures in order to determine the effects of an educational intervention. How can we estimate growth if we do not know where the students started? (See **Experimental Design.**) We can estimate relative growth without baseline measures if true random assignment of subjects to programs or "treatments" has occurred; that is, we can then infer that differences between an experimental group and a **Control Group** at **Posttest** are the result of the program or treatment. However, since random assignment does not always ensure comparable groups, subjects generally should be given a pretest as well as a posttest if the pretest to obtain baseline measures is feasible and if the pretest does not create reactive effects (see **Reactive Effects of Program and Evaluation**).

Evaluations frequently are undertaken without adequate baseline data. Sometimes, through lack of foresight, an evaluation is not envisaged until after the program is in operation (see **Ex Post Facto Design**). In other instances, a program is considered so urgent that it is implemented before an evaluation can be planned and baseline data obtained; some of the War on Poverty programs begun in the 1960s fall in this category. For whatever reason of neglect or priority, when baseline data are unavailable, evaluation results are likely to be equivocal and to stimulate considerable argument and confusion about whether the program was effective.—S. B.

Glaser, R., and Nitko, A. "Measurement in Learning and Instruction." In R. L. Thorndike (Ed.), *Educational Measurement.* (2nd Ed.) Washington, D.C.: American Council on Education, 1971. See especially page 663.

──────────────── BIAS IN TESTING ────────────────

Bias in measurement occurs when characteristics of the measures, the measurement process, or the interpretation of the results of the measurement lead to inaccurate inferences about the knowledge, skills, or other attributes of an individual or a group. In fact, the accusation of bias is most frequently made in the name of some subgroup in the tested population—a subgroup characterized by sex, ethnicity, or socioeconomic status.

Bias is really a matter of *in*validity; by definition, valid measurement cannot be biased (see **Validity**). Thus, any counsel to evaluators to ferret out biases in measurement stems from the general charge to ensure that measures used in an evaluation have sufficient validity to permit sound conclusions about the value of the education or training program. Such conclusions usually focus on whether the desired outcomes were achieved and are based on information derived from **Pretest** and **Treatment** measures as well as **Posttest** measures. If a program is directed toward heterogeneous groups of students, cautions about possible bias in the measures are especially pertinent, for it may be inappropriate for the evaluator to assume equivalence in the backgrounds of the test takers.

Bias in a measure may be attributable to the fact that the measure actually measures different things in different subgroups. For example, a test of mathematical reasoning may be just that for "majority-group" students, but it may be a test of English proficiency for Puerto Ricans or Mexican-Americans. To discount the possibility that the same instrument taps different processes in different groups, it is necessary to assess the reliability and validity of the test separately for different groups and to demonstrate the comparability of results. In this connection, the concept of construct validity is particularly critical. Bias in measures can also stem from irrelevant difficulties—for example, if the reading level required for the instructions on how to take a mathematics test is higher than the reading level of some members of the tested group. Bias can also stem from test items that are more germane to one group than another; items differentially favoring males and females, for example, have frequently been identified.

Another possible source of bias is the testing process or environment. Evaluators may assume that the testing situation will elicit maximal performance from those being tested, and, for participants from a culture where competition and achievement are stressed, this assumption is generally accurate; but if the test-taking group includes others who are not so motivated, then inaccurate measurements may be obtained. To do well, test takers must have a positive attitude toward the testing process, but members of some minority groups may enter the testing situation feeling negative and pessimistic about their chances of being accurately assessed and thus fulfill their own prophecy of bias. However, excessively motivated test takers may experience a similar decrement in performance through anxiety (see **Test Anxiety**). Varying amounts of experience in taking tests may also introduce some inaccuracies; however, there are few widely used tests on which scores appear to be susceptible to short-term improvements as the result of intensive coaching in the "tricks" of test taking (see **Test Wiseness**).

Determination of whether a given test is biased is both a

rational and an empirical process. Investigators may concentrate their attention on differences in the performance of subgroups at the item level (e.g., see Coffman), or they may be primarily concerned with differences in **Regression** equations involving total scores and an external criterion (e.g., see Cleary). It is important to note, however, that low scores per se do not necessarily indicate bias in measurement. Rather, bias may be inherent in the social, educational, or other forces that inhibited individual development.

While this discussion has focused on bias in tests, the same considerations apply to biases in other measures. As has been pointed out in many studies (e.g., see Crooks), **Ratings** are particularly subject to bias; and even self-report devices such as **Questionnaires** may be phrased in such a way that members of certain groups, wittingly or unwittingly, provide distorted pictures of themselves.

Bias is an issue, too, in measurement interpretation and use. While bias in measurement and unfairness in practice are often concomitants, they do not have to go hand in hand. Bias, perhaps unconscious, may influence evaluators to select inappropriate instruments, to ignore possible side effects attending the administration of a measure, to misinterpret the meaning or magnitude of test results (sometimes from an exaggerated expectation about the fallibility of tests), to use existing test results unwisely (or unethically) for a secondary purpose, or to apply inappropriate prediction equations to the selection or placement of students.—R. L. F., S. B. A.

Cleary, T. A. "Test Bias: Prediction of Grades of Negro and White Students in Integrated Colleges." *Journal of Educational Measurement,* 1969, *5,* 115-124.

Coffman, W. E. "Sex Differences in Response to Items in an Aptitude Test." In *18th Yearbook, National Council on Measurement in Education.* Lansing, Mich.: Evaluation Services, Michigan State University, 1961. Pp. 117-124.

Crooks, L. A. (Ed.) *An Investigation of Sources of Bias in the Prediction of Job Performance: A Six-Year Study.* Princeton, N.J.: Educational Testing Service, 1972. Proceedings of a conference held in New York City, June 22, 1972.

Humphreys, L. G. "Implications of Group Differences for Test

Interpretation." In *Assessment in a Pluralistic Society: Proceedings of the 1972 Invitational Conference on Testing Problems*. Princeton, N.J.: Educational Testing Service, 1973. Pp. 56-71.

Linn, R. L., and Werts, C. E. "Considerations for Studies of Test Bias." *Journal of Educational Measurement*, 1971, *8*, 1-4.

Messick, S., and Anderson, S. B. "Educational Testing, Individual Development, and Social Responsibility." *Counseling Psychologist*, 1970, *2*, 80-88.

Test Bias: A Bibliography. Princeton, N.J.: Educational Testing Service, 1971.

--------- CASE-STUDY METHOD ---------

A case study is an intensive, detailed analysis and description of a single organism, institution, or phenomenon in the context of its environment. The term has long been associated with law, medicine, and social work. The case study is also considered a legitimate method of inquiry in the social sciences and frequently is extended to several cases at once.

Evaluators of education and training programs may use the case-study method as their principal evaluation strategy, or they may use it in conjunction with formal evaluative research strategies. In the first instance, the evaluator is banking on the probability that a case-study (perhaps in only one or two training centers of a national program) will yield a sufficiently comprehensive picture to serve as the basis for relatively absolute judgments about the worth of the program. The methodology of the investigation may range broadly and include testing, classroom observations, content analyses of records and materials, interviews with students and staff, and descriptions of physical facilities and resources. Advocates of the case-study method point to its advantages in allowing evaluators to deal with variables that are hard to quantify —staff morale and institutional vitality, for instance.

Sometimes case studies are used as preludes to larger, more formal evaluation studies, both as the source of hypotheses that deserve investigation and for suggestions about variables and measures that should not be overlooked in the large-scale effort. Case studies are also useful as follow-ups to larger evaluation studies because they can shed light on unexplained or unexpected findings. For example, if the results of the evaluation of the reading program in a city school system indicate that students in two schools are reading much better than might have been expected on the basis of student and program characteristics, case studies might be conducted in those two schools to try to detect the reasons for their outstanding performance. If promising instructional techniques and procedures can be identified, they may then be passed on to other schools where performance was not noteworthy.

The evaluations carried out by regional accrediting associations are usually based on case studies of the schools being evaluated (see **Accreditation**). To obtain a broad, comprehensive view of the school, the accreditation process may include committee visits to the institution to make observations and to interview students and staff, as well as collection of statistical information on students, staff, and programs.—R. T. M.

Becker, H. S. "Observation: Social Observation and Social Case Studies." In D. L. Sills (Ed.), *International Encyclopedia of the Social Sciences*. Vol. 11. New York: Crowell-Collier and Macmillan, 1968. Pp. 232-238.

Dyer, H. S. "Toward Objective Criteria of Professional Accountability in the Schools of New York City." *Phi Delta Kappan*, 1970, *52*, 206-211.

Llewellyn, K. N. "Case Method." In E. R. A. Seligman (Ed.), *Encyclopedia of the Social Sciences*. Vol. 3. New York: Macmillan, 1930. Pp. 251-254.

Selltiz, C., Jahoda, M., Deutsch, M., and Cook, S. W. *Research Methods in Social Relations*. (Rev. Ed.) New York: Holt, 1960. See "The Analysis of 'Insight-Stimulating' Examples" (pp. 59-65).

Suczek, R. F. *The Best Laid Plans*. San Francisco: Jossey-Bass, 1972. An example of a case study focusing on personality growth in the first two years of college.

———————————————— CAUSALITY ————————

In evaluation causality plays a central but elusive role. The purpose of an evaluation—at least a **Summative Evaluation**—is to assign value to a program and its component parts and to make decisions about continuing, modifying, or terminating the program. It is in this decision-making phase of evaluation that causal relationships between program components and trainee achievement must be inferred.

In a well-designed experiment (see **Experimental Design**), **Variables** are manipulated in order to isolate the effects of independent variables operating on a dependent variable; disturbing influences are minimized by the use of at least one randomly selected **Control Group**; and assumptions are reduced to as few as possible. Under such conditions, causal inferences can be made with some degree of confidence. As the situation becomes more like the real world, manipulation of variables and isolation of effects become less possible, convenient comparison groups replace control groups, and more, and less plausible, assumptions have to be made. Nevertheless, almost all training and educational programs occur in the real world, where causal inferences are harder to make and the risk of making errors increases considerably. This being the case, it is essential that the nature and foundations of the inferences be clearly understood and the risk with which they are made be clearly and explicitly indicated. (See **Scientific Inquiry and Evaluation**.)

Webster's *New Collegiate Dictionary* defines *cause* as "something that occasions or effects a result; . . . esp.: an agent that brings something about." It is this "producing" component that appears to be essential to causality. Although day always follows night, we do not think of the one as causing the other. Similarly, although weight and height are significantly correlated in most groups of adults (see **Correlation**), we do not expect dieting to cause shortening. Blalock (1964, p. 9) describes this notion of "producing" as follows: "If X is a cause of Y, we have in mind that a change in X produces a change in Y and not merely that a change in X is followed by or associated with a change in Y."

It is the "producing" notion that is missing in correlation. Correlation indicates only a concurrent relationship. Two variables increase or decrease simultaneously. To ascertain that a change in one causes or produces a change in the other, more information is needed. Of course, the fact that variables are correlated gives one reason to believe that they might be causally related. If a general theory can be developed from the relationships that have been verified, it may then be possible to test several hypotheses against one another. As Stouffer (p. 296) has pointed out, "We need to look for situations where two equally plausible hypotheses deducible from more general theory lead to the expectation of different consequences. Then, if our evidence supports one and knocks out the other, we have accomplished something." Thus, the use of empirical data to identify plausible causal relationships is only one step in a process that must include the formulation and testing of explicitly stated hypotheses (see **Hypothesis Testing**).

A good explanation of the problem of identifying factors (school characteristics) that are causally related to pupil achievement is given by Dyer (p. 40):

> There is no guarantee that the school characteristics that turn up with the largest correlation coefficients or regression weights [see **Correlation** and **Regression**] are the factors that have actually produced the differences among schools in pupil performance, regardless of how elaborate the statistical procedures may be. Even were the analysis to give the teacher salary variables, for instance, a relatively large regression weight in the prediction of pupil achievement, the simple act of a salary increase in the low-achieving schools would be more likely to depress the regression weight than to elevate pupil performance. This line of reasoning is in strict accord with the classical doctrine that correlation does not necessarily imply causation. The doctrine, however, is oversimple. If indeed the data were to yield a relatively large regression weight for teachers' salaries, such a phenomenon could be translated into the not unreasonable working hypothesis that if salaries in low-achieving schools are made competitive with salaries in high-

achieving schools, then over the long haul there is at least a chance that pupil performance in the low-achieving schools will approach that in the high-achieving schools because of improved instruction.

Clearly, then, demonstrations of causality are not easy to come by. In social science research, there are so many disturbing influences to contend with that causation can only be inferred with a healthy dose of skepticism. It is this skepticism that protects us against oversimplification.—R. T. M.

Blalock, H. M., Jr. *Causal Inferences in Nonexperimental Research*. Durham: University of North Carolina Press, 1964. A good introduction to the rules of causal inference; written for the most part in nonmathematical terms.

Blalock, H. M., Jr. (Ed.) *Causal Models in the Social Sciences*. Chicago: Aldine-Atherton, 1971. A detailed and technical overview of many causal models used primarily in sociology, economics, and political science.

Coleman, J. S., Campbell, E. Q., Hobson, C. J., McPartland, J., Mood, A. M., Weinfeld, F. D., and York, R. L. *Equality of Educational Opportunity*. Washington, D.C.: U.S. Government Printing Office, 1966. Using correlational and regression analyses, relates a variety of school characteristics to pupil achievement and then, on the basis of these analyses, attempts to infer causation.

Dyer, H. "School Factors and Equal Educational Opportunity." *Harvard Educational Review*, 1968, *38*, 38-56.

Ennis, R. H. "On Causality." *Educational Researcher*, 1973, *2* (6), 4-11.

Stouffer, S. *Social Research to Test Ideas*. New York: Macmillan, 1962. A collection of the writings of Stouffer. See especially Chapter 13, on correlation analysis.

------------------------------ CEILING EFFECT ------------------------------

A test is said to have ceiling effect if many of those taking the test score at or near the maximum. Sometimes ceiling effect is due to poor test construction. If, for example, a test to assess medical students' knowledge of emergency surgical procedures does not represent the full range of difficulty of the content area but contains only relatively easy questions, then virtually all the medical students would have about the same high score, even though there may actually be considerable differences in how much they know about emergency surgical procedures. Because the test does not adequately sample the program content, the scores, bunched at the top level, are not meaningful assessments, and valid conclusions about the effectiveness of the program become impossible.

Ceiling effect can occur, however, even in well-constructed tests, in which case the scores may indeed be accurate indicators of student knowledge. An example of ceiling effect that is *not* an artifact of bad test construction occurs in **Mastery Learning** using **Criterion-Referenced Measurement**. It is quite possible that the content to be learned is finite, the students have learned all that content, and the test scores so indicate. But even when ceiling effect is not a test artifact, a problem remains. Ceiling effect reduces the variability of the scores, the **Reliability** of the measuring instrument, and the normality of the score distribution. Conventional parametric analyses of the data are sensitive to these reductions and, in general, should not be used. It may be necessary, therefore, to use **Nonparametric Statistics** instead for the analysis of data obtained under conditions of mastery learning. For example, one could compare the proportion of students achieving mastery under one program with the proportion of students achieving mastery under a different program. The point is that when assessment takes place at the end of a mastery-learning program, ceiling effect is to be expected and may be accommodated in the evaluation analysis by the use of appropriate nonpara-metric statistics.

The converse of ceiling effect is the less discussed but still important *floor effect*. A test has floor effect when those taking it score at or about the chance or minimum level. The cause of floor effect may also be poor test construction; for instance, when only the most difficult content areas in a course are covered. Floor effect also may be caused quite legitimately by the fact that few students understand what is being tested; for instance, when they are pretested in a subject area where most have received no in-struction.

Most evaluators will try to use the same test or equated tests at **Pretest** and **Posttest** for purposes of obtaining estimates of gain (or growth), because such a procedure allows the most valid inter-pretation of the results. But because floor effect is most likely to occur at pretest and ceiling effect at posttest, the choice of test needs careful consideration if problems are to be avoided. For if floor effect does appear at pretest, the evaluator will be unable to assess accurately the full impact of the program, because some of that impact will be absorbed in getting the students to a level where the test is sensitive enough to reveal growth in their achieve-ment. And, if ceiling effect occurs at posttest, the evaluator is unable to assess accurately the full impact of the program because, at least for some of the students, the test has not truly indicated the extent of their growth.

On some occasions, however, ceiling effect can appear at pretest. For example, suppose that a program for a heterogeneous group of students is being evaluated. The pretest scores might indi-cate that, at least for the better entering students, a ceiling effect already prevails. Obviously, then, with their scores already at or near the maximum, these students cannot show gain at posttest, and the evaluation will be compromised.

Such problems can be guarded against by ensuring that there are a sufficient number of relatively easy items (to provide a proper distribution of scores at pretest) and a sufficient number of relatively difficult items (to provide a proper distribution of scores at posttest).–S. B.

Anastasi, A. *Psychological Testing.* (3rd Ed.) New York: Macmil-
     lan, 1968. Contains a section on objective measurement of

difficulty (pp. 24-27); insufficient test ceiling also is mentioned (p. 6).

Blalock, H. M., Jr., and Blalock, A. B. *Methodology in Social Research.* New York: McGraw-Hill, 1968. Contains a section on floor and ceiling effects in measures of socioeconomic variables (pp. 35-36).

Diederich, P. "Pitfalls in the Measurement of Achievement Gains." In D. A. Payne and R. F. Morris (Eds.), *Educational and Psychological Measurement.* Waltham, Mass.: Blaisdell, 1967. See pp. 292-298.

CERTIFICATION

In recent years there has been increased use of assessment programs to certify and/or license a wide variety of personnel in trades and professions. Typical of such programs are the recently developed Merchant Marine Licensing Examination for use by the United States Coast Guard, the certification of general automobile mechanics by the National Institute for Automotive Service Excellence, and the certification program for members of the American Production and Inventory Control Society. While these and many similar programs were developed primarily to certify and/or license personnel in given fields, the results have a natural application to program evaluation as well.

In this entry, the recommendations for using certification and licensing examinations in evaluation of instructional programs are based on two assumptions: (1) that the best predictor of job performance is performance on similar tasks (see **Simulation** and **Situational Tests**) at the end of job training (the notion of behavioral consistency); (2) that evaluation and instructional programs should be comparable in their objectives and techniques; for example, if the examination for certification in accounting requires a student to balance a set of ledgers, the instructional program should require the student to perform similar tasks.

The type of certification examination advocated here is a special kind of **Criterion-Referenced Measurement**—namely, a minimum-competency test. Such a test meets the following requirements: (1) The content and ability that each test task is intended to measure is important to adequate job performance. (2) The set of test tasks is an adequate sample of the tasks required on the job. (3) Prepared and qualified applicants have sufficient knowledge and ability to respond correctly to each test task. (4) The minimum acceptable level of performance on each test task is established by competent job authorities.

Thus, both the instructional program and the certification examination must be based on an analysis of the occupation or job for which program and certification are designed (see **Job Analysis**). The task statements in the analysis are translated into behavioral objectives. This statement of objectives includes full descriptions of the conditions under which various performances are required and the standards that must be reached for minimum competence (see **Goals and Objectives** and **Standards**). These objectives are then used to guide the design of the instructional program.

In addition, the objectives may be classified according to their **Cognitive, Affective,** and **Psychomotor** content and turned into specifications for a test that samples occupational behavior at the appropriate level. Test items are then constructed to provide as direct a sample of job behavior as possible. For example, in certain of the trades, such as welding and carpentry, the test would involve actual welding or construction; in other instances, where predominantly cognitive activities are involved, the level of cognition required on the job would be duplicated as precisely as possible in the written examination questions.

In some occupations (e.g. law, medicine, teaching, electrical work), certification is a basic requirement before a person can legally begin work. In an attempt to ensure competency among schoolteachers, every state has adopted teacher-certification requirements. In most states the "approved-programs" approach is used. That is, teacher-education programs are approved (the institutions have been given **Accreditation**), and the graduates of these approved programs are more or less automatically certified. Accreditation is achieved through the National Council for Accreditation of Teacher Education (N-CATE). In some states an examination has to be passed (the National Teacher Examination) before a person is certified. The passing score is fixed by the state. (See Woellner.)

The results for individual candidates on the certification examination can be used not only to determine whether minimum competency has been achieved but also for diagnosis and guidance when minimum competency has not been reached. The areas in which the candidate has not demonstrated proficiency can be identified and appropriate remedial work prescribed. The results for a number of candidates who have passed through the instructional process can be used to estimate the effectiveness of the program as a whole and to suggest areas in which program improvement may be needed, as long as the evaluator takes into account the fact that beginning students differ markedly from program to program.—R. F. T., R. G. W.

Shimberg, B., Esser, B., and Kruger, D. H. *Occupational Licensing: Practices and Policies.* Washington, D.C.: Public Affairs Press, 1973.

Shimberg, B., and Thornton, R. F. *Development of Improved Examination Procedures for the Promotion of Police Officers in New York City.* Princeton, N.J.: Educational Testing Service, 1972.

Siegel, A. I., Bergman, B. A., and Federman, P. *Some Techniques for the Evaluation of Technical Training Courses and Students.* Lowry Air Force Base, Colo.: Technical Training Division, 1972. See especially the section on criterion- and norm-referenced testing (pp. 26-30).

Thornton, R. F., and Wasdyke, R. G. *A Taxonomy of Behaviors for Career Development and Measurement.* Princeton, N.J.: Educational Testing Service, 1972.

Woellner, E. H. *Requirements for Certification for Elementary Schools, Secondary Schools, Junior Colleges.* (38th Ed.) Chicago: University of Chicago Press, 1973.

—————————— CHANGE MEASUREMENT ——————————

Almost any educational program is designed to induce some type of change in the program participants: to improve reading skills, to change attitudes, to teach people a manual skill. In all such cases we want the students to be different in some way, after instruction, from the way they were prior to instruction. Thus, change measures frequently play a prominent role in evaluation studies.

Difference scores. Possibly the most intuitively natural measure of change is a simple *difference score.* When the dieter wants to know how much weight he has lost, he simply subtracts his current weight from the amount he weighed at the beginning of his diet. Similarly, the evaluator frequently subtracts a student's **Pretest** score (the score obtained prior to his experiencing the educational program) from his **Posttest** score. Unfortunately, simple difference scores have several limitations that make their appropriateness in many evaluation contexts questionable.

The use of simple difference scores implies an assumption that the scales of measurement of the pretest and the posttest are equal. When available, alternate forms of the same test would usually provide some assurance that the assumption of equal scales is reasonable (see **Equivalent Scores**). Unfortunately, alternate forms are not always available for the tests of primary concern to the evaluator.

A second limitation of difference scores is due to errors of measurement in the pretest and the posttest. The **Reliability** of the difference between two fallible measures is typically less than the reliability of either measure alone. The reliability of a difference score depends on the reliabilities of the two measures (e.g., pretest and posttest) and on the **Correlation** between them. If everything else is held constant, the reliability of the difference score decreases as the correlation between the pretest and the posttest increases. For example, if the pretest and the posttest have equal variances and both have reliabilities of .80, the reliability of the difference score would be .71 if the pretest-posttest correlation was .30, but the reliability of the difference score would be only .33 if the pretest-posttest correlation was .70.

A third limitation of difference scores is due to the well-known **Regression** effect. For evaluation studies, the regression effect is probably the most serious of the three limitations mentioned here. Stated simply, the regression effect refers to the empirical observation that, on the average, individuals who deviate from the group mean on the pretest will tend to be relatively closer to the group mean on the posttest (i.e., regress toward the mean). In other words, individuals scoring above the mean on the pretest are apt to have a lower relative position on the posttest than on the pretest, whereas individuals falling below the mean on the pretest are apt to have a higher relative position on the post-test than the pretest.

A good discussion of the regression effect in relation to measures of change may be found in Lord, and a detailed analysis of the problem will not be attempted here. However, we should call attention to the particular problem with regression effect that confronts evaluators who rely on difference scores when, by accident or design, the pretest scores of the experimental group are significantly different from those of the comparison group. Consider, for example, a compensatory education program where students are selected deliberately on the basis of low pretest scores and the program is offered to all who qualify. Available comparison groups will of necessity have higher pretest scores than students enrolled in the program (the experimental group). If the students in the experimental group exhibit greater gains from pretest to posttest than students in a comparison group, we do not know how much of that difference is due to the program and how much to regression effect. Regression effect alone may be responsible, and the conclusions about program effectiveness could be erroneous or misleading.

Groups such as classrooms or schools, rather than individual students, are sometimes the unit of analysis. For example, pretest and posttest school means may be used as the basic observations for comparisons between a group of treatment schools and a group of control schools. Under these circumstances, the problems of low reliability and of regression may be less severe; we can generally expect high reliability for the means and similar distributions of pretest means for the two groups being compared.

Residual gain. Instead of simple difference scores, *residual scores* are sometimes used as measures of change. To obtain residual-gain scores, a predicted posttest score is calculated for each pretest score from the linear regression of the posttest on the pretest. A residual gain is calculated by subtracting the predicted posttest score from the actual posttest score. Residual-gain scores provide a means of identifying individuals who have gained more than or less than expected on the basis of initial status (i.e., pretest scores). Correlates of residual gains are sometimes investigated in evaluation work. The correlation of a residual-gain score with some other variable is called a *semipartial* or a *part correlation*.

Estimated true change and base-free change. Problems of unreliability have led several investigators to propose methods of estimating *true change*; that is, the difference between the so-called true scores underlying the observed pretest and posttest scores. In Lord's procedure, estimates of the reliabilities of the pretest and the posttest are used in conjunction with the correlation between the pretest and the posttest to obtain the estimates. As noted by Cronbach and Furby, the resulting estimated true gain is as good as or better than a simple difference score.

Two components of true gains have been identified: one that is completely dependent on true initial status (i.e., true score on the pretest) and one that is completely independent of true initial status. The latter component is called a *base-free measure of change.* Such a measure, as proposed by Tucker, Damarin, and Messick (p. 457), is "primarily intended for correlational work." Thus, the base-free measure of change might be used to identify characteristics of people who gain more than expected on the basis of true pretest scores. The base-free measure of change is an estimated true residual-gain score and is better than a simple residual-gain score that does not take reliability of the measures into account.

Are change scores necessary? Although measures of change are frequently used in evaluation studies and much has been written on methodological issues in the measurement of change, it is not clear that the direct measurement of change is essential to most of the questions that are asked. In the words of Cronbach and Furby (p. 80), "Investigators who ask questions regarding gain scores would ordinarily be better advised to frame their questions in other ways." Cronbach and Furby recommend procedures that do not require the estimation of individual measures of change. Their recommended procedures enable the investigator to address the study question directly without becoming involved with the actual estimation of change scores. For example, Cronbach and Furby (p. 78) argue that there is "no need to use measures of change as dependent variables" in **Experimental** or **Quasi-Experimental** studies. They prefer analyses that treat the posttest as the dependent variable. Werts and Linn also conclude that the posttest, rather than gain or residual-gain scores, should be the dependent variable when a linear regression model is used to investigate the determinants of growth. From this perspective, initial status is best treated on an equal footing with other potential determinants of later status.—R. L. L.

Carver, R. P. "Special Problems in Measuring Change with Psychometric Devices." In *Evaluative Research: Strategies and Methods*. Pittsburgh: American Institutes for Research, 1970. Pp. 48-66.

Cronbach, L. J., and Furby, L. "How We Should Measure 'Change' —or Should We?" *Psychological Bulletin,* 1970, *74,* 68-80.

Lord, F. M. "Elementary Models for Measuring Change." In C. W. Harris (Ed.), *Problems in Measuring Change.* Madison: University of Wisconsin Press, 1963. Pp. 21-38.

Tucker, L. R., Damarin, F., and Messick, S. J. "A Base-Free Measure of Change." *Psychometrika,* 1966, *31,* 457-473.

Werts, C. E., and Linn, R. L. "A General Linear Model for Studying Growth." *Psychological Bulletin,* 1970, *73,* 17-22.

—————————————— COGNITIVE STYLES ——————————————

In recent years, several new dimensions of individual differences in the performance of cognitive tasks have been isolated. These dimensions, called cognitive styles, appear to reflect consistencies in the manner or form of cognition, as distinct from the content of cognition or the level of cognitive skill displayed. Conceptualized as information-processing habits that develop in harmony with underlying personality characteristics, cognitive styles appear in the form of stable preferences, attitudes, or habitual strategies which characterize a person's modes of perceiving, remembering, thinking, and problem solving. As such, their influence extends to almost all human activities that implicate cognition, including social and interpersonal functioning.

Some examples might be helpful in understanding these styles and their pervasive involvement in learning, thinking, and social interaction.

Field independence-field dependence refers to a preference for approaching the environment in analytical terms as opposed to a preference for experiencing events globally in an undifferentiated fashion. Field-independent (analytical) individuals tend to perceive figures as discrete from their backgrounds; they are generally facile on tasks requiring differentiation and analysis, whether in identifying the presence of logical errors or in understanding the point of a joke; this analytical penchant leads as well to a high degree of differentiation of the self from its context. Field-dependent (global) individuals, on the other hand, tend to identify with a group; they are perceptive and sensitive to social characteristics such as faces and names, susceptible to external influence, and markedly affected by isolation from other people.

Leveling-sharpening concerns individual differences in remembering, especially different tendencies to distort or modify memory traces over time. Individuals at the leveling extreme tend to blur similar memories and to merge perceived objects or events with similar, but not identical, events recalled from previous experience. Sharpeners, at the other extreme, are less prone to confuse similar objects and, by contrast, may even magnify small differences between similar memories and thereby judge the present to be less similar to the past than is actually the case.

Risk taking-cautiousness refers to consistent individual differences in willingness to take chances to achieve desired goals as opposed to a tendency to seek certainty and to avoid exposure to risky situations.

Impulsivity-reflectiveness involves individual consistencies in the speed with which hypotheses are formulated and information processed. Impulsive individuals tend to offer the first answer that occurs to them (even though it is frequently incorrect); reflective individuals tend to ponder various possibilities before deciding. (Slowness of response, however, is not necessarily indicative of reflectiveness; other evidence needs to be brought to bear before that inference is appropriate.)

Breadth of categorizing entails consistent preferences for broad inclusiveness, as opposed to narrow exclusiveness, in establishing an acceptable equivalence range for categories. Broad cate gorizers tend to include many diverse entities (objects, things, persons, or ideas) within a single category, whereas narrow categorizers require many distinct categories for classifying similar or related objects.

Other cognitive styles include *cognitive complexity versus simplicity, extensiveness versus intensiveness of scanning, constricted versus flexible control, conceptualizing styles,* and *tolerance for unrealistic experiences* (Kagan and Kogan; Messick).

From these brief descriptions, it should be clear that such styles reflect aspects of personality as well as aspects of cognition. Thus, although they function to control and regulate the course of information processing and are typically measured as response consistencies on cognitive tasks, their operation may be in the service of underlying personality traits; for such dynamic themes as anxiety over error, expectancy of success and failure, and vulnerability to distraction are central to many of the measures utilized in their assessment.

Cognitive styles differ from intellectual abilities in a number of ways. Ability dimensions essentially refer to the content of cognition, or the question of "What?"—what kind of information is being processed by what operation in what form? Cognitive styles, on the other hand, bear on the question of "How?"—that is, on the manner in which the behavior occurs. The concept of ability implies the measurement of capacities in terms of *maximal* performance, whereas the concept of style implies the measurement of preferred modes of operation in terms of *typical* performance.

Abilities, furthermore, are generally thought of as unipolar, while cognitive styles are typically considered to be bipolar. For example, the amount of mechanical aptitude that a person exhibits may range from very little to a great deal; the presence of mechanical aptitude predisposes him to achieve in certain areas, but its absence implies only that he possibly will not achieve at the same level. Cognitive styles, on the other hand, range from one extreme to the opposite extreme. Each end of the dimension has different implications for cognitive functioning. For example, an analytical, field-independent person will try to induce the inherent structure in a situation or to impose his own structure on it, rather than have structure imposed from without. At the opposite end of the dimension, a global, field-dependent person will probably prefer to have the structure provided, perhaps in the form of detailed instructions.

Another major way in which abilities differ from cognitive styles is in the values usually placed upon them. While we may tend to value high quantitative aptitude over low quantitative aptitude, for example, we would hardly have the same general preference for broad as opposed to narrow categorizing tendencies or for risky as opposed to cautious strategies. Neither end of cognitive-style dimensions is uniformly more adaptive. Their adaptiveness depends upon the nature of the situation and upon the cognitive requirements of the task at hand. Therefore, cognitive styles are usually not considered as outcome objectives of education/training programs—except possibly for younger students. (With younger students, whose habits of seeing and thinking are still relatively malleable, programs might attempt to foster student flexibility in consciously applying different stylistic approaches appropriate to the characteristics of different situations and tasks.) Rather, cognitive styles are important to consider as input **Variables** that might moderate the operation and effectiveness of education/training programs or interact with program components to produce differential results (see **Trait-Treatment Interaction**).—S. M.

Kagan, J., and Kogan, N. "Individual Variation in Cognitive Proc-
esses." In P. H. Mussen (Ed.), *Carmichael's Manual of Child
Psychology.* New York: Wiley, 1970. Pp. 1273-1365.
Messick, S. "The Criterion Problem in the Evaluation of Instruc-
tion: Assessing Possible, Not Just Intended, Outcomes." In
M. C. Wittrock and D. E. Wiley (Eds.), *The Evaluation of
Instruction: Issues and Problems.* New York: Holt, 1970.
Pp. 183-202.
Gardner, R. W., Holzman, P. S., Klein, G. S., Linton, H. B., and
Spence, D. P. "Cognitive Control: A Study of Individual
Consistencies in Cognitive Behavior." *Psychological Issues,*
1960, *2* (4).
Witkin, H. A., Dyk, R. B., Faterson, H. F., Goodenough, D. R.,
and Karp, S. A. *Psychological Differentiation.* New York:
Wiley, 1962. An extensive examination of field indepen-
dence and dependence.

───────── COGNITIVE VARIABLES ─────────

In evaluation studies, **Variables** may be categorized as input,
program, context, assessment, and outcome variables, depending
upon the purposes of measuring them. The input and outcome
variables are usually characteristics of the students and are commonly divided into the following three groups: cognitive, affective, and psychomotor (see **Affective Variables** and **Psychomotor
Variables**).

The cognitive variables are concerned with "knowing," as
distinct from "feeling" and "acting." Included are such behaviors
as perceiving, discovering, recognizing, judging, memorizing, learning, and thinking. Of course, the human process of knowing is so
rich and complex that all its components cannot possibly be identified. Nevertheless, in most training programs the trainees will
have to memorize a number of facts; they will have to read and
understand written materials; they will have to analyze and inter-

pret instructions. All these behaviors are primarily cognitive. In any evaluation, an attempt must be made to assess the extent to which the trainees develop in these areas.

The most widely used classification scheme for the cognitive variables, presented in Bloom's *Taxonomy of Educational Objectives,* groups the variables into the following six major classes: knowledge, comprehension, application, analysis, synthesis, and evaluation. *Knowledge* includes behaviors concerned primarily with remembering, as demonstrated by either recognition or recall. *Comprehension* goes somewhat further and includes the literal understanding of a written or oral communication. *Application* includes comprehension but goes beyond it in requiring the trainee to use in a related or entirely new situation what he has already comprehended. *Analysis* involves not only the appropriate generalization of what is comprehended but also the breaking down of the material comprehended into its constituent parts and the detection of the relationships of the parts to one another. *Synthesis,* on the other hand, involves the operation of combining elements and parts in such a way that a new pattern or structure becomes apparent. Finally, *evaluation* involves some combination of all the other five behaviors. It is defined as making judgments about ideas, works, solutions, methods, materials, etc., on the basis of criteria and standards. Although evaluation may focus on affective behavior when values, likes, and enjoyment play a part in the behavior, nevertheless the evaluation itself is a cognitive rather than an emotive judgment. For further details on the subdivisions of the six major classes, see Bloom's text. (See also **Taxonomies of Objectives.**)

In the past two decades a great deal of research has been devoted to the identification and measurement of cognitive variables. The *Kit of Reference Tests for Cognitive Factors* prepared by French, Ekstrom, and Price is a rich source of information about cognitive factors. Tests for imagination, originality, flexibility, and other cognitive behaviors have been developed by J. P. Guilford and his associates at the University of Southern California.

In any evaluation, a broad scope of cognitive variables must be taken into consideration. It is not sufficient simply to test trainees for recognition and recall of facts if program objectives include much more than that. Unfortunately, such oversimplified assessment of trainee behavior is not uncommon. Knowledge of facts is easy to test for. In a good training program, however, trainees will learn to do much more than memorize facts. A good evaluation must therefore assess more than mere recall.—R. T. M.

Bloom, B. S. (Ed.) *Taxonomy of Educational Objectives: Handbook I: Cognitive Domain.* New York: McKay, 1956. The basic source for the classification of cognitive variables. Examples of test items for many of the classes and subclasses are given.

French, J. W., Ekstrom, R. B., and Price, L. A. *Kit of Reference Tests for Cognitive Factors.* Princeton, N.J.: Educational Testing Service, 1963. The manual accompanying this kit gives a concise summary of the more important cognitive factors and describes the tests used to measure these factors.

Guilford, J. P. *The Nature of Human Intelligence.* New York: McGraw-Hill, 1967. The structure-of-intellect model provides a cross-classification scheme for fairly specific cognitive dimensions.

Guilford, J. P. *A General Summary of Twenty Years of Research on Aptitudes of High-Level Personnel.* Los Angeles: University of Southern California, 1969.

Thornton, R. F., and Wasdyke, R. G. *A Taxonomy for the Development of Multidimensional Test Specifications.* Princeton, N.J.: Educational Testing Service, 1973. An interesting application of a complete taxonomy to the field of career development and testing.

COHORT

The term *cohort*, as used in the social science literature, seems to owe little of its meaning to its Roman-legion origins. In his presentation of a general model for studying age and maturation, Schaie (p. 93) defined *cohort* as "the total population of organisms born at the same point or interval in time." Specifically, Schaie was concerned about disentangling the components of developmental change—the age of the person, the cohort to which he belongs (reflecting cultural impact), the time of measurement (reflecting environmental impact) and the interactions among these components. For example, his model takes account of the inherent differences between a five-year-old child in 1970 and a five-year-old in 1975, and between a five-year-old tested at the beginning of kindergarten and a child of the same age tested at the end of the kindergarten experience.

Frequently, the term *cohort* is used in designs of experimental or evaluation studies without precise concern for age. For example, it is used to describe all subjects at the same educational level or entering a particular training phase at a given time—students in grade 7 in 1973, the members of a given class at West Point, or the group beginning a navy electronics training program on a particular date. (See also **Experimental Design, Cross-Sectional Study**, and **Longitudinal Study**.)—S. B. A.

Ball, S., and Bogatz, G. A. "Summative Research of *Sesame Street*: Implications for the Study of Preschool Children." In A. D. Pick (Ed.), *Minnesota Symposia on Child Psychology*. Vol. 6. Minneapolis: University of Minnesota Press, 1972. Pp. 3-17.

Kessen, W. "Research Design in the Study of Developmental Problems." In P. Mussen (Ed.), *Handbook of Research Methods in Child Development*. New York: Wiley, 1960. Pp. 36-70.

Schaie, K. W. "A General Model for the Study of Developmental Problems." *Psychological Bulletin,* 1965, *64*, 92-107.

———————— COMMONALITY ANALYSIS ————————

Commonality analysis is a technique for investigating inter-relationships among two or more correlated **Variables** in a **Regression** analysis. In observational studies, the variables used to predict a criterion variable are often highly correlated; thus, much of the predicted **Variance** associated with one prediction variable may just as well be associated with another prediction variable. For example, if student achievement is correlated with both school and socioeconomic variables, which are themselves highly correlated, then in a regression analysis for the prediction of achievement the addition of school variables after socioeconomic variables will show little *additional* predicted variance; neither will the addition of socioeconomic variables after school variables. Commonality analysis cannot assign, a priori, the portions of predicted variance to either set of variables, but it can present such interrelations for speculation and further investigation.

Commonality analysis partitions the predicted variance into parts associated with each possible combination of predictor variables. The part of the predicted variance that is attributed to a particular variable by itself is called its "uniqueness" (used in a different sense than in **Factor Analysis**). Commonality has been generalized for treating sets of predictors as a unit and for multivariate regressions.

Commonality analysis should not be confused with "communality" as used in factor analysis.—A. E. B.

Creager, J. A., and Valentine, L. D., Jr. "Regression Analysis of Linear Composite Variance." *Psychometrika,* 1962, *27,* 31-37.

Mayeske, G. W., Wisler, C. E., Beaton, A. E., Jr., Weinfeld, F. D., Cohen, W. M., Okada, T., Proshek, J. M., and Tabler, K. A. *A Study of Our Nation's Schools.* Washington, D.C.: U.S. Department of Health, Education, and Welfare, 1972. Reanalysis of data obtained in survey of *Equality of Educa-*

tional Opportunity (Coleman and others) to "discover what characteristics of the nation's schools are most closely related to school outcomes." Authors conclude (pp. xiii-xiv) that "the common influence of the school and the student's social background exceeds either of their distinguishable features."

Mood, A. M. "Partitioning Variance in Multiple Regression Analyses as a Tool for Developing Learning Models." *American Educational Research Journal,* 1971, *8,* 191-202.

Newton, R. G., and Spurrell, D. J. "A Development of Multiple Regression for the Analysis of Routine Data." *Applied Statistics,* 1967, *16,* 51-64.

Newton, R. G., and Spurrell, D. J. "Examples of the Use of Elements for Clarifying Regression Analyses." *Applied Statistics,* 1967, *16,* 165-176.

——————— COMPENSATORY EDUCATION ———————

Compensatory education is an intervention into the lives of people who are judged to have socioeconomic handicaps that would unnecessarily limit their school achievement or life chances. Thus, it is intended to be preventive. Compensatory-education programs are generally global in nature, attempting to make up for a broad range of learning supports and experiences that are missing or deficient in the home.

In actual practice the term *compensatory* is applied rather indiscriminately to a wide variety of educational and training efforts, particularly any of those directed toward minority-group members. However, especially in the context of considering appropriate evaluation strategies, it is of more than academic interest to try to distinguish between compensatory education and efforts bearing such labels as *special* or *remedial.* Like compensatory education, special education is usually fairly comprehensive and assumes that some preventive action is needed because of a condition beyond the student's control. However, the defining condition is usually physical (e.g., deafness, blindness, brain damage, cerebral palsy). Remedial education differs in additional ways from compensatory education: the decisions to apply it are made *after* some unsuccessful attempts at regular education, it allows for the possibility that the student bears some responsibility for his failure to learn the first time around, and it usually focuses on improvement in a specific, well-defined area (e.g., reading or arithmetic skills). We find many examples of remedial-education programs in industrial and military settings (e.g., basic-skills pretraining programs for minority-group members), as well as in educational institutions.

One of the first uses of the term *compensatory education* seems to have occurred in the early 1960s in connection with the McAteer Act in California, and the frequency of use increased greatly with the implementation of the Elementary and Secondary Education Act. The ESEA also brought evaluation firmly into the picture, with requirements and guidelines for evaluation of programs funded under it. However, those who have reviewed these evaluations have been disappointed to note that a great many of them reported nothing more substantial than numbers of students enrolled, expenditures for equipment, or statements that people thought the program should continue.

Since most compensatory education is considered an intervention—an attempt to change a discouraging prediction about future success—a desirable comparison group in an evaluation study would come from the same subpopulation (judged socioeconomically "disadvantaged") as the group involved in the compensatory-education program but would not receive the program. The evaluator can ask his question in another form: Did our **Baseline Measures** for the compensated group *under*predict their later success, as compared with a comparable group of uncompensated people?

Further, if we take the notion of "compensation" seriously, the evaluator of a compensatory education program should show whether the program does in fact compensate. It is not sufficient simply to show, for example, that students gained in certain knowledges or skills. Thus, a second appropriate group against which to compare the performance of the students in a compensatory-education program is a group of students similar in age, sex, and as many other respects as possible but judged socioeconomically "advantaged" or *not* needing compensation. The results from the first comparison group ("disadvantaged" and "not treated") may also prove important in interpreting the comparison between the "advantaged" and the "compensated" groups.

A rather different kind of evaluation consideration stems from the assumption that compensatory education is a major means of breaking the poverty cycle. Specifically, the compensatory-education program tries to provide substitutes for the kinds of stimulation for personal, social, intellectual, and vocational development that are deemed to be missing in the homes of poor people. However, there are probably alternative approaches to the same general goal; for example, social-action programs might be oriented toward increasing home supports directly or toward helping the poor expand their experiences and opportunities through the use of community resources that are not based in educational institutions. Evaluative research comparing the long-term results of compensatory-education efforts with some of these alternatives should provide a very valuable base for national policy decisions oriented toward the larger problem.

Critics of the concept of compensatory education point to the dangers inherent in categorizing people for educational purposes on the basis of *non*educational variables (e.g., family income, race) and also to the fact that decisions about needs for compensatory education are generally made about groups rather than about individuals. Those charged with evaluating compensatory-education programs may be well advised to take these criticisms into account by including within their province some appraisal of the appropriateness (and consequences) of the placement of individual students in the programs.—S. B. A.

Anderson, S. B. "Educational Compensation and Evaluation: A Critique." In J. C. Stanley (Ed.), *Compensatory Education for Children, Ages 2-8*. Baltimore: Johns Hopkins University Press, 1973.

Cohen, D. K. "Politics and Research. Evaluation of Social Action Programs in Education." *Review of Educational Research*, 1970, *40*, 213-238.

Hellmuth, J. (Ed.) *Disadvantaged Child.* Vol. 3. *Compensatory Education: A National Debate.* New York: Brunner/Mazel, 1970. Section II, Testing and Evaluation, includes important discussions by Campbell and Erlebacher, Cicirelli, and Evans and Schiller on the regression artifact problem in evaluation, and a chapter by Zimiles, "Has Evaluation Failed Compensatory Education?"

McDill, E. L., McDill, M. S., and Sprehe, J. T. "Evaluation in Practice: Compensatory Education." In P. H. Rossi and W. Williams (Eds.), *Evaluating Social Action Programs: Theory, Practice, and Politics.* New York: Seminar Press, 1972. Pp. 141-185.

Roueche, J. E., and Kirk, R. W. *Catching Up: Remedial Education.* San Francisco: Jossey-Bass, 1973. A review of a number of remedial programs at the higher-education level and techniques to measure effectiveness. Recommendations for program design and implementation.

——— COMPETENCY-BASED EDUCATION/TRAINING ———

A group of lecturers at a teacher-training college in Australia used to give the trainees an extended essay examination at the end of their two-year program—a long and rigorous essay examination. And then in the four weeks it took to mark the examination papers, the students went into the schools and had their last practice-teaching experiences. Finally, they returned to the college for graduation (commencement), when special prizes and teaching certificates were awarded. One year the graduation was quite memorable. The trainee who had, in the judgment of the education lecturers, turned in the best examination paper (on teaching methods) not only received her special prize—she *also* found out that she had failed her practice teaching. In the classroom she was incompetent, but she could write a great essay.

Teacher training has been beset with the problem of how to

train (educate) teachers and, having trained the teachers, how to evaluate the program and the students in the program. These are not problems unique to teacher education. In virtually every trade and profession there is a continuing debate on how to train/educate future members. And, of late, there has been similar concern about how to certify the students and accredit the program (see **Certification** and **Accreditation**).

Within teaching, advocates of *competency-based* or *performance-based* education seek to base teacher-education programs on whatever specific competencies a teacher needs (knowledge, skills, attitudes, etc.). Consequently, they have conducted research studies to try to determine the teacher behaviors that lead to student learning. This approach also has implications for the tests used to certify teachers (see **Criterion Measurement**). If a teacher's ability to write facile prose is *not* related to student learning, why bother to teach this skill in a teacher-education program and why bother to test this skill in a certification examination? These kinds of questions ought to be in the forefront then not only for program planners but also for program evaluators—whether the program is in higher education or plumbing.—S. B.

California Teachers Association, Commission on Teacher Education. *Six Areas of Teacher Competence.* Burlingame, Calif., 1964.

Cooper, J. *Competency-Based Teacher Education.* Berkeley, Calif.: McCutchan, 1973.

Elam, S. *Performance-Based Teacher Education: What Is the State of the Art?* Washington, D.C.: American Association of Colleges for Teacher Education, 1972.

Rosner, B. *The Power of Competency-Based Teacher Education: A Report.* Boston: Allyn and Bacon, 1972.

Schmieder, A. A. *Competency-Based Teacher Education: The State of the Scene.* Washington, D.C.: American Association of Colleges for Teacher Education, 1973.

Special Issue on Competency/Performance-Based Teacher Education. *Phi Delta Kappan,* 1974, *55* (5).

COMPONENT VARIABLES ---

In the entry on **Composite Variables**, the need and method for combining variables is explained. The composite variable Y is expressed as a linear (first-degree equation) composite of its component variables: $Y = A_1 X_1 + A_2 X_2 + \ldots + A_n X_n$, where the Xs are the component variables and the As are constants which weight the contribution of each component to the total. In this case it is assumed that the components are known and that the linear composite can be formed.

In other cases, however, the components are not known, and the investigator has the task of determining what they are. Typically he would seek to identify a few broad dimensions underlying a large number of measures. Suppose, for example, we want to obtain a composite achievement score for a trainee who has taken a battery of eight mathematics tests, six verbal tests, and six tests of general knowledge. By analyzing the tests, we may find that the mathematics tests actually test two different kinds of mathematical abilities (say, quantitative reasoning and computation speed). Or we may find that the verbal and general knowledge tests are really testing a single dimension of general intelligence. In this example, there are only three components underlying the data. Every test score then can be represented as a linear composite of the three components. (If only a single dimension had been identified that accounted for most of the variance in the original scores, this dimension would be called a *principal component*.)

There are standard methods for analyzing such an array of scores and reducing them to a smaller number of components which are relatively independent of each other. **Factor Analysis** is one such method. The chief difficulty in this process is frequently that of interpreting and "naming" the components it yields.

In evaluation studies, large amounts of data often have to be reduced to a relatively small number of components and then recombined into composite variables. For example, in the *Equality of Educational Opportunity* study (Coleman et al.) many scores were grouped together and analyzed for common components. Then the various components were combined into the composite variables used in the analysis. In *A Study of Our Nation's Schools* Mayeske and his associates reduce more than four hundred variables to approximately thirty composite variables for use in an interesting reanalysis of the Coleman data.—R. T. M.

Coleman, J. S., Campbell, E. Q., Hobson, C. J., McPartland, J., Mood, A. M., Weinfeld, F. D., and York, R. L. *Equality of Educational Opportunity.* Washington, D.C.: U.S. Government Printing Office, 1966. Probably the most ambitious study of American schools ever carried out. Contains many examples of the use of composite variables.

Harman, H. *Modern Factor Analysis.* (2nd Ed.) Chicago: University of Chicago Press, 1957.

Lord, F., and Novick, M. *Statistical Theories of Mental Test Scores.* Reading, Mass.: Addison-Wesley, 1968. A good technical explanation of composite tests with the appropriate formulas for relating the statistical properties of the composite to those of its components. See especially Chapter 4.

Mayeske, G. W., Wisler, C. E., Beaton, A. E., Jr., Weinfeld, F. D., Cohen, W. M., Okada, T., Proshek, J. M., and Tabler, K. A. *A Study of Our Nation's Schools.* Washington, D.C.: U.S. Department of Health, Education, and Welfare, not dated. Includes a detailed explanation of ways of combining variables into composites.

──────────────── COMPOSITE VARIABLES ────────────────

In the general article on **Variables**, the reader will find a description of input, program, context, outcome, and assessment variables. In addition, variables are described as **Cognitive, Affec-**

tive, and **Psychomotor** in the articles under those headings. In this entry, variables are treated according to their complexity.

If the age of each trainee in a training program is known, we can speak of age as a variable. To each trainee we assign a number corresponding to his age. The number may be his actual age, or it may be a scaled score based on his age. For example, we might assign the number 1 to trainees between ages 21 and 30, a 2 to those between 31 and 40, and so on. We could also assign a number to each trainee corresponding to such characteristics as number of years of schooling, clerical speed, or height. In general, these would all be simple variables.

In addition to measures on these variables, we might be interested in obtaining for each student a measure on the more complex variable of **Socioeconomic Status**. Ordinarily, this variable is formed by combining the trainee's scores on education, family background, family income, etc. We call socioeconomic status a composite variable because it is composed of several separate **Component Variables**.

While it is possible that a composite variable could be obtained by combining the scores of its component variables in many ways, in actual practice composite variables are usually *linear* combinations only. (For example, most test scores are composite variables consisting of the sum of scores on each question.) It is common practice to weight some elements of a composite more than others. Weights are frequently determined on rational bases; for example, if a composite variable is to be composed of achievement scores in various subject areas, it may be decided that some subject areas should count more heavily than others. Weights may also be determined by more sophisticated methods where differences between observed and estimated values of the composite are taken into account.

In general, a linear composite involves a sum of weighted components. If, for example, Y is a composite variable, then $Y = A_1 X_1 + A_2 X_2 + \ldots + A_n X_n$, where the Xs represent the component variables and the As are constants which weight the contribution of each X to the total. One of the useful properties of the linear composite is that the mean and variance of the composite are related by simple formulas to the means and to the variances and covariances of the components (see **Statistics**).

It is important to take the variability of scores into account in determining weights. If component scores are to be combined into a composite score, the scores should generally be standardized before they are combined (see **Score Types**). Failure to standardize scores can result in a misleading composite score. For example, a single measure with great score variability can overpower the contributions to the composite of scores on other less variable measures.

In any evaluation that involves a large number of variables, it is almost always necessary to combine the variables into composite variables in order to summarize the large number of relationships that exist among them. In such instances the variables usually are grouped into certain logical sets; for example, characteristics of the teachers, characteristics of the student body, and characteristics of the facilities. Then the variables in the different logical sets are correlated with each other, and each correlation matrix is factor-analyzed (see **Factor Analysis**), thus permitting the investigator to represent a large number of variables by a small number of factors. The "loadings" on the factors can then be used as weights in a linear composite equation.—R. T. M.

Coleman, J. S., Campbell, E. Q., Hobson, C. J., McPartland, J., Mood, A. M., Weinfeld, F. D., and York, R. L. *Equality of Educational Opportunity*. Washington, D.C.: U.S. Government Printing Office, 1966. Contains many examples of the use of composite variables.

Lord, F., and Novick, M. *Statistical Theories of Mental Test Scores*. Reading, Mass.: Addison-Wesley, 1968. A good technical explanation of composite tests with the appropriate formulas for relating the statistical properties of the composite to those of its components. See especially Chapter 4.

Mayeske, G. W., Wisler, C. E., Beaton, A. E., Jr., Weinfeld, F. D., Cohen, W. M., Okada, T., Proshek, J. M., and Tabler, K. A. *A Study of Our Nation's Schools*. Washington, D.C.: U.S. Department of Health, Education, and Welfare, not dated. Using the Coleman data, gives a very detailed and thorough explanation of ways of combining variables into composites.

————————— COMPUTER-ASSISTED INSTRUCTION —————————

Computer-assisted instruction (CAI) uses a computer system as a means of presenting individualized instructional material to a number of students simultaneously, the students usually sitting in front of individual display consoles. The central computer acts as intermediary between the student and a body of knowledge to carry out instructional strategies planned by the teacher or by external curriculum specialists. CAI is to be distinguished from computer-managed instruction (CMI): CAI refers to the specific instructional use made of the computer as a surrogate for the classroom teacher; CMI alludes to use of the computer in monitoring achievement and diagnosing, prescribing, and reporting on student progress.

The indefatigable computer can be highly responsive to each student's needs on a continuing basis; hence, instructional programs can virtually be tailor-made. The computer's capabilities for record keeping, for scheduling the most complex assignments, for storing in its memory infinitely detailed and ordered facts about the student, and for producing on demand a record of student responses make it possible to obtain instant diagnosis of and prescriptions for student work.

As instructor and educational manager, the computer opens up exceptionally rich possibilities for the evaluator. He may observe student behavior as it is acquired. Thus, the evaluator can talk about differences in learning rates more meaningfully, since he has *direct* evidence of how students have reached a criterion performance. The evaluator is also provided with a far more precise error-detection system than he has ever had before, since the computer can furnish with lightning speed a record of individual student misinterpretations and mistakes. The computer therefore provides the evaluator with a picture of the student's processes in learning, thus clarifying the effect of a curriculum. It permits the evaluator to abandon the classical mode of assessment, his time-worn reliance on end-of-course testing. He has an instrument superbly adapted to **Formative Evaluation,** permitting the modification and revision of curriculum according to need.

The process of designing instruction for the computer forces clarification of program **Goals and Objectives** because CAI requires the most precise analysis and specification of what the student is supposed to accomplish. Since the teacher is not to be present at every moment of instruction, the curriculum writer must clearly plan and present a minutely worked-out series of "enabling" objectives—foreseeing the step-by-step processes that can lead to the ultimate attainment of goals.

Moreover, the prompt and constant feedback to the student makes possible the benefits of student *self*-evaluation—a private assessment carried out under unpressured and unthreatening conditions. The impersonality and unobtrusiveness of the computer and the anonymity of the student interacting with it have often been cited as two advantages, especially to the slow student who has often been made to suffer under the embarrassing publicity of classroom learning. CAI appreciates the dilemmas of both the slow and the gifted learner. Because of the teacher's opportunity for unremitting monitoring of program effects and auditing of the processes of goal attainment, one student can be switched to a drill-and-practice program if indicated, and another be branched off to an enriched program of complex and challenging problem solving.

This article on CAI is included here because of its relevance to specification of instructional objectives and to formative evaluation. However, we do not mean it as a blanket endorsement of CAI. Critics of computer-assisted instruction point out that the technique is generally limited to specific knowledge and skills (as opposed to creative thinking and performance), that some students may be uncomfortable in its rigid setting, and that considerable work and expense are involved in preparing and offering good programs.

Evaluations of CAI programs themselves can and do contribute to evaluative research theory. Such evaluations have shown how far we must still travel to learn with accuracy the nature and sequencing of curriculum objectives, the optimal role of the classroom teacher, and the most desirable mode of integrating CAI with regular classroom processes.—E. J. R.

Association for Educational Data Systems. *Layman's Guide to the Use of Computers.* Washington, D.C.: AEDS, 1971. Provides discussions of the history of computers in education, computer languages, and the use of computers in education and training programs. Includes a useful, nontechnical glossary.

Farr, M. J. "Computer-Assisted Instruction." *Naval Research Reviews,* Sept. 1972, pp. 8-16.

Margolin, J. B., and Misch, M. R. (Eds.) *Computers in the Classroom.* New York: Spartan Books, 1970. A comprehensive introduction to and assessment of the major issues in computer-assisted instruction.

Meredith, J. C. *The CAI Author/Instructor.* Englewood Cliffs, N.J.: Educational Technology Publications, 1971. A nontechnical discussion of CAI and techniques for creating curricula for the computer.

Suppes, P., and Morningstar, M. *Computer-Assisted Instruction at Stanford, 1966-68: Models, Data, and Evaluation of the Arithmetic Programs.* New York: Academic Press, 1972.

———————————— CONFIDENTIALITY OF DATA ————————————

There has been increasing concern in recent years about invasion of privacy and the right of individuals to be protected from disclosure of information about themselves without their consent. Public awareness of problems involving confidentiality of data has been increased by publicity given to congressional hearings, conferences sponsored by foundations, and requirements of the Department of Health, Education, and Welfare that hold its contractors responsible for safeguarding the rights and welfare of human subjects, including their right to privacy.

There are many possible motives for violation of confidentiality of data contained in the files used for evaluation studies or for routine educational/training functions. These motives may range from mere curiosity to journalistic or business enterprise. The violations may include use of educational data (such as biographical information or test scores) to compile mailing lists for commercial purposes, to discover "chiselers" on welfare rolls, to support legal actions involving alleged discrimination, to provide information to potential employers, or to provide data for educational or research purposes other than those originally intended. Some of these violations may not harm a specific individual, some may do no more than cause embarrassment, but some may do great harm. The right of the individual to choose for himself (or the right of a parent to choose for a minor child) the extent of sharing of personal information has come to be recognized as an important ethical principle, and as a result many educational and research institutions are drawing up for themselves formal statements of policies and procedures to guide decision making in the area of confidentiality of data.

Here are some examples of statements of policy regarding confidentiality of data that an educational or research organization might consider adopting for itself:

1. Individuals shall not be asked to provide information about themselves, and the files shall not contain such information, unless it is clearly relevant to the aims and functions of the institution and unless the potential harm to individuals through disclosure of information is judged to be outweighed by potential benefits to the individual or to society in general.

2. Individuals have the right to privacy with regard to information about them that is stored in the files of the institution.

3. Information provided by individuals for a designated purpose shall not be used for another purpose without their informed consent.

4. Any individual has the right to request or authorize the disclosure to specific individuals or organizations of information about himself that may be stored in the file, provided that the disclosure does not violate the right to privacy of other individuals.

5. Procedures shall be adopted that make possible the maintenance of a continuous record of all transactions involving disclosure of information from the file.

6. Any individual has the right at any time to receive for review the information about himself that is contained in the file,

and he has the right to correct errors in personal or biographical data and to request verification of test scores or other processed information.

7. Procedures shall be adopted for systematically purging from files any information that because of the passage of time is of minimal usefulness.

8. Information collected for educational purposes may be used for purposes of educational research or evaluation only if the information is treated in such a way that it cannot be identified with any individual by program personnel, including clerks and keypunch operators as well as research investigators.

9. Individuals shall be identified in research and evaluation study files only by code numbers. If it is necessary to identify individuals by name for such purposes as follow-up studies or collating new data, information linking names and code numbers shall be kept in a secure location separate from the data. When its usefulness has ended, the list linking names to code numbers shall be destroyed.

10. A committee composed of concerned, interested, and informed individuals will be formed to advise educational administrators and researchers regarding problems of confidentiality and to consider periodically the need to revise the policies of the institution regarding confidentiality of data.

In the case where the institution works with children who are too immature to make wise judgments for themselves, provision should be made, in drafting such statements of policy, for the child's parent or guardian to make judgments for the child. —N. F.

American Psychological Association. *Ethical Principles in the Conduct of Research with Human Participants.* Washington, D.C.: APA, 1973.

Guidelines for the Collection, Maintenance, and Dissemination of Pupil Records: Report of a Conference on the Ethical and Legal Aspects of School Record Keeping. New York: Russell Sage Foundation, 1970.

Katz, J. *Experimentation with Human Beings.* New York: Russell Sage Foundation, 1972. Includes experimental studies from medicine, psychology, sociology, biology, and law in exploring the problems raised by human research and the attempts that have been made to resolve them.

Kelman, H. C. "The Rights of the Subject in Social Research: An Analysis in Terms of Relative Power and Legitimacy." *American Psychologist,* 1972, *27,* 989-1016.

"Protection of Human Subjects." In *Grants Administration Manual.* Washington, D.C.: Department of Health, Education, and Welfare, 1971. Chap. 1, Section 40.

"Protection of Human Subjects." *Educational Researcher,* 1973, *2,* 10-19. (Reprinted from *Federal Register,* Oct. 9, 1973.) Proposed policy regulating research involving humans.

CONTENT ANALYSIS

Content analysis is a general assessment technique by which complex phenomena (e.g., children's compositions, adults' conversations, chemistry textbooks) can be reduced to simpler terms (e.g., word-frequency counts, categorizations of the content of conversations, readability scores). Content analysis is termed a "general" technique because it is modifiable to obtain many kinds of data that an evaluator needs.

Consider a draft of a textbook for use in introductory chemistry classes. It may be subject to **Formative Evaluation**, and content analysis can be used to answer a number of questions:

1. How readable is the textbook? Using a readability formula (e.g., the Miller-Coleman Readability Scale), an evaluator can assess the reading-difficulty level of the book. He can, for instance, count the multisyllable words, assess the average length of sentences, and find the proportion of words *not* in the most frequently used thousand words (MacGinitie). Examining prose passages with these tasks in mind is a clear use of content analysis.

2. To what extent do the test questions at the end of each chapter cover the range of objectives presented in Bloom's Taxon-

omy of Objectives? If they mostly call for memory of facts, perhaps more questions calling for evaluation of evidence and transfer of knowledge to new situations should be included. To investigate the range of the test questions, the evaluator might categorize all the questions in the draft (or some appropriate sample of them) according to Bloom's taxonomy. In this use of content analysis, some hundreds of questions are reduced to a set of percentages corresponding to the categories in the taxonomy. (See **Taxonomies of Objectives**.)

3. How appropriate is the book for teachers who use modern teaching methods? In order to use content analysis to answer this kind of vague question, an evaluator must specify what features of a textbook make it "modern." These features might include certain kinds of programmed formats, questions for group discussion, and lists of experiments that individual students can carry out at their own pace and in their own home (ready availability of the substances called for would be important here). The draft of the book could be read and instances of the sought-after features noted.

Content analysis is also the basic tool behind **Job Analysis**; in this case, the "complex phenomenon" is a specific job, and the "reduced, simpler terms" might be a listing of tasks performed in a given time period. The point is that there is a need in job analysis to discover the essential features of a job, so that instructional programs for those who want to hold that job can be better developed. In addition, measures to evaluate the effectiveness of the training can be compared with the features indicated by the job (content) analysis, which becomes the proxy criterion.

Content analysis is frequently used in an evaluation to measure the treatment being administered. The treatment may be, for example, a television program or the teaching that occurs in a given classroom, and the evaluator should be concerned with being able to specify the nature of this treatment in detail. Methods for doing so are discussed in more detail in **Treatment Measurement** and **Observation Techniques**. Most of these methods are specific applications of content analysis.

Content analysis is often used as an early phase in the development of measuring instruments such as closed-ended **Questionnaires** and structured **Interviews**. The instrument developer presents an open-ended question (e.g., "What are the major problems you encountered in applying to graduate school?") to a sample of the target population. The responses are next subjected to a content analysis. For example, a frequency count might be made of all problems mentioned, ensuring that different wordings with the same meaning are counted as the same problem (e.g., "The admissions officers were slow in responding" might be regarded as basically similar to "No one seemed to answer my letters"). Now the question can be made closed-ended (structured) for the major study to be undertaken. The wording of the question might be changed somewhat to "What are the three most important problems you encountered in applying to graduate school?" and a listing of possible responses (provided from the content analysis) would then be presented. This method of developing the options to a closed-ended question is frequently to be preferred to some inspirational technique whereby the item writer simply writes out options that he thinks *might* be forthcoming.

Thus, content analysis is a general technique adaptable for various uses in evaluation—most notably, for describing complex phenomena in terms relevant to the evaluation and for helping in the development of measuring instruments.—S. B.

Berelson, B. "Content Analysis." In G. Lindzey (Ed.), *Handbook of Social Psychology*. Vol. 1. Reading, Mass.: Addison-Wesley, 1954. Pp. 488-522. A good introduction to the techniques of content analysis.

MacGinitie, W. H. "Language Comprehension in Education." In J. R. Davitz and S. Ball (Eds.), *Psychology of the Education Process*. New York: McGraw-Hill, 1970. Includes (pp. 131-136) a clear presentation of methods of obtaining readability scores through content analysis.

Ohlsen, M. M., and Schultz, R. E. "Projective Test Response Patterns for Best and Poorest Student-Teachers." *Educational and Psychological Measurement*, 1955, *15*, 18-27. Provides an illustration of the use of content analysis as a research and evaluation tool.

———————————— CONTROL GROUP ————————————

A control group in an evaluation study generally consists of a group of students who do not receive the education/training program of interest, as contrasted with an experimental group of students who do. This is not to imply that the control group necessarily receives *no* treatment. Frequently the control group goes through a traditional course of study in the same content area as the experimental program. Or the control group may be given a "placebo" program resembling the experimental program but not presumed to have the hypothesized effect. In any case, real-world control groups are not isolated from all stimulation while the experimental group goes through the instructional program under study; at the least, people in control groups go about their daily lives, which may or may not give them the opportunity to learn some of the things that the experimental program offers.

One of the major concerns of evaluators is to keep the "contamination" of their control groups at a minimum—by such devices as keeping the students and instructors for the experimental group apart from those in the control group and not making experimental program materials available to the control group. However, even the most conscientious efforts sometimes fail. For example, in the national evaluation of *Sesame Street,* a televised instructional program for preschool children, the children in the experimental group were actively encouraged to watch the daily program segments while the children in the control group were not. Even so, subsequent interviews indicated that many so-called control children were avid viewers. This finding required a drastic reshaping of the study analyses in order to draw valid conclusions about program effects. It is incumbent upon an evaluator not only to document the application of the treatment to the experimental group (see point 1 in **Discrepancy Evaluation**) but also to investigate whether the control group may have had more access to the experimental program than was anticipated. (Access could include a *diffusion effect* based on contact with experimental-group students or instructors.)

Usually every effort is made to ensure that the control group is as similar as possible to the experimental group in important respects, with the best insurance provided by random assignment of students to one of the two conditions. However, in some cases, the control group is deliberately selected to represent a "normal" or desirable level of functioning—e.g., when middle-class children are used as the "control" against which to evaluate the effectiveness of a **Compensatory-Education** program for poor children, or when successful managers are used as the control group in an evaluation of a management-training program for new employees. Even in such cases as these, however, attempts are made to "equate" the experimental and control groups on as many other relevant demographic variables as possible; e.g., age, sex, geographical location, ethnic background.

Some researchers prefer to restrict the use of the term *control group* to groups used in true experimental designs, or at least to groups chosen to be as nearly comparable to the experimental group in *all* respects as possible. Other kinds of groups whose performance is examined in relation to the performance of the experimental group are then called *comparison groups*. (See also **Design of Evaluation, Experimental Design,** and **Quasi-Experimental Design.**)—S. B. Λ.

Ball, S., and Bogatz, G. A. *The First Year of Sesame Street: An Evaluation.* Princeton, N.J.: Educational Testing Service, 1970.

Fisher, R. A. *The Design of Experiments.* (6th Ed.) New York: Hafner, 1951. A classic discussion of the logic of "randomization" (see especially Chapter IV) in the experimenter's strategy to avoid the criticism "His *controls* are *totally* inadequate" (p. 2).

Suchman, E. A. *Evaluative Research: Principles and Practice in Public Service and Social Action Programs.* New York: Russell Sage Foundation, 1967. See the sections on the "placebo" effect (pp. 96-100) and sampling equivalent experimental and control groups (pp. 102-105).

--------------------- CORRELATION ---------------------

In mathematics, certain characteristics can be related to each other by exact formulas. For example, every child learns that the area of a circle is equal to pi times its radius squared ($A = \pi r^2$). In the behavioral sciences, relationships between characteristics of individuals (weight and height or intelligence and achievement) cannot be expressed so exactly. Nevertheless, it is generally recognized that such characteristics are related in a probabilistic sense, if not by exact formula. The *correlation coefficient* provides a means for expressing the intensity of this relationship in a quantitative manner.

In 1886, Sir Francis Galton studied the relationship between the heights of fathers and sons. He showed that, if the heights of the sons and fathers were graphed on two axes, a straight line could be used to represent the relationship. Figure 1 illustrates the type of relationship Galton found. Note that the points representing particular fathers and sons do not fall *exactly* on the line. If all the points were to fall exactly on the line, the correlation between the heights of fathers and sons would be 1. The correlation coefficient indicates how well such data can be represented by a straight line.

A formula for calculating the correlation coefficient from

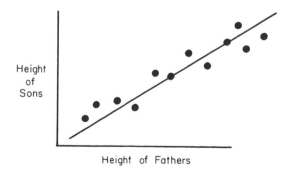

Figure 1. Illustration of Galton's data.

raw data was developed by Karl Pearson in the early 1900s. The formula deals with pairs of scores for a number of individuals; these scores are standardized. By definition, the Pearson product-moment correlation is the average of the products of the standard scores across the N pairs of scores. The formula for a standard score is $z_x = (X - \bar{X})/S$, where z_x is the standard score on some measure x, X is the actual score, $\bar{X}$ is the mean of the set of X scores, and S is the standard deviation of the set of X scores (see **Statistics**). The formula for the Pearson product-moment correlation coefficient (r_{xy}), then, is

$$r_{xy} = \frac{\sum z_x z_y}{N}$$

This formula, which corresponds directly to the definition, is seldom used actually to compute the correlation coefficient. By substituting the formulas for z_x and z_y, we obtain:

$$r_{xy} = \frac{\sum \left(\frac{X - \bar{X}}{S_x} \right) \left(\frac{Y - \bar{Y}}{S_y} \right)}{N}$$

Formulas for use in computing can then be derived rather easily (see Hays, Chapter 15).

The product-moment coefficient is the most commonly used correlation coefficient. However, it is not directly applicable to all kinds of data. For example, if scores on two characteristics are listed in rank order, the Spearman rank correlation (ρ) indicates how closely related the rankings are. The Spearman rank correlation can be calculated using the following formula:

$$\rho = 1 - \frac{6 \sum d^2}{n(n^2 - 1)}$$

In the formula, ρ is the correlation coefficient, d is the difference in ranks for each person, and n is the number of people. The following example can be used to get a rough idea of the information provided by this coefficient. Suppose that five persons are ranked from 1 to 5 on the five characteristics of height, weight, age, speed, and mathematical aptitude. These data are given in Table 1. It can be seen that the persons rank exactly the same on height and weight, exactly opposite on weight and speed, and closely on height and age. The relationship between mathematical aptitude and height seems minimal. The actual calculation yields ρ = 1 for height and weight: $\rho_{HW} = 1 - [6 (0 + 0 + 0 + 0 + 0)/5 (24)]$. For height and age, $\rho = .60$: $\rho_{HA} = 1 - [6 (1 + 1 + 4 + 1 + 1)/5 (24)]$.

Table 1

Person	Height	Weight	Age	Speed	Math. Apt.
A	1	1	2	5	3
B	2	2	3	4	1
C	3	3	1	3	5
D	4	4	5	2	4
E	5	5	4	1	2

The rank correlation between two variables is +1 if the individuals have the same rank on them; it is – 1 if the individuals have exactly reverse ranks on the variables. Other degrees of relationship yield correlations *between* +1 and – 1.

If many more persons were involved in the data, and if the actual raw scores on height, weight, age, speed, and mathematical aptitude were available, the product-moment formula would be used to calculate the correlation coefficient. It is very common to plot the actual values of the characteristics on a two-dimensional graph. When the points in the graph are examined, an indication of the magnitude of the correlation coefficient can be obtained. Typical graphs would look like those in Figure 2. In the cases where the correlation is +1 or – 1, the points lie on a straight line. For +.60 and – .60, the points lie in an ellipse. As the correlation becomes zero, the points are simply scattered in a circle on the graph.

In addition to the product-moment correlation and the Spearman rank correlation, there are several other correlation coefficients; however, they are used less commonly. Definitions of such coefficients as the tetrachoric, biserial, point biserial, phi,

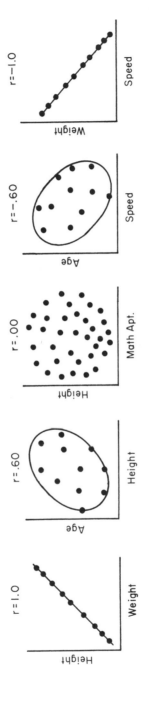

Figure 2. Graphical illustrations of correlations.
Adapted by permission from P. R. Runyon and A. Haber, *Fundamentals of Behavioral Statistics*,
Addison-Wesley, Reading, Mass., 1971.

kappa, and Kendall's tau can be found in a general statistics text. The eta coefficient, often called the correlation ratio, gives a measure of the relationship between two characteristics for which a curvilinear relationship is hypothesized. (The Pearson product-moment correlation defines a linear relationship.)

It is also possible to relate one characteristic to several other characteristics at the same time through a multiple correlation coefficient. For example, we might relate speed to both age and height. If speed and age have a correlation of -.60, speed and height have a correlation of -.70, and age and height have a correlation of .60, then the correlation between speed and a combination of both age and height can be calculated from the formula:

$$R_{S,AH} = \pm \sqrt{\frac{r_{SA}^2 + r_{SH}^2 - 2r_{AH} \cdot r_{SA} \cdot r_{SH}}{1 - r^2 AH}}$$

$$= \pm \sqrt{\frac{.36 + .49 - 2\,(.60)\,(-.60)\,(-.70)}{1 - .36}}$$

$$= \pm .73$$

By definition, the multiple correlation is the product-moment correlation between the predicted (independent) variable and the best linear composite of the predictor variables.

Finally, it may be important to know the correlation between speed and height when age is held constant, or "partialed out." The partial correlation provides a measure of the magnitude of such a relationship. It can be calculated from the following formula:

$$R_{SH,A} = \frac{r_{SH} - r_{SA}r_{HA}}{\sqrt{1 - r_{HA}^2}\,\sqrt{1 - r_{SA}^2}}$$

$$= \frac{-.70 - (-.60)\,(.60)}{\sqrt{1 - .36}\,\sqrt{1 - .36}}$$

$$= -.53$$

Thus, the original correlation of -.70 between speed and height is changed to -.53 when the effect of age is partialed out.

To summarize, the correlation coefficient gives an indication of the degree to which two variables are related. When more than two variables are involved, multiple and partial correlation coefficients can be used to indicate how one characteristic is related to a combination of two characteristics or how one characteristic is related to a second characteristic when a third is held constant. Finally, it is important to understand that correlations do not necessarily indicate causal relationships between variables (see **Causality**). Correlations at best can suggest hypotheses about causal relationship. These hypotheses then need to be tested in controlled investigations.—R. T. M.

Fisher, R. A. *Statistical Methods for Research Workers.* New York: Hafner, 1958. See especially Chapter VI.

Hays, W. L. *Statistics for the Social Sciences.* (2nd Ed.) New York: Holt, 1973. See especially Chapters 15 and 16.

Lord, F., and Novick, M. *Statistical Theories of Mental Test Scores.* Reading, Mass.: Addison Wesley, 1968. Gives theoretical foundations for many of the common correlation coefficients. See especially Chapters 12 and 15.

Maxwell, A. E. "Correlational Techniques." In H. J. Eysenck, W. Arnold, and R. Meili (Eds.), *Encyclopedia of Psychology.* Vol. 1. New York: Herder and Herder, 1972. Pp. 221-224.

McNemar, Q. *Psychological Statistics.* (4th Ed.) New York: Wiley, 1969.

— COST CONSIDERATIONS AND ECONOMIC ANALYSIS —

Much of the recent discussion of **Accountability** in education has, as an underlying premise, the assumption that improved information and reward structures can contribute to the productivity (or efficiency) of resource use in education. The entire funding structure of education/training programs at federal, state, and local levels, and in both the public and private sectors, could be based on the economic principle of return on investment. Are the benefits that result from this complex structure of education and training worth the cost involved? Specifically: (1) Can the same benefits be obtained at less cost? (2) Can greater benefits be obtained at the same cost? Attempts to apply the methods of economics to education are still young, but methods and results are becoming available that provide partial answers to these questions. In this article we shall try to provide some background in this area for evaluators of education/training programs and to introduce a few terms from economic analysis that may be useful in considering program costs and the relationships between costs and other important variables.

Many evaluation studies produce comparative results in terms of specified student/trainee outcomes; e.g., students in program A performed significantly better on criterion tests than students in program B. Decisions about terminating, modifying, or continuing these programs may then be made on the basis of such results. An underlying assumption is that the programs cost the same amounts. If the costs are indeed equal, the decision, say, to continue with A and terminate B may be a perfectly reasonable one. However, suppose that the cost of A is twice the cost of B. Now the evaluator and program director must ask: Is the difference in benefit obtained worth the difference in money invested? This is a much more difficult question than the original one: Which program resulted in greater trainee achievement? Economic analysis, using the concepts of productivity and efficiency, may offer some help in coping with the more difficult type of question.

In the usual application of economic analysis to industrial problems, production functions are developed that relate the inputs (resources) to the outputs (benefits), using market prices for all inputs and outputs. In the educational sector, it is reasonable to assume that market prices are available for some inputs (e.g., teacher time in terms of salary), but it is more difficult to assign market prices to educational outputs. What market price, for example, is to be assigned to the specific achievement level of a group of trainees or students in a particular educational or training program? The problem of assigning monetary values to the outputs of highly specific training efforts (e.g., trained pilots for commercial airlines) may be somewhat less difficult than for the outputs of general education programs (e.g., high school graduates). However, it is still of a very different order from assigning values to the products of a manufacturing process.

In light of this situation, the concepts of productivity and efficiency must be modified when applied to education/training. The problems involved in making the appropriate modifications relate to the nature of cost-benefit and cost-effectiveness analysis as mechanisms for improving efficiency. In order to illustrate how the concepts and techniques of economic analysis can be applied to education, and what modifications are specifically needed, we will first give a brief explanation of how the concepts and techniques are regularly used in economic analysis (see Arrow and Hahn, Chapter 3, for an exposition of the production theory upon which these methods are based).

Production is carried out by *firms* (used here to indicate any unit—public or private—that makes production decisions; for purposes of this discussion, schools, school districts, and training facilities may be considered firms). Each firm chooses a particular strategy for production, involving both inputs and outputs. Technically, a particular production strategy is termed an *activity vector*. A firm may have a large number of possible activity vectors, referred to as its *production-possibility set*. It chooses a particular activity vector for each time period from the possibility set. If there are n commodities in the economy, an activity vector consists of a point in the n-dimensional commodity space; negative components of the activity vector signify commodities used as inputs to the firm; positive components signify outputs of the firm. In education, the firm might be a school district; its inputs might include use of teacher time and school facilities; its outputs might include specified student competencies or changes in the levels or distributions of such competencies.

It would be ideal, of course, if a firm could choose an activity vector that had all—or almost all—positive components. But since a product cannot be created from nothing, nor can a great quantity be produced from very little, each firm has constraints on the activity vector it can choose; these constraints are delimited by the firm's production-possibility set. The production-possibility set for firm f, denoted Y_f, is the subset of the commodity space from which the firm may choose. Different firms may have different production-possibility sets because of their ownership of commodities private to the firm (e.g., managerial skills or patents). In an educational setting, corresponding commodities available to a school district might be the superintendent's skills and the students' aptitudes.

The relation between the production-possibility sets discussed here and the production-function concepts frequently used in the economics of education is straightforward. Suppose, for example, that firm f can produce commodity 3 from commodities 1 and 2 by using a particular strategy. If there exist prices for the commodities, then a *value* can be assigned to the activity vector. Since inputs are negative components of the activity vector, and outputs are positive components, the value of an activity vector (y_f)* can be expressed as the difference between the value of the outputs and the value (cost) of the inputs; it represents the gain or profit—we will use the term *gain* because of the general nature of instruction—to the firm of choosing the particular vector y_f if the prices of the components are known. A central behavioral assumption of economic theory is that firms will choose y_f so as to maximize gain at the existing prices. Of course, when the theory is applied to education, it is necessary to specify the commodities and to indicate the *extent* to which the firm is economically efficient.

Two conceptually distinct sources of economic inefficiency exist, *Pareto-inefficiency* and *allocative inefficiency*. A firm is Pareto-inefficient if it could have chosen an activity vector with a more valuable output or a less costly input (everything else being the same) but failed to do so. A school system would probably be Pareto-inefficient if it trained students for nonexistent jobs or used highly trained teachers to perform services that a clerical assistant could have performed. A Pareto-efficient activity vector is allocatively inefficient if it is possible to increase the total value of output by reallocating the output. If, for example, commodities 1 and 2 were outputs, and the total value of output could be

_____
*We use a lower-case designation for the activity vector of firm $f(y_f)$ to distinguish it from the firm's production-possibility set (Y_f). The vector y_f is, of course, a member of the set Y_f.

increased by increasing the output of commodity 1 at the expense of having less of commodity 2, then the original situation would have been allocatively inefficient. *The economic efficiency of a firm, it should be stressed, is defined in terms of the range of options open to it.* Specifying the range of options in the educational sphere is, of course, a difficult task.

Productivity, loosely speaking, is the ratio of output to input, or the amount of output per unit of input. It is a frequently used index of how well a firm is doing. Robinson Crusoe, for example, might well measure his productivity by the number of coconuts he picks per hour. A physical education teacher might measure his productivity by the number of children who learn to swim during the summer. These are simple examples, of course. Real production processes generally encompass multiple inputs and outputs, and thus it is not possible to measure productivity in units of actual output per unit of actual input (e.g., coconuts per hour, swimmers per summer). If a set of weights exists to allow aggregation of outputs into a single aggregate output and inputs into a single aggregate input, one can again construct a productivity ratio; the weights most typically used are prices, and the resulting ratio is the dimensionless number giving value of output divided by value of input. Economists term this number *total factor productivity.* Maximizing productivity (or benefit-cost *ratio*) is not necessarily desirable. It may happen that the ratio of benefit to cost is highest when both benefit and cost have minimum values, in which case gain might be very low even though productivity is high. Rather, one should be concerned with the *difference* between benefit and cost (i.e., gain), and this concern is reflected in the concept of economic efficiency.

In education, there are usually no clear prices for the outputs. Although the concept of efficiency can be applied to this case, it yields fewer results. When prices for all commodities exist, the choice of an economically efficient activity vector provides answers to two types of questions: (1) Which commodities should the firm produce, and how much of each? (2) Which inputs should be used in the production process, and how much of each should be used? Without prices for commodities that are potential outputs, it becomes impossible to provide an answer to the first question in terms of economic efficiency. It does remain possible, however, to provide an answer to the second question. The efficient choice of inputs is the one that minimizes cost, subject to the constraints that outputs reach at least some specified level. Cost-effectiveness analysis attempts to provide an answer to the question of how total cost and optimal choice of inputs vary as a function of prices and the target output. Probably the most important aspect of this approach is the creative task of generating alternative strategies. Estimating costs and setting the constraints on the output require experienced judgment. Cost-benefit analysis includes cost-effectiveness analysis but goes beyond it in attempting to assign some measure of value (benefit) to the various possible outputs. These benefits can then be compared to costs in coming to a decision concerning the optimal activity vector.

Although many program evaluators have tried to take costs into account, they have generally worked with fairly simple functions and relationships. The application of economic analysis to education/training problems should provide much more detailed information relating to costs. In spite of the very difficult problems involved in assigning costs to education/training inputs and benefits to the outputs of such programs, the use of economic techniques in studying the educational system is one of the most promising developments in education today. (See also **Systems Analysis.**)–D. J.

Arrow, K., and Hahn, F. *General Competitive Analysis.* San Francisco: Holden-Day, 1971.

Bowles, D. "Toward an Educational Production Function." In W. L. Hansen (Ed.), *Education, Income and Human Capital.* New York: Columbia University Press, 1970.

Jamison, D. "Definitions of Productivity and Efficiency in Education." Appendix A of A. Melmed, rapporteur, *Productivity and Efficiency in Education.* Washington, D.C.: Educational Panel of Federal Council on Science and Technology, Commission on Automation Opportunities in the Service Areas, 1972 (draft).

Jellema, W. W. (Ed.) *Efficient College Management.* San Francisco: Jossey-Bass, 1972.

Kennedy, C., and Thirlwall, A. P. "Surveys in Applied Economics: Technical Progress." *Economic Journal,* 1972, *82,* 11-72.

Lau, L., and Yotopoulos, P. "A Test for Relative Efficiency and Application to Indian Agriculture." *American Economic Review,* 1971, *61,* 94-109.

Levin, H. "Efficiency in Education." Paper presented at National Bureau of Economic Research Conference on Education as an Industry. Chicago, 1971.

Nadiri, M. "Some Approaches to the Theory and Measurement of Total Factor Productivity: A Survey." *Journal of Economic Literature,* 1970, *8,* 1137-1177.

Timmer, C. P. "On Measuring Technical Efficiency." *Food Research Institute Studies in Agricultural Economics, Trade, and Development,* 1970, *9,* 99-171.

—————— CRITERION MEASUREMENT ——————

The word *criterion* is usually associated with the selection process; we talk, for instance, about how well college admissions tests predict the criterion of grade-point average or how well employment tests predict criteria of satisfactory job performance. However, it is also meaningful to talk about criteria for judging the effectiveness of educational programs, usually in terms of measures of outcome **Variables** or differences between **Pretest** and **Posttest** performance. In this context, the relationship that should obtain between program **Goals and Objectives** and criterion measures is clear. Thus, the first concern of evaluators as they choose or develop criterion measures is that these measures adequately reflect the goals and objectives (i.e., criterion behaviors) of interest (see **Criterion-Referenced Measurement** and **Test Selection**). If a program seeks to improve technical-writing skills, then ideally the criterion measures should require the students to demonstrate their proficiency through actual technical writing. Measures of abilities to use the dictionary, edit manuscripts, or type, while perhaps important adjuncts to the major objective, would not in themselves constitute adequate criterion measurement.

In some cases, it is not feasible for evaluators to use measures that correspond precisely with the ultimate criteria toward which the training is directed. For example, the ultimate criterion of a training course for fighter pilots is effectiveness in combat. But the program evaluator cannot wait for combat conditions to arise, and it would be difficult to duplicate them in the classroom. The best he can probably do is use measures judged to be related to (or predictive of) combat performance. This example is an extreme one; in other instances where it is not possible to follow up all students on the jobs for which they were trained, it may be possible to follow up a sample of them and thus establish the predictive **Validity** of the measures used at the end of the training period. In these situations, the measures used at the end of the training represent *indirect* or *intermediate criteria.*

Attempts to relate measures used to evaluate general education programs to ultimate criteria are particularly troublesome conceptually and operationally. Educators are wont to say that they are trying to do much more than teach arithmetic, English, social studies, and science—that they are trying to develop the competencies needed for successful adult role functioning (see Tumin). But this ultimate criterion has never been satisfactorily delineated—perhaps it cannot be; and most evaluators of school programs must be content with measures of arithmetic, English, etc.

Investigators in the selection area have been especially concerned with the frequent discrepancy in psychometric soundness between predictor and criterion measures. They point out, for example, that those who develop predictor instruments may go to a great deal of trouble to establish their **Reliability**, content or construct validity, and other appropriate technical characteristics, only to settle for inadequate measurement of criterion behavior. They might use well-standardized aptitude tests to predict very unreliable supervisors' ratings or ill-defined grade-point averages. This kind of discrepancy is not as likely to occur between the pretest or **Baseline Measures** and the posttest measures used in evaluation of education and training programs, but it is still worth noting that measures of criterion behavior need to adhere to the same technical standards as any other measures.

As difficult as it may be to define the desirable outcomes of an instructional program and to obtain satisfactory measures, evaluators must keep still another problem in mind: Because of continuing changes in society, in people, and in job and learning environments, few measurement systems have lasting and undiminished value. Experience has shown that such systems are degradable over time unless they are periodically revitalized.—S. B. A., A. P. M.

Guion, R. *Personnel Testing.* New York: McGraw-Hill, 1965. Chapter 4 explores problems in measuring criteria and provides a listing of various available criterion measures.

MacKinney, A. C. "The Assessment of Performance Change: An Inductive Example." *Organizational Behavior and Human Performance,* 1967, *2,* 56-72.

Messick, S. "Personality Measurement and College Performance." In D. N. Jackson and S. Messick (Eds.), *Problems in Human Assessment.* New York: McGraw-Hill, 1967. Includes a discussion of the ethics of selection (pp. 840-842).

Tumin, M. M. "Evaluation of the Effectiveness of Education: Some Problems and Prospects." *Interchange,* 1970, *1* (3), 96-109.

——— CRITERION-REFERENCED MEASUREMENT ———

"Criterion-referenced" has become a catchall not only for measures appropriately described by that term but also for measures perhaps more precisely defined as content- (or objectives- or domain-) referenced or as construct-referenced. The characteristic these measures share is that students' scores on them are interpreted by rationally or empirically established **Standards** of attainment rather than comparison with the performance of some reference group of people. Criterion-referenced measurement is frequently viewed in sharp contradistinction to **Norms**-referenced measurement and sometimes with the connotation of "good" versus "bad" measurement practice. In fact, the two measurement approaches frequently overlap, and they are certainly useful supplements to each other; moreover, normative considerations, albeit usually implicitly, often underlie the choice of instrument content and performance standards for criterion-referenced tests.

It is not an accident that the three phrases used above (content-, criterion-, and construct-referenced measurement) parallel the three well-known categories of **Validity**, for validity is what good measurement is all about. However, validity is not a property of the measuring instrument per se but of the interpretations or inferences made from that measure. The distinction between criterion-referenced measurement and measurement derived from other traditions is best made in terms of the *types of interpretations* the evaluator needs to make. If he wants to know whether students have achieved minimum competency in a skills area, whether they have grasped the essence of a particular body of content, whether they are likely to perform satisfactorily on the job they are being trained for, or which of them should be classified into groups to receive specialized treatment (e.g., classes for the mentally retarded), he is less interested in how students' scores are distributed than in how they relate to specified levels of accomplishment.

We have said that the evaluator is "less interested"—not "uninterested"—in distributions of students' scores; for, as indicated earlier, almost all measurement has a normative base, even if it is an informal one. For example, we may set 50 words per minute with no more than two errors as the minimum standard for "graduation" from a three-month typing course. We do not set 10 w.p.m. or 150 w.p.m. because these speeds do not reflect typical typing requirements or average human capability—both normative notions. Furthermore, we are interested in the *distance* between students' scores and the standard, recognizing that an 80-w.p.m. graduate will probably be easier to place than a 51-w.p.m. graduate and that a student still typing 35 w.p.m. after three months will need special additional training.

What kinds of measuring instruments would be used for decisions such as those listed above?

Content-referenced measurement. Here the processes of measurement development and validation are primarily rational ones. They frequently begin with an analysis of the objectives of the education/training program (see **Goals and Objectives**). These may vary from highly specific ("Add two 2-digit numbers") to less specific ("Understand the literal meaning of typical city-newspaper articles") to not very specific ("Know the major events of United States history in the twentieth century"). Degree of specificity relates to the size of the theoretical "pool" of items or tasks that might be set to ascertain whether the objective had been met or the content "mastered." Several judges might agree that a test of only twenty problems (where the digits were systematically varied) would adequately cover the objective "Add 2-digit numbers"; that is, if a student could perform all (or nearly all) of those problems, they could agree that he had attained the objective. However, the history objective presents challenges since judges might not readily agree on the events to be regarded as "major" or on any given set of items that would constitute adequate coverage of the objective. (See the section on content validity in the article on **Validity** for some empirical approaches to this problem.)

A successful *content-referenced* instrument is one where program directors, instructors, evaluators, report readers, students, and other interested parties would say that the objective, domain, or content area of interest has been "captured" in the tasks and that the scores on the instrument have some meaning in their own right without reference to external criteria or norm distributions.

Criterion-referenced measurement. Here *criterion* is used in the more usual social science sense. As with content-referenced measures, the development of *criterion-referenced measures* frequently proceeds from the program objectives. However, these may have been derived from an analysis of the job or skills for which training is designed (see **Job Analysis**), and acceptable scores on the criterion-referenced measure are usually set in terms of the performance of successful job holders or those already deemed to have the skills the program is directed toward. Thus, a score on this type of measure draws its meaning from data collected on a criterion group, and the interpreter frequently equates the score to probability of later success. The latter is not a strict interpretation, for probability statements would be better derived from a longitudinal study (e.g., where an end-of-training measure is related to subsequent job success for the same group of students).

Construct-referenced measurement. When it is important to characterize individuals in terms of fundamental traits (e.g., intelligence, neuroticism) or to characterize situations in terms of fundamental properties (e.g., liberal, totalitarian), *construct-referenced measures* are needed. The greater the impact of the characterizations on the lives of people or institutions, the more the measures need to be grounded in strong theory and supported by firm empirical evidence. The classification of children as mentally retarded is a case in point.

A special case of construct-referenced measurement is *factor-referenced* measurement. Certain tests have been developed as references or markers for factors that have been established in the psychological literature. Such factor-referenced tests are of greatest use to the social scientist who is attempting to develop and test new theories. (See **Factor Analysis.**)

Some of the topics discussed in the literature on criterion-referenced measurement include special test-construction methodologies (e.g., rigorous specification of rules for generating items and sampling domains), the acceptable limits on indices of item difficulty and discrimination, emphasis on production as opposed to recognition of answers, and differences in the meaning of **Reliability** for criterion- versus norms-referenced measures.

Perhaps the most important inference to be drawn from this discussion is that the power and usefulness of measures increases to the extent that they allow the evaluator to make several related inferences about the phenomenon of interest. Even in a rather straightforward training situation, the evaluator will be in a better position to make recommendations if some of the measures have content, criterion, construct, *and* normative referents.—S. B. A.

Airasian, P. W., and Madaus, G. F. "Criterion-Referenced Testing in the Classroom." *NCME Measurement in Education,* 1972, *3* (4).

Ebel, R. L. "Criterion-Referenced Measurements: Limitations." *School Review,* 1971, *79,* 282-288.

Glaser, R., and Nitko, A. J. "Measurement in Learning and Instruction." In R. L. Thorndike (Ed.), *Educational Measurement.* (2nd Ed.) Washington, D.C.: American Council on Education, 1971. Pp. 625-670.

Klein, S. P., and Kosecoff, J. *Issues and Procedures in the Develop-*

ment of Criterion Referenced Tests. Princeton, N.J.: ERIC Clearinghouse on Tests, Measurement, and Evaluation, Educational Testing Service, 1973.

Popham, W. J. (Ed.) *Criterion-Referenced Measurement.* Englewood Cliffs, N.J.: Educational Technology Publishers, 1971. Five prominent authors discuss criterion-referenced measures (their development, evaluation, reporting, and interpretation) and their use in place of norms-referenced measures in education.

—————————— CROSS-SECTIONAL STUDY ——————————

The typical military training program is of short duration, generally averaging about ten or twelve weeks (Turner). For such programs, the pretest-treatment-posttest design for evaluation appears to be appropriate (see **Experimental Design**, which also discusses the importance of including control or comparison groups). Some military training programs, however, last longer (e.g., the School of Naval Warfare program, the air force program for medical laboratory specialist, and the army program in radar maintenance). For such programs, a *developmental model* of evaluation may be more appropriate; that is, a model for evaluating some aspect of growth or development. The primary application of developmental models is in measuring the academic growth of students in schools.

In general, there are three models used to assess academic attainment: (1) the "one-shot" model, (2) the cross-sectional model, and (3) the longitudinal model. The "one-shot" model simply measures the status of the group under study at a single point in time. For example, if all the fifth-grade children in the schools of a district were given a test in reading, the average scores for each school could be compared. However, the limitations of such a comparison for drawing inferences about school effectiveness are clear. It assumes that each school is working with students of equal aptitude—when, in fact, the students in the highest-scoring school might have reached their high level of reading proficiency no matter what school they attended. Thus, in order to assess growth or development, it is necessary to measure the achievement of the students as they move through different grade levels. If, for example, the same students were tested at the third grade and then again at the fifth grade, their development could be assessed. A longitudinal model of assessment is one that uses such data in determining the effectiveness of the school or program (see **Longitudinal Study**). (If the scores of students who missed one of the tests are deleted from the analysis, the remaining data are called "matched" longitudinal data; if such scores are included in the analysis, the data are called "unmatched" longitudinal data.)

The cross-sectional study is an attempt at a compromise between the "one-shot" model and the longitudinal model. That is, a test is given not to the *same* students at grades 3 and 5 but to the *current* students in these grades, and the scores of the grade-3 students are then used as proxy input scores for the grade-5 students. The assumption is that no significant changes have occurred in the population served by the school, so that the grade-3 students and the grade-5 students are comparable in economic status, etc. In other words, the present grade-3 students are like their predecessors who are now in grade 5. Students cannot be matched in cross-sectional studies; therefore, individual student growth cannot be assessed. However, average scores for grades can be used to obtain a measure of growth for a school. Again, the use of such average scores will be more or less justified by the conditions in the school. If the population is stable and students do not drop out in significant numbers, the use of average scores for different grades may be justified.

An example of a cross-sectional study is the survey of *Equality of Educational Opportunity* (Coleman et al.), in which a nationwide sample of first graders were tested at the same time as a sample of third graders, sixth graders, ninth graders, and twelfth graders. An example of a longitudinal study is the growth study conducted at Educational Testing Service (Anderson and Maier); in this study a large sample of fifth graders were tested in 1961 and then again in 1963, 1965, and 1967, as seventh, ninth, and eleventh graders, respectively.

A cross-sectional study can usually be carried out much more economically than a longitudinal study. Furthermore, although a longitudinal model seems more appealing theoretically, circumstances may render its use prohibitive. In discussing the use of cross-sectional methods in studying psychological aspects of aging, Schaie points out that no major longitudinal studies have covered an adequate enough portion of the adult age span on which to base generalizations regarding the aging process. Therefore, Schaie concludes, the use of cross-sectional methods, with appropriate techniques for adjusting for noncomparability of groups, is reasonable and fruitful. The particular circumstances involved in a study and the uses for which the information is intended will in large part shape the decision on which model is appropriate for a given situation.—R. T. M.

Anderson, S. B., and Maier, M. H. "34,000 Pupils and How They Grew." *Journal of Teacher Education*, 1963, *14*, 212-216.

Coleman, J. S., Campbell, E. Q., Hobson, C. J., McPartland, J., Mood, A. M., Weinfeld, F. D., and York, R. L. *Equality of Educational Opportunity*. Washington, D.C.: U.S. Government Printing Office, 1966.

Dyer, H. S., Linn, R. L., and Patton, M. J. "A Comparison of Four Methods of Obtaining Discrepancy Measures Based on Observed and Predicted School System Means on Achievement Tests." *American Educational Research Journal*, 1969, *6*, 591-605.

Hilton, T. L., and Patrick, C. "Cross-Sectional Versus Longitudinal Data: An Empirical Comparison of Mean Differences in Academic Growth." *Journal of Educational Measurement*, 1970, *7*, 15-24.

Schaie, K. W. "Cross-Sectional Methods in the Study of Psychological Aspects of Aging." *Journal of Gerontology*, 1959, *14*, 208-215.

Turner, C. P. (Ed.) *A Guide to the Evaluation of Educational Experiences in the Armed Services*. Washington, D.C.: American Council on Education, 1968.

————————— CULTURE-FAIR TEST —————————

The concept of culture-fair testing replaced that of culture-free testing when it was realized that the existence of test content totally free of culture is illusory (Goodenough and Harris, p. 399). To be culture-fair, then, a test should reflect comparable, rather than nonexistent, influences from various cultures, so that the test taker is not penalized because of his immersion in any particular culture or lack of opportunity to acquire certain other cultural experiences.

The issue of cultural fairness in tests is complicated by the various functions that a test can serve. If the intent of a test is to select students with necessary prerequisites for a program, then the predictor should be a sample or an approximation of the requirements for successfully completing the instruction. If that body of instruction necessarily contains elements which require background and experiences characteristic of a particular culture, then, in order to select accurately, the test should contain those elements too. In evaluation of educational programs, the intent is to determine whether students have achieved certain desired levels. Here culture fairness is less of a problem if students have had equal coverage of the content and objectives of the program.

On the other hand, tests are frequently used for a far less specific purpose, that of judging the relatively fixed ability level of an individual, where the test content has only a vague relationship to a person's future work. An example is the score derived from one of the several IQ tests (see **Intelligence Measurement**). Since such scores are often interpreted as reflections of innate and fixed ability levels, errors may occur when the testing process assumes a particular cultural background as a basis for its particular tasks but the person being tested comes from a different background. The most frequent charges of this type are levied against tests which have a heavy white-majority, middle-class orientation and yet are used to assess the ability levels of various ethnic minorities; these charges assume that the result may be a consistent underestimation of the ability of those minorities. Specifically, within educational evaluation activities, the uncritical use of student IQ scores to match experimental and **Control Groups**, especially involving ethnic mixes, can lead to inappropriate grouping and misleading results (see **Matched Sampling**).

A number of thorough studies of the predictive **Validity** of commonly used tests indicate that, when properly used, the tests predict job and school performance equally well for whites and blacks. However, this does not discount the importance of concerted efforts to include minority-oriented content in those tests, something rarely done in the past. Some *culture-specific tests* are being developed to evaluate the information a person has acquired about particular minority cultures; sometimes these tests are developed more for demonstration purposes than for practical use.

The most elaborate attempt to devise an instrument devoid of culture-specific items, either majority or minority, was that by Eells and Davis and their associates. By extensive tryouts of items on a variety of children from diverse backgrounds, they were able to collect a number of items that were equally difficult for each group. Although the product was expected to be a useful index of ability devoid of cultural influences, the scores were found to predict very little of interest, and the test generally failed to sustain its alleged culture-fair characteristics on attempted replication; thus, the tests are very little used today, and any renewed attempts to design such measures are generally agreed to be futile. The primary reason, no doubt, as Anastasi (p. 253) has suggested, is that "a test . . . equally familiar in many cultures might . . . possess little theoretical or practical value in *any* culture." *Developed* abilities are all that we *can* measure, and of course that development is influenced by the surrounding culture. Even when non-language tests are used, culture may still be influential. Consider, for example, a test composed of drawings of common objects. These supposedly common objects may be more common in some cultures than in others, and individuals from different cultures may have different skills in interpreting two-dimensional representation. Furthermore, these individuals may approach the test situation from different orientations and levels of experience.

Controversy is generated when test results are interpreted as reflecting the "worth" of the individual; cultural minorities feel unfairly treated when only things important to the majority culture are measured, rightly believing there is content of "worth" in their own culture. A true culture-fair test would be one that recognized and sampled all positive aspects of all cultures, but constructing one is probably not feasible. Again, if the test is being used to predict success in the majority culture, it must necessarily be directed toward that criterion measure.

Tests can, however, be made more accurate as measuring instruments (see **Bias in Testing**), and efforts in this direction should continue despite the unlikelihood of sizable reduction in the differential between group means. Examples of potential sources of inaccuracy include content which involves terminology that is specifically open to misinterpretation because of disparate meanings across cultures and the possibly intimidating setting within which the test is administered. However small, any differences arising from such sources should be the focus of continuing concern.—R. L. F.

Anastasi, A. *Psychological Testing.* (3rd Ed.) New York: Macmillan, 1968.

Eells, K., Davis, A., Havighurst, R. J., Herrick, V. E., and Tyler, R. W. *Intelligence and Cultural Differences.* Chicago: University of Chicago Press, 1951.

Goodenough, F. L., and Harris, D. B. "Studies in the Psychology of Children's Drawings." *Psychological Bulletin,* 1950, *47,* 369-433.

Thorndike, R. L. "Concepts of Culture Fairness." *Journal of Educational Measurement,* 1971, *8,* 63-70.

———————— CURRICULUM EVALUATION ————————

Whilc, in a sense, any evaluation of an instructional program is curriculum evaluation, the term is used most widely in connection with textbooks and other curriculum materials developed for national dissemination to schools and colleges. Some of the earliest curriculum-evaluation efforts are described in the article on **Evaluation History.**

Sputnik was the major stimulator of the great wave of curriculum reform that swept the nation in the 1960s. Concern was at first focused on curricula in the sciences and mathematics, and the Physical Science Study Committee can certainly be credited with giving the field of curriculum development a new prestige. This committee also gave evaluation a boost by including assessment of student learning in the tryouts of the new physics course and authorizing comparisons of what students learned in PSSC with what students were learning in traditional courses. There were some criticisms of the PSSC evaluation model, but, interestingly, those sponsoring new curricula in other areas began including some semblance of evaluation in their plans. This was, of course, the first time that large sums of federal and foundation money had been allocated to curriculum development, and that may have been a factor in the inclusion of sections on evaluation in the proposals and reports. Some of the better-known curriculum projects of the period were the Biological Sciences Curriculum Study (BSCS), the High School Geography Project, the work of the School Mathematics Study Group (SMSG), the Chemical Bond Approach Project, the program for Foreign Languages in Elementary Schools (FLES), and the Greater Cleveland Social Science Program.

Key figures in the curriculum-evaluation field include Ralph Tyler, Lee Cronbach, Michael Scriven, and Robert Stake. Tyler's work, going back to the 1930s, emphasizes the use of evaluation to help classroom teachers determine the effectiveness of their instruction and modify their courses accordingly. Cronbach first focused widespread attention on the logical problems involved in comparing the outcomes of a new curriculum with those of an older established curriculum when the two curricula are in fact intended to accomplish different goals. Scriven, in his efforts to clarify the role of the evaluator, has insisted that comparison is an important component of all types of evaluation and that the evaluator must attend to relative outcomes across many dimensions even if the two curricula are designed for different purposes. More important, he advances the proposition that the evaluator cannot avoid making value judgments and that any statistical indicators of program effectiveness must be considered in a judgmental framework. (See **Evaluator Role.**) Stake stresses that judgments must take into account the interactive nature of input characteristics (of students), curricula and instructional processes, and output. From these considerations and others, certain key issues in curriculum evaluation have emerged:

1. What are fair bases for comparing competing curricula when their goals are not identical? (See **Goal-Free Evaluation.**)

2. What types of evaluative information will be most useful to curriculum developers in revising their materials? (See **Formative Evaluation.**)

3. What are the strengths and limitations of behavioral objectives in the development and evaluation of curriculum materials? (See **Goals and Objectives.**)

4. What major criteria should be used in judgments about the quality of curriculum materials? The five-point model offered for **Training Evaluation** may be adaptable to materials designed for use in academic settings: validity, transfer, effectiveness, worth (cost), and acceptance. (See also **Materials Evaluation.**)

5. How should we treat intended outcomes of the program in relationship to unintended outcomes? (See **Side Effects.**)

6. How does curriculum evaluation relate to the usual concepts of research into human learning? (See **Evaluation Concepts** and **Scientific Inquiry and Evaluation.**)

As many parents and teachers have probably suffered through curriculum reform as have celebrated it. The stories of the difficulties that the "new math" presented are legion. Curriculum-evaluation efforts need to give as much attention to the process of installing and implementing a new curriculum as they do to assessment of the knowledges and skills that students apparently derive from it. Many a well-conceptualized curriculum has become something quite different in the hands of teachers who did not understand it, were intimidated by it, or deliberately sabotaged it. (See **Transactional Evaluation** and point 1 in **Discrepancy Evaluation.**)—L. S. C., S. B. A.

Cronbach, L. J. "Course Improvement Through Evaluation." *Teachers College Record*, 1963, *64*, 672-683.

Goodlad, J. I. *The Changing School Curriculum*. New York: Fund for Advancement of Education, 1966.

Scriven, M. "The Methodology of Evaluation." In *Perspectives of*

Curriculum Evaluation. AERA Monograph Series on Curriculum Evaluation, No. 1. Chicago: Rand McNally, 1967. Pp. 39-82.

Stake, R. E. "The Countenance of Educational Evaluation." *Teachers College Record,* 1967, *68,* 523-540.

Tyler, R. W. "The Function of Measurement in Improving Instruction." In E. F. Lindquist (Ed.), *Educational Measurement.* Washington, D.C.: American Council on Education, 1951. Pp. 47-67.

-------------------- DATA PREPARATION --------------------

The data collected in an evaluation have to be organized to make them readily accessible and usable. When the evaluation is small in scale (few subjects, few measures, simple design), the problems of data preparation are usually not great. However, as the size of the evaluation increases, so do the problems of data preparation. Whether data are hand-scored, keypunched, or optically scanned, they first need to be prepared to ensure good-quality data sets and efficient data analyses. Data preparation includes all steps taken to anticipate the needs of anyone working with data at some future time.

One should plan for data preparation even before data have been collected. Earlier preparatory steps can often eliminate costly problems and procedures later. Thus, measuring instruments can be designed with formats that allow easy tabulation of responses (e.g., to reduce keypunch error, keypunch columns can be indicated on the instruments); they can be structured to minimize coding after administration (e.g., multiple-choice questions can be used instead of free-response questions whenever possible); and they can be packaged for efficient administration and processing (e.g., to reduce the possibility of incomplete data sets and to facilitate keeping records of materials, all measures can be bound in a single booklet).

After data have been collected in the field, they need to be prepared by the field staff or by the person administering the tests. Preparation of data in the field can prevent the need to return incomplete data and the consequent loss of time. Preparation in the field may include hand checking all data for completeness and accuracy and returning data in whatever form will facilitate the final preparation before processing.

Once the data have been returned from the field, they have to be prepared for scoring and analysis. **Quality Control** of data by a central staff ensures uniformity of format and is often the final check of raw data. The kind of control exerted over the data depends on their amount and kind, but may include rechecking data for completeness, coding free responses, checking subject names against master rosters, and assigning identification numbers where subjects' names cannot be used. Coding is often a source of error. The work of coders should be systematically checked to ensure the maintenance of standards. If data are in a format that precludes direct keypunching or scoring, responses may have to be recorded on separate forms by hand. And if data are to be scanned, answer sheets can be checked to minimize the number of unacceptable forms.

Whatever form the raw data are put in for analysis, they have to be edited for both clerical and mechanical error. At the simplest level, data can be edited for out-of-range responses (e.g., a 5 in a column where that value is unacceptable or inconceivable) and for coding errors (e.g., a birth month of 13). The correction of miscoded or mispunched data often entails rechecking the raw data and occasionally requires calls back to the field.

Data can also be edited for "believability." For example, score distributions of samples of data can be inspected to see if they are reasonable; or the tests given by different administrators can be scored separately, and the results inspected for discrepancies which might indicate faulty administration. Correction of some errors may not be possible; e.g., if a tester gave some tests improperly and subjects cannot be retested. (See **Field Operations** and **Staff Evaluation**.) At the data preparation stage, the evaluators will frequently find it necessary to eliminate some suspect data.

The final step in data preparation is setting up data files to facilitate analysis runs. The form of these files will depend on the types of analyses to be run. However, the general objectives are data files that are easily accessible for statistical analysis and data runs that are as inexpensive as possible. For example, if analyses will frequently require group rather than individual scores, a file containing these group scores (e.g., class means) probably should be constructed at the outset.—G. A. B.

Baker, F. B. "Automation of Test Scoring, Reporting, and Analyses." In R. L. Thorndike (Ed.), *Educational Measurement.* (2nd Ed.) Washington, D.C.: American Council on Education, 1971. Explains how to develop instrumentation with later analyses in mind.

Stoker, H. W. "Automated Data Processing in Testing." In S. C. Stone and B. Shertzer (Eds.), *Guidance Monograph Series: III. Testing.* Boston: Houghton Mifflin, 1968. Useful advice on setting up data files.

DATA SOURCES

There are those who argue that the only "proof of the program" lies in changes in student behavior (see, for example, **Observation Techniques**). However, a more considered stance is probably that desired changes in student behavior are a necessary, but not sufficient, basis for praising, retaining, publicizing, and promulgating an instructional program. Program directors, sponsors, and evaluators cannot ignore such other issues as possible side effects of the program on students and others; the durability and transferability of knowledge and skills acquired by students; the acceptability of the program to students, instructors, and other interested parties; and the cost of the program in relationship to its results. (See **Side Effects**, **Training Evaluation**, and **Cost Considerations**.) Even within the general domain of intended student outcomes, there is frequently a need to look at a number of different variables that may be measured by a variety of measurement techniques.

Such comprehensive views of evaluation imply dependence on a great many sources and kinds of data. This article identifies some of these sources and kinds of data in terms of four dimensions (shown in Table 1): (1) the object of measurement (who or what is to be measured)—students or trainees, teachers or instructors, program administrators, etc.; (2) the general classes of variables to be measured (why the person or situation is to be measured)—input characteristics of students, program variables, context variables, assessment variables, outcome variables (see the article on **Variables** for a discussion of each of these classes); (3) types of measurement and data-collection instruments (how the data may be collected)—**Tests, Situational Tests** (including simulation), **Questionnaires** or inventories, logs or diaries, films or tapes, **Interviews,** archives or records (see **Unobtrusive Measures**), physical-trace measures (see **Unobtrusive Measures**), **Social Indicators, Ratings** (including **Grades**), **Observation** scales (for natural situations), clinical examinations, physiological measures; (4) sources of information (the people from whom the data may be obtained) —self, peers, students or trainees, teachers or instructors, program administrators, parents, other directly concerned adults, observer, clinician (physician, psychiatrist, psychologist, etc.).

This scheme is presented to evaluators chiefly as a reminder of the wide range of options open to them; they need not limit themselves to the usual kinds of tests and questionnaires or to obtaining information only from the students and instructors most intimately involved in the instructional program. Of course, the choice of particular measurement content and procedures must be tailored to the objectives of the instructional effort, the design of the evaluation study, and the organizational and political climate in which it is to be carried out. (For example, it would not be possible, or relevant, in some situations to obtain medical examinations of pupils; or program administrators may not be willing to submit to situational tests of their management skills.)

A possible fifth dimension of the data-collection effort is not included in Table 1. It is *where* the measurement may take place. Most data probably will be collected within the instructional environment: classrooms, laboratories, library, offices, play-

Table 1

Data Sources for Evaluation Efforts

Who or What *object of measurement*	Why *general class of variables measured*	How *likely data-collection method*[a]	From Whom *source of information*[b]
Students, trainees (adult)	I. Input, V. Outcome	A, B, C, D, E, F, G, H, K, L, M, N	1, 2, 4, 7, 8, 9
Pupils (children)	I. Input, V. Outcome	A, B, E, F, G, H, K, L, M, N	1, 2, 4, 6, 7, 8, 9
Teachers, instructors	II. Program, V. Outcome	A, B, C, D, E, F, G, H, K, L	1, 2, 3, 5, 6, 8
Program administrators	II. Program, III. Context, V. Outcome	B, C, D, F, G, K, L	1, 3, 4, 6, 7, 8
Parents of pupils	I. Input, III. Context, V. Outcome[c]	B, C, D, F, G	1, 3, 4, 5, 8
Other directly concerned adults (potential employers, supervisors, admissions officers, etc.)	III. Context, V. Outcome	C, F, G	1, 5
Classroom or direct instructional climate	II. Program	B, C, D, E, F, G, H, K, L	3, 4, 5, 6, 8
Institutional/organizational climate	II. Program, III. Context	C, D, F, G, H, K, L	3, 4, 5, 6, 7, 8
Societal climate	III. Context	C, F, G, H, J, K, L	5, 6[c], 7, 8
Data collectors	IV. Assessment	A, B, C, D, E, F, G, K, L, M, N	1, 2, 4, 5, 8
Data-collection procedures	IV. Assessment	B, C, D, E, F, G, H, K, L	4, 5, 8

[a]A—test; B—situational test; C—questionnaire; D—log, E—film, tape; F—interview; G—records; H—physical trace; J—social indicator; K—ratings; L—observation; M—clinical examination; N—physiological measure.

[b]1—self; 2—peers; 3—students; 4—teachers; 5—administrators; 6—parents (where program is for young children); 7—other adults; 8—observer; 9—clinician.

[c]Some programs, such as the parent-child centers, involve the mother as part of the instructional program. In such cases, variable class II, Program is relevant here.

ground, campus, etc. However, some instruments assessing attitudes, background, etc., can certainly be taken home to be completed by students and instructors; interviews must usually be conducted in the interviewee's home or place of business; in some instances, it is important to observe program "graduates" after they are on the jobs for which they were trained; and it is sometimes necessary to set up separate assessment centers (especially if situational tasks and complicated measurement procedures are involved).—S. B. A.

———————— DECISION-MAKING TYPOLOGY ————————

Evaluation can be viewed as one of the factors influencing decisions about education and training programs. Because evaluations are conducted to provide information for decision making, a typology of evaluation can be based on the types of decisions for which the evaluations are to be used. Four evaluation types have been identified by Guba and Stufflebeam to serve four types of decision making. This typology is not widely used among evaluators, but it may prove useful in indicating the range of activities implied by the term *evaluation*. (See also **Evaluation Concepts**.)

Context evaluation serves decision making for the planning of an ongoing program. In the continued planning of such a program, decisions have to be made in the context of the program's goals, the needs and target groups to be served by the program, and the behavioral objectives of the program. Context evaluation is diagnostic in nature and attempts to discover any discrepancies between program **Goals and Objectives** and the program's actual impact, so that planning decisions can be made or changed to produce greater correspondence between the intended and the actual outcomes (see **Discrepancy Evaluation** and **Needs Assessment**). The end products of context evaluation are program changes which presumably will result in smaller discrepancies between intended and actual outcomes.

As an example of context evaluation, the setting could be a base camp and the target group beginning trainees. A context evaluation might indicate (a) that trainees had not developed the desired amount of physical endurance after four weeks and (b) that insufficient physical exercise was provided in that period, with a great deal of time being spent at sedentary activities. These findings would imply a need for reformulating the program plans.

The method by which context evaluation is accomplished can be classified into two modes: *contingency* and *congruency*. The contingency mode of context evaluation looks outside the particular system being evaluated and is used to explore hypothetical questions such as "If an Air Force base is closed in the next year, what changes will be necessary to meet the needs of the total system?" It requires forecasts about society, its needs, and its trends. The contingency mode looks for discrepancies between a possible action (if X) and the likely results (then Y or Z). The congruency mode of context evaluation compares actual and intended program outcomes when a program is well defined and monitored. This model requires comprehensive and continual collection of data to allow comparisons between the real and the desired state of affairs. Together, the two modes of context evaluation serve both current needs and future changing needs. The congruency mode provides information for planning the program to conform to current needs, and the contingency mode provides information for planning the program to meet changing needs.

Input evaluation serves decision making concerned with making the program goals operational, where the goals were previously identified and clarified by context evaluation. In other words, input evaluation provides information about the means necessary and available to reach the ends (program goals). It describes the resources available and determines the best use of those resources in terms of costs and benefits, resulting in a design to meet the goals. As a result of input evaluation, program goals may be deemed unrealistic in terms of available resources; therefore, it may be necessary to redefine program goals and objectives. Alternatively, the decision maker may use the information in deciding what to do so that program goals and objectives can be achieved.

Specifically, input evaluation is an assessment of resources, and it results in a proposed design for implementing a program. Input evaluation provides the many answers needed to select and structure a project design. Such issues as the following arise in this type of evaluation: feasibility of accomplishing goals, availability of strategies to meet goals, potential costs of various strategies, potential advantages and disadvantages of various strategies, probability of success of various strategies based on past experiences, legality and morality of various strategies, utilization of staff, scheduling of activities, need to call on outside resources.

The methodology and techniques of input evaluation are varied and are multidisciplinary. Those that have been most fully developed include the **Program Evaluation and Review Technique (PERT)**, the **Delphi Technique**, and cost-effectiveness analyses (see **Systems Analysis** and **Cost Considerations and Economic Analysis**). Input evaluations also often rely on committee consultations, the professional literature, and judgments based on personal experiences.

Process evaluation serves the day-to-day decision-making needs required to carry out a program. It provides feedback to the producers and managers of a program, so that they can monitor the operations and detect and predict potential problems in design or implementation. The focus of process evaluation may include assessment of interpersonal relationships, logistics, and adequacy of staff performance and facilities.

A second function of process evaluation is to help program directors make decisions during the course of a program. Long-term goals are usually specified before this stage is reached, but decisions leading to the implementation of long-term goals may have to be made during the program itself. For example, at the outset a decision may have been made to implement a program in six sites. But the decision on which six sites to use may have to wait until more details about the program itself are available. As another example, a program may plan to use local people for in-service training sessions, but the actual choice of personnel, location of sessions, and topics may have to be delayed until other aspects of the program have been made final. Naturally, the clearer and more specific the input-evaluation decisions, the easier will be the task of the process evaluation. Note that this second function of process evaluation coincides with one of the functions of **Formative Evaluation.**

A third purpose of process evaluation is the recording of events through regular data collection. In this way project outcomes can be interpreted with a better understanding of what occurred during the program period.

In many programs, the program manager may function informally as the process evaluator, relying on periodic staff meetings and even on more formal means such as PERT charts and progress reports. However, a full-time process evaluator provides systematic and periodic feedback that may be essential in large-scale efforts, especially if the context and input evaluations and the ensuing decisions have been inadequately performed.

Product evaluation serves to measure and interpret program attainments; it focuses on the extent to which goals have been achieved. Whereas the product evaluation usually is identical to **Summative Evaluation,** product evaluations may also include assessments during the course of the program and thus act as a device for **Quality Control.** For example, early in a program, product evaluation might be concerned with whether intermediate goals (e.g., reading single words) are being attained. At the end of the program, the attainment of final goals (e.g., reading sentences with understanding) could also be assessed. The consequences of a product evaluation may include decisions to terminate a program, to refund and continue it, or to modify it to some degree.—G. A. B., S. B.

Guba, E. G., and Stufflebeam, D. L. *Evaluation: The Process of Stimulating, Aiding, and Abetting Insightful Action.* Monograph Series in Reading Education, No. 1. Bloomington: Indiana University, 1970.

Stufflebeam, D. L., Foley, W. J., Gephart, W. J., Guba, E. G., Hammond, R. L. Merriman, H. O., and Provus, M. M. *Educational Evaluation and Decision-Making.* Bloomington, Ind.: Phi Delta Kappan National Study Committee on Education, 1971. Presents the evaluation types in more detail than the preceding reference.

———————————— DELPHI TECHNIQUE ————————————

The Delphi technique, a method of developing and improving group consensus, was originally used at the RAND Corporation to arrive at reliable predictions about the future of technology; hence its oracular name. The technique has proved so successful in producing consensus that it has outgrown its use solely in forecasting; it is now often adopted in many different kinds of situations where convergence of opinion is advisable or desirable. Evaluators of education and training programs would find it useful in **Formative Evaluation** for arriving at goal definition, linking measurable objectives to adopted goals (see **Goals and Objectives**), or setting and defining **Standards**. Where broad representation of public points of view is sought, as in **Needs Assessment**, the Delphi technique can simplify the task of identifying and ranking needs and priorities.

Although there have been numerous adaptations and modifications, Delphi essentially refers to a series of intensive interrogations of samples of individuals (most frequently, experts) by means of mailed questionnaires concerning some important problem or question; the mailings are interspersed with controlled feedback to the participants. The responses in each round of questioning are gathered by an intermediary, who summarizes and returns the information to each participant, who may then revise his own opinions and ratings. The fact that the respondents never meet face to face has been cited as the probable reason for the efficacy of the technique, avoiding as it does the sundry prima donna behaviors that may vitiate round-table discussions. The anonymity provided for the participants apparently also encourages reflectiveness and openness to new ideas and options. For whatever causes—and however antagonistic the initial positions and complex the questions under analysis—competing opinions apparently converge and synthesize when this technique is used. Such a technique for blending diverse opinions into distinct and clearly stated majority and minority opinions is frequently an improvement over typical committee meetings and is, consequently, a boon to problem solvers and decision makers.

Some weaknesses of the Delphi technique have been cited in the literature. It is only an initial step, and it simply attempts to obtain consensus; this consensus may not necessarily be the "best" judgment. Moreover, the technique entails considerable labor, including tabulations, record keeping, and mailings. Partisans of the technique cite as supplementary benefits of Delphi its excellence as a teaching device, since the repeated rounds of feedback not only generate lively interest but may prompt deep exploration and elicit fine perceptions and distinctions.—E. J. R.

Cyphert, F. R., and Gant, W. L. "The Delphi Technique: A Tool for Collecting Opinions in Teacher Education." *Journal of Teacher Education,* 1970, *31,* 417-425.

Dalkey, N. C. *The Delphi Method: An Experimental Study of Group Opinion.* Santa Monica, Calif.: RAND Corporation, 1969.

Helmer, O. *Social Technology.* New York: Basic Books, 1966. Describes the original use of Delphi in forecasting.

Uhl, N. P. *Encouraging Convergence of Opinion, Through the Use of the Delphi Technique, in the Process of Identifying an Institution's Goals.* Princeton, N.J.: Educational Testing Service, 1971.

Weaver, W. T. "The Delphi Forecasting Method." *Phi Delta Kappan,* 1971, *52,* 267-272.

DESIGN OF EVALUATION

Evaluation, as the term is used in this book, requires some kind of measurement or data collection. The conditions and schedule under which the measures are taken or the data collected constitute the *design* of the evaluation study. The adequacy of a particular design can be judged by the extent to which the results it yields are interpretable and generalizable. In fact, the reason we design studies instead of just collect data is to increase confidence in our conclusions.

With respect to interpretability we ask of our designs: Can the findings be attributable equally well to factors *other than* the education or training program? Could the findings be attributable, for example, to:

1. World, national, or local events (for example, a television series on ecology that parallels the college course in that subject)

2. Natural biological or physiological changes, maturation (perhaps by the time he is three, Jimmy learns to climb stairs as well as Johnny, even though Johnny was given special instruction)

3. Instabilities associated with measures and sampling procedures (sample attrition, unreliability of measures, etc.)

4. Effects of initial measurement on later measurement (the student does better on the **Posttest** because of what he learned on the **Pretest,** or the pretest sensitizes him to the content and expectations of the course)

5. Variations in data-collection procedures from student to student or occasion to occasion (changes in scoring procedures, qualifications of observers, and the like)

6. Tendencies for students at the extremes of score distributions to score closer to the mean when measures are taken a second time (a particular problem with remedial or **Compensatory Education** programs when participants are selected for their very low levels of performance)

7. Differing abilities (or other characteristics) of the students in the program and the students in a comparison group— differences that are associated with the selection process (even if the students who are the better spellers are *not* given the eight-week spelling program, they may still be the better spellers after the eight weeks have passed)

8. Differing dropout rates for the students in the program and in a comparison group (if the better students drop out of the program and the poorer students drop out of the comparison group, the program may look worse than it is)

9. Relationships between the characteristics of the student group selected and other factors such as motivation and matura-

tion (if the students in the program are "volunteers" and the students in the control group, although drawn from the same general population, did not care enough about the program to volunteer, we can expect interesting differences in performance that the program itself may have had nothing to do with).

These possible alternative explanations for apparent program effects have different degrees of plausibility for different types of programs and different evaluation designs. For example, we do not worry much about significant maturation effects in navy pilot training, but we do have to take them into account in designs to evaluate a nursery school program. But let us consider one of the most widely used evaluation designs and test it against some of these possible "threats to internal **Validity**" (as the items listed above are sometimes called). Suppose that we want to evaluate the effectiveness of a six-week program designed to teach students how to administer and interpret two well-known individual **Intelligence** tests. Suppose, further, that we have measures of the kinds of skills and understandings we want students to acquire in the program. The evaluation design (called the "one-group pretest-posttest design") involves administering "before" measures (O_1) to the students at the beginning of the program (X) and "after" measures at the end (O_2): O_1 X O_2. The design permits us to measure change objectively—but can we attribute that change to the program?

Suppose that during the six-week period a major controversy about the ethics of using intelligence tests exploded in the profession and in the pages of newspapers. Might that have been more of a determiner of what students learned (or refused to learn) than the course itself? Or perhaps the "before" measure served as a stimulus for student learning from the program. At the least, the process of taking tests the first time may have had its own effect—the students learned about the test-taking procedure, how to mark answers, what to expect, etc., and thus would score better on a second testing even without the instructional intervention. We must also consider that score changes may be partially attributable to instability of the measures. Claims that the training program produced any positive changes between pretest and posttest are warranted only if such rival explanations as those suggested can be eliminated on rational and empirical grounds. This process would usually require reference to supplementary data.

Usually evaluators are interested in generalizing their results to other groups and settings. Therefore, they must be concerned not only with threats to internal validity but also with threats to external validity. Now the question becomes: Is there anything about the particular evaluation design that might make it inappropriate to assume that similar program effects would be obtained in other situations? For example:

1. Are the students in the evaluation study similar in relevant characteristics to the students to whom we wish to generalize?

2. Is the setting for the evaluation study artificial or atypical? (See **Hawthorne Effect, John Henry Effect,** and **Reactive Effects of Program and Evaluation.**)

3. Is it possible that the pretest becomes a part of the instructional program and influences the outcomes? (If so, we would not expect to get the same outcomes in a new situation where students do not receive a pretest.)

4. If evaluation results are based on multiple training procedures, are they relevant to situations where only some of the training procedures are used?

Such threats to inferences about the effectiveness of education and training programs apply to both "true" **Experimental Designs** and **Quasi-Experimental Designs.** There still exists some controversy in educational circles about whether experimental designs are necessary for program evaluation. Campbell and Stanley, undoubtedly the most influential figures in the current design scene, state unequivocally that they are "committed to the experiment: as the only means for settling disputes regarding educational practice, as the only way of verifying educational improvements, and as the only way of establishing a cumulative tradition in which improvements can be introduced without the danger of a faddish discard of old wisdom in favor of inferior novelties" (p. 172). While they do not discount the possibility that **Correlation** studies may serve as a basis for useful inferences if "very special circumstances" apply (i.e., if exposure to the program was not dependent on or correlated with prior conditions), they count such opportunities infrequent and they totally reject **Ex Post Facto Designs.**

Suppes, while generally supportive of the Campbell-Stanley point of view, still argues for "systematic examination of alternatives to experimentation" and points to "sciences like astronomy which do not engage in experimentation in any serious way and yet achieve remarkable results" (pp. 15-16). He also stresses the need for designs and associated statistical methodologies that allow estimates of the *magnitudes* of effects, not just tests for their *existence*: "If, for example, a new curriculum that costs twice as much as an old curriculum produces a measurable effect, but that measurable effect is very small in magnitude, then the practical use of this curriculum is questionable" (p. 19).

For further information about evaluation design, see **Experimental Design** and **Quasi-Experimental Design**—S. B. A.

Bracht, G. H., and Glass, G. V. "The External Validity of Experiments." *American Educational Research Journal,* 1968, *5,* 437-474.

Campbell, D. T., and Stanley, J. C. "Experimental and Quasi-Experimental Designs for Research on Teaching." In N. L. Gage (Ed.), *Handbook of Research on Teaching.* Chicago: Rand McNally, 1963. Pp. 171-246. Also published as a separate book by Rand McNally, 1966.

Campbell, D. T. "Reforms as Experiments." *American Psychologist,* 1969, *4,* 409-429. Revised and reprinted in C. H. Weiss (Ed.), *Evaluating Action Programs: Readings in Social Action and Education.* Boston: Allyn and Bacon, 1972. Pp. 187-223.

Suppes, P. *Facts and Fantasies of Education.* Technical Report No. 193, Psychological and Education Series. Stanford, Calif.: Institute for Mathematical Studies in the Social Sciences, Stanford University, 1972.

Van Dalen, D. B., and Meyer, W. J. *Understanding Educational Research: An Introduction.* New York: McGraw-Hill, 1962. See Chapters 9, 10, and 11 on patterns of historical research, descriptive research, and experimental research, respectively.

————————— DISCREPANCY EVALUATION —————————

Discrepancy evaluation refers to the search for differences between two or more elements or variables of an education/training program that, according to logical, rational, or statistical criteria, should be in agreement or correspondence. Reconciling any differences that are found may then become a major program objective. Discrepancy-evaluation efforts may focus on a wide variety of program elements or variables. Six of the most frequent areas of application are described below:

1. Discrepancies between program plans or intentions and actual program operations. Several articles in this book refer to the importance of making sure that the plans for an education or training program are, in fact, implemented. A number of nicely designed **Summative-Evaluation** studies have overlooked this simple requirement and have produced either "false negative" or ambiguous results. The television sets were not delivered until the middle of the term, teachers were able to give only one hour instead of five hours a week to an instructional segment, the program was offered to less than half of the target student population—such deviations from the paper description of the program may render the whole effort invalid. More subtle distortions can also occur, of course, and discrepancy evaluation may uncover them through the use of objective observers whose reports of what is actually happening are then compared with the stated program objectives and procedures.

2. Discrepancies between predicted and obtained program outcomes. Evaluations with this focus proceed from the question "Do the students change in the direction and amount that they were expected to change?" Expectancies may be empirically based (e.g., derived from relationships between entry or **Pretest** performance and criterion or **Posttest** performance for preceding classes of students), or they may be rationally derived. In the latter case, they frequently tend to be unrealistically high. However, in either case, identification of significant discrepancies between what was

anticipated and what was accomplished should set program directors to examining the program, analyzing the student population served, reappraising the expectancies—or all three.

3. Discrepancies between student status and desired standards of competency. Evaluation of discrepancies between the existing situation and the desired state of affairs also goes by the name of **Needs Assessment** and frequently provides the stimulus for development of new or improved educational or training programs.

4. Goal discrepancies. The term *discrepancy evaluation* is also applied to studies of consistencies (and inconsistencies) in the goal values held by different parties to an educational or training endeavor—for example, across different administrative levels in the program staff (say, teachers versus principals), between the training staff and those who receive the results of that training (e.g., military and industrial supervisors), or between the educators and taxpayers in a community. If relevant and significant groups differ widely in what they think the goals and emphases of a program should be, these differences will almost surely surface without any specific study. However, studies of discrepancies in values, if carried out in the early stages of a new education or training program, may suggest compromises which will prevent serious conflicts later. (See **Goals and Objectives** and **Transactional Evaluation**.)

5. Discrepancies between hypothetically interchangeable parts of an educational program. For example, the evaluator might look for possible differences among multiple class offerings of the same subject—say, first-year algebra. Are these offerings very similar? Do different instructors have different emphases and curriculum coverages? Is it fair to assume that all students who complete first-year algebra have comparable instructional backgrounds from which to begin the study of second-year algebra?

6. System inconsistencies. This is a more global application of discrepancy evaluation and in a sense incorporates some of the applications listed earlier. It asks whether there are inconsistencies in the logic or organization of the total program; e.g., among program objectives, instructional procedures, and measures used to assess student progress. Unfortunately, it is not unusual for a program to claim that it is fostering higher-order understandings

when, in fact, it emphasizes rote learning; or for a program oriented toward mechanical skills to limit its end-of-course testing to paper-and-pencil tests of terms and facts; or for there to be a mismatch between program requirements and staff competencies to carry them out. An external evaluator without personal investment in the training program may be in an excellent position to identify and analyze such discrepancies (see **Evaluator Role**).

The term *discrepancy evaluation* is used loosely in the literature to apply to any one of the kinds of investigations mentioned above. It is also used specifically by Malcolm Provus to apply to his model of evaluation. According to Provus (p. 12), "Evaluation is primarily a comparison of program performance with expected or designed program, and secondarily, among many other things, a comparison of client performance with expected client outcomes." His Discrepancy Evaluation Model involves the following comparisons between "reality" and some standard or **Standards**: the design of the program against a set of design criteria, the actual program operations against the input and process sections of the program design, the degree to which interim products are achieved against the hypothesized relationship between process and product, the achievement of terminal products against the specification of these products in the program design, and the cost of the program against the cost of programs having similar goals. —S. B. A., J. C. F.

Charters, W. W., Jr., and Jones, J. E. "On the Risk of Appraising Non-Events in Program Evaluation." *Educational Researcher,* 1973, *11,* 5-7.

Provus, M. *Discrepancy Evaluation.* Berkeley, Calif.: McCutchan, 1971. A plea for application of descriptive and case-study methods, as well as experimental methods, in educational program evaluation; detailed presentation of the five-stage Discrepancy Evaluation Model and its application to program improvement; critiques of the model by D. L. Stufflebeam, E. G. Guba, J. I. Goodlad, R. W. Tyler, and others.

Stake, R. E. "Objectives, Priorities, and Other Judgment Data." *Review of Educational Research,* 1970, *40,* 181-213. (See p. 202.)

───── DISSEMINATION OF EVALUATION RESULTS ─────

The dissemination problem includes the issues of who should get the results, what kinds of results should be reported for what purposes, and when and in what form results should be reported.

The "who" issue is not without its controversy. One stance is that whoever pays for the evaluation owns the results, including the right to distribute them—or withhold them. Such an arrangement is typical of many business contracts (e.g., between a company and a management consultant) and occurs most frequently when a competitive product or service is involved. It is tolerable to most evaluators only so long as (a) the results do not appear to have any significant implications beyond the particular program involved and (b) the client honors any obligations that have been made to disseminate information to program students or staff (such obligations may derive from the evaluation as well as the program itself). The skepticism of evaluators about proprietary use of their findings no doubt stems from the fact that most of them are social scientists first, steeped in the traditions of humanism and full disclosure. If the developers of *Sesame Street,* a nationally televised instructional program for preschoolers, had been unwilling to subject the results of the evaluation to public scrutiny, they would probably have had great difficulty in persuading a good outside evaluator to take on the job. The same would be true for many programs that use public money, can be expected to be widely disseminated (e.g., the Physical Science Study Committee course and other major school-curriculum efforts), affect "vulnerable" societal groups (e.g., poverty groups or very young children), or promise some results that bear generally on human learning and development (i.e., offer the opportunity for evaluative research, not just evaluation of the particular program).

In any case, dissemination arrangements (who is to have the right to disseminate the results—and to whom) should be worked out explicitly and in advance of the evaluation. If a contract is involved, these arrangements should be included in its terms. The audiences for evaluation reports will, of course, vary with the nature of the program and the evaluation effort. However, the following list may serve as a reminder of the kinds of groups that are candidates for information: current and prospective students (or their parents or guardians if the students are children); instructors; agencies who funded the program; members of the evaluator's profession (e.g., social scientists); directors of similar education/training efforts; interested community members, if a program is of local concern; local, state, and national media; members of the professions concerned with program content (e.g., modern languages, mathematics, electrical contracting).

Accepted guidelines for technical reports in the social sciences are also appropriate guidelines for formal reports of evaluation studies. Basically such reports should include complete and unvarnished accounts of the program, the evaluation procedures, and the outcomes. Furthermore, the ethical standards of the social science professions generally suffice to identify the kinds of information (records of individual students, information obtained in confidence, etc.) that should *not* be revealed in evaluation reports (see also **Confidentiality of Data**). The trouble with many technical reports, however, is that they effectively conceal information from some people who need to have it or could profit from it. What is intelligible to colleagues back at the university may be imponderable or ponderous to laymen or people from other disciplines. (Even reports written for university colleagues may be more obscure than they need to be, but that is not the issue here.) Therefore, evaluation reports should be targeted to the intended audiences. Instructors may profit most from having evaluation results described to them in informal discussion, with an eye to instructional improvements suggested by the results. Newspapers will pay attention to tidy releases, but their writers will seldom wade through long technical reports. Parent groups may deserve still other specially designed reporting procedures. And so on.

Finally, evaluation results need to be issued in time to do some good. Unfortunately, there are many stories about mismatches between action deadlines and information-release dates: the report on the effects of busing on primary-grade children that came out two weeks after the school board had to decide whether to continue or discontinue the program; the analysis of effective sequences in the first segments of an instructional television series that was not completed until the whole season's run had been taped; the recruitment of two new and hopeful groups into the high school equivalency program while the report showing its invalidity was delayed. In some evaluation projects, compromises may have to be made between completeness and timeliness; e.g., statistical analyses and release of results may be ordered so that the most telling ones for project decisions are made available first. At the same time, the evaluator must use good judgment about when *not* to disseminate evaluation results; e.g., if he suspects that they may be inaccurate or would be misleading.

Evaluators who have gone to a great deal of trouble to conduct a sound investigation of the effectiveness of an education/ training program and to report the results in timely and appropriate fashion may be discouraged to find that policy decisions may be made with slight reference to the empirical evidence they have produced. This is particularly the case with large-scale social-action programs, where politics and ideology tend to prevail over more rational processes and where, in fact, evaluation studies may be commissioned primarily to provide a gloss of scientific respectability. Cain and Hollister suggest that "a first step toward creating a more favorable atmosphere for evaluation studies is to recognize that they will not be the final arbiters of the worth of a program" (p. 135). Perhaps we should be content in many instances if evaluation evidence will merely "lessen the role of 'hearsay' testimony in the decision process" (p. 136).—S. B. A.

Cain, G. G., and Hollister, R. G. "The Methodology of Evaluating Social Action Programs." In P. H. Rossi and W. Williams (Eds.), *Evaluating Social Programs: Theory, Practice, and Politics.* New York: Seminar Press, 1972. Pp. 109-137.

Hawkridge, D. F., Campeau, P. L., and Trickett, P. K. *Preparing Evaluation Reports: A Guide for Authors.* AIR Monograph No. 6. Pittsburgh: American Institutes for Research, 1970.

———————————— EQUIVALENT SCORES ————————————

Most test users are reluctant to employ the same form, or edition, at different administrations of a test, and prefer instead to introduce different forms at different times. Their reluctance is understandable. Continued reuse of the same forms invites collection of student files of test questions and makes it possible for some students to acquaint themselves in advance with the questions that will appear on the test. This practice invalidates their performance on the test and is clearly unfair to students who have not had access to the questions. There are other problems too. For example, if an instructor wants to assess growth over time, he is hesitant to use the same measure twice because he will not know how much the results of the second administration are attributable to the training and how much they are attributable to recollection of questions asked on the first test. Although such problems can be circumvented by using different test forms at different administrations, the practice brings with it other problems that also require solution. In any testing program which makes use of a number of different forms of the same test, there will inevitably be variations in difficulty from form to form. Therefore, if the scores of individuals who take the different forms are to be compared to one another for the evaluation of their relative ability, it is necessary in the interests of equity to calibrate, or "equate," the scores on the different forms.

The process of equating, or the development of equivalent scores, is a statistical one which ultimately yields an equation or a table for converting scores on one form to scores on the other form. The sense of this conversion is that if the two forms are measuring the same ability, then it is not unreasonable to translate scores which are expressed in terms of the units of one test to scores in terms of units of the other test. This translation or conversion of scores from one form to the other is precisely parallel in its intent to the conversion of the measurements of temperature from the scale of centigrade to the scale of Fahrenheit. Here too the two measurements relate to the same dimension (temperature) and differ only with respect to the scale of measurement on the two types of instruments. In educational and psychological measurement it is possible, once an appropriate conversion has been made from one scale to the other, to compare the performances on the two different instruments as though they had been originally observed on the same instrument. Thus, just as it is possible to compare the temperatures in New York City (as they are observed on the Fahrenheit scale) with temperatures in Berlin (which have been observed on the centigrade scale), so it is possible to compare the performance of a student on one form of a test with the performance of the same student or some other student on a different form of that test. In both instances, all that is needed is an appropriate conversion of scales and the expression of both scores on the same, or equivalent, score scale.

The subject of equating is a large and complicated area of study in the field of psychometric theory. A number of methods of equating have been developed over the last thirty years. Briefly, most of the methods require (a) that the test forms to be equated be administered to random halves of a large group of individuals, sometimes with an additional "calibration test," and (b) that appropriate statistical procedures be applied. A variety of procedures are available for a corresponding variety of situations. All procedures, however, are intended to serve the same purpose: to provide a system of equivalent scores by which scores earned on different forms of a test are rendered interchangeable.

It is important for those who use score equivalencies to assure themselves that (a) adequate experimental samples were used in the equating, (b) the equating method was reliable and appropriate, and (c) the tests that were equated are truly "parallel forms" of the same psychological function. The fact that two tests may be called by the same name is obviously not sufficient; only a careful content analysis and a statistical analysis for parallelism will tell whether they are indeed as parallel as their names may imply.

The availability of equivalent scores on different forms of a test may be helpful in the conduct of evaluation studies. Such studies frequently call for the administration of one form of the test prior to the educational "treatment" and a second form at the conclusion of the treatment (see **Experimental Design**). Unless the two forms are carefully equated in the sense described above, score gains earned by the students during the intervening period will either be exaggerated or underestimated—in either case, misrepresented. (An alternative procedure is to administer both forms of the test at **Pretest** and at **Posttest**; that is, at pretest administer Form A to half the students and Form B to the other half, and then at posttest reverse the assignment of test forms.) The availability of equated scores also makes it possible to compare score gains from one evaluation study to another and to make generalizations with regard to the efficacy of the education/training program under study.

Equivalent scores are more broadly useful, indeed necessary, when there is a need for multiple forms of a test; when students who have taken different forms are to be compared—for selection, placement, guidance, remediation, sectioning, and credit; and when institutional and population analyses are to be made. In sum, the availability of a constant metric, made possible by a sophisticated system of equivalent scores, is not only one of the marks of a mature science; it is indispensable in the conduct of studies of the educational process.—W. H. A.

Angoff, W. H. "Scales, Norms, and Equivalent Scores." In R. L. Thorndike (Ed.), *Educational Measurement*. (2nd Ed.) Washington, D.C.: American Council on Education, 1971. Pp. 508-600.

Levine, R. S. *Equating the Score Scales of Alternate Forms Administered to Samples of Different Ability*. Research Bulletin 55-23. Princeton, N.J.: Educational Testing Service, 1955.

Lord, F. M. "Equating Test Scores—A Maximum Likelihood Solution." *Psychometrika*, 1955, *20*, 193-200.

───────────── EVALUATION CONCEPTS ─────────────

What should evaluation of education/training programs encompass? Who should engage in the process? When should it be applied? The answers given to these questions by experts in this relatively new field vary widely. Sometimes the points of conflict are chiefly semantic; for example, one man's *context evaluation* (see **Decision-Making Typology**) may be another man's **Needs Assessment**, and **Formative Evaluation** does not seem substantially different from the *developmental testing* referred to by representatives of industry. However, variations in definitions and specifications may also reflect fundamental differences in philosophical and methodological postures. At the extremes, a few evaluators would stop at the level of subjective description of the program, and a few others would insist that efforts bearing the evaluation label be as scientifically rigorous in design and execution as any research in the behavioral sciences. It is possible, nevertheless, to list some characteristics of evaluation on which there is wide, if not universal, agreement; these are the characteristics implied by most uses of the term in this book:

1. The primary purpose of evaluating an education or training program is to provide information for decisions about the program. Thus, an evaluation study should be planned with relevant alternative decisions in mind.

2. Evaluation results should be useful for program-improvement decisions, not just for decisions about continuation or termination.

3. Evaluation information should be provided in time to be useful for such decisions. (This point may seem gratuitous, but the number of unused—and unusable—evaluation reports on shelves is dusty testimony to the need to spell it out.)

4. Evaluation is a human judgmental process applied to the results of program examination. (It is important to note that judgmental processes and the value systems which influence them are, themselves, subject to systematic examination.) Measurement is not evaluation, but it can provide useful data for evaluation.

5. Evaluation efforts should take into account the long- and short-term objectives of the program. It is also desirable for evaluators to be alert to any unintended effects that a program might have. (See **Goals and Objectives, Medical Model of Evaluation,** and **Side Effects.**)

6. Just as it is important to consider effects that a program was not necessarily designed to foster, so it is important to delineate the events *other than the program* that might have produced any effects that are discerned. Eliminating plausible alternative explanations for the results is a key consideration at the design phase (see **Design of Evaluation**). In this connection, the evaluator should also not lose sight of the possible effects of the very processes designed to collect data for the evaluation (see **Reactive Effects of Program and Evaluation**).

7. It is difficult to conceive of a useful model for evaluation of education/training programs that is not multivariate in nature. Human behavior, including that exhibited in such programs, is complex and multiply determined. Related to this point is the importance of determining whether a program is differentially effective for different groups of people. (See **Systems Analysis** and **Trait-Treatment Interaction.**)

8. The processes of obtaining information for evaluation should meet appropriate criteria of objectivity, reliability, validity, practicality, utility, and ethical responsibility (see **Reliability, Validity,** and **Confidentiality of Data**). Although data may be—and usually are—collected on individuals, the focus of evaluation efforts is on the program. Thus, the measurement and interpretation systems involved have different requirements from systems designed for selection, placement, or guidance.

Beyond these broad principles, evaluators may conceptualize their tasks and roles quite differently and still produce useful data and judgments. For example, their efforts can be based on such apparently opposing strategies as:

a. Formative vs. summative—focusing primarily on feedback for program improvement versus evaluation of the overall outcomes of the program. (See **Formative Evaluation** and **Summative Evaluation.**)

b. Comparative vs. absolutist—judging results in comparison with performance of another group (or earlier performance by the same group) versus judging results in terms of some performance standard related to program objectives. (See **Control Group, Mastery Learning,** and **Standards.**)

c. Internal vs. external—conducted by members of the program staff versus outside evaluators. (See **Evaluator Role.**)

d. Evaluation vs. evaluative research—where the latter implies hypothesis testing and searches for explanation and generalizability beyond those characteristic of typical applied evaluation efforts. Suchman makes a somewhat different distinction. He says that while evaluation "implies some logical or rational basis for making . . . judgments, it does not require any systematic procedures for marshaling and presenting objective evidence to support the judgment," and his use of evaluative research is "restricted to the utilization of scientific research methods and techniques for the purpose of making an evaluation" (p. 7). "Evaluative research refers to those procedures for collecting and analyzing data which increase the possibility for 'proving' rather than 'asserting' the worth of some social activity" (p. 8). (See also **Scientific Inquiry and Evaluation.**)

e. Experimental vs. quasi-experimental—the "true" controlled experiment versus designs with inevitable equivocality caused by the absence of randomization. (See **Experimental Design** and **Quasi-Experimental Design.**)

f. Extended vs. constrained—where the evaluator feels a freedom (or even obligation) to go beyond the immediate time span and assumptions of the particular program to be evaluated versus efforts restricted to established conditions, assumptions, and "real" program time. (See **Goal-Free Evaluation** and **Time-Series Analysis.**)

All these views have merit under particular circumstances and, at the least, deserve better representations than we can provide here. Therefore, we depart from our self-imposed limit of five references per entry and present an extended list to the reader interested in pursuing definitions and philosophies of "evaluation."—S. B. A.

American Institutes for Research. *Evaluative Research: Strategies and Methods.* Pittsburgh: American Institutes for Research, 1970. An interesting collection of papers with a "formal" evaluation emphasis. See especially the first chapter (by

G. H. Johnson), "The Purpose of Evaluation and the Role of the Evaluator," and the comments by A. A. Lumsdaine.

Astin, A. W., and Panos, R. J. "The Evaluation of Educational Programs." In R. L. Thorndike (Ed.), *Educational Measurement.* (2nd Ed.) Washington, D.C.: American Council on Education, 1971. Pp. 733-751.

Bergman, B. A., and Siegel, A. I. *Training Evaluation and Student Achievement Measurement: A Review of the Literature.* Lowry Air Force Base, Colo.: Technical Training Division, Air Force Human Resources Laboratory, 1972.

Bloom, B. S., Hastings, J. T., and Madaus, G. F. *Handbook on Formative and Summative Evaluation of Student Learning.* New York: McGraw-Hill, 1971. Emphasizes evaluation in the classroom; includes chapters by eleven different authors on evaluation of learning in different school areas—preschool, language arts, social studies, industrial education, etc.

Crawford, M. P. *Research in Army Training: Present and Future.* Washington, D.C.: HumRRO, 1967.

Cronbach, L. J. "Course Improvement Through Evaluation." *Teachers College Record,* 1963, *64,* 672-683. Discusses evaluation in the service of course improvement, decisions about individuals, and administrative regulation; argues on the side of absolutist rather than comparative evaluation.

Denny, T. (Issue Ed.) "Educational Evaluation." *Review of Educational Research,* 1970, *40* (2), 181-324. Contains particularly important papers by Stake and by David Cohen, the latter on politics and research.

Glaser, R. (Ed.) *Training Research and Education.* New York: Wiley, 1965. Excellent sections on skills training, proficiency measurement, and coordination of training research and practice.

Guba, E. G., and Stufflebeam, D. L. *Evaluation: The Process of Stimulating, Aiding and Abetting Insightful Action.* Monograph Series in Reading Education, No. 1. Bloomington: Indiana University, 1970.

Stake, R. E. "The Countenance of Educational Evaluation." *Teachers College Record,* 1967, *68,* 523-540. A "must" in the evaluation literature. Distinguishes between informal and formal evaluation and outlines the potential contributions of the latter; emphasizes the role of judgment; discusses absolutist versus comparative evaluation.

Suchman, E. A. *Evaluative Research: Principles and Practice in Public Service and Social Action Programs.* New York: Russell Sage Foundation, 1967. A comprehensive treatment of evaluative research from historical, administrative, social, and methodological perspectives—in 178 well-written pages.

Tyler, R. W. (Ed.) *Educational Evaluation: New Roles, New Means. The Sixty-Eighth Yearbook of the National Society for the Study of Education, Part II.* Chicago: University of Chicago Press, 1969. Includes examples of specific evaluation efforts in schools.

Tyler, R. W., Gagné, R. M., and Scriven, M. *Perspectives of Curriculum Evaluation.* AERA Monograph Series on Curriculum Evaluation, No. 1. Chicago: Rand McNally, 1967. Scriven's contribution to this volume is the most quoted one and includes arguments for comparative and comprehensive evaluation; Tyler's is more historical and instruction-oriented; Gagné's is well worth reading for the emphasis he places on precision of specifying and measuring outcomes.

Wittrock, M. C., and Wiley, D. E. (Eds.) *The Evaluation of Instruction: Issues and Problems.* New York: Holt, 1970. Derives from a symposium held at UCLA. Includes papers on evaluation theory (Bloom, Glaser), instructional variables (Gagné), contextual variables (Lortie), criterion variables (Messick, Alkin), and methodological issues (Wiley, Trow), along with comments by other leaders in the field.

--------------------- EVALUATION HISTORY ---------------------

Evaluation poses a problem to the historian, since it has been a shifting concept. As Merwin (p. 6) has observed, "Concepts of evaluation have changed over the years. They have changed in relation to such issues as who is to be evaluated, what is to be evaluated, and how evaluations are to be made." In this book we are concerned principally with evaluation of programs; and this area has received considerable attention since the early 1950s, when the curriculum reform movement began.

However, the roots of program evaluation go deeper. Concern with judging the worth of programs developed with the offering of any public services (e.g., public health, education, and welfare). As the public service movement grew, so did the demands to justify the expenditures. Evaluation represented a response to these demands. After all, it behooved public servants to "account" for the ducats and justify programs supported by public purses by providing evidence of program effectiveness. But such early evaluative enterprises constituted little more than descriptions—in effect, countings and recountings of services rendered. The reports took their place beside the other file-and-forget documents held together with red ribbons and left in archives to document more the history of bureaucracy than the utility of programs.

Obviously, answers to queries about the merit of education/training programs could not be supplied by routine statistics. More sophisticated measurement techniques and procedures were needed. Thus, some have equated the history of program evaluation with the history of educational measurement. (See Ebel's succinct annotation of the highlights of measurement history.) However, evaluation is more than measurement (see **Evaluation Concepts**), although evaluators were slow to perceive this truth and lagged in defining their field and its distinctive features.

In the mid-nineteenth century the newly created Federal Bureau of Education (later the United States Office of Education) was directed to "show the condition of progress of education in the several states" (Cronbach and Suppes, pp. 37-44). The resulting surveys probably had their usefulness in encouraging schools to keep accurate records and in providing a rough listing of services that educational institutions could and should offer. Nevertheless, in concentrating attention on the inputs and processes of education, the surveys supplied little assessment of *outcomes,* few answers to the perennial question: What return are the community and the nation getting for their investment in the schools? When such surveys were used in the search for answers about the worth of schools, the conclusions were frequently erroneous or misleading. For example, in 1909 Leonard Ayres surveyed school records and government statistics, counted numbers of children promoted per dollars of expenditures, and drew the conclusion that schools were filled with "retarded" children (i.e., children who were over-age for their grade levels). He neglected to observe that the schools were crowded with newly arrived immigrant children and that the situation was therefore hardly surprising and certainly no reflection on the schools or on the students. Uncritical use of simple counts also led to such absurdities as assessing the comparative quality of schools by summing academic credits earned or courses passed by the students. It is small wonder that "evaluations" of this kind led to wholesale student promotions and, in later years, to a grave misuse of educational-test results solely to placate restive taxpayers. Callahan (p. 100) quotes the typical remark of a harried superintendent: "The results of a few well-planned tests would carry more weight with the businessman and the parent than all the psychology in the world." Such primitive evaluations were also often used to make decisions about the school curriculum. Thus, in the 1909 survey already noted, Ayres considered his data on "retardation" sufficient evidence to call for a change of curriculum to accommodate the masses of "slow" children he was convinced were languishing in the schools.

Studies of curricula and the educational value of the various subject matters were, however, important contributions of the pioneers of American educational research. E. L. Thorndike, for example, exploded the idea that the so-called "difficult" studies (e.g., Latin) automatically developed intellectual power. He also performed an early example of **Materials Evaluation**, analyzing the adequacy of arithmetic textbooks. In another study, Thorndike investigated the usefulness of arithmetic drill exercises. A landmark in curriculum evaluation was the effort of J. M. Rice, who attempted a first-hand appraisal of public education. In 1892 Rice visited thirty-six cities, talked with 1200 teachers, and wrote a classic of the Muckraking Era—a criticism of the banality of the curriculum and of the politicization of the schools. When he turned his attention to the incompetence of instruction, blasting the mindless drill and interminable rote repetition of daily lessons, he carried out what was probably the first serious study that took careful account of educational outcomes. He administered his own spelling tests to 33,000 pupils and showed that achievement had no relationship to the amount of time spent in spelling drill. (See Cremin; Cronbach and Suppes.)

Still another trail blazer was G. Stanley Hall, who developed the use of **Questionnaires** in educational research and who founded the child-study movement. Hall conducted research in the service of curriculum revision and assistance to teachers. In a forerunner of **Formative Evaluation**, he investigated what children knew about common things, places, and objects in their everyday life. He found, for example, that his subjects knew that milk came from cows, but they did not know that animals were the source of leather. As Boring notes, Hall's investigations led to the idea that teachers must not take what children know for granted, or assume that children necessarily perceive relationships among the facts they already know. Relationships would also have to be taught.

In the early decades of this century, new tests were created along with the technology of objective scoring, item scaling, and test norming. Measurement was developing its capacity to answer the question: How much? Evaluation was aided by the growing strength and sophistication of the measurement movement, especially as it inculcated a healthy respect for the **Reliability** and **Validity** of measures the evaluator must use. Evaluators were, however, constrained by the lack of instruments in many important areas, for practitioners tended to develop measures in areas in which they felt most secure.

The work of Ralph W. Tyler during the 1930s laid the foundations for the evaluation movement as we now know it. It was Tyler who advocated a much broader range of student assessment and influenced testers to concern themselves not only with **Cognitive Variables** but also with **Affective Variables**. Tyler's views are embodied in the Eight-Year Study of the Progressive Education Association, which demonstrated the possibilities for new types of instrumentation and coverage (see Smith and Tyler). Probably Tyler's major contribution was his insistence on defining the **Goals and Objectives** of programs in behavioral terms and making them the basis of instrument development and evaluation. The work that ensued in the 1940s and 1950s was particularly concerned with helping teachers formulate their objectives in order to improve their tests and adapt their instruction to the needs of individual pupils.

During the 1940s strides also were made in training evaluation. Massive recruitment of personnel into the military services and defense industries during World War II, and the resultant crash training programs, spurred the search for optimal training results through the most efficient and economical methods possible. Industry and the military were, of course, veteran trainers of personnel, but their past efforts had largely emphasized selection—the matching of the right man to the right job. In times of emergency, however, such as the war years presented, with shortages of instructors and materiel and the critical problem of readying raw recruits for unfamiliar and complex technical jobs, training often had to substitute and compensate for deficiencies in trainees' educational backgrounds, aptitudes, and skills.

Wartime pressures made it impossible for needed skills to be fostered gradually through traditional classroom procedures. Consequently, novel instructional methods were devised and repeatedly evaluated in order to improve their effectiveness. Mechanical devices, for example, were developed to train in a variety of perceptual-motor skills (flying an aircraft, operating radar, firing at rapidly moving targets, etc.). (See Fattu.) These devices were designed to simulate actual materials and situations. In this way, lives would not be lost nor would equipment be ruined by inevitable student mistakes or ineptitude. Training was not restricted, of course, to the perceptual-motor areas. It was found, for example, that mechanical training devices (such as language laboratories and teaching machines) could be used in teaching a variety of cognitive skills, and evaluators investigated which devices produced the best results. In concert with the instructors, they looked for suitable criterion measures that reflected course objectives, basing their evaluations on the measurement of objectives that were defined and stated in behavioral terms. Frederiksen (p. 345) has summarized the methods used in training evaluation: "soliciting opinions . . . , using attitude scales, measuring knowledge of facts and principles, eliciting for observation behavior which is logically related to the desired outcome, eliciting behavior in the 'What would you do?' situation, eliciting lifelike behavior in situations which simulate real life, and observing real-life behavior." The last is rarely a good technique because control of the situation is lacking, he cautions, and recommends instead eliciting lifelike behavior in simulated situations. (See **Situational Tests** and **Observation Techniques**.)

More gains for program evaluation were recorded during the post-Sputnik drive to revise and update school curricula in science, mathematics, and, to some extent, the humanities (see **Curriculum Evaluation**). Evaluation received further impetus when Title I of the Elementary and Secondary Education Act of 1965 authorized federal money to be allotted to schools for special programs for "disadvantaged" children and required annual evaluation of the effectiveness of the programs. Centers were established throughout the country to assist the schools in their efforts, and the literature began to swell with new models and taxonomies of evaluation. State departments of education wishing to receive money from Title III of the ESEA were required to conduct a **Needs Assessment**, and this activity in turn intensified an interest in evaluating the level of education in the individual states.

The proliferation in the 1950s and 1960s of new technological aids to education and training (television, tape recordings, films, computers) spurred studies of their value in assisting, supplementing, and, in some cases, supplanting traditional classroom instruction.

More recent developments in education/training evaluation or applications of techniques from other areas are treated in detail under specific headings in this book: **Adversary Model, Criterion-Referenced Measurement, Decision-Making Typology, Discrepancy Evaluation, Formative Evaluation, Goal-Free Evaluation, Item Sampling, Medical Model of Evaluation, Path Analysis, Secondary Evaluation, Summative Evaluation, Trait-Treatment Interaction, Transactional Evaluation, Unobtrusive Measures.** Some of these will no doubt assume historical significance in the field; others may not appear in future encyclopedias of evaluation.—E. J. R.

Boring, E. G. *A History of Experimental Psychology.* (2nd Ed.) New York: Appleton-Century-Crofts, 1957. See page 568.

Callahan, R. E. *Education and the Cult of Efficiency.* Chicago: University of Chicago Press, 1962. Views some aspects of educational research and evaluation as an outcome of the drive for economy and efficiency in the schools at the turn of the century, in imitation of methods used in business and industry.

Cremin, L. A. *The Transformation of the School.* New York: Knopf, 1961. Sees the development of educational research in the context of progressivism in the early twentieth century.

Cronbach, L. J., and Suppes, P. (Eds.) *Research for Tomorrow's Schools: Disciplined Inquiry for Education.* New York: Macmillan, 1962. See especially Chapter 2, "American Scholars and Educational Progress: 1858-1958."

Ebel, R. L. *Essentials of Educational Measurement.* Englewood Cliffs, N.J.: Prentice-Hall, 1972. See especially Chapter 1.

Fattu, N. A. "Training Devices." In C. W. Harris (Ed.), *Encyclopedia of Educational Research.* (3rd Ed.) New York: Macmillan, 1960. Pp. 1529-1534. A discussion of mechanized training devices used during World War II and the research and development of such devices in the years immediately following the war.

Frederiksen, N. "Proficiency Tests for Training Evaluation." In R. Glaser (Ed.), *Training Research and Evaluation.* Pittsburgh: University of Pittsburgh Press, 1962. Pp. 323-346. Gives examples of interesting new developments in simulating life-like situations for the purpose of measuring student/trainee accomplishment.

Merwin, J. C. "Historical Review of Changing Concepts of Evaluation." In R. W. Tyler (Ed.), *Educational Evaluation: New Roles, New Means. The Sixty-Eighth Yearbook of the National Society for the Study of Education, Part II.* Chicago: University of Chicago Press, 1969.

Smith, E. R., and Tyler, R. W. *Appraising and Recording Student Progress.* New York: Harper, 1942. A report of the Eight-Year Study.

Suchman, E. A. *Evaluative Research: Principles and Practice in Public Service and Social Action Programs.* New York: Russell Sage Foundation, 1967. See Chapter II.

——————— EVALUATOR ROLE ———————

To indicate the kinds of work a teacher does, educational sociologists have developed lists of roles the teacher plays. There is the teacher as purveyor of knowledge, as the pure representative of society, as the principal's pawn, as student confidant, as group leader, etc. Each role is a unidimensional caricature emphasizing the essence of one aspect of the teacher's task. However, these educational sociologists also explain that, in reality, a teacher adopts many of these roles, creating an individual professional identity by emphasizing some, adapting others to his own personality, and neglecting still others. By looking over the "shopping list" of roles, a prospective teacher has the opportunity to analyze and discuss ways that teachers behave in their professional life, noting that some roles are appropriate in one situation while others are appropriate in other situations.

No one, up to now, has provided this kind of service for evaluators, and so we intend to fill the gap. Note, however, that there is no effort to order these roles by appropriateness, because many of them (but not all) will be appropriate, depending on the situation and the personalities of the participants. (See also **Evaluation Concepts.**)

Evaluator as judge. This role is relatively passive. The evaluator as judge does not actively develop an evaluation design, nor does he collect data. Rather, he looks over the information presented to him (or reanalyzes and rethinks evaluations already conducted) and then passes sentence. An evaluator who assumes this role should be either somewhat brash and presumptuous or else experienced and venerated. In either case, if the judge is censorious, he will be feared and perhaps resented. If an evaluator wants to bring out defensiveness in program developers, he should play the judge role with as authoritarian a manner as Charles Laughton playing Captain Bligh in *Mutiny on the Bounty*. However, defensiveness will occur whichever way the role is played. (See **Audit of Evaluation** and **Secondary Evaluation.**)

Evaluator as juror. This role is similar to the judgeship. It also involves a passive role in evidence gathering. However, unlike the judge, the juror simply says that the program is guilty or not guilty (it does not work or it does). The evaluator as juror does not pass a specific sentence but leaves it to higher authority to decide what to do next. Some jurors will recommend that mercy be shown the program and that it be sent to reform school (where the rate of recidivism is notoriously high). Other jurors will be less merciful and will recommend capital punishment for the program (an action that is sure to lead the program's defenders to plead that their program's death would be cruel and unusual). The state will respond that killing the program certainly cuts down on recidivism; but, of course, the ultimate decision is not the jury's domain.

A few evaluation jurors are beginning to show frustration. It seems, even if there is no recommendation for mercy, that the guilty program is soon out on parole, committing further crimes against students. Appeals by the jurors to the justice department seem to go unheeded—apparently the jails are already overcrowded with bad programs. The evaluator as juror has little responsibility for the ultimate disposition of a program; so, if it is a self-selected role, he should not complain about lenient parole boards or organized crime buying executive clemency.

Evaluator as defendant. (Some people prefer to call the defendant the perpetrator, but we assume his innocence until he is found guilty.) How, you may ask, can an evaluator get himself so caught up in a program (so "ego-involved" as the court psychologist testified) that the program and evaluation merge? The answer lies in one of two processes. Perhaps the evaluator becomes caught up while working enthusiastically on the **Formative Evaluation.** He has provided the program's producers with such good advice that the program must be worth fighting for. Sometimes the defendant pleads guilty to the lesser charge of being an accomplice to the crime of imposing a futile program on hapless students. The sentence is less, but the guilt is still present. Either way, formative evaluators find involvement an occupational hazard, and for this major reason we argue that formative evaluation is not sufficient evaluation and that the person in charge of the formative evaluation of a program should be different from the one in charge of the **Summative Evaluation.**

A second possibility is that the evaluator simply loses his scientific cool. He finds himself evaluating some program that strikes him personally as being worthwhile—but before the evidence is available and prepared. No one is immune to this possibility. A good, liberal evaluator sees lots of money being spent on poor, undernourished children. Before you can say "Head Start" he is there defending the program. This may be a noble role, but not for an independent evaluator.

Evaluator as attorney. These remarks apply to the evaluator as either prosecutor or defense counsel. Either of these roles may seem, at first glance, to be appropriate, at least *after* the evaluation has been carried out. Thus, if the evaluation is generally negative, why shouldn't the evaluator take on the role of prosecutor? The answer lies as much in the judicial system as it does in the scientific method. Legal people in their professional roles become advocates of a special position and take up adversary relationships. The prosecutor is there to prosecute; the defense counsel is there to defend. The scientist, on the other hand, is on a personal search for truth. A program has good points and bad points. Gray is a permissible color. We presume, therefore, that a scientific evaluator will present the mixture of black and white he finds in a program and will not sacrifice the exceptions to the general picture he sees, in order to make the best possible case for the prosecution—or the defense. (See **Adversary Model of Evaluation**).

Evaluator as expert witness. A certain status is attached to this role. The court will listen attentively to the evaluator, and the years of graduate school seem at last to be worth something. But the role has its problems too. After the expert has given his testimony, there is the cross-examination by a possibly hostile attorney. Some evaluators are so afraid of hostile attorneys that they severely limit their expert witnessing. If that sounds like cowardice, it is at least cowardice tempered by realism. What kinds of testimony can the evaluator give? No evaluation is perfect—free from interpretation by alternate hypotheses. It is rare to see a true score; even if a true score were to confront us, we might not see it as different from its erring brothers. We can never be sure that a test is assessing the variable we want it to assess—and only that variable. (See **Design of Evaluation, Reliability**, and **Validity**.)

So the knowledgeable evaluator is a humble evaluator, and he realizes the imprecisions of his profession. As an expert witness he presents his best judgments based on his admittedly fallible evidence. A glib but hostile attorney may be able to make the evaluator's testimony resemble the output of a shredding machine. And that can be distressing to the evaluator. Nonetheless, we advocate the role of expert witness as a proper one for an evaluator. To hide one's results and conclusions for fear of attack is regrettable; to hide them and then criticize the final decisions is deplorable; but to present them voluntarily, honestly, and openly—that seems to us the mark of a professional.

Evaluator as detective. This kind of evaluator is big on "law and order." He knows that crimes are committed every hour of every day, that innocent students are victimized, and that the way courts are these days it's hard to get a conviction. But it won't be through lack of his trying. The final report he submits to his superior officer will detail all the evidence against the program he can possibly collect. Unfortunately, there will be no benefit of the doubt, because in the detective's mind there is no doubt. Failure to get positive results means the program's "a no-good bum."

The detective is very useful at times. No one puts anything over on him, and crooked data gatherers work in fear of him; for if there's a criminal to be caught, our detective will do it. His methods are rough sometimes, and his net brings in some good-guy programs too –but he gets his man.

Some people think the detective is down on programs that are trying to go straight because he secretly yearns to develop programs himself. However, when he was in high school, his guidance counselor said he was not creative enough, so he became an evaluator. The detective could probably use some therapy. When he sees himself in a better light, but at the same time accepts the limitations on his own talents, he will be less critical and more open and objective about programs.

Evaluator as social worker. This evaluator is almost the opposite of the detective evaluator. "There is good in every program," our social worker is fond of sighing, "and with my help we'll find it and build upon it, won't we?" Many producers of programs find the social worker a bore, but they keep him around anyway. He has never yet said anything really bad about a program.

Judges of supreme funding-agency courts sometimes call in

the social worker evaluator too—especially when they need a summative evaluation of some two-time loser they've previously aided and now are about to resentence. "Of course, I'll be pleased to help," says the social worker. "Rehabilitation, not incarceration, is my motto."

The social worker points with pride to a number of rapacious programs who have now settled down to useful lives. He is less likely to point to other occasions when, on a social worker's testimony alone, thieving and murderous programs have been let out on bail to continue their antisocial behaviors.

The social worker's most distressing moment was in court a few weeks ago. He gave testimony quite opposite from the detective's testimony and the judge threw them both out.

Evaluator as court reporter. This kind of role is still prized by some evaluators. It involves the evaluator in recording all the proceedings but *not* in passing judgment. Thus, the evaluator will report the number of witnesses to a program, what they said they saw, how they responded to the questions posed to them, etc. However, the court reporter evaluator does not place values on the evidence. He leaves that to others. An evaluator who places no values is like a pest exterminator who does not exterminate pests. He may perform other useful services around the house but not the one he is supposed to. Thus, the court reporter evaluator produces massive documentation, millions of words, hundreds of pages—and nowhere can anyone tell what he thinks of the program.—S. B., S. B. A.

Dyer, H. S. "The Mission of the Evaluator." *Urban Review,* 1969, *3* (4), 10-12.

Waller, W. *The Sociology of Teaching.* New York: Wiley, 1965. Pages 375-440 present roles teachers play. First published in 1932, this book is a classic.

———————————— EXPECTANCY TABLES ————————————

    Expectancy tables describe the relationship between a predictor score and a criterion measure. Such tables are arranged in a way that will permit statements regarding the likelihood that a person with a given score will achieve a particular level of proficiency on the criterion. If one imagines a two-way scatter diagram of test scores against course grades (as in Table 1, for example), one can think of this diagram as consisting of a series of distributions of course grades, one for each of a corresponding series of intervals of test scores. (In order to simplify the illustration, the number of cases in each distribution has been deliberately chosen to be a round number.)

    The actual, or raw, frequencies in each of these distributions may be converted to *relative* frequencies by dividing each frequency by the total number of cases in its distribution to achieve the results shown in parentheses.

Table 1

Frequency Distributions of Course Grades

		Test Score (Predictor)					
		0-9		10-19		20-29	...
		freq.	(%)	freq.	(%)	freq.	(%)
	A						
	A−					1	(1)
	B+			1	(2)	7	(7)
Course	B	1	(2)	2	(4)	13	(13)
Grade	B−	2	(5)	7	(14)	18	(18)
(Criterion)	C+	6	(15)	9	(18)	22	(22) ...
	C	7	(18)	12	(24)	18	(18)
	C−	8	(20)	9	(18)	13	(13)
	D+	7	(18)	7	(14)	7	(7)
	D	6	(15)	2	(4)	1	(1)
	D−	2	(5)	1	(2)		
	F	1	(2)				
	Totals	40	(100)	50	(100)	100	(100) ...

These relative frequencies are then cumulated to produce a table (Table 2) that will indicate the likelihood, or expectation, of a student with a test score in a given interval of score earning a course grade as high as or higher than some value. For example, a student with a score of 15 (interval 10-19) is likely to have 80 chances in 100 of earning C– or higher; 20 chances of earning B– or higher; but only 2 chances in 100 of making at least B+. To the extent that the likelihood, or expectation, of earning a given grade increases sharply with score level and to the extent that the distributions for each test-score group are short and not widely dispersed, the correlation between test scores and course grades (i.e., the empirical **Validity** of the test) is high. This validity is ordinarily expressed in the form of a **Correlation** coefficient, which describes the strength of the relationship between scores and grades and the precision with which course grades can be predicted from knowledge of the test scores.

Expectancy tables have the very great advantage of making clear the strengths, limitations, and effective use of test scores in prediction. The upward gradient of the distributions of course grades indicates graphically the fact that scores *are* predictors of course grades. On the other hand, the dispersion of grades at each interval of score suggests that the prediction is imprecise and that other factors besides test scores also affect performance in school. Finally, the presentation of the predictions in the form of likeli-

Table 2

Cumulative Frequency Distributions of Course Grades

	Test Score			
	0-9	*10-19*	*20-29*	*etc.*
A				
A–			1	
B+		2	8	
B	2	6	21	
B–	7	20	39	
C+	22	38	61	
C	40	62	79	
C–	60	80	92	
D+	78	94	99	
D	93	98	100	
D–	98	100		
F	100			

hoods or probabilities of performance makes clear to the counselor as well as to the student that the prediction is only a prediction and not an unalterable decree.

Expectancy tables are useful principally in connection with selection programs—where there is a clear and generally accepted criterion of satisfactory performance, and a test, or battery of tests, is used to predict that criterion. These tables are also used occasionally, however, in connection with evaluation studies, when the scores obtained at the conclusion of an evaluation study are themselves used as predictors of future performance. In such instances it should be expected that the criterion performance would change as a function of the changed test performance, since many training programs are primarily designed to change the prediction of criterion behavior.

In most predictions of criterion performance, we deal with intermediate criteria as realistic substitutes for ultimate criteria, which are seldom, if ever, available. In most instances the ultimate criteria take too long to develop to be of value in the evaluation study. Often, too, ultimate criteria elude satisfactory definition. (See **Criterion Measurement**.) However, even with these restrictions, expectancy tables are useful in describing the predicted outcomes and the degree to which changes in those outcomes are likely to take place as a result of an educational program. —W. H. A.

Bingham, W. V. "Great Expectations." *Personnel Psychology*, 1949, *2*, 397-404.

Lawshe, C. H., and Bolda, R. A. "Expectancy Charts. I: Their Use and Empirical Development." *Personnel Psychology*, 1958, *11*, 353-365.

Lawshe, C. H., Bolda, R. A., Brune, R. L., and Auclair, G. "Expectancy Charts. II: Their Theoretical Development." *Personnel Psychology*, 1958, *11*, 545-559.

Madaus, G. F. *The Development and Use of Expectancy Tables for the Graduate Record Examinations Aptitude Test*. Special Report No. 66-1. Princeton, N.J.: Educational Testing Service, 1966.

Schrader, W. B. "A Taxonomy of Expectancy Tables." *Journal of Educational Measurement*, 1965, *2*, 29-35.

————————— EXPERIMENTAL DESIGN —————————

In the article on **Design of Evaluation**, we discussed the possible threats to interpretability and generalizability of results that must be considered with any design. However, to the extent that "true" experimental designs are used in evaluation studies, these threats are minimized.

The three classical experimental designs discussed here depend in their most precise form on *random assignment* of students or units of concern (e.g., classrooms) to experimental and control groups (see **Control Group**). (It should be pointed out that the unit that is assigned randomly should then be the unit of analysis.) When random assignment is not administratively feasible, evaluators use various methods of ensuring that the experimental and control groups are as equivalent as possible. Sometimes they may resort to selective matching of students or classes. However, as Campbell and Stanley (p. 176) note, "The value of this process has been greatly oversold, and it is more often a source of mistaken inference than a help to valid inference." (While they state (p. 185) that "matching as a substitute for randomization is taboo," they cite situations where statistical precision is gained by using matching as an *adjunct* to randomization.) (See also **Matched Sampling.**)

Pretest-posttest control group design. In this design both groups are given "before" measures (O_1). Then the experimental group is exposed to the education or training program (X), and the control group is not. Following the program, both groups are given "after" measures (O_2) that are comparable to the initial measures. The design may be schematized as follows:

$$E: \quad O_1 \quad X \quad O_2$$
$$C: \quad O_1 \qquad\quad O_2$$

The basic test of program effectiveness is indicated by the difference between $(O_2 - O_1)$ for the E group and $(O_2 - O_1)$ for the C group.

The design can be extended to cover more than one education or training program, thus:

$$
\begin{array}{llll}
\text{E1:} & O_1 & X_1 & O_2 \\
\text{E2:} & O_1 & X_2 & O_2 \\
\text{C:} & O_1 & & O_2
\end{array}
$$

If every effort is made to keep the experimental and control groups from having contact with each other, and if administrations of the measures are as nearly comparable as possible for the E and C groups, the pretest-posttest control group design rules out most of the danger of mistakenly attributing changes to the program when in fact they were due to some other factors. For example, it can be assumed that extraneous events occurring between the before and after measures contributed equally to score differences obtained for the E and C groups, as would such factors as maturation or other normal physiological changes, test practice effects, and possible instabilities in the measures.

However, even though the evaluation study is carefully executed according to this design, it may not be possible to generalize the results to other students and settings. For example, the evaluator may worry that the pretest sensitizes students to the education or training program in important ways, so that the evaluation results would not hold in a situation where there was no pretest. The next design attempts to cope with this possibility.

Solomon four-group design. This design adds two groups to the preceding design. One of these groups is exposed to the program but given the after measure only; thus, performance on the posttest cannot be influenced by the pretest. The last group does not receive anything but the after measure.

$$
\begin{array}{llll}
\text{E1:} & O_1 & X & O_2 \\
\text{C1:} & O_1 & & O_2 \\
\text{E2:} & & X & O_2 \\
\text{C2:} & & & O_2
\end{array}
$$

Scores obtained from this design can be analyzed to determine the effects of all of the variables involved (program, pretesting, intervening events, etc., and their interactions)—from comparisons between E1 and C1 results; the effects of the program alone—from comparisons between E2 and C2 results; the effects of the pretest alone—from comparisons between C1 and C2 results; the interaction between pretesting and the instructional program—from comparisons between E1 results and a combination of C1 and C2 results.

Posttest-only control group design. This design corresponds to the last two rows of the Solomon design:

$$E: \quad X \quad O_2$$
$$C: \qquad\;\; O_2$$

It dispenses with a pretest on the assumption that true random assignment of students to the experimental and control conditions suffices to ensure equivalence of the groups. The significance tests that the evaluator applies to the differences between the results for the E and C groups are based in probability theory and allow him to take account of chance differences.

Some social scientists are so wedded to the notion of the pretest and distrustful of the process of randomization that they tend to reject this design. Actually it may be superior to the pretest-posttest control group design in that it controls for pretest-program interaction. Furthermore, there are some situations where the use of pretests in the usual sense is inappropriate; for instance, pretests in French competency cannot very well be given to students who are just beginning the study of that language. Not the least of the recommendations for the posttest-only design is that it may be more convenient to implement and somewhat less expensive than the two preceding designs. However, if randomization is not possible, dependence on this design is misplaced, since without a pretest there is no way of determining whether the two groups were comparable *before* the program began.

There are two other design strategies that are frequently described in the evaluation literature: the *one-shot case study* and the *one-group pretest-posttest design.* Some of the severe limitations of the latter ($O_1 \; X \; O_2$) are mentioned in the article on **Design of Evaluation.** The former, consisting only of treatment and measure for one group ($X \; O$), borders on the "unethical," in Campbell and Stanley's view. Suchman (pp. 93-94) points out that this design frequently "gives rise to testimonial evidence in favor of a program. . . . This is largely what happens in various 'faith' cures. . . . While this design can reassure the program administrator that his activities are being well received by his clients, it really provides little evidence as to its actual effectiveness."

Many experts agree with Stanley (p. 104) that "there is a definite though by no means unlimited place in evaluation for controlled, variable-manipulating, comparative experimentation." However, when experimental designs are not possible, evaluators are directed by Campbell (p. 191) to "self-critical use of quasi-experimental designs. We must do the best we can with what is available to us." (See **Quasi-Experimental Designs**.)—S. B. A.

Campbell, D. T. "Reforms as Experiments." In C. H. Weiss (Ed.), *Evaluating Action Programs: Readings in Social Action and Education.* Boston: Allyn and Bacon, 1972. Pp. 187-228. Revised from an earlier paper in *American Psychologist,* 1969, *24,* 409-429.

Campbell, D. T., and Stanley, J. C. "Experimental and Quasi-Experimental Designs for Research on Teaching." In N. L. Gage (Ed.), *Handbook of Research on Teaching.* Chicago: Rand McNally, 1963. Pp. 171-246.

Isaac, S., and Michael, W. B. *Handbook in Research and Evaluation.* San Diego: Robert R. Knapp, 1971. See pages 36-43 for tabular descriptions of the designs mentioned in this chapter.

Stanley, J. C. "Controlled Experimentation: Why Seldom Used in Evaluation?" In *Toward a Theory of Achievement Measurement. Proceedings of the 1969 Invitational Conference on Testing Problems.* Princeton, N.J.: Educational Testing Service, 1970. Pp. 104-108.

Suchman, E. A. *Evaluative Research: Principles and Practice in Public Service and Social Action Programs.* New York: Russell Sage Foundation, 1967. See Chapter VI, "The Evaluative Research Design."

———————————— EX POST FACTO DESIGN ————————————

The phrase *ex post facto design* commonly refers to attempts to *simulate* a research/evaluation design after the fact. Consider, for example, this situation: One group of people complete a Bachelor of Arts program in the traditional four years; a second group, through an accelerated program in the same institution, obtain B.A.s in three years. Several years later a university official asks, "Did it make a difference—have students who went through the accelerated program fared as well as students who didn't?"

The first problem inherent in the official's question is what is meant by "faring well," but let us suppose that some definition made up of annual salary and career satisfaction can be agreed upon. On what basis can one infer that any salary or satisfaction differences that may be found between the two groups of graduates are attributable to differences in their undergraduate schedules? An examination of the students' entering records would probably reveal that the two groups were different to start with; perhaps the people in the three-year group were more hard pressed economically, and the group included a larger proportion of men. Furthermore, on the average, members of the four-year group took more courses than required, married later, and attended graduate school in larger numbers. The entering characteristics might have been the major determiners both of the choice of the three-year over the four-year program and of the later measures of success. And different experiences of members of the two groups following graduation certainly might have been related to salary and satisfaction. In other words, going through college in three versus four years may have had no effect *in itself*.

One approach that is sometimes suggested to the problem of teasing out causes and effects in an ex post facto situation is to match students on the basis of background characteristics and compare students *within* defined subsets (see Chapin). An attempt would be made to use all background characteristics thought to be relevant. Thus, in the example, we might identify all the low-socioeconomic-status (SES) males in the three-year group who took the same number of undergraduate courses, married at approximately the same age, and did not attend graduate school and compare them with a similar sample of males in the four-year group; or we might compare females in the two groups who were of similar SES, took the same number of undergraduate courses, had not married, and had attended graduate school. It can be seen that the sample sizes for each of the pairs of comparison groups would probably become quite small.

Another approach to handling the data is somewhat more sophisticated: the "matching" variables would all be used as covariates in a multiple covariate analysis of covariance (see **Multivariate Analysis**). With either approach, however, *under*matching is almost bound to occur because it is virtually impossible to include *all* student characteristics that contributed to selection of the alternate programs or to the later measures of success or to both.

In many attempts at ex post facto analyses, investigators are not even as lucky as in the example here. There are no preprogram records to refer to, and estimates of what students were like before the program have to be obtained from recollections provided by the students in postprogram interviews—frequently after a considerable period of time has elapsed. Such recollections are seldom very reliable or accurate. Even if preprogram records exist, they are often incomplete or in error; or they are not relevant because they were set up for purposes other than program evaluation. How much better it is to design evaluation studies at the time a new program is conceived—or, better, collect data on relevant student and program variables *routinely,* so that they can be compiled at any point in order to monitor or evaluate the program (see Messick).—S. B. A.

Campbell, D. T., and Stanley, J. C. "Experimental and Quasi-Experimental Designs for Research on Teaching." In N. L. Gage (Ed.), *Handbook of Research on Teaching.* Chicago: Rand McNally, 1963. Pp. 171-246 (especially 240-241).

Chapin, F. S. *Experimental Designs in Sociological Research.* (Rev. Ed.) New York: Harper, 1955. See Chapter V, "Ex Post Facto Experimental Design: From Present to Past."

Messick, S. "Research Methodology for Educational Change." In

Educational Change: Implications for Measurement. Proceedings of the 1971 Invitational Conference on Testing Problems. Princeton, N.J.: Educational Testing Service, 1972. Pp. 69-81.

Rubin, S., and Asher, W. "Comment on 'Intellectual Differences in Five-Year-Old Underprivileged Girls and Boys with and Without Pre-Kindergarten Experience.' " *Psychological Reports,* 1969, *25,* 297-298. Critique of an ex post facto study.

Westinghouse Learning Corporation and Ohio University. *The Impact of Head Start: An Evaluation of the Effects of Head Start Experience on Children's Cognitive and Affective Development.* Contract OEO B89-4536. Washington, D.C.: Office of Economic Opportunity, 1969. A report by Cicirelli and others of a controversial study using an ex post facto design.

---------------------- FACTOR ANALYSIS ----------------------

Factor analysis is a technique used to summarize data and to identify structures in the data that may not be immediately evident. In the entry on **Statistics,** we explain how large bodies of data are summarized in terms of measures of central tendency and dispersion. The summarization effected by factor analysis is a much more ambitious undertaking than that involved in a simple statistical summary. In factor analysis, an attempt is made to summarize and clarify *all* the interrelationships among the variables involved in a study. Since the general statistic used to indicate relationships between any two variables is the **Correlation** coefficient, factor analysis is ordinarily used to summarize and clarify the correlations among a large set of variables. Factor analysis was originally developed as part of a psychological theory to explain cognitive behavior. Its development as a statistical technique has been recent (see Lawley and Maxwell).

Although there are many technical methods for carrying out the factor analysis, the concept itself is not a very difficult one. In his classic work *The Vectors of the Mind,* L. L. Thurstone presented the case for the theory of multiple factors that are common to and underlie much of human behavior. Thurstone posited the existence of certain primary mental abilities that he suggested would be able to account for much of man's intellectual behavior. His theory appeared quite plausible, and he attempted to work out the accompanying mathematical techniques needed to discover the primary abilities underlying various sets of observable behaviors.

The notion of hypothetical constructs that underlie observable behavior is central to the theory of multiple factor analysis. It seems self-evident that much of our personal observable behavior is the manifestations of a relatively few stable and interrelated factors in our personality or cognitive makeups. For example, it seems likely that a variety of mathematical behaviors will be the observable manifestations of some underlying mathematical ability that is common to all or many of the observed behaviors.

Charles Spearman developed the first generally accepted theory of a factor structure underlying test behavior. The tests used by Spearman were generally homogeneous, and he was able to account for observed test scores in terms of a common factor underlying all the behaviors and a specific factor unique to each test. Thurstone, on the other hand, used more complex batteries of tests and developed a psychological theory of a small number of factors underlying the observed test behaviors. In particular, Thurstone generalized Spearman's *zero tetrad difference criterion* to a *zero determinant criterion* which is related to the rank of a matrix. (See the introduction in Harman's book for a brief discussion of this history.) Using a small number of related traits, Thurstone demonstrated a clear and reasonable summarization of large bodies of observable test data.

In order to perceive how factor analysis may be used in real-world settings, consider the following study by Mulaik, carried out in connection with a research project designed to predict the reactions of soldiers to combat stress. The researchers hypothesized that an individual soldier's reaction to combat stress would depend upon the degree to which he responded emotionally to the potential danger of a combat situation and the degree to which he nevertheless felt he could successfully cope with the situation. The researchers attempted to construct fourteen seven-point adjectival rating scales to measure the emotional concern for threat and the degree of optimism in coping with the situation. Seven scales were constructed for each behavior. At the outset, the researchers were not certain to what extent the scales actually measured two distinct dimensions of the kind intended.

In the study, 225 soldiers in basic training were asked to rate the meaning of "firing my rifle in combat" using the fourteen scales. The soldiers made the ratings on five separate occasions over a two-month period. The correlation between each pair of scales was calculated using the soldiers' ratings. The correlations are given in Table 1. Note that there are 91 correlations to summarize and clarify. Can these data be accounted for by a single factor underlying all fourteen scales? If not, can they be accounted for by two underlying factors? Three? How many? Mulaik found the rotated factors given in Table 2. This matrix of loadings can be used to numerically approximate the correlation matrix in Table 1. How close the approximation is will indicate how completely the factors can explain the data. (Rotation involves transforming the factors to satisfy some agreed-upon criterion and to make them more interpretable. The technical details of the factor-analytic method and of rotation can be found in Harman's text.) Can Mulaik's two factors be interpreted? It can be seen from Table 2 that variables 1, 3, 5, 7, and 11 have high loadings on factor 1 and variables 2, 4, 6, 12, and 14 have high loadings on factor 2. (The numbers in Table 2 are called *loadings* because they tell how strongly the variable depends on or "loads" on the factor. See Harman, p. 290, for a brief discussion of the term *loading*.) In Figure 1, the fourteen variables are plotted. Note that oblique axes may be passed through the clusters of points to give a relatively simple structure underlying the data. The factor in the second quadrant (lower right) would be associated with fear response, and the factor in the fourth quadrant (upper left) would be associated with optimism regarding outcome. The analysis shows that some of the scales are not unambiguous measures of the intended dimensions. Such scales might be discarded in constructing a final set of scales for measuring the intended dimensions.

Table 1

Interrelations Among 14 Scales

	1	2	3	4	5	6	7	8	9	10	11	12	13	14	Scale
1	1.00														Frightening
2	-.20	1.00													Useful
3	.65	-.26	1.00												Nerve-shaking
4	-.26	.74	-.32	1.00											Hopeful
5	.71	-.27	.70	-.32	1.00										Terrifying
6	-.25	.64	-.30	.68	-.31	1.00									Controllable
7	.64	-.30	.73	-.34	.74	-.34	1.00								Upsetting
8	-.40	.39	-.44	.40	-.47	.39	-.53	1.00							Painless
9	-.13	.24	-.11	.24	-.16	.26	-.17	.27	1.00						Exciting
10	-.45	.36	-.49	.42	-.53	.39	-.53	.58	.32	1.00					Nondepressing
11	.59	-.26	.63	-.31	.32	-.32	.69	-.45	-.15	-.51	1.00				Disturbing
12	-.30	.69	-.35	.75	-.36	.68	-.39	.44	.28	.48	-.38	1.00			Successful
13	-.36	.35	-.50	.43	-.42	.38	-.52	.45	.20	.49	-.45	.46	1.00		Settling (vs. Unsettling)
14	-.35	.62	-.36	.65	-.38	.62	-.46	.50	.36	.51	-.45	.67	.49	1.00	Bearable

Source: By permission from S. A. Mulaik, *The Foundations of Factor Analysis.* McGraw-Hill, New York, 1972.

Table 2
Rotated Factors

		1	2
1	Frightening	.83	−.10
2	Useful	− .11	.85
3	Nerve-shaking	.84	−.16
4	Hopeful	− .17	.87
5	Terrifying	.86	−.14
6	Controllable	− .18	.80
7	Upsetting	.89	−.22
8	Painless	− .50	.44
9	Exciting	−12	.34
10	Nondepressing	− .57	.43
11	Disturbing	.67	−.29
12	Successful	− .24	.85
13	Settling	− .48	.43
14	Bearable	− .33	.76

Source: By permission from S. A. Mulaik, *The Foundations of Factor Analysis.* McGraw-Hill, New York, 1972.

This example shows how the data available on fourteen scales are really a manifestation of behavior in two underlying dimensions: fear of potential danger and optimism about coping ability. The original data can be used with the results of the factor analysis to obtain factor scores for each soldier. Thus, in this particular example, 3150 units of data (225 $\times$ 14) are reduced to 450 units (225 $\times$ 2), and the underlying structure of two dimensions is clearly identified.

In most evaluation studies, the situation will be similar to this; that is, measures on many variables will be available. Factor analysis is a useful tool for summarization, so that the evaluation may then concentrate on the important and pervasive factors in the programs being evaluated.

Although the principal application of factor analysis will probably continue to be in the reduction and clarification of correlations among measures on persons, the technique may also be applied to the *correlations of attributes within one person* (*P* technique), *the correlations among persons* (*Q* technique), the *correlations among occasions for one person* (*O* technique) or *among occasions for many persons* (*T* technique), and the *correlations between two persons on their reactions to a single stimulus (test) on a series of occasions* (*S* technique). These extensions of factor

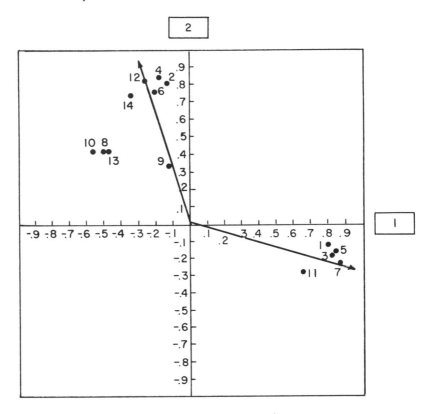

Figure 1. Plot of fourteen variables on rotated factors 1 and 2.
By permission from S. A. Mulaik, *The Foundations of Factor Analysis.*
McGraw-Hill, New York, 1972.

analysis to different situations are explained more fully in the
Cattell reference. The general factor technique illustrated in the
body of this entry is referred to as the R technique.

Finally, Ledyard Tucker has developed techniques for extending factor analysis to three-dimensional matrices (three-mode
factor analysis). In this extension, for example, if a set of persons
were given a set of tests on a number of occasions, one mode
would be the sample of persons, the second mode would be the
battery of tests, and the third mode the set of occasions. If the
test scores were arranged in a rectangular table with rows for
individuals and columns for tests, the array would be termed a
two-mode matrix. If the occasions were then constructed verti-

cally on the person X text matrix, the arrangement of the data in the resulting rectangular three-dimensional figure would be termed a three-mode matrix. Further details on this extension may be found in the Tucker references.—R. T. M.

Cattell, R. B. "The Three Basic Factor Analytic Research Designs —Their Interrelations and Derivations." *Psychological Bulletin,* 1952, *49,* 499-520.

Harman, H. H. *Modern Factor Analysis.* (2nd Ed.) Chicago: University of Chicago Press, 1957.

Lawley, D. N., and Maxwell, A. E. *Factor Analysis as a Statistical Method.* London: Butterworth, 1963.

Mulaik, S. A. *The Foundations of Factor Analysis.* New York: McGraw-Hill, 1972. One of the most recent summaries of the theory and methods of factor analysis.

Thurstone, L. L. *The Vectors of the Mind.* Chicago: University of Chicago Press, 1935.

Thurstone, L. L. *Multiple Factor Analysis.* Chicago: University of Chicago Press, 1947.

Tucker, L. R. "Experiments in Multi-Mode Factor Analysis." In *Proceedings of the 1964 Invitational Conference on Testing Problems.* Princeton, N.J.: Educational Testing Service, 1965.

Tucker, L. R. "Some Mathematical Notes on Three-Mode Factor Analysis." *Psychometrika,* 1966, *31,* 279-311.

―――――――――――― FADE-OUT ――――――――――――

If the term *fade-out* applied only to such familiar consequents of education or training programs as forgetting verbal materials or slowing down in motor skills with age or lack of practice, we probably would not bother to enter it in this book on evaluation. Rather, we are concerned with a particular demonstration of fade-out, one that disturbs program directors, educational philosophers, politicians, and evaluators alike.

Unfortunately, most educational interventions are not evaluated in any systematic way at all; when evaluations *are* carried out, however, they generally stop at the point at which students complete the program. Very seldom are the students followed up to see what happened to them later, especially as compared with another group of students who did not receive the intervention. But when students are followed up, the results are frequently disappointing. Measures two or three years later show smaller differences between the "treated" and "untreated" groups than do the immediate posttests.

In programs such as Head Start (see **Compensatory Education**), the documentation of fade-out after a year or more has led some critics to label such interventions as failures and/or to interpret the results as supportive of innate group differences (e.g., Jensen). The countercritics, especially Donald Campbell, argue that fade-out effects, although regrettable, are consistent with conventional learning theory, do not indicate that the initial gains were artifacts or unreal, and do not in themselves cast doubt on the appropriateness of the intervention. Ball and Bogatz have noted, for example, that "such interventions as *Sesame Street* are useful if they have good *short-term* effects" and question expectations for anything more from such efforts. "Education, like morphine, is not likely to have a long-term 'high' (effect) through a one-shot deal, whether it is mainlined or sent out on VHF. If compensatory education is to have a permanent effect, it must be a constant input" (see Stanley, p. 2).

In some instances, special programs are directed specifically toward trying to minimize fade-out effects. Follow Through programs in grades K-3 after Head Start at preschool are an example. Stanley is not very hopeful about such attempts to maintain gains: "It seems to me quite doubtful that most children whose cognitive abilities at age four or five are truly low will learn to read with average or better comprehension by the end of third grade under any regime now known" (p. 8). He calls instead for a drastic reorganization of the educational system, with longitudinal teaching teams who provide children with appropriate sequential learning experiences. Presumably neither "remedial reading" nor "fade-out" would be pertinent concepts in such a system.—S. B. A.

Alter, M. "Retention as a Function of Length of Retention Interval, Intelligence, and Training Time." *Journal of Programmed Instruction,* 1963, *2,* 7-17.

Anastasi, A. "Training and Individual Differences." In *Differential Psychology.* (3rd Ed.) New York: Macmillan, 1958. Pp. 189-215.

Campbell, D. T., and Frey, P. W. "The Implications of Learning Theory for the Fade-Out of Gains from Compensatory Education." In J. Hellmuth (Ed.), *Disadvantaged Child.* Vol. 3: *Compensatory Education: A National Debate.* New York: Brunner/Mazel, 1970. Pp. 455-463.

Jensen, A. R. "How Much Can We Boost IQ and Scholastic Achievement?" *Harvard Educational Review,* 1969, *39,* 1-123.

Stanley, J. C. (Ed.) *Compensatory Education for Children, Ages 2 to 8.* Baltimore: Johns Hopkins University Press, 1973.

--------------------------- FIELD OPERATIONS ---------------------------

Field operations involve the implementation of the study design, sampling, and data-collection procedures in program evaluations. The word *field* implies the place or places where the evaluation is conducted, and the word *operations* implies whatever happens in the field. Field operations thus are the systems and people that make an evaluation work. Depending on the nature of a study, field operations may include such practical activities as obtaining permission to collect data in a site, selecting and training a field staff, obtaining and testing study subjects, and maintaining the support of the community, field staff, and subjects throughout the study.

Obtaining permission to collect data in a site can be a simple matter of telephoning the principal of a school or the director of a training program. Or it may be very complex—depending on the nature and scope of the evaluation. Whatever the situation, permission is usually needed from some person or group in authority to conduct a study in the field. (See also **Confidentiality of Data**.)

Whether the evaluation is being conducted in a structured setting like a school or in a completely unstructured environment like individuals' own homes, the investigator might run into many problems when trying to enter a community. The investigator must in fact sell a product, the study, to the people in authority, since it is their school, community center, or training facility that will be involved. Often, the difficulty of the "sales" job is compounded by an initial distrust of research and evaluation felt by persons whose work or products are being evaluated. For example, to a local community, investigations of any kind may be seen as threats to the status quo (which community leaders and authorities usually are interested in maintaining and defending). The very existence of a program that is financially or politically rewarding may be threatened by negative research findings. Similarly, those in authority may feel that evaluation is unnecessary, since they think they already know the answers. They may also argue that evaluation rarely gives simple or complete answers, that evaluators may wrongly conclude that their programs or schools or people are somehow inferior to others, and that the study may even be harmful to the subjects involved. (See **Politics of Evaluation**.)

In order for evaluators to work in the field, the concerns of those in authority must somehow be relieved. Certain provisions can be built into a research design that make the evaluation rewarding to those involved. These include monetary rewards such as employing local people to collect data and purchasing project materials in the local community. Perhaps most important, the evaluation results can and should reward the local community by providing data feedback, so that recommendations can be transformed into action and improvement at the local level.

Local authorities may be willing to support an evaluation but still may be hesitant to comply with some of its requirements —most notably, when the evaluation design includes random assignment of groups to treatments where one group will be denied something of potential value (see **Experimental Design** and **Sampling**). For example, the evaluation of a new television program in classrooms may require that some classes be denied television sets that other classes are given; or an evaluation of income maintenance may necessitate giving money to some groups and not to others. Such random assignment may seem unjust to local people, and the evaluator will have to convince them that it is an absolutely necessary procedure.

To facilitate field operations, the investigator might approach other groups in addition to the structured lines of authority. In a community, these include the leaders of ethnic or religious groups who have immediate and informal access to the local people and who may ease entrance into local areas. In studies where door-to-door surveying is to occur, the permission of the local police is sometimes necessary to prevent such legal complications as having interviewers arrested for soliciting without a license. In general, the larger the community or organization involved, the more complicated are the procedures one must go through to obtain permission to work in an area.

Selecting a field staff is a necessary part of field operations whenever the evaluation calls for the collection of more data than can be collected by the investigator alone. In a structured environment like a school or training program, the field staff might be instructors, substitute teachers, or the evaluators themselves. The primary qualifications for field staff in this type of setting are experience in working with subjects and possibly with administering tests or conducting observations.

While knowledge of research procedures and experience in testing are desirable in any field staff, these qualifications sometimes become less important when data are collected from local residents in their own homes. In these instances, members of the field staff should be people who are familiar with the locality and the area's prevailing power structure and who are not perceived as "foreign" by local residents. The ideal situation would be to find a trained researcher in the local community to serve as a member of the evaluation staff. However, such fortunate coincidences are rare, and in their absence it is frequently wiser to use local people trained to canvass door to door than to depend on outside researchers who might not get beyond the first front door they approach.

There are problems inherent in using local people as field staff. These include (a) the need to give them extensive (and expensive) training in research techniques, (b) the possible need for new rounds of hiring and training staff if attrition results because of flagging interest or if opportunities for more permanent employment arise, and (c) the likelihood of having to restructure data-collection instruments in order to make them usable by field staff without much background in evaluation and measurement. These problems exist with any field staff but are compounded when local people inexperienced in research are employed.

The *training of a field staff* in sampling and data-collection procedures is necessary to ensure that standard procedures are followed. While no two people will ever administer a test (or other instrument) in exactly the same way, thorough training will minimize some of the more obvious pitfalls for testers, observers, and interviewers. Often a discussion of procedures is insufficient, and films of actual test situations and trial runs with sample subjects will ease the transition from training to actual field testing. But even after the most thorough and tedious training, periodic observations of field staff during data-collection phases are advisable to detect and correct inappropriate procedures. (See **Staff Evaluation.**)

Obtaining study subjects in the field may be synonymous with gaining cooperation from those in authority. For example, if the study subjects are students in a class, they are in effect captive subjects with little or no right of refusal. On the other hand, obtaining study subjects in a large-scale evaluation may require door-to-door canvassing to locate subjects and obtain their permission to be studied. In door-to-door canvassing, members of the field staff often need identification, both for themselves and for the research project, so that prospective subjects can substantiate facts and figures. Printed pamphlets describing the project may successfully encourage residents to feel that the study is a legitimate operation. (See **Survey Methods.**)

Problems may arise during the *collection of data* if the interviewer is of a different race from the subject or if the interviewer is of a different sex (many women will refuse to open the door to a strange man, no matter what his identification). The use of residents as field staff might circumvent some of these problems, but their use in sampling and testing may create other difficulties. If field people feel that participation in the evaluation study could benefit the subjects, they may canvass friends and relatives in a given area and ignore others; they may also ignore friends if they feel that participation in the study might somehow be harmful or an invasion of privacy. Parenthetically, this bias may affect local authorities asked to assign groups or subjects to one or another treatment. During all data-collection phases (interviewing, observing, or testing), local people may be more inclined than trained researchers to ignore standardized directions and assist respondents, either because of a "vested" interest in the study's outcome or because altruistic instincts prevail.

During an evaluation, the *support and cooperation of local authorities, field staff, and subjects* must be maintained. Local authorities or school administrators may want to make changes in the program, product, or design that would invalidate the evaluation effort. For example, a principal might decide during an evaluation that the experimental treatment is sufficiently rewarding to warrant its introduction into all classes, including those designated to be the **Control Group.** Thus, when initial cooperation is arranged, the full implications of participation must be agreed upon, with the understanding that field problems and suggestions from participants will become part of the final evaluation report.

The field staff employed in an evaluation may lose interest or take other jobs if the evaluation plan necessitates intermittent stretches of unemployment between testings or interviews. Maintaining a stable field staff may require payment even when the workload is small. Otherwise, the evaluator may be constantly recruiting and training new staff members.

Maintaining the subjects' support is most vital of all. Population mobility will account for losses, some of which can be prevented by tedious investigation through post offices and local agencies. However, subjects may also be lost if they fear that the data they provide will not remain confidential or if they feel that the study is more bother to them than it is worth. Monetary payment prevents some of these losses, as does keeping requests (to complete forms or to answer questions) at a minimum. If the subjects in a study are teachers or others in some role of authority, they may refuse continued cooperation if they begin to feel threatened by the possibility of negative findings that could reflect on them personally. (See **Reactive Effects of Program and Evaluation.**)

The logistics of field operations are dependent on the complexity of the study and its duration. In large studies, the organization of field operations may require great administrative expertise on the part of both the field staff and the investigator. If many communities or agencies are involved, both in-house and on-site personnel may be required to schedule work among field-staff members, monitor data collection, and oversee the distribution and retrieval of data forms. A coordinator may also be required to serve as liaison among the field staff, research staff, and community organizations.

Field operations in an evaluation study require not only evaluation skills but also knowledge of budgetary matters and community politics and skills in administration, coordination, and communication. Perhaps above all, field operations require flexibility of all concerned in meeting the inevitable "crises" that require adjustments in even the best-designed and best-researched evaluation plan.—G. A. B.

Anderson, S. B. "From Textbooks to Reality: Social Researchers Face the Facts of Life in the World of the Disadvantaged." In J. Hellmuth (Ed.), *Disadvantaged Child.* Vol. 3: *Compensatory Education: A National Debate.* New York: Brunner/Mazel, 1970. Pp. 226-237.

Caro, F. G. *Readings in Evaluation Research.* New York: Russell Sage Foundation, 1971. See the articles by C. Argyris, ("Creating Effective Research Relationships in Organizations"), J. Mann ("Technical and Social Difficulties in the Control of Evaluation Research"), and F. G. Caro ("Evaluation in Comprehensive Urban Anti-Poverty Programs").

Rossi, P., and Williams, W. (Eds.) *Evaluating Social Action Programs: Theory, Practice, and Politics.* New York: Seminar Press, 1972. See the articles by P. Rossi and W. Williams ("Testing for Success and Failure in Social Action") and D. N. Kershaw ("Issues in Income Maintenance Experimentation").

Trow, M. "Survey Research and Education." In C. Glock (Ed.), *Survey Research in the Social Sciences.* New York: Russell Sage Foundation, 1967. Pp. 315-375.

Weinberg, E. *Community Surveys with Local Talent: A Hand-*

book. Chicago: National Opinion Research Center, 1971. Offers guidelines for conducting field interviews based on NORC's experience in health-center surveys.

——————— FORMATIVE EVALUATION ———————

Evaluation research has been categorized into two types—formative and summative (see **Summative Evaluation**). Formative evaluation essentially is concerned with helping the developer of programs or products (curricula, books, television shows, etc.) through the use of empirical research methodology; summative evaluation is concerned with evaluating the overall program after it is in operation. Ideally, the formative evaluator will work along with the developer from the outset of his work. Therefore, at the same time as development planning is taking place, the problems related to personnel, cost, and procedures of formative evaluation should also be solved.

Examples of the kinds of evaluation research conducted by the formative evaluator include:

1. *Materials pretesting.* As components of a program or product (e.g., lesson units in a curriculum, chapters in a book) are produced, the formative evaluator tries them out on a small sample of the intended users. Through such techniques as **Observation** and **Tests,** the evaluator is able to report to the producer on such factors as whether the component gained and held the attention of the sampled group, whether learning (or whatever other intended outcome) took place, and whether the component was easily used or administered. On the basis of this reporting, the component may be revised, and then the revised component is pretested. And so the process continues until both producer and formative evaluator are satisfied.

2. *Target-group description.* Frequently the producer may be insufficiently informed about a target population's character-

istics. For example, a medical educator writing pamphlets about drug abuse may want to know more about the urban adolescent's current slang terminology for drugs, a producer of a television show aimed at first graders may want to know what the commonly held interests of this group are, or a writer of a general science textbook may want to know the extent of ninth-grade girls' knowledge of and interest in automobile engines. This part of the formative evaluator's work is similar to needs assessment performed in a somewhat different context.

3. *Goal definition.* Those who initiate the development of a program or a product are often unsophisticated in goal definition (see **Goals and Objectives**). The formative researcher should, therefore, make sure that a goals statement is drawn up, with the goals operationally defined. Goal definition is frequently an iterative process in the early stages. The goal is vaguely conceptualized; the formative evaluator provides an operational definition; and this definition is rejected by the developer, who produces his own revised version of the goal. The formative evaluator may then show that this revised goal is unattainable for the target population or too open to multiple interpretations, and so the process continues until consensus is reached. As part of the process of selecting goals among a number of competing goals, the formative evaluator may suggest bringing together a panel of experts to help reach consensus. Special psychometric techniques such as rating scales (see **Ratings**) and the **Delphi Technique** may be used with the panels in the process.

4. *Special studies.* Research into basic processes and relationships is not usually considered part of formative evaluation; but for ongoing programs it may be included, especially when the program is innovative or the target group's major characteristics are unknown. For example, problems of how to change certain attitudes of those experimenting with hard drugs may best be solved only after a sample of hard-drug experimenters have been subjected to a series of studies on influence processes. However, political considerations may require that a drug program begin before the results of the studies are available. Research on the problems can still proceed while the program is in operation, and, since the program is a continuing one, the results can be fed into the program as they are obtained. In this case, formative evalua-

tion can help improve a program and contribute to the body of basic psychological and sociological knowledge as well.

Since most formative evaluation provides short-term feedback, especially in the materials-pretesting area, much of its work is perforce hurried. A program producer may not have time for a highly sophisticated statistical analysis or for a complex sampling procedure to be carried out. This is not to say that formative evaluations are completely exempt from scientific rigor but rather that they may be simplified, more error-prone versions of later summative evaluations. Thus, the generalizability of formative-evaluation findings is reduced, and one would, therefore, usually expect formative evaluation to occur with each new program or product development.

An important feature of formative evaluation as distinct from summative evaluation is that formative evaluation must occur in close collaboration with program or product development. The formative evaluator is a part of the development process, and it is not unreasonable for him to become as ego-involved in the program as his scientific demeanor will allow. The summative evaluator, on the other hand, should be, and should seem to be, independent of developer, product, and program. Thus, the person who carries out the formative evaluation may be of considerable help to the summative evaluator (in terms of problems of measurement, etc.), but probably the formative evaluator should not become the summative evaluator. (See **Evaluator Role** and **Goal-Free Evaluation**).—S. B.

Bloom, B. S., Hastings, J. T., and Madaus, G. F. *Handbook on Formative and Summative Evaluation of Student Learning.* New York: McGraw-Hill, 1971. Contains references to formative evaluation in many different kinds of programs.
Reeves, B. F. *The First Year of "Sesame Street": The Formative Research.* New York: Children's Television Workshop, 1970. Presents some good examples of how formative research can help improve a program.
Rossi, P. H. "Practice, Method and Theory in Evaluating Social Action Programs." In J. L. Sundquist (Ed.), *On Fighting Poverty: Perspectives from Experience.* New York: Basic Books, 1969. Pp. 217-234.

Scriven, M. "The Methodology of Evaluation." In *Perspectives of Curriculum Evaluation.* AERA Monograph Series on Curriculum Evaluation, No. 1. Chicago: Rand McNally, 1967. Pp. 39-82. An historically important article, being one of the first references to formative evaluation.

Weiss, C. H. "The Politicization of Evaluative Research." *Journal of Social Issues,* 1970, *26* (4), 57-68.

--- GOAL-FREE EVALUATION ---

Goal-free evaluation is an approach proposed by Michael Scriven as a means of ensuring that evaluators take into account the *actual* effects and not just the *intended* effects of education and training programs. It derives from his growing uneasiness about the separation of goals and side effects. (See **Goals and Objectives** and **Side Effects.**) Some programs, Scriven notes, achieve their goals in exemplary fashion but are terminated because of particularly adverse side effects, while other programs make little or no progress toward intended outcomes but are implemented because of important unintended gains. Under such circumstances, it makes little sense to perpetuate a distinction between intended and unintended outcomes since the final appraisal should focus on importance and value, not intention; and it may be misleading and mischievous to give special attention to one type of effect in an evaluation effort merely because it was anticipated in advance as a "goal." Special emphasis upon goals is appropriate in evaluating a proposal, but not in evaluating a process or product.

Indeed, Scriven feels that the whole language of "side effects" or "secondary effects" or "unanticipated effects" tends to detract from what might in fact be the critical program achievements. He concludes that "consideration and evaluation of goals [are] an unnecessary but also a possibly contaminating step." He

offers as an alternative approach goal-free evaluation, "the evaluation of *actual* effects against . . . a profile of *demonstrated* needs"
in the area of education under consideration (p. 1). In this approach, the evaluator would make a deliberate attempt not to be
co-opted by the rhetoric of program goals, which are viewed as
appropriate targets in program planning and development but not
in evaluation. He would gather data bearing on a broad array of
actual effects and would evaluate the importance of these effects
in meeting educational needs (or producing educational or personal harm). To be sure, the program goals could usually be
induced from this array of actual effects, but this step is viewed as
unnecessary. If the array does not turn out to include all the major
goals, the program developer might be tempted to view the whole
enterprise as irrelevant, but he would usually be better served to
recommend revising the program and even modifying its goals,
possibly to capitalize upon side effects documented in the evaluation effort.—S. M.

Scriven, M. "Pros and Cons about Goal-Free Evaluation." *Evalua-
    tion Comment,* 1972, *3* (4), 1-4.

———————————— GOALS AND OBJECTIVES ————————————

The terms *goals* and *objectives* are often used interchangeably. In some cases, however, it is useful to distinguish between
them, and the distinction adopted here rests in the level of generality of each kind of statement. Goals are logically stated first;
they are concerned with ultimate outcomes and are usually
phrased in general or global terms. Objectives are narrower and
usually short-range; they are statements of student behaviors that,
taken together, are thought to contribute to the envisioned final
goals. Examples of goals and objectives, and their translation into
behavioral objectives and measures, are provided in Table 1, which

Table 1

Examples of Goals and Objectives and Their Translation into
Behavioral Objectives and Measures[a]

Domain: Music	Ends (for students)	Means (to be employed by education/training agents)
Goals	I. Perform a musical piece, theme, or figure in any medium.	Offer a two-year music course for junior high school students.
	II. Read the standard musical notation scheme and its accompanying figures, numbers, and verbal symbols.	Provide trained instructors with adequate planning time.
	III. Listen to music with understanding.	Provide relevant audiovisual materials: tape equipment, records, record players, sheet music, pictures of instruments, recorders, pianos, etc.
	IV. Be knowledgeable about composers, performers, periods, styles, instruments, and works and about the place of music in Western culture.	Provide appropriate space and facilities.
	V. Seek musical experiences.	Provide appropriate credit and institutional rewards for students and instructors.
	VI. Develop preferences and make judgments about music and its performance.	Facilitate access to live musical performances.
Objectives (See Goal III above)	A. Recognize and identify instruments, musical forms, and particular works—by sound.	Provide a balanced mix of instruction and practice in the following areas:
	B. Perceive the unity of musical selections and gross and subtle changes in musical performance.	Perceiving (becoming aware of) aspects of musical selections and performance.
	C. Discriminate between different related aspects of music—by sound.	Discriminating between similar musical forms and experiences.
	D. Attend to simple and complex pieces of music.	Recognizing and naming standard musical instruments, forms, and works.

Domain: Music	Ends (for students)	Means (to be employed by education/training agents)
Behavioral Objectives (See Objective C above)	1. Distinguish the following: voice (male or female), pitch (up or down), volume (louder or softer), melody (steps or skips), rhythm (waltz or march), speed (faster or slower), singing (unison or harmony), mode (major or minor), voice (soprano or alto, tenor or bass), instruments of the same class (e.g., French horn, trombone, trumpet).	Explain what is meant by pitch, volume, rhythm, etc. Demonstrate variations in these characteristics through live and recorded performance. Have students reproduce the variations of interest through humming, playing, and singing; have them record and play back their productions.
	2. Discriminate variations on a theme: Is this sample a variation on a given theme? Is this sample more of a variation than that one?	Explain and demonstrate what is meant by variations on a musical theme, moving from simple variations to more complex ones. Have students try to invent variations on simple themes.
Measurement (See Behavioral Objectives 1 and 2 above)	Student performs successfully on a multiple-choice test: 5-10 items on each variation of interest under Behavioral Objective 1 (presented by tape)—student marks answer sheet (male or female voice; trombone, trumpet, or French horn; etc.); 10-15 items (also presented by tape) where student marks whether sample is or is not a variation on a comparison theme; 10-15 items requiring finer distinctions among variations. (Minimum standards of successful attainment of objectives have been specified in advance.)	Develop measuring instrument, using skilled professionals. Set standards for attainment. Administer, score, analyze results. Provide feedback helpful to students, instructors.

[a]Many entries in this table are adapted from *Phase I, National Assessment* (Princeton, N.J.: Educational Testing Service, 1965), pp. 42-56.

shows how curriculum planners might proceed in formulating their aims, at each level of generality, for a two-year course in music. Statements of behavioral objectives stand last, at the level of maximum specificity; derived from an analysis of the more general objectives, behavioral objectives specify the sought-for behaviors in greater detail, sometimes including specification of the level of performance expected of the student and the context in which that performance is expected. They may differ from the first set of objectives in their concentration on *measurable* performance by the learner.

Program planners often confuse goals and objectives for students with those for the educational agency. The confusion, essentially, is one between outcome and support goals. Thus, one may encounter statements about what the education/training agency intends to do in support of goal attainment. For example, an intent to hire guidance counselors or to purchase audiovisual equipment is not, properly speaking, an ultimate goal in the sense intended here; rather, it is a statement about means to that end (see Table 1). The means are of course vital, but they are, in our view, ancillary to the chosen outcomes.

During the last few decades, stating objectives in terms of measurable student behavior has gained both support and opposition. Proponents of the approach maintain that stating objectives in terms of observable behaviors offers clear-cut targets that can be used by teachers to plan their instruction and by students to guide their study. They maintain also that assessment of the effectiveness of learning is facilitated, because behavioral objectives provide the evaluator with specific information about what is to be measured. They insist that, since the purpose of education is to change the behavior of the learner, the objectives of instruction should be stated in terms of that behavior.

Opponents of behavioral objectives argue that the method focuses principally on the teaching of facts at the expense of more complex and higher-level behavior. They consider the concept dehumanizing and inflexible, tending to discourage creativity and spontaneity in the classroom. They are also unwilling to accept specified performance as the sole criterion of learning.

Although the controversy is not over, some compromises are being made and a substantial number of educators probably would agree on these points: (1) Objectives expressed in measurable, behavioral terms are appropriate for basic skills and for other areas when there is agreement about the components of an instructional program. (2) For most purposes, behavioral objectives need not be reduced to trivial detail. The degree of specificity may vary and should relate to the purpose of instruction and the understanding of students and instructors. (3) The use of behaviorally stated objectives should be contained in an instructional model which recognizes and provides for individual differences. (4) Complex and long-range objectives should be included in a set of objectives, even though they cannot be described in precise terms or measured with a high degree of accuracy. (5) Educational objectives must be appropriate to the social milieu at a given time, and students should participate with their instructors in finding objectives that make sense to them. (6) In times like the present, when technological and social changes are rapid and the future is uncertain, the desired behaviors should be adaptable to situations other than the existing one. The ultimate usefulness of behavioral objectives will depend upon how effectively they may be adapted to quite different learning needs and situations.

To the evaluator, objectives expressed in terms of specific student behaviors are highly desirable, since they represent a first step in the development or selection of measurement instruments. If statements of objectives are not highly specific, the evaluator will inevitably have to infer by himself how the attainment of such skills and knowledge may be measured.

It has been suggested that the special skills of evaluators should be used to develop a comprehensive pool of objectives encompassing a wide range of specific and complex behaviors. Teachers would select from this pool those objectives which fit their purposes and their students' learning capabilities and interests. Others believe that the process of setting objectives is an essential part of instructional planning and should not be simply a matter of selection from a "catalog" prepared by others.

Evaluation is part of the whole process of setting objectives and measuring how well those objectives have been reached. In the beginning, evaluation tools are used to analyze subject matter to be taught and to determine the status of the learner. During instruction, tests or other evaluation instruments measure progress and provide feedback on changes which should be made in the learning situation (see **Formative Evaluation**). At the conclusion of the instructional unit, progress toward the achievement of objectives and goals is assessed (see **Summative Evaluation**).—E. J. R., A. Z. S.

Gagné, R. M., and Kneller, G. P. "Behavioral Objectives? Yes or No?" *Educational Leadership,* 1972, *19,* 394-400.

Krathwohl, D. R., and Payne, D. A. "Defining and Assessing Educational Objectives." In R. L. Thorndike (Ed.), *Educational Measurement.* (2nd Ed.) Washington, D.C.: American Council on Education, 1971. Pp. 17-45.

Lindvall, C. M. (Ed.) *Defining Educational Objectives.* Pittsburgh: University of Pittsburgh Press, 1964. A report of the 1963 Regional Commission on Educational Coordination. Includes papers by C. M. Lindvall, David Krathwohl, Robert M. Gagné, Robert Glaser, James H. Reynolds, and Ralph W. Tyler.

Mager, R. F. *Preparing Objectives for Programmed Instruction.* Belmont, Calif.: Fearon, 1962. A step-by-step description of how to specify objectives. Illustrations included.

Popham, W. J. *Establishing Instructional Goals.* Englewood Cliffs, N.J.: Prentice-Hall, 1970. A collection of self-instructional programs dealing with various aspects of instruction that can be used in decision making. The programs focus on the selection and statement of instructional goals.

GRADES

Grades, the symbols or marks given by teachers to indicate an individual's degree of accomplishment in a course of instruction, are dependent upon whatever measurement processes have been carried out by the teacher and therefore suffer from all the errors of measurement that are involved in those measurement processes. For example, a grade of *A* in mathematics, based on a teacher's subjective judgment that the student was "performing very well," would be likely to suffer from all the problems of subjective judgments, including conscious and unconscious biases of the teacher, lack of clear criteria of what constitutes "performing very well," and low levels of **Reliability** and **Validity**.

Grades have a simplicity that charms many people. They also have problems that cause discomfort in many measurement experts. The popularity of grades stems in part from the fact that simply one letter (or number) is used to summarize a student's achievement in a subject area, and that is a nice reduction of a complex issue. However, it would make more sense to use many letters (or numbers)—indicating, for example, that the student has mastered this element, needs further practice in this skill, is trying hard to overcome that deficiency, etc. Some educators have argued that at least two grades should be given for each subject area—one to indicate level of achievement (current status) and the other to indicate amount of effort being expended or amount of progress being made. A student who is performing a little above average and trying hard is different from the one who is achieving at the same level but apparently not trying. When a single grade is given for a course, it is often difficult to know whether the grade indicates level of performance, effort, or some combination involving perhaps a rating of progress as opposed to status.

Grades impart a sense of fixed and final judgment. Thus, there is comfort in knowing that Junior is an *A* student in English; and wrath can be righteous if he is pronounced only a *D* student in French. Let us for the moment suspend reality and assume that those grades represent truth untarnished by errors of measurement and judgment. Even so, the level of performance or effort of an *A* student in one situation is not necessarily the same as that of an *A* student in another. The point is that grades rarely have absolute meaning. Rather, they are quite commonly relative to a reference group—the class, the other trainees, the rest of the school, etc. An *A* in Introductory Psychology at East-West Community College is not the same as an *A* in Introductory Psychology at Highly Selective University. The best students at East-West would probably perform at about the same level as the poorest students at Highly Selective. Statewide surveys based on **Standardized Tests** indicate that a student in the top 10 percent of students in a high school serving a disadvantaged area performs at a level corresponding to the bottom 10 percent for some high schools serving advantaged communities. Or, as another example of the relativity of grades, one finds that among those responsible for graduate school admissions, a *B* average from one college will be treated as *better* performance than an *A* average from some other college with lower academic standards.

The meaning of a particular grade is also affected by differing abilities of groups over time. For example, a grade of A in the class of 1973 may be the equivalent of a grade of B in the class of 1968 if the level of ability of the student body has dropped in the intervening years (Hills and Gladney). This problem may be exacerbated when instructors grade students "on the curve"; that is, give grades to students on some prearranged basis whereby, for instance, 7 percent receive A, 24 percent B, 38 percent C, 24 percent D, and 7 percent F—where A = at least 1.5 standard deviations (SDs) above the mean; B = .5 to 1.5 SDs above the mean; C = .5 below to .5 SDs above the mean; D = 1.5 to .5 SDs below the mean; F = more than 1.5 SDs below the mean (see the normal curve at the top of Figure 1 in Score Types). Ironically, grading students "on the curve" represents an attempt to be fair—to ensure that the distribution of grades is about the same for each class regardless of whether the teacher is an easy or a hard marker. Indeed, it does ensure that, and it can be modified so that a class with higher average attainments gets better grades than one with lower average attainments. But if, over time, there is a gradual change in the quality of the student body, or if the quality of instruction varies from class to class, one student's A may not be comparable to another's A, and marking on the curve may be a factor contributing to the problem of interpreting grades.

Grades are, at best, a contaminated measure of achievement. What are some of the factors that contaminate the measure? One seems to be a sex bias favoring attractive females. Another seems to be a personality factor (called Machiavellianism) in which the student consciously or unconsciously seeks to manipulate the teacher's gradings by such techniques as sitting in the front of the class, asking questions, visiting the teacher after class, and feigning interest in the classwork.

Grades remain popular in education and training programs because they allow teachers to make personal evaluations of students. However, they have lost some ground over recent years. They have been eliminated entirely in a few colleges, and in others the pass-fail option has been increasingly adopted. These changes have occurred partly because of the realization of technical problems involved in the use of grades (some of which have been presented here) and partly because of a philosophical disagreement with their use. This disagreement is especially strong among progressive educators (e.g., Holt) and activist student groups. The substance of the argument is that grades—and working for grades—(a) pervert the educational process by narrowing the focus of students and teachers, (b) create harmful anxieties, and (c) present artificial, extrinsic motives for learning at the expense of more "moral" motives that are intrinsic to the learning task (such as learning for the pleasure it brings).

In response to these arguments, it might be pointed out that the imperfect feedback provided by grades is still generally better than no feedback. Further, if grades are culpable because they are based on unreliable and invalid examinations, let us develop better examinations rather than do away with grades. Finally, if grades represent levels of performance on tests that have validity (especially construct validity), working for a good grade involves the same processes as working to accomplish the goals of the program. That can hardly be considered reprehensible.

The pros and cons of grades as a technique in individual assessment and evaluation can be argued at much greater length. What needs further elaboration here is the use of grades in the evaluation of programs. In program evaluation, students' grades sometimes are used as an outcome (dependent) variable. Thus, one program is proclaimed better than some other because the students in the first program get better grades than those in the second. If this sort of evaluation seems primitive and unlikely, consider that high school programs are frequently judged on the basis of how well students do in college—on *grade*-point average!

There are other more reasonable uses of grades in an evaluation. One is as a covariate when students have been randomly assigned to treatments. Random assignment does not ensure equal groups at the start of the treatments; some inequality is almost certain. Grades are readily available from school records and, as a covariate, allow an analysis that tells about treatment effects if treatment groups had been equal with respect to previous grades. A second reasonable use of grades is as a moderator variable. Here the evaluator asks, for example, whether students at various letter-grade levels are differentially affected by the treatment. If a comparison of two methods of teaching Intermediate French were being undertaken, students in the two treatments might be "blocked" into subgroups according to the grade received in Introductory French and the analysis conducted accordingly. Perhaps those who obtained *A*s and *B*s in Introductory French (better-motivated or better-achieving students—or some combination) do better with one method, and perhaps the situation is reversed for students who obtained *C*s and *D*s. (See **Variables** and **Trait-Treatment Interaction.**)

When grades are used to evaluate an individual, they are open to criticism and are only as valid and reliable as the assessments and measurement processes on which they are based. When grades are used in the evaluation of a program, they should rarely be used as the sole outcome variable but might prove useful as covariates or as moderator variables.—S. B.

Ebel, R. L. *Essentials of Educational Measurement.* Englewood Cliffs, N.J.: Prentice-Hall, 1972. See Chapter 12 ("Marks and Marking Systems"), a well-reasoned presentation, setting the problems of grades in a realistic perspective.

Hills, J. R., and Gladney, M. B. "Factors Influencing College Grading Standards." *Journal of Educational Measurement,* 1968, *5,* 31-39.

Holt, J. *How Children Fail.* New York: Pitman, 1968. Argues that grades have an undesirable influence on the educational process.

Rothney, J. W. M. *Evaluating and Reporting Pupil Progress.* What Research Says to the Teacher, No. 7. Washington, D.C.: National Education Association, 1955.

Singer, J. E. "The Use of Manipulative Strategies: Machiavellianism and Attractiveness." *Sociometry,* 1964, *27,* 128-150.

—————————————— HALO EFFECT ——————————————

Whenever judges rate people on a series of traits or behaviors, there is a possibility that they will make their judgments on the basis of global impressions of the people rather than on the specific traits. This widely encountered phenomenon in the rating process has been termed the *halo effect.*

The effect, a form of bias or generalized set, can work to produce either high or low **Ratings** or **Observation** records. A student who reads well, for example, may also be rated by a teacher as high on such other characteristics as attentiveness, neatness, or cooperativeness. In contrast, a teacher may assume that a poor speller cannot be good at other verbal tasks. Halo effects, of course, are not limited to ratings of students; they frequently occur in employee or **Staff Evaluation.**

The presence of "halo" is suspected when there are unusually high intercorrelations among scales purporting to measure different aspects of behavior. In this case, the stabilities of ratings and observations are also likely to be spuriously high, since a first favorable (or unfavorable) impression may persist when a second observation or rating must be made of the same person.

The halo effect was first identified more than a half century ago, and the literature abounds in examples of the problems it creates for the **Validity** and **Reliability** of ratings. Medley and Mitzell cite a typical example of its operation: School administrators were asked to rank teachers according to (a) their general merit as teachers and (b) the administrator's estimate of their intellectual capacity. The two rankings correlated .71. However, when more objective measures of intelligence were used, the correlations between intelligence scores and ratings of teaching effectiveness were substantially reduced. (See **Correlation.**)

Since the halo effect is partially a function of preconceptions or the amount of prior information judges have about the object or person to be rated, the evaluator may wish to seek independent, external ratings. Unfortunately, use of external raters does not guarantee the bypassing of halo effect. However, investigators have found that if the variable to be rated is carefully defined so as to provide sufficient specificity and clarity, halo error can be greatly diminished. For example, instead of being asked to respond to a vague, global category such as "leadership," a rater might be asked to rate trainees on more specific categories such as "initiates structure in group discussions," "suggests new approaches to problems," "peers turn to him for advice on actions to be taken," "volunteers for new assignments." Thus, the rater is forced away from general impressions into more careful and objective analysis.—E. J. R.

Cahen, L. "An Experimental Manipulation of the Halo Effect." Unpublished doctoral dissertation, Stanford University, 1966. Contains a thorough review of the literature on halo effect.

Coffman, W. E. "Essay Examinations." In R. L. Thorndike (Ed.), *Educational Measurement*. (2nd Ed.) Washington, D.C.: American Council on Education, 1971. Pp. 271-303. Contains discussion of the influence of halo effect on reliability of scoring essay examinations.

Crissy, W. J. E., and Regan, J. J. "Halo in the Employment Interview." *Journal of Applied Psychology*, 1951, *35*, 338-341.

Medley, D. M., and Mitzel, H. E. "Measuring Classroom Behavior by Systematic Observation." In N. L. Gage (Ed.), *Handbook of Research on Teaching*. Chicago: Rand McNally, 1963. Pp. 305-306.

Scannell, D. P., and Marshall, J. C. "The Effect of Selected Composition Errors on Grades Assigned to Essay Examinations." *American Educational Research Journal*, 1966, *3*, 125-130.

———— "HARD" AND "SOFT"—SHIBBOLETHS ————
IN EVALUATION

In general, hard evaluation is regarded as rigorous by its friends and trivial by its enemies. Soft evaluation is regarded as sensitive by its friends and unscientific by its enemies. A few brave people obliquely challenge these assertions, saying that there is no such thing as hard or soft evaluation—only hard or soft evaluators. Like most shibboleths (pet phrases that help distinguish adherents of different parties or sects from one another),* the terms *hard* and *soft* have often been applied thoughtlessly. In common parlance, a hard evaluation usually involves (1) a research design capable of discerning causal relationships (see **Causality**); (2) the collection of data that are objective, reliable, and valid; (3) the analysis of these data by sophisticated statistical techniques. (Examples of such hard evaluations are the *Sesame Street* and *Plaza Sesamo* evaluation studies—see Bogatz and Ball; Diaz-Guerrero and Holtzman.) A soft evaluation usually involves (1) a research design that, at most, can point to correlationships; (2) data that are subjective and judgmental; (3) an absence of sophisticated statistical analyses of the data. (Many evaluations based on the **Case-Study Method** exemplify soft evaluation, as do many of the efforts carried out as part of an **Accreditation** process.)

James C. Stone (University of California, Berkeley) in a personal communication has used the term *phenomenological evaluation* to label one kind of soft evaluation. Here the personal viewpoints, reactions, and experiences of participants are collected, and the interaction between and among them is documented; the process may involve logs, diaries, informal feedback, self-reports, and observations (see **Data Sources**). The evaluator becomes a participant-observer in phenomenological evaluation,

---

*Scott wrote that knaves and fools invent catchwords and shibboleths to keep honest people from coming to a just understanding.

identifying with the participant and systematically recording his or her own reactions as well as those of the participants.

The degrees of difference between hard and soft evaluation are shown in Figure 1, a simple scheme based on some of the major components involved. The hardest kind of evaluation (the front lower-left-hand cube) is a sophisticated statistical analysis of objective data obtained from a true **Experimental Design**. The softest kind of evaluation (the back upper-right-hand cube) is an unsophisticated statistical analysis of subjective data obtained from a nonexperimental evaluation design. In practice, evaluations may include a number of these "cubes"; and on the basis of the "cube," with the appropriate reasoning, a piece of *evidence* is established. Since evaluators will usually want to present a variety of evidence, evaluation might include both objective and subjective data; and some of these data may be presented at the descriptive level, while others may be subjected to a more sophisticated level of statistical analysis (e.g., **Multivariate Analysis**).

Extremists in the hard-evaluation camp view soft evaluation as indicative of soft-headedness and insufficient training on the part of the evaluator. They further agree that the results of a soft evaluation are not open to **Replication** and that subjectivity is so rampant that it is impossible to tell what are legitimate conclusions and what are the formal statements of prejudgments or chance occurrences. Extremists in the soft-evaluation camp look with similar disfavor on hard evaluation. They claim that hard evaluations miss the essence of a program's impact; ignore the variables that currently available objective measures cannot assess adequately; and are mechanistic, basing conclusions on statistical tests of relatively trivial data rather than on intelligent judgments.

A major issue in all of this is the kind of evidence an evaluator finds acceptable. Which is a more acceptable kind of evidence: a statistically significant higher mean gain by an experimental group (compared with a **Control Group**) on a standardized achievement test, or a consistent report by the experimental students that they feel they are learning more? If there is no statistically significant difference between the achievement of students taught by Method A as compared with Method B, but teachers prefer to teach by Method A, which piece of evidence (which "cube") should an evaluator prefer?

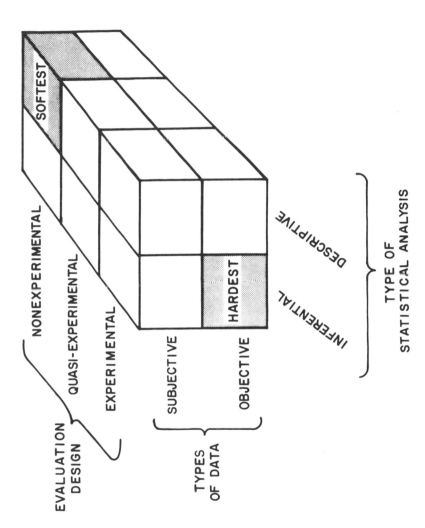

Figure 1. Components involved in hard and soft evaluations.

The word *acceptable* implies that there is some purpose for the evaluation. Thus, the kind of evidence that an evaluator finds acceptable is in part dependent on what he wants to find out. (The term *evidence* is used here to include the data, design, and analysis.) If he wants to find out which method has the greatest impact on student attainment, he will not be substantially helped by evidence on teachers' preferences; if he wants to find out whether the school system is successful in retaining staff, he will not regard students' scores as useful evidence. In short, the evidence—whether based on objective or subjective data, whether collected within an experimental, quasi-experimental, or nonexperimental design, whether statistically analyzed or not—should be *appropriate* to the question being asked.

Furthermore, as evaluators we should obtain the best evidence that it is *feasible* to obtain. Considerations here include practicality and cost. Thus, it may not be practical to assign subjects randomly to treatments and construct a true experiment. Computer technology in a school system may not be capable of handling an analysis of covariance. The cost of obtaining objective observational data may be too great for the evaluation budget. Demanding a particular kind of evidence that cannot be obtained is tantamount to saying that no evidence will be presented. Usually, it is better to have tried and got some evidence than never to have tried at all.

Finally, the questions about the *technical quality* of the data cannot be ignored; that is, whether the data are objective or subjective, they still have to meet reasonable criteria of **Reliability** and **Validity**. One must also demand that the design and analyses be properly carried out. An unreliable judgment in a case study is as bad as an inappropriate error term in an analysis of variance.

In general, the hard-versus-soft argument would suggest that objective measures are probably more reliable than subjective measures but that subjective measures may be more valid than objective measures. But this kind of argument can too easily be misinterpreted. Both objective and subjective measures must have sufficient reliability in an evaluation to ensure the possibility of obtaining reliable assessments across groups. If we are assessing a relatively stable characteristic (children's achievement in mathematics, adults' skill in typing), an unreliable measure, no matter how "sensitive," cannot be valid. The presence of either validity or reliability cannot make up for the absence of the other. It is incumbent on both the soft and hard evaluators to indicate how reliable and valid their data are.

In short, it is imprudent to prejudge and stereotype "hard" and "soft" evaluation. These are extreme forms of a continuum that enmeshes design, data, and analysis. There are good hard and good soft evaluations (appropriate to the questions raised, feasible, and technically sound). And, just as clearly, there are bad hard and bad soft evaluations. But most comprehensive evaluations, of necessity, include both hard and soft components; and both are almost bound to find their critics as well as their praisers.—S. B.

Bogatz, G. A., and Ball, S. *The Second Year of Sesame Street: A Continuing Evaluation*. Princeton, N.J.: Educational Testing Service, 1971.
Diaz-Guerrero, R., and Holtzman, W. H. "Learning by Televised *Plaza Sesamo* in Mexico." *Journal of Educational Psychology,* in press.
Spielberg, H. *Phenomenology in Psychology and Psychiatry*. Evanston, Ill.: Northwestern University Press, 1972.

HAWTHORNE EFFECT

Hawthorne effect refers to changes in behavior that occur when the subjects in an experiment or evaluation are aware of their special status. Students work more eagerly or teachers teach more enthusiastically perhaps because they feel that they are especially chosen. Although the new program gets the credit for their performance, it is the awareness of the participants—and not the program as such—that has improved the performance of those involved. In a new program for training radio operators, for example, those responsible for the training may decide to use the new program with only a proportion of the trainees and to evaluate its use relative to the old program. In such circumstances, it is quite likely that the trainees and trainers using the new program will be aware of their special status. Because of this *awareness*, they may perform better in their respective roles; and it may then seem that the new program is more effective than the old one, although there may in fact be no difference in the real effectiveness of the two programs. The true state of affairs may become apparent as the "newness" of the new program wears off.

In order to be sure in an evaluation that Hawthorne effect is not operating to make a newly adopted program seem better than previous programs, it is best to disguise or minimize the newness of the program under study. Alternatively, both the experimental *and* the control groups can be made to feel that they have some special experimental status. Perhaps both groups get new books even though the **Control Group** could have continued to use the somewhat worn ones of the previous year. In drug research, for example, the experimental group gets the new drug. The control group also gets a pill that looks exactly the same as that given the experimental group; but this pill, unknown to the subjects, contains only a neutral substance—a placebo. Often this placebo has clear effects on the subjects, depending on what they expect it to do to them. Hawthorne effect is basically the same process as that which occurs in drug research when a placebo produces results that it would not normally be expected to produce.

The Hawthorne experiments were conducted by investigators from the Massachusetts Institute of Technology for the National Research Council and the Illuminating Engineering Society. The experiments, begun in 1924, were conducted in a number of plants, including the Hawthorne, Illinois, plant of Western Electric Company. The question was whether degree of lighting in the plant affected productivity. It seemed that whenever a new degree of lighting was tried (higher *or* lower), production increased. In reporting this effect in the Hawthorne plant, Snow (p. 282) added: "Any investigation attempting to evaluate definitely the effect of illumination or some such influence must take the greatest of pains to control or eliminate all factors but the one being studied. Many of them can be controlled or eliminated, but the one great stumbling block remaining is the problem of the psychology of the human individual." Roethlisberger and Dickson conducted many more experiments at the Hawthorne plant and found that even when women employees were put on a 48-hour week with no rest period or lunch, there was an upward trend in productivity, provided the women were aware that they were subjects in an experiment.

Hawthorne effect was first used in the terminology of evaluation by French in 1953. French was interested in educational experiments in a field setting as opposed to laboratory settings. He argued that those conducted in field settings were less subject to artificiality and, therefore, were more generalizable. The exception, he pointed out (p. 101), "is well illustrated in the Hawthorne experiments. From a methodological point of view, the most interesting finding is what we might call the *Hawthorne effect.*"

The question of whether Hawthorne effect necessarily operates in an educational setting has been raised. Cook, for example, has had some difficulty in reproducing a Hawthorne effect in his relatively extensive programmatic research. However, at this point, it would seem prudent for evaluators to assume the existence of a Hawthorne effect and to guard against it by the use of strategies presented earlier in this article.

Some educators in recent years have talked about harnessing the Hawthorne effect. If this awareness can improve performance, they argue, why not introduce change into educational systems and study the effects of the change—thereby deliberately creating a Hawthorne effect and improving the performance of those under study? This, the argument goes, should be done even if the change itself has no great merit. The counterargument is that if change and experimentation were the rule rather than the exception, Hawthorne effect would probably not occur. In any event, this kind of manipulation of a school system by educational administrators, however useful it might be, still does not make for proper evaluation. The evaluator must be on guard against Hawthorne effect, thereby ensuring that the results of the study being conducted are caused by the actual treatment and not by the spurious factor of the subjects' realizing that they are part of an experiment.—S. B.

Carey, A. A. "The Hawthorne Studies: A Radical Criticism." *American Sociological Review,* 1967, *32,* 403-416.

Cook, D. L. "The Hawthorne Effect in Educational Research." *Phi Delta Kappa,* 1962, *44,* 116-122. Reprinted in W. H. MacGinitie and S. Ball (Eds.), *Readings in Psychological Foundations of Education.* New York: McGraw-Hill, 1968.

Cook, D. L. *The Impact of the Hawthorne Effect in Experimental Designs in Educational Research.* Cooperative Research Project No. 1757. Washington, D.C.: United States Office of Education, 1967.

French, J. R. P., Jr. "Experiments in Field Settings." In L. Festinger and D. Katz (Eds.), *Research Methods in the Behavioral Sciences.* New York: Dryden Press, 1953. Chapter 3.

Roethlisberger, F. J., and Dickson, W. J. *Management and the Worker.* Cambridge, Mass.: Harvard University Press, 1941.

Snow, C. E. "Research on Industrial Illumination." *Tech Engineering News,* 1926, *8,* 257-282.

Trow, M. "Methodological Problems in the Evaluation of Innovation." In F. G. Caro (Ed.), *Readings in Evaluation.* Rensselaer, N.Y.: Russell Sage, 1971.

——————————— HYPOTHESIS TESTING ———————————

In **Scientific Inquiry and Evaluation,** the general nature of probability is treated, as well as its relationship to prediction and the testing of models and theories. *Hypothesis testing* is used here in a restricted sense to refer to statistical tests of carefully worded statements (hypotheses). Is program A better than program B? This is a valid question, but it is not a hypothesis. A hypothesis would be the following: Program A *is better* than Program B.

In most evaluations it is reasonable to hypothesize that some program is superior to that being used with a **Control Group.** Frequently this hypothesis is implicit; that is, the evaluator may not present it as a formal, explicit hypothesis. In order to test the hypothesis that the new program is superior, the technically appropriate procedure is to state a *null hypothesis* (that the programs are equally effective). A statistical test will then indicate the probability that a difference exists; and we may, on that basis, be able to reject the null hypothesis and assert that the original hypothesis is verified.

In testing the hypothesis that there is no significant difference (see **Statistical Significance**) between the mean performance of two groups (one group in each program), we do not expect to find a difference of exactly zero. Rather, the question is whether the difference we find could have occurred simply by chance. The t statistic may be used to answer this question. If, for example, we compare the means for two groups of 120 persons and find that the value of the t statistic is 2.00, then the difference in mean scores would be significant at the .05 level of significance (critical value = 1.98) but not at the .01 level (critical value = 2.62). That is, if we were able to repeat the study with many new samples, such a difference would occur by chance less than five times out of one hundred; but it *could* occur by chance more than once in one hundred instances.

Our choice of .05, .01, or .001 as the level of significance is dependent upon the amount of error we are willing to tolerate. If we accept .05 as our level, then about five times in one hundred we will incorrectly reject the null hypothesis when it is, in fact, true. This type of error is known as a *Type I error*. If the level of significance is .01, then the probability of our making a Type I error is only 1 percent. We can make the probability of making a Type I error arbitrarily small; as the level of significance is set lower, however, the likelihood of making a Type II error increases.

A *Type II error* refers to failure to reject the null hypothesis when it is, in fact, false. As the probability of making a Type I error goes down, the probability of making a Type II error goes up. The lower the probability level is set for rejecting the null hypothesis, the more willing the investigator is to err in the direction of failing to claim a result rather than in the direction of claiming a result when he is wrong. The investigator has to weigh the risks involved in making one or the other type of error. Ordinarily, the probability of making a Type I error is specified before the experiment is begun. The probability of making a Type II error is ordinarily not known, and it is frequently very large.

While the concepts of level of significance and Type I and Type II errors are somewhat complex, the user of evaluation results should at least be aware of their bearing on the confidence with which results of evaluation studies can be interpreted. If the level of significance is set low (say, .01) and yet a significant result is obtained, conclusions can be drawn with a high degree of confidence.—R. T. M.

College Entrance Examination Board. *Introductory Probability and Statistical Inference.* New York: College Entrance Examination Board, 1959. See especially Chapter 7 for a relatively simple treatment of hypothesis testing.

Edwards, A. L. *Experimental Design in Psychological Research.* New York: Holt, 1959. See Chapters 2 and 7.

Fisher, R. A. *Statistical Methods for Research Workers.* New York: Hafner, 1958. See especially Chapter 5.

Hays, W. L. *Statistics.* New York: Holt, 1963. See especially Chapters 9 and 10.

Lindquist, E. F. *Design and Analysis of Experiments in Psychology and Education.* Boston: Houghton Mifflin, 1953. See especially pages 66-72, on types of errors.

Runyon, R. P., and Haber, A. *Fundamentals of Behavioral Statistics.* Reading, Mass.: Addison-Wesley, 1967. See especially the second part of the text, on inferential statistics.

---------------------------- INDEPENDENCE ----------------------------

Statistical independence. The concept of independence plays an important role in many statistical techniques. In some instances, assumptions of the independence of variables are essential to the derivation of a technique. In other cases, the primary

interest is in the possible association (or lack of association) between two variables, and a statistical test may be used to test for
independence. (See **Statistical Analysis.**) Two variables are statistically independent if the distribution of one variable has nothing
to do with the other variable; the probability of the occurrence of
one event does not in any way affect the probability of occurrence
of another event. More formally, the variables x and y are said to
be statistically independent if, and only if, the joint probability
function $f(x, y)$ is equal to the product of the marginal probability functions $f(x)$ and $f(y)$.

It is sometimes assumed that *statistically independent* and
uncorrelated are interchangeable terms. However, these terms are
not equivalent. Statistically independent variables are uncorrelated, but uncorrelated variables are not necessarily statistically
independent. (See **Correlation**).

Experimental independence. Observations (made with tests,
questionnaires, and other measures) are experimentally independent if they are operationally distinct and do not influence
each other by virtue of being obtained in the same experimental
situation. The elimination or modification of one experimental
observation has no effect on the outcome of another observation
if they are independent. Experimentally independent observations
are not necessarily statistically independent; but if there is a statistical association between the events, it is not due to experimental
constraints.

Observations are sometimes experimentally dependent because of constraints in the experimental situation and sometimes
because of the way in which scores are derived. For example, if
the same judge is used to rate a person in two situations, the
ratings might be considered experimentally dependent because
those given in one situation may influence the ratings in the second situation (see **Halo Effect** and **Ratings**). Dependence caused
by the computations applied to the observations frequently occurs
when several scores are derived from the same set of observations.
For example, a test may yield several subscores and a total score
equal to the sum of the subscores; the total score and each sub-
score are dependent because of the way the scores are derived, and
the use of these scores in statistical analyses could lead to misleading results. For instance, if the total score and the subscores in the

above example were all included in a **Factor Analysis**, the built-in dependence between the total score and the subscores is likely to yield a factor which is nothing more than an artifact of the way in which the scores are defined.—R. L. L.

INSTITUTIONAL EVALUATION

Institutional evaluation addresses the question of what an institution *is*: what it does, how it does it, and how well it does it. Although the term has been associated primarily with higher education, the processes are equally applicable to other types and levels of institutions dedicated to education or training.

There are inherent difficulties in the notion of assessing the overall functioning of an institution. Many argue that any attempt to attach a single label to such a complex entity ignores the probable fact that any institution that has existed for a period of time has some good and some bad features. Others suggest that there *is* some central concept or quality that can be assessed and can express rather well the totality of the institution; for example, its fiscal status and policies, its impact on its students, or a still elusive concept called vitality.

The history of efforts to achieve institutional evaluation suggests at least five critical and interrelated aspects of the problem: who is to do it, why it is to be done, the level of objectivity to be employed, the breadth of the focus, and whether the institution is to be compared with other institutions.

With regard to the first aspect (who does it), different strategies will certainly be used by evaluators from different disciplines—by educational historians, management efficiency experts, department chairmen, educational research specialists. Whether the evaluators come from inside or outside the institution can make a difference too.

With regard to the second aspect (why the institutional evaluation is being done), a self-study committee fighting for accreditation and recognition inevitably will have different immediate goals from those, say, of a funding agency attempting to determine whether continued investment in the institution is worthwhile. The purposes of the evaluation must be made honestly explicit at the outset.

The level of objectivity employed has major implications. Highly objective procedures, involving quantification of structural or behavioral indices, permit reliable and replicable measurement. However, at the extreme, insistence on objectivity can lead to neglect of important institutional variables just because they cannot be precisely weighed or counted. Some **Accreditation** efforts (a form of institutional evaluation) have been based almost exclusively on information about such characteristics as plant value, operating budget, endowment income, growth rates, number of library volumes, and faculty credentials. But what an institution has and what it achieves are not necessarily synonymous. In order to capture many important institutional qualities (some of which are subtle), evaluators may have to use some subjective procedures, even though these may be prone to bias.

Coupled with the issue of objectivity is the precision and rigor of the evaluation design in which the measures are to be employed (see **Design of Evaluation**). Precise specification of institutional goals, assessment of how well they are met (which may require repeated measures of outcomes over time), the use of **Control Groups**, and the partialing out of personal factors (e.g., scholastic ability of entering students) to isolate institutional factors must all enter into consideration.

The breadth of focus of evaluation is dependent upon the goals of the evaluators, the needs of the institution, and the time and money available. It may encompass physical facilities; several populations (faculty, administrators, students, alumni, trustees, and others); a number of different characteristics of those populations (e.g., faculty research contributions, attitudes of students and alumni, student achievement, administrative "styles"); curricula, instructional procedures, and learning resources; and administration policies, rules, and procedures. Or the target may be more specific; for example, an institution with a continuing history of fiscal soundness and growth may place its evaluational focus on what and how well it provides for its students and faculty. However, even with a relatively limited focus, institutional evaluation, by definition, requires consideration of more than one component of the institution and the interaction between components. An evaluation of a library of an institution is just that—not an evaluation of the institution.

A comparative evaluation approach places observations in context, but it is not always easy to identify comparison groups of institutions having similar goals and capabilities. Such an approach also restricts measurement to only those indices that may be readily available for other institutions: ability of entering students, proportion of Ph.D.s on faculty, etc. A noncomparative approach, while permitting consideration of a broader range of variables, may erroneously attribute positive or negative effects to institutional functioning when they have resulted from noninstitutional factors—or may identify apparently laudable results that are mediocre compared with the achievements of other institutions.

Modern approaches to institutional evaluation probably began with the challenge of Jacob's *Changing Values in College*. Jacob attested, not without subsequent attack, that it was difficult to prove that colleges had any effects on students in some of the areas stressed in undergraduate education. Sanford's work lent respectability to the proposition that the college is a legitimate object of evaluative research by social scientists, and, starting about 1960, many colleges began to open offices of institutional research. The increasing evaluation activity at the level of the individual institution has been paralleled by the development of systems for analyzing data across institutions. The work of institutional measurement specialists at the National Merit Scholarship Center typifies this trend (see Astin's *Who Goes Where to College*).

Important and useful instruments and procedures for institutional evaluation are now available, many of them stemming from the pioneering work of Pace and Stern at Syracuse University—work that produced the College Characteristics Index and the Activities Index (attempts to deal with the dichotomy of student need versus environmental press)—and from the efforts of the Institutional Research Program in Higher Education (IRPHE) at Educational Testing Service. IRPHE measures focus on such variables as institutional goals and institutional environment as perceived by faculty (or as reflected in faculty attitudes and behavior).—J. A. D.

Astin, A. *Who Goes Where to College?* Chicago: Science Research Associates, 1965.

Dressel, P. L., and Associates. *Institutional Research in the University: A Handbook.* San Francisco: Jossey-Bass, 1971.

Feldman, K. A., and Newcomb, T. M. *The Impact of College on Students.* San Francisco: Jossey-Bass, 1969. 2 vols. Volume 1 contains an analysis of four decades of research on college students. Volume 2 contains summary tables.

Jacob, P. E. *Changing Values in College: An Exploratory Study of the Impact of College Teaching.* New York: Harper, 1957.

Sanford, N. (Ed.) *The American College: A Psychological and Social Interpretation of the Higher Learning.* New York: Wiley, 1962.

Stone, J. C. *Breakthrough in Teacher Education.* San Francisco: Jossey-Bass, 1968. An interesting discussion of a variety of teacher-training institutions, as viewed by an external evaluator.

INTELLIGENCE MEASUREMENT

Intelligence is an abstract construct relating to abilities to reason and comprehend. Like other constructs in the behavioral sciences, intelligence cannot be measured directly. We can only make inferences about a person's intelligence by observing his behavior when he is confronted with certain kinds of situations (tasks).

It is generally conceded that the scope of human mental ability is so large that no single problem task can adequately sample all its characteristics. Therefore, intelligence tests usually include a diversity of tasks, although the particular combination varies, depending on the developer's definition of intelligence. The acknowledged complexity of mental functioning and the attempts to include within intelligence tests tasks designed to tap several aspects of it would seem to argue against reporting global estimates of intelligence. For example, is it sensible to add an estimate of spatial reasoning abilities to an estimate of verbal reasoning abilities to produce a single index of a person's intelligence? Most people are probably more "intelligent" in one of these areas than the other, and the summation obscures such differences. However, many intelligence tests do yield such summary intelligence scores, and they are widely used.

Since intelligence tests are typically collections of diverse subtests, it is not unusual to find similar subtests used in measures bearing other titles. For example, the type of intelligence-test question that asks for the next entry in a series of numbers (e.g., 2, 4, 6, 8, 10, ?) is also found in mathematical aptitude tests, mathematical achievement tests, and tests of aptitude for computer programming. There is very little material which is exclusively intelligence-testing material.

The distinction between individually administered and group-administered tests is an important one. The first intelligence test, developed by Binet and Simon in 1904, was an individually administered test; that approach is continued in the Stanford-Binet and the tests developed by Wechsler. A disadvantage of individual administration is the time required. However, individual tests can offer more interesting tasks, and the diversity of tasks is usually greater than in group tests, allowing a broader sampling of mental abilities. Individual tests also permit, by virtue of their setting, observational insights by school psychologists and other clinically oriented test administrators. Thus, the individually administered approaches are sometimes considered superior and are frequently pointed to as validating scales for the group techniques (see **Validity**). Nonetheless, the correlations between individual and group tests are high, and general surveys of group characteristics are more economically and frequently just as reliably carried out by paper-and-pencil techniques than by extensive and expensive individually administered tests.

No discussion of intelligence measures can avoid a brief comment on the so-called **Intelligence Quotient**. As originally conceived, this quotient attempted to characterize mental development in relation to age. The individual's performance was first scaled as a *mental age*; that is, if a person's test performance was about equal to the average performance of eight-year-old children, then the person was given a mental age score of 8. The IQ was based on the ratio MA/CA, where MA = mental age and CA = chronological age. If a "chronological" four-year-old had the mental age of an eight-year-old, the IQ would be 200; if a chronological sixteen-year-old had the mental age of an eight-year-old, the IQ would be 50. (The ratio is multiplied by 100 to remove the decimal point.) The concept becomes unworkable with adults since mental growth does not follow a regular and continuous pattern throughout life. For this and other technical reasons, Wechsler introduced the so-called *Deviation IQ,* in which the mean ability of each age group is established to be 100 and a performance which is one standard deviation above or below the mean is taken as an IQ of 115 or 85, respectively. (See **Score Types.**)

Estimates of intelligence demonstrate quite high **Reliability** over time. Retests with alternate forms of intelligence tests after intervals of five to ten years result in retest reliability coefficients of about .70. These findings, together with reported differences in intelligence for racial groups, have been used to support theories of the genetic base for intelligence and have led to analyses of test results into components attributable to genetic and to cultural influences. To date, no one of these theories has been accepted, and in general it does not seem appropriate to draw inferences about genetic "intelligence" from the results of current tests. Rather, a concept of intelligence as a reasonably stable developed ability that is complexly determined by genetic *and* cultural factors but is far from unchangeable seems most appropriate. (See **Culture-Fair Test** and **Bias in Testing.**)

Few educational evaluations treat intelligence as an outcome variable (see **Variables**). However, intelligence results sometimes must be used in evaluation designs so that individual or group differences in intelligence may be controlled for when the results of other variables are evaluated. In many instances, however, it would be preferable to use tests of specific cognitive abilities as "matching" variables or covariates (see **Matched Sampling** and the discussion of covariance in **Multivariate Analysis**).—T. F. D.

Anastasi, A. *Psychological Testing.* (3rd Ed.) New York: Macmillan, 1968. Part 2 (Tests of General Intellectual Development) is an excellent general survey of intelligence tests.

Butcher, H. J. *Human Intelligence.* London: Methuen, 1968. A comprehensive discussion of the concept of intelligence. Chapters 8 and 9 focus on appraisal instruments, but with a British flavor and with less depth than the Anastasi or Cronbach surveys.

Cronbach, L. J. *Essentials of Psychological Testing.* (3rd Ed.) New York: Harper, 1970. Chapters 7, 8, and 9 review general-ability tests. End-of-chapter "suggested readings" offer suggestions for further explorations.

——————————————— INTERACTION ———————————————

Interaction effect is the term used to describe results attributable to certain *combinations* of treatments or **Variables**. The presence or absence of interaction effects will influence the interpretation of the results of an experiment or the evaluation of a training program. A simple hypothetical example illustrates the importance of the interaction effect in the design and analysis of a study. Suppose we want to compare two methods of instruction being used in a training program for male and female recruits. We represent the two methods of instruction as the column treatment in Table 1 and the sex of the trainee as the row treatment. For the evaluation, one hundred men and one hundred women are assigned to the study; fifty trainees in each group are taught by Method I, and fifty are taught by Method II. After the program has been completed, each trainee is given a proficiency test. The mean scores for the four groups are given in Table 1. (In this example, the fifty women in the group taught by Method I received a mean score of 60, etc.) The numbers to the right are row averages, and the numbers at the bottom are the column averages.

Table 1

Mean Scores for Trainees

(N = 50 per cell)

		Method		
		I	II	
Sex	Women	60	70	65
	Men	80	50	65
		70	60	

Three questions can be answered from these data: (1) Is there a systematic effect due to the method of instruction alone (column effect)? (2) Is there a systematic effect due to the sex of the trainees alone (row effect)? (3) Is there a systematic effect due only to the combination of a particular sex group with a particular method of instruction (interaction effect)? The first question is answered by considering the column means. Note that the one hundred trainees who were instructed by Method I scored higher on the average than those instructed by Method II. The row means are both 65, which indicates that no difference exists between men and women in performance on the proficiency test. However, it is obvious from the cell entries that women do better when instructed by Method II and men do better when instructed by Method I. There is a very strong interaction effect due to the particular combinations of sex and method. Thus, if the sex of the trainees were not known, all trainees might be assigned to Method I, because the data show that Method I gives a higher mean score than Method II over both sexes. However, if the sex of trainees is known, then the males should be assigned to Method I and the females to Method II.

In evaluation, interaction effects are usually tested for first. If no interaction effect is present, then main effects may be interpreted simply for all levels of the other variables involved in the evaluation. However, if an interaction effect is detected, then the effects attributed to one factor must be interpreted for specific levels of the other factor (see Trait-Treatment Interaction).

In this simple illustration, only two levels of each of two factors were given. It is possible, of course, to have more than two factors, with each factor having more than two levels. The number of possible combinations may become large and unwieldy. For example, in an experiment with two levels of each of three factors, there are eight (2 X 2 X 2) combinations to be considered; and, in general, for two levels of n factors, there would be 2^n combinations to be considered. When the number of interactions is large, the investigator may try to eliminate some of the interaction effects while looking for main effects. The use of randomized groups, randomized blocks, the crossover design, latin squares, and balanced incomplete block designs can often allow the experimenter to eliminate some interaction effects from the overall experiment.

Because interactions can be so complex and can so drastically change the interpretation of results, possible interactions and their effects must be fully discussed in reports of evaluation studies. The user of the evaluation results, fully informed and aware of the significance of these effects for his interpretations, is then better equipped to make sound decisions on the merits, or otherwise, of the procedures, methods, or treatments evaluated in the report.—R. T. M.

Campbell, D. T., and Stanley, J. C. "Experimental and Quasi-Experimental Designs for Research on Teaching." In N. L. Gage (Ed.), *Handbook of Research on Teaching*. Chicago: Rand McNally, 1963. Pp. 171-246.

Cochran, W. G. "Experimental Design: The Design of Experiments." In D. L. Sills (Ed.), *International Encyclopedia of the Social Sciences*. Vol. 5. New York: Crowell-Collier and Macmillan, 1968. Pp. 245-254.

Cox, D. R. *Planning of Experiments*. New York: Wiley, 1958. See especially Chapter 6 on the basic ideas of factorial experiments.

Edwards, A. *Experimental Design in Psychological Research*. New York: Holt, 1960. See especially Chapter 13, "Complex Factorial Designs."

—————————— INTEREST MEASUREMENT ——————————

A person's interests are reflected in his tendencies to seek or avoid certain kinds of activities. We assess the interests of our friends and acquaintances informally by observing how they spend their free time, what rewards and incentives seem to motivate them, how often certain topics arise in their conversation, and what they say they are interested in when asked. The formal measurement of interests takes similar approaches but, of course, involves greater structure and an attempt to attain more objective observations.

The most frequently used formal method of measuring interests is a paper-and-pencil inventory. Examples include the Strong Vocational Interest Blank (SVIB) and the three major Kuder Interest Inventories. The SVIB contains some four hundred items, and the respondent is asked to indicate whether he likes, dislikes, or is indifferent to the activity specified in the item. Examples of items are adding numbers, buying a new house, or chairing a meeting. The responses are then compared with those obtained from members of more than fifty different occupations. Thus, the respondent can see how his interests compare with those of artists, bankers, psychologists, real estate salesmen, lawyers, carpenters, etc.

The Kuder Interest Inventories include an instrument to assess vocational interests (e.g., outdoor, scientific, clerical, persuasive), one to assess occupational interests (e.g., pharmacist, travel agent, photographer), and one to assess personal interests (e.g., sociable, practical, theoretical). Each item presents three activities such as "go for a ride in the country," "go to an art gallery," "go to church." The respondent marks the one he would like to do most and the one he would like to do least. (See **Ipsative Measures**.)

In addition to these two interest inventories, a large number of other paper-and-pencil interest measures are commercially available; and many others have been developed for use in research and evaluation studies (see **Test Selection**). The evaluator frequently finds it necessary, however, to develop his own interest measure, or at least to adapt one already developed, since the purposes of the program being evaluated are unlikely to be identical to those of other programs. Quite basic changes in the wording of items may be required just to fit the program and sample characteristics (e.g., level of vocabulary, name of the program).

A respondent can fake his responses on interest inventories; a key issue, then, is whether the respondent would have good reason to want to fake. If he thinks that getting a job depends on his responses, faking may occur. However, if he feels that no such decision is dependent on his responses, but rather that the responses will be used to help him (e.g., in guidance or counseling), then faking is less likely to occur.

Less frequently used measures of interest are behavior checklists and **Observation Techniques**, including those used in simulated settings (see **Situational Tests**). The rationale behind such measures is that through a person's behavior we can identify his interests. This approach is especially appropriate for estimating the interests of young children who cannot express their interests verbally. It is also useful in estimating the interests of adolescents and adults in a situation where it would be advantageous for them to fake their responses on a paper-and-pencil measure. Observations can be made and simulated settings can be established so that the assessment is carried out by **Unobtrusive Measures**. For example, the examiner might observe the kinds of books borrowed from a library or the magazines read in a waiting room where a variety of magazines are available.

Among adolescents and adults, interests show considerable stability over time. It has also been shown that scores on interest inventories are related to job satisfaction. Note, however, that interests and ability are not necessarily related. Someone with ability to do a job may have little interest, and someone with pronounced interest may have insufficient ability. Interest measurement is not a good substitute for achievement or ability measurement.

Interests might be measured as part of an evaluation for a variety of reasons. Interests might be considered as dependent **Variables**. The evaluator may want to know whether an educational program designed to affect trainees' interests actually does so. Or interests might be considered as possible interactive factors (see **Interaction**); for instance, an evaluator may want to know whether a program will benefit those with one set of interests but will harm (or not affect) those with a different set of interests. In this case, the interests of trainees should be measured before they enter the program. Evaluators may also wish to assess interests as a possible side effect of a program (see **Side Effects**). For example, consider a continuing-education program instituted to develop professional-level medical officers. In assessing the success of the program, the evaluator should determine not only (a) whether it did, in fact, turn out competent medical officers but also (b) whether the trainees gained or lost interest in health as a career field.—S. B.

Buros, O. K. (Ed.) *The Mental Measurements Yearbook.* Highland Park, N.J.: Gryphon Press, 1938, 1941, 1949, 1953, 1959, 1965, 1972. The last edition cites over sixty published measures of interests.

Getzels, J. W. "The Problem of Interests: A Reconsideration." In H. A. Robinson (Ed.), *Reading: Seventy-Five Years of Progress.* Supplementary Educational Monographs No. 96. Chicago: University of Chicago Press, 1966. An in-depth discussion of the concept of interests.

Gronlund, N. E. *Measurement and Evaluation in Teaching.* New York: Macmillan, 1965. Includes (pp. 351-354) a general discussion of interest inventories.

Tyler, L. E. *The Psychology of Human Differences.* New York: Appleton-Century-Crofts, 1965. See Chapter 8 for a good review of the research done on the interest preferences, especially the occupational interests, of adults.

Witty, P. "A Study of Children's Interests: Grades 9, 10, 11, 12." *Education,* 1961, *82,* 39-45, 100-110, 169-174. A comprehensive review of the research literature on children's interests, with some coverage of the research methods used.

INTERVIEWS

An interview, which may be thought of as an oral questionnaire, is a conversation wherein an interviewer tries to obtain information from—and sometimes impressions about—an interviewee. (The processes of developing interviews and questionnaires are very similar; the reader should consult the entry on **Questionnaires** for further information about their construction.)

The interview may be used as a measurement technique in evaluating a person: to help make decisions for selecting and promoting employees, for counseling employees and students with problems, and for reviewing on-the-job or in-school performance (see Fear). Even though interviews are commonly used in personal evaluations, this article, in harmony with the purpose of this book, will focus only on interviews in program evaluation.

In program evaluation, the interview may be used as a means of obtaining data on student background variables (e.g., family, education, interests, attitudes) and on student reactions to the program, its materials, and the instructor. In addition, instructors, other program personnel, and other concerned parties can be interviewed for their reactions to the program and for information about the content, context, and conduct of the program. Interviews may be conducted with groups as well as with individuals, but special techniques are needed to encourage full participation by all group members, and special interviewer skills are required (see, for example, Green and Stone).

Interviews in program evaluation may be structured or unstructured. The structured interview has its content and procedures standardized in advance. It is quite like an objective, self-response questionnaire where the response options are listed (except that it is administered orally by an interviewer). Options to the questions may be presented to the respondent either orally or visually (display cards). The unstructured interview is rather like a free-response or open-ended questionnaire, except that the interview allows greater flexibility, since the interviewer can adapt the questions to preceding responses. Thus, responses might indicate that a particular line of questioning is proving fruitful and the interviewer may choose to extend it.

There are continuing arguments over the relative merits of self-response questionnaires and interviews in evaluative research. Questionnaires are certainly less expensive to administer per subject and are generally preferred when large samples are sought. However, the choice of technique is dictated not only by cost but also by the content of information being sought and the level of education of the respondents. If the information is likely to cause embarrassment or defensiveness (e.g., if it pertains to sex behavior, racial attitudes, drug-taking activities), an anonymous questionnaire might be a better technique. If the respondents are functionally illiterate, an interview would probably yield more valid responses. In addition, interviews allow observation of the respondent—and sometimes of his home, work, or other environment. McLean's comparison of interviews and self-response questionnaires is shown in Table 1.

The selection and training of interviewers are crucial matters if the interview results are to be believable. The interviewer, obviously, should have desirable personal characteristics (he should be personable, tactful, attentive to detail, honest, etc.). In addition, the interviewer may have to be chosen in light of the characteristics of those to be interviewed (e.g., it is better for some purposes to have interviewers of the same sex and same race as those interviewed). Training should be used not only to familiarize the interviewer with the questions, formats, options, etc., but also to ensure that standard procedures of questioning and recording prevail in all interviews. Otherwise, a respondent's reply might become a function of the interviewer assigned to him. A supervisor should examine data from each of the interviewers to see whether they obtained a similar range and variety of answers for comparable interviewees. (See **Field Operations**.) And, as a check on interviewers, the supervisor should ask some of those interviewed whether, in fact, the interview took place and what procedures were followed. The test-retest **Reliability** of some of the items on the interview can be established through the supervisor's reinterview.

One of the major problems of the interview is that, no

Table 1

Comparison of Interview and Questionnaire Techniques

Interview	*Questionnaire*
Advantages	
1. Does not require reading or writing by the respondent.	1. Cheaper and easier to administer.
2. Adaptable to unforeseen circumstances.	2. Impersonal, anonymous.
3. Provides greater opportunity to obtain a representative sample of respondents.	3. Completed at subject's convenience.
4. Allows for interviewer check on responses.	4. Guaranteed uniform presentation.
5. Permits study of complex and sensitive topics.	
6. Allows the responding environment to be structured somewhat.	
Disadvantages	
1. Requires trained interviewers.	1. Generally low return.
2. Subject to variable and unpredictable interviewer bias.	2. Must be entirely self-motivating.
3. Volume of responses tends to be large and difficult to structure.	3. Uncertain identification of respondent.
	4. Does not permit any easy verification of responses.

matter how well trained the interviewers, interviewer characteristics may systematically affect the responses obtained. In some instances the interviewer misperceives what the person being interviewed is saying; in other instances the person being interviewed misperceives what the interviewer is asking. This *interviewer bias* can be minimized by careful interview construction, by training procedures which make the interviewers aware of the possible problems, and sometimes by matching interviewer characteristics to characteristics of the sample being interviewed. Of course, the less the interviewer bias, the greater the **Validity** of the data. —S. B., M. R.

Fear, R. A. *The Evaluation Interview.* (2nd Ed.) New York: McGraw-Hill, 1973. Concentrates on the use of interviews in personal evaluation.

Green, J. L., and Stone, J. C. "Developing and Testing Q-Cards and Content Analysis in Group Interviews." *Nursing Research,* 1972, *21,* 342-347.

McLean, L. D. "Research Methodology in Educational Psychology." In J. R. Davitz and S. Ball (Eds.), *Psychology of the Educational Process.* New York: McGraw-Hill, 1970. Includes (pp. 584-589) a concise discussion of advantages and disadvantages of interviews versus questionnaires and of interviewer bias.

Mouly, G. J. *The Science of Educational Research.* (2nd Ed.) New York: Van Nostrand Reinhold, 1970. Includes (pp. 263-276) a discussion of the interview as a research and evaluation tool.

Parker, C. A. "Questions Concerning the Interview as a Research Technique." *Journal of Educational Research,* 1957, *51,* 215-221.

Zamoff, R. B. *Guide to the Assessment of Day Care Services and Needs at the Community Level.* Washington, D.C.: Urban Institute, 1971. Provides an example of the use of interviews as a part of the evaluational process.

―――――――――――――― IPSATIVE MEASURES ――――――――――――――

Ipsative measures or scores are encountered far less often in education and psychology than normative measures or scores, and their properties are not as well understood. An ipsative score describes a level on one variable (or characteristic) relative to another (or others); thus, the focus of ipsative scores is on comparisons *within* an individual in marked contrast to the normative scores produced by most **Standardized Tests**, which reflect, in a more or less absolute sense, the level of performance on a given characteristic and are customarily used to make comparisons *between* individuals. Thus, with ipsative scores, we might say that Smith's clerical interest score is 40 and his mechanical interest score is 60; therefore his mechanical interest is stronger. With normative scores, however, we might say that Smith's reading score is 50, and Brown's is 70; therefore Brown reads better than Smith. (See also **Norms** and **Score Types**.)

The hallmark of an ipsative measure is that the sum of scores for a set of variables is the same for each person. For example, Smith's clerical and mechanical interest scores are 40 and 60, respectively; Walton's are 25 and 75; and Reed's are 95 and 5—each totals 100.

Ipsative scores may stem from (a) tests and measures that rely on special procedures for producing such scores directly or (b) statistical methods that transform normative scores. (Whichever approach is taken, the scores have a number of characteristics in common.) Among the special procedures used to produce ipsative scores are ranking, paired comparisons, and many forced-choice methods, which are employed on such popular devices as the All-port-Vernon-Lindzey Study of Values, Edwards Personal Preference Schedule (EPPS), and Q sorts. Ideally, statistical ipsatization involves two steps: First, scores for the normative variables are standardized so that they all have the same mean and standard deviation (see **Statistics**). Second, a constant is added to the scores for each person, in order to make the sum of scores the same for everyone. For example, if four variables are involved and they total 200 for Harrison and 280 for Martin, a constant of 25 may be added to each of Harrison's scores and 5 to each of Martin's scores, so that the scores for each individual sum to 300.

Ipsative scores have a number of unusual mathematical and statistical properties that are generally not recognized, although these characteristics have important implications for the use of the scores in both research and practice. One is that the matrix of intercorrelations among the scores obtained from a single ipsative measure has no inverse, and, hence, standard methods for computing multiple correlations, factor analyses, and other multivariate statistics cannot be applied to such matrices (see **Correlation**, **Factor Analysis**, and **Multivariate Analysis**). This problem is readily solved, however, by dropping one of the variables; interestingly, the results will be the same regardless of which variable is eliminated. Another property of the intercorrelation matrix is that the upper and lower limits of the mean correlation for the set of scores are $(n-4)/n$ and $-1/(n-1)$, where n is the number of scores. As an illustration of this general phenomenon, the mean correlation in the EPPS manual between the fifteen scales is $-.071$, precisely the value of the lower limit. Thus, the extent of correlation between ipsative scores is dependent on the number of variables involved. A related characteristic is that the correlations of a set of ipsative scores with a normative variable sum to zero, provided the ipsative variables have equal variances. According to the EPPS manual, the mean of the correlations between the EPPS scales and the Agreeableness, Cooperativeness, and Objectivity scales of the Guilford-Martin Personnel Inventory are .00, $-.06$, and $-.16$, respectively. The validity of ipsative scores is constrained in complicated ways.

Because of the distinctive rationales underlying ipsative and normative scores, the scores have different meanings and cannot be interpreted in the same way. Two people with an identical normative score on a variable may vary markedly in their ipsative scores on that variable because of differences on one or more of the other variables in the ipsative format. Interpreting the relationship between an ipsative and a normative variable is complicated.

Ipsative scores are particularly valuable, even indispensable, in certain situations. In counseling, guidance, and similar settings where the focus is on the individual and the aim is to identify his best-developed interests, comparative strengths and weaknesses in his abilities and achievements, etc., ipsative scores are the simplest and most direct way of providing this information. Ipsative scores are also useful for tests and rating procedures that employ forced-choice methods to reduce social-desirability **Response Sets**, faking, and other kinds of distortion. Forced-choice methods, insofar as they succeed in eliminating from the ipsative scores the distorting influences present in normative scores, might be expected to result in greater **Validity** than the customary normative procedures. Only limited data on this question are currently available. However, some systematic comparisons of normative and ipsative versions of personality inventories suggest that they have roughly the same validity.—L. J. S.

Cattell, R. B. "Psychological Measurement: Normative, Ipsative, Interactive." *Psychological Review,* 1944, *51,* 292-303.

Clemans, W. V. "An Analytical and Empirical Examination of Some Properties of Ipsative Measures." *Psychometric Monographs,* 1966, No. 14.

Gleser, L. J. "On Bounds for the Average Correlation Between Subtest Scores in Ipsatively Scored Tests." *Educational and Psychological Measurement,* 1972, *32,* 759-765.

Radcliffe, J. A. "Some Properties of Ipsative Score Matrices and Their Relevance for Some Current Interest Tests." *Australian Journal of Psychology,* 1963, *15,* 1-11.

Scott, W. A. "Comparative Validities of Forced-Choice and Single-Stimulus Tests." *Psychological Bulletin,* 1968, *70,* 231-244.

---------------------------- ITEM SAMPLING ----------------------------

Item-sampling (or matrix-sampling) techniques were first advocated as a way of getting more representative test **Norms.** For example, a publisher or personnel officer might be able to get five hundred students or employees each to take a random set of five items from a hundred-item test, whereas he might not be able to get all of them to take the whole test. Studies have indicated that this approach of breaking up a longer test into a number of shorter tests and administering them at random to examinees indeed results in good estimations of the test mean and, in most cases, of the variance. (It is not satisfactory to break up in this way speeded tests or tests where item performance is assumed to be dependent on the context in which the items are presented. If a test has heterogeneous items and item-sampling techniques are used with it, estimates of variance suffer.)

Item-sampling techniques can be a boon to evaluators of education/training programs where (a) they are interested only in group data and not in assessment of individuals, (b) there is a broad range of materials covered in the program, and/or (c) it is desirable to measure change with comparable measures over time. In the last case, for example, it would be possible to obtain data on all one hundred items of a test several times during a course or program without any student's necessarily taking the same item twice.

It is not sensible to use item-sampling techniques if an examiner wants to obtain the intercorrelations among a large pool of items; in such instances, it would be better to give all items to all examinees. However, an investigator could test a few hypotheses about item interrelationships within an item-sampling model. Thus, if he is interested in relationships among items 3, 5, and 9, he might write the specifications for item sampling so as to have item 3 appear with item 5 in one subset, with 9 in another, etc.

Versions of item sampling have been used successfully in a number of studies, including the National Longitudinal Study of Mathematical Abilities, the National Assessment of Educational Progress, and test norming efforts (e.g., at Educational Testing Service and Sandia Corporation).—S. B. A.

Barcikowski, R. S. "A Monte Carlo Study of Item Sampling (Versus Traditional Sampling) for Norm Construction." *Journal of Educational Measurement,* 1972, *9,* 209-214.

Cahen, L. S., Romberg, T. A., and Zwirner, W. "The Estimation of Mean Achievement Scores for Schools by the Item-Sampling Technique." *Educational and Psychological Measurement,* 1970, *30,* 41-60.

Husek, T. R., and Sirotnik, K. "Matrix Sampling." *Evaluation Comment,* 1968, *1* (3).

Lord, F. M. "Estimating Norms by Item Sampling." *Educational and Psychological Measurement,* 1962, *22,* 259-267.

Plumlee, L. B. "Estimating Means and Standard Deviations from Partial Data—an Empirical Check on Lord's Item Sampling Technique." *Educational and Psychological Measurement,* 1964, *24,* 623-630.

Shoemaker, D. M. *Principles and Procedures of Multiple Matrix Samples.* Technical Report No. 34. Inglewood, Calif.: Southwest Regional Laboratory for Educational Research and Development, 1971.

—————————————— JOB ANALYSIS ——————————————

Job analysis seeks to delineate the duties, requirements, and conditions of jobs in a systematic way. Four key terms in the literature and practice of job analysis are *task* (a unit of work), *position* (the work of one worker on a set of tasks), *job* (a group of similar positions in an organization), *occupation* (a group of similar jobs found across a number of organizations or establishments).

Job analysis is useful in identifying both instructional components and effectiveness criteria for training programs. In order to train a person for a job, it is important to know what tasks he will have to perform and what specific skills, knowledge, and other characteristics are required to perform them. These job components can then be organized in a meaningful way to form the basis for the training curriculum. Measures developed to evaluate the effectiveness of the training strategies would focus on the same job-important tasks and skills.

Until recently, job analysis was used more frequently by industry and the military for personnel selection and placement and for job and employee evaluation than in training and training evaluation. However, with shifts in the nature of training demands and with current emphasis on "training by objectives," competency/performance-based education (particularly teacher education), and **Criterion-Referenced Measurement,** the importance of the kinds of specific data provided by job analysis has been increasingly recognized.

Job-analysis methods include questionnaires, interviews, observations, work participation, diaries, and expert opinion. **Questionnaires** may be relatively unstructured (job incumbents are asked to provide information about themselves and their jobs in their own words) or so structured that workers are given lists of possible tasks and characteristics and are asked only to check the tasks they perform and the characteristics of their jobs. The less structured the job questionnaire, the less useful it is with workers who lack verbal facility and the more difficult it is to analyze. On the other hand, checklists (which are more easily administered to large groups and are certainly easier to analyze) require a great deal of preliminary work in order to derive appropriate task statements.

Interviews, if they are well designed and structured, are likely to provide more complete pictures of jobs than questionnaires. (Interviews are also useful as a first step in developing statements of job characteristics to be used in questionnaires.) However, the procedure can be costly and time-consuming. Interviews may be conducted with individual workers, selected as representative of those on particular jobs, or with a number of employees in a group setting. Usually such interviews for job analysis are conducted outside the actual job setting, but with "observation interviews" the interviewer collects data from the worker *while* the worker performs the job. This special interviewing technique may produce a very accurate and complete job description, but it also runs the risk of interfering with normal work operations and hence producing a distorted description.

In other instances, there is no interview, and the worker is simply observed on the job; such a procedure must be handled carefully, however, if the worker is to believe that the observer is concerned with the nature of the job and not with the quality of the worker's performance. Observations also have the disadvantage of being even more costly and time-consuming than interviews. However, for jobs such as teaching, where very subtle and complex skills and interactions are involved, observations may provide the only means of "capturing" the nature of the job and its requirements. (See **Observation Techniques** and **Reactive Effects of Program and Evaluation.**)

In still other cases, the job analyst himself performs the job in order to gather firsthand information about its requirements. This method is impossible or unproductive, however, if the task requirements are beyond the immediate capabilities of the analyst.

In the diary approach to job analysis, workers are asked to keep a written running account of their job activities. This technique can provide valuable information if workers can and do keep accurate logs. However, it is sometimes criticized because it takes up too much employee time.

Job Title: BAKER
Alternate Title: BREAD BAKER
Industry: Hotels and Restaurants
Job Summary:
  Bakes bread, rolls, muffins, and biscuits for consumption in dining rooms of hotels
  or restaurants, mixing ingredients to make dough, and cutting and shaping dough
  by hand or machine.
Work Performed:
  1. Studies requirements for day and day following, and plans production in order
     to have bread, rolls, biscuits, and muffins freshly baked when wanted and in
     quantities specified.
  2. Mixes (develops) dough according to recipe: Weighs and sifts flour into a bowl
     or mixer, adds shortening, yeast or baking powder, seasoning, and water or milk
     of desired temperature; either starts electric motor actuating beater that mixes
     and beats ingredients to form dough, or kneads dough by hand; places dough in
     a greased mixing bowl or proofing trough and allows it to ferment (rise or proof);
     may place dough in a proof box to ferment.
  3. Cuts and shapes dough, sprinkling flour on work bench to prevent sticking:
      a) Flattens and distributes dough in floured pan and places it in manually
         operated divider which cuts the dough into sections of equal size; may cut
         dough to size with knife or biscuit cutter; molds all cut dough into desired
         shapes, by hand; may place butter, jelly, poppy seeds, or other topping on
         rolls.
      b) For muffins: Pours batter directly into greased muffin pans.
      c) For bread: Cuts off portion of dough with a scraper or heavy knife; weighs
         each portion to ensure uniformity of size; roughly shapes each portion by
         hand, and either places it in a greased pan or mold, or in the case of "hearth"
         breads (rye, French, Vienna, etc.), on a large, flat, greased pan.
  4. Places pans in proof box where the dough further rises. The length of time that
     dough is proofed depends on the recipe used (amount of yeast, water, and salt),
     type of flour, heat of proof box, and to some degree on the policy of the estab-
     lishment or technique of the individual worker.
  5. Bakes dough: Puts pans on peel and places them in oven; places hearth breads
     directly on hearth, using no pans; sets thermostatic temperature control or regu-
     lates fuel supply or draft to control oven temperature; may turn hand valve to inject

Figure 1.
From J. Tiffin and E. J. McCormick, *Industrial Psychology* (5th ed.).
Prentice-Hall, Englewood Cliffs, N.J. © 1965.

Some job-analysis methods do not require direct contact
with workers but depend upon information provided by secondary
sources. For example, supervisors may meet with the job analyst
and describe the job being studied, or supervisors may be asked to
recount critical incidents of success or failure on the job. Secondary sources of information about jobs are useful to the extent that
they have extensive and recent knowledge of the job being studied. (The critical-incident technique, it might be noted, may provide an accurate picture of key aspects of a job, but probably will
not provide an integrated picture of the job.)

steam into oven, moistening crust to prevent it from becoming too hard or brown; observes progress of baking, noticing the color of dough, smelling it, and pinching or pricking it with a fork; removes baked rolls, bread, muffins, or biscuits from oven with peel or rake, or with heavy gloves.

6. Places baked products on a rack to cool.
7. Supervises a BAKER HELPER who cleans utensils and performs miscellaneous other tasks such as cutting dough.

Equipment:

Mixer; proof box; oven; proofing trough; divider; peel; rake; mixing bowls; scraper; rolling pins; biscuit cutter; work bench; refrigerator; scales; measuring cups and spoons; sifter; pans and molds for bread, biscuits, rolls, and muffins; knives.

Material:

Flour; shortening; yeast; baking powder; baking soda; milk; water; seasoning; and other ingredients used to make bread, rolls, biscuits, and muffins.

Working Conditions:

Surroundings: Inside; hot.
Hazards: Minor burns from oven or hot pans.

Specialized Qualifications:

Worker must be able to bake all kinds of bread.
Ability to bake previously prepared pastries, and make special types of breads such as cornbread and Danish pastries, may be required of worker.

Special Physical Requirements:

Strength: To lift heavy bags of flour, weighing as much as 100 pounds. Keen sense of taste and smell to determine whether ingredients are properly seasoned and sufficiently baked.

Test Standards (for use in selection of inexperienced workers for training)

Test (from USES
General Aptitude
Test Battery)

	Minimum Score
Intelligence	75
Form Perception	80
Finger Dexterity	70
Clerical Perception	80

Figure 1. (Continued)

The product of a job analysis is generally a *job description,* which usually contains information on materials and equipment used, working conditions, organizational settings, responsibilities, and desirable employee characteristics. A sample job description is shown in Figure 1. The implications of such a description for the contents of a training program for bread bakers and for measures used to evaluate the effectiveness of such a program are straight-forward.

The principles of job analysis are not limited to employees or prospective employees. Educators can, for example, analyze the "job" of second-year algebra and direct their first-year algebra teaching toward proficiencies required to perform second-year tasks.—M. R., S. B. A.

McGehee, W., and Thayer, P. W. *Training in Business and Industry.* New York: Wiley, 1961. See especially Chapters 2, 3, 4, and 9.

Miller, R. "Task Description and Analysis." In R. Gagné (Ed.), *Psychological Principles in System Development.* New York: Holt, 1962. Pp. 187-228.

Special Issue on Competency/Performance-Based Teacher Education. *Phi Delta Kappan,* 1974, *55* (5).

Tiffin, J., and McCormick, E. J. *Industrial Psychology.* (5th Ed.) Englewood Cliffs, N.J.: Prentice-Hall, 1965. See especially Chapter 3.

United States Employment Service (Bureau of Employment Security). *Training and Reference Manual for Job Analysis.* Washington, D.C.: U.S. Government Printing Office, 1965.

——————————— JOHN HENRY EFFECT ———————————

When a **Control Group** is placed in competition with an experimental group which is using an innovative procedure that threatens to replace the customary (control) one, the members of the control group may perform more competently or enthusiastically or speedily than they ordinarily do. This kind of overperformance is known as the *John Henry effect*—a reactive effect that may occur in control groups just as the **Hawthorne Effect** may occur in experimental groups.

The phenomenon of the overperforming control group derives its name from the American folk hero John Henry, a fabled black railroad worker who, having heard that the steam drill is to replace human steel drivers, sets himself to compete with the machine. Through prodigious exertion he exceeds the machine's performance—although the effort finally kills him.

Saretsky discusses the John Henry effect in the context of an experiment in **Performance Contracting** conducted by the Office of Economic Opportunity, where there were above-average control-group gains in achievement (up to 1.6 years) in a majority of the eighteen experimental sites. Since these gains went far beyond normal expectations, the question arose as to whether the control teachers were performing atypically, extending themselves in what they felt was a threatening situation. Interviews with the project directors and inspection of the typical performance of the teachers' classes in two previous years appeared to confirm the impression that the teachers *were* distinctly "trying harder."

So far, the effect has not been widely discussed in the literature, although other evaluators probably have encountered or will encounter this form of competitive behavior and the resultant overachievement of control groups. Since the John Henry effect may make experimental treatments appear spuriously ineffective, it would be well for evaluators to be on the alert for any unusually large gains by control groups. The entry on **Hawthorne Effect** provides suggestions about how to counter experimentally induced reactive effects. (See also **Reactive Effects of Program and Evaluation.**)—E. J. R.

Battelle Memorial Institute. *Interim Report on the Office of Economic Opportunity Experiment in Educational Performance Contracting.* Columbus, Ohio: Battelle, 1972.

Saretsky, G. "The OEO P.C. Experiment and the John Henry Effect." *Phi Delta Kappan,* 1972, *53,* 579-581.

Zdep, S. M., and Irvine, S. H. "Reverse Hawthorne Effect." *Journal of School Psychology,* 1970, *8* (2), 89-95.

——————— JOHNSON-NEYMAN TECHNIQUE ———————

One of the primary purposes of evaluation is to identify particularly effective programs of instruction. Suppose, for example, that two innovative training programs are being compared for possible widespread adoption. The classical **Experimental Design** would entail a random assignment of trainees to the two programs and the subsequent assessment of the achievement of the two groups. We are interested in testing whether one program is better than the other (see **Hypothesis Testing**). We do this by assuming that the difference between the achievement levels of the two groups is not significant (null hypothesis) and trying to reject that assumption. If the null hypothesis is rejected, then we state that the difference in mean achievement between the two groups is statistically significant (see **Statistical Significance**).

In some cases, although the difference in mean achievements between the two groups will not prove significant, the differences between subgroups (for instance, low-aptitude, middle-aptitude, and high-aptitude subgroups in each of the two main groups) may be significant (see **Interaction** and **Trait-Treatment Interaction**). The Johnson-Neyman technique can be used to identify the subgroups for which differences will be significant. The identification is carried out by determining the permissible values on extraneous variables that will lead to significant differences on the criterion variable. For example, Johnson and Neyman showed that suitable restrictions on the chronological and mental ages of two groups of students would determine groups with significant differences in achievement in social studies, even though the original total groups did not differ significantly in their mean achievements.

The use of the Johnson-Neyman technique has been extended to include more than two variables for creating the subgroups. The extension is explained in the references cited. In general, the user of evaluation results should know that the method leads to a way of identifying subgroups that will differ significantly in their mean values on the criterion variable.—R. T. M.

Abelson, R. P. "A Note on the Neyman-Johnson Technique." *Psychometrika*, 1953, *18*, 213-217.

Cahen, L. S., and Linn, R. L. "Regions of Significant Differences in Aptitude-Treatment-Interaction Research." *American Educational Research Journal*, 1971, 8, 521-530.

Johnson, P. O., and Fay, L. "The Neyman-Johnson Technique, Its Theory and Applications." *Psychometrika*, 1950, *15*, 349-367.

Johnson, P. O., and Neyman, J. "Tests of Certain Linear Hypotheses and Their Applications to Some Educational Problems." *Statistical Research Memoirs*, 1936, *1*, 57-93.

Potthoff, R. F. "On the Johnson-Neyman Technique and Some Extensions Thereof." *Psychometrika*, 1963, *29*, 241-256.

─────────── LONGITUDINAL STUDY ───────────

In a longitudinal study, repeated measurements are taken of the same subjects, usually over a considerable period of time. Longitudinal designs have been used far more often in research on human development than in program evaluation; however, they should be considered for the latter when there is concern with continuous monitoring of an ongoing program or with long-term program effects. For example, with many ongoing programs it would be undesirable to wait until the program has been completed before finding out whether it is having any effects on students. The simplest version of a longitudinal design might look like this:

$$O_1 \quad X \quad O_2 \quad X \quad O_3 \quad X \quad O_4$$

Os are repeated observations of students, and X is the program. Although this design contains some confounding (e.g., the results obtained at O_2 may be attributable to *both* the first program segment *and* the experience of O_1), it should be generally helpful in a **Formative Evaluation**, provided the results of the successive observations are fed back to the program director promptly.

If the evaluator wants to eliminate the type of confounding described above and estimate the effects of the observations on the students, **Control Groups** may be added, thus:

$$
\begin{array}{llllllll}
\text{E:} & O_1 & X & O_2 & X & O_3 & X & O_4 \\
\text{C1:} & O_1 & & O_2 & & O_3 & & O_4 \\
\text{C2:} & & & O_2 & & & & \\
\text{C3:} & & & & & O_3 & & \\
\text{C4:} & & & & & & & O_4 \\
\end{array}
$$

While the results of O_4 for the E group reflect the combined influence of the program and the previous observations, the results of O_4 for C1 reflect effects of previous observations but not the program, and O_4 for C4 should yield results not influenced by either factor.

If the object of the evaluation is to estimate long-term as well as short-term program effects, the data-collection schedule for the experimental group might look like this:

$$O_1 \quad X \quad O_2 \quad \ldots \quad O_3 \quad \ldots \quad O_4$$

O_2 is taken at the completion of the program, and O_3 and O_4 are taken after intervals of time have passed.

An alternative strategy for assessing long-term program effects involves random selection of subgroups of students and administration of postprogram measures at different times:

$$
\begin{array}{llllll}
\text{E1:} & O_1 & X & O_2 \\
\text{E2:} & O_1 & X & \ldots & O_3 \\
\text{E3:} & O_1 & X & \ldots & \ldots & O_4 \\
\end{array}
$$

This approach reduces the likelihood that the evaluator will attribute the long-term effects to the program when, in fact, they were due to other factors, such as experience with the repeated postprogram measurements (see **Design of Evaluation**). The design is strengthened still further by the addition of control groups of students who receive the preprogram and the postprogram measurements but are not exposed to the instructional program.

Whenever the results of successive measurements are to be used to document change, the measurements should be as comparable as possible. The evaluator must attend to comparability both in the instruments and in the data-collection schedule and procedures. For example, one publisher's vocabulary test may not be comparable to another's (even two equated test forms from the same publisher may differ enough to seriously upset a study of gains); measurements taken just before an important holiday may not be comparable to measurements taken during a more normal period; interviews in the home may not be comparable to interviews at the training facility. The problem of obtaining comparable measures over time is exacerbated in studies of young children, where it may not be possible to use the same types of measures across age levels or where the same measures may have different meanings at different age levels. In such cases, investigators frequently use measures at earlier ages that are considered to be predictors or precursors of measures used at later ages; for example, children might be given visual and auditory discrimination tests when they are five years old and reading-comprehension tests when they are seven. Some purists argue, however, that a true longitudinal study cannot tolerate changes in instrumentation across successive measurements. One approach to this dilemma is to administer measures according to an overlapping pattern (see Figure 1).

A number of variations in longitudinal designs are described in the literature. For example, there are longitudinal designs that utilize more than one **Cohort** (Schaie), and there are combinations of longitudinal and **Cross-Sectional** designs (see, for example, the discussion of the "patched-up" design in **Quasi-Experimental**

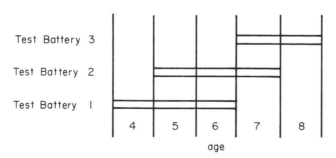

Figure 1. Tests administered in overlapping pattern for a longitudinal study.

Design). Study of some of these variations should alert the evaluator to both theoretical and practical means of increasing the precision of his designs and thus reducing the equivocality of his conclusions.—S. B. A.

Campbell, D. T., and Stanley, J. C. "Experimental and Quasi-Experimental Designs for Research on Teaching." In N. L. Gage (Ed.), *Handbook of Research on Teaching.* Chicago: Rand McNally, 1963. Pp. 171-246.

Glennan, T. K., Jr. "Evaluating Federal Manpower Programs: Notes and Observations." In P. H. Rossi and W. Williams (Eds.), *Evaluating Social Programs: Theory, Practice, and Politics.* New York: Seminar Press, 1972. Pp. 187-220. See especially the section on longitudinal versus retrospective studies (pp. 202-204).

Hand, H. H., and Slocum, J. W. "A Longitudinal Study of the Effects of a Human Relations Training Program on Managerial Effectiveness." *Journal of Applied Psychology,* 1972, *56* (5), 412-417.

Schaie, K. W. "A General Model for the Study of Developmental Problems." *Psychological Bulletin,* 1965, *64,* 92-107.

Suchman, E. A. *Evaluative Research: Principles and Practice in Public Service and Social Action Programs.* New York: Russell Sage Foundation, 1967. See the section on longitudinal-study design (pp. 100-102).

———————————— LORD'S PARADOX ————————————

In an evaluation it is often important to compare the performance of two groups—for example, a group in an experimental program and a **Control Group** in the regular program. A problem occurs when the groups are different to start with (at **Pretest**). If there are differences at the completion of the program (at **Post-**

test), are they due to the experimental program or simply to the differences noted at pretest? One way of overcoming this problem is to use a statistical technique called *analysis of covariance,* in which an adjustment is made for initial differences (see **Statistical Analysis**). Sometimes, however, an analysis of covariance can produce quite misleading and even absurd results. The term *Lord's paradox* is used to refer to such instances and is so named after Frederic M. Lord, who first drew attention to it. He has written the remainder of this entry, thereby providing the reader with greater detail than this overview.

Lord's paradox relates to a common problem in group comparison: We observe that group A is better than group B on measurement y (on a posttest score, for example). However, we also have data showing that group A is or was better than group B on measurement x (pretest score). Is it statistically plausible that the observed difference on y is attributable to the difference on x?

Logically, an investigator cannot assert that a group difference on y is or is not plausibly attributable to a preexisting difference on x unless he first knows something about how a change in x would affect y. Unfortunately, in evaluation studies the investigator usually does not have such information. Nevertheless, in practice, in order to be able to proceed, he usually makes some plausible assumption about the effect of x on y. There may well be other equally plausible assumptions, however, that lead to contradictory conclusions. This is the source of Lord's paradox (Lord, 1967, 1969), illustrated by Figure 1. The x and y variables in the figure represent (say) body weight in September and in the following June, respectively. The mean of each group (large dot) lies on the 45-degree line through the origin O, indicating that there was no change in mean weight between September ($\bar{x}$) and June ($\bar{y}$) for either group. For each group, the frequency distribution of body weight is exactly the same in June as it was in September. There is no reason to suspect any differential dietary or other effect occurring between September and June. The June sex difference appears simply to be the same sex difference that already existed in September.

The sophisticated statistical technique used for group comparisons involving pre and post measurements is commonly an analysis of covariance. It is assumed in such analyses that if there

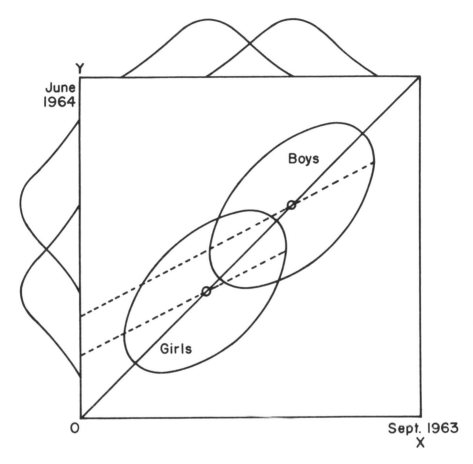

Figure 1. Lord's paradox.

is no treatment effect, the group means will both fall on the same within-group **Regression** line (the two within-group regression lines will in this case coincide). As is apparent from the figure (where the regressions are shown as broken lines), the boys' mean lies above the girls' regression line. If there are enough cases, the analysis of covariance will necessarily "show" that after "adjusting" for initial (September) differences, the boys' adjusted final (June) mean weight is significantly higher than the girls'.

This is an absurd conclusion in view of the fact that, as a group, the boys showed no gain or loss or any change at all over the period studied, and the girls likewise. The foregoing is the first part of the paradox. Now, consider a subgroup of boys chosen only on the basis of initial weight, and consider a similarly chosen subgroup of girls having the same frequency distribution of initial weight. It is visually obvious from the figure that, even though boys and girls both showed no overall gain or loss, the subgroup of boys is going to gain substantially more than the subgroup of girls, no matter what the distribution of initial weight. This completes the remainder of the paradox.

Suppose the ellipse representing the boys' scatterplot were moved upward (or downward) in the figure, making $\bar{y}$ greater (less) than $\bar{x}$ while leaving everything else unchanged. Given enough cases, one then would surely say that the boys had gained (lost) more than the girls. Thus, for these data we have made an implicit assumption, involving the 45-degree line, very similar to the assumption made in the analysis of covariance, involving the within-group regression line. For these data, the 45-degree line seems so natural as to rule out any alternative. For many problems, however, there is no clear justification for preferring one such assumption to another.

The paradox is not just an amusing statistical puzzle. Its purpose is to call attention to a common flaw in certain types of research. For example, consider the problem of evaluating federally funded special educational programs. A group of disadvantaged children are pretested in September, then enrolled in a special program, and finally posttested in June. A control group of children are similarly pretested and posttested but not enrolled in the special program. Since the most disadvantaged children are selected for the special program, the control group (like the boys in Figure 1) will typically have higher pretest scores than the disadvantaged group. As in Figure 1, an investigator using analysis of covariance will tend to conclude that the control group gains more than the other group "after adjusting for preexisting differences." Campbell and Erlebacher pointed out this flaw in the widely publicized Westinghouse study of the Head Start program. (See also **Compensatory Education**.)

The illustrative example of Figure 1 was purposely explained here in terms of physical weight, rather than in terms of test scores or other ratings of educational performance or of social value, in order to make clear that the difficulty need not be due to errors of measurement. Methods suggested by Lord (1960) for dealing with errors of measurement in analysis of covariance may not touch the main problem faced here. There simply is no way to adjust y for preexisting between-group differences on variable x unless we know how variable x affects variable y.—F. M. L.

Campbell, D. T., and Erlebacher, A. "How Regression Artifacts in Quasi-Experimental Evaluations Can Mistakenly Make Compensatory Education Look Harmful." In J. Hellmuth (Ed.), *Disadvantaged Child.* Vol. 3. New York: Brunner/Mazel, 1970. Pp. 185-210.

Lord, F. M. "Large-Sample Covariance Analysis When the Control Variable Is Fallible." *Journal of the American Statistical Association,* 1960, *55,* 307-321.

Lord, F. M. "A Paradox in the Interpretation of Group Comparisons." *Psychological Bulletin,* 1967, *68,* 304-305.

Lord, F. M. "Statistical Adjustments When Comparing Preexisting Groups." *Psychological Bulletin,* 1969, *72,* 336-337.

Westinghouse Learning Corporation and Ohio University. *The Impact of Head Start Experience on Children's Cognitive and Affective Development.* Contract OEO B89-4536. Washington, D.C.: Office of Economic Opportunity, 1969. A report by Cicirelli and others.

——————————— MASTERY LEARNING ———————————

The concept of mastery implies that there is some identifiable and circumscribed body of skills or knowledge that an instructional program attempts to foster in all students, that there is some agreement about the levels of performance that indicate mastery of the skills or content areas, and that there is some means of determining whether mastery levels are attained. Thus, it involves program **Goals and Objectives, Standards,** and special problems of measurement.

Some educators hold the view that almost all instruction should be based on a mastery-learning model (see, for example, Block, Bloom). However, such a model is probably more generally applicable to training in specific skills than to general education efforts as we usually think of them. Cronbach (p. 53), for example, says, "I see educational development as continuous and open-ended. 'Mastery' seems to imply that at some point we get to the end of what is to be taught."

Mastery tests are a special case of **Criterion-Referenced Measurement**. Specifications for their development may be derived from judgments about what constitutes mastery in the area, from analysis of a criterion task for which mastery is sought (see, for example, **Job Analysis**), from evidence about the performance of a "successful" comparison group, or from some combination of these. Sometimes mastery standards are superimposed on an existing test or other measure which may have been developed for other purposes. For example, a group of instructors might agree that a score of sixty items right on a particular standardized spelling test constitutes mastery of the subject in terms of their instructional objectives.

We do not expect a good mastery test to have the same statistical properties as a test designed to discriminate between individuals and rank them on a continuum. Rather, a mastery test should serve to separate students into two fairly distinct groups: those who have clearly reached the predetermined standard of competency and those who have not. Frequently mastery tests belie their name and are no more than minimum-competency tests (see **Certification**).

If the mastery standards are precisely defined and the attainment measures well constructed, the evaluator of a mastery-oriented program may have an easier time of it than his colleagues working in more ambiguous situations. The success score for the program can be simply the proportion of students who achieve the mastery standard—in a reasonable period of time and at an acceptable cost.—S. B. A.

Block, J. H. (Ed.) *Mastery Learning: Theory and Practice.* New York: Holt, 1971. Contains selected papers by Block, B. S. Bloom, J. B. Carroll, and P. W. Airasian and an annotated bibliography. See especially Carroll's chapter, "Problems of

Measurement Related to the Concept of Learning by Mastery."

Bloom, B. S. "Mastery Learning and Its Implications for Curriculum Development." In E. W. Eisner (Ed.), *Confronting Curriculum Reform.* Boston: Little, Brown, 1971. Pp. 17-49.

Cronbach, L. J. "Comments on 'Mastery Learning and Its Implications for Curriculum Development.' " In E. W. Eisner (Ed.), *Confronting Curriculum Reform.* Boston: Little, Brown, 1971. Pp. 49-55.

Davis, F. B. "Item Selection Techniques." In E. F. Lindquist (Ed.), *Educational Measurement.* Washington, D.C.: American Council on Education, 1955. See pages 266-267, 315.

Mehrens, W. A., and Lehmann, I. J. *Measurement and Evaluation in Education and Psychology.* New York: Holt, 1973. See the discussion of mastery testing (p. 65 ff.).

MATCHED SAMPLING

Matched sampling (or matching) is often used in an attempt to reduce bias in nonrandomized studies and to reduce variance in nonrandomized studies and experiments. Matching in an experiment involves the pairing (or *blocking,* as it is often called in experimental-design literature) of two units because they are similar, followed by the random assignment of one treatment to one member of the pair and another treatment to the other member of the pair. If the units really are similar, such matching will increase the precision of the experiment.

As has been pointed out by many writers since Fisher, randomization of treatments to subjects is a powerful tool for eliminating systematic sources of bias. If randomization is absent, it is virtually impossible in many practical circumstances to be convinced that the estimates of the effects of treatments are unbiased. That is, other variables (besides the treatment) that affect the dependent variable may be differently distributed across treatment groups, and thus any estimate of the treatment effect is confounded by effects due to these extraneous variables. (See **Experimental Design** and **Quasi-Experimental Design**.)

In nonrandomized studies, matching is often used to reduce the bias due to these extraneous variables. Classic examples of nonrandomized studies are those in which one member of a pair of identical twins is exposed to one treatment (e.g., a rich home environment) and the other member to another treatment (e.g., a deprived home environment). In practice, matching more commonly involves finding pairs of subjects who are similar in many important aspects (e.g., sex, age, parental occupation) and exposing the two members of each pair to different treatments.

Given the choice between a nonrandomized study and an essentially equivalent experiment, one would prefer the experiment. Thus, in the Report of the President's Commission on Federal Statistics, Light, Mosteller, and Winokur urge greater efforts to use experiments in evaluating public programs and in social research, despite the practical difficulties. Often, however, random assignment of treatments to units is not feasible, as in studies of the effects of smoking on health, of complications of pregnancy on children, or of long-term exposure to doses of radiation on uranium mine workers. Also, as in these examples, one might have to wait many years for the results of an experiment, whereas other relevant data might be at hand. Hence, although inferior to an equivalent experiment, a nonrandomized study may be superior to, or useful in conjunction with, a marginally relevant experiment. For example, assume that we want to estimate the effects of a compensatory reading program on young children, and there are relevant data (pretest and posttest data for groups of "similar" children exposed and not exposed to the special program) and marginally relevant experimental data (data on long-term memory from an experiment on the effects of the general method of teaching on older children). Both sets of data are useful for decisions about the utility of the program. In addition, the analysis of data from nonrandomized studies can be useful in isolating those treatments that appear to be successful and thus worthy of further investigation by experimentation, as when studying special teaching methods for underprivileged children.

Hence, a basic step in planning an observational study is to list the major confounding variables, design the study to record them, and use some such method as matched sampling for removing or reducing the biases that they may cause. In addition, when summarizing the evidence on any differential effects of the treatments, the evaluator should speculate about the size and direction of any remaining bias. (See the discussion of threats to the internal and external validity of studies in **Design of Evaluation.**)

An alternative to matching is to adjust for the confounding variables after the samples have been drawn. That is, random samples are drawn, and the estimates of the treatment are adjusted by means of a model relating the dependent variable y to the confounding variables x. When y and x are continuous, this model usually involves the **Regression** of y on x. A third strategy is to control bias due to the x variables by both matched sampling and statistical adjustment. Notice that the statistical adjustment is performed after all the data are collected, whereas matched sampling can take place before the dependent variable is recorded.

A recent summary of statistical work on the effectiveness of matching in reducing bias in nonrandomized studies is given by Cochran and Rubin. They conclude that regression adjustment alone is generally superior to matching alone but that the combination of matching and regression adjustment generally appears to be better than either alone. However, much work remains to be done, especially on nonlinear multivariate cases.—D. B. R.

Campbell, D. T., and Stanley, J. C. "Experimental and Quasi-Experimental Designs for Research on Teaching." In N. L. Gage (Ed.), *Handbook of Research on Teaching.* Chicago: Rand McNally, 1963. Pp. 171-246.

Cochran, W. G. "Observational Studies." In T. A. Bancroft (Ed.), *Statistical Papers in Honor of George Snedecor.* Ames: Iowa State University Press, 1972. Pp. 77-90.

Cochran, W. G., and Rubin, D. B. "Controlling Bias in Observational Studies: A Review." *Sankhya-A,* 1974, 1-30.

Fisher, R. A. *Statistical Methods for Research Workers.* London: Oliver & Boyd, 1925.

Light, R. J., Mosteller, F., and Winokur, H. S. "Using Controlled Field Studies to Improve Public Policy." *Federal Statistics* (Report of the President's Commission), 1971, *2,* 367-402.

Rubin, D. *Estimating Causal Effects of Treatments in Experimental and Observational Studies.* Princeton, N.J.: Educational Testing Service, 1972.

———————— MATERIALS EVALUATION ————————

A multitude of educational materials are marketed to schools and to other education and training institutions. It is important to know how effective these materials are in helping teachers teach and learners learn. Unfortunately, in most cases, gaining knowledge about effectiveness is something that users of educational materials have to do on their own. (See **Pretest** and **Formative Evaluation** for a discussion of what ought to be done before materials are marketed.) A recent analysis of the sixty "best sellers" among textbooks has shown that less than 10 percent were field-tested before publication (Komoski). According to the same survey, barely 7 percent of 633 programmed instructional materials in major curriculum areas had empirical support, and only about 1 percent of 233 materials used in broadcast television instruction had been learner-tested.

There is a widespread need to determine among the ever increasing quantity of educational materials which ones are of high quality. This need is especially acute in the case of textbooks in states with statewide adoption policies. Educational consumers of instructional materials should not have to assume the whole task of ascertaining the relative effectiveness of materials they are considering for adoption and purchase. However, information is not generally available to enable consumers of education/training products to judge whether a given product can be expected to facilitate learning. Sometimes it is even difficult to judge whether materials are readily adaptable to the local situation.

In order to encourage those who should be assembling information on product effectiveness and usability to do so, educational consumers should press for hard evidence, emphasizing that such evidence is critical for their decisions. At the same time, educators and trainers should be willing to offer their institutions to developers and publishers as sites for product-evaluation studies and thus contribute to the assemblage of product knowledge for their own use and use by others. Meanwhile, however, much of the materials evaluation that occurs will be done by educator consumers as they face the task of selecting new acquisitions.

One of the most serious faults with current instructional materials is that their development is too far removed from the classroom teacher and the "operational" learning situation. Consequently, many innovative materials do not receive widespread use. Some publishers, however, are now using teachers as an integral part of both the development and the evaluational processes, and *adaptation* by the teacher rather than *adoption* by the school is becoming the ultimate objective of the vendor. More flexibility and less uniformity seem to be hallmarks of successful adoptability.

Whether materials evaluation is accomplished by developer or user, the first questions that need to be raised have to do with the relationship between the materials and instructional *goals*. The evaluator may begin with rational analyses of the content, difficulty, and appropriateness of the materials in light of instructional objectives and the characteristics of the student population to be served. (See **Goals and Objectives** and **Content Analysis**.)

However, the evaluator will also want to turn to empirical data to gauge the *effectiveness* of the product. Here it is necessary to look in two directions: indications of gains or change in the direction of stated goals, and separate indications of change in directions not anticipated or in populations not expected to be affected (see **Side Effects**). Test data gathered in the course of verification studies provide the most consequential "hard" evidence—especially where the sample is both adequate in size and representative of the target population, where the tests are reliable and valid, where experimental and control groups are fitted into a sound study design, and where the pre-post gains are substantial (see **Design of Evaluation**). As additional indicators, the performance of the product during field trials may be gauged by teacher-student acceptance and by interest expressed by users in continued use. Supplementary background evidence may be sought on product quality, the quality of previous products of the same developer, and similar indicators of probable failure or success.

A major step forward in the measurement of effectiveness would call for product field testing and verification to be done beyond the influence of the product developer. It is only natural for evaluation done by developers on their own products to be lacking in objectivity, the inclination being to test only what is taught. An independent evaluator can be expected to view a product in a broader perspective. Separating **Summative Evaluation** of a product from both its development and formative evaluation is not a new idea. As early as 1961, Brickell distinguished among design and development, evaluation, and demonstration and dissemination, and urged that the three functions be carried out by different groups. However, over the past decades the development, evaluation, and dissemination functions have usually been carried out by the same organization and often by the same people.

An additional criterion, *adoptability,* may be measured by the ready availability of the product for use in an institution or agency which wishes to adopt it. At the high end of the scale, a product would be immediately available in virtually unlimited quantities. At the other extreme, the potential user may have access only to a sample or a description of the product or a report on the results of its field trials. An additional set of considerations concerning adoptability relates to changes needed at the site where the product will be used, such as structural or utilities modifications in teaching/learning space, special needs for teacher training, and advance-planning requirements. Ideally, a product should be adoptable with a modest planning and preparation effort.

Adequate indicators of *costs* of adoption and use are almost as important as measures of effectiveness. They are also apt to be as elusive, for true costs are quite different from quoted costs, and initial costs sometimes are but a small percentage of ongoing costs. In any event, both introduction of the product *and* its continued use come into account in estimating costs, as do indirect costs such as those imposed by heavy demands on human and material resources. The important dollar components of costs include purchases for the initial adoption, resupply of expendables each year, supplementary purchases, in-service training, changed staffing requirements, repair and maintenance, and facilities use. There are also important components of cost that it is not easy to put dollar values on; e.g., disruptions (–) or new efficiencies (+) brought through adoption of the product; opposition (–) or enthusiastic response (+) by community, parents, students, and teachers; and time wasted (–) or saved (+) attributable to the product's use.

Evaluation of instructional materials used in education/ training programs is seen in the main as a matter of applying a set of criteria in the context of a given product's use; estimating the extent to which each criterion is met; and, with the resulting set of sometimes complex interrelationships in mind, making an overall judgment about that product's efficacy. If judgments are to be made about competing products, comparable dimensions and criteria should be used.—W. W. W.

Brickell, H. M. *Organizing New York State for Educational Change*. Albany, N.Y.: State Education Department, 1961. See especially the discussion of three phases of instructional innovation and their "irreconcilable distinctions" (pp. 62-71).

Educational Products Information Exchange. *Evaluating Individualized Materials*. New York: EPIE Institute, 1972.

Komoski, P. K. Testimony Before the Select Education Subcommittee of the Education and Labor Committee of the U.S. House of Representatives. *Congressional Record,* May 11, 1971.

Scriven, M. *Evaluation Skills* (tape 6B). An instructional cassette recording produced by W. J. Popham. Washington, D.C.: American Educational Research Association, 1971. A convenient device for helping people improve their skills in materials evaluation.

Walton, W. W., Epstein, M. G., Margosches, E. H., and Schrader, W. B. *Selection of Products for Focused Dissemination*. Princeton, N.J.: Educational Testing Service, 1971. A substantive and procedural analysis of the first comparative evaluation of educational products conducted on a nationwide basis. The evaluation was done for the National Center for Educational Communication in connection with the dissemination programs of the U.S. Office of Education.

———————— MEDICAL MODEL OF EVALUATION ————————

Of the many ways to carry out evaluation studies, the most typical involves a simple comparison of average gains for different groups, some of which have been exposed to the educational treatment or training program of interest. This approach has been called the *engineering model* of evaluation: it focuses upon input-output differences, frequently in relation to cost. It provides information necessary for assessing the overall significance or impact of a treatment or program but not sufficient for developing or revising the program. If evaluative research is to provide a base of knowledge and understanding that will not only permit systematic program improvement but also justify extrapolations of the findings to other settings and problem areas and point to needed program modifications to cope with changing conditions, then the form it takes and the kinds of questions it asks must go beyond the typical engineering approach to a more complex research paradigm. This more complex approach, which has been called the *medical model* of evaluation, goes beyond the engineering approach in several ways.

To begin with, the medical model explicitly recognizes that prescriptions for treatment and the evaluation of their effectiveness should take into account not only reported symptoms but other characteristics of the organism and its ecology as well. This is essentially a call for a **Systems-Analysis** approach to educational evaluation—that is, dealing empirically with the interrelatedness of all the factors (psychological, social, environmental, and educational) which may affect performance.

Another obvious derivative of the medical model is a concern for monitoring possible **Side Effects** of the treatment. In addition to the *intended* outcomes of a program, we should also assess a wide range of *possible* outcomes; for in the process we may uncover some consequences that ought to be considered in reaching a final appraisal of the program's value. A further implication is that feelings and reactions should be assessed periodically throughout the course of the treatment and not just at the beginning and the end. As is the custom in exemplary medical practice, we should be concerned about attitudes toward the treatment itself.

And, of course, underlying the entire metaphor is the notion that whenever possible in evaluating educational programs, as in evaluating drugs, we should go beyond a simple assessment of the size of effects to an investigation of the processes that produce the effects. It is only through an understanding of these processes that we will be able to develop a rational basis for changing programs if conditions change and for identifying the types of potential side effects that should be monitored.

Thus, according to the medical model, educational research and evaluation should focus not only upon the outcomes of education but also upon the process and the context of education, thereby encompassing several broad areas of measurement concern—input, program, context, and outcome (see **Variables**). In addition, it is frequently wise to extend the range of the evaluation even further in time. As in a medical case study, measures of antecedent conditions should be included as well as follow-up measures of the consequences both of the treatment and of the termination of treatment.

This approach emphasizes the importance of comparative longitudinal data in evaluating the effectiveness of educational treatments and stresses the need for multivariate analytical procedures that properly take into account those student-process-environment interactions that produce differential results (see **Longitudinal Study** and **Multivariate Analysis**).—S. M.

Messick, S. "Evaluation of Educational Programs as Research on the Educational Process." In F. F. Korten, S. W. Cook, and J. I. Lacey (Eds.), *Psychology and the Problems of Society.* Washington, D.C.: American Psychological Association, 1970. Pp. 215-220.

Messick, S. "The Criterion Problem in the Evaluation of Instruction: Assessing Possible, Not Just Intended, Outcomes." In M. C. Wittrock and D. E. Wiley (Eds.), *The Evaluation of Instruction: Issues and Problems.* New York: Holt, 1970. Pp. 183-202.

Scriven, M. "Student Values as Educational Objectives." In *Proceedings of the 1965 Invitational Conference on Testing Problems*. Princeton, N.J.: Educational Testing Service, 1966. Pp. 33-49.

Scriven, M. "The Methodology of Evaluation." In *Perspectives of Curriculum Evaluation*. AERA Monograph Series on Curriculum Evaluation, No. 1. Chicago: Rand McNally, 1967. Pp. 39-83.

─────────────── MOTIVATION ───────────────

The concept of motivation is used in the explanation of a great number of diverse behaviors—from searching for food by a hungry rat or curling up in defense by a fearful inchworm, to long hours of work by a physicist or gang warfare by groups of ghetto youth. Motivation is concerned with the *arousal, direction,* and *continuance* of behavior. It is an omnibus word carrying many different psychological processes as passengers.

In education, motivation often has a rather specialized meaning. As many teachers see it, a student is motivated if the student wants to do the things that the teacher thinks he should want to do. If a student is attentive and persistent in his schoolwork, if he shows respect and tries hard to please the teacher, then he is thought to be motivated. Similarly, a teacher may look upon an avid basketball player who hates schoolwork as unmotivated. In fact, *both* students are motivated—but toward different things. (From a psychologist's viewpoint, the term *motivation* is often used inappropriately by educators.)

Motivation cuts across many aspects of program evaluation. Here is a short list and accompanying discussion of important aspects to be considered by the program evaluator.

Measurement of motivation. Wherever motivation is to be assessed in an evaluation, its measurement becomes a problem.

Motivation is a concept or variable without physical reality. We do not see motivation; we see behavior. We cannot measure persistence; we can measure only the results of persistent behavior. Thus, the measurement of motivation is indirect, just as is our measurement of other psychological constructs; e.g., attitudes, interests, and values (see **Attitudes, Interest Measurement,** and **Values Measurement**). Properly constructed, however, measures of motivation can be shown to have **Validity** and **Reliability**, and the evaluator should look for this evidence before adopting a particular measure of motivation.

The fact that motivation encompasses many processes has already been emphasized. The implication for measurement is that motivation can be assessed through a variety of measures covering a variety of motivational constructs. For students in a classroom, five distinct motivational factors have been noted: (1) positive orientation toward school-related learning, which involves persistence, high need for achievement, high level of aspiration, and positive academic self-concept and feelings about past experiences in school; (2) need for social recognition, which may involve seeking social reinforcement from the teacher and being academically competitive with classmates; (3) motive to avoid failure, which involves fearing failure and being worried about examinations (see **Test Anxiety**); (4) curiosity about things (perceptual curiosity) and about relationships (epistemic curiosity); (5) conformity, which may involve working in class because it is expected of the student by teachers or parents or engaging in other behaviors because they are expected by peers. In short, to measure motivation the evaluator has to choose from among a list of motives such as this and decide which to use. A guiding criterion should be relevance to the program.

Motivation as an outcome (dependent) variable. In the **Medical Model of Evaluation,** motivational change probably would be considered an output **Variable;** for even if motivational change is not an intended outcome, it is likely to be a possible **Side Effect.** The problem for the evaluator is which aspect of motivation should be measured. Clearly this will depend upon the goal or possible side effect to be assessed. In a comparison of two training programs for typists, one based on group classroom instruction and the other on individualized programmed instruction, the evaluator might consider measuring the trainee's persistence on the job as an outcome variable. On the other hand, in an evaluation of two different teaching styles ("authoritarian" and "democratic") for a program in Chinese language at a naval intelligence school, curiosity levels might be the motivational variable to be measured (i.e., those with "democratic" teachers might become more curious about Chinese culture). As a third example, in an evaluation of a program for potential high school dropouts, level of aspiration, need for achievement, and academic self-concept might be chosen as outcome motivational variables to be measured.

Motivation as an input variable. In evaluating the effects of a program, a frequently neglected but nevertheless useful procedure is to examine possible interactive effects between program and type of student (see **Trait-Treatment Interaction**). One of the domains in which students may be "typed" is motivational. Again, the choice of the specific aspect of motivation will be a problem, but it can be solved through a judgmental analysis of the likely motives that would interact with the program. Thus, highly structured programs might work well for rather anxious students; open, individualized, project-work programs might work poorly for anxious students but well for confident and curious students; programs with a moderate risk level (for instance, where failure rate is known to be about 25 percent) will probably be found most compatible for students with a high need for achievement; and programs with teacher-dominant classrooms will probably work best with conforming students.

Motivation and data collection. The motivations of those collecting the data may have profound effects upon the kinds of data collected (see **Field Operations, Interviews, Evaluator Role,** and the eight articles on Reactive Concerns). Motivations affect what data we look at (direction), what we notice (arousal), and what we pursue (continuance). Many people who study evaluation processes recommend, therefore, that evaluators try to state explicitly their motives (and the motives of their data collectors) that may have influenced the evaluation (e.g., the evaluator thinks that closing the gap between lower- and middle-class children is of paramount importance, or the evaluator considers annual income a more useful measure of success than degree of job satisfaction). Of course, the same degree of explicitness should be required in a **Secondary Evaluation.**

This does not exhaust all possible relationships between

motivation and program evaluation. The literatures on motivation and on evaluation are extensive, but rarely do they intersect. The references provided here are for books on motivation—there are no books that specifically relate motivation to program evaluation.—S. B.

Advertising Research Foundation. *A Bibliography of Theory and Research Techniques in the Field of Human Motivation.* Westport, Conn.: Greenwood, 1972.
Brown, R. *Social Psychology.* New York: Free Press, 1965. See Chapters 4 and 9-13, where such topics as need for achievement, attitude change, and conformity are discussed.
Cofer, C. N., and Appley, M. H. *Motivation: Theory and Research.* New York: Wiley, 1964. The most comprehensive book available on the psychology of motivation.
Fowler, H. *Curiosity and Exploratory Behaviors.* New York: Macmillan, 1965. Has implications for program development and program evaluation.
McClelland, D. "What Is the Effect of Achievement Motivation Training on the Schools?" *Teachers College Record,* 1972, *74,* 129-145.
Stacey, C. L., and DeMartino, M. F. *Understanding Human Motivation.* New York: World, 1965. A fine general overview of motivation as it applies to human behavior.

MULTIVARIATE ANALYSIS

Multivariate analysis refers to a series of statistical techniques used for analyzing a set of **Variables** observed on a number of students or experimental subjects. The variables being analyzed are called *dependent variables* (or *outcome variables* or *criteria*). The dependent variables are analyzed with reference to one or more *independent variables* (or *program variables* or *carrier vari-*

ables or *predictors*). Multivariate analyses are usually generalizations of such univariate analyses as multiple regression, differing in that univariate analyses have only one dependent variable no matter how many independent variables. (See **Statistical Analysis.**)

A frequent assumption of multivariate analysis is that p (dependent variables) may be expressed as weighted sums of m (independent variables and residuals), as in the matrix equation $Y = XB + E$, where Y is an $N \times p$ matrix (N = number of observations) containing the measures of the dependent variables, X is an $N \times m$ matrix containing the measures of the independent variables, B is an $m \times p$ matrix of weights, and E is an $N \times p$ matrix of residuals (or error). Y and X are known, whereas B and E are unknown values which must be estimated. It is also useful to assume that the residuals are normally distributed and that although the residuals for different variables for an individual may be correlated, knowledge of the residuals for one person gives no information about the residuals for other persons.

Important purposes of multivariate analysis are (1) to find an estimate $\hat{B}$ of the weights B that fit the data as well as possible in the sense of making the sum of squared residuals as small as possible—these weights may be used in predicting the values of Y from given values of X; (2) to make an estimate ($\hat{\Sigma}$) of the variances and covariances of the residuals—this is a measure of how well the weighted sums fit or predict Y; (3) to test hypotheses that some or all of the weights in $\hat{B}$ are not significantly different from hypothesized values (usually zero). **Hypothesis Testing** is useful, for example, if an experimenter wishes to test whether certain independent variables are useful in prediction of the dependent variables. There are a number of different ways to approach multivariate hypothesis testing.

A number of techniques under the general heading of multivariate analysis are of interest to the evaluator or educational researcher: canonical correlation, Hotelling T^2, Mahalanobis D^2, Manova, Manocov, and discriminant analysis.

Canonical correlation. Canonical correlation is a measure of the interrelationship between two sets of variables. Essentially, a separate set of weights is found for each set of variables such that, if these weights are used to find weighted sums of each set, the two weighted sums will be correlated as highly as possible. If batteries of predictor tests and criterion tests are subjected to canonical analysis, the weighted sum of the criteria will be the most predictable possible combination of criteria; hence, Hotelling termed this function the "most predictable criterion." A complete canonical analysis will find as many canonical correlations as dependent variables (or independent variables if there are fewer); the largest canonical correlation corresponds to the most predictable criterion, the second-largest canonical correlation is the highest possible correlation of the residuals after the first canonical variable is removed, and so forth. Canonical correlations can be subjected to significance tests in the same way as in the multivariate analysis of variance (see below).

Since correlation analysis is symmetric, the results are the same whether a set of variables is considered dependent or independent. If one of the sets of variables has but one member, then the canonical correlation is the same as the multiple correlation between that variable and the other set; if both sets have but one member, then the canonical correlation is the Pearson product-moment correlation coefficient (see **Correlation**).

Hotelling T^2, Mahalanobis D^2. The Hotelling T^2 statistic is a generalization of Student's t statistic, which is used to test hypotheses that the means or differences between means of a set of variables are simultaneously equal to a set of known constants (usually zero). The Mahalanobis D^2 statistic is a measure of the distance between the set of means and the set of constants or of the difference between two sets of group means. These statistics may be used to measure and test the significance of the differences between two groups in their performance on a series of educational tests. The T^2 test is usually more appropriate than a series of separate t statistics for a set of educational tests given to two groups of students. (See **Statistical Analysis**.)

If Hotelling's T^2 is used when there is but one variable instead of a set of variables, Hotelling's T^2 is identical to the square of Student's t.

Multivariate analysis of variance (Manova) and covariance (Manocov). Manova is the multivariate analogue of the analysis of variance (Anova) in univariate statistics and is most commonly used in testing the differences among means measured on independent groups of subjects (see **Statistical Analysis**). Manova applies to sets of means; whereas a one-way Anova tests the differences among the means of, say, five experimental groups, a one-way Manova can test the differences among sets of means of several different variables. For example, we might compare the differences on reading, arithmetic, *and* science achievement for five experimental groups. Manova can give one overall significance statistic for the group differences.

Manocov is the multivariate analogue of the analysis of covariance (Anocov) and is most commonly used for testing the differences among multivariate regression planes. One may test whether or not multivariate regression planes for independent groups can be presumed to be sampling fluctuations from a common plane. Manocov may also be used to test multivariate regression planes for common intercepts (adjusted means) assuming common slopes.

Manova is strictly comparable to Anova as is Manocov to Anocov, and the techniques are equivalent if there is only one dependent variable. Either may be used for crossed and/or nested experimental designs (see Winer). Manocov is also subject to the inference problems associated with **Lord's Paradox.**

Discriminant analysis. Discriminant analysis is a statistical technique used to find the linear combinations of variables which best discriminate among a set of predefined groups. This type of analysis may be used in educational research to find out in which ways the students in several different experimental groups are most dissimilar (or similar) on a given set of variables. The weights computed in discriminant analyses have been used in educational guidance to measure the similarity of individuals to members of occupational and educational groups. Discriminant analysis is very similar to Manova, and the hypothesis test from Manova is appropriate for testing the significance of group differences.—A. E. B.

Anderson, T. W., Das Gupta, S., and Styan, G. P. H. *A Bibliography of Multivariate Statistical Analysis.* New York: Wiley, 1972.

Cooley, W. W., and Lohnes, P. R. *Multivariate Procedures for the Behavioral Sciences.* New York: Wiley, 1962.

Dempster, A. P. *Elements of Continuous Multivariate Analysis.* Reading, Mass.: Addison-Wesley, 1969.

Morrison, D. F. *Multivariate Statistical Methods.* New York: McGraw-Hill, 1967.

Winer, B. J. *Statistical Principles in Experimental Design.* New York: McGraw-Hill, 1962.

──────────────── NEEDS ASSESSMENT ────────────────

The process by which one identifies needs and decides upon priorities among them has been termed *needs assessment.* In the context of education and training programs, a need may be defined as a condition in which there is a discrepancy between an *acceptable* state of affairs and an *observed* state of affairs. Needs assessment may be applied to individuals, groups, or institutions.

The extent of discrepancy may be either objectively measured or subjectively estimated. In the first case, the level of measured performance is compared with the level judged acceptable. In the second case, selected judges are asked to indicate the extent to which needs exist in a given area. However, the line between the two approaches is somewhat blurred, for a value judgment is necessary in either case (in the setting of the acceptable level or in the rating of the degree of need), and objective measurement may be used in the so-called "subjective" approach.

An "objective" needs assessment usually passes through these steps:

1. Identify the goal areas considered important to the educational system (school, class, training program, etc.).
2. Select or develop measures (indicators) for these goal areas.
3. Set acceptable levels on the measures.
4. Administer the measures.
5. Compare obtained levels against the acceptable levels. If

the obtained levels are less than the acceptable levels, a need is indicated.

A "subjective" needs assessment usually consists of the following steps:

1. Identify the goal areas considered important to the educational system.
2. Optional: Select or develop measures for these goal areas and administer them. This step may be used to provide formal evidence for consideration in judging need.
3. Develop a rating scale for judging the degree to which present performance in the goal area is acceptable. Goal areas could be rank-ordered according to the acceptability of performance, or the acceptability of performance in each goal area could be rated on an interval scale. (If step 2 been used, summaries of the data are given to judges for their consideration in making their ratings.)
4. Obtain the ratings from a group of judges and average the ratings to obtain indices of need. It is useful to keep points of view separate here if the responses of some judges are clearly different from those of other judges.

It is possible to have various combinations of "objective" and "subjective" needs assessments. Judges may, for example, defer to their own opinions as well as to the formal evidence. Thus, opinions of colleagues, the remarks of students, etc., may be considered as well as what is measured. (Of course, opinions may be collected formally by questionnaires and as such become "measured.") Judges could also be asked to consider only formal evidence, in which case the difference between the two procedures would be only that, in the second procedure, setting acceptable levels would be bypassed in favor of judging needs directly.

Whichever approach is adopted (the "subjective" or the "objective"), the next step is to assess the priorities among needs for the purpose of defining action programs.

Several factors affect decisions about need priorities and may be considered either when establishing needs or at a later time. One factor is the judged importance of the goal areas. Given two goal areas, discrepancies in the high-importance areas may be attacked before discrepancies in the low-importance areas. The number of persons demonstrating a need may also be taken into consideration. The decision maker must determine whether it is preferable to attack intense needs demonstrated by only a few persons or to deal with less intense needs that are, however, pervasive. For example, is it better for an instructor to spend most of his instructional time helping a few students who are failing a course of study, or instructing many others in useful skills that they would not otherwise learn? A third factor that affects the ordering of need priorities is the feasibility of initiating programs to eliminate the need. Even though a need might be important and pervasive, if the decision maker cannot see a ready way to attack it, it might be assigned a lower priority than a need considered less vital but about which something can be done. For example, it is certainly more feasible for a school to try to improve children's low reading scores than to try to improve the educational levels of their parents—even though the latter may be recognized as a major source of the children's reading problem. In some cases, it may be possible to conduct research to find ways to deal with important but stubborn needs. However, the delays attendant on a long-term research effort must be weighed against the short-term effect of directly attacking a less important need. These and other factors make the task of assigning priorities among needs a very complicated endeavor.

Complex mathematical models have been used to aid the decision maker both in identifying needs and in setting priorities. These can be useful as long as the decision maker understands what assumptions underlie the analysis model and realizes where judgment enters into the mathematical formulations. (See **Systems Analysis**.)

Needs assessment is likely to play a dual role in an evaluator's life. His special skills and experience in formulating goals, and in the selection, application, and construction of measuring instruments, etc., fit him particularly for involvement in needs assessment. But more important, perhaps, needs assessment is itself a valued tool for him, not only in the initial design of programs and evaluation studies but also for monitoring any changes in the needs that programs are meant to serve.—G. L. M.

Center for the Study of Evaluation. *CSE Elementary School Evaluation Kit: Needs Assessment.* Boston: Allyn and Bacon, 1973. Covers the goal-selection process, test selection, data collection, and the selection of critical need areas.

Feldmesser, R. A. *Educational Goal Indicators for New Jersey.* Princeton, N.J.: Educational Testing Service, 1973. Description of a rationale for the needs-assessment program carried out by the State Education Department of New Jersey.

Florida Educational Research and Development Council. *Plan for Study of the Educational Needs of Florida.* Gainesville: University of Florida, College of Education, 1968.

Harless, J. H. "An Analysis of Front-End Analysis." *Improving Human Performance—A Research Quarterly,* Winter 1973.

--- NONPARAMETRIC STATISTICS ---

One of the most frequently asked questions in program evaluation is whether the difference between an experimental group and a control group on some criterion variable is statistically significant. The meaning of **Statistical Significance** is explained under that heading, and various tests of significance (e.g., t and F tests) are discussed in **Statistical Analysis.** Those tests of significance are based on the properties of the normal distribution (see **Statistics**).

There are some cases, however, when the distribution of the data is either unknown or not normal. Rank data are an illustration of data that are not normally distributed. If one hundred persons are ranked from 1 to 100 on some variable, then the frequency of each rank is 1 (assuming no ties). The frequency histogram (see **Statistics**) for these data would simply be a rectangle with a height of 1; for this reason, the data are said to have a rectangular distribution. The tests of significance based on the normal distribution use the parameters of a normal distribution in the formulas for the tests and are therefore called *parametric tests.* Nonparametric tests of significance, by contrast, are tests that are not dependent on the parameters of any particular distribution. Consequently, they are also called *distribution-free tests of significance*. By extension, nonparametric statistics refers to that class of statistical methods that are distribution free. Since the nonparametric methods are based on weaker assumptions than the classical parametric procedures, the tests are generally not as powerful as the parametric tests. If data are normally distributed, but a distribution-free statistical test is used, generally the null hypothesis will not be rejected as often as it would be by the more appropriate parametric test (see **Hypothesis Testing**). Since the detection of significant differences ordinarily starts with the rejection of the null hypothesis, the use of a nonparametric test when a parametric test could be used might result in wrongly concluding that a program is ineffective. For this reason, a parametric test is preferred when its use can be justified.

Nonparametric tests can be used to determine (1) the probability that a given sample could not have come from a specified population (e.g., the chi-square goodness-of-fit test). Other applications of nonparametric techniques include (2) evaluating whether two samples of data could have come from populations having different characteristics (e.g., the sign test, Wilcoxon matched-pairs signed-ranks test, Mann-Whitney U test) and (3) evaluating paired observations for significant association or correlation (e.g., chi-square contingency analysis, Fisher exact test, Spearman rank correlation coefficient, Kendall tau rank correlation coefficient). The most common nonparametric tests are those used on ranked data, and they will be briefly illustrated in this entry. A comprehensive treatment of the subject can be found in Walsh's three-volume *Handbook of Nonparametric Statistics*.

1. The term "being from a specified population" is ordinarily used to set up the null hypothesis. For example, if it is suspected that the frequency of school visits of mothers is related to the amount of maternal education, the null hypothesis can be stated as follows: There is no difference in frequency of school visits among mothers with differing amounts of education. In order to test this hypothesis, it is assumed that all the mothers come from a population in which the number of school visits is not related to maternal education. Siegel (pp. 180-184) gives a simple example using artificial data for forty-four moth-

ers. Four categories for maternal education are used. The median number of visits for the forty-four mothers is determined. Then, if maternal education does not affect the number of visits, we would expect the number of mothers above and below the median in each category to be approximately equal. If education does make a difference, then the observed frequencies will differ significantly from the expected frequencies. Chi square can be used to test the significance of such differences between observed frequencies and expected frequencies. If the differences are small, then the chi-square value will be small. As the frequencies become more disparate, the chi-square value becomes larger, and it becomes more likely that the observed frequencies did not come from the population on which the null hypothesis was based. Tables that give the chi-square values for hypothesis rejection are readily available. (See Siegel for tables and further details, pp. 180-184.)

2. Evaluators sometimes attempt to control for effects of extraneous variables—that is, variables not associated with the educational treatment—by "matching" students on such variables (background characteristics, etc.). Typically, one student in each matched pair is assigned to one treatment and the other student in the pair to another treatment (or to a control group). Similarly, school classes rather than individuals may be matched on a set of extraneous variables. (See **Matched Sampling**.)

The sign test may be applied to two sets of scores (e.g., on an achievement measure) that are arranged in matched pairs, provided the scores within each pair can be ordered. Then we focus only on the *direction* of the difference for each pair. If the first member of the pair is greater than the second member, the sign is positive; if the second member is greater than the first, the sign is negative. Under the null hypothesis, we expect half of the signs to be positive and half negative. Therefore, the null hypothesis is rejected if too few of either sign occur. Tables are available (Siegel) for testing the significance of the proportion of one sign in an application of the test. An illustration of the application of the sign test is given in Table 1. In this case, the number of pairs of classes is 8 and the number of minus signs is 3. Three out of eight minus (or plus) signs has a probability of .363 of occurring by chance (from Table D in Siegel), and the null hypothesis cannot be

Table 1

**Mean Achievement Scores for "Matched" Classes
Taught by Method A and Method B (Sign Test)**

Method A	Method B	Sign
80	64	+
84	69	+
85	72	+
70	61	+
65	76	−
60	68	−
73	66	+
71	74	−

rejected at either the .05 or .01 level. Thus, we cannot conclude that Method A was associated with higher achievement.

The Wilcoxon sign test is different from the sign test in that the *magnitudes* of the differences between the matched pairs are used. The test gives more weight to a pair which shows a large difference than to a pair which shows a small difference. Using the same data as in Table 1, Table 2 illustrates the use of the Wilcoxon sign test. Differences are computed and ranked without respect to sign, with the smallest difference being ranked as one. Now the sum of the ranks of positive differences (T) and the sum of the ranks of negative differences (S) are computed:

$$T = 8 + 7 + 6 + 4 + 2 = 27$$
$$S = 5 + 3 + 1 = 9$$

Tables are available for testing the significance of the smaller sum for samples of different size. (Under the null hypothesis, the sums should be equal.) For this example, with $n = 8$ and $S = 9$, the null hypothesis cannot be rejected at the .05 level of significance.

When the two samples are independent and cannot be arranged in matched pairs, the Mann-Whitney U test may be used to test whether the two samples have been drawn from the same population. First, the data in both samples are arranged in order of magnitude and each score is replaced by its rank. Using the data from Table 1, for example, and assuming we had no advance basis for assigning the sixteen classes to eight pairs, we would begin our

Table 2

Application of Wilcoxon Sign Test to Data from Table 1

Method A	Method B	Difference	Rank of Difference
80	64	16	8
84	69	15	7
85	72	13	6
70	61	9	4
65	76	−11	5
60	68	− 8	3
73	66	7	2
71	74	− 3	1

inquiry as in Table 3. The statistic U is the total number of times an A score precedes a B score. For B = 61, one A score precedes it. For B = 64, one A score precedes it. For B = 66, two A scores precede it, etc. In this example, $U = 1 + 1 + 2 + 2 + 2 + 4 + 5 + 5 = 22$. The sampling distribution of U under the null hypothesis is known, and therefore a test for the significance of the U value for various sizes of samples can be found in available tables. In this example, for two samples of size 8, $U = 22$. Using Table J from Siegel, we find that the probability of getting a U of 22 is .164 when there is, in fact, no difference. Thus, the null hypothesis cannot be rejected at the .05 level.

The Mann-Whitney U test can also be used with samples that are of different sizes. As the size of the two samples increases beyond 20, the sampling distribution of U rapidly approaches the normal distribution. In such cases, the z values associated with the normal distribution can be used to test for significant differences (see **Statistical Significance**).

3. The most commonly used correlation coefficient is the Pearson product-moment correlation coefficient. The interpreta-

Table 3

Data Used to Compute the Mann-Whitney U Test

Score	60	61	64	65	66	68	69	70	71	72	73	74	76	80	84	85
Sample	A	B	B	A	B	B	B	A	A	B	A	B	B	A	A	A
Rank	1	2	3	4	5	6	7	8	9	10	11	12	13	14	15	16

tion of this measure of the relationship between two sets of scores is based on the assumption that the two sets of scores are from normally distributed populations. The nonparametric correlation coefficients are not dependent on underlying normal distributions. One such correlation, the Spearman rank correlation coefficient, may be calculated by the following formula: $\rho = 1 - [6\Sigma D^2/n\ (n^2 - 1)]$. In this formula, D is the difference in rank for each subject (or class or group) on the two variables and n is the number of subjects. An example using the Spearman rank correlation coefficient is given in the article on **Correlation**. For $n = 8$, the rank correlation must be at least .643 to be significant at the .05 level.

There are advantages and disadvantages of nonparametric methods. The primary advantage is that they are usually simpler than the classical parametric tests and thus can be understood and applied more easily. In addition, they are not dependent on the distributions of the populations from which the data are drawn. On the negative side, the nonparametric tests are generally less efficient. Efficiency (or power) relates in this instance to the amount of information that can be obtained from a sample. To say that one statistical test is twice as efficient as another statistical test means that the first can provide the same information as the second using a sample of only half the size. For very small samples, the sign tests have an efficiency of about 95 percent as compared with a t test. As the sample size increases, the efficiency decreases. The efficiency of the sign test decreases to about 63 percent for large samples. In other words, if the data *were* from a normal distribution, the appropriate classical test would be just as effective with a sample 37 percent smaller.—R. T. M.

Greenwood, E. R., Jr. *A Detailed Proof of the Chi-Square Test of Goodness of Fit.* Cambridge, Mass.: Harvard University Press, 1940. Attempts to "bridge the gap between what is known as the chi-square test of goodness of fit and the actual mathematical curve, the chi-square curve," a gap that is "very annoying to anyone with any mathematical curiosity."

Moses, L. E. "Nonparametric Statistics for Psychological Research." *Psychological Bulletin,* 1952, *49,* 122-143.

Siegel, S. *Nonparametric Statistics for the Behavioral Sciences.*

New York: McGraw-Hill, 1956. A good summary of the main nonparametric tests, with clear illustrations of how to use them.

Walsh, J. E. *Handbook of Nonparametric Statistics.* New York: Van Nostrand, 1962. 3 vols.

Wilcoxon, F. "Individual Comparisons by Ranking Methods." *Biometrics Bulletin,* 1945, *1,* 80-82.

NORMS

Although the dictionary definition of *norm* is "a set standard of development or achievement," the word *norms* as used in evaluation generally applies to an empirically derived distribution of scores on a test. Such a distribution is a description of how a defined group of people performed on the test and does not carry in itself any value judgments about "good" or "bad" performance. From a norms table alone, we can say only that these are the highest, or lowest, or middle scores in *this* group. And we must recognize that a given score representing a low level of performance in one norms group (e.g., college sophomores) may represent a high level of performance on the same test in another group (e.g., high school dropouts) because of the different ability levels represented in the two groups.

A good norms table is accompanied by a clear description of (a) the group on which it is based (e.g., a national sample of tenth graders, a sample of entering female college freshmen in the eastern states, all the Naval Reserve officers in a given year, all the fourth graders in this school), (b) the way in which the sample was selected, the number of students and institutions involved, and the date of testing, and (c) any special conditions under which the tests were administered. The table sets forth a list of scores obtainable on the test and the percentile rank associated with each score for the specified group. A percentile rank describes the test standing of an individual with respect to the other members of the norms group; for example, if a student has a percentile rank of 80 on some test, this means that his score is better than the scores of 80 percent of the students in the norms group. (There are two other definitions of *percentile rank*: the percentage of scores that fall (a) at or below the given score or (b) below the midpoint of the given score interval. See the Ebel reference.) Table 1 provides a rather typical example of entries in a norms table. The example is based on 300 students. A person consulting the table for aid in interpreting a student's score of 156 would note that 91 percent of students in the norms group earned scores lower than that—or this student's score is in the top 10 percent with respect to students in this norms group. Means and standard deviations of scores are additional accompaniments to most norms distributions (see **Statistics**).

The three most frequent kinds of test norms are *age norms,* where scores are classified by the average ages of the people who earned them (used by Binet originally and still characteristic of many **Intelligence** tests); *grade norms,* where score distributions are given separately for students in different grades, or scores are converted into grade equivalents or average scores earned by students at different grade levels (characteristic of most school and college achievement tests); and *occupational norms,* where score

Table 1

Entries in a Norms Table

Score	Frequency[a]	Cumulative Frequency	Percentile Rank
170-171	1	300	99
168-169	0	299	99
166-167	1	299	99
164-165	2	298	98
162-163	3	296	98
160-161	5	293	97
158-159	8	288	95
156-157	13	280	91
154-155	16	267	86
etc.			

[a]Number of people obtaining the score.

distributions are given for members of occupational groups (frequently used for interest inventories). Publishers' age and grade norms are usually based on **Cross-Sectional** rather than **Longitudinal** samples. (See **Score Types**.)

The existence of well-documented norms is the major criterion justifying the application of the adjective *standardized* to a test (see **Standardized Tests**). However, although very relevant to interpreting the score of an individual for guidance purposes, norms are generally more useful indirectly than directly in evaluating the effectiveness of a program for a group of students. For example, they may be helpful in suggesting the levels of performance that program directors might reasonably aspire to, and they may offer some clues about the meaning and importance of gains that students may show in a program.

Norms groups can seldom be made to stand alone as the appropriate comparison groups against which to appraise the progress of students in specified curricula or training programs. The misuse of norms in this way can lead to the following kind of dilemma: The national fall norms averages for a mathematics test are 49 and 54 for fifth and sixth graders, respectively; fifth graders in a special mathematics program in a given suburb earn average scores of 52 at the beginning of the course and 60 at the end. Should the program director congratulate himself on his students' eight-point gain in contrast to the five-point difference between the national groups? Are the suburban students comparable to the national groups? Does the slight discrepancy in time of second testing make a difference? Is it harder to go from 49 to 54 than, say, from 52 to 57? Should the suburban students have gained *more* than they did if the program is to be labeled effective? The norms reference alone does not answer these questions. On the other hand, the program director in this instance would probably be hard pressed to defend the continuance of his program if the students had gained fewer than five points—or had declined in the skills measured by the test—if the test content was judged important. So references to national norms for standardized tests are frequently useful in evaluation studies—if for no other reason than to indicate that the program did not put the students behind their **Cohorts** who received more traditional instruction.—S. B. A.

Angoff, W. H. "Scales, Norms, and Equivalent Scores." In R. L. Thorndike (Ed.), *Educational Measurement*. (2nd Ed.) Washington, D.C.: American Council on Education, 1971. Pp. 533-562.

Ebel, R. L. *Essentials of Educational Measurement*. Englewood Cliffs, N.J.: Prentice-Hall, 1972. See page 286.

Lorge, I., and Thorndike, R. L. "Procedures for Establishing Norms." In *Technical Manual, Lorge-Thorndike Intelligence Tests*. Boston: Houghton Mifflin, 1954. Reprinted in D. N. Jackson and S. Messick (Eds.), *Problems in Human Assessment*. New York: McGraw-Hill, 1967. Pp. 791-793.

Schrader, W. B. "Norms." In C. W. Harris (Ed.), *Encyclopedia of Educational Research*. (3rd Ed.) New York: Macmillan, 1960. Pp. 922-926.

———————————— OBSERVATION TECHNIQUES ————————————

Direct observation has for years been one of the **Job-Analysis** methods used in industry for the assessment of efficiency in production. In recent years more attention has been given to applying the idea within education. Traditionally, the effects of a teaching situation or a training program have been measured without observing the teaching process or, at best, with only enough observation to make a rating of the teacher's ability. With the advent of newer observation instruments based upon systematic recording of observable behaviors, a more precise data-based orientation toward the teaching-learning process is possible.

Observation techniques comprise such divergent forms of data collection as **Ratings**, systematic-observation instruments, and sequential narratives of everything that happens to an individual during an observation session. Mechanical means such as audio- or videotaping are also used. The data collected through direct observation vary in objectivity and immediate availability for data analysis. Ratings, since they already represent a summary judgment, are the most readily usable, but the behaviors upon which the judgment is based may be obscured. More objective data are collected by systematic-observation instruments which indicate the presence of—or tally the occurrences of—specific, predetermined, low-inference items of behavior. Such instruments tend to be precoded or require a minimum of coding time before being processed. Many may be directly keypunched, or optically scanned and read onto tape, before being summarized by the computer. A videotape is the ultimate in objective recording of behavior, but care must be taken to assure that the focus of the camera will be on those behaviors relevant to a specific problem. The data are not quickly available for analysis, however, since the videotape must be subsequently reviewed and the recorded behaviors coded just as in observing live performance (See **Content Analysis**.)

The remainder of this entry will be concerned primarily with *systematic-observation instruments* because of their advantages for research and evaluation. Such instruments are built by selecting variables thought to be relevant, describing those variables behaviorally, and developing a system for automatically recording them. Two kinds of recording systems are used, sign systems and category systems.

Sign systems describe the teaching situation as a snapshot describes a view. Typically, the instrument consists of a relatively large number of variables (perhaps sixty to one hundred or more) defined behaviorally (e.g., student gives direction; teacher criticizes). After a period of observation, of two to five minutes or more, all those behaviors that have occurred are checked. Behaviors that occur more than once during an observation period are checked only once. Repeated observations give additional still pictures of the classroom. Given the large amount of data collected by this type of system, the number of variables is generally reduced by summing items on a rational basis or through **Factor Analysis**.

Category systems generally deal with a more restricted number of variables (categories), but they are recorded continuously, as often as they occur, to produce an ongoing, moving record of behaviors. A category system is like a moving picture, its emphasis is on continuous action. To keep such a record, however, the observer cannot be burdened by a large number of categories. The action must be somewhat confined. The observer's job is to categorize and record behavior as it occurs, perhaps every three seconds or oftener.

The proliferation of systematic-observation instruments in the past decade has blurred somewhat the distinction between the sign and category systems, but the rationale remains. Each of the systems has its advantages and disadvantages: broad versus narrow focus, static versus dynamic representation. Each system attempts to have the observer become a recorder rather than an evaluator of events, and to make recording as immediate, direct, and simple a process as possible. To the extent that developers of observation instruments are successful in meeting these objectives, the problems of training observers are reduced. However, even with the most apparently straightforward system, the evaluator should budget some time for training and then take periodic samples of the forms or protocols produced by observers on the job as a check on their accuracy and consistency (see **Quality Control**).

Reliability and validity are as important for observation instruments as for any other kind of measurement—and typically harder to come by and prove than with many of the testlike instruments. **Reliability** is always a measure of consistency. In systematic observation one must be concerned not only with the consistency of recording of data within observers (intraobserver reliability) and between observers (interobserver reliability) but also with the stability of the behavior being recorded. The most stringent definition of reliability in classroom observation is based on the concept that the mean differences of repeated measures obtained within classrooms will be smaller than the mean differences between classrooms. Consistency of recording and consistency of behavior both enter into such a reliability measure, which may be derived from a repeated-measures analysis of variance (see **Statistical Analysis**). However, few investigators have reported such data, most opting instead to report a measure of observer agreement.

The most stringent definition of **Validity** of a systematic observation measure for program evaluation requires a significant **Correlation** between the measure and an outside criterion, generally a measure of student achievement or gain. This requirement is based on the belief that teaching effectiveness must be defined by the effect on students (i.e., by changes in student behavior). Although face validity, or other kinds of validity, may be useful, depending on the purposes of the observation, research on the teaching process should base validity of its measurements on correlation with changes in student behavior.

The potential of systematic-observation instruments for usefulness in educational research and training is enormous. In addition to using observational data as measures of classroom process and as outcome measures in planned change, we may use observation data to provide feedback in teacher training or to describe the classroom process existing within a school or training facility. Observation instruments can readily be used for comparison of behaviors across grade levels or programs. One can only hope that the proliferation of instrumentation for research involving systematic observation will be followed by systematic use of the most valid and reliable instruments to measure and evaluate the teaching process across all levels and kinds of education and training.

(See also **Reactive Effects of Program and Evaluation** and **Unobtrusive Measures**.)—M. E. R.

Furst, N. J. "Systematic Classroom Observation." In L. Deighten (Ed.), *Encyclopedia of Education*. New York: Macmillan, 1971. Pp. 168-183.

Medley, D. M., and Mitzel, H. E. "Measuring Classroom Behavior by Systematic Observation." In N. L. Gage (Ed.), *Handbook of Research on Teaching*. Chicago: Rand McNally, 1963. Pp. 247-328.

Rosenshine, B. *Teaching Behaviors and Student Achievement*. Windsor, Berkshire, England: National Foundation for Educational Research in England and Wales, 1971. A review of students involving systematic-observation data or ratings in which teaching behaviors were related to student achievement.

Rosenshine, B., and Furst, N. "The Use of Direct Observation to Study Teaching." In R. M. Travers (Ed.), *Second Handbook of Research on Teaching*. Chicago: Rand McNally, 1973. Pp. 122-183.

Simon, A., and Boyer, E. G. (Eds.) *Mirrors for Behavior: An An-*

thology of Classroom Observation Instruments. 14 vols., plus summary vol. and supplementary vols. A and B. Philadelphia: Research for Better Schools, 1967, 1970. As comprehensive a collection of observation instruments as can be found.

———————————— PATH ANALYSIS ————————————

Path analysis is a technique for investigating the interrelationships of a set of variables within the context of a causal model (see **Causality**). It was originated by a geneticist, Sewall Wright, more than fifty years ago. Largely unknown to social scientists for years, it has recently received a great deal of attention within the social sciences, especially sociology. Much of the recent popularity might be attributed to an influential paper by Duncan in 1966 and to the related work of Blalock and Simon (see Blalock).

The method of path analysis "is based on the construction of a qualitative diagram in which every included variable, measured or hypothetical, is represented (by arrows) either as *completely* determined by certain others (which may be represented as similarly determined) or as an *ultimate* factor" (Wright, p. 190). Where a variable cannot be represented as completely determined by known factors, a residual factor is assumed that is uncorrelated with any of the factors having causal connections to that variable. Given a complete causal model, the linear relationships among the variables are analyzed, with the direction of the causation taken into account; the result is a set of path coefficients that indicate the strength of each causal path.

Some investigators have high regard for path analysis; others view it with great skepticism. Much of the appeal of path analysis probably stems from the mistaken notion that it is a technique for identifying the causal determinants of a set of correlations. On the other hand, the skepticism stems from the well-known fact that the mere existence of a correlation between A and B does not permit us to know whether A causes B, or whether B causes A, or whether the relationship is due to some other factor. Both views of path analysis miss the point that it is a hypothetico-deductive system wherein causal connections are hypothesized and the resulting model is then applied to the data to determine the logical consequences of the hypotheses (see **Scientific Inquiry** and **Evaluation**). If the model is an accurate reflection of reality, path analysis can provide estimates of the strength of the causal connections or provide a test of a given connection within the model. It cannot generate the correct causal model from the data, however.

Although a sharp distinction is sometimes made between path analysis and the simultaneous equation methods used by economists, the two methods are quite similar. Where the econometrician uses unstandardized regression coefficients, the path analyst prefers standardized coefficients. However, both rely on the same basic equations and linear regression techniques. (See **Correlation** and **Regression**.)

One of the great advantages of a technique such as path analysis over the more traditional correlational analyses used by educational researchers is that the investigator is forced to make his assumptions explicit. This sometimes can expose rather fuzzy thinking that lurks behind seemingly lucid discussions of large sets of correlation coefficients. Causal interpretations "must rest on assumptions—at a minimum, the assumption as to the ordering of the variables, but also assumptions about the unmeasured variables. . . . The great merit of the path scheme, then, is that it makes the assumptions explicit and tends to force the discussion to be at least internally consistent so that mutually incompatible assumptions are not introduced surreptitiously into different parts of an argument extending over scores of pages" (Duncan, p. 7).—R. L. L.

Anderson, J. G., and Evans, F. B. "Causal Models in Educational Research: Recursive Models." *American Educational Research Journal*, 1974, *11*, 29-39.
Blalock, H. M. (Ed.) *Causal Models in the Social Sciences*. Chicago: Aldine-Atherton, 1971. Deals with a variety of causal models and structural systems of equations. Part II contains

articles on path analysis by Malcolm Turner and Charles
Stevens, Sewall Wright, Otis Dudley Duncan, and Blalock.

Duncan, O. D. "Path Analysis: Sociological Examples." *American Journal of Sociology,* 1966, *72,* 1-16.

Jencks, C., Smith, M., Acland, H., Bane, M. J., Cohen, D., Gintis, H., Heynes, B., and Michelson, S. *Inequality: A Reassessment of the Effect of Family and Schooling in America.* New York: Basic Books, 1972. Examples of the use of path analysis in estimating the heritability of IQ scores (Appendix A) and the determinants of educational attainment, occupational status, and income (Appendix B).

Wright, S. "Path Coefficients and Path Regressions, Alternative or Complementary Concepts?" *Biometrics,* 1960, *16,* 189-202.

PERFORMANCE CONTRACTING

Performance contracting, an application to education of methods sometimes used in administering manufacturing contracts, has received widespread attention as a possible crash method of improving educational processes and outcomes. In this respect, performance contracting is closely related to the concept of educational **Accountability**. The terms are, however, not interchangeable. Performance contracting is properly viewed as one means of stimulating and accomplishing the purpose of accountability: acceptance of the obligation to improve the effectiveness of public schools with all pupils, no matter what their backgrounds.

Performance contracting was originally used as an educational technology by the Job Corps. By 1970-71, at least 100 performance contracts were in operation across the United States, and in 1970 the Office of Economic Opportunity decided to institute a thoroughgoing test of the concept, by establishing projects in eighteen widely scattered school districts. The results, as reported, were inconclusive.

A performance contract is a legal pact between an educational agent (such as a school board) and a contractor (usually private business firms or divisions of private corporations selling educational hardware, textbooks, and other educational products and services; sometimes teachers' associations and, in a few cases, individual teachers). The contractor signs an agreement to improve student performance by specified amounts in certain basic skills. He is paid according to his success in bringing the performance of the students up to those prespecified levels. If the contractor succeeds with the students, he makes a profit. The profit motive is thus enlisted to increase efforts on behalf of students. In some cases, performance contracts also contain "turnkey" provisions: the contractor assumes responsibility for teaching regular staff to use his methods and materials, so that the program can be conducted by the school system itself in subsequent years and/or extended to a larger number of students. Performance contracts have dealt with a wide variety of grade levels (from kindergarten to high school) and subjects, but reading and mathematics are the most common subjects contracted for, partly because they are valued as basic skills on which future learning depends and partly because they are relatively easy to measure.

Within guidelines established by the educational agent, the contractor is usually free to use whatever methods he feels can be most effective—teaching machines, individualized instruction, incentive systems, audio-visual aids. Contractors may use their own instructors and paraprofessional personnel or use teachers already in the school. They may also make use of extrinsic rewards to students such as transistor radios, trading stamps, candy, or free time during class period for recreational activities (the profit motive at work on the students). Incentives are sometimes also offered to teachers and parents.

Payment is based on the differences between the results of pretests and posttests administered to the students (see **Pretest** and **Posttest**). Typically, a base payment (e.g., $50 per student) is made for one grade level of improvement in one year, with a guaranteed level or minimum gain below which no payment is made, and a bonus paid for additional measured gains (e.g., $20 for each month beyond a year).

Since results must be certified, an evaluator is employed as an impartial agency to measure the learning achievements on which the contractor's payments are to be based. An auditor may then be employed to verify the work of the evaluation agency, in the manner of a fiscal auditor; but if the educational agency has sufficient confidence in the evaluator, it may dispense with the audit (see **Audit of Evaluation**). A management support group may also be employed at the outset to deal with the intricacies of awarding contracts, to evaluate and choose the final bidders, and to act as a liaison agency.

In the course of attempts to certify payments to contractors, many problems of measurement have arisen:

1. For pupils with severe deficiencies (those scoring far below the mean), few **Standardized Tests** are accurate. For example, when a sixth-grade student scores very low, it is hard to tell whether he is at a 4.0 or a 2.5 grade-equivalent level (see **Score Types**).

2. **Regression** effects work to the benefit of performance contracts oriented toward low-scoring students. Whether or not the contractor effects "real" improvements, such students are likely to score somewhat higher on retest.

3. There is the distinct possibility that contractors may "teach to the test" or, worse, "teach the test" (direct coaching). Ever since the first problem of this nature was uncovered in a performance contract in Texarkana, Arkansas, most contracts have included provisions to prevent the contractor from knowing which test will be used to determine payments, as well as provisions for heavy penalties if test items are discovered in the instructional program. It is recognized, of course, that in the interests of fairness the testing ought not to be too different from the instruction.

4. There is a controversy over basing payments on individual score gains versus gains in group means. Differences in individual scores, taken a year apart and converted into grade levels, are not considered sufficiently reliable. On the other hand, use of group means opens up the possibility that contractors will work intensively with a few students able to achieve large gains and neglect the students who would contribute little to an increase in the mean. Other types of change measures might be considered, of course (see **Change Measurement**). Still another solution might be to write contracts for a minimum of three years, so that the possibility of individual score gains would be greater and the differences more reliable.

5. Criterion-referenced tests rather than standardized norms-referenced tests are often preferred by school systems and contractors, but such tests present special problems of construction and interpretation (see **Criterion-Referenced Measurement** and **Norms**). From the standpoint of the community, such tests do not allow for comparisons with students in other schools in other parts of the country and hence may be less reassuring.

6. The use of control groups would seem to be almost a necessity to protect both the contractor and the educational agent. Without a **Control Group**, the contractor could be penalized for results attributable more to the low input level of the students than to the efficacy of the program, while the educational agent could be asked to pay for gains that might have been produced equally well by conventional methods—or by no intervention at all. Apparent gains could also be attributable to **Regression** effect, **Hawthorne Effect**, or **John Henry Effect**. On the other hand, even when control groups are used, criticisms can arise about their selection. The control groups must be selected appropriately and "contamination" avoided.

At present the legal status of performance contracting is complicated and unresolved. There are political conflicts involving teachers' associations, which fear competition and loss of tenure, and various factions of the community, which are demanding better student performance or lower taxes or both.

So far, most contracts have stressed a few narrowly defined skills because reliable measures are available for testing them. Performance contracts are not being used in noncognitive areas such as social maturity, self-esteem, and civic responsibility, nor in relation to many broader educational objectives. Nevertheless, the performance-contracting experiments have at least helped focus the attention of industry and the public on the futility of hoping to change social-economic deficiencies by improvements in reading and mathematics scores alone. Performance contracting has also shown that educators are now ready to listen to and work with outsiders (some precedent having been set for contractual arrangements with such outside agencies as museums, public service groups, and private companies); educational technologists have gained more confidence in their products (at the least, some companies have become involved in how their products are used); and there have been some innovations in instructional systems.

An earlier meaning for the term *performance contract* was the teacher-student contract under which students contracted with teachers to produce a written report, carry out a project, or pass a test on specified subject material in a certain period of time in exchange for credit points or grades. Currently, because of the trend toward individualized instruction and nontraditional study, the use of similar kinds of "contracts" has been increasing.—A. H. W.

Feldmesser, R. *Performance Contracting in Principle and Practice.* TM Report No. 20. Princeton, N.J.: ERIC Clearinghouse on Tests, Measurement, and Evaluation, 1972.

Hall, G. R., Carpenter, P., Haggart, S. A., Rapp, M. L., and Summer, G. C. *A Guide to Educational Performance Contracting.* Santa Monica, Calif.: RAND Corporation, 1972. A summary of research findings and coverage of the performance-contract concept, legal requirements, contractor selection, organization and monitoring of programs, validating achievement, and settling of contracts.

Levine, D. M., and Uttal, B. "Performance Contracting Policy: Motivational Problems and New Models." *Teachers College Record*, 1973, *74*, 317-355.

Mecklenburger, J. A. *Performance Contracting.* Worthington, Ohio: Charles A. Jones, 1972. Puts performance contracting in perspective and reports in depth on the Banneker experiment at Gary, Indiana, the Texarkana model, the OEO experiment, and some interesting variations.

Sigel, E., and Sobel, M. *Accountability and the Controversial Role of the Performance Contractors: A Critical Look at the Performance Contracting Phenomenon.* White Plains, N.Y.: Knowledge Industry Publications, 1971. An evaluation of the economic, legal, political, and measurement pitfalls of performance contracting, as well as the areas of promise it offers.

————————— PLANNING AND PRIORITIES —————————

Planning the instructional program and planning the evaluation of that program are—or usually should be—closely interlinked. When time and resources are unlimited and all parties to the endeavor are in complete agreement, the problem of priorities becomes one simply of the appropriate sequence of activities. However, these ideal conditions hardly if ever obtain, and both directors and evaluators of education/training programs are faced with deciding among alternatives what to emphasize, which activities to undertake, how to undertake them, and whom to please. In practice, priority decisions are frequently made accidentally or by default. This article argues for conscious efforts to specify alternatives and make priority decisions *before* the program or evaluation study is in full motion.

Here are some examples of the kinds of priority decisions that program directors might be faced with:

1. Should the program attempt to cover all the **Goals and Objectives** originally stated for it, or should it treat a few intensively? Which ones?

2. If parents and school board members (or industrial supervisors and training officers, or other groups with vested interests in the program) differ in their views about what the program should emphasize, whose view should prevail? Or can they be compromised? (See point 4 in **Discrepancy Evaluation**.)

3. Should we use an older curriculum or teaching method that instructors are familiar with, or should we adopt a new one that is heralded as better but requires complete retraining of the staff?

4. Within a given staff budget, what should be the ratio of skilled instructors to paraprofessionals?

5. Should the program be offered initially on a large scale (say, to all who are eligible) or on a small scale (so that it can be evaluated before it is made generally available)?

6. Should program evaluation be included in the overall plans? What will we accept as evidence of program success or failure?

7. How much money can we spend on evaluation relative to the cost/importance of the instructional effort?

8. Which will help us most—a **Summative Evaluation** of the overall effectiveness of the program or a **Formative Evaluation** that will help us improve the program as we go along? Can we afford to obtain both? Can we afford not to obtain both?

9. Is it feasible politically to follow the evaluator's advice and assign some students at random to the program while withholding it from others? (See **Field Operations.**)

The evaluator, for his part, must decide—within the limits of his charge, budget, schedule, and the "climate" of the situation—such questions as these:

1. Is it better to draw a representative or a purposive sample of program sites or classrooms? (See **Sampling** and **Site Selection.**)

2. Should we assess a small sample intensively or a large sample extensively?

3. Should we train local people to collect data or bring in already skilled outsiders? (See **Field Operations.**)

4. If we cannot measure achievement toward all of the program objectives, which ones should we choose?

5. What criteria of program success other than student/trainee achievement are relevant? Are we obligated to obtain evidence about **Side Effects?** Long-term effects? Transferability? Acceptability? Costs? (See **Training Evaluation** and **Cost Considerations.**)

6. Can we afford to dispense with a **Pretest?**

7. Would it be better to use less-than-relevant measures "off the shelf" or to go to the time and expense of developing custom-tailored ones? (See **Achievement-Test Construction** and **Test Selection.**)

8. Should we risk going into the field with a precise **Experimental Design** that may be invalidated in implementation, or should we use a less precise design that may be easier to execute? (See **Field Operations.**)

9. Should we report data that we have not fully analyzed because they are needed for immediate decisions by the program sponsors? (See **Dissemination of Evaluation Results.**)

In other words, priority decisions must usually be made about every aspect of instructional programs and the studies designed to evaluate them. For programs, these aspects include goals and objectives, staff (including selection, training, and assignment), facilities, materials and equipment, student evaluation, and needs for program evaluation, as well as—in many cases—recruitment, selection, and placement of students. For evaluation studies, areas of key consideration may be summarized to correspond to the headings listed in the "Classification of the Articles" at the beginning of this volume: choice of the appropriate *evaluation model(s)* and the appropriate evaluation personnel; definition of the *functions and targets* of the evaluation, in terms of *program objectives and standards*; recognition of the *social context* for the evaluation and appreciation of the need to take it into account at all stages of the effort; *planning and design,* including sample selection; consideration of *systems technologies* that may support the effort; identification of *variables* to be assessed; development/ selection of *measurement approaches and types,* in light of *technical measurement considerations*; data collection, with concern for possible *reactive effects*; *analysis and interpretation* of the data and dissemination of the results.—S. B. A.

PLANNING-PROGRAMMING-BUDGETING SYSTEM (PPBS)

In 1961, Charles Hitch began the development of a program structure for the Department of Defense designed to link the mission planning with the fiscal planning. It departed from the former long-range plans, which were usually "unrealistic, infeasible, and unbalanced" (Hitch, p. 466), and imposed instead realistic planning with a sensitivity to the resource and fiscal constraints of the Department. The success of these efforts in the Department of Defense is attested to by the Executive Order issued by President Johnson on August 25, 1965, that program budgeting would be introduced in all Federal Government departments and agencies—a procedure that is still followed.

Program budgeting involves both long-range substantive plans of an organization and annual budgets. It considers the policy objectives in terms of present and future economic costs. Because there are inevitably more programs competing for limited resources than those resources can support, it is necessary to make compromises among the various objectives; this is the function of a planning-programming-budgeting system. The programs or activities may be so diverse that there is no way to compare them except to express each of them in a common metric—namely, dollars. Only by such means can federal programs involving defense and education be compared. The comparisons cannot be limited to these quantitative data, of course, but the quantitative information can provide insight into the consequences of spending money on one or another program. A PPB system would allocate all the resources and dollars necessary to carry out the programs of an organization; and, by linking substantive and fiscal planning, it can go a long way toward making the entire planning process feasible and balanced. (See **Cost Considerations and Economic Analysis.**)

The enormously complicated job of managing large, complex organizations (governmental or military entities, universities, or industrial concerns) makes administrators increasingly aware of the value of having more and better facts for decision making (even if political considerations weigh heavily). Through the use of the kind of information made available in a PPB system, the decision maker can be more effective in applying his judgment. Program budgeting and sophisticated planning make for sounder analysis of alternative courses of action. The principal advantage of the system is that it permits more rational decisions and better management of those decisions. (See also **Systems Analysis.**)—H. H. H.

Cook, D. L. *Educational Project Management.* Columbus, Ohio: Merrill, 1971. A comprehensive view of the science of project management as it relates to educational research and development.

Hartley, H. J. *Educational Planning-Programming-Budgeting: A Systems Approval.* Englewood Cliffs, N.J.: Prentice-Hall, 1968.

Hitch, C. J. "What Are the Programs in Planning, Programming, Budgeting?" *Socio-Economic Planning Sciences,* 1969, *2,* 465-472.

National School Public Relations Association. "PPBS and the School." In *Education U.S.A.* Washington, D.C.: NSPRA, 1972. P. 56.

Novick, D. (Ed.) *Program Budgeting.* Cambridge, Mass.: Harvard University Press, 1965. See especially Part I (three chapters) devoted to the government decision-making process and the role of budgeting in that activity.

Parden, R. J. "Planning, Programming, and Budgeting Systems." In W. W. Jellema (Ed.), *Efficient College Management.* San Francisco: Jossey-Bass, 1972.

Rivlin, A. M. *Systematic Thinking for Social Action.* Washington, D.C.: Brookings Institution, 1971. See especially the introductory chapter, in which the role of PPBS in government decision making is indicated.

Special Issue on the Principal and PPBS. *National Association of Secondary School Principals Bulletin,* October 1972, *56.*

─────────────── POLITICS OF EVALUATION ───────────────

When numbers of human beings are commonly involved in a program aimed at achieving certain sets of goals, they are likely to have at least somewhat differing versions of which goals are most and which least important, which values are to be preserved and which can be sacrificed, what is the acceptable ratio of cost and effort to gain and achievement, what will determine whether the program has succeeded or failed, and who shall make such judgments.

These conflicting views are likely to be brought out sharply when it is proposed that the program be evaluated to determine its relative degree of success and failure. At that point, those involved in the program are likely to become partisans with regard to the desirability, quality, and purposes of the evaluation, and they are likely to bring to bear their own partisan viewpoints to influence the "evaluation" to the extent possible—even in extreme cases, trying to prevent any evaluation from taking place. The politics of evaluation refers to all such partisan activities directed at influencing the conduct of evaluation in line with partisan preferences.

Teachers, principals, and program directors who try to shape the evaluation of educational or training programs so as to shed honor upon their classes or schools are examples of the politics of evaluation in action. In short, the politics of evaluation refers to the contest of power and wills in the evaluation situation, aimed at securing credit for success or avoiding blame for failure of ongoing programs, or at assisting or preventing the institution of new programs.

So understood, political considerations may and almost always do enter into evaluation at every stage, starting with the initial question "Does an activity or program need to be evaluated?" and including such other questions as "What shall be evaluated? Who shall do the evaluating? What should be the scope of the evaluation? How much should insiders participate? What will be taken as an adequate form of evaluation? What shall be done about a program after it has been evaluated? How public shall the results of the evaluation be?"

While these questions are complex enough, they are relatively simple compared to the summary evaluative question "Are the measured benefits of the program worth the costs, relative to possible alternative programs (including existing practices)?" This type of question permits maximum entrance of political considerations, for it involves judgments on which it is extremely difficult to bring decisive evidence to bear. How, for instance, can one decide whether a program that produces an increment of n units of self-esteem and $n + 5$ units of academic achievement is better or worse than one that produces an increment of $n + 5$ units of self-esteem but only n units of academic achievement? In such judgments, the weights previously assigned to these various outcomes shape the final answer, and those weights tend to be functions of personal values and preferences rather than something demonstrably superior about the educational program. The numerous conflicts in urban schools today revolve around just such issues.

Political factors are inimical to the evaluation process when they interfere in a negative way with the scientific conduct of evaluation. Such scientific evaluation is indispensable if one is to achieve the closest possible approximation to an objective and reliable estimate of the effectiveness of programs, whether this is being done retrospectively or concurrently with the program or prospectively. Since the politics of evaluation may thus be seen as a potential obstacle to conducting evaluations, those concerned with evaluation must perforce be concerned with political factors and prepared to deal with them.

In the effort to reduce the distorting influences of political factors, one may be guided by a checklist of frequently employed techniques of distortion. Suchman (p. 143) has classified these into six major types as follows: (1) "eye-wash," selecting for evaluation only those aspects of a program that appear to be successful; (2) "white-wash," covering up program failure by avoiding objective appraisal and securing "testimonials" from partisans; (3) "submarine," attempting to torpedo or destroy a program, regardless of its worth, because of power interests within the administration or system; (4) "posture," making gestures toward "objective evaluation" which, however, are not carried through and which are designed only to promote a favorable image; (5) "postponement," seeking to delay or prolong the evaluation as much as possible in the hope that concern about the program will dissipate over time; and (6) "substitution," attempting to shift attention from an essential part of the program that has failed to a minor part of the program that has succeeded.

Also useful to the scientific evaluator is a checklist of rationalizations frequently used to try to prevent evaluation from taking place. These include contentions that since the effects of the program are long-range ones, their effectiveness cannot be measured in the short range; or that the effects of the program are too complex to be susceptible to accurate measurement; or that the results are small but significant and cannot be measured by available instruments.

Still other rationalizations are employed to "explain away" negative findings of evaluation. These include the contentions that while some persons in the program did not benefit, others did, and they could not have done so if there had not been a program; or that the absence of different results for experimental and control groups proves the need for greater doses of the experimental treatment; or that the effectiveness of the program cannot really be estimated because those who most needed the services provided in the program did not participate. Perhaps the most frequently employed tactic for avoiding "external" evaluation, or for rejecting such evaluation once completed, is the insistence that only intensely involved participants can really estimate the effects of a program. This is the classic instance of the "insider" versus the "outsider" argument, one version of which is the claim that only teachers of the same race as students can teach those students effectively, especially if the students belong to minority groups.

Experienced investigators, who have encountered the many frustrations in store for anyone who attempts to conduct scientific evaluations of educational programs, strongly admonish evaluators to be involved in the new program from the outset. Moreover, evaluators are exhorted to seek a pre-experiment understanding with all interested and effective authorities regarding the conditions that they (the evaluators) will require for their tasks. While there is no assurance that such agreements will be kept, the agreements make it more likely that one will be able to conduct scientific evaluation relatively free of political distortions, or at least within previously known limits of predictable political distortion. By contrast, an investigator who agrees to evaluate programs ex post facto faces the often insoluble problem of determining what experimental inputs might have influenced the outcome (see **Ex Post Facto Design**). While some of these are determinable after the fact, many are not; one must therefore be prepared to report that much of the variance in the outcomes will have to be left unexplained.

Some evaluation specialists believe that the evaluation situation can be used as a learning process for the participants, so that the participants may discover for themselves that they cannot be even minimally sure that their efforts have yielded any desired results. Then and only then are they likely to appreciate the value of scientific evaluation. This view thus envisages evaluation as a several-stage process, in which the first stages are devoted to enabling participants to discover the value of scientific evaluation, and the later stages then take place in accordance with the canons of scientific procedure. By this process, political considerations that would have otherwise prevented or distorted scientific evaluation might be attenuated or eliminated.

Since adequate scientific evaluation requires the involvement of the evaluator from the outset, especially in experimental programs, there has been a growth in awareness of the need to include the costs of evaluation in project proposals. However, contrary pressures to reduce program costs often force the elimination of any budgetary provisions for evaluation, and the results of development projects are disseminated without any evidence of their effectiveness. The high rate of attrition among nonevaluated programs, however, suggests that failing to provide for scientific evaluation may be uneconomical in the long run.

Economic and political considerations become especially powerful in shaping program development when there is considerable political pressure to "get something done." The impatience of the lay public and their legislative representatives at all levels of government often results in a downgrading of the importance of evaluation. The result may be a series of failures of program innovations, which because of political imperatives are often *overclaimed* at the outset and which inevitably fail when measured by the initial claims made on their behalf. The Peace Corps, the Teacher Corps, Vista, and Head Start programs are outstanding examples of overclaimed programs that are eminently susceptible to the judgment of "failure." Partisans of these programs, however, point to certain "serendipitous" (i.e., unanticipated) results that are judged positive and valuable, such as the training of substantial numbers of people in new and important skills and attitudes.

A distinction has been made by Suchman between *evaluation* (the general process of judging the worth of some activity regardless of the method employed) and *evaluative research* (the specific use of the scientific method for the purpose of making an evaluation). One might therefore formulate the goal of scientific inquirers as the attempt to make the greatest use of evaluative *research* in the context of evaluation (see **Scientific Inquiry and Evaluation**). Seen this way, the politics of evaluation concerns all those factors present in any evaluation situation which may impede or influence the use of evaluative research. (See also **Dissemination of Evaluation Results, Evaluation Concepts, Evaluator Role,** and **Field Operations.**)—M. M. T.

Borgatta, E. F. "Research Problems in Evaluation of Health Service Demonstrations." *Milbank Fund Quarterly,* 1966, *44* (Part 2).

Campbell, D. T. "Reforms as Experiments." *American Psychologist,* 1969, *24,* 409-429.

Suchman, E. A. *Evaluative Research.* New York: Russell Sage Foundation, 1967. See especially Chapter VIII, "Evaluation and Program Administration."

Tumin, M. M. "Evaluation of the Effectiveness of Education." *Interchange,* 1970, *1* (3), 96-109.

Weiss, C. H. (Ed.) *Evaluating Action Programs.* Boston: Allyn and Bacon, 1972. See especially P. H. Rossi, "Booby Traps and Pitfalls in the Evaluation of Action Programs" (pp. 224-235).

POSTTEST

A posttest is the test administered at the end of the data-gathering sequence of an evaluation study; that is, when the program or part of the program being evaluated has been completed. The posttest is an essential element in most evaluation designs (see **Design of Evaluation**). Without it, the evaluator would not be able properly to assess a program's impact.

A question about posttests that is given relatively little attention is this: How long after the program is over should the posttest be given? Usually the posttest is given as soon afterward as possible—thus providing the evaluator with a maximum estimate of the impact because the least amount of forgetting will have occurred. However, many evaluations are primarily concerned with longer-term effectiveness of programs, in which case the posttest should be delayed somewhat. Another possibility—to have both an immediate and a delayed posttest—would be clearly valuable if it were suspected that a program had special, long-term motivational properties or provided the student with new insights and approaches to the subject matter. For example, in some evaluations that called for the comparison of a direct-teaching technique with a discovery-learning technique, it was found that the direct-teaching technique showed a stronger immediate impact than that obtained with discovery learning. However, at the delayed posttest some six weeks after the programs were over, the group who had experienced the discovery learning had experienced comparatively little **Fade-Out** and now surpassed the performance of the group that had learned under the direct teaching. (See **Longitudinal Study.**)

One potential danger of having both an immediate and a delayed posttest (especially when a **Pretest** has also been administered) is that of **Practice Effect**. An evaluator can reduce practice effect by using equivalent forms of a test (to reduce specific memory effects) or by choosing a research design in which only a random subset of the members of the experimental and control groups are tested at the immediate posttest, with the rest being tested at the delayed posttest.—S. B.

Kersh, B. Y., and Wittrock, M. C. "Learning by Discovery: An Interpretation of Recent Research." *Journal of Teacher Education*, 1962, *13*, 461-468.

———————————— PRACTICE EFFECT ————————————

Practice effect refers to the fact that taking a test on one occasion often improves subsequent scores on that test or, to a lesser extent, on a similar test. (See also **Equivalent Scores.**) Presumably, the person who takes a test becomes familiar with the format of the test and even remembers some of the test items; as a result, the test taker's scores will improve if he takes the test, or a similar test, again.

Most of the research on practice effect has been conducted with intelligence, aptitude, and achievement tests. It has shown that practice effect is most pronounced when the test taker is inexperienced in test taking and when the test is timed (speeded). (See **Test Wiseness**.) Moreover, practice effect usually is dissipated if more than three months have elapsed from the first to the second testing. Thus, the amount of practice effect will vary depending on the type of test, the sophistication of the test taker, and the amount of time between the two testings. Practice effect usually improves scores at the second testing by no more than one fifth of a standard deviation—on the average. For example, it would be relatively rare for the average IQ score of a group to improve by more than three points because of practice effect, and it would be relatively rare for the average College Entrance Examination Board score of a group to improve by more than twenty points. Generally average gains due to practice effect are not large, but in critical individual cases practice effect can make an important difference.

Practice effect can be especially troublesome in evaluation unless the evaluation design is constructed to overcome it (see **Design of Evaluation**). Suppose, for example, a simple evaluation were being conducted of a new program in basic reading for young adults who are semiliterate. Using a standardized reading test as the measure, the evaluator administers a **Pretest** to the class (at the beginning of the course) and a **Posttest** a month later (at the end of the course). The results indicate a substantial improvement over the month. How much of this improvement is due to the program and how much to practice effect? It is impossible to say. Since only one month had elapsed between testings and since the subjects in the evaluation were young adults whose test-taking skills were probably "rusty," a considerable portion of the improvement could have been caused by practice effect. Practice effect could probably be reduced somewhat by using alternate forms of the test for pretest and posttest, but an even better way to overcome the problem of practice effect in an evaluation would be to use a **Control Group** comparable to the group being evaluated. The control group would not receive the program but would take both the pretest and the posttest. Both groups would then be affected by practice effect, and differences between the groups would presumably be due primarily to program effects.

Sometimes it is impossible to obtain a comparable control group. Perhaps all those who are eligible to participate in a program are placed in the program. In such a case, or if the cost of testing a control group is too great, an expedient worth using is to randomly assign some of the people in the program to a posttest-only testing condition, while the rest are both pretested and posttested. The pretest-posttest group provides an estimate of baseline (pretest) performance from its pretest scores; the difference between the two groups at posttest is an estimate of practice effect; and the posttest-only group provides an estimate, unbiased by practice effect, of the status of program participants after undergoing the program.–S. B.

Campbell, J. T., Hilton, T. L.. and Pitcher, B. *Effects of Repeating on Test Scores on the Graduate Record Examinations.* GRE Special Report 67-1. Princeton, N.J.: Educational Testing Service, 1967.

Knapp, R. R. "The Effects of Time Limits on the Intelligence Test Performance of Mexican and American Subjects." *Journal of Educational Psychology,* 1960, *51,* 14-20.

Stanley, J. C., and Hopkins, K. D. *Educational and Psychological Evaluation.* Englewood Cliffs, N.J.: Prentice-Hall, 1972. Includes (pp. 138-140) a discussion of practice effect and the effects of coaching on tests.

Weiss, R. A. *The Effects of Practicing a Test: A Review of the Literature.* Princeton, N.J.: Educational Testing Service, 1961.

PRETEST

The term *pretest* has different meanings depending on whether it is used in association with instructional materials, with subjects (trainees or students), or with test and questionnaire items and formats.

When used with instructional materials, a pretest involves

trying out the materials (or portions of the materials) to see whether they have the desired characteristics; for instance, whether they hold the attention of the learner or effectively teach the target audience the facts they are designed to teach. The pretesting of materials is one of the functions of **Formative Evaluation**. It is a very important aspect of curriculum and program development but is often neglected, especially in textbook writing. Techniques of materials pretesting are described in **Materials Evaluation**.

Pretest has quite a different meaning when it is used in conjunction with the trainees or students in an evaluation. The pretesting of subjects is frequently an integral part of an evaluation design (see **Design of Evaluation**). It provides information about the subjects *before* the program begins and, with data from the **Posttest**, allows the evaluator to make inferences about the effects of the program. (See also **Baseline Measures**.)

The third use of *pretest* is with test and questionnaire items and formats. Here pretesting involves trying out items and formats on a small group of people similar to those who will be involved in the evaluation (see **Achievement Test Construction**). This kind of pretest will enable the evaluator to determine the suitability of the formats (Did they cause confusion? Were they readily understood?) and the item characteristics (Were items too easy or too hard? Did an item correlate with other items developed to measure the same area of knowledge?). Typically, pretest results are analyzed to yield data about difficulty, speededness, item discrimination, item homogeneity, **Reliability**, and sometimes **Validity**.—S. B.

--------- PROGRAM EVALUATION AND REVIEW ---------
TECHNIQUE (PERT)

PERT, a systematic timetabling and programming technique, was developed in 1958 and 1959 to measure and control the development and progress of the Polaris Fleet Ballistic Missile

program. The successful coordination of the several thousand contractors and agencies involved in the Polaris program is credited
with advancing the completion date by more than two years. Although PERT was originally applied in managing a research and
development program, it has since been used in the management
of a wide variety of military and industrial projects that involve
many interrelated activities.

One major advantage of this technique is that the planning
required to develop a PERT chart contributes to a clearly defined
program and to the successful control of the program. Each individual accomplishment (event) in a program is the result of one or
more tasks (activities). An event occurs at a particular instant in
time and is the result of the completion of all activities leading up
to the event. The event must occur before any activities following
it and based upon it can begin. The first step in applying PERT is
to define the events necessary for the completion of the project,
determine the activities required for each event, and specify the
interrelationships. The next step is to obtain estimates of the
length of time each activity is expected to take. Each estimate is
made by the person who will be responsible for performing the
activity. From this information, a chart (see Figure 1) can be
made. The letters in the chart represent events. The relationships
between the events (activities) are represented by the lines and
arrows. The numbers above the activity lines represent the expected time durations (days, in this example). Event H cannot

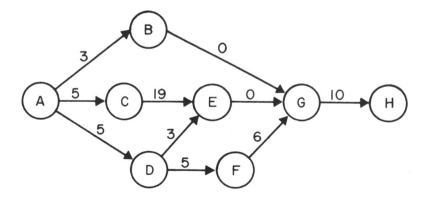

Figure 1. A PERT chart.

occur until the activity G-H, which requires 10 days, has occurred. Event G cannot occur until events B, E, and F have occurred. In this example, there are four "paths" from A to H. The path A-C-E-G-H has a total expected duration of 34 days (5 + 19 + 0 + 10). This path, which has the longest total expected duration of all the paths, is called the "critical path." No delay or "slippage" can occur in the activities along the critical path if the project is to finish on time. Path A-B-G-H has an expected duration of 13 days (3 + 0 + 10); therefore, activity A-B may be started as much as 21 days after activity A-C (34 − 13 = 21) without delaying the expected completion date. This 21 days is called the "slack" of activity A-B. Any activity on the critical path will have a slack of zero. Ordinarily, PERT allows the estimator to submit three time estimates for each activity: optimistic, most likely, and pessimistic. The discrepancies among the three time estimates are a "measure of uncertainty" of the activity.

PERT enables the project manager to determine the probability of meeting specific deadlines (calculated from the three time estimates of each activity). It identifies activities which are most likely to be bottlenecks and, consequently, should be closely monitored as the project progresses to assure that no slippages occur. PERT also enables the manager to evaluate changes in the project.

The PERT system should be updated and reviewed at frequent intervals so that the manager can take appropriate action. If, for example, it appears that activity C-E on the chart is going to require 21 days rather than 19, the manager must decide whether additional resources or funds should be made available to avoid lengthening the critical path.

PERT has many advantages. The chart gives a picture to both participants and managers of how their efforts are related to the total project. Not only does each individual see how his efforts tie into the overall project, but communication lines across the project organization are frequently improved. Management is able to spot potential trouble and take corrective action to make the best possible use of resources for achieving the overall goal.

PERT can be applied both to training programs themselves and to evaluation of such programs. In either case its usefulness is largely a function of the complexity of the program; the more elements involved, the more likely it is that PERT will help.

The act of PERTing a training or education program may serve to clarify **Goals and Objectives** and requirements. Its application during the progress of the program can help identify areas where slippage is occurring and thus where revision or unusual effort is needed (see **Formative Evaluation**). Furthermore, the job of those evaluating a training program is greatly facilitated if the activities, schedule, and other aspects of the program are clearly identified in PERT terms.

Whether or not PERT is applied to the development and implementation of the program, it can still be a useful aid to the director of a large-scale evaluation where many components must be coordinated—for example, pilot studies, test construction, staff selection and training, literature reviews, contacts with subjects and clients, and preparation of data-analysis procedures.—M. B.

Case, C. M. "The Application of PERT to Large-Scale Educational and Evaluation Studies." *Educational Technology,* Oct. 1969, *9*, pp. 79-83.
Cook, D. L. *Program Evaluation and Review Technique Applications in Education.* Washington, D.C.: U.S. Government Printing Office, 1966.
Special Projects Office, Department of the Navy. *PERT Summary Report, Phase I.* Washington, D.C.: U.S. Government Printing Office, 1962.

---------- PROJECTIVE TESTS ----------

A projective test is one in which the person being tested is given some ambiguous or unstructured stimulus (such as an ink-blot, an incomplete sentence, or a picture) and is asked to create his own response—to "project" his own feelings and thoughts. For example, he may be asked to tell what he "sees" in the inkblot, to end the incomplete sentence, or to make up a story to explain what is happening in the picture. These responses are then interpreted as projections of the person's thoughts and feelings.

Projective tests are used almost exclusively to assess variables in the personality domain; for example, such personality characteristics as introversion, anxiety, need for affiliation, need for achievement. There are a great many projective tests, but Lindzey has classified five main types: associations to words or inkblots, story construction, sentence or story completion, choice or arrangements of pictures or stories, and free expression through drawing, acting, or play.

Two of the most widely used projective tests are the Rorschach Inkblot Test and the Thematic Apperception Test (TAT). With the Rorschach, the subject is shown a series of inkblots and asked to state what he sees in them. The tester notes the content of the response and also such details as whether all the inkblot is used by the subject and whether the subject "sees" movement or color in it. With over 3000 publications available about the Rorschach, it is one of the best documented measurement techniques. It also typifies more than any other projective test the problems and virtues of this particular kind of measurement technique.

The Thematic Apperception Test is made up of a series of pictures, which are shown one at a time to the respondent. One picture, for example, shows two women—one woman seated and looking straight ahead, and an older woman standing behind her. The older woman is clad in black and her head is cupped in her hand. Her fingers are long and thin. The respondent is then asked to tell a story about the picture—what is happening, what the women are thinking, etc. The story obtained in response to a TAT may be scored for a number of different characteristics such as need for achievement and need for affiliation.

Other characteristics of projective tests are that there are no right or wrong answers, and the respondent is usually not aware of how his responses are being scored or exactly what is being assessed. Projective tests are valued in many clinical settings not only for the scores they provide but also for the insights the clinician may gain from interactions with the responder during the administration.

There are a number of problems associated with the use of a projective test in evaluations. Often there is disagreement by experts on how any specific test response should be scored. Still another major problem is that projective tests have low test-retest **Reliability**. Thus, for example, the need-for-affiliation scores obtained from administering the TAT have quite low correlations with the scores obtained on a second administration with the same subjects a few weeks later. Perhaps because of their relatively low reliability, projective tests often have low predictive powers. For example, people with high need-for-achievement scores on the TAT do not usually perform much better in achievement-oriented tasks than their counterparts with low need-for-achievement scores.

The use of projective tests in evaluation is not generally recommended—especially if the evaluation involves many subjects. The administration and scoring of projective tests usually require a considerable amount of training and a great deal of time. Since these tests usually have to be individually administered and scored by a highly skilled person, the cost is high. If a projective test is used in an evaluation, it is advisable to use other personality measures (e.g., inventories, questionnaires) as additional means of assessing the variable of interest.—S. B.

Eysenck, H. J. "Rorschach Review." In O. K. Buros (Ed.), *The Fifth Mental Measurements Yearbook*. Highland Park, N.J.: Gryphon Press, 1959. Pp. 276-278. Includes critical examination of projective tests generally.

Goldfried, M. V., Stricker, G., and Weiner, I. B. *Rorschach Handbook of Clinical and Research Applications*. Englewood Cliffs, N.J.: Prentice-Hall, 1971. A comprehensive description and discussion of the Rorschach test.

Lindzey, G. "On the Classification of Projective Techniques." *Psychological Bulletin*, 1959, *56*, 159-168.

Stanley, J. C., and Hopkins, K. D. *Educational and Psychological Measurement and Evaluation*. Englewood Cliffs, N.J.: Prentice-Hall, 1972. See pages 396-402 for a pointed discussion of the problems of projective tests.

Vernon, P. E. *Personality Assessment: A Critical Survey*. London: Methuen, 1963. See Part II ("The Clinical Psychologist's Understanding of Personality"), especially Chapter 10 ("Projective Techniques").

——————— PSYCHOMOTOR VARIABLES ———————

Psychomotor (also referred to as *motor, sensory-motor,* or *perceptual-motor*) variables comprise the third broad area of educational objectives proposed by Bloom and his associates, although the taxonomy of these variables has yet to appear (see **Taxonomies of Objectives, Cognitive Variables,** and **Affective Variables**). The psychomotor domain is concerned with muscular activities—with those movements of the body, limbs, or other body parts (e.g., fingers) necessary for a given action. To move from the relatively simple action of sharpening a pencil to, say, the very complicated one of flying a modern jet aircraft calls into play the psychomotor skills and abilities of the individual in an increasingly complex coordination of eye, hand, and mind.

At one time, psychomotor skills were considered as largely indicative of general intelligence—so much so that early tests of mental functioning were heavily dependent upon psychomotor skills. In the late 1890s, however, Binet concluded that the connection between these skills and general mental functioning was not clear; consequently, he separated these two broad areas of abilities. Today, it is acknowledged that a complex interrelationship exists between cognitive, affective, and psychomotor skills.

A distinction must be made between skills and abilities, as used here. *Abilities* may be regarded as general traits of the individual. They develop at different rates, are mostly the result of learning, and are usually acquired by adolescence. By adulthood, they tend to be set to such an extent as to resist change, and are important primarily as they are available to the individual in the learning of new tasks. *Skill* pertains to the level of proficiency attained in a task. (Some authorities—Seashore, for example—define as many as four, rather than just two, subcategories: ability, skill, aptitude, and capacity.)

A distinction also needs to be made between *fine* and *gross* motor skills, since research suggests that there are some important differences between them. Gross motor skills or coordination usually involve large body movements, with strength the prevailing factor. Fine motor skills, as might be expected, depend less upon strength and more upon speed, precision, or delicacy of much smaller movements, frequently manipulative and restricted to the arms, hands, and fingers.

These distinctions made, let us consider some of the directions that measurement of psychomotor skills might take in relationship to education/training programs. One might wish to analyze an entirely new task to discover the abilities necessary to master it (there were few precedents, for example, for the piloting of a space capsule until recently) and to establish the desired level of mastery; to evaluate the basic ability of an individual to undertake a new task; or, finally, to evaluate how highly developed the student's skills have become after training and practice. The effects of different teaching methods appear to interact with individual differences to produce large variations in learning (see **Trait-Treatment Interaction**). And, although a variety of Tests (using apparatus ranging from the uncomplicated pegboard to quite complex devices) have been devised, the results can sometimes be unexpected. Tests that seem to reproduce accurately the important elements of a task may not, in fact, have much predictive value. Others, of equal face **Validity**, do an excellent job. These apparently contradictory findings probably stem from failures of test developers and users to understand and include the most relevant psychomotor factors. It is often more important to design tests that adequately sample the underlying psychomotor factors than to be overly concerned with presenting a job sample that encompasses obvious aspects of the job. For example, Fleishman (1969), long associated with the development of selection tests in the psychomotor area for the United States Air Force, points out that the Complex Coordination Test is a valid predictor that does closely resemble a pilot's task, whereas the Rotary Pursuit Test, also a valid predictor, does not in any way duplicate a pilot's job. The success of both tests, so different superficially, lies in their ability to tap the abilities necessary for success as a pilot.

Research has already uncovered many significant psychomotor factors, too many to discuss individually here. Fleishman (1969) lists some twenty psychomotor abilities; *finger dexterity, reaction time,* and *gross body coordination* are typical identifying labels that illustrate the range.

It is interesting to note that as one becomes more practiced at a task, there is frequently a change in the precise combination of psychomotor abilities with other abilities needed for performance. Nonmotor abilities, such as spatial relations or verbal ability, may be the predominant factors during the early stages of learning a task. As learning progresses, the role of these nonmotor abilities diminishes, and performance becomes more dependent upon psychomotor abilities. This effect is important, since knowledge of the abilities necessary at different levels of learning has obvious implications for the development and evaluation of effective training programs.—G. S.

Ammons, R. B., and Ammons, C. H. "Skills." In C. W. Harris (Ed.), *Encyclopedia of Educational Research.* (3rd Ed.) New York: Macmillan, 1960. Pp. 1282-1287.

Fleishman, E. A. "The Description and Prediction of Perceptual-Motor Skill Learning." In R. Glaser (Ed.), *Training Research and Education.* Pittsburgh: University of Pittsburgh Press, 1962. Pp. 137-175.

Fleishman, E. A. "Motor Abilities." In R. L. Ebel (Ed.), *Encyclopedia of Educational Research.* (4th Ed.) London: Macmillan, 1969. Pp. 888-895.

Johnson, B. L., and Nelson, J. K. *Practical Measurements for Evaluation in Physical Education.* Minneapolis: Burgess, 1969. A comprehensive compilation of measures with accompanying norms intended mainly for use up to adolescence; i.e., during the years when psychomotor abilities are being developed.

Seashore, R. H. "Work and Motor Performance." In S. S. Stevens (Ed.), *Handbook of Experimental Psychology.* New York: Wiley, 1951. Pp. 1341-1362. Contains, in addition to Seashore's chapter, other useful sections on learning and human performance, each with a comprehensive bibliography.

Thornton, R. F., and Wasdyke, R. G. *A Taxonomy for the Development of Multidimensional Test Specifications.* Princeton, N.J.: Educational Testing Service, 1973. An interesting application of a complete taxonomy, including psychomotor skills, to the field of career development and testing.

———————————— QUALITY CONTROL ————————————

The term *quality control* is ordinarily used in conjunction with the term *acceptance sampling*. We want to judge whether or not an entire group of products (physical objects, test scores, computations, etc.) is acceptable. For example, a potential large purchaser of light bulbs might want evidence of the quality he can expect in shipments. Suppose his specifications call for bulbs that will last up to 1000 hours of use. To determine whether a particular light bulb will indeed burn for 1000 hours, it is necessary to use the bulb until it burns out. To test a shipment of, say, 10,000 bulbs, the usual procedure would be to select a sample of the bulbs for testing. Suppose the buyer is willing to accept shipment of 10,000 bulbs if he can have some confidence that less than 5 percent will burn for fewer than 800 hours. He is willing to make his decision on the basis of tests of a random sample of 100 bulbs. If fewer than five of the 100 bulbs burn for less than 800 hours, he will accept the entire shipment. This is an example of *acceptance sampling*. The manufacturer who performs a similar checking procedure *before* distributing his product is using a *quality-control* procedure. If the procedure shows that more than 5 percent of the sample are of inferior quality, an examination of the manufacturing process is made to try to determine the source of the problem.

The methods by which the sample is selected and its quality tested are *statistical quality-control methods*. The development of this field was considered so important during World War II that, between 1943 and 1945, the Office of Production Research and Development of the War Production Board established throughout the country thirty-three intensive courses on statistical quality control. It was estimated in 1957 that statistical quality control was saving American industry at least four billion dollars each year.

In evaluation studies, data correspond to the light bulbs in the industrial example. In a set of test scores, for example, a number of the scores may be incorrect because of scoring, coding, or keypunching errors. In this case, a sample of the test scores will be checked independently against a standard specified by the investigator. He may require that no more than one score in 1000 be in error (a tolerance level of .1 percent for accepting the entire set of data). If the sample drawn gives evidence of a higher rate of error, then the source of the error should be identified and the scores corrected. It may happen, for example, that a large number of test scores have been incorrectly keypunched by an inexperienced keypunch operator. The work of this one operator could be redone, and the data again examined for quality. If possible, quality-control procedures should be used early in any operation, so that errors can be identified before they are allowed to persist.

In evaluation, data are usually collected by **Tests, Interviews, Observation Techniques,** and **Ratings.** For quality control in evaluation, therefore, these data must be examined to see whether they are judged sufficiently free of error to be worthy of further analysis. Data may be examined for errors in a variety of ways, some of them very expensive. Frequently an ongoing inspection scheme is established, whereby a deviation from some set value gives a warning that an adjustment is needed. For example, in a quality-control situation for coding an assessment instrument, a sample of each coder's work will be recoded by an independent coder. A tolerance level for errors will be set. If the frequency of errors for a particular coder is greater than the acceptable level, all of the instruments coded by that individual are recoded. The individual may be retained or replaced. Then the process continues.

In national surveys employing interviews, it is common practice to review 15 percent of the interviews by telephone as a check on quality. Ordinarily, the information obtained is used to identify ineffective interviewers, who are then replaced. Other procedures for checking on the quality of interview data include comparing refusal rates which different interviewers may encounter (this may indicate a biased sample of respondents), checking the number of omitted responses after the data are coded, and using the computer to check out-of-range values and other coding and keypunching errors. If the number of errors is large, additional efforts (often with specially trained interviewers) can be made to reinterview certain groups of respondents. (See **Field Operations.**)

In evaluation studies, quality-control procedures should be used routinely from the very first phase of data collection through to the last stages of analysis.—R. T. M.

College Entrance Examination Board. *Introductory Probability and Statistical Inference for Secondary Schools.* New York: CEEB, 1957. See especially Chapter 7 for a simple and interesting discussion on statistical quality control.

Hamaker, H. C. "Quality Control, Statistical: Acceptance Sampling." In D. L. Sills (Ed.), *International Encyclopedia of the Social Sciences.* Vol. 13. New York: Crowell-Collier and Macmillan, 1968. Pp. 225-230.

Page, E. S. "Quality Control, Statistical: Process Control." In D. L. Sills (Ed.), *International Encyclopedia of the Social Sciences.* Vol. 13. New York: Crowell-Collier and Macmillan, 1968. Pp. 230-233.

Phillips, B. N., and Weathers, G. "Analysis of Errors Made in Scoring Standardized Tests." In D. N. Jackson and S. Messick (Eds.), *Problems in Human Assessment.* New York: McGraw-Hill, 1967. Pp. 794-796. (Reprinted from *Educational and Psychological Measurement,* 1958.)

——————— QUASI-EXPERIMENTAL DESIGN ———————

To paraphrase Campbell and Stanley, there are many education and training situations in which the evaluator can introduce something like **Experimental Design** but where he lacks control over *when* students are exposed to the program or *which* students are exposed to it, including the inability to assign students at random to experimental and control groups (see **Control Group**). Collectively, such situations may require the use of compromise procedures called *quasi-experimental designs.*

In the article on **Design of Evaluation,** we discussed some of the problems that evaluators may encounter in trying to interpret and generalize their findings. The implication was that the reason we *design studies,* rather than just *collect data,* is to anticipate such problems and avert as many threats to the validity of our conclusions as possible.

In this article, we shall discuss three classes of quasi-experimental designs useful in various practical evaluation situations. There are others, but these should serve to illustrate the possibilities available to the ingenious and sensitive evaluator working under less than perfect conditions (in the sense of true experimental control).

Time-series designs. Frequently a new instructional program is applied to all eligible students. It is either politically or practically not feasible to establish a control group, or the program administrator may never have thought about it. Frequently, too, in these situations the evaluator is called in after the fact. If there is some record of several relevant measurements taken over a period of time before the introduction of the new program, then a time-series design may provide a useful framework for evaluating program effects. We can schematize this design as follows, where Os represent comparable measures taken over time and X represents the inception of the program of interest:

$$O_1 \quad O_2 \quad O_3 \quad X \quad O_4 \quad O_5 \quad O_6$$

The number of Os before and after X is not fixed and will vary with the situation, but usually the more the better.

Let us see how the time-series design might be applied in the evaluation of a new third-grade reading program. Suppose there is a record of reading scores on a standardized test administered at the end of the third grade for the three years preceding installation of the new program. And suppose the evaluator is able to obtain scores on the same test for the next three groups of third graders who receive the new program. He might find one of the patterns shown in Figure 1, where the new reading program was introduced at the beginning of the year following O_3. Note that the score "gain" between O_3 and O_4 is the same in all the examples. However, only pattern I gives much cause for rejoicing about the effectiveness of the special reading program. (Actually, from pattern I, it looks as if the program gets better after its first year of installation; perhaps it took awhile for the instructors to feel comfortable with the new program and get some of the "bugs" out.) Even with pattern I, however, the evaluator is well advised to obtain additional information to rule out the possibility that some other event occurring between O_3 and O_4 (and having long-range consequences) might be responsible for the apparent increase in reading competence of the third graders. One such event might be a shift in the population of third graders served by the school—in the direction of a larger proportion of verbally facile children.

A pattern such as II might cause the evaluator to wonder about **Hawthorne Effect** in the first year of the new program's operation. At any rate, the gains were apparently not maintained. Patterns III and IV should not encourage the evaluator to infer any program effect. However, if the evaluator had had access only to the before (O_3) and after (O_4) measures, he might have been erroneously tempted to do so.

The example here involves measurement of different groups of students, presumably from the same population. A longitudinal study design in which repeated measures are taken of the same students is a special case of time-series design and is discussed in more detail under **Longitudinal Study**.

A refinement of the time-series design adds a control group that is judged comparable to the experimental group but does not receive the special instructional intervention:

$$\text{E:} \quad O_1 \quad O_2 \quad O_3 \quad X \quad O_4 \quad O_5 \quad O_6$$
$$\text{C:} \quad O_1 \quad O_2 \quad O_3 \quad \quad O_4 \quad O_5 \quad O_6$$

In the example of the evaluation of a third-grade reading program, the control group might consist of successive classes of third graders in elementary schools with similar populations where no special program was introduced. If the experimental group shows a gain between O_3 and O_4 and the control group does not, confidence is increased that the program and not some other event caused the result. (See also **Time-Series Analysis**.)

Pretest-posttest nonequivalent group designs. Frequently in the real world of education/training, where it is not possible to assign students at random to experimental and control groups, it is

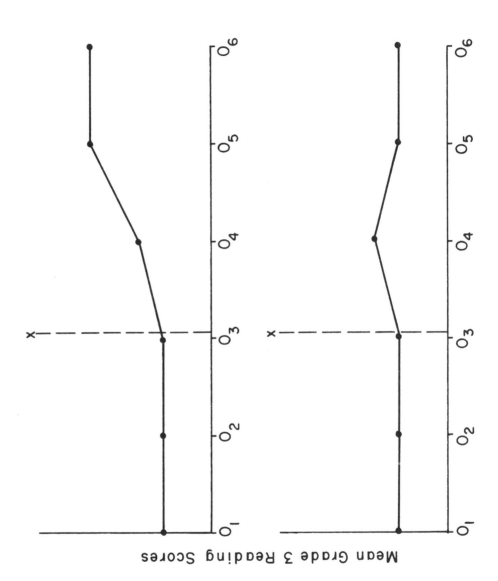

Mean Grade 3 Reading Scores

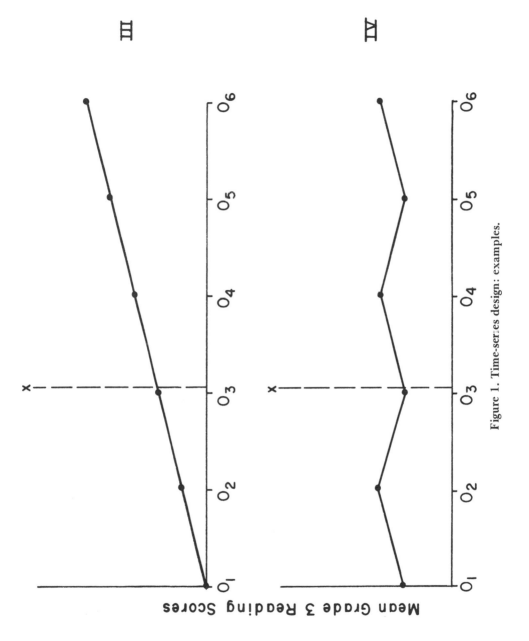

Figure 1. Time-series design: examples.

possible to assign instructional treatments at random to intact groups of students judged to be roughly comparable. Thus, a design that looks like the pretest-posttest control-group design (see **Experimental Design**) may be used:

$$\begin{array}{llll} \text{E:} & O_1 & X & O_2 \\ \text{C:} & O_1 & & O_2 \end{array}$$

Since students are not assigned randomly, however, there are more threats to the internal validity of the conclusions. Results from such a design usually are open to a variety of conflicting interpretations; the equivalence of the groups cannot be assured by matching or related procedures (see **Matched Sampling**); analysis of covariance and regression techniques do not necessarily provide the proper adjustment for those variables on which the experimental and control groups differ (see **Lord's Paradox**). However, as Campbell and Stanley point out, this design is still preferable to the design that involves only pretest and posttest with one group.

A variation on this design (which Campbell and Stanley call "patched-up") assumes that there are two student groups judged to be roughly comparable, and that one of these groups has just received the instructional program and the other is about to be exposed to it. Such a situation might arise with successive classes of entering trainees.

$$\begin{array}{lllll} \text{E1:} & X & O_1 & & \\ \text{E2:} & & O_1 & X & O_2 \end{array}$$

(To maintain the comparability of the groups, the calculation of the difference $O_2 - O_1$ for E2 should be based only on students who complete the course or program.) If the training program has an effect, it will be documented by positive differences, as follows: O_1 for the first group (E1) will be greater than O_1 for the second group (E2), and O_2 will be greater than O_1 for the second group (E2). The difference between O_2 for the second group and O_1 for the first group provides information about the effects of the pretest on the posttest. Evaluators considering this design should consult Campbell and Stanley (p. 229) for variations in the testing pattern that can make the design more robust in terms of causal inferences and should add little to the cost of the evaluation.

Regression-discontinuity design. This relatively powerful design is applicable to situations where (a) resources are scarce and education/training can be given only to the "most deserving"—at either the high or the low end of the scale—and (b) it would not be feasible or justifiable to withhold the program from groups of students who qualify. Consider, for example, a program to be offered only in schools with high percentages of poverty-level children or a fellowship program for outstanding graduate students in physics. If all who qualify are to receive the program, it would not be sensible in either case to try to set up a control-group design: schools *without* high percentages of poor children (or graduate students *below* the standard for "outstanding") could hardly be considered equivalent groups. However, the regression-discontinuity design offers a way out of the dilemma if scores can be assigned on the priority dimension to those who are and are not admitted to the program. For example, we could give a score to each school in the district corresponding to average family income, or we could use the scores on the fellowship examination for graduate students in physics.

Let us develop further the illustration from compensatory education. Suppose that there are twelve schools (A-L) in the district, and the special program (say, in basic skills) is given in the six with the lowest economic levels (A-F). If we plot average scores on a criterion achievement measure (taken after the program has been in operation for some time) against average family income, we might get results such as those shown in Figure 2. Pattern I very clearly suggests an effect of the compensatory program. After exposure to the program, students in schools C-F scored as well as or better than students in the most nearly comparable school (in terms of parental income) without the program. More important, the program has apparently indeed compensated; the students in schools A-F are performing better than their economic level would have predicted. Results corresponding to pattern II do not warrant positive conclusions about the program. In fact, the evidence is negative in cost-benefit terms if the special program is more expensive than the regular program.

A general principle underlying this discussion of quasi-experimental designs is that the weaker the evaluator's design control, the more important it is for him to collect *a broad range of data* by *multiple methods* from *multiple sources*. For example, if

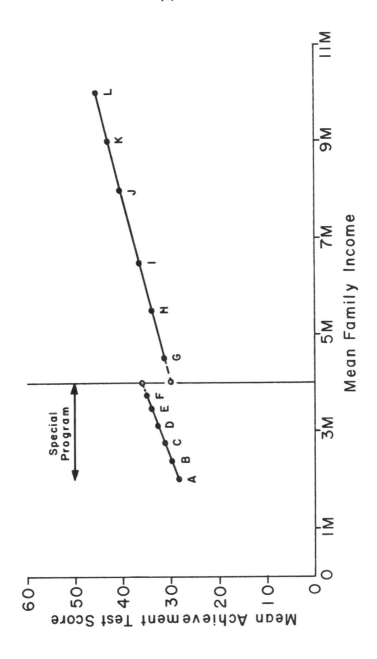

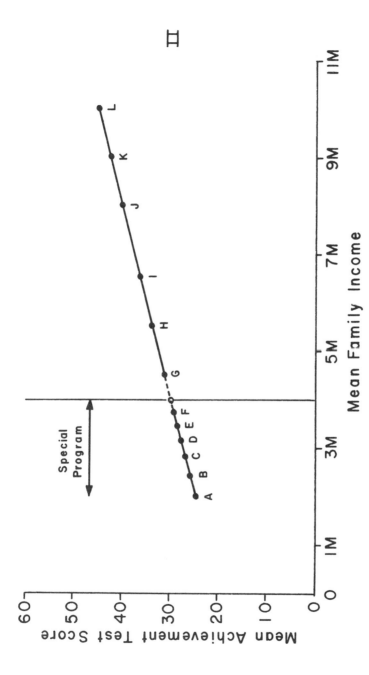

Figure 2. Regression-discontinuity design: examples.

he suspects that home conditions may have as much to do with student achievement as the instructional program, he should attempt to measure home influence directly and take account of it as best he can in interpreting the evaluation results; and, if he must use subjective ratings about program effectiveness, he should try to obtain these ratings from several different groups involved in the program (instructors, students, and administrators, say) and supplement them with additional (and ideally nonreactive) kinds of measures that would appear to bear on the same question. As Webb (p. 34) has noted, the "most persuasive evidence and the strongest inference" frequently comes from such a "triangulation of measurement processes." (See also **Reactive Effects of Program and Evaluation** and **Unobtrusive Measures**.)—S. B. A.

Campbell, D. T. "Reforms as Experiments." In C. H. Weiss (Ed.), *Evaluating Action Programs: Readings in Social Action and Education*. Boston: Allyn and Bacon, 1972. Pp. 187-228. Revised from an earlier paper in *American Psychologist*, 1969, *24*, 409-429.

Campbell, D. T., and Stanley, J. C. "Experimental and Quasi-Experimental Designs for Research on Teaching." In N. L. Gage (Ed.), *Handbook of Research on Teaching*. Chicago: Rand McNally, 1963. Pp. 171-246. Also published as a separate book by Rand McNally, 1966.

Isaac, S., and Michael, W. B. *Handbook in Research and Evaluation*. San Diego: Robert R. Knapp, 1971. See Design 5 (nonrandomized control-group pretest-posttest design, p. 43) and Designs 7 and 8 (one-group and control-group time-series designs, pp. 46-47).

Messick, S., and Barrows, T. S. "Strategies for Research and Evaluation in Early Childhood Education." In I. J. Gordon (Ed.), *Early Childhood Education: The Seventy-First Yearbook of the National Society for the Study of Education*. Chicago: NSSE, 1972. Pp. 261-290.

Webb, E. J. "Unconventionality, Triangulation, and Inference." In *Proceedings of the 1966 Invitational Conference on Testing Problems*. Princeton, N.J.: Educational Testing Service, 1967. Pp. 34-43.

──────────── QUESTIONNAIRES ────────────

A questionnaire is a group of printed questions used to elicit information from respondents by means of self-report. The questions may be open-ended, requiring respondents to answer in their own words, or fixed choice, requiring respondents to select one or more answers from among those provided (see **Achievement-Test Construction**). The respondents may also be provided with checklists or rating scales. Questions may be concerned with the respondent's personal background, factual knowledge, or attitudes and opinions.

Self-report questionnaires have several advantages over **Interviews**: (1) Questionnaires may be relatively inexpensive to administer, since they are completed by the respondent without an interviewer present. (2) They can be distributed to respondents quickly and inexpensively through the mail, or they can be administered to an assembled group of people (such as a class of students or a group of teachers) at one time. (3) They can be answered by each respondent at his own pace. (4) They often can be designed to maintain respondents' anonymity; thus, respondents are reassured that their answers will not be used against them in any way and presumably will respond with greater honesty than might otherwise be the case. (5) They can be standardized, so that all respondents are given exactly the same printed questions to answer; in an interview, a respondent's answers may be influenced by the way the interviewer asks questions.

The ease with which questionnaires can be administered has contributed to their widespread use. However, questionnaires have all the limitations of other self-report measures. The primary problem is that responses may not be truthful or accurate, and it is often difficult, expensive, or impossible for the investigator to determine their **Validity**. A respondent may make careless errors (e.g., writing in an incorrect number, checking the wrong response); he may make purposeful errors in the hope of conveying a favorable impression and avoiding embarrassing admissions; or he may make unintentional errors because he misinterprets questions or does not understand his attitudes, feelings, or actions well enough to answer questions accurately. Invalid responses are often associated with questions dealing with attitudes, but they may also occur when questions require factual data that can be verified. For example, a respondent may inflate his report of such things as the frequency with which he votes in national and local elections, the amount of his charitable contributions, or the number of books he reads yearly, and he may deflate his report of such things as the frequency with which he watches television or the amount of food he consumes.

Another problem with questionnaires—especially those that are mailed—is the possibility of a low rate of response, resulting in a biased sample. Except in cases where questionnaires are distributed and collected from a captive audience, response rates from initial distributions of questionnaires can run quite low. General mail surveys often have response rates as low as about 20 percent. To ensure a high response rate, paying respondents or following up the initial distribution with phone calls and personal visits is suggested. If response rates are still low, nonrespondents should be sampled and interviewed to see if their responses differ in systematic ways from the responses of those who responded voluntarily. All these problems greatly increase the cost of questionnaire administration, so that populations that are likely to yield low response rates may perhaps be more efficiently questioned through personal or telephone interviews.

Other problems with questionnaires may be less important but need to be recognized. Whereas questionnaires normally allow respondents to answer at their leisure, this also means that respondents will answer at different times, on different days, and in different circumstances—and that their responses may be subject to situationally induced differences. The use of a standardized questionnaire is not the same as a standardized testing situation. Additionally, with no time limits imposed, respondents may vary considerably in the amount of time and care they take in answering questions. A questionnaire administration must be limited to people who can read and write. In studies involving teachers or college graduates, this may be an insignificant problem, but in a survey of the U.S. adult population, a substantial proportion of people will be unable to respond to any but the most simply worded questionnaires.

Steps taken in the construction of a questionnaire are similar to those used to develop most tests. They include deciding what information is needed and what is not needed for the study (possibly by constructing mock tables beforehand to see the relationships and information that will be useful), deciding whether the questionnaire items should be structured (fixed choice) or unstructured (open-ended), drafting and reviewing the items, pretesting, and possibly interviewing some respondents to discover problems that typical analyses will not uncover, and revising the instrument on the basis of all these inputs. An additional step in developing questionnaires is often precoding of the items to indicate column numbers for keypunching, so that the questionnaire can be processed almost immediately after administration.

To reduce later processing costs, open-ended questions should be used sparingly to reduce the amount of coding and follow-up interviewing. In addition, to increase response rates, questionnaires should be attractively laid out, should include information about the study to make people feel their responses will be useful, should include information about the study's sponsors to enable respondents to verify its legitimacy, should avoid questions that may be seen as invasions of the respondent's privacy, should be as short and as easy to complete as possible, and should be easy to return. Note, too, that to increase the likelihood of valid responses, questions should be as specific as possible to avoid respondents' putting their own meaning to words. For example, "How many hours did you watch television yesterday?" is preferable to "How many hours a day do you usually watch TV?" because the former asks for recall of a specific, recent incident and is more likely to produce accurate answers than a request for "average" or "typical" behavior. "How many books have you read in the past month?" is preferable to "Do you read many books?" because the word *many* may mean one book to some people and twenty books to another. Similarly, "How many days were you absent from school in the last month?" is preferable to "Are you often, rarely, or never absent from school?" because days absent is a unit understandable to everyone, whereas the terms *often* and *rarely* are likely to be interpreted differently by different people.

To reduce the number of omissions, questions should appear nonthreatening to the respondent. As well as promising anonymity, the questionnaire constructor should phrase questions that avoid moral or ethical judgments. For example, "Are you ever absent from school because you pretended to be sick?" might be a threatening admission for a school child to have to make, whereas "How often do you pretend to be sick so you can stay home from school?" implies some acceptance and recognition of such behavior and may not be seen by the respondent as threatening. The latter form still leaves the opportunity for the respondent to deny such behavior.—G. A. B., S. B.

Helmstadter, G. C. *Research Concepts in Human Behavior.* New York: Appleton-Century-Crofts, 1970. Includes (pp. 70-77) a clear discussion of questionnaire construction.

Mouly, G. J. *The Science of Educational Research.* New York: Van Nostrand Reinhold, 1970. Provides (pp. 241-263) a summary of how and when to use questionnaires.

Riley, M. W. *Sociological Research II: Exercises and Manual.* New York: Harcourt, Brace, 1963. See Section I ("Gathering the Data") for discussion and exercises related to questionnaire construction and use.

Selltiz, C., Jahoda, M., Deutsch, M., and Cook, S. *Research Methods in Social Relations.* (Rev. ed.) New York: Holt, 1960. See Chapter 7 ("Data Collection: Questionnaires and Interviews") for advantages and disadvantages of questionnaire use; and see Appendix C for steps in questionnaire construction.

Stanley, J. C., and Hopkins, K. D. *Educational and Psychological Measurement and Evaluation.* Englewood Cliffs, N.J.: Prentice-Hall, 1972. Includes (pp. 297-298) a brief discussion of the advantages and disadvantages of questionnaires.

—————————————— RATINGS ——————————————

Ratings are subjective assessments made on an established scale. Although measures based on ratings provide only rough information about particular programs and persons, they are easy to obtain and often are the only means available for assessing performance—especially on-the-job performance, where the observable cues indicating the presence of a trait are too numerous to actually record. Ratings, then, serve as rough appraisals of behavior.

Ratings must be interpreted with care because they tend to be unreliable, biased, and contaminated. Bergman and Siegel list the following as factors which can contribute to poor or inadequate ratings: (a) friendship, (b) quick guessing, (c) jumping to conclusions, (d) first-impression responses, (e) appearance, (f) prejudices, (g) halo effects, (h) errors of central tendency, and (i) leniency. The first six of these have obvious effects on ratings. A **Halo Effect** occurs when a rater allows his general impression to influence his judgment of each separate trait on a rating scale. Errors of central tendency and leniency occur when the rater tends to use only the middle or the upper portion of the rating scale, respectively (see **Response Sets**). Many sources of bias can be avoided, however, by appropriate selection and training of the raters.

Although the rater may write an essay on the individual or program that he is rating, the more common method involves rating various competency items by checking such terms as *outstanding, above average, average, below average,* and *unsatisfactory.* Other methods for structuring the scale include numbers increasing from 1 (indicating very poor) up to 5, 7, or more (indicating very good). Ordinarily, a rating form will include certain statements that specify the behaviors corresponding to the various points on the rating form. A typical rating form is shown in Figure 1; it was designed for supervisors' ratings of employees in school food services jobs. Such rating forms are in very common use in evaluating training performance, student achievement, or job behavior. Although there are problems involved in using such rating

PERSONNEL PROGRESS REPORT

Name of Employee _____ Classification _____ School _____

1 – LEADERSHIP

Unsatisfactory	Below Average	Average	Above Average	Outstanding
Lacking in leadership and/or respect.	Some indication of lack of leadership and/or respect.	Good leader but neither looked up to nor down upon.	Good leader and well regarded by employees.	Marked traits of leadership. Enjoys high regard of employees.

2 – DEPENDABILITY

Unsatisfactory	Below Average	Average	Above Average	Outstanding
Requires constant supervision. Difficulty in following directions.	Requires considerable supervision. Does not always follow directions.	Requires average or normal supervision.	Can usually be depended upon.	Needs very little supervision. Reliable.

3 – INTEREST

Unsatisfactory	Below Average	Average	Above Average	Outstanding
No enthusiasm for work.	Interest spasmodic, never great. Rarely enthusiastic.	Normal amount of interest in job. Some enthusiasm.	Interested in job. Usually enthusiastic.	High interest in job. Very enthusiastic.

4 – ATTITUDE TOWARD SCHOOL POLICIES

Unsatisfactory	Below Average	Average	Above Average	Outstanding
Continually complains about school policies.	Usually accepts school policies but requires considerable "selling".	Usually accepts school policies.	Accepts school policies willingly.	Is sympathetic to school policies and their purposes.

5 – ATTITUDE TOWARD SUPERVISION

Unsatisfactory	Below Average	Average	Above Average	Outstanding
Resents any supervision.	Does not always accept constructive supervision.	Has about the average viewpoint toward supervision.	Willing to accept suggestions and constructive criticism.	Appreciates help of supervision.

6 – ATTITUDE TOWARD FELLOW EMPLOYEES

Unsatisfactory	Below Average	Average	Above Average	Outstanding
Selfish, jealous, fault finding, uncooperative.	Not consistent in relation to others. May be quarrelsome at times.	Has no serious differences with others.	Cooperative, friendly and helpful	Goes out of her way to be cooperative, helpful, friendly to others.

7 – PERSONAL APPEARANCE

Unsatisfactory	Below Average	Average	Above Average	Outstanding
Wears soiled uniforms. Slovenly in appearance.	Careless in appearance and cleanliness of uniform.	Usually wears clean white uniforms. Presents mediocre appearance.	Wears clean white uniforms. Presents attractive appearance.	Wears clean white uniform. Unusually well-groomed.

8 – HEALTH

Unsatisfactory	Below Average	Average	Above Average	Outstanding
Seems physically unable to carry full load of job.	Usually slow or awkward because of health or age. Often sick or tires quickly.	Able to do normal amount of work without tiring easily. Has little extra.	Health-Generally good. Seldom ill and does not tire easily.	Very energetic. Has marked endurance and is rarely sick.

9 – FOOD PREPARATION

Unsatisfactory	Below Average	Average	Above Average	Outstanding
Unsatisfactory. Gives no attention to appearance and taste of food.	Fair food preparation.	Usually serves attractive and tasty food.	Very good.	Outstanding

10 – ORDERLINESS

Unsatisfactory	Below Average	Average	Above Average	Outstanding
Sloppy as to cleanliness and orderliness of kitchen and storerooms.	Frequently fails to maintain station clean and orderly.	Usually keeps kitchen and store rooms in clean and orderly condition.	Kitchen and storeroom seldom dirty and out of order.	Always keeps kitchen and store rooms clean and orderly.

Figure 1. Graphic scale performance-evaluation report.
By permission from F. M. Lopez, *Evaluating Employee Performance*,
International Personnel Management Association, Chicago, 1968.

forms, they should be used by trained observers when more objective methods of measuring performance are not available.

In developing scales, it is important to consider the setting in which the rating takes place. For example, the person being rated must have an opportunity to perform the activities on which he is being rated. In addition, the rater must be able to observe the behavior to be rated. In the rating form shown in Figure 1, the employee's attitude toward fellow employees is rated. If conditions do not allow for interaction among employees, or for supervisor observation of such interaction, that particular scale should be deleted from the rating form. Also, if the rating is to be effective and accepted, both those who use it and those who will be judged by it should participate in its design, installation, administration, and review. By such a cooperative effort, ambiguities can often be avoided. For example, the employer and the employee may differ on the meaning of leadership and on the interpretation of the various categories involved in rating it. Whether an employee is looked up to or looked down upon may not be an easy decision to make, depending on the signs that one is willing to accept as indications of esteem or lack of esteem.

In evaluation, especially of training programs with small numbers of trainees, the raw data will often be in the form of ratings. To be useful, then, the ratings should be gathered with care for the considerations outlined in this entry.—R. T. M.

Bergman, B. A., and Siegel, A. I. *Training Evaluation and Student Achievement Measurement: A Review of the Literature.* Lowry Air Force Base, Colo.: Technical Training Division, 1972. See especially pages 13 and 14.

Festinger, L., and Katz, D. (Eds.) *Research Methods in the Behavioral Sciences.* New York: Dryden, 1953. See especially Chapter 9, on the observation of group behavior.

Gessner, P. K. "Evaluation of Instruction." *Science,* 1973, *180,* 566-570. Student ratings of instruction are positively related to class performance on national normative examinations: the higher the student ratings of the instruction they receive, the higher the class score relative to a nationwide norm.

Lopez, F. *Evaluating Employee Performance.* Chicago: Public Personnel Association, 1968. Discusses the principles, techniques, and problems of planning, designing, installing, operating, and reviewing an effective employee performance-evaluation program.

REACTIVE EFFECTS OF PROGRAM AND EVALUATION

Reactive effects are those effects that occur because of the program or measurement but are not related to the substance of the instruction or evaluation. The classic example of a reactive program effect is the **Hawthorne Effect.** (Investigators at the Hawthorne plant of Western Electric concluded that the cause of increased productivity was not planned variations in working conditions but a feeling that, because of these variations, management was really concerned about the workers.) Program innovators in many areas have been elated by the enthusiasm and apparent success marking the first year of an effort, only to find a subsequent rapid return to *pre*innovation levels. Some educators have even suggested a continuing commitment to change, primarily to capitalize on Hawthorne effects (see Trow).

Other variables that may contribute positively or negatively to outcomes but are not part of the intended instructional treatment—and thus interfere with generalizations of conclusions to other settings—include instructor expectations for students (the so-called *Pygmalion effect*), peer pressures, extraordinary efforts to beat a competitive program or student group (see **John Henry Effect**), deliberate attempts to scuttle the program, or cheating to make it look better than it is (e.g., teaching the test).

The measurements used by the evaluator may also produce reactive effects that decrease the validity of the results. Evaluators who come from the physical sciences will recognize the analogy to the Heisenberg principle of uncertainty: It is impossible to make a

precise determination at the same time of both the position and
the velocity of an electron. Similarly, the very process of measuring student knowledge or other characteristics may affect those
characteristics—or at least the responses from which they are inferred. Webb and his colleagues have provided an excellent delinea-
tion of possible reactive measurement effects. They include:

> The "guinea-pig" effect—awareness of being tested or ob-
> served. They hasten to point out that this awareness "need
> not, by itself, contaminate responses . . . but the probability
> of bias is high in any study in which a respondent is aware
> of his subject status" (p. 13).
>
> Role selection. This is not a question so much of dishonesty
> or inaccuracy on the part of the respondent as of selection
> of responses perceived as "proper" or expected in the situa-
> tion.
>
> Real changes in the characteristics being measured. For
> example, initial questions on a test may lead to a change in
> understanding that will improve later responses on the test—
> **Pretests** may influence **Posttest** performance. (See **Design of
> Evaluation.**)
>
> **Response Sets.** Personality-based or instrument-induced
> tendencies of students to respond in irrelevant but con-
> sistent ways.

Student responses may be influenced too by the characteristics of the data collectors—testers, interviewers, etc. Various
studies have reported on spurious results attributable to race, age,
religion, and sex of data collectors and interactions of these characteristics with characteristics of the subjects in an investigation
(e.g., male interviewers may obtain fewer responses from male
interviewees than from female interviewees; see **Interview**). Other
variables that can change the kinds of responses students give include the competence of the data collector, how the data collector
filters the student's response if, as in an interview, he has the job
of recording or coding it, and even the expectations of the data
collector.

If students and instructors did not know that they were involved in a program being evaluated, some of the sources of inva-

lidity of data described here would disappear. Although it is seldom possible to keep them in the dark, it may be possible in some cases at least to keep them from knowing whether they are in the experimental or the **Control Group**. John Tukey has suggested (in informal discussion) that "equally elegant-*appearing* treatments" be given to the two groups; e.g., the new math program might be given in the experimental group and new art supplies provided for the control group. Suchman discusses this issue in relationship to placebo experiments in medicine. However, he concludes realistically that the notion of setting up "dummy" programs and utilizing double-blind designs is largely hypothetical for the evaluation of public service programs.

Webb and his associates pin their hopes for eliminating many reactive effects on the use of nonreactive measures: records, hidden observation, etc. (see **Unobtrusive Measures**). However, the majority of investigators feel that a giant step will have been taken when evaluators are simply aware of possible reactive effects of programs and evaluation and alert to signs of them in the programs and measures they are concerned with. Then they may be less tempted to attribute effects to programs when the effects might, in fact, be attributable to some of the peculiar reactive effects discussed here.—S. B. A.

Baker, J. P., and Crist, J. L. "Teacher Expectancies: A Review of the Literature." In J. D. Elashoff and R. E. Snow (Eds.), *Pygmalion Reconsidered*. Worthington, Ohio: Charles A. Jones, 1971. Pp. 48-64.

Finn, J. D. "Expectations and the Educational Environment." *Review of Educational Research*, 1972, *42*, 387-410.

Suchman, E. A. *Evaluative Research: Principles and Practice in Public Service and Social Action Programs*. New York: Russell Sage Foundation, 1967. See the section on the "placebo" effect (pp. 96-100).

Trow, M. "Methodological Problems in the Evaluation of Innovation." In M. C. Wittrock and D. E. Wiley (Eds.), *The Evaluation of Instruction: Issues and Problems*. New York: Holt, 1970. Pp. 289-305. Comments and discussion follow (on pp. 305-331).

Webb, E. J., Campbell, D. T., Schwartz, R. D., and Sechrest, L. *Unobtrusive Measures: Nonreactive Research in the Social Sciences.* Chicago: Rand McNally, 1966. See especially the section on sources of invalidity of measures (pp. 12-27).

REGRESSION

The term *regression* was introduced into statistics by Galton. In comparing the heights of fathers and their adult sons, Galton found that the mean height of the sons of tall fathers was less than the mean height of the fathers themselves and that the mean height of sons of short fathers was greater than that of their fathers. For fathers of a given height, the mean of their sons always "regressed" toward the overall mean of all fathers.

Regression effect refers to the phenomenon that the values of variables tend to move toward the mean on subsequent evaluations. In proficiency tests given across time, the regression effect is manifested in the tendency of trainees who score either above or below the mean on a test to score closer to the mean on a subsequent equivalent test. Thus, if a new training program is given to those students who score low on a pretest, an evaluator must take the regression effect into consideration in interpreting the scores on the posttest. What look like improved scores may simply be artifacts due to the regression effect. However, regression artifacts may tend to mask the effects of a training or educational program. Campbell and Erlebacher have shown that the selection of a **Control Group** from a generally more advantaged population made the Head Start program look bad in the Westinghouse-Ohio University evaluation. If a control group had been chosen from a generally less able population, the program would have probably looked good. (See Campbell and Erlebacher for a more detailed explanation of this type of regression artifact.)

The term *regression* is also applied to a statistical technique used to develop an equation for predicting one variable from the known value of a second variable. In studying the relationships between the heights of fathers and sons, we can plot the heights of fathers on one axis and the heights of sons on the other axis. If the heights of sons are plotted on the Y-axis and the heights of fathers on the X-axis, we can obtain a scatterplot of X and Y values. If a straight line is fitted to the data in such a way as to minimize the sum of the squares of the vertical distances of the points from the line, we call the line thus defined the *regression line*. If Y represents the heights of sons and X the heights of fathers, then the equation $Y = a + bX$ gives the linear relationship between Y and X. If a number of actual values of X and Y are available, then estimates of a and b can be found easily. The value of a gives the Y-intercept of the regression line; b, the coefficient of X, is called the *regression coefficient*. It is related to the correlation between X and Y. If the X and Y values are considered a set of sample values from some population of X and Y values, then the regression line can be considered an estimate of the relationship that exists in the population. In this case the population value corresponding to b is β (beta). It is possible to test whether β differs significantly from zero; i.e., whether the slope of the line differs significantly from the horizontal. The test of the significance of β is related to testing whether X and Y are significantly correlated.

If the data are represented by a straight line (or an estimated curve), then the value of Y for any given X can be esti-

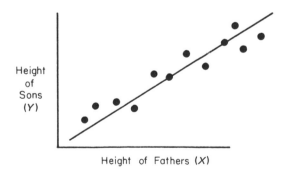

Figure 1. Illustration of Galton's data.

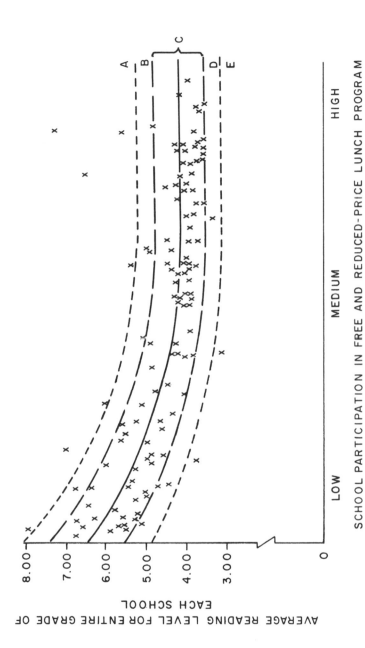

Figure 2. Illustrative scattergram of reading-test scores (for fifth grades in all schools of a large urban system). By permission from Bayla F. White. Signals devised to reveal school performance. In *Search*. The Urban Institute, Washington, D.C., January, 1973.

mated. This use of the regression line to estimate values of the dependent variable for a given value of the independent variable is one basis for measuring the effectiveness of a program or institution in terms of its difference from the value estimated by the regression line. If a program is represented by a point above the line, it is doing a better job than was expected on the basis of the critical variables in the system.

Multiple regression is the extension of the regression technique to the case when more than one variable is used to predict the dependent variable. If more than one independent variable is used to estimate Y, the first-degree equation is called a *regression surface*. For example, if $Y = a + bX + cZ$, Y is a linear combination of X and Z. The constants b and c are the regression coefficients or weights.

The example given in Figure 1 is an illustration of linear regression. In Figure 2, an example of *curvilinear regression* is given. In this study in a public school system, the curve in the center is the best-fitting second-degree curve. Curves B and D give boundaries for points less than a specified distance from the regression curve. Points in the region between A and B and between D and E are farther from the curve. Points outside A and E are farthest from the curve.

Cases outside the two outer curves may be considered *outliers* in the sense that they are far from the center of the distribution. Often, in evaluation, such outliers will be used in case studies in an attempt to discover the reasons for their deviating so far from the mean values (see **Case-Study Method**).—R. T. M.

Campbell, D. T., and Erlebacher, A. "How Regression Artifacts in Quasi-Experimental Evaluations Can Mistakenly Make Compensatory Education Look Harmful." In J. Hellmuth (Ed.), *Disadvantaged Child.* Vol. 3: *Compensatory Education: A National Debate.* New York: Brunner/Mazel, 1970.

Hays, W. L. *Statistics.* New York: Holt, 1963. See especially Chapters 15 and 16.

Urban Institute. "Signals Devised to Reveal School Performance." *Search,* January-February 1973, pp. 5-8.

—————————— RELIABILITY ——————————

In evaluation, the information on which judgments are based is obtained in many ways. Persons are interviewed, programs are observed, teachers are rated, and students are tested. The evaluator must be concerned about the quality of the techniques and instruments used in the interviews, observations, ratings, and tests; and "quality" is usually defined in terms of **Validity** and reliability. Validity is the more important of these two concepts, but reliability is a necessary, if not sufficient condition, for validity. A reliable measure is one that provides consistent and stable indications of the characteristic being investigated. The issue is complicated because the characteristic being measured (aptitude, skill, attitude, etc.) may itself be unstable and/or the measurement instrument or procedure may change from one application to another. These conditions may give rise to variations in the results of the measurement.

If we could measure a given characteristic of an individual or situation many, many times, we could then take the average of the measurements as a "true" measure of the characteristic. If the variation of the measurements from their average was small, we would consider the measurement reliable. If the variation was large, we would consider the measurement unreliable. The standard error of measurement is defined, theoretically, as the square root of such a variance (i.e., the standard deviation—see **Statistics**) and would provide the most direct index of reliability. However, in practice, it is not usually feasible or sensible to take repeated measurements of the same characteristic of an individual or situation, and the standard error of measurement is commonly estimated from group data. The estimate may be based on the typical index of reliability, the *reliability coefficient.*

Consider, for example, the case where it is possible to take two measures of a characteristic for each individual in a group. If the measures of the characteristic are reliable, we would expect the individuals to retain about the same rank in the group on each measure. We might express this relationship by a **Correlation** coefficient, which indicates how two sets of "scores" are related. If the correlation is high, the measurement instruments and procedures are considered reliable. Of course, an underlying assumption here is that the characteristic measured on the two occasions is stable. If the characteristic is unstable, then the rank of an individual might change from one occasion to the next, and the correlation would be lowered. The degree to which the assumption of characteristic or trait stability is tenable should influence the choice of the method used to determine the reliability coefficient of a test or other measurement procedure. Four common methods of obtaining reliability coefficients are described below.

1. *Test-retest method.* The same test (or other measurement device) is given to a group of individuals on two different occasions, and the correlation between their scores is computed. This method is appropriate for skills measures such as typing tests. It is less appropriate for such measures as multiple-choice tests of knowledge and understanding, because individuals may simply remember the choices they marked the first time and repeat them on the second occasion. The effect of this memory factor would be to provide an inflated estimate of the reliability of the measures. On the other hand, if a long period of time were allowed between the two measurements in order to reduce the influence of memory, the abilities or other characteristics being measured might themselves change. Then the test-retest method might produce an underestimate of the reliability of the measure. Since differences at retesting may represent true changes in unstable traits (such as attitudes or opinions) rather than measurement errors, the test-retest method of estimating reliability is not recommended for instruments designed to measure such traits.

2. *Alternate-forms method.* Alternate (or parallel) forms of a test or other measure are administered to the same people, and the correlation between the scores obtained is the reliability coefficient. Alternate forms of a test are built to measure the same abilities or other characteristics, but they are composed of different questions. The reliability coefficient provides evidence of the success of the test maker in sampling the same domain with two different instruments. The use of the alternate-forms method of estimating reliability overcomes the memory problem associated with the test-retest method.

3. *Split-half method.* If only one test is given, it may be divided into two "equivalent" halves and the reliability coefficient computed on the basis of the scores obtained on the two halves. Items may be assigned to the two halves on rational, systematic (e.g., the odd-numbered items in one half and the even-numbered items in the other half), or random bases. When investigators would like to estimate what the reliability coefficient for the measure would be if students' total (instead of half) scores had been used in the calculations, they frequently use the Spearman-Brown formula: $r = 2r'/(1 + r')$, where r' is the correlation between scores on halves of the test and r is the *adjusted* reliability coefficient.

4. *Internal-consistency methods.* When only one measure is given and it contains many questions or items, estimates of reliability (or, more accurately, internal consistency) can be based on the item statistics. Two commonly used coefficients are based upon total number of items, the standard deviation of the test, and either the average item variance (Kuder-Richardson Formula 20) or the test mean (Kuder-Richardson Formula 21)—see Gulliksen, pp. 220-225. Another widely used index of the homogeneity of the items in a test (the degree to which they measure the same underlying characteristic) is Cronbach's "alpha" coefficient.

One of the major factors that may influence the reliability of a measure is its length. As the number of items increases, the chance factors which enter into the test score tend to balance out. The Spearman-Brown formula mentioned above, in its general case, allows investigators to estimate the reliability of a new test formed by increasing or decreasing the number of items in an existing test (see, for example, Cronbach, p. 168 ff.).

Reliabilities can also be computed for differences between scores. Ordinarily, the differences between scores are less reliable than the scores themselves. This tendency for difference scores to be relatively unreliable poses a problem for the evaluator who wishes to use the gain between pretest and posttest as a measure of the effectiveness of a program (see **Change Measurement**).

Some adjustments have to be made in the usual kinds of estimates of test reliability when they are applied to criterion-referenced measures (see **Criterion-Referenced Measurement**). In general, because of differences in purpose and developmental procedures, criterion-referenced tests have lower score variability than norms-referenced tests (see **Norms**). Since estimates of reliability

are dependent on score variability, estimates of reliability for criterion-referenced tests may appear to be low even though the tests
are internally consistent. Livingston has derived a generalized formula for the reliability coefficient of criterion-referenced tests,
based on deviations of obtained scores from a criterion score
rather than from the mean score.

The concept of reliability is applicable to all kinds of measurement, although the concept has been most thoroughly ex-
plored and developed in connection with tests. Of particular concern to many evaluators is the consistency of ratings or observations. There are really two issues here: the consistency with which
a single judge (rater, observer) acts, and the consistency of the
responses of two or more judges to the same phenomena. A commonly used index of intrajudge or interjudge agreement is the simple "percent agreement" (see Dyer and King, p. 12 ff.). Or investigators may determine the correlation between sets of ratings.

Unfortunately, reliabilities of conventional rating procedures, as estimated by the correlation between ratings given by
two independent judges, are generally low (see Thorndike, p. 362).
However, it is possible to pool the ratings of a number of independent judges and substantially increase the reliability of the ratings. The pooling functions in the same way as lengthening a test.

Reliabilities can also be computed for mean scores of groups
of students or trainees. The mean scores are ordinarily more stable
than individual scores, and the reliability coefficients based on
group means are consequently higher than those based on individual scores. Consider, for example, this case: Two students take a
test with a reliability coefficient of .50 (based on individual
scores); if one student scores at the fiftieth percentile and the
other at the seventy-fifth percentile on the first administration of
the test, the probability that their standings will be reversed in a
second administration of the test is about .37. On the other hand,
if the two initial scores were the *means* for two groups of twenty-
five students each, the chances that they will reverse in a second
administration are less than .05. (See Thorndike and Hagen, p.
194.) Thus, while a test with low reliability may be a poor instrument for drawing conclusions about individuals, it may be adequate for drawing conclusions about groups. This is obviously an
important consideration for evaluators of education/training pro-

grams, where decisions frequently are made on the basis of group results. (The evaluator should be reminded that most of the reliability coefficients given in test manuals are based on individual scores and thus normally underestimate the reliability of group means.)

In evaluation studies, it is important that the measures used be reliable. However, just as a measure may be valid for some groups and purposes (and according to some definitions) and not for others, a measure may be reliable enough for some applications and decisions and not for others. For example, the same test might provide reliable measurement of the mathematical abilities of high school freshmen but not of fifth graders; or the results of a questionnaire may be reliable when averaged across responders but may not provide a very reliable description of any one responder. —R. T. M.

Cronbach, L. J. *Essentials of Psychological Testing.* (3rd Ed.) New York: Harper, 1970. See especially Chapter 6.

Dick, W., and Hagerty, N. *Topics in Measurement: Reliability and Validity.* New York: McGraw-Hill, 1971. See especially Chapters 1 through 3.

Dyer, H. S., and King, R. G. *College Board Scores: Their Use and Interpretation.* Princeton, N.J.: Educational Testing Service, 1955.

Gulliksen, H. *Theory of Mental Tests.* New York: Wiley, 1950. See especially Chapters 15 and 16.

Livingston, S. A. "Criterion-Referenced Applications of Classical Test Theory." *Journal of Educational Measurement,* 1972, *9* (1), 13-26.

Thorndike, R. L. "Reliability." In D. N. Jackson and S. Messick (Eds.), *Problems in Human Assessment.* New York: McGraw-Hill, 1967. Pp. 217-240.

Thorndike, R. L., and Hagen, E. *Measurement and Evaluation in Psychology and Education.* (3rd Ed.) New York: Wiley, 1969.

———————————— REPLICATION ————————————

Replication involves the attempt to do again what has been done before, and in the sciences it refers specifically to carrying out an experiment or study previously carried out. There are degrees of replication. In a "direct" (Sidman) or "literal" (Lykken) replication, the second study is exactly imitative of the first. In a "systematic" (Sidman) or "operational" (Lykken) replication, the second study tries to duplicate exactly the procedures of the first study but allows other features to vary. Finally, in a "constructive" (Lykken) replication, the second study avoids imitation of the first study's procedures, measures, etc., and uses quite different techniques in an attempt to establish the same conclusions.

In the physical sciences, the replication or repetition of experiments is commonly carried out. In the social sciences, it is relatively rare, perhaps because duplicating treatments, measurements, and populations is difficult and journal editors seem to prefer new studies.

The advantage of an exact replication which produces results similar to those obtained from the first study is that one can be more confident of the validity of those results. For example, consider a computer-aided instructional program given under specified conditions to a random sample of the entering freshmen in a service academy; if this procedure were replicated with the same procedures and with a second random sample of the same population, and if the results obtained were similar in both instances, then one would be more confident of the results than if the replication had not taken place. Too often in education and training, the positive results of a single evaluation study are accepted as the basis for costly program changes with no attempt made to substantiate the initial results through replication.

Exact replication permits substantiation, but it does not permit greater generalization of results. That is, when an evaluation is replicated and the replication yields similar results, we can be more confident that the results are valid—but we cannot say that the results can be generalized to variations on the treatment or to different populations. Yet, in the evaluation of training and educational programs, such generalization may be crucial; for our populations are constantly changing, along with our needs to extend our instructional innovations. In order to make needed generalizations, we require other kinds of replication. For example, a new training program might be tested on recruits in different base camps, or a television program to teach reading might be evaluated across a number of sites. If the program seems to work in one site or one grade and not another, the degree to which we can or cannot generalize conclusions about the effectiveness of the program is made clearer. In another situation, we might want to try to keep the student population and our measurements the same but make some variations in teaching techniques. Then, if we got similar results, we might conclude that the basic program was effective even under such variations as we imposed.—D. A. T., S. B.

Lykken, D. T. "Statistical Significance in Psychological Research." *Psychological Bulletin.* 1968, *70,* 151-159.

Shaver, J. P., and Larkins, A. C. "Research on Teaching Social Studies." In M. M. W. Travers (Ed.), *Second Handbook of Research on Teaching.* Chicago: Rand McNally, 1973. Replication is discussed (pp. 1252-1254) in the context of research and evaluation in social studies programs.

Sidman, M. *Tactics of Scientific Research: Evaluating Experimental Data in Psychology.* New York: Basic Books, 1960. See discussion of replication as a tool of inquiry (pp. 73-111).

———————— REQUEST FOR PROPOSAL (RFP) ————————

The Request for Proposal (or RFP) is a popular technique used by government agencies, military units, large city school systems, state departments of education, and other groups to solicit research, development, dissemination, and evaluation services at a reasonable price. An RFP is generally developed by the agency staff or consultants. It consists of statements outlining the job to be done, the time schedule, and any specific constraints under which the contractor will have to work (e.g., staff commitments, personnel policies, cost ceilings). It is issued to a selected list of possible contractors, with a date by which proposals must be submitted. Sometimes there is a public announcement (in newspapers or the *Commerce Business Daily*) of the availability of the RFP; sometimes, too, a bidders' conference is held between the date of the issuance of the RFP and the due date for the proposal, with agency personnel available to answer questions about the work and intent.

Occasionally, an RFQ (Request for a Statement of Competency and Qualifications) precedes the issuance of an RFP. This enables the agency to narrow the RFP mailing list to an appropriate group of potential bidders; marginally relevant organizations then will not need to go to all the trouble of preparing formal proposals, and the requesting agency will not waste time reviewing them.

In principle, the RFP is a very fair way of giving many groups an opportunity to bid on a project and giving the issuing agency data on which to make informed decisions about competency to perform. In practice, RFPs, or the agencies responsible for them, have been criticized on a number of grounds: (1) lack of specificity in the RFP or, conversely, too much specificity, so that there is little room left for any creative problem solving on the part of the potential contractor; (2) requirements that reveal failure on the part of the RFP authors to understand technical or practical aspects of the work they are requesting; (3) issuance of an RFP when in fact the agency is already leaning toward—or, even worse, actually committed to—a particular bidder; (4) the equally questionable practice of providing one or more groups with advance information about the RFP so that they can get ahead on the preparation of the proposal; (5) issuance of a vague RFP with the intention not of actually letting a contract but of getting ideas for a more specific RFP to be put out later for bids; (6) failure to make the selection criteria clear (e.g., selecting only on the basis of cost when it had been implied that quality would be given equal consideration) or to obtain competent reviews of the proposals submitted. Many complaints of these types come no doubt from unsuccessful and disgruntled bidders. Some, however, are justified, and it is incumbent on the agency issuing the RFP to assign knowledgeable people to prepare it, to leave some room for input from the contractor (in the long run this should result in a more imaginative product or service), to make the selection procedure as clear and valid as possible, and certainly to be—and appear to be—above suspicion of bias or devious motives.

Strangely, the "how-to-do-it" literature seems to provide more help for the writer of the proposal than for the writer of an RFP. Several useful guides to proposal development are listed at the end of this article. Unfortunately, such guides frequently fail to cover what the proposer is to do when he feels that he cannot comply fully with the terms of the RFP. He may see serious technical or procedural problems with the requirements. For example, he may feel that the evaluation design specified provides an inappropriate basis for the inferences to be made about the value of the instructional program. Or he may recognize that the time allowed for carrying out certain activities is inadequate. The bidder may be able to work out such problems with the issuing agency, but, in any case, he should propose only what he can in good conscience do. However, he should clearly *label* the parts of his proposal that deviate from the terms of the RFP (otherwise he may be considered unresponsive to it) and give reasons for the changes. Issuing agencies have even been known to welcome such feedback from bidders and to change their own requirements accordingly.

Bidders also have a right to protect the original contents of their proposals from misuse such as that suggested earlier (in item 5). One rather straightforward way of calling attention to this right is to include a statement in the proposal to the effect that the information furnished is to be used only to evaluate the offeror's proposal. When a proposal is accepted by the issuing agency, other rights remain to be negotiated at contract time. These include the copyrighting and future use of products and publications resulting from the work performed.—S. B. A.

American Association of School Administrators. *The School Executive's Guide to Performance Contracting.* Washington,

D.C.: AASA, 1972. Appendix B (p. 40) includes a sample RFP.

Hall, M. *Developing Skills in Proposal Writing.* Corvallis, Ore.: Office of Federal Relations, Oregon State System of Higher Education, 1971. Includes a section on the preproposal phase and sources of ideas (including RFPs) and a section on writing the proposal (choosing a title; preparing budgets, timetables, deadlines).

Jacquette, F. L., and Jacquette, B. L. "What Makes a Good Proposal?" *Foundation News,* 1973, *14,* 18-21.

Krathwohl, D. R. *How to Prepare a Research Proposal: Suggestions for Those Seeking Funds for Behavioral Science Research.* Syracuse, N.Y.: Syracuse University Book Store, 1966. The table of contents serves as a checklist to analyze a proposal's strengths and weaknesses with respect to problem statement, procedure, design, facilities, personnel, budget, etc. An appendix on special kinds of studies is also included.

Urgo, L. A. *A Manual for Obtaining Government Grants.* Boston: Robert J. Corcoran Co., 1972. Includes model letters (from the initial inquiry to the letter requesting specific reasons for not funding), instructions for preparing an abstract, tips on proposal writing and a list of typical shortcomings, a list of government criteria for training programs, model evaluation sheets, and material on the interdisciplinary approach and federal funds.

———————————— RESPONSE SETS ————————————

The responses a person makes to a test may be determined not only by item content but also by the form of item used and other aspects of the test situation. The item form or the test directions, for example, may induce temporary strategies or preferences that systematically influence responses, such as the tendency to respond quickly rather than accurately. In addition, the examinee may characteristically bring to tests of certain forms various test-taking attitudes and habits, such as a tendency to respond "true" or to agree when in doubt, that produce a cumulative effect on his score. Properties of test form, then, may differentially influence an individual's mode of item response and may also permit the operation of preferred or habitual styles of response. These stylistic response consistencies are called *response sets*. A response set is a habit or temporary disposition that causes a person to respond to test items differently from the way he would respond if the same content were presented in a different form or context.

Thus, a test presumed to measure one characteristic (such as knowledge or ability or interests) may also be measuring another characteristic (response set) that might not have been reflected in the score if some other form of test had been administered. The term *form* is here used loosely to include all aspects of the test situation to which the examinee may react, including the item type, the tone of its statement, the number and nature of response alternatives provided, the test directions, instructions for guessing, and the presumed use to which the scores will be put.

Response-set variance is of two major types: (1) transitory consistencies limited to a particular test or to a single testing session and (2) reliable, stable consistencies with some generality over tests and situations. Two types of stable consistencies may also be distinguished in turn: (a) the type that reflects durable but relatively trivial individual differences (perhaps in language usage or expressive habits) and (b) the type that reflects significant aspects of personality. Since this latter type of stable response-set variance may be of special importance as a potential indicator of personality characteristics, it has been given the distinctive label of *response style*. A response style is a consistency in the manner of response to some aspect of test form other than *specific* item content; it is relatively enduring over time and displays some generality in responses both in other tests and in nontest behavior (Jackson and Messick).

Some of the major kinds of response sets that have been identified in the literature include:

1. *Tendency to gamble or guess*—reliable individual differ-

ences in the tendency to guess when in doubt, varying from a tendency to respond only when certain, to a penchant for attempting every item.

2. *Speed versus accuracy*—reliable differences in preference for responding rapidly, as opposed to carefully and accurately.

3. *Evasiveness, indecision, and indifference*—the inclination to use the noncommittal middle category on a variety of response options, such as the neutral category on attitude scales, the "?" on the "yes-?-no" format, or the "indifferent" choice on the "like-indifferent-dislike" option.

4. *Interpretation of judgment categories*—reliable preferences for particular response options, due at least in part to stable differences in viewpoint about the meaning and score of the judgment categories provided; e.g., two persons with the same "real" pattern of interests would receive quite different scores if one consistently interpreted the "like" category in a "like-indifferent-dislike" format to include anything that he did not dislike, while the other limited its application to those things that he actively desired or advocated.

5. *Extremeness*—consistent tendencies to mark extreme categories as opposed to more moderate ones on rating scales. (In addition to its possible occurrence as a result of differences in the interpretation of judgment categories, the tendency to respond extremely may also stem from a "desire for certainty" or may reflect self-confidence in expressing opinions.)

6. *Confidence*—the consistent tendency, independent of ability or knowledge, to select options such as "Correct answer not given" or "None of the above" on multiple-choice items.

7. *Inclusiveness*—the tendency to give many responses as opposed to few when no specific limit is placed on the number of responses required (as in the instructions to "List the activities that interest you" or "Mark those statements that reflect your attitudes").

8. *Criticalness*—consistent differences in the strictness of evaluating the equivalence of objects or their acceptability in terms of some standard; e.g., the tendency to respond "different," as opposed to "same," in appraising the equivalence of two possibly equivalent alternatives.

9. *Acquiescence*—reliable tendencies to answer "true" on

true-false examinations or to respond "agree," "like," and "true" on personality, interest, and attitude questionnaires when the respondent lacks knowledge or certainty about his answers.

10. *Tendency to respond desirably*—the tendency to respond not to specific item content but to a more general connotation of an item's meaning—namely, its desirability. This tendency apparently stems not so much from a deliberate attempt to put oneself in a favorable light as from an unwitting bias in self-regard.

11. *Tendency to fake*—the tendency to distort responses in order to bias the impression given to the examiner. This bias in self-report, which seems to be at least partially deliberate, is usually detected on items having a marked discrepancy between the judged desirability of the characteristic described and its frequency of occurrence. A variety of detection or "validity" scores, such as the *Lie* scale on the Minnesota Multiphasic Personality Inventory, are included in standard personality questionnaires.

12. *Tendency to deviate*—consistent tendencies to respond atypically, to give a response deviant from the judged modal response of some reference group.

The operation of response sets may either increase or decrease the **Reliability** and empirical **Validity** of scores. However, since they cause individuals with the same "true" trait or ability level to receive different test scores, response sets seriously attenuate logical or construct validity and complicate interpretations. Thus, response sets tend to introduce errors of measurement that should be avoided or controlled.

Procedures for controlling response sets include (a) changing the test form to prevent their occurrence (e.g., using multiple-choice instead of true-false items to preclude acquiescence), (b) modifying directions to reduce their operation (e.g., providing explicit instructions on guessing, such as "Be sure to answer every item"), and (c) using special response-set scores to correct or partial out their influence (see **Achievement Test Construction**). If fixed response categories are used, the alternatives should be defined as clearly and as objectively as possible. Whenever the occurrence of a particular response set is thought likely, the instructions should be written to provide more structure and to reduce ambiguity, thereby increasing the likelihood of consistent interpretation of the items by individuals. When a response set is used as a measure of personality, of course, such control procedures should be avoided and the test conditions should be designed to elicit the response tendencies of interest and to heighten their influence.—S. M.

Berg, I. A. (Ed.) *Response Set in Personality Assessment.* Chicago: Aldine-Atherton, 1967. A general treatment of the response-set problem, with particular emphasis on the meaning and control of acquiescence, desirability, and deviation tendencies.

Cronbach, L. J. "Response Sets and Test Validity." *Educational and Psychological Measurement,* 1946, *6,* 475-494.

Cronbach, L. J. "Further Evidence on Response Sets and Test Design." *Educational and Psychological Measurement,* 1950, *10,* 3-31.

Jackson, D. N., and Messick, S. "Content and Style in Personality Assessment." *Psychological Bulletin,* 1958, *55,* 243-252.

Messick, S. "Response Sets." In D. L. Sills (Ed.), *International Encyclopedia of the Social Sciences.* Vol. 5. New York: Macmillan and Free Press, 1968. Pp. 492-496.

--------------------------------- SAMPLING ---------------------------------

A *census* studies all elements of a population. A *sample* comprises some (but generally not all) of the elements of a population selected for study. Sampling refers to the techniques and procedures involved in selecting elements from a population and to the particular methods of data analysis appropriate to the sample-selection method. Investigators frequently sample from a population rather than conduct a census if sampling will meet the precision requirements of the investigation. Sampling is also undertaken in the interests of (a) speedy conduct of the study, (b) low cost of operations, and sometimes (c) data collection where a census might be preferred but either cannot be done at all or cannot be done well. If the intent of an evaluation is to characterize part or all of a population, then sampling should be considered.

A *population* is a set (or collection) of all elements possessing one or more attributes of interest. Examples are (a) the set of all men who enlist in the navy on a given day, (b) the set of all flashlights of the same type produced by a company in a given fiscal year, (c) the set of all students enrolled in a given course of instruction, and (d) the set of all rounds of ammunition for a given piece of ordnance. A population may be of *finite size* (contain a finite number of elements) or of *infinite size* (contain an infinite number of elements). Examples a, b, and c above illustrate finite populations; example d is infinite in size if it is intended to consist of all rounds that have been produced and, additionally, of all that might be produced in the future.

The exact procedure for selecting elements from any given population must be designed to fit the specific circumstances of the study. The design should be developed with care, for the kind of sample will determine many attributes of the resulting data. Samples may be considered to belong to one of two broad categories: subjective or objective.

Subjective samples, also called purposive samples, are those having elements selected because of their perceived importance or utility (for example, an expert may be asked to apply his judgment in designating which elements of a population should be selected) or the administrative ease of data collection (students in the closest classroom or the first box of items completed in a manufacturing production run). Subjective samples can be useful, and inferences regarding the attributes of the population can be made, provided sufficient consideration is given to the relevant factors and well-informed judgments are applied to the selection process. Subjective samples, however, often raise concerns that the considerations have been insufficient and that the judgments have not been as informed as the problem requires. The prevalence of such concerns has tended to diminish the use of subjective sampling in formal studies of population characteristics.

Objective samples are obtained by procedures which attempt to avoid the biases often encountered in subjective sampling. Objective sampling begins by constructing a *frame* for the population. The frame is as complete a list as possible of all elements in the population, often consisting of identification numbers or names and addresses (see **Confidentiality of Data**). Once a frame has been constructed, elements are selected from it for inclusion in the study. If the selection is properly executed, characteristics obtained from the resulting sample may be inferred to be characteristics of all elements named in the frame. However, inference usually is not extended to the population, since segments of the population may have been impossible to frame or may have been inadvertently omitted from the frame, a condition which might be termed *underregistration*. *Overregistration* occurs whenever inappropriate elements (elements from another population than that of interest) are framed. In large-scale projects it is not unusual for both overregistration and underregistration to occur. Since inference is generally limited to the frame, considerable effort should be expended to obtain a frame as free of under- and overregistration as possible.

There are a great variety of objective sampling procedures. *Systematic* samples are those obtained by selecting every kth element of a population, such as every tenth folder from a filing cabinet (where the set of all folders is the frame). The process is often fast and accurate but sometimes results in unanticipated biases arising from the systematic arrangement of subpopulations within the population. Selection of every fifth student from a classroom could, for example, exclude everyone except students who sit in the front row, and selection of every fifth house on a street could greatly overrepresent corner houses. Some of these problems may be overcome by dividing the frame into groups and selecting a first element from each group through the use of a random number between 1 and k (using a random-number table) and selecting every kth element thereafter. Such samples are termed *systematic random samples*. Systematic samples, random or otherwise, make certain combinations impossible.

The *simple random sample* is selected by first framing the population and then selecting the desired number of elements, n, as the first n distinct random numbers (from a random-numbers table) less than or equal to the frame size. This procedure allows every element of the population to have the same probability of being selected into the sample. Simple random samples avoid most of the problems mentioned earlier. This kind of sample is the simplest fully randomized one and is probably more frequently used than any other objective kind.

When a population is characterized by great variability in the attributes of interest, it is sometimes possible to divide the population into mutually exclusive subpopulations so that, within each subpopulation, there is relatively little variability. Then *stratified random sampling* procedures, which involve selecting a simple random sample from each stratum (mutually exclusive subpopulation), can be used. When stratified random sampling procedures are applied appropriately, the characteristics of the population can be estimated with greater precision than if a simple random sample of the same size had been selected from the unstratified population.

Sometimes it is convenient to select the sample in stages, using simple random sampling at each stage. One might, for example, select a few schools at random (from a defined population of schools), then select a few classrooms at random (from the population of classrooms in each selected school), then select a few students at random (from the population of students in each selected classroom). Such samples are called *multistage random samples* (in this example, three-stage). The elements of the first stage (in the example, schools) are called *primary sampling units* or PSUs. Elements of other stages are similarly numbered (e.g., secondary sampling units). In the example above, it might have been preferred to select all students in each selected classroom. Such a sample, selecting all elements within the next-to-last stage, is termed a *cluster sample*.

Cluster sampling is very often used in education evaluation projects where there are natural clusters of schools and people within them. In a survey of secondary school principals, for example, school districts might be selected as PSUs, followed by the selection of all principals in each of the selected districts; again, in a survey of teachers, the districts and schools might be selected in the first two stages, followed by selection of all teachers within the selected schools. When natural clusters are present, it is often easier to administer evaluative instruments by cluster sampling than by other approaches; thus, the administration of a test to all students in a classroom is often easier to accomplish properly than would be the selection of (and subsequent administration to) a random sample of the students within the classroom, especially if statistically unsophisticated staff must perform the selection. However, proper design of a cluster sample (to ensure precise estimates of population characteristics) is often a difficult and complicated process; so the presence of natural clusters and ease of administration should not be the sole determiners of the choice of cluster sampling.

Multistage random samples and cluster samples do not require complete frames, and generally framing is done only where appropriate. Thus, in the example, students would be listed only for the selected classrooms in selected schools. This feature is of great economic benefit in *area-frame sampling* (generally a form of multistage sampling), in which, for example, a large number of counties might be selected at the first stage; voting precincts within in selected counties might be selected at the second stage; and, at the third and final stage, a door-to-door census might be conducted within the areas (precincts) to frame households or individuals, thereby avoiding the necessity of making a census of the nation in order to construct a frame.

Sampling procedures have also been applied to the **Quality Control** of production processes, generally by the periodic random selection of a few items from each production lot. After some history of sampling has been generated, the production-quality level can be monitored through classification of the results of a single sample as within control limits (acceptable quality) or out of control (excessive quality or inadequate quality). *Acceptance sampling* is a variant of this procedure: If the number of defective items selected is excessive (in statistical terms), the entire lot would be rejected as of inferior quality; otherwise, the entire lot would be accepted.

Certain biases, called *nonresponse biases*, may occur in samples unless every designated element of the sample is actually included in the study. For this reason, strong efforts to obtain high rates of response are to be preferred to the practice of drawing a too-large sample in anticipation of a low response rate. The latter strategy is a poor one, since it encourages the presence of bias. In some circumstances, where small amounts of bias are innocuous, the ideal 100-percent response rate may be slightly relaxed. In *quota sampling,* for example, a worker is assigned a list of elements to obtain for the study, and a quota (usually a preestablished proportion) of these elements must be obtained. When high quotas are set, potential biases are small and good results have been obtained. Low quotas, on the other hand, have been associated with highly biased results.

In many sampling designs the user is faced with a choice among the ways in which the desired number of sample elements may be allocated to sections of the population. In a stratified random sample having four strata, from which a fixed total number of elements are to be selected, one may consider at least three methods of allocating subsample sizes to the four strata. The simplest procedure would be to draw an equal number of elements at random from each stratum.

If the strata are of unequal sizes (contain different numbers of elements), or if they differ in the degree of variability within the strata, such a method would be inefficient. To avoid the first problem, one might employ *proportional allocation*; i.e., select a number of elements from each stratum proportional to the size of the stratum, using the same proportion for all strata. If there are appreciable differences in variability, proportional allocation may be replaced by *optimum allocation,* a generic term referring usually to methods of maximizing precision of estimates, minimizing costs, or to combinations of cost-precision considerations. A maximum-precision approach, for example, consists of allocating sample elements to strata in numbers proportional to the variances of the strata.

A relatively new method, that of allocating observations with probabilities proportional to size, has improved the precision of some sample estimates of population characteristics. In this method, data already available are used to assign a "measure of size" to each element of the population. The probability that a given element will be selected is then determined, based on the sample design and the number of observations required, so that the probability of selection is proportional to the "measure of size." If the measure of size is strongly related to the actual size of the element, estimates of population size are facilitated. To illustrate, suppose we wish to select a sample of counties. If we take the measure of county size to be the number of inhabitants as of the latest census, and if we allocate the sample across the population of counties so that larger (more populous) counties have higher probabilities of being selected (i.e., if the probability that a county will be selected is proportional to the population size of that county), then estimates of the population size of the frame of counties can usually be derived from the sample with good precision.

In practice, decisions about sample designs and methods of allocating observations are frequently not as clear-cut as this discussion might suggest. Compromises associated with developing the **Survey Methods** to be used in a given survey often control or affect sampling strategies that can be employed, and frequently a combination of strategies is required. Furthermore, many sample designs, especially the more complicated ones, require that a series of adjustments be made on the data before meaningful estimates of population parameters can be obtained (a procedure referred to as *weighting*). Such designs also tend to involve biased estimators (i.e., statistics which do not, on the average, equal their corresponding population parameters); the biases are often so small as to be inappreciable, and there may be compensatory improvements in precision or reductions in cost. Nonetheless, such factors as bias, weighting, allocation, and sample plan tend to act in concert to produce an intricate problem which must be carefully considered before the sample is actually drawn.—F. R. C.

Cochran, W. G. *Sampling Techniques.* (2nd Ed.) New York: Wiley, 1963. A comprehensive, technical introduction to sampling.

Johnson, N. L., and Smith, H., Jr. (Eds.) *New Developments in Survey Sampling.* New York: Wiley, 1969. A collection of papers presented at a symposium on survey sampling. Highly technical but of interest to the advanced, statistically oriented student.

Kish, L. *Survey Sampling.* New York: Wiley, 1965. Another comprehensive, technical introduction to sampling.

Stephan, F. F., and McCarthy, P. J. *Sampling Opinions.* New York: Wiley, 1958. Part I provides an introduction to the nature and role of sampling.

SCALES

The term *scale,* in the measurement sense, comes from the Latin word *scala,* meaning "ladder" or "flight of stairs." Hence, anything with gradations can be thought of as "scaled." We use scales to provide a standard of reference to measure the properties of an object or event.

There are different kinds of scales; and these different kinds of scales can themselves be ordered. The ordering of scales is sometimes referred to as *levels of measurement.* There are four of these levels: nominal, ordinal, interval, and ratio.

The most primitive level is the *nominal* scale. We have a nominal scale when objects or events are merely classified (see qualitative **Variables**). Numbers can be assigned to the classification; e.g., subjects in an evaluation may be classified as 1 (male) or 2 (female), or curriculum materials may be classified from 1 to 12, depending on the grade in school in which they are usually introduced. There is little that one can do arithmetically or statistically with such nominal-scale numbers. It makes little sense to add a 1 (male) and a 2 (female)—and arrive at a 3. However, a nominal scale does facilitate sorting and counting objects or events (especially when computers and related technology are used). And the frequency counts obtainable can be analyzed by such techniques as chi square (see **Nonparametric Statistics**).

The next scale, or next level of measurement, is the *ordinal* scale, used when the objects or events to be measured can be arranged from least (smallest, etc.) to most (largest, etc.). Rankings such as percentiles (see **Score Types**) are examples of an ordinal scale. As with the nominal scale, one cannot legitimately add, subtract, multiply, or divide numbers from an ordinal scale. Consider a student who obtained a percentile rank of 99 on the midterm exam and 59 on the final; consider another student who received a percentile of 79 on both tests. These numbers are rankings—they merely indicate the ordering of the students who took the test. As an exercise, assume that these percentiles (99,

59; 79, 79) correspond to CEEB scores. Is the total CEEB score over both tests the same for both students? (*If* the percentiles were added, each student would have a "total" percentile of 158.) Look at Figure 1 in **Score Types** to work out your answer.

We can perform some statistical analyses with ordinal data; e.g., we can use rank-correlation techniques to assess the relationship between the rankings of an experimental group on a pretest with their rankings at posttest (see **Nonparametric Statistics** and **Correlation**).

The next level of measurement is the *interval* scale, and the highest level is the *ratio* scale. An interval scale allows us to say how far apart two scores are, because adjoining units on the scale are always equidistant from each other, no matter where they are on the scale. A ratio scale shares this property and, in addition, has a true zero. The Fahrenheit thermometer represents an interval scale: The difference between 58°F and 59°F is the same as the difference between 97°F and 98°F, but 0°F does not mean zero heat. A foot rule represents a ratio scale: the inch difference between 6″ and 7″ is the same as the difference between 9″ and 10″, and here 0″ does mean absence of length. With the ratio scale it makes sense to say that 6″ is twice as long as 3″. It is not true, however, that 100°F is twice as warm as 50°F—though it is 50°F warmer. Thus, addition and subtraction are proper procedures with both interval and ratio scales; but only with ratio scales should one use multiplication and division.

The distinctions among these scales have more than academic interest. They determine the kinds of statistical treatments we can use on our data; for example, the appropriate measure of central tendency for use with a nominal scale is the mode, whereas the median may be used with an ordinal scale, and the mean with an interval or ratio scale (see **Statistics**).

We clearly recognize that most of our measures of achievement, aptitude, etc., do *not* have ratio scales; for example, we reject the absurd notion that the person who gets a zero score on a vocabulary test has no vocabulary. We tend to think of such measures as having interval scales. However, there is some controversy on this point, with one school of thought maintaining that, at best, we have ordinal scales. On the one hand, one can argue that the difference between IQs of 99 and 100 is not necessarily the same as that between 129 and 130—and that all the IQ scale does is *order* the persons taking the test. On the other hand, one may argue that these differences *can* be treated as equal and that even physical measures, which appear to have interval-scale properties, do not have these properties in some absolute sense; for example, it may involve a lot more energy and effort to increase the heat in a house from 75°F to 76°F than from 65°F to 66°F, and it may be more difficult to increase typing speed from 50 to 55 words per minute than from 30 to 35 words per minute.

Tyler advises us to assume that we have an interval measure when using achievement and aptitude scores and to assume that the interval-scale assumption is a "model" to be used in the same way a geologist uses a model to study mountain ranges. As long as the model leads to conclusions that are useful and appear to be valid, we continue to employ it. But a caution is still in order. While it may be statistically convenient to continue to assume that our test scores derive from an interval scale, the assumption may sometimes present us with conceptual difficulties. Consider this example: After two months, a middle-class group of sixth graders gains six months in achievement in an experimental reading program (from a grade equivalent score of 7.0 to 7.6) and a lower-class group of sixth graders also gains six months (from 3.0 to 3.6). Assuming that we have proper controls in our design, can we conclude that the program is equally effective with both groups? Probably not. It would be better to conclude only that the program was effective for both groups.

(And now remember the problem posed earlier in this article. The total CEEB score would be substantially greater for the student with the percentiles of 99 and 59.)—S. B., A. Y.

Stevens, S. S. *Handbook of Experimental Psychology.* New York: Wiley, 1951. See the chapter on mathematics, measurement, and psychophysics for a discussion of levels of measurement as used in psychology.

Thorndike, R. L. *Educational Measurement.* (2nd Ed.) Washington, D.C.: American Council on Education, 1971. See the chapters by L. V. Jones and W. H. Angoff.

Tyler, L. E. *Tests and Measurements.* (2nd Ed.) Englewood Cliffs, N.J.: Prentice-Hall, 1971. Chapter 1 has a clear presentation of levels of measurement.

———————— SCIENTIFIC INQUIRY AND EVALUATION ————————

Evaluation, as we have defined it, bases its methodology on the social sciences (see **Evaluation Concepts** and **Adversary Model of Evaluation**). In this article, some of the major tenets of scientific inquiry, especially as they relate to the social sciences, will be presented.

A science in its most primitive stages consists of a collection of descriptions of events. An example of such a description is the following: "Joey learned his lessons very quickly when he was allowed to watch television immediately thereafter." More methodological sophistication is required and a greater body of data must be known before the following general statement can justifiably be made: "Learning occurs faster when a reward immediately follows the response to be learned."

The second statement is more than a description—it is a *hypothesis,* and it provides an *explanation.* The greater power of an explanation lies in its capacity for generalization and prediction. Once such a hypothesis is confirmed, it may be applied to future events and stated in a specific form, such as "Billy will learn to play the oboe more quickly if, as soon as he has finished practicing, he is given a piece of his favorite pie." To be able to draw inferences, to make predictions, and to have such predictions come true is one of the primary goals of science.

A generalized statement or set of statements which provides an explanation for a class of events is called a hypothesis or a theory. The distinction between the two is not well defined. Often we speak of a hypothesis as a generalization, but one which is not quite so general as a theory.

Theory is often used to refer to an explanation entailing many very general hypotheses comprising a system of basic axioms or postulates. These axioms are the higher-level laws of the system. They express relations between concepts (theoretical constructs) which are not in themselves observable. "Electrons" and "intelligence" are examples of theoretical constructs. Lower-level laws or hypotheses are specific instances (initial conditions) deduced from the axioms. The advantage of such an axiomatic system is that it can be reduced to a minimal number of general laws from which all specific cases can be derived and tested. The general hypothesis from learning theory which was stated earlier could be an axiom from which statements about specific children and specific learning situations could be derived.

A theory must be *testable* in principle. Just what evidence would count against it must be clear. Suppose I were to propose the following hypothesis: "An invisible five-headed leprechaun lives in the corner of my living room and eats newspaper print." If you were a patient and tolerant person, you would then ask me what evidence I have that such a creature exists. I would say that I have none—I just know it is there. You again patiently point out that we cannot hear, feel, or smell the leprechaun. I reply that it is very quiet; it moves away when we move toward it, and it has no smell. You proceed to show me that no newspapers are missing, nor has any print come off the ones that are here. I again formulate an ad hoc hypothesis. And we go on indefinitely until you give up and decide that I have lost all sense of reason. The "theory" of the leprechaun is at best useless, and some would say it is meaningless. Such "theories" lurk in the corners of all sciences.

It has been argued by some that theories are not necessary in science. They are, of course, not necessary unless we wish to draw inferences, generalize, and make predictions. In recent years, models have often been used as alternatives to theories. *Model* has much the same meaning as it does in ordinary language: a system or theory that is well developed in one discipline is applied to another which is less well understood. The function of the brain is less well understood than that of a computer. A computer is in many ways similar to a brain: it takes in information, processes it, stores it, retrieves it, and outputs it in some form. In those respects in which one system resembles another, it is said to model the other. If specific brain functions can be modeled by the basic axioms of computer-system theory, then because of the deductive structure of the theory, specific relations pertaining to brain function can be inferred.

At some point, however, a model generally breaks down— the model and the system modeled are not necessarily equivalent.

The brain is not the same thing as a computer (unless we have a very loose definition of "computer"); the nervous system is not an electric circuit, but it behaves in many ways like one; traffic is not a fluid, but the principles of fluid mechanics can be applied to traffic flow.

We may use a set of mathematical equations, a purely formal system, to relate quantities in the physical world in order to provide a mathematical model of a physical system. One must be cautioned, however, that the property of logical necessity inherent in a mathematical system is not inherent in any physical system.

An education/training program is usually developed on the basis of some theoretical position, though the theory may be implicit rather than explicit. In a sense, then, the evaluation consists of the testing of a hypothesis based on that theory. Thus, if the hypothesis is verified (e.g., if the program is shown to be superior to one based on a different theory), we can draw inferences, generalize, and make predictions (e.g., we may predict that the program will be effective with other groups of students). Note that the evaluator, unlike the social scientist in other applied areas, usually does not have the opportunity to develop the major hypotheses; instead, the program and the hypotheses related to it are the province of the program developer.

How do we confirm or verify a hypothesis? The philosophical problem is the same whether the hypothesis pertains to the physical sciences ("Pressure is proportional to temperature") or the behavioral sciences ("A child learns faster if he is rewarded"), or whether the hypothesis states the expected results of an evaluation ("Language course Q is superior to other language courses"). (See **Evaluation Concepts.**) An evaluation may be viewed philosophically as a particular kind of procedure for formulating and testing hypotheses; as such, it may be crucial to the verification of certain theories (see **Hypothesis Testing**). What does verification entail? In order to confirm a universal proposition (a statement that generalizes to all cases for all time), we would have to test it for all cases over all time. This is clearly impossible in principle as well as in practice. The problem of induction, as this dilemma is called, was recognized at least as early as the eighteenth century. Inferences to general statements can never be made deductively from specific statements. Only after a great many special cases

have been observed can one begin to generalize. Even then there is
no point at which we can say how certain we are that the statement is truly general. (See **Case-Study Method.**)

Let us look further at the process of verification. Many students during the course of their education learn that "scientific
method" is a definite steplike procedure that starts somehow with
the formulation of a hypothesis and ends with a full-blown confirmed theory. This is both naïve and inaccurate. The process, to
begin with, is a cyclic one—it has no first step. We have all made
observations. We make them all the time. We observe traffic when
we cross the street; we notice that a child learns to count exceptionally well when he uses an abacus. It is after we have made
many such observations that we begin to generalize—to form
hypotheses. The critical observer will not stop at this point. He
knows that his observations may be biased or that he may have
certain motives for wanting to generalize. This observer will want
to test his hypothesis.

To do so may require a sophisticated experimental design.
Regardless of the design, if his conclusions support his hypothesis,
we say that it has been confirmed or verified. We know, however,
that if a similar experiment is later performed, and most likely it
will be, the results may be different because of uncontrolled influences that did not exist in the first experiment. No experiment,
survey, or evaluation can be replicated identically. (See **Replication.**)

That phase of verification involving the formulation of a
hypothesis is the *inductive* phase. Testing it is the *deductive* phase.
From a general hypothesis and specific initial conditions we
deduce an expected outcome. Observations of actual outcome
may strengthen our hypothesis or force us to modify it. Rarely do
we discard a hypothesis or theory entirely. That fact is often not
recognized by the layman. Newtonian physics was not disproved
by relativity; instead, a very important correction factor was
added. To show that a particular teaching method does not live up
to one's expectations does not prove that the method is entirely
worthless; nor does success in one instance prove that the teaching
method is beyond reproach.

The cyclic process of repeatedly modifying hypotheses,
deducing their implications, and testing those implications is called

the *hypothetico-deductive method* and is seen to operate most clearly in the physical sciences.

From this procedure, it is evident that we never reach a point where a theory is finally confirmed in any absolute sense. Perhaps we would like to be able to say that it is 95 percent confirmed. But we cannot assign a number to the degree of confirmation. It is not the same thing as "confidence" in the statistical sense. We cannot assign a probability other than zero or one to a universal proposition. We can never be sure that a hypothesis of the form "All P are Q" is true. It is false if we find one counterexample. To test a probabilistic statement, "95 percent of all P are Q," involves the same problems. For a finite population, if 94 percent of all P are Q, the hypothesis has been disproved. Even if we confirm it in the finite case, we cannot generalize to an infinite population or to the future without an inductive leap. We are left with the question "How do we measure the degree of confirmation of the statement '95 percent of all P are Q'?" (See **Statistical Inference** and **Statistical Significance**.)

This leads us into the subject of the meaning of probability. Whether probability means relative frequency in the long run (such as actuarial statistics), degree of confirmation (some hypothesis is "probably" true), degree of certainty ("the probability of rain is 80 percent"), degree of truth ("true 90 percent of the time"), best betting odds ("odds of tossing a head are 50:50"), or any of a number of other definitions is an unsettled issue. It seems that we should, however, distinguish at least two types of probability. The first is *a priori probability*: the probability that we know without having to conduct an experiment. We know, for example, that the probability of tossing a head with an unbiased coin is one half. We know from the structure of the coin that there are only two possible outcomes and that, because we have no other information, those two alternatives are equally likely. The second type is *empirical probability*. In order to know the probability that I will live at least sixty-five years, I must observe how many people in the past have lived that long and what factors are related to longevity. I would then predict on the basis of these data the probability of my living beyond sixty-five. For more detailed discussions of the philosophical foundations of probability, see Carnap (1950) or Reichenbach; probability as a statistical problem is discussed by Feller.

This article has touched very briefly on a number of complex philosophical issues: scientific explanation, the role of theories and models in science, the problems of induction and confirmation, and the nature of probability. No attempt was made to give a thorough and exhaustive account of any of these issues. Evaluation is seen as one kind of procedure for formulating and testing hypotheses (not restricted to statistical **Hypothesis Testing**). It can be an important step in the process of theory verification. (See also "Hard" and "Soft"—Shibboleths in Evaluation.)—J. G.

Carnap, R. *Logical Foundations of Probability*. Chicago: University of Chicago Press, 1950. A different viewpoint from Reichenbach's.

Carnap, R. "The Two Concepts of Probability." In H. Feigl and M. Brodbeck (Eds.), *Readings in the Philosophy of Science*. New York: Appleton-Century-Crofts, 1953.

Feller, W. *An Introduction to Probability Theory and Its Application*. New York: Wiley, 1966.

Hempel, C. G. "The Theoretician's Dilemma: A Study in the Logic of Theory Construction." In H. Feigl, M. Scriven, and G. Maxwell (Eds.), *Minnesota Studies in the Philosophy of Science*. Vol. 2: *Concepts, Theories, and the Mind-Body Problem*. Minneapolis: University of Minnesota Press, 1958.

Hempel, C. G., and Oppenheim, P. "The Logic of Explanation." In H. Feigl and M. Brodbeck (Eds.), *Readings in the Philosophy of Science*. New York: Appleton-Century-Crofts, 1953. A classic in the philosophy of science; somewhat technical.

Nagel, E. *The Structure of Science*. New York: Harcourt, Brace, 1961. A popular introduction to the philosophy of science.

Pap, A. *An Introduction to the Philosophy of Science*. New York: Free Press, 1962. Somewhat more rigorous than Nagel but quite readable; well documented.

Reichenbach, H. *The Theory of Probability*. Berkeley: University of California Press, 1949. A different viewpoint from Carnap's.

─────────────────── SCORE TYPES ───────────────────

A score is a number derived from a measure, but that number has, of itself, little meaning. In order to interpret that number, we have to know the *type* of score the number represents. Consider, for example, a score of +2.0. If this were a standard *z* score (see below), it would indicate that only about 3 percent of those taking the test obtained a better score. On the other hand, if the score +2.0 represented a percentile, it would mean that about 98 percent of those taking the test obtained a better score.

In this article a number of different types of scores will be presented. Some are quite familiar to the lay reader; others are more technical. Some can be readily used in statistical treatments of data; some are not as useful for statistical purposes but are very useful for the presentation of easily understood descriptions of program effects. In an evaluation, the type of score should be chosen with consideration of the purposes for which the scores will be used. Of course, the evaluator is not restricted to one type of score; in fact, if time and budget permit, it may be best to use, for example, one during the initial data collection, another for descriptive display in the report, and a third in the statistical analyses.

Raw score. A raw score, as the name suggests, is the number of points (usually the number of correct answers) obtained on a measure. Raw scores are valuable because they are basic; that is, they can be translated into other types of scores, either by the evaluator or by someone who wishes to study further the evaluator's work. If evaluators do not present all the individual raw scores in their reports, they should at least consider presenting summaries of these raw scores (e.g., means and standard deviations—see **Statistics**). Raw scores are amenable to statistical treatment. Some statistical analyses require that the scores be distributed normally (see **Statistics**), but even skewness in the distribution of raw scores can be overcome by a mathematical transformation. Thus, from a statistical viewpoint raw scores are particularly valuable.

Raw scores have a potential major disadvantage for an evaluation report. They can readily be misinterpreted by the lay reader. For example, a raw score of 70 on a 100-item test may be seen as barely passing, because many people have been led to think that 70 percent correct is a minimum passing score. The sophisticated reader, however, would first want to know more about the difficulty of that test, and what ranking a student with a score of 70 would have among other students taking the test. In a test of **Mastery Learning**, a raw score of 70 out of 100 at **Posttest** might be considered a poor score; however, the same score obtained on a **Pretest** in a new subject area would be quite differently interpreted.

Because it is rare for two tests to be of the same difficulty level, it is usually unreasonable to compare raw scores obtained on different tests. Consider a program to improve the basic educational skills (reading and arithmetic) of trainees. At the end of the program, the trainees on the average obtain 70 correct answers on a 100-item reading test and 60 correct on a 100-item arithmetic test. This does not necessarily mean that the trainees are better at reading than at arithmetic. It might mean that the reading test is an easy one and the arithmetic test relatively difficult. Therefore, the evaluator should not assume that the reading program is more successful than the arithmetic program.

Raw scores obtained on **Criterion-Referenced** measures usually can be more readily interpreted than raw scores from **Standardized Tests** because raw scores on a criterion-referenced measure have some meaning in their own right without reference to a **Norms** group or any external criterion. Consider, for example, a raw score of 15 out of 26 correct on a criterion-referenced letter-naming test. The meaning of this score cannot be specified exactly (we do not know which letters the student was unable to name), but its general import is clear. The score indicates that the person named 15 of the 26 letters correctly. We still do not know whether this is a "good" or "bad" result in relationship to the performance of the student's peers. Thus, raw scores can be interpreted only in the light of other information such as the type of test, its difficulty level, and the scores obtained by other comparable students.

Before one can legitimately compare scores from one test with scores from another test, the raw scores have to be converted to a common metric. The most usual attempts of such conversions involve standard scores, percentile scores, grade-equivalent scores, and age-equivalent scores. In each of these instances, raw scores are interpreted in terms of the performance of some reference group.

Standard score. A standard score is a score coming from an array with a prearranged, arbitrary mean and standard deviation. If the value for the mean is zero and if the value for the standard deviation is 1, we have a standard score known as a z score. Standard z scores can be calculated by the formula $z = (x - \bar{x})/S$, where x is a given raw score, $\bar{x}$ is the raw-score mean of the scores under consideration, and S is the standard deviation of the raw scores under consideration. (See **Statistics**.) A z score indicates the number of standard deviations above (+) or below (–) the mean for a given raw score.

To explain this further, let us return to raw scores. Raw scores have varying means and standard deviations from test to test, even when the number of items in the tests is constant. Thus, it is difficult, as we pointed out earlier, to compare a trainee's score of 70 on a 100-item reading test with his score of 60 on an arithmetic test of the same length. Let us suppose we know that the mean raw score on the first test is 60 and the standard deviation is 10. Then a raw score of 70 is equal to a z score of $(70 - 60)/10 = 10/10 = +1.0$. Let us suppose that the mean raw score on the second test is 40 and the standard deviation is 5. Then a raw score of 60 on the second test is equal to a z score of $(60 - 40)/5 = 20/5 = +4.0$. In short, a raw score on the first test of 70 is equal to a z score of $+1.0$, and a raw score of only 60 on the second test is equal to a z score of $+4.0$. The first test was much easier, and the trainees' scores were more scattered. Standard scores, unlike raw scores, take the mean and the dispersion (scatter) of scores into account. Therefore, standard scores can legitimately be compared from test to test provided they are based on the same population or on a comparable population.

Another commonly used standard score is the IQ. The IQ, as developed for most IQ tests, has a mean of 100 and a standard deviation usually of 15. Thus, for example, the mean raw score on an IQ test is converted to an IQ of 100, and a raw score that is one standard deviation below the mean is converted to an IQ of 85.

The reason for the IQ score having this particular mean and standard deviation is historical, stemming from the time when an actual intelligence quotient was calculated by the formula CA (chronological age)/MA (mental age) X 100 (the multiplication by 100 got rid of fractions).

There are many other standard scores—among them, the College Entrance Examination Board (CEEB) scores, with a mean of 500 and standard deviation of 100; *T* scores, with a mean of 50 and a standard deviation of 10; the Iowa Tests of Educational Development (ITED) scores, with a mean of 15 and a standard deviation of 5; and stanines, with a mean of 5 and a standard deviation of 2.

Percentile. One of the most commonly used score types is the percentile. It indicates the percentage of students whose scores fall *below* a given score. There are other, though similar, definitions (see Ebel, p. 286)—among them, the definition that a percentile indicates the percentage of students whose scores fall *at or below* a given score. The percentile provides a ranking. If a raw score of 27 is given a percentile rank of 85, it simply means that 85 percent of the raw scores in a certain group fall below 27. It does *not* mean that the person with a raw score of 27 has 85 percent of the answers correct. A major advantage of percentiles is that they are easily understood and readily calculated.

Percentile conversion tables can be developed for various reference groups so that a person's raw score can be compared with scores earned by those in each group. The person's raw score might correspond to a percentile of 55 for students in that person's class, to a percentile of 75 for all people in his program, or to a percentile of 40 for college graduates in the program. Thus, a percentile becomes meaningful only when the reference group is known. (See **Norms.**)

A major problem with percentiles is that percentile units have different meanings depending on where they lie in the scale 0-99. This is so because raw scores usually are bunched in the middle of the distribution. A small increase in the number of correct answers for an average student might easily move his percentile ranking on the test from, say, 45 to 55, while a corresponding increase in raw score for a student whose score is among the lowest (or highest) in the group would produce a much smaller change in the percentile rank (see Figure 1).

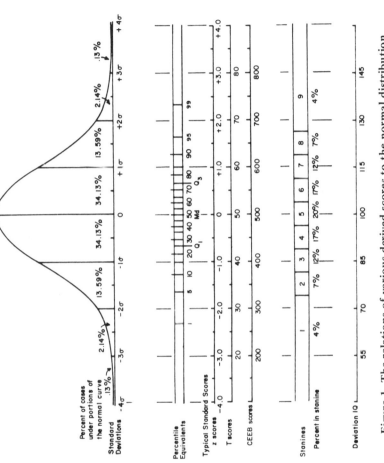

Figure 1. The relations of various derived scores to the normal distribution and to each other. (Courtesy of the Psychological Corporation.)

One use of percentiles in an evaluation is in describing effects on students' relative rankings. For example, in an evaluation of a basic education program for high school dropouts entering the army, it might make sense to indicate their percentile ranks (in terms of the total group of army recruits) in arithmetic and reading before the program and after the program. Assuming the evaluation design is appropriate, then higher percentiles at posttest might be interpreted as indicative of the effects of the program.

Grade-equivalent score. In subject areas that are studied in elementary and high school, it is possible to establish levels of performance to be expected at each grade level. For example, on a sixty-item test in arithmetic a given raw score (say, 30 correct) might be typical of an average beginning sixth-grade student and a raw score of 50 typical of a beginning seventh grade-student. In this fashion it is possible to convert raw scores on the test to a grade-equivalent score (grade plus number of months in that grade).

An apparent virtue of grade-equivalent scores is this simplicity. Suppose that new multigrade classrooms are tried out in a school district and that some children are randomly assigned to these classrooms while others remain in conventional single-grade classrooms. Suppose further that the two groups of children were comparable at the start of the year and that at the end of the year the results look like the presentation of hypothetical data in Table 1.

A lay reader would readily understand from this display that the multigrade experience seems to benefit the fourth graders

Table 1

Average Grade-Equivalent Scores (Hypothetical Data)

	Conventional Grades[a]			Multigrade[b]		
	4th	*5th*	*6th*	*4th*	*5th*	*6th*
Arithmetic Computation	4.6	5.7	6.7	5.9	6.1	6.7
Arithmetic Concepts	4.7	5.8	6.5	5.2	6.0	6.4
Word Knowledge	4.5	5.6	6.7	5.7	5.9	6.6
Reading Comprehension	4.6	5.9	6.8	4.9	5.9	6.7

[a]There were three classes in each of grades 4, 5, and 6.
[b]There were nine classes, each composed of fourth, fifth, and sixth graders in equal one-third proportions.

but may have deleterious effects for the sixth graders. Further, it may be seen that the fourth graders in a new program benefit mainly in arithmetic computation and word knowledge. Even if the scores of the conventional (control) classes were not available, the same conclusions might be reached, though with less confidence. The point is that a **Control Group** already exists—the group of classes who were used initially to obtain the grade-equivalent norms. Note that the conclusions reached here are not based on statistical tests. They are simply based upon judgments made by inspection of mean performances presented in terms of grade-equivalent scores. This is not a technically precise procedure, but it is more readily understood by a lay reader than, for example, the results of a **Multivariate Analysis** of variance based on the raw scores. An evaluator might well consider carrying out and reporting the multivariate analysis of variance *and* displaying the results in terms of grade-equivalent scores.

There are some problems in the use of grade-equivalent scores. One problem is that extreme scores are readily misinterpreted. Extreme scores, no matter what the type of score used, tend to be less reliable than scores in the middle range. But grade-equivalent scores that are extreme suffer in still another way. A beginning second-grade student may obtain an arithmetic score of 3.8, and although this score may correspond to the average score of third graders tested in April, it does not mean that the second-grade student's knowledge of arithmetic is directly comparable with that of a typical third grader. Their individual knowledge and the specific items correctly answered could be quite different.

Another quite common misinterpretation is that grade-equivalent scores represent some kind of standard (see **Standards**). A politician who says "I want every child in my district to be reading above his grade level" probably does not understand what he is asking for. A grade-equivalent score indicates typical performance —not necessarily good or bad performance. If *all* children could be raised in their achievement levels, then the grade-equivalent norms would have to be raised too, so that they could continue to indicate typical performance.

A third problem with the interpretation of grade-equivalent scores lies in the fact that different tests have different score scatters. For example, third graders who read well for their grade frequently perform on reading tests at about the level of a typical sixth grader. Once the basic reading skills have been attained, students can move ahead in reading quickly on their own. In arithmetic, however, performance is more heavily dependent upon classroom instruction. It is quite rare for a third grader to be able to perform in arithmetic at the level of a typical sixth grader. On one frequently used standardized achievement-test battery, a child at the beginning of fourth grade who was at the 88th percentile for fourth graders would have a grade-equivalent score of 6.0 in paragraph meaning but a grade-equivalent score of 4.9 in arithmetic computation. If a child were still closer to the top of his fellow beginning fourth graders (say, at the 96th percentile), he would have a grade-equivalent score of 6.9 in paragraph meaning and 5.3 in arithmetic computation. Thus, as with raw scores, one must be careful in comparing the grade-equivalent scores on one test with those on another.

Grade-equivalent scores are developed by a process of *extrapolation* and *interpolation* and should therefore be interpreted warily. Suppose that a reading test is developed for fourth and fifth graders. The final version of the test will *not* be given to a sample of children in every grade at every month. Rather, it will be given mainly to a sample of children in fourth and fifth grades during some specified period of the school year. The scores are plotted for those months in those grades and a curve then fitted to the plot marks. When the grade-equivalent tables are subsequently constructed, some of the grade-equivalent scores will correspond exactly to actual grade and months when the norms group was tested. The other grade-equivalent scores will be obtained by reference to the fitted curve. Extreme scores (those estimated from outside the grade range tested) are said to be extrapolated. Scores estimated for months within the grade tested are said to be interpolated. The point is, however, that no matter how good the **Sampling**, some grade-equivalent scores are simply estimates.

Age-equivalent score. Age-equivalent scores are similar to grade-equivalent scores in both their development (one looks here for typical performance at various age levels) and interpretation. Thus, they have advantages and disadvantages similar to those of grade-equivalent scores. Age-equivalent scores are more likely to be developed for aptitude tests than for achievement tests. Mental-age scores developed for intelligence tests are the most common examples.

Grade-equivalent scores divide the grade into ten parts to correspond with the ten months in school (presumably, little learning occurs in the two summer-recess months). Age-equivalent scores are divided into twelve parts to correspond to the calendar year. Thus, an age-equivalent score of 9.11 refers to the typical performance of children who are nine years and eleven months of age.

A comparison of standard-score and percentile-score systems can be seen in Figure 1, which assumes a normal distribution. Note, however, that age- and grade-equivalent scores and raw scores cannot readily be plotted on this figure.—S. B.

Angoff, W. H. "Scales, Norms, and Equivalent Scores." In R. L. Thorndike (Ed.), *Educational Measurement*. (2nd Ed.) Washington, D.C.: American Council on Education, 1971. Pp. 508-600. An excellent technical presentation of types of scores.

Downie, N. M. "Types of Test Scores." In S. C. Stone and B. Shertzer (Eds.), *Guidance Monograph Series: III. Testing*. Boston: Houghton Mifflin, 1968.

Ebel, R. L. *Essentials of Educational Measurement*. Englewood Cliffs, N.J.: Prentice-Hall, 1972. See Chapters 11 and 19 for a general discussion of types of scores.

Gronlund, N. E. *Measurement and Evaluation in Teaching*. New York: Macmillan, 1965. See Chapter 14 for a discussion of how to interpret various types of scores.

SECONDARY EVALUATION

Secondary evaluation occurs when the data and/or the reports of an evaluation are studied and reported upon by another evaluator. Secondary evaluation is sometimes referred to as "metaevaluation" because it is a process that occurs "above and be-yond" the primary evaluation. Secondary evaluation is akin to **Audit of Evaluation**, but audits have a different professional con-notation and usually involve activity concurrent with, rather than subsequent to, the primary evaluation.

A secondary evaluation may simply be a critical review of the primary evaluation. This review is especially useful if the pri-mary evaluation employs a complicated research design or com-plex statistical procedures. Then the educated lay reader not only has the report of the primary evaluator to rely on, but also a sec-ond opinion (from the secondary evaluator) on the adequacy of the primary evaluation.

Another kind of secondary evaluation (and one that is more costly) involves reanalysis of the data from the primary evaluation. This reanalysis may be performed to check for accuracy and to test the reasonableness of the results and conclusions from the pri-mary evaluation by using a different method of analysis. It may also seek answers to questions not asked in the primary evaluation; the problem here is that the new questions may be unanswerable in terms of the original measures and design. Care should be taken not to blame the primary evaluation for its failure to provide all the data that might happen to interest a secondary evaluator.

Secondary evaluations have some values. They are usually less tied to the original program and therefore can be more objec-tive. Because time constraints are less pressing, due consideration can be given to worrisome points—there is rarely a deadline by which a secondary evaluation must be finished. Secondary evalua-tions gain, too, from added perspective. Primary evaluations are frequently conducted under political and other pressures that force quick decisions on such issues as data collection and analysis (see **Politics of Evaluation** and **Field Operations**). The effects of these extraneous influences can sometimes best be assessed at a later time by a secondary evaluator.

The secondary evaluator inevitably has the opportunity for displaying his greater "hindsight" wisdom—and hindsight always has 20-20 vision. Therefore, the conclusions from the secondary evaluation may well conflict with those of the primary evaluation. This conflict is most likely if the primary evaluation has egregious flaws; but then almost any practical evaluation effort has *some* flaws. Secondary evaluations might, therefore, be judged in part on the balance between the positive and negative conclusions they contain. If the conflict between the evaluators is intense and if both evaluations have attained prominence, the conflict will eventually be settled by professional peer reviews.—S. B.

Elashoff, J. D., and Snow, R. E. *Pygmalion Reconsidered.* Worthington, Ohio: Charles A. Jones, 1971. A number of secondary evaluations and tertiary evaluations (evaluations of secondary evaluations) are included.

Mayeske, G. W., Wisler, C. E., Beaton, A. E., Jr., Weinfeld, F. D., Cohen, W. M., Okada, T., Proshek, J. M., and Tabler, K. A. *A Study of Our Nation's Schools.* Washington, D.C.: U.S. Department of Health, Education, and Welfare, undated. Reanalysis and reconceptualization of data from the Coleman survey of *Equality of Educational Opportunity* to demonstrate school influences.

Mosteller, F., and Moynihan, D. P. *On Equality of Educational Opportunity.* New York: Vintage Books, 1972. The Coleman study revisited *again.*

Rosenthal, R. R., and Jacobsen, L. *Pygmalion in the Classroom.* New York: Holt, 1968. Contains a primary evaluation of teacher-expectancy effects in classrooms.

Rosenthal, R. R., and Rubin, D. B. "Pygmalion Reassessed." In J. D. Elashoff and R. E. Snow, *Pygmalion Reconsidered.* Worthington, Ohio: Charles A. Jones, 1971. Pp. 139-155. A tertiary evaluation of Elashoff and Snow's secondary evaluation of Rosenthal and Jacobsen's *Pygmalion in the Classroom.*

———————————— SIDE EFFECTS ————————————

As is pointed out in the article **Medical Model of Evaluation,** we should try to assess not only the *intended* outcomes of a program but also a wide range of *possible* outcomes. These possible but unintended outcomes may be referred to as the program's potential side effects.

Side effects may be positive or negative. For example, a staff program in a government department may achieve its intended outcome of providing selected clerical employees with skills enabling them to work at higher-level administrative positions. A positive side effect might be a reduction in absenteeism among the selected clerical employees. A negative side effect might be an increase in absenteeism among clerical employees not selected for this program.

Some side effects may be so crucial that they outweigh the impact of the intended outcomes. A dramatic illustration of this occurred in drug evaluation, where thalidomide was evaluated for its intended outcome and found to be an effective tranquilizer. Later, however, the drug proved to have a negative side effect with pregnant women, causing the death or radical deformity of fetuses. Negative side effects, although not so obviously tragic, occur as well in educational programs—most notably in the affective domain. For example, consider the children who learn arithmetic skills (intended outcomes) but also learn to hate arithmetic and to consider themselves without talent in that subject (negative side effects). To ignore the possibility of such side effects in an evaluation is to carry out an incomplete evaluation.

Sometimes the finding of positive side effects is used to bolster a decision to continue a program, even though the intended outcomes do not occur. For example, a new program for training high school dropouts to become proficient telegraph operators may prove no more effective than the older program for achieving the intended proficiency outcome. But positive side effects are noted, indicating that the trainees in the new program like the work better and are more likely to seek jobs as telegraphists. If the new program costs no more and has no apparent negative side effects, it would seem sensible to adopt it—on the basis of its superior positive side effects.

There are two major problems to be considered in planning the assessment of side effects: (1) *Which* potential side effects should be assessed? (2) *Who* makes the decision? The problem of *which* side effects to investigate out of the myriad possibilities is not an easy one to resolve. Choices have to be made and priorities set in light of the type of program being evaluated, the students for whom it is intended, the coverage of the intended goals, and the potential interactive problems that the presence of specific side effects might create.

If the intended effects are confined to the **Cognitive** or **Psychomotor** domains, it would be wise to assess side effects involving **Attitudinal** and **Affective** changes. In education programs, and to a lesser extent in training programs, the evaluator should be concerned not only with cognitive variables and psychomotor variables as outcomes but also with outcomes related to the feelings and attitudes of those in the program. It may not be worthwhile to learn mathematics if a side effect is to *hate* mathematics.

An evaluation is most likely to register side effects in outcomes closely related to the intended effects of the program. For example, we might expect training in Italian to have some transfer value for Spanish comprehension but little for Hungarian; or an algebra course to affect attitudes toward mathematics but not toward English. When the evaluator is trying to decide which candidate side-effect variables to measure, he may be able to eliminate some on the basis of such judgments about unlikely transfer effects. However, any decision to measure certain possible side effects and ignore others runs the risk of being wrong. The evaluator's best initial strategy is probably to focus major attention on intended effects and a few obvious and important possible side effects. If the evaluation shows that the program has merit and if the program is continued, the next evaluation can simply monitor the achievement of the intended outcomes while engaging in a more elaborate assessment of possible side effects.

The problem of *who* decides which side effects to assess is not easily solved. In general, the program developer can and should specify the intended outcomes of the program, but greater responsibility should be placed on the evaluator to specify the side effects to be assessed. The program developer is too often open to charges of wanting to minimize or eliminate any investigation of negative side effects to save himself from professional embarrassment. And he might be accused of trying to focus the investigation of positive side effects on those that are closely related to the intended outcomes. (See also **Goal-Free Evaluation**.)—S. B.

Messick, S. "The Criterion Problem in the Evaluation of Instruction: Assessing Possible, Not Just Intended Outcomes." In

M. C. Wittrock and D. E. Wiley (Eds.), *The Evaluation of Instruction: Issues and Problems.* New York: Holt, 1970. Pp. 183-202.

Scriven, M. "The Methodology of Evaluation." In *Perspectives of Curriculum Evaluation.* American Educational Research Association Monograph Series on Curriculum Evaluation. Chicago: Rand McNally, 1967. Pp. 39-83.

Suchman, E. A. *Evaluative Research.* New York: Russell Sage Foundation, 1967. Pp. 126-128.

---------------------------- SIMULATION ----------------------------

In its general sense, simulation may be described as any act of assuming an "appearance of" without the reality. The "playing-house" world of the child or the adult make-believe world of the stage are thus encompassed by this definition. In its more restrictive, scientific usage, simulation may be defined as "the act of representing some aspects of the real world by numbers or other symbols that can be easily manipulated in order to facilitate its study" (Harman). This approach to the study of large-scale problems was enhanced by the analogue computers of the 1930s, but the truly great strides were made in very recent years with the widespread availability of electronic digital computers. The new approaches—involving scientific **Systems Analysis** and simulation techniques—first were applied to military problems, but more recently have been used to explore problems associated with industrial, health, and educational systems.

If a system is to be simulated for ease of study, a selection must be made of elements from the real system for representation in the simulation model. Depending on the degree of abstraction from the real-life system, the simulation model varies in its complexity; this complexity, however, bears no direct relationship to the possible conclusions that might be drawn about the system. On the surface, using the real system as the "model" would seem to be direct and simple; but such a procedure usually proves neither practical nor feasible. At the other extreme, a complete mathematical model of the real system is equally impractical (even if a solution for a complex set of equations can be obtained by analytical methods, there would always be the question of the validity of the model).

Simulations employed by psychologists, sociologists, and educators frequently involve human beings in the "feedback loops" and may or may not involve computers. Usually, the simulation is conducted in the laboratory. Important features of the actual system are represented (simulated), but often symbolic representations suffice (e.g., reports of an activity rather than the activity itself).

For example, in a training program for school administrators on assessment and evaluation in educational planning, an entire school district—its physical facilities, teacher and pupil populations, budgetary as well as instructional problems, etc.—was simulated (i.e., represented in the laboratory), so that the real-life school people could consider and evaluate alternative approaches to problems without trial-and-error experimentation on their own school districts. Simulations of the "stock market" and "grant proposals" have been used as instructional tools in graduate courses in psychology. Other examples of laboratory simulations have involved the study of information-processing systems, the training of military personnel in an air defense operation, and the training of business executives and business school students. Another procedure, closely related to laboratory simulation, is the **Situational Test**. For example, a person's knowledge of a job can be evaluated by observing and grading his performance on an "in-basket" test, which simulates various day-to-day tasks typical of the job. Similarly, the effectiveness of a training program may be investigated by using simulated tasks as evaluation instruments and performance on them as criteria.

Perhaps the most common type of simulation is a computer model of a real system, and this is the sense in which the term *simulation* is used by most operations researchers and economists. In an all-computer simulation there is no place for human beings or real hardware components; all aspects of the system must be reduced to logical decision rules and operations that can be programmed as part of the model. Such simulation models play a crucial role in cost-benefit analysis (see **Cost Considerations and Economic Analysis**). Simulation can be useful in evaluating alternative policy decisions in such diverse aspects of the educational enterprise as changes in the curriculum of an entire public school system, control of college faculty turnover and tenure, and improvements in specific technical training programs. Simulation provides a decision maker with a "laboratory" in which he can try out his ideas for evaluation of alternatives (by changing the parameters in the model according to his insights and experience). This simulated evaluation can be done before resources are committed to costly operational programs.—H. H. H.

Carter, L. F. *The Systems Approach to Education—The Mystique and the Reality.* Santa Monica, Calif.: Systems Development Corporation, 1969.

Harman, H. H. "Simulation: A Survey." Paper presented at the Joint IRE-AIEE-ACM Computer Conference, Los Angeles, 1961.

Parsons, H. M. *Man-Machine System Experiments.* Baltimore: Johns Hopkins University Press, 1972. A comprehensive survey of large-scale man-machine system experiments that involved elaborate simulation, usually computer-based but including actual people operating actual machines. See especially Chapter 2, "Problems of Method" (section on simulation, pp. 49-70), and Chapter 24, "Man-Machine System Experiments in Systems Research: Commentary" (a review of published views on the nature of simulation, its purposes, its advantages and limitations, and its methods).

Proceedings of the Symposium on Operations Analysis of Education. *Socio-Economic Planning Sciences,* 1969, *2,* 105-520. See especially R. L. Sisson, "Can We Model the Educational Process?"

——————————— SITE SELECTION ———————————

Suppose that a basic-training program in use in many government offices throughout the nation is to be evaluated. Or suppose that an educational television program on a national network is to be evaluated. With such widespread programs, the evaluator will probably have to choose only a few sites in which to work, since the cost of evaluating in every potential site would be enormous.

There are two major approaches to site selection. One is to sample systematically from among a listing of all sites. The systematic **Sampling** of sites would be carried out if, for example, unbiased estimates of the effects of some program on the population are required. Sites might then be stratified by size, region, etc., and randomly sampled within each stratum. However, to obtain a satisfactory sample, a relatively large number of sites probably would have to be chosen; and, again, the cost of the evaluation would probably be considerable if not prohibitive.

A second and more frequent approach is to select a few sites deliberately (nonrandomly), although subjects can still be selected at random within the site or sites chosen. In general, the selection of a few sites requires the investigator to make judgments about the desirability and feasibility of working in any given area. If money and other factors limit the number of sites but allow work to be conducted in more than a single place, geographic spread may be desirable. Depending upon the populations to be studied, other factors—such as the size, ethnic composition, and the urban or rural nature of the community—might also be considered.

The most important factor in choosing a site may be the willingness of local people to participate (see **Field Operations**). Another major consideration is the generalizability of the site (whether the community and program are in some ways typical or prototypical of the communities and programs the investigator is interested in). In an evaluation of a welfare program, for example, an investigator might favor a site where many people receive welfare; however, the city that had the greatest proportion of welfare recipients might be atypical in other respects and, if selected, might not produce results that would be at all applicable to other cities. Although there is no such thing as an average or typical city, the selection process might consider the effects of choosing obviously unusual sites.

In some studies, sites may be selected that have distinctive characteristics. For example, the evaluation of a program that has been in operation for some time may be most usefully conducted in the few sites where the program is about to be instituted and so enable the collection of preprogram **Baseline Measures**.

Whenever sites are selected rather than systematically sampled, the reasons for making the choices should be clearly and completely specified so that others may be aware of the factors considered (as well as those not considered). Also, a thorough description of the sites should be included as part of the evaluation report. The physical, economic, cultural, and political attributes of the sites selected for an evaluation should be presented, so that others may make an informed judgment about the generalizability of results.—G. A. B.

SITUATIONAL TESTS

A situational test is a type of performance test in which tasks are presented in a setting that approaches the authenticity of real life. The test is standardized in the sense that all examinees are given identical problems under identical conditions (see **Standardized Tests**). The examinee is instructed to behave as though he were actually in a real-life situation. One rather elaborate situational test requires examinees to participate in the operation of an air defense direction center. A less elaborate, but still realistic, test measures the performance of an administrator in responding to items that have supposedly collected in his in-basket. Other situational tests have been developed for use in medical education to measure skills in differential diagnosis and patient management; and the technique was pioneered successfully during World War II as part of officer-selection procedures. (See also **Assessment** and **Simulation**.)

Measurement of behavior in real-life situations that correspond to the test situations is theoretically possible. The advantage of the situational test over real life is that the nature of the problems and the situation in which they are presented can be controlled. In real life, we might have to wait a long time for opportunities to observe the behavior we wish to measure; and when the opportunities do arise, they are likely to involve different contexts and conditions. The hardest problems may, for example, be given to the most able people, thus violating a basic requirement for a test. Thus, in certain important respects, situational tests may be superior to real life as a source of measurement data.

A possible disadvantage of the situational test, especially when we wish to measure behaviors that occur spontaneously, as in measuring personal or social characteristics, is that the examinee may respond in ways that he believes are desired by the examiners. For example, if the examinee believes that a situational test is supposed to measure social skills, he may utter many polite expressions and otherwise behave in a manner in accordance with his view of the purpose of the test. (See **Reactive Effects of Program and Evaluation**.) On the other hand, behavior based on ability to solve problems is not so easily under voluntary control, and tests intended to measure this ability are therefore less susceptible to *desirability bias*. Appropriate instructions may help to minimize desirability bias in taking the test. For example, when the purpose of the test is to find out how often a particular kind of behavior will occur spontaneously, the instructions may avoid reference to the specific behavior of interest and simply give examinees a general direction to "try to do a good job."

Since situational tests may be difficult to administer and score, one would not usually employ an elaborate situational test to measure abilities that can be measured adequately by using a simpler format, such as a simple performance test or a multiple-choice test. For example, one would not need to simulate the job of an accountant to measure arithmetic ability; but if one wants to find out how well an accountant detects subtle errors in applications of accounting procedures when his attention is not directed to this aspect of the problem, a situational test might be very appropriate.

The development of methods for scoring a situational test may require some thought and ingenuity. For example, it may be necessary to do a content analysis of responses in order to devise a suitable checklist or score sheet for scoring. On the other hand, if the test is intended to elicit a particular type of performance, it may be easy to provide a method for scorers to record the number of instances of that kind of behavior. (See **Content Analysis.**)

The usual psychometric criteria for evaluating a test should be applied to situational tests (see **Reliability** and **Validity**). Validation is a problem, as it is for any test, because of the difficulty of finding suitable criterion measures. The earlier comments about the advantages of situational tests over real-life observations suggest that the use of real-life data as criteria may pose problems; the situational test may sometimes provide a better criterion than the records of real-life behavior. Indeed, a well-conceived situational test may possess such a high degree of "face" validity that one might reasonably use it, at least provisionally, as a criterion measure. (See **Criterion Measurement.**)—N. F.

Damrin, D. E. "The Russell Sage Social Relations Test: A Technique for Measuring Group Problem-Solving Skills in Elementary School Children." *Journal of Experimental Education,* 1959, *28,* 85-99.

Frederiksen, N., Jensen, O., and Beaton, A. E. *Prediction of Organizational Behavior.* New York: Pergamon, 1972. Methods of data collection in social-psychological research. See especially Chapter 2.

Guetzkow, H. (Ed.) *Simulation in Social Science: Readings.* Englewood Cliffs, N.J.: Prentice-Hall, 1962. Contains readings illustrating a variety of situational tests used in research.

McGuire, C. H. "An Evaluation Model for Professional Education —Medical Education." In *Proceedings of the 1967 Invitational Conference on Testing Problems.* Princeton, N.J.: Educational Testing Service, 1968.

Weislogel, R. L., and Schwartz, P. A. "Some Practical and Theoretical Problems in Situational Testing." *Educational and Psychological Measurement,* 1955, *15,* 39-46.

———————————— SOCIAL INDICATORS ————————————

A social indicator is a measure of a social condition, a measure derived from the "real-life" behavior of large numbers of people rather than from the behavior of subjects in experimental or controlled situations. By virtue of this derivation, an indicator has an intrinsic meaning which is usually lacking in the score on a test or an attitude scale. The inspiration for the concept came from economics, where indicators of economic conditions, such as the Gross National Product and the Consumer Price Index, were found to be useful as the bases of policy decisions and as ways of monitoring broad trends and informing the general public in readily understandable terms about important but complex matters. It has, therefore, seemed logical to transfer the concept to other, noneconomic domains (although many social indicators have major economic components, and vice versa, so that the distinction between economic and noneconomic indicators can hardly be made any longer). Actually, some social indicators (such as birth rates and crime rates) have long been familiar, but many proposals have recently been made for an expansion of their coverage and refinements in their precision, to satisfy the growing needs for early identification of potentially troublesome social trends and for the reliable determination of the outcomes of social-intervention programs.

The defining characteristics of indicators imply that they are most useful in the evaluation of large-scale programs expected to have their effects through the cumulated acts of many people over a relatively long period of time. An illustration would be an effort to improve traffic safety through a public-education campaign, for which one indicator of success might be a reduction in the number of injury-producing accidents per million vehicle miles of travel during a specified unit of time in a specified area.

But the same characteristics also suggest some of the major limitations of this type of measure. One is that the magnitude of any one indicator is affected by many forces that are extraneous to the condition they are supposed to reflect. Thus, the considerable reduction in the homicide rate in the past fifty years might seem to indicate that the tendency toward violent crime has declined, but the factor probably most responsible for this reduction has been the improvement in medical care, which has prevented many murderous assaults from resulting in death. Similarly, traffic-accident rates are influenced by changes in highway and automobile construction, traffic densities, traffic-control devices, licensing regulations, law enforcement, etc. Thus, was the lowering of the death toll on the roads during the 1974 gas shortage due to lower driving speeds, fewer miles traveled, or both, or to a truckers' strike that occurred at the same time? Such extraneous forces clearly affect the validity of indicators and may even overwhelm any effects of the program being evaluated.

Other limitations are that some indicators are based on the behavior of more or less self-selected groups—e.g., the divorce rate as an indicator of the stability of family life—and thus may be seriously biased; and that they often rely on reported rather than (the possibly quite different) actual numbers of incidents—e.g., venereal-disease rates. To compound the difficulties, the forces affecting self-selection and reporting may themselves be changing while the program being evaluated is in operation, so that the indicator may change independently of the condition being measured. For reasons such as these, an indicator is best regarded as an indirect measure; and it is generally urged that, where indicators are used, several be used at the same time, in order to ensure against the inadequacies of any one. This solution, however, creates problems of its own, as when different indicators show different trends.

Probably the most common sources of data for indicators are the statistical publications of government agencies. These have the advantage of low cost to the evaluator, and they are sometimes thought also to have the advantages of being objective as well as unobtrusive and nonreactive (see **Unobtrusive Measures**). However, a degree of caution is called for. Where data have been collected by an agency whose own performance may be reflected therein, subtle distortions of many kinds can creep in. For example, crime statistics issued by a law-enforcement agency may well appear to tell a different story from those prepared by an independent group. Furthermore, many of these data are gathered in questionnaire surveys (e.g., the Census enumerations) and so are not truly unobtrusive; and as the data become more widely used for indicator purposes, they may lose their nonreactiveness.

On the whole, while indicators have attractive features and are applicable to some phenomena that cannot be measured in any other equally satisfactory way, they also have weaknesses which are the reverse of their strengths—in particular, the lack of control over relevant variables and over the attributes of the "subjects." Their precision also continues to leave much to be desired, although progress can be expected in the near future. Meanwhile, an evaluator would be well advised to restrict their role to that of supplementary measures, to be used in conjunction with more direct measures wherever possible. An indicator may suggest whether an educational program is having its final desired impact; it will not show whether the content of the program is being effectively taught.—R. A. F.

Bauer, R. A. (Ed.) *Social Indicators.* Cambridge, Mass.: MIT Press, 1966. Essays, with many examples, on what social indicators might accomplish for the nation, on the dimensions of system structure and performance that should be measured, and on the organizational problems of gathering and using social-indicator data. The pioneering classic of the field.

Gross, B. M. (Ed.) *Social Intelligence for America's Future: Explorations in Societal Problems.* Boston: Allyn and Bacon, 1969. Aimed at formulating a "strategy for developing social intelligence." First three chapters provide an overview, some valuable warnings about social measurement, and a discussion of feedback problems; other chapters deal with particular areas of measurement, concentrating on conceptual rather than technical issues. Synopses of all chapters are included.

Sheldon, E. B., and Moore, W. E. (Eds.) *Indicators of Social Change: Concepts and Measurements.* New York: Russell

Sage Foundation, 1968. Detailed considerations of the problems and prospects of social-indicator measurements in a dozen fields, ranging from education and economic growth to religion and leisure.

Toward a Social Report. Washington, D.C.: U.S. Department of Health, Education, and Welfare, 1969. A concise discussion of what social indicators reveal about the quality of life in the United States, what they fail to reveal, and how they might be improved.

Wilcox, L. D., Brooks, R. M., Beal, G. M., and Klonglan, G. E. (Eds.) *Social Indicators and Societal Monitoring: An Annotated Bibliography.* San Francisco: Jossey-Bass, 1972. An introductory essay on the history and present state of the social-indicators field; a listing of more than one thousand items, about half of them classified and annotated; an author index and a key-word index to the items; and an address list of individuals and institutions active in the development of social indicators.

SOCIOECONOMIC STATUS (SES)

Socioeconomic status (SES) is a key notion in sociology that has been found useful in psychology, education, and other related fields. The essence of SES is that individuals differ in their position in a social hierarchy, as a result of a large variety of determinants, and that their social position has profound behavioral consequences. SES is not well defined, either conceptually or empirically. Conceptually, social theorists have distinguished among a host of related constructs, the most influential scheme being Weber's triad of prestige or status, wealth, and power.

A plethora of standardized and ad hoc measures purporting to assess SES exists, varying greatly in **Reliability, Validity,** and ease of use. Almost without exception, these indexes deal with the prestige dimension; other potentially important aspects have received little attention. Since nearly all the measures were developed with whites, it is uncertain that the indexes function in the same way for blacks; in the absence of convincing data on this issue, caution should be exercised in using such indexes with non-whites. Finally, the measures do not provide a satisfactory way of classifying people as "upper class," "middle class," or "working class," although some do attempt to make such familiar categorizations.

Many measures consist of single variables, such as occupation (scaled to reflect prestige), education, income, and possessions. Indexes based on occupation are the most popular, and several factor analyses indicate that occupation is, indeed, the best single measure of SES. Hollingshead and Duncan provide the most useful procedures for assessing occupation. The use of the Hollingshead scale requires relatively little training, and the coding is quick as well as direct, but necessitates an appreciable amount of judgment. The Duncan SEI measure requires more extensive training, and several steps are involved in the coding, but the entire process is comparatively objective and requires a minimum of judgment. Both measures were originally developed for coding occupational information obtained from open-ended questions or existing records, but the Duncan device is readily adaptable to a multiple-choice format.

A number of multiple indexes also exist. The best known are Warner's Index of Status Characteristics (a combination of occupation, source of income, type of house, and type of neighborhood) and Hollingshead's Two-Factor Index of Social Position (a merger of occupation and education). Such devices have been widely criticized because the selection of the variables and the weights assigned to them are based on experience in particular (and often atypical) communities at a certain time (usually some date in the distant past), and, hence, these measures may not apply to individuals living in other towns and cities now. Additionally, most of the multiple indexes give the largest weight to occupation, indicating that they are tapping relatively little besides whatever is already accounted for by occupation.

The use of SES indexes presents a number of problems in practice. Some variables, notably occupation, are especially difficult to code from available data. Obtaining data may be difficult.

For example, information about the head of the household is often essential because, typically, every member of the family is assigned the socioeconomic status of the head. Yet this information may have to be obtained from someone else who may not be able to give accurate answers. Additionally, other kinds of information (e.g., income) may be difficult to procure because the individual is reluctant to divulge it. Finally, the head of the house may not be readily identifiable in broken or disorganized families.

Despite their many drawbacks, SES measures serve as important **Variables** in a wide variety of research and evaluation settings. They are used as descriptive variables in reporting relevant background or input characteristics of subjects, as control variables in eliminating variance considered to be extraneous in a particular comparison (e.g., the achievement of northern versus southern students, holding SES constant), as independent variables (e.g., occupational aspirations associated with SES), and as dependent or outcome variables (e.g., learning characteristics of the home environment within different SES groups).

SES measures are substantially related to a host of variables in sociology, psychology, and education. Among the more important relationships in the educational sphere, SES is positively associated with school achievement, ability-test performance, language acquisition, educational aspirations, and achievement motivation. Researchers differ in their views of such relationships. By and large, sociologists view SES as an interesting variable in its own right, whereas psychologists and educators tend to see it as a surface or carrier variable that reflects the operation of psychological and educational variables that need to be isolated and studied by themselves. For example, sociologists might be content to demonstrate that SES is related to academic success. Psychologists and educators, on the other hand, might wish to follow up this result to uncover the relevant psychological and educational variables associated with SES (e.g., student ability and motivation, characteristics of the home, nature of pupil-family and pupil-teacher interactions) that underlie such a finding.

In view of the demonstrated importance of SES, a clear need exists for the development of standardized measures that can be used to assess the major dimensions in this domain for the diverse groups in modern society.—L. J. S.

Duncan, O. D. "A Socioeconomic Index for All Occupations." In A. J. Reiss, Jr., O. D. Duncan, P. K. Hatt, and C. C. North, *Occupations and Social Status.* New York: Free Press, 1961. Pp. 109-138.

Hollingshead, A. B. *Two Factor Index of Social Position.* New Haven, Conn.: Author, 1957. A comprehensive guide for coding occupation and education, and combining them into a single index.

Svalastoga, K. *Social Differentiation.* New York: McKay, 1965. See especially Chapter 5 ("Life Chances, Life Style, Innovation, and Deviance") for a review of major correlates of SES.

Warner, W. L., Meeker, M., and Eells, K. *Social Class in America.* Chicago: Science Research Associates, 1949. See especially Chapter 8 ("Computing the Index of Status Characteristics") and Chapter 9 ("The Characteristics and the Seven-Point Scales for Measuring Them") for a complete description of the procedure for obtaining and using the Warner index.

Weber, M. "Class, Status, Party." In H. H. Gerth and C. W. Mills (Eds.), *From Max Weber: Essays in Sociology.* New York: Oxford University Press, 1946. Pp. 180-195.

——————— STAFF EVALUATION ———————

The evaluator of an education/training program may be concerned with two entirely different staff groups: the staff of the instructional program and the staff conducting the evaluation study. In the first case, he is interested in the effectiveness of administrators and instructors in delivering the program to students, a *crucial* program **Variable**. In the second case, he is interested in the efficiency, integrity, and accuracy with which evaluation data are collected and processed. In either case, failure to secure some information about the quality of staff performance might result in erroneous conclusions about how the program worked.

The first question the evaluator must answer about program staff is whether they, in fact, implemented the planned instructional activities. The dangers of assuming that, because a program was intended to operate in a certain way, it *did* operate in that way are pointed out in the article on **Discrepancy Evaluation**. At the next level, the evaluator may direct his attention toward the adequacy of the performance of the program staff, usually the instructors. As many investigators have pointed out (e.g., Medley and Mitzel, McDonald), it is far easier to obtain indirect information about teaching ability than to obtain direct measures of teaching performance. Thus, teachers are usually evaluated by such devices as tests of knowledge about the subject matter they are supposed to teach, administrators' ratings, self-report instruments covering what they do in the classroom, and sometimes ratings made by students or trainees. Measures of on-the-job performance are difficult to obtain because, for example, the behavior to be evaluated is complex; teacher performance may not be comparable from one classroom to another; direct observations are expensive, and time-sampling techniques frequently fail to capture the full range of behaviors of interest; and the presence of an observer may drastically alter the instructor's customary approach to his task (see **Observation Techniques**). Nevertheless, it is frequently important for the evaluator of an education/training program actually to get into the classrooms or other training settings to find out what is going on. In some instances, when program directors seemed unable to state their **Goals and Objectives**, evaluators have even been forced to try to deduce the objectives of a program from direct observation.

In evaluating program staff, an evaluator may seek to discover any difficulties administrators or instructors are having in implementing the program—especially difficulties that might be corrected through staff training, modification of materials, etc. (see **Formative Evaluation**)—and/or to identify any possible explanations for the apparent effectiveness or ineffectivenss of the program as judged by student outcomes (see **Summative Evaluation**).

The importance and difficulty of evaluating the work of the

evaluation staff increases, of course, with the size and nature of that staff and the complexity of the evaluation-study design. If the staff is small and well trained, the director of the evaluation project may be content with informal observations. However, in a large-scale study, he may want to collect systematic data about the performance of the evaluation staff in implementing the **Experimental Design** (e.g., assigning students at random to programs if that is required); adhering to the data-collection schedule (e.g., giving the **Pretest** before the program begins); administering data-collection instruments skillfully and according to prescribed procedures; securing the cooperation of program staff and students; and organizing, processing, and analyzing data (see **Field Operations** and **Quality Control**). In cases where the evaluator must depend on members of the instructional program staff to provide the data he needs, the importance of finding out how accurately and well they perform these tasks is great. However, he must employ great subtlety and tact in evaluating their performance or run the risk of obtaining no data at all.

A number of techniques for employee appraisal have been developed for use in business, industry, and the military. Some of these may be applicable to evaluation of program staff and the staff of the evaluation study, depending upon the nature of the evaluation. For example, when formal evaluation is undertaken, it should probably begin with identification of the dimensions of the job (see **Job Analysis**) and of criteria for assessing performance on the dimensions. In some cases, objective indices of performance (e.g., number of interviews completed by evaluation field staff) can be developed. In most cases, however, it will probably be necessary to develop judgmental rating forms. (See the separate article on **Ratings** for a discussion of various types and their advantages and limitations.)—M. R., S. B. A.

Glaser, R., and Short, J. "Training in Industry." In B. von H. Gilmer (Ed.), *Industrial and Organizational Psychology.* New York: McGraw-Hill, 1971. Pp. 382-427.

McDonald, F. J. "Evaluation of Teaching Behavior." In W. R. Houston and R. B. Howsam (Eds.), *Competency-Based Teacher Education.* Chicago: Science Research Associates, 1972. See especially the discussion of problems of direct

measurement of skills and knowledge and the present state
of the art (pp. 58-61).

Medley, D. M., and Mitzel, H. E. "Measuring Classroom Behavior
by Systematic Observation." In N. L. Gage (Ed.), *Handbook
of Research on Teaching.* Chicago: Rand McNally, 1963.
See especially Chapter 6.

Quirk, T. J. "Some Measurement Issues in Competency-Based
Teacher Education." *Phi Delta Kappan,* 1974, *55,* 316-319.
See also the critique of Quirk's article by Richard Cox in
the same issue.

Tiffin, J., and McCormick, E. J. *Industrial Psychology.* (5th Ed.)
Englewood Cliffs, N.J.: Prentice-Hall, 1965. See Chapter 9
("Performance Appraisal") and Chapter 10 ("Training").

—————————— STANDARDIZED TESTS ——————————

Some criticisms of testing stem from a view that testing is
motivated by a mechanistic philosophy whereby all people are cast
into one mold, without regard for their essential individuality.
Test makers, on the other hand, insist that they do *not* disregard
essential differences among individuals—that, in fact, these differences are precisely what they seek to understand. Through standardized tests they attempt to provide for measurement of individual differences in as unambiguous ways as possible. Thus, the process of standardization permeates all aspects of testing: construction, administration, scoring, reporting, and interpretation of
results.

The construction effort is oriented toward presenting questions that fairly sample or cover a domain of interest and that give
every examinee an equal opportunity to demonstrate or express
his skills, knowledge, understandings, attitudes, or other processes
the test is designed to measure. In attempting to obtain fair assessment of the domain, test makers may rely on counsel by experts

(content validity) and/or on research on the underlying psychological processes, including whether the test measures the same
thing for different groups of people (construct validity). The
process of ensuring that every examinee is given an equal opportunity to demonstrate his abilities includes efforts to eliminate
such irrelevant difficulties as these: requiring an examinee to *read*
instructions for a task intended to assess listening-comprehension
ability, an answer-marking procedure that is almost as difficult as
the problems posed by the test itself, a severely restrictive time
limit, or items that are more germane to one group than another.
Adequate pretesting of test items and analysis of the results are
key parts of the construction process. (Note that "pretest" is used
in a different sense here from **Pretest** in evaluation designs.)

In specifying the conditions and procedures for test administration, the developer of a standardized test strives not only for
uniform directions for all examinees but also for favorable environmental conditions (proper light, ventilation, etc.); a nonthreatening atmosphere which will tend to reduce **Test Anxiety** or alien-
ation; and adequate "practice" with the test materials, so that
differences in **Test Wiseness** will not influence examinees' opportunities to show what they know or can do. At the same time, the
instructions for administering the test should not be so restrictive
as to sacrifice test validity. For example, if persistence or speed is
not a factor that the test is designed to measure and if examinees
grow tired, it may be more important to give them a rest break
and allow them to return to the test later instead of carrying on
doggedly. Allowing for intelligent deviation from "cookbook"
instructions is especially important in testing young children,
adults in continuing-education courses, and other examinees who
are not regular players of the "testing game."

The maker of a standardized test seeks almost perfect scoring reliability uncontaminated by irrelevant or biasing factors; and
the scoring principles must be clearly spelled out, so that scores
are reproducible by other scorers or machines. This does not imply
that a standardized test must consist entirely of multiple-choice or
other kinds of objective items. In numerous instances standardized
tests require constructed responses that call for subjectivity in
scoring. For such tests, however, the task of defining scoring specifications and setting uniform standards is more difficult. (See
Achievement Test Construction.)

Two other key steps in standardization are developing an appropriate score-scale system and establishing relevant norms. Scaling techniques are used principally to adjust for possible differences in difficulty between alternate forms of a test. Scores on the various forms are equated—or "calibrated"—and converted to a common reporting scale. Then, within the limitations imposed by the reliability of the equating method, we can be confident that an examinee's score was not significantly affected by the particular test form he took. Such equating has particular advantages for evaluation studies when it is desirable to study trends or to compare groups tested at different times. (See **Scales** and **Equivalent Scores**.)

Norming (see **Norms**) involves administering the test to obtain reference data for appropriate groups of examinees. Norms-referenced tests are distinguished from **Criterion-Referenced** measures, but the latter frequently have some normative reference, even if it is informally derived.

Finally, the maker of a standardized test is obligated to present to users a detailed accounting of the characteristics of the test: the use for which it is intended or recommended, a clear outline of test content, information on **Reliability** and standard errors of measurement, **Validity** information, item difficulties and discrimination indices, etc. The American Psychological Association (APA), the American Educational Research Association (AERA), and the National Council on Measurement in Education (NCME) have set down these requirements in *Standards for Educational and Psychological Tests*. (These standards place responsibilities on test users as well as test developers; users are admonished not to destroy the value of tests through inappropriate applications.)

Standardized tests are a valuable aid to evaluators of educational and training programs if they are good tests and if they measure some of the program **Goals and Objectives**. By enabling evaluators to make comparisons of a target group with other groups of students, standardized tests provide some insurance against idiosyncracy in program efforts and help to put educational evaluation on firmer scientific ground.—S. B. A.

American Psychological Association. *Standards for Educational and Psychological Tests*. Washington, D.C., 1974.

Angoff, W. H., and Anderson, S. B. "The Standardization of Educational and Psychological Tests." *Illinois Journal of Education,* Feb. 1963, pp. 19-23. Reprinted in D. A. Payne and R. F. McMorris (Eds.), *Educational and Psychological Measurement.* Lexington, Mass.: Xerox College Publishing, 1967. Pp. 9-14.

Messick, S., and Anderson, S. B. "Educational Testing, Individual Development, and Social Responsibility." *Counseling Psychologist,* 1970, *2,* 80-88.

STANDARDS

One of the dictionary definitions of *standard* conforms well to the meaning of *standard* in the context of education or training programs: "a degree or level of requirement, excellence, or attainment." Standards for students or trainees may be set in terms of test scores (in some terminologies "cutting scores"), other quantitative measures of competence (e.g., speed of assembly, number of exercises completed satisfactorily), ratings assigned by supervisors or instructors, or performance profiles based on several measures. We can speak of *minimum* standards (the standard expected of everyone who completes the program or course), and we can speak of standards that demarcate *levels* of proficiency (traditionally, the standard for a course grade of *A* is different from the standard for a course grade of *B,* etc.). In some situations, different standards on essentially the same dimension(s) may be applied to different population groups; e.g., length of golf drive for women versus men, typing speed for clerks versus secretaries, English-language proficiency for native-born versus foreign-born speakers.

All standards are matters of judgment. However, the bases for judgments vary from "hard" to "soft." And the question of *whose* judgment is paramount and recurrent.

Sometimes standards are primarily data-based; i.e., set in relationship to performance of a reference group (relative standards). For example, standards for a training program oriented toward a licensed occupation might be set in terms of the performance of a sample of people who are already licensed. If all those who now have a license can be considered qualified, then the standard could be set at the lowest level of performance in this reference group. However, if some of the licensed group are not considered qualified, then the standard would be set at an appropriately higher point on the performance dimension.

Similarly, standards for educational achievement may be set in relationship to the performance of other students at the same educational level. For example, standards for acceptable performance in geometry might be set on the basis of the performance of students in previous classes who have been considered successful. Frequently public school personnel set standards in terms of the scores of national norms groups on standardized tests; e.g., a minimum reading-comprehension standard for third graders corresponding to the twenty-fifth percentile in the **Norms** group.

Problems in setting and using relative standards arise to the extent that the student group to which they are being applied is different from the reference group on which they are based. Last year's geometry class may have had a better mathematical background than this year's class. A minimum standard of the twenty-fifth percentile for a national population may be inappropriately low for students in "gifted" classes. In many cases, too, relative standards must be adjusted to the needs and task requirements of the times; good performance of a decade ago might be considered barely acceptable today—or vice versa.

Standards may be set on rational as well as empirical grounds—on consideration of what the student group in question should know or be able to do after completing the training or educational sequence. Such standards are sometimes called *absolute standards*. For example, standards of successful completion of job training may be derived from analyses (formal or informal) of the skills and knowledge that the job requires (see **Job Analysis**). Standards for traditional courses of study may be developed from **Content Analyses** of the subject matter; e.g., students should be able to identify forty out of fifty specified stock figures in Western literature, or to identify two out of three "unknowns" in elementary chemistry. In these examples, "perfect" performance is not

expected; some allowance for task ambiguity and normal variations in student acuity and attention is frequently made in setting
absolute standards. This is especially important when standards are
set in terms of performance on a conventional ability or achievement test, which usually contains a large number of items from
diverse domains. A useful way of setting absolute standards on
such an instrument is to have judges estimate the probability that
a student of a given level of competency would answer each test
item correctly. Then item probabilities are averaged and summed
across the relevant items.

   Criterion-referenced measures are generally more compatible with absolute standards and norms-referenced measures with
relative standards. However, neither criterion-referenced measures
nor absolute standards are completely without some normative
considerations, although such considerations may be more implicit
than explicit; e.g., we just do not set a speed of 100 w.p.m. as a
standard in a six-week typing course. (See **Criterion-Referenced
Measurement** and **Norms.**)

   The difficulties of obtaining agreement about standards are
very like the difficulties of obtaining some consensus about educational or training **Goals and Objectives,** and some of the same procedures and cautions noted for goals and objectives are equally
applicable to standards: all relevant groups (instructors, program
administrators, program sponsors, and in some cases community
members, parents, and students) should have an opportunity to
participate in the process of setting standards; definitions of standards should be stated in as clear and unambiguous terms as possible; and specific provision should be made for review and revision
of standards as situations change.

   Some program-evaluation models stress the importance of
comparing obtained student performance with predetermined standards. If student performance does not come up to the standards,
then the program has not been effective or the standards were
unrealistic—or both. Cronbach, for example, urges such a design for
evaluation studies oriented toward course improvement, as long as
measures are taken of possible **Side Effects** as well as of a broad range
of objectives. This evaluation strategy is to be contrasted with strategies where performance of the group in the program is compared
with that of a **Control Group.** (See also **Mastery Learning.**)

This article has focused on standards for students or trainees. The term *standards* is also used in relationship to the education/training program itself and to the evaluation. Thus, we may have standards for program facilities (e.g., state laws about per-pupil space requirements and safety standards for schools), standards for program development (such as those prepared by the Operations Department of AT&T), and standards for evaluation methodology (e.g., *Standards for Educational and Psychological Tests*). Some suggest that *guidelines* might be a better word than *standards* in the last two instances.—G. L. M., S. B. A.

American Psychological Association. *Standards for Educational and Psychological Tests.* Washington, D.C., 1974.

American Telephone and Telegraph Company. *Training Development Standards: Quick Reference Guide.* New York: AT&T Training and Research Group, 1972.

Cronbach, L. J. "Course Improvement Through Evaluation." *Teachers College Record,* 1962, *64,* 672-683.

Hills, J. R. "Use of Measurement in Selection and Placement." In R. L. Thorndike (Ed.), *Educational Measurement.* (2nd Ed.) Washington, D.C.: American Council on Education, 1971. Pp. 680-732.

Popham, W. J., and Baker, E. L. *Establishing Instructional Goals.* Englewood Cliffs, N.J.: Prentice-Hall, 1970. Pp. 59-77.

Thorndike, R. L. "Marks and Marking Systems." In R. L. Ebel (Ed.), *Encyclopedia of Educational Research.* (4th Ed.) New York: Macmillan, 1967. Pp. 759-766.

──────────── STATISTICAL ANALYSIS ────────────

In any evaluation study, there will be one or more sets of data to be summarized and analyzed. The data will usually be collected from a sample of the population which we are interested in studying and to which we expect to apply the evaluation results. The objective is to make inferences about the population from this sample. Some statistical techniques used in relating sample information to the entire population are explained in **Statistical Inference** and **Statistical Significance.**

In this entry several of the most important statistical techniques for the analysis of data will be described. These techniques are based upon two distributions in common use in evaluation studies—t and F distributions. Statistical tests which are based on these distributions and which meet certain assumptions are known as *exact* tests because we can find the exact probability that the test statistic will fall in some critical region if the null hypothesis is true (see **Hypothesis Testing**). Hence, if the test statistic (say, the t or the F) falls outside this region, we reject the null hypothesis. Frequently in an evaluation we cannot assume that the assumptions underlying the t or F distributions hold exactly in our population—e.g., perhaps the scores are *not* normally distributed. In such instances we can still use the t or F tests, but then the statistical test is *approximate*. The tests are "robust" in the sense that approximation will generally be reasonable.

We do not intend in this article to provide a full description of the mathematics behind the t and F distributions; nor do we intend to provide complete descriptions of how to calculate t and F. However, we do want to explain some of the uses of the t and F tests; an evaluator who needs more information should consult a statistician or the references provided at the end of this article.

The t test is used mainly to test hypotheses about the difference between two means. For example, an evaluator may hypothesize that program A leads to greater student achievement than program B. This hypothesis can be statistically tested using means and standard deviations of the achievement scores of the students in the two programs. (See **Statistics.**) In an evaluation, the t test is usually used to test whether an experimental program is better than a control program.

If two samples are drawn randomly from two normal populations, the following formula provides a t value for testing that the two populations have the same mean. The value can then be looked up in a table of t values to find the significance level (see, for example, Edwards, Table V, or Walker and Lev, Table IX): $t =$

$(\bar{X}_1 - \bar{X}_2)/S_{(\bar{X}_1 - \bar{X}_2)}$, where $\bar{X}_1$ and $\bar{X}_2$ are the sample means and $S_{(\bar{X}_1 - \bar{X}_2)}$ is the standard error of the mean differences (calculated using the sample sizes and the standard deviations). If $\bar{X}_1$ and $\bar{X}_2$ are substantially different from each other in relation to the standard-error term (the denominator), then t will be large—either positive or negative—and will probably be statistically significant. The statistic is sensitive to the number of scores that make up the two means. Thus, the larger the number of students in the two samples (say, experimental and control samples), the more "powerful" the test of the significance of the difference between their scores. An example using the t test is provided in **Statistical Significance**.

Incidentally, the t distribution is sometimes called "Student's Distribution." It was developed by a British statistician, William Sealy Gosset, who worked for Guinness Brewery in Dublin. His employer would not allow Gosset to use his own name in his research writings, so he adopted the pseudonym "Student."

The F test (based on the F distribution) can be thought of as an extension of the t test. It is used when we want to extend the t test to a situation where there are more than two independent random samples of some normally distributed population. Suppose, for example, that there are three methods of training Morse code operators and we wish simply to find out whether any one of the methods is superior. Given three random samples of students (each trained by a different method), we might try to use three t tests. We might compare method 1 against method 2, method 1 against method 3, and method 2 against method 3. But, under three separate null hypotheses, the probability that at least one of these comparisons would be statistically significant is greater than the probability that any particular one of the three comparisons, if tested alone, would be significant. Such a procedure, therefore, would improperly increase the probability of rejecting the null (no significant difference) hypothesis.

When more than two sample means are the focus of attention, the F rather than the t distribution should be used—at least first. This allows for statistical testing in more complex evaluation designs. Thus, if three training methods are being compared, we may also want to see how the methods interact with some other student variable such as sex. A design such as the following allows us to see whether the main effect of method is significant (X_a vs. X_b vs. X_c), whether the main effect of sex is significant (X_m vs. X_f), and whether there is a significant interaction between teaching method and sex of student—e.g., perhaps method A works best for males, and B for females:

	Method A	Method B	Method C	
Male Students	$\overline{X}_{am}$	$\overline{X}_{bm}$	$\overline{X}_{cm}$	$\overline{X}_m$
Female Students	$\overline{X}_{af}$	$\overline{X}_{bf}$	$\overline{X}_{cf}$	$\overline{X}_f$
	$\overline{X}_a$	$\overline{X}_b$	$\overline{X}_c$	

Again, it is not our purpose to teach the reader how to perform the necessary computations. Conceptually, the basis for the F test is to be found through an examination of variance (the square of the standard deviation—see **Statistics**). In a simple case, if the variance of the scores *within* the groups being compared is much greater than the variance *between* those groups, then the F statistic will be small and not significant because F = mean square (variance) between groups/mean square (variance) within groups.

Not surprisingly, this procedure is called *analysis of variance* (Anova or ANOVA). The logic of analysis of variance can be captured intuitively if we think about particular instances. Let us imagine that we have three groups of five students. Each group is taught by a different method. Here are the students' scores at posttest:

	Method A	Method B	Method C	
	6	35	3	
	26	5	31	
	13	5	24	
	19	20	10	
	16	10	17	
Mean	16	15	17	Grand Mean = 16

There is little variance here between (among) the three groups (means of 16, 15, and 17) but great variance within each of the groups. Ask yourself, in this situation, whether these findings reflect a substantial difference among the methods. Hardly. Consider, alternatively, another set of results:

	Method A	Method B	Method C	
	25	15	9	
	27	16	8	
	26	14	7	
	28	15	6	
	24	15	5	
Mean	26	15	7	Grand Mean = 16

Now the variance between (among) the group means is large (26, 15, and 7), but within each group the variance is small. Such results might very well reflect a significant difference among the methods.

Like the t statistic, the F statistic is sensitive to sample sizes —both the number of groups being compared and the number of subjects (scores) in each group. Most statistics textbooks have a table of F values that can be used to determine the significance of a given F statistic (see, for example, Walker and Lev, Table X).

The F test can also be used in an extension of analysis of variance—*analysis of covariance*. Suppose that two groups of trainees (1 and 2) are tested for achievement after they have been exposed to two different training programs (A and B). Group 2 obtains a mean score which is significantly greater than that of Group 1 at the .05 level of significance (see **Statistical Significance**). It might, therefore, be concluded that program B is a better program than program A. However, suppose that a program auditor (see **Audit of Evaluation**) points out that the two groups already differed significantly on a test of reading ability *before* the start of the two programs (at pretest). After additional analysis (analysis of covariance), he asserts that the statistically significant result at the end of the program is just a reflection of this original difference, and, in fact, the two programs do not have differential effects. If the two groups had not differed on reading ability, they would not have differed significantly in achievement after the programs. This assertion is based on an analysis of covariance.

An evaluator may undertake an analysis of covariance when he suspects that (a) some variable other than the educational program (e.g., pretest scores or IQ or socioeconomic status or number of books in the home) may be affecting the outcome and (b) the groups he is comparing differ in this characteristic. Covariance adjusts for such differences, in a sense presenting the case for what would be the outcome if those differences were nonexistent. The technique of covariance involves adjustment of dependent variable scores (e.g., achievement test scores at the end of the program) using the linear relationship between the dependent variable and some covariate (e.g., pretest scores, SES).

There are problems in the covariance technique (and the subsequent use of the F test)—see, for example, **Lord's Paradox**. In general, it should not be used to compare quite different groups— groups from different populations. It would be improper to covary height to see whether the Giants is a better basketball team than the Pygmies. On the other hand, if the evaluator of a reading program had randomly assigned students to treatments but later found that one of the treatment groups was better prepared or had somewhat higher aptitude than the others, the analysis of covariance technique might be a reasonable procedure to adopt. —R. T. M., S. B.

Edwards, A. L. *Experimental Design in Psychological Research.* New York: Holt, 1950. See especially Chapters 8, 9, 10, and 17.

Ferguson, G. A. *Statistical Analysis in Psychology and Education.* (3rd Ed.) New York: McGraw-Hill, 1971. See especially Chapters 15, 16, 17, and 20.

Fisher, R. A. *Statistical Methods for Research Workers.* New York: Hafner, 1958. (A revised edition of Fisher's original 1925 text.) See especially Chapters 7 and 8.

Lindquist, E. F. *Design and Analysis of Experiments in Psychology and Education.* Boston: Houghton Mifflin, 1953. See especially Chapter 14, on the analysis of covariance.

Snedecor, G. W. *Statistical Methods.* (4th Ed.) Ames: Iowa State College Press, 1946. See especially Chapters 10, 11, and 12.

Walker, H. M., and Lev, J. *Statistical Inference.* New York: Holt, 1953. See statistical tables IX and X for t and F values.

STATISTICAL INFERENCE

Statistical inference is the process of drawing conclusions about a population from a sample or group of samples (see **Sampling**). In the evaluation of training programs, we ordinarily attempt to identify a program that works well for particular trainees, with the expectation that the program will also work well for other trainees not involved in the evaluation. For example, if program A is judged to be better than program B for trainees who studied at several centers in the South, we would like to predict that program A will also be better than program B for all trainees in the South.

Before we can confidently make such a prediction, we must determine whether our sample is really representative of the overall population. For example, we may ask whether the achievement scores of the groups are such that they appear to be from the same overall population. To test this, each sample is used to estimate the various statistical properties (parameters) of the population, and an underlying distribution for the population is assumed. The normal distribution (see **Statistics**) is the distribution most frequently employed as a model. The mathematical properties of this model are well known. The probability of drawing a sample of size n, with an arbitrary mean (say $\overline{X}$), from a population of size N, with a mean of μ, is known and is given in readily available tables (see Hays, Table 1). If a very large number of samples of size n are taken from a population of size N, the means of the samples will themselves form a normal distribution, with the average of the means equal to the mean of the population, and the standard deviation of the sample means equal to the standard deviation of the population divided by the square root of n. This standard deviation of the sample means is called the *standard error of the mean*.

To illustrate the use of statistical inference, first assume that the population mean (μ) and standard deviation (σ) are known: $\mu = 40$ and $\sigma = 10$. Suppose that we then select random groups of size 100 from the population. The means of the samples will themselves form a normal distribution with mean $\overline{X} = 40$ and standard deviation $\sigma_{\overline{X}} = 10/\sqrt{100} = 1$ (the standard error of the mean). Now, suppose that a group of trainees in the South has a mean score of 43. What is the probability that this group of trainees is a random sample from the overall population of trainees? This is determined by calculating the quantity z (see **Score Types**) as follows: $z = (\overline{X} - \mu)/\sigma_{\overline{X}} = (\overline{X} - \mu)/\sigma_{\sqrt{n}} = (43 - 40)/1 = 3.00$. The probability of selecting a sample of trainees with this score or a higher score by chance is slightly greater than .001. If the hypothesis (see **Hypothesis Testing**) being tested is that the mean of the population from which this sample is drawn is 40, we could reject that hypothesis at the .01 level of significance (see **Statistical Significance**). In fact, any z value that is more than +2.58 or less than −2.58 will allow us to reject the hypothesis being tested at the .01 level. It is easy to derive the critical region by using these values of z in the equation and solving for $\overline{X}$. For example, in this illustration, when $z = -2.58$, then $\overline{X} = 40.00 - 2.58 = 37.42$. When $z = +2.58$, then $\overline{X} = 40.00 + 2.58 = 42.58$. The region between 37.42 and 42.58 contains the range of values that allow for acceptance of the hypothesis.

Now, suppose that the parameters of the population are not known. Then we use the sample values to estimate the parameters of the population, state a range of values within which we are confident the parameter falls (confidence interval), and express that confidence as a probability level (level of confidence). Using the example already given, assume that we have 100 trainees with an average score of 43 and a standard deviation of 8. Our best estimate of the mean of the population from which this sample was chosen is the average score of the sample, 43. However, if the population mean was actually 42, this might still be a likely sample. The inference problem is to determine those values for the mean of the population that would not lead to the rejection of the hypothesis that the sample was drawn from the population. We could work the z formula backward if we knew $\sigma_{\overline{X}}$. If we assume that the standard deviation of the sample is a good estimate of the standard deviation of the population, the $\sigma_{\overline{X}}$ equals the standard deviation of the sample divided by the square root of 100. Thus, $\sigma_{\overline{X}} = 8/10 = .8$. For the .01 level of significance we know that z must be less than −2.58 or greater than +2.58 in order to reject the hypothesis being tested. If z is between $-$ 2.58 and $+$ 2.58, the hypothesis is not rejected. Using $z = (\overline{X} - \mu)/\sigma_{\overline{X}}$, $-$ 2.58 = (43 $-$ μ_1)/0.8, μ_1 = 43 + 2.1, and 2.58 = (43 $-$ μ_2)/0.8, μ_2 = 43 $-$ 2.1. Therefore, based on the sample of size 100 with mean 43, the confidence interval for the mean of the population is from 40.9 to 45.1 at the .01 level of significance. Thus, based on the sample, it is possible to infer the mean of a population within some range with some level of confidence.—R. T. M.

Edwards, A. L. *Experimental Design in Psychological Research.* New York: Holt, 1950.

Fisher, R. A. *Statistical Methods for Research Workers.* New York: Hafner, 1958. See especially Chapter 5.

Hays, W. L. *Statistics.* New York: Holt, 1963. See especially Chapters 7 through 10.

Huntsberger, D. V. *Elements of Statistical Inference.* Boston: Allyn and Bacon, 1961. See especially Chapters 6 and 7.

Runyon, R. P., and Haber, A. *Fundamentals of Behavioral Statistics.* Reading, Mass.: Addison-Wesley, 1967. See especially the second part of the text, on inferential statistics.

STATISTICAL SIGNIFICANCE

A statistically significant event is an "event" that is unlikely to occur by chance. Events include such things as the sequence of numbers showing on several consecutive rolls of a die, a difference between the mean values of two sets of scores on a test, and a relationship between two variables, such as income and age.

In evaluation, the investigator frequently attempts to find statistically significant differences between groups of trainees on outcome variables. Important conclusions and decisions will be based on these differences. Consequently, the user of evaluation results should know what is meant when he is told that program A is better than program B, based on a difference in trainee achievement that is statistically significant at the .05 level, say. (See **Hypothesis Testing.**)

In the entry on **Statistical Inference**, the distribution of sample means for samples of a given size is explained. Suppose that there are 30 trainees in program A and 30 trainees in program B. On a given test, the mean score for the trainees in program A is 39; for those in program B the mean score is 43. Is the difference $(43 - 39 = 4)$ statistically significant at the .05 level? That is, does this difference of 4 have less than a 5 percent probability of occurring *by chance,* based on what we know about sampling? An answer to this question is based on theoretical consideration of all pairs of samples of size 30 that can be chosen from populations with means of μ_1 and μ_2 and standard deviations of σ_1 and σ_2. The differences between the means of the samples will form a normal distribution with a mean of $\mu_1 - \mu_2$ and a standard deviation equal to the square root of the sum of the squared standard deviations of the samples $(\sigma = \sqrt{\sigma_1^2 + \sigma_2^2})$. To test for a significant difference between means at a given level, the Student t test may be used:

$$ t = \frac{(\bar{X}_1 - \bar{X}_2) - (\mu_1 - \mu_2)}{S_{(\bar{X}_1 - \bar{X}_2)}} $$

The value of t is based on the means of the samples $(\bar{X}_1, \bar{X}_2)$, the means of the populations from which the samples are drawn, and the standard deviation of the distribution of mean differences $S_{(\bar{X}_1 - \bar{X}_2)}$. It has a known probability of occurring under certain conditions, depending upon the sizes of the samples and the assumption of normally distributed populations. It can therefore be used to test whether an obtained value of t in a given case would occur by chance at some level, say the 5 percent level.

If the null hypothesis is that the two samples come from the same population, then $\mu_1 - \mu_2 = 0$. Suppose for our two groups of trainees $S_{(\bar{X}_1 - \bar{X}_2)} = 10$, then $t = (43 - 39)/10 = .40$. To determine whether this value of t is likely to occur by chance (at the .05 level, or 5 times in 100 instances), one can consult readily available tables of the t distribution (see Edwards, Table V). For this illustration, the t value for the .05 level of significance is 2.00.

Since .40 is less than 2.00, the null hypothesis cannot be rejected. Thus, as far as this analysis is concerned, there is not a significant difference between the achievements of the two groups.

If two variables are normally distributed in the population under study, then it is also possible to determine the probability that obtained **Correlations** between them could have occurred by chance. These values, too, are listed in readily available tables (see Edwards, Table VI). For example, for the Pearson product-moment correlation, for a group of 100 persons a correlation of .20 would be significantly different statistically from zero at the .05 level of significance (the critical value is .1946). This means that if the correlation was really zero, this correlation of .20 would occur by chance fewer than 5 times in 100 instances.

The users of evaluation should have a general knowledge of what statistical significance means and of its close relationship to chance occurrences. If a single event is studied and is found to be statistically significant at the .05 level, we conclude that the result is unlikely to have occurred by chance. However, if 100 events are studied and 5 of them are found to be statistically significant at the .05 level, the findings are consistent with what would be expected merely by chance. If a lower, more conservative level of significance (say, .01 rather than .10) is used to interpret significant differences, more confidence can be placed in statistically significant results.—R. T. M.

Edwards, A. L. *Experimental Design in Psychological Research.* New York: Holt, 1950. See especially Chapter 8.

Fisher, R. A. *Statistical Methods for Research Workers.* New York: Hafner, 1958. See especially Chapter 5.

Hays, W. L. *Statistics.* New York: Holt, 1963. See especially Chapters 9 and 10.

Runyon, R. P., and Haber, A. *Fundamentals of Behavioral Statistics.* Reading, Mass.: Addison-Wesley, 1967. See especially the second part of the text, on inferential statistics.

———————————— STATISTICS ————————————

Statistics as applied to evaluation includes two main fields: (a) *descriptive statistics,* which is concerned primarily with summarizing data systematically for ease of comprehension, and (b) *inferential statistics,* which is concerned with using data as the basis for making certain generalizations and interpretations.

A very simple example serves to illustrate various common terms used in statistics. The example is not meant to be realistic, for descriptive statistics is concerned with summarizing data and the small set of data used in this illustration would hardly need summarization. However, for demonstrating the concepts, this simple example should be sufficient. The following is a set of nine scores of trainees on an achievement test: 45, 30, 35, 40, 40, 50, 45, 35, 40. These are called *raw data* because they appear just as they have been gathered. The simplest thing that might be done with data like these is to arrange them in increasing or decreasing order. In increasing order, the data become 30, 35, 35, 40, 40, 40, 45, 45, 50. The difference between the largest and smallest numbers (50 – 30 = 20) is called the *range.* If there were a large number of scores, they would ordinarily be arranged in a *frequency table,* which simply gives the number of scores lying in specified intervals. Table 1 shows the nine scores as they might be arranged in a frequency table.

Table 1

Frequency Table

Score Interval	Frequency
30-34	1
35-39	2
40-44	3
45-49	2
50-54	1

A very common practice in descriptive statistics is to represent the data as a frequency *histogram* or a frequency *polygon*. histogram is just a set of rectangles, with the height of each rectangle corresponding to the numbers of scores in a given interval. A frequency histogram for this example is given in Figure 1. If the midpoints of the tops of the rectangles are connected, the resulting figure is called a *frequency polygon* (see Figure 2).

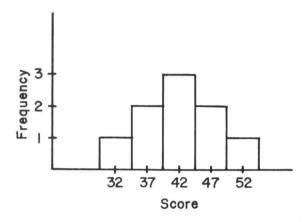

Figure 1. Frequency histogram.

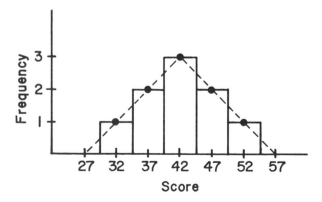

Figure 2. Frequency polygon.

When a very large number of cases are involved in the data, a frequency polygon (as shown in Figure 2) tends to become a smooth curve. This smooth curve is called a *frequency curve.* Three *frequency curves,* described in terms of their shapes, are given in Figure 3. As Figure 3 shows, some frequency curves are

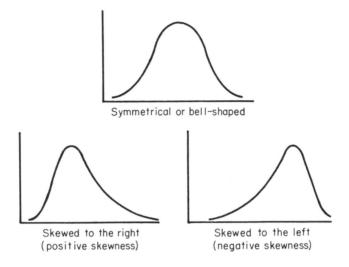

Symmetrical or bell-shaped

Skewed to the right (positive skewness)

Skewed to the left (negative skewness)

Figure 3. Frequency curves.

lopsided, or skewed, with the scores piled up toward one end of the distribution. As the peak of the curve moves to the left, the tail or the slope of the curve to the right becomes relatively longer and gentler; this is called *positive skewness.* Conversely, a shift in the peak to the right results in a longer and gentler slope or tail to the left, or *negative skewness.*

Data also may be represented by *cumulative-frequency* tables and curves. *Cumulative frequency* simply means that the frequencies are added together up to the boundary of any interval. For example, the cumulative-frequency table corresponding to Table 1 is given in Table 2. The *cumulative-frequency curve* is shown in Figure 4.

When we are dealing with large sets of data, two descriptive properties are particularly important: (1) Around what score do the data tend to center? (2) How spread out are the scores? Several common statistics are used to describe the central tendency of a

Table 2
Cumulative-Frequency Table

Score	Frequency	Percent
less than 34	1	11.1
less than 39	3	33.3
less than 44	6	66.6
less than 49	8	88.8
less than 54	9	100.0

set of scores: *mean, median,* and *mode.* The *mean* is the arithmetic average of the scores. The *median* is the score in the middle, so that half of the scores are equal to or less than the median. If there are an even number of scores, the average of the two middle scores is usually taken as the median. The *mode* is the score with the highest frequency. In our simple example of nine scores, the mean, median, and mode are all 40. In the set of five scores 1, 1, 2, 5, and 6, the mean is 3, the median 2, and the mode 1.

Similarly, several common statistics are used to describe the *dispersion* of the scores: *range, variance,* and *standard deviation.* The *range* is simply the difference between the highest and lowest scores. The *standard deviation* and the *variance* are a little more complicated. In the set of scores given in the example, where the mean is 40, the deviation of each score from that mean could be

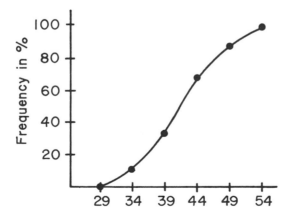

Figure 4. Cumulative-frequency curve.

computed and the average taken. However, because some of the numbers are above and some below the mean, the deviations will be both positive and negative. To eliminate the problem of plus and minus signs, each difference can be squared before the average is taken; the square root of the average is then used as the final statistic. The average of the squared deviations is called the *variance* of the scores. The positive square root of the variance is called the *standard deviation* of the scores. The calculation of the variance and standard deviation for the data given earlier is shown in Table 3.

Table 3
Calculation of Variance and Standard Deviation

Score	Deviation from Mean	Squared Deviation
30	−10	100
35	− 5	25
35	− 5	25
40	0	0
40	0	0
40	0	0
45	5	25
45	5	25
50	10	100

Average of squared deviations = 300/9 = 33.3 (variance)

Square root of variance = $\sqrt{33.3}$ = 5.8 (standard deviation)

Theoretical (i.e., mathematical) distribution functions can be very useful in describing the characteristics of a population, since empirical data often behave like such a theoretical distribution. The most common mathematical function—with roots in the scientific observations of errors of measurement in physics and astronomy—is the well-known, bell-shaped *normal distribution,* as represented in Figure 5.

Inferential statistics provide means of using data collected in specified ways to test statistical hypotheses and to evaluate the precision of estimates based on descriptive statistics (see **Statistical Inference, Statistical Significance, Statistical Analysis,** and **Multivariate Analysis**). In statistical inference, a group for which data

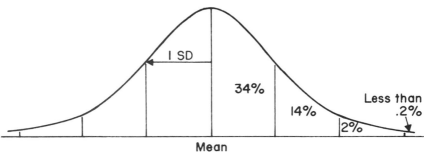

Figure 5. Normal distribution, showing percentage of cases
falling in each region.

are available is regarded as a sample drawn from an underlying
population (see **Sampling**); statistical inference makes it possible
to describe the population by using the sample data and a suitable
mathematical model. Such general information about the population is useful in interpreting results for a number of samples. For
example, suppose that mean gains obtained by one method of
teaching sixth-grade reading are higher than those obtained by an
alternative method for a particular sample. Any generalizations
from this experiment will depend on estimates of the probability
that the observed difference is attributable to a real difference in
the effectiveness of the two methods rather than to sampling fluctuations. Differences which are unlikely to have arisen by chance
are designated *statistically significant* and are given special attention in the interpretation of the results.

The requirements for effective statistical inference have
strong implications for the way that data are collected. As a result,
the design of evaluation experiments or surveys calls for careful
consideration of the requirements of statistical inference, as well
as the methodological requirements of the particular research
focus of the study. This planning should be done *before* any data
are collected. (See **Experimental Design** and **Quasi-Experimental
Design.**) Details on the statistical aspects of experimental design
can be found in the Winer reference.—W. B. S., R. T. M.

Edwards, A. L. *Statistical Analysis.* (3rd Ed.) New York: Holt,
        1969. Covers the basic concepts and methods of statistics,
        with minimum emphasis on mathematics and calculation.

Kish, L. A. *Survey Sampling.* New York: Wiley, 1965. A balanced treatment of statistical and methodological aspects of sample surveys.

McNemar, Q. *Psychological Statistics.* (4th Ed.) New York: Wiley, 1969. A comprehensive treatment of statistical methods used in measurement and evaluation, with special emphasis on the interpretation of statistical results.

Winer, B. J. *Statistical Principles in Experimental Design.* (2nd Ed.) New York: McGraw-Hill, 1971. A systematic treatment of the principles and methods of statistical inference in experimental designs useful in the behavioral sciences.

———————— SUMMATIVE EVALUATION ————————

Evaluation research may be categorized under two major headings—**Formative Evaluation** and summative evaluation. The purpose of summative evaluation is to assess the overall effectiveness of a program, whereas the purpose of formative evaluation is generally to help in the development of the program.

Another major distinction between formative and summative evaluation concerns the audience for whom the work is intended. The results of formative evaluation are intended primarily for those who are working on the development of the program. Summative-evaluation reports are directed primarily toward those who set policy at various levels—e.g., who decide whether to continue to fund a national program or, at the local level, whether to use the program with students in their school system. Thus, summative evaluation is the assessment of an already developed program. The summative evaluator gets into the major phase of his work as the formative evaluator finishes his.

The implications of these distinctions for professional relationships are important. The formative researcher and the program developer are interdependent. The program developer needs the formative researcher for the performance of a number of crucially important functions (see **Formative Evaluation** for a detailed account). On the other hand, the summative researcher should be independent of the program, its developers, and those who assist the developers. Through an independent relationship, the summative evaluator can not only *be* objective about the program being evaluated but also *seem* to be objective. Both being objective and seeming to be so are important if the conclusions reached by the summative evaluator are to be valid and believable.

Summative evaluations may vary considerably in scope, complexity, and cost, but in each instance it is almost certain that the evaluator will have to consider a number of major areas including program **Goals and Objectives, Sampling, Test Selection, Design of Evaluation,** and **Statistical Analysis.** (See also on **Planning and Priorities** and "Hard" and "Soft"–Shibboleths in Evaluation.)

Because summative evaluation means assessing the impact of a program, the researcher has to be concerned with the question "Impact with respect to what?" Most evaluation experts would look for an answer by focusing on both the intended and the unintended goals of the program. (See **Medical Model of Evaluation** and **Side Effects** for discussions of this issue.) There is some dispute, however, and other experts suggest that the summative evaluation should be a **Goal-Free Evaluation**; i.e., the evaluator should not be overconcerned with the stated goals of the program, which might be unnecessarily and defensively restrictive. In any case, after the criteria by which the impact will be assessed have been determined, the summative evaluator will have to choose appropriate measures—presumably, measures that will reflect the criteria chosen as most important (see **Criterion Measurement**).

In addition, in the early planning phase of the summative evaluation, decisions will have to be made about target populations, the sampling plan, and the design of the study. If the proper lead time is given the summative evaluator, these early decisions and the subsequent activities can be carried out with proper technical expertise. Summative evaluation, given adequate time and funds, can and should be technically excellent research. Much of this book is devoted to furthering this principle.

Typically, the product of the summative research will be a report (see **Dissemination of Evaluation Results**). If all has gone well, the report will indicate areas of program success (intended outcomes attained, positive but unintended outcomes attained) and areas of program failure (intended outcomes not attained, negative unintended outcomes noted). The study should also be sufficiently sophisticated to allow the evaluator to point to the program features that seemed to influence success or failure. That is, good summative evaluation may well have formative implications.—S. B.

Bloom, B. S., Hastings, J. T., and Madaus, G. F. *Handbook on Formative and Summative Evaluation of Student Learning.* New York: McGraw-Hill, 1971. A wide-ranging and intensive treatment of the topic.

Rossi, P. H. "Practice, Method and Theory in Evaluating Social Action Programs." In J. L. Sundquist (Ed.), *On Fighting Poverty: Perspectives from Experience.* New York: Basic Books, 1969.

Scriven, M. "The Methodology of Evaluation." In *Perspectives of Curriculum Evaluation.* AERA Monograph Series on Curriculum Evaluation, No. 1. Chicago: Rand McNally, 1967. Pp. 39-82. An historically important article, being one of the first references to formative evaluation.

Suchman, E. A. *Evaluative Research.* New York: Russell Sage Foundation, 1967. A clear presentation of the work involved in summative evaluation.

—————————— SURVEY METHODS ——————————

The diverse techniques and procedures used to obtain information about a population, usually a human population in the real world rather than in a laboratory, have become collectively known as *survey methods.* A survey generally begins with an explicit statement of the problem: the goals of the study, the population of interest, the information to be obtained, and the resources necessary and available to do the work. In cases where a problem is difficult to conceptualize or where novel solutions must be employed, unusual approaches such as brainstorming or the **Delphi Technique** may be employed. Once the problem has been explicated, however, the general direction for its solution should be apparent. A planning phase typically follows.

During the planning phase, schedules of costs and events must be prepared. In larger studies, the development of such schedules can be facilitated by the use of such computerized aids as the **Program Evaluation and Review Technique (PERT).** An organizational structure for the conduct of the study must also be designed and personnel requirements established so as to delineate the areas of authority and responsibility. The basic format of data-collection instrumentation must be established; e.g., it must be determined whether data will be gathered through electronic or mechanical means (such as automated recorders or computers), whether skilled observers or interviewers will be used, whether questionnaires will be mailed. The concomitants of each alternative must also be considered. If, for example, automated recorders are desired, how many will be required? Where can they be procured? What will they cost? How quickly can they be obtained? How reliable are the recorders? What are the operating costs, in money and manpower? If plans call for the use of interviewers, how many will be required? Where will they be obtained? What educational or cultural background should they have? How are they to be trained? How are they to be managed? How many additional interviewers will be necessary to ensure against absenteeism and resignations during the study? How much, how often, and by what formula should interviewers be paid, and how should their pay be delivered to them? If the survey covers a large geographic region, lines of supply and communication may be overextended. How can this be avoided? Through redundancy? Increasing channel capacity? Increasing channel reliability?

During the planning phase, extensive thought must also be devoted to the kinds of information to be gathered. What demographic data must be retrieved to characterize the respondents? What attitudes must be assessed? Which cognitive skills? Which personality factors? How reliable must the instruments be? Which of the variables of interest can be measured through the use of instruments already available? For which kinds of information must new instruments be developed?

Some attention must be devoted to assuring a high response rate from the selected respondents. How many call-backs will an interviewer be required to make? How many follow-up questionnaires will be sent a respondent? How will the responses be monitored? What schedule will be used for follow-up mailings? Will respondents be paid or rewarded for their participation in the survey? If so, how much will they be paid or how will they be rewarded—and how will the payment or reward be delivered?

Plans associated with theories to be tested or plans associated with **Experimental Design** and **Sampling** are primary to the survey effort; consequently, they typically underlie all other survey plans and are reflected in them. At the conclusion of the planning phase, it is often judicious to review the plans and procedures to ensure that these more theoretical concerns have not been overlooked or modified in some improper way. Once the plans and procedures for the conduct of the study have been completed, the first steps toward implementation may be taken.

Implementation often begins simultaneously in several directions. Personnel must be assembled, fitted into the organizational format, and trained for their jobs. Unless experienced survey staff are already available, administrators, clerical staff, secretaries, interviewers, and technical staff (computer programmers, keypunch operators, sociologists, psychologists, education specialists, statisticians, printers, test and questionnaire specialists, and others) may have to be recruited, selected, and trained for the jobs to be done.

Concurrently, sampling activities may begin. These include completing the sample design, assembling the sample frames, and selecting the sample of respondents from those listed on the frames (together with any replacements that may be necessary).

Test and questionnaire development, as well as the procurement of other instruments already available, also takes place at this time. When all instruments have been obtained, the data-collection phase of the survey may begin. In this phase the instruments are administered to the selected elements of the population and the necessary call-backs and follow-ups are made to obtain the desired response rates and as complete data as possible.

The data must then be prepared for analysis. **Data Preparation** often include editing, coding, keypunching or keytaping, verification, and construction of a computer data file. The files produced are then analyzed according to the experimental design and sampling design used for the study. In many cases, the complexity of this task requires that a statistician be available for consultation, if not to manage and supervise the data-analysis effort. Interpretation of the results of the analysis almost always requires the capabilities of a professional whose field of interest relates to the topic of the study. Ideally, the professional should be familiar with the assumptions and characteristics of the analysis applied to the data; if he is not, he should work closely with a statistician in interpreting the results of the analysis. The conclusion of a survey is at hand when the results are finally reported. Typically, reporting includes the technical documentation of the study and indicators of the successfulness of the effort (such as response rates and considerations of nonresponse-bias effects), in addition to reporting the goal-oriented information which was the purpose of the study.

The expenditures of effort described here are almost certain to reduce mistakes and improve the usefulness of the final results. Extensive training of interviewers, for example, reduces interviewer variability, and coding data twice (checking for discrepancies between coders) results in more stable data. Since practically all surveys are conducted within constraints of time and money, these scarce resources must be apportioned to the stages of the survey in a series of compromises to obtain, overall, the highest-quality result.—F. R. C.

Glock, C. Y. (Ed.) *Survey Research in the Social Sciences.* New York: Russell Sage Foundation, 1967. See pages 315-377 for a discussion of survey research in the field of education.

Lansing, J. C., and Morgan, J. N. *Economic Survey Methods.* Ann Arbor: Institute for Social Research, University of Michigan, 1971. Covers design, sampling, data-collection methods, and data analysis, as well as financing, organization, and use of survey research.

Miller, D. C. *Handbook of Research Design and Social Measurement.* New York: McKay, 1964. Provides reference materials in research design and sampling, statistical analysis, selection of sociometric scales or indexes, and research costing and reporting.

Phillips, B. S. *Social Research: Strategy and Tactics.* New York: Macmillan, 1966. See Chapter 6, "Interviews, Questionnaires, and Surveys."

Sjoberg, G., and Nett, R. *A Methodology for Social Research.* New York: Harper, 1968. See the section on structured interviews (pp. 193-211).

-------------------- SYSTEMS ANALYSIS --------------------

In the context of evaluation of education/training programs, the concept *systems analysis* can be employed usefully in a rather broad sense, encompassing several meanings that might be distinguished for other purposes. Basically, systems analysis is a tool available to the executive in making decisions based (almost always) on incomplete information. More specifically, it is designed to assist a decision maker in identifying a preferred (or optimum) choice among possible alternatives. By this somewhat crude definition many analytical procedures would be included under systems analysis.

At least one popular method—**Program-Planning-Budgeting System**—is specifically excluded. It is considered distinct from systems analysis because either method can be used without the other. As used in the Department of Defense—where these methods had their full realization—program budgeting (or Five Year Program) covers the entire Department, while systems analysis (or cost-effectiveness or cost-benefit analysis) is applied only to certain problems of choice. It is also true that cost-effectiveness studies had been successfully developed before the ideas of program budgeting were conceived.

In a very general way, systems analysis may be viewed as a way of looking at problems, without necessarily making use of

analytical aids or computing devices. If a set of elements are sufficiently numerous, share some common purpose, and involve interactions and interdependencies, they may be considered a "system." The behavior of such a system is the subject under study.
Because of its inherent variables and their interdependencies, we
would expect that different outputs would be produced if the
basic inputs and constraints were altered. To help make decisions
about such a system, the systematic array of possible alternatives
and subjective judgments about their outcomes could be very useful even if no further analytical work were done.

Systems analysis, as most commonly used, tries to arrive at
some kind of optimal solution of a decision problem. It usually
consists of an attempt to *minimize* dollar *costs* for any *specified
outcome* or, conversely, to *maximize benefits* for a *given cost*.

The analysis proceeds by making explicit a number of feasible alternative ways that might achieve some stated objectives,
and, by estimating their associated costs and expected benefits, it
provides a means for selecting an optimal alternative. A formal
conceptualization of a cost-benefit analysis is represented in Figure 1. Probably the most important aspect of this approach is the
creative task of generating alternative programs. (The mathematical models may be highly theoretical and complex, while estimates
of costs and anticipated benefits may be difficult to come by and
require experienced judgment; but all the technical expertise
applied to the program cannot offset the omission of a viable alternative program.) The several programs are rank-ordered according
to a single (composite) criterion, usually after several iterations
based on revised estimates of costs and anticipated outcomes in
the feedback loops, so that ultimately a decision can be made
regarding preferred programs.

When a formal cost-benefit analysis is done, the results can
be exhibited as in Figure 2. This kind of presentation brings the
alternative programs into juxtaposition on a common metric of
benefits, with associated costs on the other axis. A program represented by a line with a small slope will yield very large benefits for
relatively small costs, while a program with a steep slope requires
high costs to accomplish relatively small benefits. In Figure 2 the
several programs are arranged in cost-benefit order. Given a fixed
level of resources, the program to be implemented is indicated by

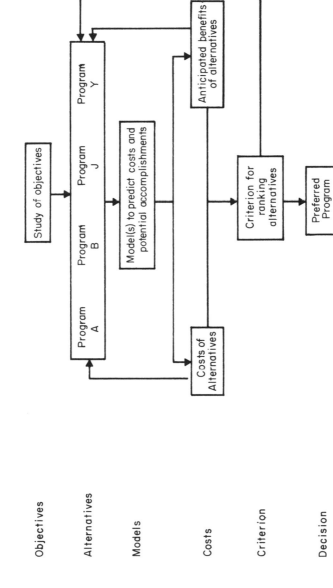

Objectives

Alternatives

Models

Costs

Criterion

Decision

Study of objectives

Program A   Program B   Program J   Program Y

Model(s) to predict costs and potential accomplishments

Anticipated benefits of alternatives

Costs of Alternatives

Criterion for ranking alternatives

Preferred Program

Figure 1. Simple model of a cost-benefit analysis.

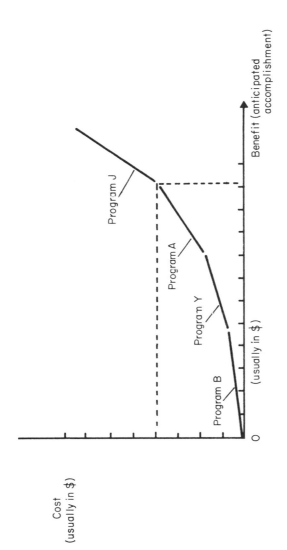

Figure 2. Results of a cost-benefit analysis.

drawing a horizontal line from that fixed level of resources to the curve. The anticipated benefits are indicated by dropping a vertical line to the benefit axis. (It should be noted here that benefits as well as costs are usually expressed in dollar values.)

The fact that costs and potential benefits of a program are considered does not make a cost-benefit analysis. The important component trade-off must also be present. In other words, if someone simply investigates the costs of introducing a new remedial-reading program, and compares the reading accomplishments (benefits) that accrue from this program with the accomplishments of students not given this treatment, he is not conducting a "cost-benefit study." The foregoing comparison might help him make a more valid assumption about expected benefits of the proposed programs. But in a cost-benefit analysis, the proposed reading program would be put in competition with other programs (not necessarily restricted to reading), and decisions would be made regarding their *relative* merits in consideration of both costs and benefits of each.

Cost-effectiveness studies in education are frequently regarded with the same kind of suspicion that was prevalent in the military establishment. Many military men believed that cost-effectiveness studies put "dollars before national security" and violated the dictum "nothing but the best for our boys." The educational argument goes: "If national defense is far too important a matter to be inhibited by cost, so certainly is the education of our citizens." The point both camps seem to miss is that cost resources are never unlimited; if we use more resources for one worthy purpose, less remains for other worthy purposes. Trade-offs are inevitable, but there is a need to ground trade-off decisions in as rational a context as possible. (See also **Simulation** and **Cost Considerations and Economic Analysis**.)—H. H. H.

Carter, L. F. *The Systems Approach to Education—The Mystique and the Reality*. Santa Monica, Calif.: System Development Corporation, 1969.

Churchman, C. W. *The Systems Approach*. New York: Delacorte Press, 1968. This book questions whether any single approach—systems, humanist, religious, etc.—is the "correct" approach to understanding the complex systems in which we live. The author concludes that *the* systems approach consists of a continuing debate among those with various attitudes toward society.

Hitch, C. J. *Decision-Making for Defense.* Berkeley: University of California Press, 1966. See especially Chapter III ("Cost-Effectiveness"), where cost-effectiveness studies are considered synonymous with "systems analyses."

"Proceedings of the Symposium on Operations Analysis of Education." *Socio-Economic Planning Sciences,* 1969, *2,* 105-520. Discussion and exchange of information between educators/educational researchers and those who have applied the techniques of operations analysis to educational problems.

Rivlin, A. M. *Systematic Thinking for Social Action.* Washington, D.C.: Brookings Institution, 1971. A book addressed to making government decisions more rationally. Chapter 3 discusses the need for identifying the objectives of social-action programs and the helpfulness of cost-benefit analysis in reaching decisions about them.

─────────── TAXONOMIES OF OBJECTIVES ───────────

One of the most durable principles in creating curricula for education/training programs (and in developing evaluations of the programs) is that the planners must first decide upon the outcomes being sought. But curriculum planners may find themselves wondering, after generating dozens of specific objectives for a course, whether they have totally covered a field or how all the selected objectives interrelate. They ask themselves (and each other) which course objectives ought to come first, which should receive major instructional emphasis or only a minor effort, which objectives must be accomplished as a preparation or prerequisite for other objectives, and which seem to be duplicates and might therefore be dropped altogether. Such concerns have led to the creation of taxonomies of objectives.

Scientists had already created taxonomies for the biological and physical sciences, classifying phenomena according to their properties and relationships. (The biological taxonomy, for example, classifies animals into class, order, family, genus, and species.) Educators hoped, similarly, to find a way to order and classify objectives that would rest on educational, logical, and psychological principles; could be empirically verified; would be consistent with educational and psychological theory; and perhaps even (as in the more exact sciences) point logically to phenomena as yet undiscovered. Thus, the deliberations over a number of years of many educational theorists and practitioners resulted in two pioneering (and probably the best-known) taxonomies of objectives in the cognitive and affective domains (see Bloom, 1956, and Krathwohl et al.). While lacking the extensive validation of their counterparts in the exact sciences, these taxonomies have aided significantly in the classification and description of educational outcomes.

The following advantages have been claimed for the taxonomies, although many investigators have been disappointed in their attempts to use them: (1) The analysis and sorting of objectives facilitate the preparation of clear statements of goals for programs. (2) The conceptual frameworks highlight the interrelationships of objectives and discourage atomistic approaches to instruction. (3) The detailed coverage of the objectives stimulates the development of improved and more comprehensive curricula. (4) Accuracy of communication is furthered, since scholars and practitioners from many different settings are provided with a shared, carefully defined vocabulary. (5) New ideas, materials, and economies of effort have been stimulated. (6) Test construction is improved, since test items can be based on operationally defined objectives. (7) Classroom instructors are given new perspectives on the range of course coverage and on desirable emphases in curriculum.

Bloom and Krathwohl and associates decided to divide the taxonomies into three "domains," the cognitive, affective, and psychomotor, recognizing nevertheless that the domains overlap. Handbook I, *The Cognitive Domain* (the largest of the taxonomies), deals with solving intellectual tasks—from the simple recall of facts to original ways of combining, synthesizing, and evaluating new ideas and materials. Handbook II, *The Affective Domain,* includes objectives dealing with attitudes, values, interests, appreciation, and social-emotional adjustment. A taxonomy for the psychomotor domain (see **Psychomotor Variables**) has not yet been completed by Bloom and his associates, although others (see, for instance, Thornton and Wasdyke) have developed taxonomies in that domain.

There are six main categories of objectives in the taxonomy for the cognitive domain (knowledge, comprehension, application, analysis, synthesis, evaluation) and five in the affective domain (receiving or attending, responding, valuing, organization, and characterization by a value complex). The organizing principle for the cognitive domain is "complexity"; i.e., each category is assumed to involve behavior more complex and abstract than the previous category. The organizing principle for the affective domain is "internalization," or how fully and deeply an emotion, attitude, or appreciation has become "part" of a person.

The following outline is a condensed version of the taxonomy for the cognitive domain (Bloom, 1956) and for the affective domain (Krathwohl et al.). (See also **Affective Variables** and **Cognitive Variables.**)

Taxonomy for the Cognitive Domain

1.00 Knowledge
... involves the recall of specifics and universals, the recall of methods and processes, or the recall of a pattern, structure, or setting.
1.10 Knowledge of specifics
    1.11 Knowledge of terminology
    1.12 Knowledge of specific facts
1.20 Knowledge of ways and means of dealing with specifics
    1.21 Knowledge of conventions
    1.22 Knowledge of trends and sequences
    1.23 Knowledge of classifications and categories
    1.24 Knowledge of criteria
    1.25 Knowledge of methodology

1.30 Knowledge of the universals and abstractions in a field
    1.31 Knowledge of principles and generalizations
    1.32 Knowledge of theories and structure
2.00 Comprehension
. . . represents the lowest level of understanding.
2.10 Translation
2.20 Interpretation
2.30 Extrapolation
3.00 Application
The use of abstractions in particular and concrete situations.
4.00 Analysis
The breakdown of a communication into its constituent elements or parts such that the relative hierarchy of ideas is made clear and/or the relations between the ideas expressed are made explicit.
4.10 Analysis of elements
4.20 Analysis of relationships
4.30 Analysis of organizational principles
5.00 Synthesis
The putting together of elements and parts so as to form a whole.
5.10 Production of a unique communication
5.20 Production of a plan, or proposed set of operations
5.30 Derivation of a set of abstract relations
6.00 Evaluation
Judgments about the value of material and methods for given purposes.
6.10 Judgments in terms of internal evidence
6.20 Judgments in terms of external criteria

Taxonomy for the Affective Domain

1.0 Receiving (attending)
. . . concern that the learner be sensitized to the existence of certain phenomena and stimuli; that is, that he be willing to receive or to attend to them.
1.1 Awareness
1.2 Willingness to receive
1.3 Controlled or selected attention

2.0 Responding
    ... concern with responses that go beyond merely attending
to the phenomenon. A person is actively attending.
   2.1 Acquiescence in responding
   2.2 Willingness to respond
   2.3 Satisfaction in response
3.0 Valuing
    ... behavior ... is motivated by the individual's commitment
to the underlying value guiding the behavior.
   3.1 Acceptance of a value
   3.2 Preference for a value
   3.3 Commitment
4.0 Organization
    For situations where more than one value is relevant, the nec-
essity arises for (a) the organization of the values into a system, (b) the determination of the interrelationships among
them, and (c) the establishment of the dominant and pervasive one.
   4.1 Conceptualization of a value
   4.2 Organization of a value system
5.0 Characterization by a value or value complex
    ... the values already have a place in the individual's value
hierarchy, are organized into some kind of internally consistent system, have controlled the behavior of the individual
for a sufficient time that he has adapted to behaving this
way; and an evocation of the behavior no longer arouses emotion or affect except when the individual is threatened or
challenged.
   5.1 Generalized set
   5.2 Characterization

Other psychologists, too, have attempted taxonomic systems based on different sortings and hierarchical principles (see
Stones and Anderson) and are attempting to validate the taxonomies through extensive research (see Cox and Unks).

The taxonomies typically contain a clear definition of each
category, a selection of illustrative objectives for each, a discussion
of problems in testing the objective, and sometimes a set of illustrative test items that will elicit the desired behaviors. The significance of the taxonomies for evaluators is principally that they

force attention upon selection of a full range of objectives, from "lower" to "higher"; they may also suggest to program designers the choice of learning experiences likely to promote the objectives they have selected and appropriate evaluation instruments for each kind of learning or performance which the program hopes to evoke.—E. J. R.

Bloom, B. S. (Ed.) *Taxonomy of Educational Objectives. Handbook I: Cognitive Domain.* New York: McKay, 1956.

Cox, R. C., and Unks, N. J. *A Selected and Annotated Bibliography of Studies Concerning the Taxonomy of Educational Objectives: Cognitive Domain.* Pittsburgh: University of Pittsburgh, Learning Research and Development Center, 1967.

Gagné, R. M. *The Condition of Learning.* New York: Holt, 1965. An eight-level taxonomic model which shows types of learning that are ancillary to other learnings, proceeding from simple to complex behaviors.

Krathwohl, D. R., Bloom, B. S., and Masia, B. B. *Taxonomy of Educational Objectives. Handbook II: Affective Domain.* New York: McKay, 1964.

Stones, E., and Anderson, D. *Educational Objectives and the Teaching of Educational Psychology.* London: Methuen, 1972. For an extensive discussion of the several taxonomies that have been constructed, see pages 17-27 and 194-205.

Thornton, R. F., and Wasdyke, R. G. *A Taxonomy for the Development of Multidimensional Test Specifications.* Princeton, N.J.: Educational Testing Service, 1973. An interesting application of a complete taxonomy to the field of career development and testing.

---------------------------------- TEST ANXIETY ----------------------------------

The concept of anxiety was formalized as a psychological construct by Freud and has played a central role in the behavioral sciences ever since. Manifestations include both physiological responses (e.g., palm sweating) and affective responses (ranging from vague feelings of uneasiness to feelings of dread and terror). Most theorists agree that it is important to distinguish between anxiety as a *transitory state* and anxiety as a *continuing personality trait* and that at least the first kind of anxiety is strongly situation-dependent. Testing is one kind of situation that seems to arouse anxiety states in some people some of the time.

Evaluators of education and training programs are concerned about anxiety chiefly as it may affect the meanings of test scores and thus inferences about the effectiveness of a program. The problem is not a simple one, especially when we consider that anxiety may serve as a facilitator of performance as well as a debilitator. For example, it has been noted that high anxiety may be debilitating in complex tasks but facilitating in simpler tasks.

There are two approaches to dealing with test anxiety in an evaluation study. The first is to try to reduce the likelihood of its occurring at a serious enough level to substantially depress or compromise the results. The second is to try to assess test anxiety directly and then take its influence into account in analyses and interpretations.

If anxiety is associated with worry about the testing process, then the kinds of actions suggested in the article on **Test Wiseness** may tend to alleviate it. If anxiety is based on fear of negative personal evaluation, anonymity for responders and/or emphasis on the fact that only the program is being evaluated and not the students should help. For some students (young children especially), anxiety seems to be reduced in the presence of a warm, sympathetic examiner. However, even the best-meant attempts to reduce test anxiety may actually increase it in some students.

The second approach to handling test anxiety is hampered by the scarcity of adequate measures of state, as opposed to trait, anxiety and by lack of understanding of the relationships between them. A number of trait-anxiety measures, beginning with the work of Taylor and Spence, have been developed and refined (e.g., the Children's Manifest Anxiety Scale by Castanada, McCandless, and Palermo; Sarason's General Anxiety Scale for Children; and the Alpert-Haber Achievement Anxiety Test). However, correlations between scores on such measures and scores on achievement and ability tests are generally small. So, not incidentally, are many of the correlations between anxiety scores derived from different measures.

In the face of all these difficulties, evaluators are probably well advised to take both approaches when test anxiety is seen as a potentially serious problem.—S. B. A.

Alpert, R., and Haber, R. N. "Anxiety in Academic Achievement Situations." *Journal of Abnormal and Social Psychology,* 1960, *61,* 207-215.

Sarason, S. B., Davidson, K. S., Lighthall, F. F., Waite, R. R., and Ruebush, B. K. *Anxiety in Elementary School Children.* New York: Wiley, 1960. See especially Chapter 2 ("Hypotheses"), Chapter 3 ("Review of Literature"), Chapter 4 ("The Anxiety Scales"), Chapter 7 ("Interfering and Facilitating Effects of Anxiety").

Taylor, J. A. "A Personality Scale of Manifest Anxiety." *Journal of Abnormal and Social Psychology,* 1953, *48,* 285-290.

Tobias, S., and Hedl, J. J., Jr. *Test Anxiety: Situationally Specific or General?* Tech. Memo No. 49, Project NR 154-280. Tallahassee: Computer Assisted Instruction Center, Florida State University, 1972.

Wine, J. "Test Anxiety and Direction of Attention." *Psychological Bulletin,* 1971, *76,* 92-104.

TESTS

Test is one of those words we take for granted. We seldom look it up in *Webster's Collegiate*: "test (Educ.)" = "any series of questions or exercises or other means of measuring the skill, knowledge, intelligence, capacities, or aptitudes of an individual or group." We tolerate much narrower definitions (e.g., those limited to paper-and-pencil examinations) and also much broader ones (e.g., sometimes we apply the word *test* to comprehensive **Assessment** of an individual or to an entire program-evaluation effort). The common elements seem to be (a) an experience that is reproducible across two or more people or groups and (b) some means of characterizing individuals or groups in comparable terms on the basis of that experience.

Many articles in this book have the word *test* in their titles (**Achievement Test Construction, Bias in Testing, Culture-Fair Test, Pretest, Projective Tests, Test Wiseness,** etc.), and many more use the word extensively in the text. The purpose of the present entry is simply to review in one place some of the diverse and frequently overlapping bases for describing or classifying tests. The following list contains some of the important dimensions:

1. *Proposed use of the results.* **Formative** or **Summative Evaluation** of programs, research, **Needs Assessment,** individual diagnosis, guidance, placement, selection, job advancement, **Certification,** self-assessment, etc. The concept of validity is central here.

2. *Whether test-based decisions are to be made about individuals (as in selection) or groups (as in program evaluation).* This dimension has important implications for test construction, test administration (e.g., see **Item Sampling**), and requirements for **Reliability.**

3. *Construct measured:* personality characteristics, aptitudes, mental abilities, perceptual-motor skills, interests, attitudes, etc.

4. *Subject matter or content:* mathematics, history, auto mechanics, shorthand, art, etc.

5. *Whether the focus is on maximal or typical performance* —on the best performance the student is capable of or on the level and quality of performance exhibited under ordinary circumstances. Most tests in cognitive areas are intended to measure maximal performance. However, especially when decisions about instructional intervention strategies for individual students are involved, it may be useful to try to assess both and study any discrepancies between them (see Anderson and Messick, pp. 12-14; Lyman, p. 4).

6. *Homogeneity of the items or tasks*—the degree to which the test items tend to measure the same construct or domain versus several constructs or domains. The attempts at development of factor-dominant tests, such as the Tests of Primary Mental Abilities, mark one end of this continuum (see **Factor Analysis**), while many standardized achievement tests are deliberately designed to survey a number of different domains (see **Standardized Tests**). Sometimes tests are assembled into batteries to cover several related areas.

7. *Supporting data base:* score or performance interpreted in terms of rational analyses of the test content or domain, subjectively established **Standards** (as in tests of **Mastery Learning**), reference to external criteria (see **Criterion-Referenced Measurement**), and/or **Norms**.

8. *Type of response student gives:* production or performance (e.g., an essay, a recipe, a musical performance, or driving an automobile); recognition (e.g., in true-false, multiple-choice, or matching items). (See **Achievement Test Construction**.)

9. *Type of scoring:* objective vs. subjective (judgmental), machine vs. hand, global (e.g., an overall rating) vs. analytic (e.g., ratings of discrete aspects of performance), quantitative (where the score indicates more or less of a characteristic) vs. qualitative (where the score indicates a classification of a student—e.g., "interested in people" or "interested in things").

10. *Whether there are standards for the acceptability of responses*—standards in terms of correctness, gradations of quality, etc. The usual achievement and ability tests have correct or "best" answers, while many tests of attitudes or opinions do not.

11. *Congruency of the perceptions of the tester and the student about the purposes of the measurement.* For most tests used in evaluation of education/training programs, what the student thinks he is being tested on and what the tester thinks he is testing for are the same thing. However, in some tests—especially those used in clinical settings—the purpose of the test is disguised to the subject; e.g., he might think he is doing classification tasks when he is really being scored on impulsivity (see **Projective Tests**).

12. *When the instrument is administered:* **Pretest** (before the instructional program), **Posttest** (at the end of the program), etc.

13. *Emphasis on speed of response*—usually defined along the dimension "speeded" to "power," with power tests having generous time limits or none at all.

14. *Whether the test is given to only one person at a time or to a group.* The individual-administration mode is characteristic of many clinical tests (see **Intelligence Measurement**); however, most educational, industrial, and military tests are group tests.

15. *Who constructs the test.* Some measurement books treat teacher-made tests and commercial or published tests separately. The distinction is trivial in itself. However, commercial publishers often have more resources and expertise to put into the development process and access to a large and representative norms sample. The critical consideration in evaluation is the fit of the tests to the program objectives and evaluation design. In any comprehensive evaluation study, it is likely that a variety of tests will be used, including both standardized ones and tests constructed especially for the project.—S. B. A.

Anderson, S., and Messick, S. "Social Competency in Young Children." *Developmental Psychology,* 1974, *10* (2), 282-293.
Campbell, D. T. "A Typology of Tests, Projective and Otherwise." In D. N. Jackson and S. Messick (Eds.), *Problems in Human Assessment.* New York: McGraw-Hill, 1967. Pp. 190-194.
Cronbach, L. J. *Essentials of Psychological Testing.* (3rd Ed.) New York: Harper, 1970. See the chapter on purposes and types of tests (pp. 22-43).
Lyman, H. B. "Intelligence, Aptitude, and Achievement Testing." In S. C. Stone and B. Shertzer (Eds.), Guidance Monograph Series: III. *Testing.* Boston: Houghton Mifflin, 1968.

Thorndike, R. L. "Educational Measurement for the Seventies." In R. L. Thorndike (Ed.), *Educational Measurement.* (2nd Ed.) Washington, D.C.: American Council on Education, 1971. Pp. 3-14.

————————————— TEST SELECTION —————————————

It is unfortunate that many people have equated "evaluation" with "testing," for evaluation encompasses much more than measurement. Furthermore, too close an association of evaluation with tests—especially paper-and-pencil tests—could lead to neglect of many important variables simply because there are no tests for them.

However, many skills and achievements that instructional programs are designed to foster can be measured by Tests, and there are many tests available. It is sensible for evaluators to investigate the possibility that relevant tests already exist for their purposes before they decide to undertake the difficult and expensive task of developing new instruments. More important, the use of common measures allows some comparisons across programs, and the resulting accumulation of knowledge can be useful.

There are more than thirty publishers in the United States who issue test catalogs, and a list of them is given in Table 1. The most ambitious attempt to provide comprehensive and critical information about all published tests has been Buros's *Mental Measurement Yearbooks,* published in 1938, 1941, 1949, 1953, 1959, 1965, and 1972. The literature also contains a number of reviews of measures in particular fields (see, for example, the test-review references at the end of this article). Educational Testing Service, Princeton, New Jersey, maintains a very large collection of tests and is an especially useful source of information about instruments that have gone out of print. The ERIC (Educational Resources Information Center) system is another repository of information about some measuring instruments.

Table 1

Major U.S. Publishers of Standardized Tests

American College Testing Program (ACT)
P. O. Box 168
Iowa City, Iowa 52240
319-351-4470

American Guidance Service, Inc.
Publishers' Building
Circle Pines, Minnesota 55014
612-786-4343

The Bobbs-Merrill Company
4300 West 62nd Street
Indianapolis, Indiana 46268
317-291-3100

Bureau of Educational Measurements
Kansas State Teachers College
Emporia, Kansas 66801
316-343-1200

Bureau of Educational Research & Service
C-20 East Hall
The University of Iowa
Iowa City, Iowa 52240
319-353-3823

CTB/McGraw-Hill
Del Monte Research Park
Monterey, California 93940
408-373-2932

Committee on Diagnostic Reading Tests, Inc.
Mountain Home, North Carolina 28758
704-693-5223

Consulting Psychologists Press, Inc.
577 College Avenue
Palo Alto, California 94306
415-326-4448

Cooperative Tests and Services—see Educational Testing Service

Educational and Industrial Testing Service
P. O. Box 7234
San Diego, California 92107
714-488-1666

Educational Records Bureau
Box 619
Princeton, New Jersey 08540
609-921-9000

Educational Test Bureau—see American Guidance Service, Inc.

Educational Testing Service
Princeton, New Jersey 08540
609-921-9000

Follett Publishing Company, A Division of Follett Corporation
P. O. Box 5705
Chicago, Illinois 60680
312-666-5855

Ginn and Company—see Personnel Press

Grune and Stratton, Inc.
111 Fifth Avenue
New York, New York 10003
212-260-4900

Guidance Testing Associates
6516 Shirley Avenue
Austin, Texas 78752
512-452-6969

Harcourt Brace Jovanovich, Inc.
757 Third Avenue
New York, New York 10017
212-572-5000

Houghton Mifflin Company
Pennington-Hopewell Road
Hopewell, New Jersey 08525
609-466-1950

Institute for Personality and Ability Testing (IPAT)
1602 Coronado Drive
Champaign, Illinois 61822
217-352-4739

Martin M. Bruce, Publishers
340 Oxford Road
New Rochelle, New York 10804
914-235-4450

Table 1 (Continued)

McGraw-Hill Book Company—*see* CTB/
McGraw-Hill

Personnel Press
Education Center
P. O. Box 2649
Columbus, Ohio 43216
    614-253-8642

Priority Innovations, Inc.
P. O. Box 792
Skokie, Illinois 60076
    312-729-1434

The Psychological Corporation
304 East 45th Street
New York, New York 10017
    212-679-7070

Psychological Research Services
Case Western Reserve University
1695 Magnolia Drive
Cleveland, Ohio 44106
    216-368-3536

Psychological Test Specialists
Box 1441
Missoula, Montana 59801

Psychologists and Educators Inc.
Suite 212
211 West State Street
Jacksonville, Illinois 62650
    217-243-2135

Psychometric Affiliates
Box 3167
Munster, Indiana 46321
    219-836-1661

Richardson, Bellows, Henry and Com-
    pany, Inc.
1140 Connecticut Avenue, N.W.
Washington, D.C. 20036
    202-659-3755

Scholastic Testing Service, Inc.
480 Meyer Road
Bensenville, Illinois 60106
    312-766-7150

Science Research Associates, Inc.
259 East Erie Street
Chicago, Illinois 60611
    312-266-5000

Sheridan Psychological Services, Inc.
P. O. Box 6101
Orange, California 92667
    714-639-2595

Stoelting Company
1350 South Kostner
Chicago, Illinois 60623
    312-522-4500

Teachers College Press
Teachers College
Columbia University
New York, New York 10027
    212-870-4215

University Bookstore
Purdue University
360 State Street
West Lafayette, Indiana 47906
    317-743-9618

Western Psychological Services
12031 Wilshire Boulevard
Los Angeles, California 90025
    213-478-2061

*Sources of Information About Employ-
ment Tests*

Industrial Relations Center
University of Chicago
1225 East 60th Street
Chicago, Illinois 60637

Psychological Institute
O'Rourke Publications
Box 1118
Lake Alfred, Florida 33850

Stevens, Thurow and Associates, Inc.
105 West Adams Street
Chicago, Illinois 60603

Test catalogs and reviews are helpful in identifying promising candidates for use in evaluation studies. However, final selection must rest on examination of the instruments themselves, along with relevant manuals and technical reports.

The American Psychological Association, the American Educational Research Association, and the National Council on Measurement in Education have recommended technical standards for educational and psychological tests. These recommendations specify the essential information about validity, reliability, norms, etc., that test publishers should provide to enable potential users to judge the merits of the tests. Of these, the most important for those selecting tests for use in evaluation studies are *content* and *construct* **Validity.**

If an achievement instrument is sought, does its coverage correspond closely with the subject matters and skills stressed in the instructional program—or a relevant subset of them? (If the latter, additional measures for the other areas may have to be found or developed.) Any achievement-test-selection procedure that does not involve item-by-item review cannot claim to have answered this question about coverage.

If an instrument is sought to measure a general psychological trait (such as self-concept or analytical reasoning) which the program is attempting to influence, what is the evidence for assuming that a candidate instrument measures it? What other measures purporting to tap the same trait does it correlate with? What measures purporting to tap antithetical traits does it relate negatively to? What measures that are designed to measure independent traits does it show little or no relationship with?

Some degree of **Reliability** of measurement is, of course, essential for validity. The potential user of a test for evaluation purposes must consider the reliability evidence presented for the test on two grounds: whether the conclusions he wishes to draw from the evaluation study will require reliable measurement of individuals as well as groups (in the former case he needs higher reliability coefficients) and whether the type of validity information is relevant to his purposes (e.g., if he is planning to use alternate forms of the test for **Pretest** and **Posttest,** he would be especially interested in the correlation between scores on the two forms). The existence of equated test forms is itself a major selection criterion for some evaluation-study designs. (See **Equivalent Scores.**)

While an evaluator may not plan actually to use test **Norms** to interpret the results of an evaluation study, information about the characteristics and performance of various groups to whom a test has been administered can be very useful in helping to judge the appropriateness of the test for students or trainees in the particular program being evaluated: difficulty level of the items, relevance of the content to student backgrounds, etc. (see **Standardized Tests**).

In addition to looking at the technical characteristics of individual tests, the evaluator must, of course, be concerned with fit and feasibility. He usually has a broad range of variables to contend with and limited time and money. Any individual measure must be considered in terms of its contribution to the total assessment. Thus, in some cases a factor in the selection of a test might be its amenability to item-sampling procedures (see **Item Sampling**). Or a major impetus for seeking a test in the first place might be to reduce overdependence on other forms of data collection (questionnaires, etc.).—S. B. A.

American Psychological Association. *Standards for Educational and Psychological Tests.* Washington, D.C., 1974.

Cronbach, L. J. *Essentials of Psychological Testing.* (2nd Ed.) New York: Harper, 1960. See especially Chapter 6 and Tables 14 and 15.

Fitzpatrick, R. "The Selection of Measures for Evaluating Programs." In *Evaluative Research: Strategies and Methods.* Pittsburgh: American Institutes for Research, 1970. Pp. 67-81.

Guion, R. M. *Personnel Testing.* New York: McGraw-Hill, 1965. A comprehensive treatment of measurement in employment situations, with relevance for evaluation of industrial training efforts.

Katz, M. *Selecting an Achievement Test: Principles and Procedures.* Princeton, N.J.: Educational Testing Service, 1958. An excellent guide based on study of "own" school characteristics and testing needs in relationship to characteristics and capabilities of available tests.

Test-Review References

Beatty, W. *Improving Educational Assessment and an Inventory of Measures of Affective Behavior.* Washington, D.C.: Association for Supervision and Curriculum Development, National Education Association, 1969.

Berger, B. *An Annotated Bibliography of Measurements for Young Children.* New York: Center for Urban Education, 1969.

Bonjean, C. M., Hill, R. J., and McLemore, S. D. *Sociological Measurement: Inventory of Scales and Indices.* San Francisco: Chandler, 1967.

Buros, O. K. (Ed.) *Reading Tests and Reviews.* Highland Park, N.J.: Gryphon Press, 1968.

Buros, O. K. (Ed.) *Personality Tests and Reviews.* Highland Park, N.J.: Gryphon Press, 1970.

Buros, O. K. (Ed.) *The Seventh Mental Measurements Yearbook.* Highland Park, N.J.: Gryphon Press, 1972.

Cattell, R. B., and Warburton, F. *Objective Personality and Motivation Tests.* Urbana: University of Illinois Press, 1967.

Farr, R., and Anastasiow, N. *Tests of Reading Readiness and Achievement: A Review and Evaluation.* Newark, Del.: International Reading Association, 1969.

Hoepfner, R. (Ed.) *CSE Elementary School Test Evaluations.* Los Angeles: Center for the Study of Evaluation, UCLA Graduate School of Education, 1970.

Hoepfner, R., Stern, C., and Nummedal, S. G. (Eds.) *CSE-ECRC Preschool/Kindergarten Test Evaluations.* Los Angeles: Center for the Study of Evaluation and Early Childhood Research Center, UCLA Graduate School of Education, 1971.

Johnson, O., and Bommarito, J. W. *Tests and Measurements in Child Development: A Handbook.* San Francisco: Jossey-Bass, 1971.

Kaya, E. *Review of Preschool Tests, 1965-69.* New York: Hofstra University, 1969.

Shaw, M. E. *Scales for the Measurement of Attitudes.* New York: McGraw-Hill, 1967.

Simon, A., and Boyer, E. G. (Eds.) *Mirrors for Behavior: An Anthology of Classroom Observation Instruments.* Philadelphia: Research for Better Schools, 1967-1970. A fifteen-

volume series including analyses of the state of the art of
classroom observation, seventy-eight observation instruments, and many references.

Straus, M. A. *Family Measurement Techniques: Abstracts of Published Instruments, 1935-1964.* Minneapolis: University of Minnesota Press, 1969.

Wylie, R. C. *The Self-Concept: A Critical Survey of Pertinent Research Literature.* Lincoln: University of Nebraska Press, 1961.

TEST WISENESS

Changing attitudes toward test wiseness parallel changing attitudes toward failure to learn. It is recognized that the burden for students' failure to learn falls as much upon the school or program as upon the student. And—especially in evaluation studies—test wiseness should be more a concern of the instrument developer and administrator than the test taker. Instruments and the accompanying conditions for their administration should be designed so that differential advantages deriving from previous experience with similar materials or knowledge of testing conventions will be minimal. When this is not the case, there are serious threats to the **Validity** of the measurement; the interpreter cannot tell the extent to which score differences reflect differences in the abilities the test was designed to measure, as opposed to differences in test-taking sophistication.

Recognizing that to some people (e.g., very young children, adults in continuing-education programs, students from other nations) taking a test may be a new or not recently practiced activity, what are some of the steps that testers can take to reduce the influence of test wiseness on test scores? They fall into two classes:

1. Steps to make all test takers "wise": clear directions for preparing for the test, if preparation is required; generous use of practice materials; clear and relevant examples of question types

and response procedures; simple response procedures; easy-to-read-and-follow formats; similar formats throughout a test battery, to reduce the necessity for changing mental sets and learning new mechanical procedures; and—in the case of multiple-choice items—specific instructions about guessing. (On the last point, the fairest procedure seems to be to tell all test takers *to guess*.) Ebel (p. 206) has suggested that "more error in measurement is likely to originate from students who have too little, rather than too much, skill in taking tests."

2. Steps to avoid flaws in the development of the measures that favor those who have learned to capitalize on them: for example, unequal distribution of correct answers (e.g., a disproportionate number of correct responses in the fourth position of five-choice items), responses containing such words as *always* or *never* (the experienced test taker has learned that these can usually be eliminated as incorrect or false), differences in lengths of item options that correlate with correctness, and "kangaroo" options (those that are so different in kind or grammar from the other options in a set that they stand out as either right or wrong). (See **Achievement Test Construction**.)

It is important to note that **Test Anxiety** is not the opposite of test wiseness, although some of the steps taken to remove the influence of the latter from the scores may also help alleviate the former. (See also **Practice Effect**.)—S. B. A.

Anderson, S. B., Katz, M., and Shimberg, B. *Meeting the Test.* New York: Four Winds Press, 1965. Descriptions of a number of different kinds of educational and vocational tests, with many examples of the types of questions that appear in them. Chapter 13 is entitled "Hints to the Test Taker—How to Do Your Best."

Bennett, G. K., and Doppelt, J. E. *Test Orientation Procedure.* New York: Psychological Corporation, 1967. A kit of information and practice materials to familiarize job applicants with the kinds of tests commonly used in business and industrial organizations.

Ebel, R. L. *Measuring Educational Achievement.* Englewood Cliffs, N.J.: Prentice-Hall, 1965. See the sections on test wiseness and test anxiety (pp. 205-207).

Millman, J., Bishop, C. H., and Ebel, R. "An Analysis of Test-Wiseness." *Educational and Psychological Measurement,* 1965, *25,* 707-726.

Millman, J., and Pauk, W. *How to Take Tests.* New York: McGraw-Hill, 1969. Gives suggestions on preparing for examinations, taking examinations, and answering special types of test items.

------------------- TIME-SERIES ANALYSIS -------------------

A time series is a set of observations taken at specified times, usually at equal intervals. By considering a variable across time, the investigator is able to evaluate program effects without being misled by fluctuations that may be due, for example, to the manner in which the current testing was carried out or to a recent event that has a noticeable but short-term effect on the variable. Movements that are simply irregular can be sorted out when a phenomenon is studied over a sufficiently long time span. (See **Quasi-Experimental Design.**)

An example of a graph of a time series is given in Figure 1. The characteristic movements of a time series may be classified into four main types: (1) long-term movements, (2) cyclical movements, (3) seasonal movements, and (4) irregular or random movements. *Long-term* movements refer to the general direction in which the graph of a time series appears to be going over a long interval of time. The long-term movement is generally indicated by a *trend curve.* In Figure 1, the line of dashes is a trend curve for the cattle-population data. *Cyclical movements* refer to long-term oscillations about the trend line or curve. In Figure 1, the heavy curve shows the cyclical movements of the time series about the trend curve. *Seasonal movements* refer to identical, or almost identical, patterns which a time series appears to follow during corresponding months of successive years. In Figure 1, no seasonal

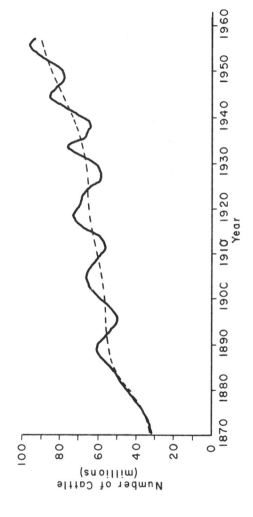

Figure 1. Cattle population of the United States, 1870-1960.

movements are present. Seasonal movements can be extended to include periodicity over any interval of time; e.g., daily, hourly, weekly. *Irregular or random movements* refer to sporadic motions of a time series due to chance events.

The analysis of time series consists in investigating the factors listed above and is often referred to as the decomposition of a time series into its basic component movements.

A common procedure used in smoothing out a time-series curve with many strong fluctuations is the technique of computing moving averages. A moving average of order n is defined as a sequence of arithmetic means (see **Statistics**). For example, for the sequence of numbers 5, 3, 1, 8, 6, 4, 2, a sequence of moving averages of order 3 is obtained as follows: $(5 + 3 + 1)/3$, $(3 + 1 + 8)/3$, $(1 + 8 + 6)/3$, $(8 + 6 + 4)/3$, $(6 + 4 + 2)/3 = 3, 4, 5, 6, 4$. If the data corresponded to monthly values, then the moving averages would be called *three-month moving averages*. The moving averages tend to reduce the amount of variance in the data and thus are often used to eliminate unwanted fluctuations.

Few of the testing programs in evaluation studies are used long enough to establish time series over a span of years. While this is not surprising, given the rapid changes that take place in the programs themselves, it makes experimental inference very difficult. Without an extended time frame in which to interpret results, it is possible to interpret a seasonal effect too strongly. For example, if students are tested in the fall of the year, there may be an effect due to "forgetting" over the summer.

When data are collected over time, comparison groups can be used quite effectively. For example, if growth curves for an experimental group and a comparison group (say, a random sample of the population) are available, it is possible to detect deviations from the "normal" growth, or trend, curve that may occur with the experimental group during a period of treatment. (See **Quasi-Experimental Design.**)

The user of evaluation results should be aware of the necessity to interpret results in a time frame, for it is in a time frame that the results will have to be applied. If time is neglected as an essential component of evaluation, interpretation of the results of the evaluation usually will be greatly oversimplified.— R. T. M.

Bock, R. D. "Conditional and Unconditional Inference in the Analysis of Repeated Measurements." Paper prepared for the Symposium on the Application of Statistical Techniques to Psychological Research, Canadian Psychological Association, York University, June 4, 1969.

Campbell, D. T. *Time-Series of Annual Same-Grade Testings in the Evaluation of Compensatory Educational Experiments.* Duplicated memorandum. Evanston, Ill.: Northwestern University, 1970.

Campbell, D. T., and Stanley, J. C. "Experimental and Quasi-Experimental Designs for Research on Teaching." In N. L. Gage (Ed.), *Handbook of Research on Teaching.* Chicago: Rand McNally, 1963. Pp. 171-246. Reprinted as *Experimental and Quasi-Experimental Design for Research.* Chicago: Rand McNally, 1966.

Glass, G. V., Willson, V. L., and Gottman, J. M. *Design and Analysis of Time-Series Experiments.* Boulder, Colo.: Laboratory of Educational Research, University of Colorado, 1972. A summary of seven years of work in time-series analysis, stemming from the Campbell and Stanley work in experimental and quasi-experimental design.

Harris, C. W. (Ed.) *Problems in Measuring Change.* Milwaukee: University of Wisconsin Press, 1967. See especially Chapters 5 and 12.

Spiegel, M. R. *Theory and Problems of Statistics.* New York: Schaum, 1961. Chapter 16 provides many examples of time series.

---------------------- TRAINING EVALUATION ----------------------

Training programs, as contrasted with broader educational programs, are ordinarily thought of as having relatively immediate and limited objectives; e.g., to help the trainee gain the competencies needed for work, military service, or other defined roles in society. However, many training programs include or espouse some objectives frequently associated with more academic programs; e.g., some of the executive-development programs offered in industry and the military. And many programs conducted in conventional educational institutions are oriented, usually among other things, toward immediate job-related competencies; teacher education is a notable case in point. Some of the current controversy about competency/performance-based teacher education probably stems from the traditional dual nature of the process (see the *Phi Delta Kappan* reference).

As we suggested in the introduction to this book, there is seldom any useful purpose served by trying to force a distinction between training and education. However, there are some strategic consequences for evaluation in distinguishing between instructional programs conducted or sponsored by organizations primarily *to serve their own needs* and programs with more general personal-societal goals. This article focuses on evaluation of the former, which include most in-service programs for teachers and typical military and industrial training programs.

Initially, the evaluator tends to direct attention toward whether the program is accomplishing its objectives. This implies that the intended objectives have been made explicit (see **Goals and Objectives** and **Taxonomies of Objectives**), that valid measurement of the objectives is possible, and that the evaluation design takes account of (1) the initial status of trainees (if they were not far advanced, then the training can be expected to have a measurable effect; if they were already quite proficient, then not much change can be expected, and the evaluator cannot claim that the proficiency was a *result* of the training) and (2) the possibility that changes that appear to be the result of training might very well have occurred if trainees had simply stayed on the job (to check this point, it is good practice to set up a **Control Group** which does not receive the training; see also **Design of Evaluation**).

J. H. Harless (Harless Performance Guild, Inc., McLean, Va., personal communication) calls this process of testing whether the program meets its objectives *program validation* (which relates to but is not identical with notions of measurement validation; see **Validity**). Harless argues, however, that program validation is not enough. Those evaluating an organizational training program must also look into *transfer* (Do the skills/knowledge learned in the training get exhibited on the job?) and *effectiveness* (Does the instruction solve the performance problem it was intended to solve?). The process of evaluating transfer and effectiveness may include consideration of whether the objectives of the training program are compatible with the larger goals of the organization and whether organizational barriers exist to the ability of trainees to apply what they have learned. For example, does the trainee have an opportunity to use his newly developed skills immediately after he returns to the job, or are time and events allowed to intervene so that he may forget what he learned?

Two other essential factors to consider in the evaluation of organization-based programs are *worth* and *acceptance*. There are limits to the amount of money that any organization responsible to stockholders, taxpayers, or its own profit motive can spend on training, no matter how well the program meets both specific and general objectives. Even within acceptable cost ceilings, most organizations want to know that they are getting the best training for their money, that the training is cost effective. In other words, are the benefits accruing to the organization from the training program worth the expense? (Have we spent $1 on a 10¢ problem?) This aspect of training evaluation may include comparative studies of alternative training approaches bearing different price tags.

The definition of *acceptance* used here encompasses both the technical accuracy of the training and the reactions of trainees and supervisors to it. The former is frequently assessed by content examination by subject-matter specialists; the latter, by critiques and questionnaires. Training directors are well aware that a poor program can gain acceptance; they are also aware that if supervisors dislike a program or feel it is not useful, the chances are high that the program will be ignored or scuttled. (See **Transactional Evaluation.**) Acceptance testing has acquired a bad name in some training circles, because the "smiles test" has sometimes been the only form of training evaluation that has taken place. However, specific assessment of acceptance is frequently a useful adjunct to measures of the validity, transfer, effectiveness, and worth of an organization-based training effort.—S. B. A., A. P. M.

Bray, D. W., Campbell, R. J., and Grant, D. L. *Formative Years in Business: A Long-Term AT&T Study of Managerial Lives.*

New York: Wiley, 1974. Stresses (pp. 59-60) the importance of feedback to trainees about their performance and
apparent potential, as these factors may bear on their progress in the organization.

Glaser, R. (Ed.) *Training Research and Education.* New York:
Wiley, 1965. See especially Chapters 11 and 12.

Harless, J. H. "An Analysis of Front-End Analysis." *Improving
Human Performance—A Research Quarterly,* Winter 1973.

Sills, D. L. (Ed.) "Evaluation Research." *International Encyclopedia of the Social Sciences.* Vol. 5. New York: Macmillan
and Free Press, 1968. P. 198.

Special issue on competency/performance-based teacher education. *Phi Delta Kappan,* 1974, *55* (5).

─────────── TRAINING OF EVALUATORS ───────────

Just as a house painter's house is often the one most in need
of painting, so too there is a general neglect of the training of evaluators by the evaluators of training programs. There is no Accreditation of existing programs because there is no accrediting agency.
There is no accrediting agency because there is no professional
organization that primarily represents program evaluators. In practice, many program evaluators who receive specific training in
their work get this training in graduate programs in education,
psychology, or sociology. It has been suggested that those from
education programs tend to work more in the genre of "soft" evaluation; those from psychology programs tend to work more in the
genre of "hard" evaluation (see "Hard" and "Soft"—Shibboleths
in Evaluation); and those from sociology programs tend to work
more in the genre of discussing evaluation. Many program evaluators also come from schools of business, departments of economics, and operations-research programs.

Obviously, the type of training influences the type of evaluation carried out (see **Evaluator Role**); and the type of evaluation carried out influences the type of training program for evaluators that is advocated. Nonetheless, certain areas of need in the evaluator's training program seem important: measurement, statistics, and research design (to provide technical background); philosophy and history of education and of science (to understand the evaluator's place and role); psychology (to understand the learner and processes of learning and development); education (to understand the teacher and teaching processes); sociology (to understand the relationship between the evaluation product and the decision-making process in a social setting). Most training programs labeled "evaluation" stress the technical (measurement, statistics, design) aspects of the job, relegating the courses in psychology, education, and sociology to adjunct roles.

The need to consider the training of program evaluators arose in the 1960s, when the demand for them became strong. At that time, the United States Office of Education was funding a large array of Research and Development Centers (including the Center for the Study of Evaluation at the University of California, Los Angeles) and Regional Laboratories. At about the same time, the United States Office of Education was funding many new programs in elementary and secondary schools (e.g., education for the disadvantaged, audio-visual services) and requiring the evaluation of these programs. Because of the critical shortage of evaluators, the United States Office of Education then funded training programs for evaluators. Most of those programs are no longer available, their funding having ceased; but the need for evaluators remained strong as the **Accountability** movement took hold.

A census of program evaluators has never been undertaken; we do not know how they were trained or even whether most program evaluations are conducted by people who think of themselves as program evaluators (rather than educational psychologists, professors of measurement, etc.). Presumably, as time passes and program evaluation becomes a more mature field, an association for evaluators will develop, and the training of evaluators will receive systematic attention.—S. B.

——————— TRAIT-TREATMENT INTERACTION ———————

Education has had a long and discouraging history of searching for the one best instructional treatment or method for everyone. The continuing battle over the best way to teach reading (e.g., phonics versus "look-say") is a case in point. Thus, the concept of trait-treatment interaction (TTI) has received an enthusiastic reception from theoreticians and practitioners alike. Simply stated, TTI implies that different learners with different characteristics may profit more from one type of instruction than from another, and that therefore it may be possible to find the best match of learner characteristics and instructional method in order to maximize learning outcomes. (See also **Interaction.**)

The notion is not limited to education. In medicine, patients with the same diagnosed affliction but with different medical histories may need very different medications. Mental patients with different personality patterns may respond quite differently to different types of therapy. High school freshmen may profit more from the help of one counselor, while high school seniors may profit more from the help of another. Military trainees with almost identical aptitude patterns may, because of differences in their interest patterns, perform better in certain training programs than in others, depending on the emphases in the instruction.

Trait-treatment interaction has also been labeled *aptitude-treatment interaction* (ATI), but the term *trait* is preferred by many because it is more general. *Trait* can be used to designate any clearly identifiable and relatively stable characteristic of the learner, including level of achievement or developed ability, **Cognitive Styles**, other aspects of personality, interests, social class (see **Socioeconomic Status**), ethnic background, and the usual academic and vocational "aptitudes." *Treatment*, too, has broad connotations and can encompass the nature of the content to be learned, various approaches to instruction, teacher characteristics, the course schedule, and even the system of rewards and punishments associated with performance in the program.

Figures 1, 2, and 3 illustrate three possible relationships between a trait measure (e.g., reading ability) and an outcome measure (e.g., score on the final course examination) when two different treatments are applied. These relationships are discussed here with reference to decisions about appropriate assignment of students to programs. Figure 1 shows no interaction between treatment and trait; treatment 1 is superior to treatment 2 at all levels of the trait measure (e.g., no matter whether students are the best or the poorest readers in the group). Therefore, other things being equal, the best decision rule for future students is to assign them all to treatment 1. Figure 2 displays an *ordinal interaction*: while treatment 1 appears to be more effective generally, there may be a point on the trait score scale where it would not make much difference whether learners were assigned to treatment 1 or treatment 2. If one treatment were significantly more costly than the other one, the decision maker might choose to assign all students with trait scores of 6 or below to the less expensive treatment. Figure 3 shows a *disordinal interaction*; i.e., the lines showing the relationships between trait and outcome measures for the two treatments cross. It can be seen from Figure 3 that students with trait scores above 9 might better be assigned to treatment 1, while students with trait scores below 9 could be expected to profit more from treatment 2. Lubin provides an excellent discussion of the use of interactions in the interpretation of data for decision making.

While a great deal of attention has been paid to the notion of TTI, relatively few investigators have designed their studies or analyzed their data with the identification of possible interactions in mind. The few who have investigated the phenomenon have only occasionally found significant interactions, and some of these have not held up in **Replication**. There are probably several overlapping reasons for this state of affairs. First, the conceptualization, design, and conduct of TTI research is complex, requiring attention to multiple input, context, program, and outcome **Variables** and use of **Multivariate Analyses**. Second, TTI is probably a relatively subtle effect. The measures and descriptors of both students and programs that are used in much evaluative research may be too gross to reveal it. Finally, of course, no matter how appealing the notion of trait-treatment interaction is, it simply may not

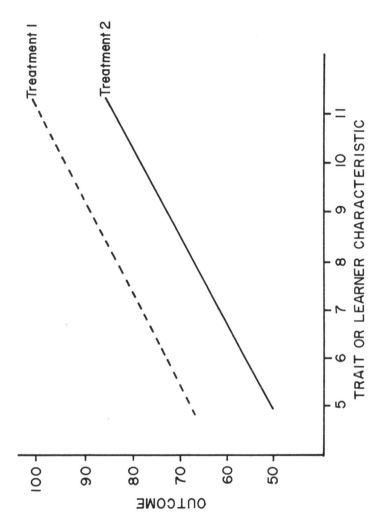

Figure 1. No interaction.

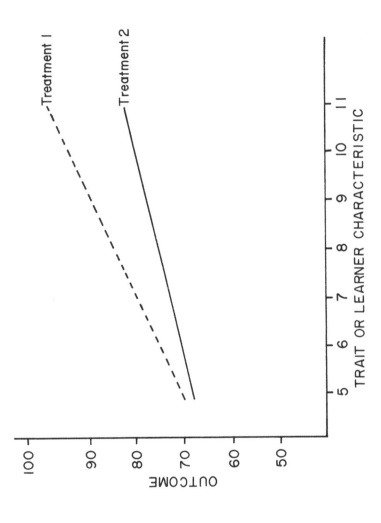

Figure 2. Ordinal interaction.

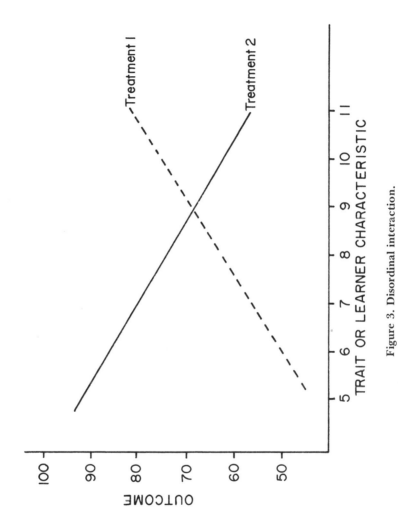

Figure 3. Disordinal interaction.

exist in many practical situations or with most students (e.g., most students may be flexible enough to benefit from either treatment, or treatments may be so eclectic that they include "something for everyone"). Certainly further empirical investigations and theoretical analyses of the concept are needed at this stage. However, the lesson for evaluators is clear: they should at least look for differential effects of a program on subgroups of students. A program may appear to have no effect if the evaluator simply looks at average gains, whereas a closer inspection of the data might reveal that the program had significant benefits for some learners. Or evaluators and program sponsors might rejoice at the apparent success of a program only to find that it had detrimental effects on a few students. An initial indication of such discrepant effects may be provided by significant differences in the correlations between student traits and gains in achievement for different programs (see Correlation).—L. S. C.

Berliner, D. C., and Cahen, L. S. "Trait-Treatment Interactions and Learning." In F. N. Kerlinger (Ed.), *Review of Research in Education*. Itasca, Ill.: Peacock, 1973.

Bracht, G. H. "Experimental Factors Related to Aptitude-Treatment Interactions." *Review of Educational Research*, 1970, *40*, 627-645.

Cronbach, L. J. "How Can Instruction Be Adapted to Individual Differences?" In R. M. Gagné (Ed.), *Learning and Individual Differences*. Columbus, Ohio: Merrill, 1967. Pp. 353-379.

Glaser, R. "Individuals and Learning: The New Aptitudes." *Educational Researcher*, 1972, *1* (6), 5-13.

Lubin, A. "The Interpretation of Significant Interaction." *Educational and Psychological Measurement*, 1961, *21*, 807-817.

─────────── TRANSACTIONAL EVALUATION ───────────

In addition to **Formative Evaluation** and **Summative Evaluation,** a new aspect of educational evaluation has emerged that emphasizes the implementation of change. Transactional evaluation attempts to apply systems-theory principles to the area of program innovation.

Many constructive changes never take place within an organization—not because they lack merit but because they meet with covert as well as overt resistance from the members of the organization, the participants in the system. Since change often brings the system into disequilibrium, thereby forcing participants to compete once again for the system resources, proposed changes often are threatening to those involved. The defensive reactions precipitated by this threat are largely responsible for the mildly subversive acts that can cause a proposed change to die before its merits have been tested. If methods of implementing change do not consider the impact of the change on the existing system, they are almost bound to fail. Transactional evaluation is designed to minimize the disruption of the reallocation process and thereby minimize personal threat and subsequent defensiveness felt by the system participants.

How does transactional evaluation work? First of all, the need for a change is indicated either by the availability of new ideas or by a dysfunction in the existing system. If the goal is to implement new ideas, the transactional evaluator begins by distributing a detailed description of the proposed change to those who will be affected by the change (e.g., administrators, teachers, and students). Each participant is asked to submit an anonymous written response to the proposed change. If the goal is to deal with a system dysfunction, the evaluator asks for a brief, anonymous, written report on what is wrong with the present system. The evaluator uses the information from the reports to prepare a questionnaire of scaled agreement responses that represents the various viewpoints expressed. This questionnaire is then distributed throughout the system, and its results are tabulated and returned to all the system participants.

Up to this point, it has been the aim of transactional evaluation to prevent any direct confrontations between disagreeing parties. However, after the questionnaire results are dispersed, proponents and antagonists of the major conflicting views are brought together. By delaying actual confrontation, the evaluator has prefocused the group's attention on the issues that have a major bearing on the potential conflict. At this point, a specialist skilled in interpersonal group communications is used to moderate the discussion.

Following the initial group discussion, a pilot test of the proposed change is begun. Those members of the group who are most favorably disposed toward the change act as change proponents. Those members of the group who oppose the change act as critics. Now the strengths and weaknesses of the innovation can be openly discussed while the legitimacy of the arguments is being concurrently tested in a practical situation. In this way, much of the energy previously used to subvert the change may be channeled into constructive evaluation of the program. Defensiveness can be played down, agreement need not be required, and questions can be substituted for arguments. Group impasses are referred to an impartial observer for arbitration.

After the pilot program has had time to stabilize, its overall success is reevaluated by the confrontation group. At this time, any decision about implementing the change on a wider scale has a much greater chance of being decided on rational grounds. If the change is implemented, it also has a much better chance of survival.

Since transactional evaluation must be tailored to the needs of a specific system, its use is limited to cases where an appropriate combination of transactional-evaluation and interpersonal-communication skills can be obtained. Furthermore, each situation requires a new transactional process, since the standardization of one group's problems would be meaningless in a different situation. Since transactional evaluation is directed at the field situation, controlled studies of its effectiveness are difficult. Transactional evaluation would also seem to be limited to those organizations that are old enough and mature enough to have sufficient internal strength to deal with the human relationships among their members. At the present time, although the methodology is largely unproved, the technique may still be worth serious consideration by an organization seeking to implement change without disruption.—T. W. D.

Rippey, R. M. (Ed.) *Studies in Transactional Evaluation.* Berkeley, Calif.: McCutchan, 1973. Fifteen authors discuss the emerging role of transactional evaluation from both the theoretical and practical perspectives. Several examples of how the process has been implemented are discussed.

————————— TREATMENT MEASUREMENT —————————

Most evaluations pay great attention to outcome (dependent) variables and to input (independent) variables (see **Variables**). The adequacy of the measures used to assess these variables is of considerable concern to the evaluator, and the final evaluation report will often present detailed evidence on their **Reliability**, **Validity**, and other technical characteristics.

Unfortunately, the same attention is far less frequently paid to the instructional treatment being evaluated. One of the best illustrations of the neglect of program or treatment variables is provided by studies conducted to evaluate the effectiveness of new science and mathematics curricula, developed after Sputnik. Great care was taken with the **Evaluation Designs** and the selection of appropriate outcome measures; the treatment (the specific program) was randomly assigned to one set of classes while the **Control Group** continued with the old, conventional program. But it was *assumed* that the classes in the new program were indeed receiving a different treatment from the control classes—after all, the textbooks and teacher guides were different, and usually the teachers had undergone in-service courses on the rationale behind the new program and how to implement it. However, Gallagher was intrigued by the equivocal results from such evaluations. He studied the classroom behaviors of teachers of the new science program, Biological Sciences Curriculum Study (BSCS). He found that, from an operational viewpoint, there was no such thing as a standard BSCS program in the schools. There were instead quite different versions, depending on the teacher's interpretations; and the program, therefore, came in many different levels of abstraction and with different kinds of content.

Evaluators should always be alert to such problems, and consideration should be given to the measurement of the treatment. It is *not* sufficient to assume that what are supposed to be the experimental and the control treatments are in fact occurring. If the evaluator is assessing the differential impact of specific preschool programs (e.g., Montessori versus Bereiter-Englemann), part of the measurement procedure should consist of documenting empirically that the two programs are indeed different in certain ways. It is not enough simply to list how the two programs are theoretically supposed to be different.

How is measurement of the treatment to be accomplished? A number of techniques are available. If the treatment is a program to be taught by a teacher, at least two elements should be assessed: the content of the program (through **Content Analysis**) and the actual presentation of the program (by one or more **Observation Techniques**). By comparing the results of the content analysis with the results of the observations, the evaluator can see whether the program is actually being implemented as intended.

The necessity to measure the treatment is strong even when the treatment is quite clear and not mediated by a teacher who might alter it. Consider a film program on health for naval recruits. The objectives of the film program may be clearly stated, and the film producers may indicate that specific amounts of time in the film are devoted to specific objectives. However, the evaluator's independent assessment of the film might show that most of the time supposedly devoted to certain objectives is actually spent on attention-holding techniques, with relatively little content being presented. It might also show that certain objectives are indeed given the amount of time indicated by the producers but that the mode of film presentation is relatively bland (e.g., a doctor lecturing on the topic), whereas the mode of presentation for other objectives is an interesting use of animation.

Since the situation in which the treatment occurs may be considered a part of the treatment and since it may have consequences of its own, it too should be assessed. Thus, programmed instruction for children seems to be more effective when an adult is present. A basic adult-education program with self-pacing materials seems to work better when administered in a group setting than in the learner's home via correspondence.

In general, if the treatment is not measured, it is difficult to interpret the results of an evaluation; for it is difficult then to specify the characteristics of the agent presumed to have caused the result. We can still say that differences occurred—if they did—but we cannot say much beyond that. If the treatment is measured, there still may be doubt about which specific factors were causal agents, but at least the evaluator and the program director have some information to guide future program examination.—S. B.

Charters, W. W., and Jones, J. E. "On the Risk of Appraising Non-Events in Program Evaluation." *Educational Researcher,* 1973, *2,* 5-7.

Gallagher, J. J. "Teacher Variation in Concept Presentation in the BSCS Curriculum Program." *BSCS Newsletter,* 1967, *30,* 8-18.

Jacobs, P. I., Maier, M. H., and Stolurow, L. M. *A Guide to Evaluating Self-Instructional Programs.* New York: Holt, 1966. Demonstrates that programmed instruction can be differentially effective depending on how it is presented.

———————— UNOBTRUSIVE MEASURES ————————

The usual measures of the success of education/training programs take the form of **Interviews, Questionnaires,** or **Tests.** Since all these techniques run the risk of evoking responses which are uncharacteristic of behavior outside the assessment situation, they may lead to equivocal interpretations. Distortions may result from the respondent's well-intentioned attempt to create a good impression (of himself or of the program) and from such other factors as deliberate inaccuracy or dishonesty, negative personal reactions to the interviewer or administrator of the measure, **Response Sets** (e.g., tendencies to acquiesce to any point of view presented by an "authority" or to mark the last choice in multiple-choice items), or even real changes in perception or cognition brought about by the measurement experience itself (see **Reactive Effects of Program and Evaluation**). The possibilities of such distortion have led many investigators to explore and use unobtrusive measures.

There are three general types of these measures: physical traces, archives, and observations. Physical trace measures include such varied indicators as the rate of floor-tile replacement around instructional exhibits, wear on library-book pages (or dust on a particular collection of books), consumption of scratch pads or other program-related materials, and number of different fingerprints on a training device (to find out how many different students practiced with it). Some of these are examples of erosion measures (based on selective wear on some material); others are examples of accretion measures (based on deposits on materials).

The kinds of archives or records that might be of interest to program evaluators include such things as records of class attendance; records of books checked out of the library; requests for transfer, student-instructor conferences, or counseling; lists of dropouts; purchase requisitions; records of salary increases, promotions, arrests, or other events following training; student notebooks or even "doodles" during lectures. Of course, as with more conventional measures, a good case must be made for the relevance and relative unambiguity of meaning of any unobtrusive measures used.

Observations are an especially pertinent form of data collection for evaluators who want to know what is going on in an instructional program and what students' spontaneous reactions to it are. At the least, the evaluator must establish that the planned instructional program was in fact implemented at the level intended. Discrepancies between the paper descriptions of a program and its real-world execution (see **Discrepancy Evaluation**) can lead to "strange" evaluation results—not to mention synthetic conclusions.

Observations can be collected directly by human observers; or, if the magnitude and importance of the program warrant it, observers can be supplemented or replaced by mechanical or electronic devices. Human observers must have a clear idea of what they are looking for; mechanical observations must be precisely defined and focused. In either case, it is desirable to check on the reliability of the observations through the use of independent records of the same event.

Some of the hardware developments that have facilitated observations of programs include tape recorders, still cameras, television and movie cameras (infrared techniques have been used in darkened film theaters to record audience reactions), electrical or mechanical devices to record body movement (e.g., audience fidgeting), "electric eyes" (e.g., to collect data on the number of people attending a presentation), and devices to measure physiological reactions such as perspiration and heart beat. The substitution of hardware for human observers, of course, does not minimize the importance of human judgment in the application and interpretation of the measures.

Observations are subject to exceptional ethical as well as methodological problems. On one hand, the presence of an observer (or a television camera) can substantially alter the behavior of instructors or students. On the other hand, problems of morale and morality can attend deception about the presence of purposes of observation. Many investigators compromise by making it known that observations are taking place and then attempting to introduce these observations in such a way that they will come to be ignored—or accepted as a normal part of the program routine or furnishings.

The word *unobtrusive*, as applied to trace, archival, and observation measures, is actually somewhat confusing. For although such measures are not as directly reactive as a test or interview, they can still elicit distortions in normal behavior if the subjects know that data are being collected. It may be helpful to think of two measurement dimensions here, leading to four classification cells: obtrusive-unobtrusive (referring to the general measurement situation) and reactive-nonreactive (referring to the specific measurement task). Thus, an achievement test would typically be obtrusive and reactive, standardized **Situational Tests** observed through one-way screens would be unobtrusive and reactive, observations in the natural setting with the observer present would be obtrusive and nonreactive, and measures taken from earlier records would be unobtrusive and nonreactive.

A persuasive argument for using unconventional measures such as those discussed here is to supplement other measures of the same variables. Almost all measures leave something to be desired, and it is naïve to put all our faith in any single measure of a phenomenon. Social scientists call the process of using multiple measures, which overlap in theory but not in inferential weaknesses, "triangulation." If we think of a variable as occupying some logical space, the problem is to locate (explain) that variable as precisely as possible. Any single measure, subject as it is to error and contamination, is likely to miss the mark in some unknown direction and leave us with an incomplete or erroneous explanation.—S. B. A.

Anderson, S. B. "Noseprints on the Glass—or How Do We Evaluate Museum Programs?" In E. Larrabee (Ed.), *Museums and Education*. Washington, D.C.: Smithsonian Institution Press, 1968. Pp. 115-126.

Selltiz, C., Jahoda, M., Deutsch, M., and Cook, S. W. *Research Methods in Social Relations*. New York: Holt, 1959. See especially Chapter 6 ("Observational Methods") and Chapter 9 ("The Use of Available Data as Source Material").

Webb, E. J. "Unconventionality, Triangulation, and Inference." In *Proceedings of the 1966 Invitational Conference on Testing Problems*. Princeton, N.J.: Educational Testing Service, 1967. Pp. 34-43.

Webb, E. J., Campbell, D. T., Schwartz, R. D., and Sechrest, L. *Unobtrusive Measures: Nonreactive Research in the Social Sciences*. Chicago: Rand McNally, 1966. An exciting presentation of information about collection of social science data by means other than interviews, questionnaires, or tests. Discusses sources of invalidity of measures (including reactive measurement effects) and the uses of physical-trace, archival, and observational measures.

———————————— VALIDITY ————————————

The evaluation of an education or training program is, in itself, a validating process—an attempt to demonstrate the worth of the program in attaining its objectives, and sometimes to substantiate or refute the claims made for it by its sponsors. However, the word *validity* is used more specifically in two aspects of evaluation studies: the design and the measurement. Validity of evaluation designs (defined in terms of the interpretability and generalizability of conclusions) is discussed in **Design of Evaluation**. The present article will focus on validity as applied to the tests, questionnaires, observations, ratings, and other measurement procedures used in evaluation designs. The two topics are related, however, for sound conclusions about program effectiveness cannot be drawn from good designs that use poor measures any more than from poor designs using the best of measures.

Most measurement textbooks have a definition of test validity that goes like this: A test is valid if it measures what it purports to measure. However, it is more meaningful to talk about the validity of *inferences* based on results obtained from tests and other measures than about the validity of the instruments themselves. The most crucial inferences in evaluation studies have to do usually with whether a desired outcome was achieved and sometimes with how much of it was achieved. However, such inferences are seldom made on the basis of results of outcome measures alone; the evaluator is frequently concerned with the quality of measurements of input, program, context, and assessment variables as well (see **Variables**). In each case, he wants to be confident that the measure adequately reflects and represents the domain of interest and that it is not equally or more likely to be a measure of something else. For example, scores on an achievement measure in auto mechanics should be indicative of competence in maintaining and repairing vehicles, not of personality traits or verbal skills.

The measurement literature is full of adjectives associated with various conceptions of validity: concurrent, congruent, construct, content, convergent, criterion, discriminant, ecological, face, factorial, intrinsic, job-analytic, population, predictive, pseudo, rational, substitutive, synthetic, etc. A few of these cannot be incorporated into any technical definition of "validity," although they may represent reasonable measurement concerns. For example, the APA *Standards* (p. 26) statement about face validity emphasizes that "the mere appearance of validity is not an acceptable basis for interpretive inferences from test scores"; however, practical evaluators know that what a test appears to measure may affect its acceptability to students, instructors, and policy makers.

For the sake of simplicity, validity will be discussed in this article under three main headings, corresponding to the categories used in the APA *Standards for Educational and Psychological Tests*. These categories, however, are far from independent.

1. *Construct validity* refers to the degree to which scores on a measure permit inferences about underlying traits. Can we infer from a score on a measure that a person is creative, analytical, persistent, mechanically competent, or motivated to achieve? Or that the climate of a classroom is democratic or autocratic? Are the measurement results better accounted for by these constructs than by theoretically different constructs? Do higher scores on the measure indicate more of the trait and lower scores less? Do the trait characterizations derived from the measure hold up in other situations? Construct validity is usually estimated from patterns of correlations of the measure in question with other measures: scores on the measure should be significantly related to scores on theoretically relevant measures (*convergent validity*) and should show no significant relationship to scores on theoretically unrelated measures (*discriminant validity*). Two other subcategories of construct validity that should be of special concern to those evaluating education/training programs offered on a wide scale are population and ecological validity: Does a measure have the same meaning—measure the same processes or traits—in different population groups (as defined by region, sex, age, ethnic group, etc.)? Does a measure have the same meaning in different environmental settings —can we generalize the results to different situations?

Some psychologists say that construct validity is a powerful enough conception to suffice, that other categories of validity are simply special cases of construct validity. Their argument is especially cogent in relation to the next kind of validity to be discussed, content validity, for a test interpreter is rarely willing to limit his conclusions to the particular content of a measure. Rather, he tends to talk about reading comprehension in a global sense rather than about performance on a particular group of items.

2. *Content validity,* however, is a very important notion for the measures of skill and knowledge that are frequently employed in evaluation studies. In this context, content validity usually refers to the degree to which a measure captures a program objective (or objectives). If a student performs well on the measure, can we say that he attained the objective? Evidence for content validity may be rational and/or empirical. For example, if a training program is designed to ready students for jobs as auto mechanics, then the program outcome measure should include a good representation of the tasks that students will be expected to perform on the job. The content specifications for the measure would probably come from a **Job Analysis.** Or, as another example, if one objective of a reading program is to increase reading speed, then the evaluator may point to exercises requiring various reading rates as evidence of the content validity of his measure. Content validity is easier to come by when the performance domain of interest is relatively finite and unambiguous; e.g., arithmetic addition, typing. With an amorphous domain such as social studies achievement or literature appreciation, it is more difficult to show a logical relationship between the measures and the achievement desired. Good measurement developers approach the problem by specifying subdomains (or subobjectives) of interest, but even then the test tasks they choose to set in any one subdomain may be only the smallest fraction of all the test tasks they might set. In these instances, empirical evidence of content validity is especially relevant. For example, separate test forms can be constructed independently from the same test specifications, and scores on them can be compared. If the correlations are high, we have evidence at least that two (or more) people have similar conceptions of the domain to be sampled. Other useful empirical information is provided by the intercorrelations of items designed to assess the same objective or content area. (See **Achievement Test Construction.**)

The notions of content validity and **Criterion-Referenced**

Measurement are particularly compatible, in spite of the semantic difficulty which might suggest that criterion-referenced measurement is more closely related to the next kind of validity.

3. *Criterion-related validity* refers to the degree to which scores on a measure relate to scores on an external criterion. For example, we may talk about the validity of a paper-and-pencil test of mechanical understandings in terms of the relationship between scores on that test and ratings of actual mechanical performance. Or we may talk about the relationship between scores on measures at the end of training and later measures of on-the-job success. In other words, criterion-related validity studies are concerned with two kinds of variables: (a) the data-collection method (e.g., paper-and-pencil test versus performance ratings) and (b) the interval of time between administration of the measure of interest and the criterion measure (if they are given at about the same time, we can talk about *concurrent validity*; if the criterion measure is given later, we are usually focusing on *predictive validity*). Evidence for criterion-related validity is highly situation-bound; e.g., the relationships between test scores and freshman grade-point averages may vary widely from college to college—or from year to year in the same college. Thus, it is not safe for an investigator to claim criterion-related validity for a measure unless a significant relationship between the measure and the criterion is established in a situation clearly comparable to the one in which the measure is being used.

In most textbook discussions of validity, predictive validity dominates. And there are a few people who are willing to accept high correlations between any two scores as ample evidence of validity, even if they are not able to suggest a rational explanation for the relationship (e.g., between mathematical aptitude and success as a highway patrolman.) However, this position is incomprehensible to social scientists seeking to understand human learning and development, and it is not very practical in the real world of education and training programs, where students and policy makers alike are demanding "relevance."

As the preceding discussion has suggested, the usual indicators of validity are **Correlation** coefficients. To those who ask "How high should the correlations be?" or "What level of relationship is acceptable?" the only appropriate answer is "It depends."

As Cronbach (p. 496) points out, "This depends not just on the correlation between test and criterion, but also on the importance of the decision. . . . A test of modest validity that provides information not otherwise available is worth using." His argument is especially pertinent in the evaluation area, where the evaluator is concerned with reflecting a wide range of program objectives and background conditions in his measures, and where decisions are usually to be made about the program rather than about the futures of individual students.—S. B. A.

American Psychological Association. *Standards for Educational and Psychological Tests.* Washington, D.C., 1974.

Bechtoldt, H. F. "Construct Validity: A Critique." *American Psychologist,* 1959, *14,* 619-629.

Cronbach, L. J. "Test Validation." In R. L. Thorndike (Ed.), *Educational Measurement.* (2nd Ed.) Washington, D.C.: American Council on Education, 1971. Pp. 443-507.

Dick, W., and Hagerty, N. *Topics in Measurement: Reliability and Validity.* New York: McGraw-Hill, 1971. A programmed text.

Loevinger, J. "Objective Tests as Instruments of Psychological Theory." In D. N. Jackson and S. Messick (Eds.), *Problems in Human Assessment.* New York: McGraw-Hill, 1967. Pp. 78-123. Includes a fundamental treatment of validity issues.

———————— VALUES MEASUREMENT ————————

Each individual has an implicit set of values which, along with many other pressures (e.g., group norms, personal abilities), help to determine his behavior. Values, interests, attitudes, and beliefs are terms with overlapping referents; but values, in general, refer to relatively stable elements in one's overall belief system. Attitudes and interests stem from and are indicative of the values that are held. Thus, values are more central, general, and stable than attitudes or interests. Note, however, that these terms are used loosely, and even the best-known measure of values (Allport, Vernon, and Lindzey) uses *values, interests,* and *attitudes* almost interchangeably.

One useful way to indicate what is meant by values is to list the names of values assessed by various measures. The Allport, Vernon, and Lindzey scale provides a profile on six value dimensions: theoretical (dominant interest is truth), economic (dominant interest is usefulness), aesthetic (dominant interest is form and harmony), social (dominant interest is love of people), political (dominant interest is power), and religious (dominant interest is unity and the mystical). The Differential Value Profile (Thomas) also has six factors: aesthetic (valuing form, symmetry, beauty), humanitarian (valuing people), intellectual (valuing rationality), material (valuing money), power (valuing authority and dominance), and religious (valuing commitment to a Higher Purpose).

Values help define what is good and right. They influence and help organize our thoughts, feelings, and behavior. It is perhaps surprising, therefore, that there has been relatively little work done in measurement of values. The two measures mentioned in the previous paragraph constitute the major instruments available. There are, of course, other measures that might bear indirectly on values (e.g., a measure of some personality characteristic such as open- versus closed-minded, liberal versus conservative, present- versus future-oriented). These personality measures typically examine one dimension only. That dimension may be a useful one for the evaluator, who can obtain information about pertinent measures from reference sources such as those edited by Buros (see **Test Selection**).

The measurement of values typically involves the development of individual profiles of values. A person's values are consonant with his personality characteristics, attitudes, interests, and motives; thus, in general, it would be unwise for an evaluator to become immobilized through undue concern with the semantic problem. If no useful values scale is available, he might also consider attitude or interest measures which seem to reflect the set of values of concern to him. If the evaluator wishes to develop a measure of values, he can avail himself of several possible measurement techniques. (See **Attitudes**.)

In program evaluation designs, values can be assigned various roles. Evaluators can measure values as outcome **Variables** (e.g., in a training program for Army chaplains) or as possible **Side Effects** (e.g., of four years of college). However, program directors and evaluators may frequently be disappointed if they expect significant changes in values as intended outcomes or side effects of short-term programs. It is unlikely that such stable traits will be influenced by efforts that are not long-term and targeted.

Values can also be treated as input or moderator variables if evaluators suspect that students with different values may react differently to the program. For example, some evidence indicates that most students who choose to enter a particular course of study (e.g., theology or business) are fairly homogeneous in their values, and programs may be geared toward such students; those students whose values are different from the average may react quite differently to a program. A program in humanities might work out well for students with high aesthetic values scores but poorly for students with high political-economic values scores. (See **Trait-Treatment Interaction.**)

Values may affect the evaluator as well as the students and programs in the evaluation. The evaluator's values will help determine what is assessed, what is analyzed, how it is analyzed, and what is concluded. (See also **Motivation.**)—S. B.

Allport, G. W., Vernon, P. E., and Lindzey, G. *A Study of Values: A Scale for Measuring the Dominant Interests in Personality.* Boston: Houghton Mifflin, 1960.

Raths, L. E., Harmin, M., and Simon, S. B. *Values and Teaching.* Columbus, Ohio: Merrill, 1966. Suggests how values may be clarified, made explicit, and modified through classroom experiences.

Rokeach, M. *The Nature of Human Values.* New York: Free Press, 1973. A comprehensive, scholarly discussion of topics related to values (e.g., measurement, behavior, long-term change).

Stanley, J. C. "Insight into One's Own Values." *Journal of Educational Psychology,* 1951, *42,* 399-408.

Thomas, W. L. *The Differential Value Profile.* Grand Rapids, Mich.: Educational Service Company, 1967.

Thurstone, L. L. "The Measurement of Values." In *The Measurement of Values.* Chicago: University of Chicago Press, 1959. Pp. 182-194. A collection of twenty-seven of Thurstone's papers on measurement topics.

VARIABLES

Variables are the stuff of all empirical investigation; but the number and complexity of the variables that have to be dealt with usually increase dramatically as the investigation moves from the domain of basic or laboratory research to studies in the real world. Evaluations of education/training programs certainly fall in the latter category.

A type of information can be a variable in one investigation and a constant (or fixed characteristic) in another. For example, in an evaluation of one electronics training program, number of previous courses in electronics may be an important student variable; for another training program, where students are required to have the same number of prerequisite courses for admission, amount of previous training may be considered a constant. Variables may be *qualitative* or *quantitative*. Examples of qualitative variables are geographical region (Northeast, Midwest, etc.), marital status (single, married, divorced, etc.), and instructional approach (e.g., lecture or programmed instruction). Examples of quantitative variables are city size, number of years married, and number of hours spent in instruction per day. Quantitative variables can be further classified as *continuous* (if fractional units are meaningful) or *discrete*. For example, age is usually considered a continuous variable, while class size may be reported only in whole numbers and thus be considered discrete. For some comparative purposes, of course, evaluators may want to force continuous variables into discrete categories; e.g., students over eighteen and students under eighteen.

Specific attention to the nature of each candidate variable for an evaluation study is important, because the variable type relates to the choice of measurement technique and, in turn, to the analytic procedures applied. For example, if the evaluator is concerned about only two levels of competency of entering trainees, he would not need to use a measuring instrument that provides very fine discriminations among trainees. And, at the analysis stage, the techniques employed for correlating discrete variables would be different from the ones used with continuous variables. (See Correlation.)

Investigators may manipulate some variables (e.g., put students through training courses of different lengths) and try to control others (i.e., neutralize or equate their effects), but they usually want to measure or describe *all* variables that might be important. In evaluation studies these include:

1. *Input characteristics of students:* age, sex, amount of previous training, economic level, race, physical condition, verbal ability, etc. Such variables go by many different names in the literature—antecedent, background, precondition, etc.

2. *Program variables:* materials used, classroom activities, group structure, program duration, physical facilities, costs, instructor characteristics (including teaching styles), etc. Such variables may receive a number of different labels; e.g., process, independent, treatment, experimental, stimulus.

3. *Context variables:* relevant characteristics of the general setting in which the program takes place; e.g., community attitudes and resources, the national political climate, the unemployment rate in the occupation toward which the training is directed.

4. *Assessment variables:* characteristics of the instruments or data-collection procedures that might affect results and lead to erroneous interpretations about program effects; e.g., sex, race, and competence of interviewers; relaxed or stressful testing conditions. Variables in categories 3 and 4 are sometimes described as *intervening* (Suchman); however, in psychological research that adjective has another meaning—a meaning associated with hypothetical constructs such as learning and motivation that are not subject to direct measurement or observation.

5. *Outcome variables:* student achievement and attitudes, parent involvement, employer satisfaction with program "gradu-

ates," number of trainees completing the program, etc. Such variables are also frequently referred to as dependent, output, response, criterion, or consequent.

This listing of variables under five categories does not imply that a particular variable is relegated to the same category for all times and under all conditions. For example, an outcome variable for one instructional sequence may become an input variable for the next sequence. Moreover, although variables are measured or described separately, they may interact in important ways in instructional situations. For example, program outcomes may be different for male and female students; two program variables may interact to produce results that are not predictive from either variable alone; and relationships between program characteristics and student outcomes may be different for high-ability than for low-ability students (student ability in this case is sometimes referred to as a *moderator variable*). (See **Interaction** and **Trait-Treatment Interaction**.)

The translation of variables into measures is one of the most important—and difficult—tasks for the evaluator. Some variables, such as length of employment or rate of pay, are, of course, relatively straightforward and have widely accepted forms of measurement. For example, length of employment can be measured in years or fractions of years and rate of pay in dollars per week. It is even possible to change the measures of such variables somewhat without jeopardizing understanding of their meaning. For example, length of employment can be reported in weeks and rate of pay to the nearest $1000 per year.

However, other variables central to program and evaluative concerns do not have universally accepted definitions—variables such as intelligence, problem-solving ability, attitudes, satisfactions, and even skills levels. It is incumbent on evaluators to specify the precise set of operations they use to measure such abstract variables. The specification of such a set of operations is known as an *operational definition*. For example, one evaluator might define "intelligence" in terms of scores on a given intelligence test; another might define it as amount of formal education completed. "Student satisfaction with the instructional program" might be defined in terms of a specified set of responses to a particular questionnaire or dropout rate from the program or some combination of these two measures.

Unless the evaluator presents such operational definitions of his variables along with his findings, the findings stand a good chance of being misinterpreted—or overinterpreted. For example, a conclusion that intelligence does not seem to be related to student satisfaction with the program might have a very different meaning under the different operational definitions of "intelligence" and "satisfaction" mentioned above. Precision of definition of variables is also essential to any generalization or replication of the results of evaluative research efforts.—S. B. A.

Fox, D. J. *The Research Process in Education.* New York: Holt, 1969. See Chapter 5, "The Nature of Variables and Data" (pp. 138-166).

Kaplan, A. "Definition and Specifications of Meaning." *Journal of Philosophy,* 1946, *43,* 281-288.

Messick, S., and Barrows, T. S. "Strategies for Research and Evaluation in Early Childhood Education." In I. J. Gordon (Ed.), *Early Childhood Education. The Seventy-First Yearbook of the National Society for the Study of Education.* Chicago: University of Chicago Press, 1972. Pp. 261-290. Those evaluating programs at other levels should not be deterred by the title of this article from reviewing the excellent list of possible measurement domains (pp. 265-268).

Saunders, D. R. "Moderator Variables in Prediction." In D. N. Jackson and S. Messick (Eds.), *Problems in Human Assessment.* New York: McGraw-Hill, 1967. Pp. 362-371. Originally published in *Educational and Psychological Measurement,* 1958.

Siegel, A. I., Bergman, B. A., and Federman, P. *Some Techniques for the Evaluation of Technical Training Courses and Students.* Lowry Air Force Base, Colo.: Technical Training Division, 1972. See the straightforward discussion of interaction (pp. 89-91).

Suchman, E. A. *Evaluative Research: Principles and Practice in Public Service and Social Action Programs.* New York: Russell Sage Foundation, 1967. See the discussions of independent, intervening, and dependent variables (pp. 83-88, 105-111, 171-176).

—————————————— VARIANCE ——————————————

Variance is the term used to describe the dispersion or spread in a set of measures (see **Statistics**). In evaluation, the primary concern is ordinarily focused on the central tendency of a set of measures, usually the mean; e.g., the mean performance of an experimental group in comparison with the mean performance of a **Control Group**. In some contexts, however, interest may be focused on variability itself, with questions of central tendency relegated to secondary importance. Consider a situation where training is conducted under stressful conditions; well-prepared trainees may be stimulated to perform even better, while poorly prepared trainees may be upset by the stress, and their performance may deteriorate even further. If two groups are trained under different conditions of stress, their mean performance may be the same, while pronounced differences in variability may occur. In many cases, all trainees may improve, but the mean and the variance may increase at different rates, so that the differences between two groups of trainees (e.g., those who performed well and poorly initially) may become even greater.

Thus, variability is an important object of attention in its own right. If the purpose of a program is to decrease the differences among students, then variance rather than mean achievement may be the more appropriate variable. Neglecting to recognize this fact has led to confusion in interpreting the results of many evaluations of compensatory-education programs (see **Compensatory Education**). Programs aimed at assisting weak students may do so. However, they may assist strong students even more, so that in the final analysis differences between the two groups may in fact increase rather than decrease.

In addition to studying changes and differences in variance as a variable in its own right, investigators often study the amount of variance in a set of measures in an attempt to identify the sources of the variation. In order to understand this use of variation, it is necessary to understand what is meant by variation "within" training programs in contrast to variation "between" training programs. Suppose, for example, two programs are compared in terms of the achievement of the trainees in each program. In program A, twenty trainees receive scores which vary from 30 to 50 with a mean of 40. In program B, twenty trainees receive scores from 35 to 55 with a mean of 45. The differences among the trainees in the same program are called "within-group" differences. The difference between the trainees in program A and the trainees in program B is called the "between-group" difference. Of course, the set of scores for all forty students will have its own variance, related to the overall mean of the forty scores. It is easy to show that this overall variance is exactly the sum of the "within-group" variance and the "between-group" variance. In general, if there is more than one group, the total variance can be "partitioned" into that within the groups and that between (or among) the groups. If every trainee in group A had received a score of exactly 40, and every trainee in group B had received a score of exactly 45, then all of the variance (100 percent) would be between-group variance and none (0 percent) would be within-group variance. On the other hand, if every student in group A could be matched with a student in group B who received exactly the same score on the test, then all (100 percent) of the variance would be within groups and none (0 percent) between groups. If the amount of between-group variance is 0 percent, then the groups have achieved identically and there are no program effects. If all of the variance is between-group variance, then the program differences would appear to be independent of trainee differences. In the real situation, of course, a certain percentage of the variance will be between-group variance, and it is this variance that is of interest in attempting to attribute effects to programs. (See the discussion of analysis of variance in **Statistical Analysis.**)

In the *Equality of Educational Opportunity* survey, a composite measure of school achievement was used as the criterion measure. It was found that approximately 70 percent of the variance in the total group of students was within-school variance and approximately 30 percent was between-school variance. It was this 30 percent of the variance that was then analyzed for school effects. Similarly, the between-group variance will be the object of major analysis in evaluations of the effects of specific programs.

Thus, when a group of trainees is used as a unit, only a portion of the variance is being studied. If this portion is small, then overall program effects are small, and the investigator should look for differential effects of the program on individual students or subgroups of students. (See **Interaction, Trait-Treatment Interaction, Johnson-Neyman Technique.**)

Once the variance has been partitioned into "between" and "within" components, various elements of the program can then be correlated with the mean achievement for the groups in an attempt to account for the variation. For example, in the *Equality of Educational Opportunity* study, such characteristics of the schools as percentage of teachers certified, educational background of the principal, types of instructional methods, and extent and quality of physical facilities were related to the achievement of the students. Of course, these characteristics are all related among themselves and do not affect student achievement independently of each other. It may be that teacher characteristics can account for 80 percent of the variance in school means while program characteristics can account for 70 percent of the variance. Obviously, the two together do not account for 150 percent of the variance. Rather, the two sets of characteristics will account for some of the variation in conjunction with each other. Such variance, called *shared variance,* sometimes lies behind conflicting interpretations of the effectiveness of specific educational components. A full discussion of the problem of "multicollinearity" among variables is beyond the scope of this entry. More detail can be found in the references. (See **Regression** and **Causality.**)
—R. T. M.

Coleman, J. S., Campbell, E. Q., Hobson, C. J., McPartland, J., Mood, A. M., Weinfeld, F. D., and York, R. L. *Equality of Educational Opportunity.* Washington, D.C.: U.S. Government Printing Office, 1966.

Mayeske, G. W. "Teacher Attributes and School Achievement." In *Do Teachers Make a Difference?* Washington, D.C.: U.S. Government Printing Office, 1970. Pp. 100-119. A brief overview of the issue of partitioning variance; based on the Coleman data.

McDonald, F. J., Forehand, G. A., Marco, G. L., Murphy, R. T., and Quirk, T. J. *A Design for an Accountability System for the New York City School System.* Princeton, N.J.: Educational Testing Service, 1972. See especially Chapters 6, 7, 13, 14, and 15.

Mosteller, F., and Moynihan, D. P. *On Equality of Educational Opportunity.* New York: Random House, 1972. A collection of papers deriving from a Harvard University seminar on the Coleman report. See especially the section on variance (pp. 15-19).

Mood, A. M. "Macro-Analysis of the American Education System." *Operations Research,* 1969, *17,* 770-784. A relatively simple explanation of the problem of relating educational inputs to outputs.

BIBLIOGRAPHY

Abelson, R. P. "A Note on the Neyman-Johnson Technique." *Psychometrika,* 1953, *18*, 213-217.

Advertising Research Foundation. *A Bibliography of Theory and Research Techniques in the Field of Human Motivation.* Westport, Conn.: Greenwood, 1972.

Airasian, P. W., and Madaus, G. F. "Criterion-Referenced Testing in the Classroom." *NCME Measurement in Education,* 1972, *3* (4).

Allport, G. W., Vernon, P. E., and Lindzey, G. *A Study of Values: A Scale for Measuring the Dominant Interests in Personality.* Boston: Houghton Mifflin, 1960.

Alpert, R., and Haber, R. N. "Anxiety in Academic Achievement Situations." *Journal of Abnormal and Social Psychology,* 1960, *61*, 207-215.

Alter, M. "Retention as a Function of Length of Retention Interval, Intelligence, and Training Time." *Journal of Programmed Instruction,* 1963, *2*, 7-17.

American Association of School Administrators. *The School Executive's Guide to Performance Contracting.* Washington, D.C., 1972.

American Institutes for Research. *Evaluative Research: Strategies and Methods.* Pittsburgh, 1970.

American Psychological Association. *Ethical Principles in the Conduct of Research with Human Participants.* Washington, D.C., 1973.

American Psychological Association. *Standards for Educational and Psychological Tests.* Washington, D.C., 1974.

American Telephone and Telegraph Company. *Training Development Standards: Quick Reference Guide.* New York: AT&T Training and Research Group, 1972.

Ammons, R. B., and Ammons, C. H. "Skills." In C. W. Harris (Ed.), *Encyclopedia of Educational Research.* (3rd Ed.) New York: Macmillan, 1960.

Anastasi, A. "Training and Individual Differences." In *Differential Psychology.* (3rd Ed.) New York: Macmillan, 1958.

473

Anastasi, A. *Psychological Testing.* (3rd Ed.) New York: Macmillan, 1968.

Anderson, J. G., and Evans, F. B. "Causal Models in Educational Research: Recursive Models." *American Educational Research Journal,* 1974, *11,* 29-39.

Anderson, R. C. "How to Construct Achievement Tests to Assess Comprehension." *Review of Educational Research,* 1972, *42,* 145-170.

Anderson, S. B. "Noseprints on the Glass—or How Do We Evaluate Museum Programs?" In E. Larrabee (Ed.), *Museums and Education.* Washington, D.C.: Smithsonian Institution Press, 1968.

Anderson, S. B. "From Textbooks to Reality: Social Researchers Face the Facts of Life in the World of the Disadvantaged." In J. Hellmuth (Ed.), *Disadvantaged Child.* Vol. 3: *Compensatory Education: A National Debate.* New York: Brunner/Mazel, 1970.

Anderson, S. B. "Accountability: What, Who and Whither?" *School Management,* 1971, *15* (9), 28-29, 50.

Anderson, S. B. "Educational Compensation and Evaluation: A Critique." In J. C. Stanley (Ed.), *Compensatory Education for Children, Ages 2-8.* Baltimore: Johns Hopkins University Press, 1973.

Anderson, S. B., Katz, M., and Shimberg, B. *Meeting the Test.* New York: Four Winds Press, 1965.

Anderson, S. B., and Maier, M. H. "34,000 Pupils and How They Grew." *Journal of Teacher Education,* 1963, *14,* 212-216.

Anderson, S. B., and Melville, S. D. *Making Your Own Tests: Planning; Construction; Analysis.* A series of three filmstrips with sound. Princeton, N.J.: Educational Testing Service, 1963.

Anderson, S. B., and Messick, S. "Social Competency in Young Children." *Developmental Psychology,* 1974, *10* (2), 282-293.

Anderson, T. W., Das Gupta, S., and Styan, G. P. H. *A Bibliography of Multivariate Statistical Analysis.* New York: Wiley, 1972.

Angoff, W. H. "Scales, Norms, and Equivalent Scores." In R. L. Thorndike (Ed.), *Educational Measurement.* (2nd Ed.) Washington, D.C.: American Council on Education, 1971.

Angoff, W. H., and Anderson, S. B. "The Standardization of Educational and Psychological Tests." *Illinois Journal of Education,* Feb. 1963, 19-23. Reprinted in D. A. Payne and R. F. McMorris (Eds.), *Educational and Psychological Measurement.* Lexington, Mass.: Xerox College Publishing, 1967.

Arrow, K., and Hahn, F. *General Competitive Analysis.* San Francisco: Holden-Day, 1971.

Association for Educational Data Systems. *Layman's Guide to the Use of Computers.* Washington, D.C., 1971.

Astin, A. *Who Goes Where to College?* Chicago: Science Research Associates, 1965.

Astin, A. W., and Panos, R. J. "The Evaluation of Educational Programs." In R. L. Thorndike (Ed.), *Educational Measurement.* (2nd Ed.) Washington, D.C.: American Council on Education, 1971.

Baker, F. B. "Automation of Test Scoring, Reporting, and Analyses." In R. L. Thorndike (Ed.), *Educational Measurement.* (2nd Ed.) Washington, D.C.: American Council on Education, 1971.

Baker, J. P., and Crist, J. L. "Teacher Expectancies: A Review of the Literature." In J. D. Elashoff and R. E. Snow (Eds.), *Pygmalion Reconsidered.* Worthington, Ohio: Charles A. Jones, 1971.

Ball, S., and Bogatz, G. A. *The First Year of Sesame Street: An Evaluation.* Princeton, N.J.: Educational Testing Service, 1970.

Ball, S., and Bogatz, G. A. "Summative Research of *Sesame Street*: Implications for the Study of Preschool Children." In A. D. Pick (Ed.), *Minnesota Symposia on Child Psychology.* Vol. 6. Minneapolis: University of Minnesota Press, 1972.

Barcikowski, R. S. "A Monte Carlo Study of Item Sampling (Versus Traditional Sampling) for Norm Construction." *Journal of Educational Measurement,* 1972, *9,* 209-214.

Barro, S. M. "An Approach to Developing Accountability Measures for the Public Schools." *Phi Delta Kappan,* 1970, *52,* 196-205.

Battelle Memorial Institute. *Interim Report on the Office of Economic Opportunity Experiment in Educational Performance Contracting.* Columbus, Ohio: Battelle, 1972.

Bauer, R. A. (Ed.) *Social Indicators.* Cambridge, Mass.: MIT Press, 1966.

Beatty, W. *Improving Educational Assessment and an Inventory of Measures of Affective Behavior.* Washington, D.C.: Association for Supervision and Curriculum Development, National Education Association, 1969.

Bechtoldt, H. F. "Construct Validity: A Critique." *American Psychologist,* 1959, *14,* 619-629.

Becker, H. S. "Observation: Social Observation and Social Case Studies." In D. L. Sills (Ed.), *International Encyclopedia of the Social Sciences.* Vol. 11. New York: Crowell-Collier and Macmillan, 1968.

Bennett, G. K., and Doppelt, J. E. *Test Orientation Procedure.* New York: Psychological Corporation, 1967.

Berelson, B. "Content Analysis." In G. Lindzey (Ed.), *Handbook of Social Psychology.* Vol. 1. Reading, Mass.: Addison-Wesley, 1954.

Berg, I. A. (Ed.) *Response Set in Personality Assessment.* Chicago: Aldine-Atherton, 1967.

Berger, B. *An Annotated Bibliography of Measurements for Young Children.* New York: Center for Urban Education, 1969.

Bergman, B. A., and Siegel, A. I. *Training Evaluation and Student Achievement Measurement: A Review of the Literature.* Lowry Air Force Base, Colo.: Technical Training Division, Air Force Human Resources Laboratory, 1972.

Berliner, D. C., and Cahen, L. S. "Trait-Treatment Interactions and Learning." In F. N. Kerlinger (Ed.), *Review of Research in Education.* Itasca, Ill.: Peacock, 1973.

Bingham, W. V. "Great Expectations." *Personnel Psychology,* 1949, *2,* 397-404.

Blalock, H. M., Jr. *Causal Inferences in Nonexperimental Research.* Durham: University of North Carolina Press, 1964.

Blalock, H. M., Jr. (Ed.) *Causal Models in the Social Sciences.* Chicago: Aldine-Atherton, 1971.

Blalock, H. M., Jr., and Blalock, A. B. *Methodology in Social Research.* New York: McGraw-Hill, 1968.

Block, J. H. (Ed.) *Mastery Learning: Theory and Practice.* New York: Holt, 1971.

Bloom, B. S. (Ed.) *Taxonomy of Educational Objectives.* Handbook I: *Cognitive Domain.* New York: McKay, 1956.

Bloom, B. S. "Mastery Learning and Its Implications for Curriculum Development." In E. W. Eisner (Ed.), *Confronting Curriculum Reform.* Boston: Little, Brown, 1971.

Bloom, B. S., Hastings, J. T., and Madaus, G. F. *Handbook on Formative and Summative Evaluation of Student Learning.* New York: McGraw-Hill, 1971.

Bock, R. D. "Conditional and Unconditional Inference in the Analysis of Repeated Measurements." Paper prepared for the Symposium on the Application of Statistical Techniques to Psychological Research, Canadian Psychological Association, York University, June 4, 1969.

Bogatz, G. A., and Ball, S. *The Second Year of Sesame Street: A Continuing Evaluation.* Princeton, N.J.: Educational Testing Service, 1971.

Bonjean, C. M., Hill, R. J., and McLemore, S. D. *Sociological Measurement: Inventory of Scales and Indices.* San Francisco: Chandler, 1967.

Borgatta, E. F. "Research Problems in Evaluation of Health Service Demonstrations." *Milbank Fund Quarterly,* 1966, *44* (Part 2).

Borich, G. D. (Issue Ed.) *Journal of Research and Development in Education,* 1971, *5* (1), 1-96.

Boring, E. G. *A History of Experimental Psychology.* (2nd Ed.) New York: Appleton-Century-Crofts, 1957.

Bowles, D. "Toward an Educational Production Function." In W. L. Hansen (Ed.), *Education, Income and Human Capital.* New York: Columbia University Press, 1970.

Bracht, G. H. "Experimental Factors Related to Aptitude-Treatment Interactions." *Review of Educational Research,* 1970, *40,* 627-645.

Bracht, G. H., and Glass, G. V. "The External Validity of Experiments." *American Educational Research Journal,* 1968, *5,* 437-474.

Bray, D. W., Campbell, R. J., and Grant, D. L. *Formative Years in Business: A Long-Term AT&T Study of Managerial Lives.* New York: Wiley, 1974.

Bray, D. W., and Grant, D. L. "The Assessment Center in the Measurement of Potential for Business Management." *Psychological Monographs,* 1966, *80.*

Brickell, H. M. *Organizing New York State for Educational Change.* Albany, N.Y.: State Education Department, 1961.

Browder, L. H. (Ed.) *Emerging Patterns of Administrative Accountability.* Berkeley, Calif.: McCutchan, 1971.

Brown, R. *Social Psychology.* New York: Free Press, 1965.

Buros, O. K. (Ed.) *Reading Tests and Reviews.* Highland Park, N.J.: Gryphon Press, 1968.

Buros, O. K. (Ed.) *Personality Tests and Reviews.* Highland Park, N.J.: Gryphon Press, 1970.

Buros, O. K. (Ed.) *The Mental Measurements Yearbook.* Highland Park, N.J.: Gryphon Press, 1938, 1941, 1949, 1953, 1959, 1965, 1972.

Butcher, H. J. *Human Intelligence.* London: Methuen, 1968.

Cahen, L. "An Experimental Manipulation of the Halo Effect." Unpublished doctoral dissertation, Stanford University, 1966.

Cahen, L. S., and Linn, R. L. "Regions of Significant Differences in Aptitude-Treatment-Interaction Research." *American Educational Research Journal,* 1971, *8,* 521-530.

Cahen, L. S., Romberg, T. A., and Zwirner, W. "The Estimation of Mean Achievement Scores for Schools by the Item-Sampling Technique." *Educational and Psychological Measurement,* 1970, *30,* 41-60.

Cain, G. G., and Hollister, R. G. "The Methodology of Evaluating Social

Action Programs." In P. H. Rossi and W. Williams (Eds.), *Evaluating Social Programs: Theory, Practice, and Politics.* New York: Seminar Press, 1972.

California Teachers Association, Commission on Teacher Education. *Six Areas of Teacher Competence.* Burlingame, Calif., 1964.

Callahan, R. E. *Education and the Cult of Efficiency.* Chicago: University of Chicago Press, 1962.

Campbell, D. T. "A Typology of Tests, Projective and Otherwise." In D. N. Jackson and S. Messick (Eds.), *Problems in Human Assessment.* New York: McGraw-Hill, 1967.

Campbell, D. T. *Time-Series of Annual Same-Grade Testings in the Evaluation of Compensatory Educational Experiments.* Duplicated memorandum. Evanston, Ill.: Northwestern University, 1970.

Campbell, D. T. "Reforms as Experiments." In C. H. Weiss (Ed.), *Evaluating Action Programs: Readings in Social Action and Education.* Boston: Allyn and Bacon, 1972. Revised from an earlier paper in *American Psychologist,* 1969, *24,* 409-429.

Campbell, D. T., and Erlebacher, A. "How Regression Artifacts in Quasi-Experimental Evaluations Can Mistakenly Make Compensatory Education Look Harmful." In J. Hellmuth (Ed.), *Disadvantaged Child.* Vol. 3: *Compensatory Education: A National Debate.* New York: Brunner/Mazel, 1970.

Campbell, D. T., and Frey, P. W. "The Implications of Learning Theory for the Fade-Out of Gains from Compensatory Education." In J. Hellmuth (Ed.), *Disadvantaged Child.* Vol. 3: *Compensatory Education: A National Debate.* New York: Brunner/Mazel, 1970.

Campbell, J. T., Hilton, T. L., and Pitcher, B. *Effects of Repeating on Test Scores on the Graduate Record Examinations.* GRE Special Report 67-1. Princeton, N.J.: Educational Testing Service, 1967.

Campbell, D. T., and Stanley, J. C. "Experimental and Quasi-Experimental Designs for Research on Teaching." In N. L. Gage (Ed.), *Handbook of Research on Teaching.* Chicago: Rand McNally, 1963. Reprinted as *Experimental and Quasi-Experimental Design for Research.* Chicago: Rand McNally, 1966.

Carey, A. A. "The Hawthorne Studies: A Radical Criticism." *American Sociological Review,* 1967, *32,* 403-416.

Carnap, R. *Logical Foundations of Probability.* Chicago: University of Chicago Press, 1950.

Carnap, R. "The Two Concepts of Probability." In H. Feigl and M. Brodbeck (Eds.), *Readings in the Philosophy of Science.* New York: Appleton-Century-Crofts, 1953.

Caro, F. G. *Readings in Evaluation Research.* New York: Russell Sage Foundation, 1971.

Carter, L. F. *The Systems Approach to Education—The Mystique and the Reality.* Santa Monica, Calif.: Systems Development Corporation, 1969.

Carver, R. P. "Special Problems in Measuring Change with Psychometric Devices." In *Evaluative Research: Strategies and Methods.* Pittsburgh: American Institutes for Research, 1970.

Case, C. M. "The Application of PERT to Large-Scale Educational and Evaluation Studies." *Educational Technology,* October 1969, *9,* 79-83.

Cattell, R. B. "Psychological Measurement: Normative, Ipsative, Interactive." *Psychological Review*, 1944, *51*, 292-303.

Cattell, R. B. "The Three Basic Factor Analytic Research Designs—Their Interrelations and Derivations." *Psychological Bulletin*, 1952, *49*, 499-520.

Cattell, R. B., and Warburton, F. *Objective Personality and Motivation Tests.* Urbana: University of Illinois Press, 1967.

Center for the Study of Evaluation. *CSE Elementary School Evaluation Kit: Needs Assessment.* Boston: Allyn and Bacon, 1973.

Chapin, F. S. *Experimental Designs in Sociological Research.* (Rev. Ed.) New York: Harper, 1955.

Charters, W. W., Jr., and Jones, J. E. "On the Risk of Appraising Non-Events in Program Evaluation." *Educational Researcher*, 1973, *2*, 5-7.

Churchman, C. W. *Prediction and Optimal Decision.* Englewood Cliffs, N.J.: Prentice-Hall, 1961.

Churchman, C. W. *The Systems Approach.* New York: Delacorte Press, 1968.

Cleary, T. A. "Test Bias: Prediction of Grades of Negro and White Students in Integrated Colleges." *Journal of Educational Measurement*, 1969, *5*, 115-124.

Clemans, W. V. "An Analytical and Empirical Examination of Some Properties of Ipsative Measures." *Psychometric Monographs*, 1966, No. 14.

Cochran, W. G. *Sampling Techniques.* (2nd Ed.) New York: Wiley, 1963.

Cochran, W. G. "Experimental Design: The Design of Experiments." In D. L. Sills (Ed.), *International Encyclopedia of the Social Sciences.* Vol. 5. New York: Crowell-Collier and Macmillan, 1968.

Cochran, W. G. "Observational Studies." In T. A. Bancroft (Ed.), *Statistical Papers in Honor of George Snedecor.* Ames: Iowa State University Press, 1972.

Cochran, W. G., and Rubin, D. B. "Controlling Bias in Observational Studies: A Review." *Sankhya-A*, 1974, 1-30.

Cofer, C. N., and Appley, M. H. *Motivation: Theory and Research.* New York: Wiley, 1964.

Coffman, W. E. "Sex Differences in Response to Items in an Aptitude Test." In *18th Yearbook, National Council on Measurement in Education.* Lansing, Mich.: Evaluation Services, Michigan State University, 1961.

Coffman, W. E. "Essay Examinations." In R. L. Thorndike (Ed.), *Educational Measurement.* (2nd Ed.) Washington, D.C.: American Council on Education, 1971.

Cohen, D. K. "Politics and Research. Evaluation of Social Action Programs in Education." *Review of Educational Research*, 1970, *40*, 213-238.

Coleman, J. S., Campbell, E. Q., Hobson, C. J., McPartland, J., Mood, A. M., Weinfeld, F. D., and York, R. L. *Equality of Educational Opportunity.* Washington, D.C.: U.S. Government Printing Office, 1966.

College Entrance Examination Board. *Introductory Probability and Statistical Inference for Secondary Schools.* New York, 1957.

College Entrance Examination Board. *Introductory Probability and Statistical Inference.* New York, 1959.

Commission on Elementary Schools. *A Guide to the Evaluation and Accreditation of Elementary Schools.* Atlanta: Southern Association of Colleges and Schools, 1971.

Cook, D. L. *Program Evaluation and Review Technique Applications in Education.* Washington, D.C.: U.S. Government Printing Office, 1966.

Cook, D. L. *The Impact of the Hawthorne Effect in Experimental Designs in Educational Research.* Cooperative Research Project No. 1757. Washington, D.C.: United States Office of Education, 1967.

Cook, D. L. "The Hawthorne Effect in Educational Research." *Phi Delta Kappan*, 1962, *44*, 116-122. Reprinted in W. H. MacGinitie and S. Ball (Eds.), *Readings in Psychological Foundations of Education.* New York: McGraw-Hill, 1968.

Cook, D. L. *Educational Project Management.* Columbus, Ohio: Merrill, 1971.

Cooley, W. W., and Lohnes, P. R. *Multivariate Procedures for the Behavioral Sciences.* New York: Wiley, 1962.

Cooper, J. *Competency-Based Teacher Education.* Berkeley, Calif.: McCutchan, 1973.

Cox, D. R. *Planning of Experiments.* New York: Wiley, 1958.

Cox, R. C., and Unks, N. J. *A Selected and Annotated Bibliography of Studies Concerning the Taxonomy of Educational Objectives: Cognitive Domain.* Pittsburgh: Learning Research and Development Center, University of Pittsburgh, 1967.

Crawford, M. P. *Research in Army Training: Present and Future.* Washington, D.C.: HumRRO, 1967.

Creager, J. A., and Valentine, L. D., Jr. "Regression Analysis of Linear Composite Variance." *Psychometrika*, 1962, *27*, 31-37.

Cremin, L. A. *The Transformation of the School.* New York: Knopf, 1961.

Crissy, W. J. E., and Regan, J. J. "Halo in the Employment Interview." *Journal of Applied Psychology*, 1951, *35*, 338-341.

Cronbach, L. J. "Response Sets and Test Validity." *Educational and Psychological Measurement*, 1946, *6*, 475-494.

Cronbach, L. J. "Further Evidence on Response Sets and Test Design." *Educational and Psychological Measurement*, 1950, *10*, 3-31.

Cronbach, L. J. "Course Improvement Through Evaluation." *Teachers College Record*, 1963, *64*, 672-683.

Cronbach, L. J. "How Can Instruction Be Adapted to Individual Differences?" In R. M. Gagné (Ed.), *Learning and Individual Differences.* Columbus, Ohio: Merrill, 1967.

Cronbach, L. J. *Essentials of Psychological Testing.* (3rd Ed.) New York: Harper, 1970.

Cronbach, L. J. "Comments on 'Mastery Learning and Its Implications for Curriculum Development.'" In E. W. Eisner (Ed.), *Confronting Curriculum Reform.* Boston: Little, Brown, 1971.

Cronbach, L. J. "Test Validation." In R. L. Thorndike (Ed.), *Educational Measurement.* (2nd Ed.) Washington, D.C.: American Council on Education, 1971.

Cronbach, L. J., and Furby, L. "How We Should Measure 'Change'—or Should We?" *Psychological Bulletin*, 1970, *74*, 68-80.

Cronbach, L. J., and Suppes, P. (Eds.) *Research for Tomorrow's Schools: Disciplined Inquiry for Education.* New York: Macmillan, 1962.

Crooks, L. A. (Ed.) *An Investigation of Sources of Bias in the Prediction of Job Performance: A Six-Year Study.* Princeton, N.J.: Educational Testing Service, 1972.

Cyphert, F. R., and Gant, W. L. "The Delphi Technique: A Tool for Collecting Opinions in Teacher Education." *Journal of Teacher Education*, 1970, *31*, 417-425.

Dalkey, N. C. *The Delphi Method: An Experimental Study of Group Opinion.* Santa Monica, Calif.: RAND Corporation, 1969.

Damrin, D. E. "The Russell Sage Social Relations Test: A Technique for Measuring Group Problem-Solving Skills in Elementary School Children." *Journal of Experimental Education,* 1959, *28,* 85-99.

Davis, F. B. "Item Selection Techniques." In E. F. Lindquist (Ed.), *Educational Measurement.* Washington, D.C.: American Council on Education, 1955.

Dempster, A. P. *Elements of Continuous Multivariate Analysis.* Reading, Mass.: Addison-Wesley, 1969.

Denny, T. (Issue Ed.) "Educational Evaluation." *Review of Educational Research,* 1970, *40* (2), 181-324.

Diaz-Guerrero, R., and Holtzman, W. H. "Learning by Televised *Plaza Sesamo* in Mexico." *Journal of Educational Psychology,* in press.

Dick, W., and Hagerty, N. *Topics in Measurement: Reliability and Validity.* New York: McGraw-Hill, 1971.

Diederich, P. "Pitfalls in the Measurement of Achievement Gains." In D. A. Payne and R. F. Morris (Eds.), *Educational and Psychological Measurement.* Waltham, Mass.: Blaisdell, 1967.

Downie, N. M. "Types of Test Scores." In S. C. Stone and B. Shertzer (Eds.), *Guidance Monograph Series. III: Testing.* Boston: Houghton Mifflin, 1968.

Dressel, P. L., and Associates. *Institutional Research in the University: A Handbook.* San Francisco: Jossey-Bass, 1971.

Duncan, O. D. "A Socioeconomic Index for All Occupations." In A. J. Reiss, Jr., O. D. Duncan, P. K. Hatt, and C. C. North, *Occupations and Social Status.* New York: Free Press, 1961.

Duncan, O. D. "Path Analysis: Sociological Examples." *American Journal of Sociology,* 1966, *72,* 1-16.

Dunn, T. F., and Goldstein, L. G. "Test Difficulty, Validity, and Reliability as Functions of Selected Multiple-Choice Item Construction Principles." *Educational and Psychological Measurement,* 1959, *19,* 171-179.

Dyer, H. "School Factors and Equal Educational Opportunity." *Harvard Educational Review,* 1968, *38,* 38-56.

Dyer, H. S. "The Mission of the Evaluator." *Urban Review,* 1969, *3* (4), 10-12.

Dyer, H. S. "Toward Objective Criteria for Professional Accountability in the Schools of New York City." *Phi Delta Kappan,* 1970, *52,* 206-211.

Dyer, H. S., and King, R. G. *College Board Scores: Their Use and Interpretation.* Princeton, N.J.: Educational Testing Service, 1955.

Dyer, H. S., Linn, R. L., and Patton, M. J. "A Comparison of Four Methods of Obtaining Discrepancy Measures Based on Observed and Predicted School System Means on Achievement Tests." *American Educational Research Journal,* 1969, *6,* 591-605.

Ebel, R. L. *Measuring Educational Achievement.* Englewood Cliffs, N.J.: Prentice-Hall, 1965.

Ebel, R. L. "Criterion-Referenced Measurements: Limitations." *School Review,* 1971, *79,* 282-288.

Ebel, R. L. *Essentials of Educational Measurement.* Englewood Cliffs, N.J.: Prentice-Hall, 1972.

Educational Products Information Exchange. *Evaluating Individualized Materials.* New York, 1972.

Educational Testing Service. *Multiple-Choice Questions: A Close Look.* Princeton, N.J., 1963.

Edwards, A. L. *Statistical Analysis.* (3rd Ed.) New York: Holt, 1969.

Edwards, A. L. *Experimental Design in Psychological Research.* (4th Ed.) New York: Holt, 1972.

Eells, K., Davis, A., Havighurst, R. J., Herrick, V. E., and Tyler, R. W. *Intelligence and Cultural Differences.* Chicago: University of Chicago Press, 1951.

Elam, S. *Performance-Based Teacher Education: What Is the State of the Art?* Washington, D.C.: American Association of Colleges for Teacher Education, 1972.

Elashoff, J. D., and Snow, R. E. *Pygmalion Reconsidered.* Worthington, Ohio: Charles A. Jones, 1971.

Ennis, R. H. "On Causality." *Educational Researcher,* 1973, 2 (6), 4-11.

Eysenck, H. J. "Rorschach Review." In O. K. Buros (Ed.), *The Fifth Mental Measurements Yearbook.* Highland Park, N.J.: Gryphon Press, 1959.

Farr, M. J. "Computer-Assisted Instruction." *Naval Research Reviews,* September 1972, 8-16.

Farr, R., and Anastasiow, N. *Tests of Reading Readiness and Achievement: A Review and Evaluation.* Newark, Del.: International Reading Association, 1969.

Fattu, N. A. "Training Devices." In C. W. Harris (Ed.), *Encyclopedia of Educational Research.* (3rd Ed.) New York: Macmillan, 1960.

Fear, R. A. *The Evaluation Interview.* (2nd Ed.) New York: McGraw-Hill, 1973.

Feldman, K. A., and Newcomb, T. M. *The Impact of College on Students.* San Francisco: Jossey-Bass, 1969. 2 vols.

Feldmesser, R. *Performance Contracting in Principle and Practice.* TM Report No. 20. Princeton, N.J.: ERIC Clearinghouse on Tests, Measurement, and Evaluation, 1972.

Feldmesser, R. A. *Educational Goal Indicators for New Jersey.* Princeton, N.J.: Educational Testing Service, 1973.

Feller, W. *An Introduction to Probability Theory and Its Application.* New York: Wiley, 1966.

Ferguson, G. A. *Statistical Analysis in Psychology and Education.* (3rd Ed.) New York: McGraw-Hill, 1971.

Festinger, L., and Katz, D. (Eds.) *Research Methods in the Behavioral Sciences.* New York: Dryden, 1953.

Finley, C. J., and Berdie, F. S. *The National Assessment Approach to Exercise Development.* Denver: National Assessment of Educational Progress, 1970.

Finn, J. D. "Expectations and the Educational Environment." *Review of Educational Research,* 1972, 42, 387-410.

Fishbein, M. (Ed.) *Readings in Attitude Theory and Measurement.* New York: Wiley, 1967.

Fisher, R. A. *Statistical Methods for Research Workers.* London: Oliver & Boyd, 1925.

Fisher, R. A. *The Design of Experiments.* (6th Ed.) New York: Hafner, 1951.

Fitzpatrick, R. "The Selection of Measures for Evaluating Programs." In *Eval-*

uative Research: Strategies and Methods. Pittsburgh: American Institutes for Research, 1970.

Fleishman, E. A. "The Description and Prediction of Perceptual-Motor Skill Learning." In R. Glaser (Ed.), *Training Research and Education.* Pittsburgh: University of Pittsburgh Press, 1962.

Fleishman, E. A. "Motor Abilities." In R. L. Ebel (Ed.), *Encyclopedia of Educational Research.* (4th Ed.) London: Macmillan, 1969.

Florida Educational Research and Development Council. *Plan for Study of the Educational Needs of Florida.* Gainesville: College of Education, University of Florida, 1968.

Fowler, H. *Curiosity and Exploratory Behaviors.* New York: Macmillan, 1965.

Fox, D. J. *The Research Process in Education.* New York: Holt, 1969.

Frederiksen, N. "Proficiency Tests for Training Evaluation." In R. Glaser (Ed.), *Training Research and Evaluation.* Pittsburgh: University of Pittsburgh Press, 1962.

Frederiksen, N., Jensen, O., and Beaton, A. E. *Prediction of Organizational Behavior.* New York: Pergamon, 1972.

French, J. R. P., Jr. "Experiments in Field Settings." In L. Festinger and D. Katz (Eds.), *Research Methods in the Behavioral Sciences.* New York: Dryden Press, 1953.

French, J. W., Ekstrom, R. B., and Price, L. A. *Kit of Reference Tests for Cognitive Factors.* Princeton, N.J.: Educational Testing Service, 1963.

Furst, N. J. "Systematic Classroom Observation." In L. Deighten (Ed.), *Encyclopedia of Education.* New York: Macmillan, 1971.

Gadway, C. J. *Reading and Literature: General Information Yearbook.* Denver: National Assessment of Educational Progress, 1972.

Gagné, R. M. *The Condition of Learning.* New York: Holt, 1965.

Gagné, R. M., and Kneller, G. P. "Behavioral Objectives? Yes or No?" *Educational Leadership,* 1972, *19,* 394-400.

Gallagher, J. J. "Teacher Variation in Concept Presentation in the BSCS Curriculum Program." *BSCS Newsletter,* 1967, *30,* 8-18.

Gardner, R. W., Holzman, P. S., Klein, G. S., Linton, H. B., and Spence, D. P. "Cognitive Control: A Study of Individual Consistencies in Cognitive Behavior." *Psychological Issues,* 1960, *2* (4).

Gessner, P. K. "Evaluation of Instruction." *Science,* 1973, *180,* 566-570.

Getzels, J. W. "The Problem of Interests: A Reconsideration." In H. A. Robinson (Ed.), *Reading: Seventy-Five Years of Progress.* Supplementary Educational Monographs No. 96. Chicago: University of Chicago Press, 1966.

Glaser, R. (Ed.) *Training Research and Education.* New York: Wiley, 1965.

Glaser, R. "Individuals and Learning: The New Aptitudes." *Educational Researcher,* 1972, *1* (6), 5-13.

Glaser, R., and Nitko, A. J. "Measurement in Learning and Instruction." In R. L. Thorndike (Ed.), *Educational Measurement.* (2nd Ed.) Washington, D.C.: American Council on Education, 1971.

Glaser, R., and Short, J. "Training in Industry." In B. von H. Gilmer (Ed.), *Industrial and Organizational Psychology.* New York: McGraw-Hill, 1971.

Glass, G. V. "The Many Faces of Educational Accountability." *Phi Delta Kappan,* 1972, *53,* 636-639.

Glass, G. V., Willson, V. L., and Gottman, J. M. *Design and Analysis of Time-*

Series Experiments. Boulder, Colo.: Laboratory of Educational Research, University of Colorado, 1972.

Glennan, T. K., Jr. "Evaluating Federal Manpower Programs: Notes and Observations." In P. H. Rossi and W. Williams (Eds.), *Evaluating Social Programs: Theory, Practice, and Politics.* New York: Seminar Press, 1972.

Gleser, L. J. "On Bounds for the Average Correlation Between Subtest Scores in Ipsatively Scored Tests." *Educational and Psychological Measurement,* 1972, *32,* 759-765.

Glock, C. Y. (Ed.) *Survey Research in the Social Sciences.* New York: Russell Sage Foundation, 1967.

Goldfried, M. V., Stricker, G., and Weiner, I. B. *Rorschach Handbook of Clinical and Research Applications.* Englewood Cliffs, N.J.: Prentice-Hall, 1971.

Goodenough, F. L., and Harris, D. B. "Studies in the Psychology of Children's Drawings." *Psychological Bulletin,* 1950, *47,* 369-433.

Goodlad, J. I. *The Changing School Curriculum.* New York: Fund for Advancement of Education, 1966.

Green, J. L., and Stone, J. C. "Developing and Testing Q-Cards and Content Analysis in Group Interviews." *Nursing Research,* 1972, *21,* 342-347.

Greenwood, E. R., Jr. *A Detailed Proof of the Chi-Square Test of Goodness of Fit.* Cambridge, Mass.: Harvard University Press, 1940.

Gronlund, N. E. *Measurement and Evaluation in Teaching.* New York: Macmillan, 1965.

Gross, B. M. (Ed.) *Social Intelligence for America's Future: Explorations in Societal Problems.* Boston: Allyn and Bacon, 1969.

Guba, E. G., and Stufflebeam, D. L. *Evaluation: The Process of Stimulating, Aiding and Abetting Insightful Action.* Monograph Series in Reading Education No. 1. Bloomington: Indiana University, 1970.

Guetzkow, H. (Ed.) *Simulation in Social Science: Readings.* Englewood Cliffs, N.J.: Prentice-Hall, 1962.

Guidelines for the Collection, Maintenance, and Dissemination of Pupil Records: Report of a Conference on the Ethical and Legal Aspects of School Record Keeping. New York: Russell Sage Foundation, 1970.

Guilford, J. P. *The Nature of Human Intelligence.* New York: McGraw-Hill, 1967.

Guilford, J. P. *A General Summary of Twenty Years of Research on Aptitudes of High-Level Personnel.* Los Angeles: University of Southern California, 1969.

Guion, R. *Personnel Testing.* New York: McGraw-Hill, 1965.

Gulliksen, H. *Theory of Mental Tests.* New York: Wiley, 1950.

Hall, G. R., Carpenter, P., Haggart, S. A., Rapp, M. L., and Summer, G. C. *A Guide to Educational Performance Contracting.* Santa Monica, Calif.: RAND Corporation, 1972.

Hall, M. *Developing Skills in Proposal Writing.* Corvallis, Ore.: Office of Federal Relations, Oregon State System of Higher Education, 1971.

Hamaker, H. C. "Quality Control, Statistical: Acceptance Sampling." In D. L. Sills (Ed.), *International Encyclopedia of the Social Sciences.* Vol. 13. New York: Crowell-Collier and Macmillan, 1968.

Hand, H. H., and Slocum, J. W. "A Longitudinal Study of the Effects of a Human Relations Training Program on Managerial Effectiveness." *Journal of Applied Psychology,* 1972, *56* (5), 412-417.

Harless, J. H. "An Analysis of Front-End Analysis." *Improving Human Performance—A Research Quarterly*, Winter 1973.

Harman, H. H. *Modern Factor Analysis.* (2nd Ed.) Chicago: University of Chicago Press, 1957.

Harman, H. H. "Simulation: A Survey." Paper presented at the Joint IRE-AIEE-ACM Computer Conference, Los Angeles, 1961.

Harris, C. W. (Ed.) *Encyclopedia of Educational Research.* (3rd Ed.) New York: Macmillan, 1960.

Harris, C. W. (Ed.) *Problems in Measuring Change.* Milwaukee: University of Wisconsin Press, 1967.

Harrocks, J. E. *Assessment of Behavior.* Columbus, Ohio: Merrill, 1964.

Hartley, H. J. *Educational Planning-Programming-Budgeting: A Systems Approval.* Englewood Cliffs, N.J.: Prentice-Hall, 1968.

Hawkridge, D. G., Campeau, P. L., and Trickett, P. K. *Preparing Evaluation Reports: A Guide for Authors.* AIR Monograph No. 6. Pittsburgh: American Institutes for Research, 1970.

Hays, W. L. *Statistics.* New York: Holt, 1963.

Hays, W. L. *Statistics for the Social Sciences.* (2nd Ed.) New York: Holt, 1973.

Hellmuth, J. (Ed.) *Disadvantaged Child.* Vol. 3: *Compensatory Education: A National Debate.* New York: Brunner/Mazel, 1970.

Helmer, O. *Social Technology.* New York: Basic Books, 1966.

Helmstadter, G. C. *Research Concepts in Human Behavior.* New York: Appleton-Century-Crofts, 1970.

Hempel, C. G. "The Theoretician's Dilemma: A Study in the Logic of Theory Construction." In H. Feigl, M. Scriven, and G. Maxwell (Eds.), *Minnesota Studies in the Philosophy of Science.* Vol. 2: *Concepts, Theories, and the Mind-Body Problem.* Minneapolis: University of Minnesota Press, 1958.

Hempel, C. G., and Oppenheim, P. "The Logic of Explanation." In H. Feigl and M. Brodbeck (Eds.), *Readings in the Philosophy of Science.* New York: Appleton-Century-Crofts, 1953.

Hills, J. R. "Use of Measurement in Selection and Placement." In R. L. Thorndike (Ed.), *Educational Measurement.* (2nd Ed.) Washington, D.C.: American Council on Education, 1971.

Hills, J. R., and Gladney, M. B. "Factors Influencing College Grading Standards." *Journal of Educational Measurement*, 1968, *5*, 31-39.

Hilton, T. L., and Patrick, C. "Cross-Sectional Versus Longitudinal Data: An Empirical Comparison of Mean Differences in Academic Growth." *Journal of Educational Measurement*, 1970, *7*, 15-24.

Hitch, C. J. *Decision-Making for Defense.* Berkeley: University of California Press, 1966.

Hitch, C. J. "What Are the Programs in Planning, Programming, Budgeting?" *Socio-Economic Planning Sciences*, 1969, *2*, 465-472.

Hoepfner, R. (Ed.) *CSE Elementary School Test Evaluations.* Los Angeles: Center for the Study of Evaluation, UCLA Graduate School of Education, 1970.

Hoepfner, R., Stern, C., and Nummedal, S. G. (Eds.) *CSE-ECRC Preschool/Kindergarten Test Evaluations.* Los Angeles: Center for the Study of Evaluation and Early Childhood Research Center, UCLA Graduate School of Education, 1971.

Hollingshead, A. B. *Two Factor Index of Social Position.* New Haven, Conn., 1957.

Holt, J. *How Children Fail.* New York: Pitman, 1968.

Humphreys, L. G. "Implications of Group Differences for Test Interpretation." In *Assessment in a Pluralistic Society: Proceedings of the 1972 Invitational Conference on Testing Problems.* Princeton, N.J.: Educational Testing Service, 1973.

Huntsberger, D. V. *Elements of Statistical Inference.* Boston: Allyn and Bacon, 1961.

Husek, T. R., and Sirotnik, K. "Matrix Sampling." *Evaluation Comment,* 1968, *1* (3).

Isaac, S., and Michael, W. B. *Handbook in Research and Evaluation.* San Diego: Robert R. Knapp, 1971.

Jackson, D. N., and Messick, S. "Content and Style in Personality Assessment." *Psychological Bulletin,* 1958, *55,* 243-252.

Jackson, D. N., and Messick, S. (Eds.) *Problems in Human Assessment.* New York: McGraw-Hill, 1967.

Jacob, P. E. *Changing Values in College: An Exploratory Study of the Impact of College Teaching.* New York: Harper, 1957.

Jacobs, P. I., Maier, M. H., and Stolurow, L. M. *A Guide to Evaluating Self-Instructional Programs.* New York: Holt, 1966.

Jacquette, F. L., and Jacquette, B. L. "What Makes a Good Proposal?" *Foundation News,* 1973, *14,* 18-21.

Jamison, D. "Definitions of Productivity and Efficiency in Education." Appendix A of A. Melmed, rapporteur, *Productivity and Efficiency in Education.* Washington, D.C.: Educational Panel of Federal Council on Science and Technology, Commission on Automation Opportunities in the Service Areas, 1972 (draft).

Jellema, W. W. (Ed.) *Efficient College Management.* San Francisco: Jossey-Bass, 1972.

Jencks, C., Smith, M., Acland, H., Bane, M. J., Cohen, D., Gintis, H., Heynes, B., and Michelson, S. *Inequality: A Reassessment of the Effect of Family and Schooling in America.* New York: Basic Books, 1972.

Jensen, A. R. "How Much Can We Boost IQ and Scholastic Achievement?" *Harvard Educational Review,* 1969, *39,* 1-123.

Johnson, B. L., and Nelson, J. K. *Practical Measurements for Evaluation in Physical Education.* Minneapolis: Burgess, 1969.

Johnson, N. L., and Smith, H., Jr. (Eds.) *New Developments in Survey Sampling.* New York: Wiley, 1969.

Johnson, O., and Bommarito, J. W. *Tests and Measurements in Child Development: A Handbook.* San Francisco: Jossey-Bass, 1971.

Johnson, P. O., and Fay, L. "The Neyman-Johnson Technique, Its Theory and Applications." *Psychometrika,* 1950, *15,* 349-367.

Johnson, P. O., and Neyman, J. "Tests of Certain Linear Hypotheses and Their Applications to Some Educational Problems." *Statistical Research Memoirs,* 1936, *1,* 57-93.

Kagan, J., and Kogan, N. "Individual Variation in Cognitive Processes." In P. H. Mussen (Ed.), *Carmichael's Manual of Child Psychology.* New York: Wiley, 1970.

Kaplan, A. "Definition and Specifications of Meaning." *Journal of Philosophy,* 1946, *43,* 281-288.

Katz, J. *Experimentation with Human Beings.* New York: Russell Sage Foundation, 1972.

Katz, M. *Selecting an Achievement Test: Principles and Procedures.* Princeton, N.J.: Educational Testing Service, 1958.

Kaya, E. *Review of Preschool Tests, 1965-69.* New York: Hofstra University, 1969.

Kelman, H. C. "The Rights of the Subject in Social Research: An Analysis in Terms of Relative Power and Legitimacy." *American Psychologist,* 1972, *27,* 989-1016.

Kennedy, C., and Thirlwall, A. P. "Surveys in Applied Economics: Technical Progress." *Economic Journal,* 1972, *82,* 11-72.

Kersh, B. Y., and Wittrock, M. C. "Learning by Discovery: An Interpretation of Recent Research." *Journal of Teacher Education,* 1962, *13,* 461-468.

Kessen, W. "Research Design in the Study of Developmental Problems." In P. Mussen (Ed.), *Handbook of Research Methods in Child Development.* New York: Wiley, 1960.

Kish, L. *Survey Sampling.* New York: Wiley, 1965.

Klein, S. P., and Kosecoff, J. *Issues and Procedures in the Development of Criterion Referenced Tests.* Princeton, N.J.: ERIC Clearinghouse on Tests, Measurement, and Evaluation, Educational Testing Service, 1973.

Knapp, R. R. "The Effects of Time Limits on the Intelligence Test Performance of Mexican and American Subjects." *Journal of Educational Psychology,* 1960, *51,* 14-20.

Komoski, P. K. Testimony Before the Select Education Subcommittee of the Education and Labor Committee of the U.S. House of Representatives. *Congressional Record,* May 11, 1971.

Kourilsky, M. "An Adversary Model for Educational Evaluation." UCLA *Evaluation Comment,* 1973, *4* (2), 3-6.

Krathwohl, D. R. *How to Prepare a Research Proposal: Suggestions for Those Seeking Funds for Behavioral Science Research.* Syracuse, N.Y.: Syracuse University Book Store, 1966.

Krathwohl, D. R., Bloom, B. S., and Masia, B. B. *Taxonomy of Educational Objectives.* Handbook II: *Affective Domain.* New York: McKay, 1964.

Krathwohl, D. R., and Payne, D. A. "Defining and Assessing Educational Objectives." In R. L. Thorndike (Ed.), *Educational Measurement.* (2nd Ed.) Washington, D.C.: American Council on Education, 1971.

Kruger, W. S. "Program Auditor: New Breed on the Education Scene." *American Education,* 1970, *6,* 36.

Lansing, J. C., and Morgan, J. N. *Economic Survey Methods.* Ann Arbor: Institute for Social Research, University of Michigan, 1971.

Lau, L., and Yotopoulos, P. "A Test for Relative Efficiency and Application to Indian Agriculture." *American Economic Review,* 1971, *61,* 94-109.

Lawley, D. N., and Maxwell, A. E. *Factor Analysis as a Statistical Method.* London: Butterworth, 1963.

Lawshe, C. H., and Bolda, R. A. "Expectancy Charts. I: Their Use and Empirical Development." *Personnel Psychology,* 1958, *11,* 353-365.

Lawshe, C. H., Bolda, R. A., Brune, R. L., and Auclair, G. "Expectancy

Charts. II: Their Theoretical Development." *Personnel Psychology*, 1958, *11*, 545-559.

Lessinger, L. M. "Engineering Accountability for Results in Public Education." *Phi Delta Kappan*, 1970, *52*, 217-225.

Lessinger, L. M. *Every Kid a Winner: Accountability in Education*. Palo Alto, Calif.: Science Research Associates, 1970.

Levin, H. "Efficiency in Education." Paper presented at National Bureau of Economic Research Conference on Education as an Industry. Chicago, 1971.

Levine, D. M., and Uttal, B. "Performance Contracting Policy: Motivational Problems and New Models." *Teachers College Record*, 1973, *74*, 317-355.

Levine, M. "Scientific Method and the Adversary Model: Some Preliminary Suggestions." UCLA *Evaluation Comment*, 1973, *4* (2), 1-3.

Levine, R. S. *Equating the Score Scales of Alternate Forms Administered to Samples of Different Ability*. Research Bulletin 55-23. Princeton, N.J.: Educational Testing Service, 1955.

Lieberman, M. "An Overview of Accountability." *Phi Delta Kappan*, 1970, *52*, 194-195.

Light, R. J., Mosteller, F., and Winokur, H. S. "Using Controlled Field Studies to Improve Public Policy." *Federal Statistics* (Report of the President's Commission), 1971, *2*, 367-402.

Lindquist, E. F. *Design and Analysis of Experiments in Psychology and Education*. Boston: Houghton Mifflin, 1953.

Lindvall, C. M. (Ed.) *Defining Educational Objectives*. Pittsburgh: University of Pittsburgh Press, 1964.

Lindzey, G. "On the Classification of Projective Techniques." *Psychological Bulletin*, 1959, *56*, 159-168.

Linn, R. L., and Werts, C. E. "Considerations for Studies of Test Bias." *Journal of Educational Measurement*, 1971, *8*, 1-4.

Livingston, S. A. "Criterion-Referenced Applications of Classical Test Theory." *Journal of Educational Measurement*, 1972, *9* (1), 13-26.

Llewellyn, K. N. "Case Method." In E. R. A. Seligman (Ed.), *Encyclopedia of the Social Sciences*. Vol. 3. New York: Macmillan, 1930.

Loevinger, J. "Objective Tests as Instruments of Psychological Theory." In D. N. Jackson and S. Messick (Eds.), *Problems in Human Assessment*. New York: McGraw-Hill, 1967.

Lopez, F. *Evaluating Employee Performance*. Chicago: Public Personnel Association, 1968.

Lord, F. M. "Equating Test Scores—A Maximum Likelihood Solution." *Psychometrika*, 1955, *20*, 193-200.

Lord, F. M. "Large-Sample Covariance Analysis When the Control Variable Is Fallible." *Journal of the American Statistical Association*, 1960, *55*, 307-321.

Lord, F. M. "Elementary Models for Measuring Change." In C. W. Harris (Ed.), *Problems in Measuring Change*. Madison: University of Wisconsin Press, 1962.

Lord, F. M. "Estimating Norms by Item Sampling." *Educational and Psychological Measurement*, 1962, *22*, 259-267.

Lord, F. M. "A Paradox in the Interpretation of Group Comparisons." *Psychological Bulletin*, 1967, *68*, 304-305.

Lord, F. M. "Statistical Adjustments When Comparing Preexisting Groups." *Psychological Bulletin*, 1969, *72*, 336-337.

Lord, F. M. "Significance Tests for Partial Correlation Corrected for Attenuation." *Educational and Psychological Measurement*, 1974.

Lord, F. M., and Novick, M. R. *Statistical Theories of Mental Test Scores.* Reading, Mass.: Addison-Wesley, 1968.

Lorge, I., and Thorndike, R. L. "Procedures for Establishing Norms." In *Technical Manual, Lorge-Thorndike Intelligence Tests.* Boston: Houghton Mifflin, 1954. Reprinted in D. N. Jackson and S. Messick (Eds.), *Problems in Human Assessment.* New York: McGraw-Hill, 1967.

Lubin, A. "The Interpretation of Significant Interaction." *Educational and Psychological Measurement*, 1961, *21*, 807-817.

Lykken, D. T. "Statistical Significance in Psychological Research." *Psychological Bulletin*, 1968, *70*, 151-159.

Lyman, H. B. "Intelligence, Aptitude, and Achievement Testing." In S. C. Stone and B. Shertzer (Eds.), *Guidance Monograph Series.* III: *Testing.* Boston: Houghton Mifflin, 1968.

McClelland, D. "What Is the Effect of Achievement Motivation Training on the Schools?" *Teachers College Record*, 1972, *74*, 129-145.

McDill, E. L., McDill, M. S., and Sprehe, J. T. "Evaluation in Practice: Compensatory Education." In P. H. Rossi and W. Williams (Eds.), *Evaluating Social Action Programs: Theory, Practice, and Politics.* New York: Seminar Press, 1972.

McDonald, F. J. "Evaluation of Teaching Behavior." In W. R. Houston and R. B. Howsam (Eds.), *Competency-Based Teacher Education.* Chicago: Science Research Associates, 1972.

McDonald, F. J., Forehand, G. A., Marco, G. L., Murphy, R. T., and Quirk, T. J. *A Design for an Accountability System for the New York City School System.* Princeton, N.J.: Educational Testing Service, 1972.

McGehee, W., and Thayer, P. W. *Training in Business and Industry.* New York: Wiley, 1961.

MacGinitie, W. H. "Language Comprehension in Education." In J. R. Davitz and S. Ball (Eds.), *Psychology of the Educational Process.* New York: McGraw-Hill, 1970.

McGuire, C. H. "An Evaluation Model for Professional Education—Medical Education." In *Proceedings of the 1967 Invitational Conference on Testing Problems.* Princeton, N.J.: Educational Testing Service, 1968.

MacKinney, A. C. "The Assessment of Performance Change: An Inductive Example." *Organizational Behavior and Human Performance*, 1967, *2*.

McLean, L. D. "Research Methodology in Educational Psychology." In J. R. Davitz and S. Ball (Eds.), *Psychology of the Educational Process.* New York: McGraw-Hill, 1970.

McMorris, R. F., Brown, J. A., Snyder, G. W., and Pruzek, R. M. "Effects of Violating Item Construction Principles." *Journal of Educational Measurement*, 1972, *9*, 287-295.

McNemar, Q. *Psychological Statistics.* (4th Ed.) New York: Wiley, 1969.

McReynolds, P. (Ed.) *Advances in Psychological Assessment.* Palo Alto: Science and Behavioral Books, 1968, 1971. San Francisco: Jossey-Bass, 1974.

Madaus, G. F. *The Development and Use of Expectancy Tables for the Grad-*

uate Record Examinations Aptitude Test. Special Report No. 66-1. Princeton, N.J.: Educational Testing Service, 1966.

Mager, R. F. *Preparing Objectives for Programmed Instruction.* Belmont, Calif.: Fearon, 1962.

Margolin, J. B., and Misch, M. R. (Eds.) *Computers in the Classroom.* New York: Spartan Books, 1970.

Maxwell, A. E. "Correlational Techniques." In H. J. Eysenck, W. Arnold, and R. Meili (Eds.), *Encyclopedia of Psychology.* Vol. 1. New York: Herder and Herder, 1972.

Mayeske, G. W. "Teacher Attributes and School Achievement." In *Do Teachers Make a Difference?* Washington, D.C.: U.S. Government Printing Office, 1970. Pp. 100-119.

Mayeske, G. W., Wisler, C. E., Beaton, A. E., Jr., Weinfeld, F. D., Cohen, W. M., Okada, T., Proshek, J. M., and Tabler, K. A. *A Study of Our Nation's Schools.* Washington, D.C.: U.S. Department of Health, Education, and Welfare, 1972.

Mayor, J. R. *Accreditation in Teacher Education: Its Influence on Higher Education.* Washington, D.C.: National Commission on Accrediting, 1965.

Mecklenburger, J. A. *Performance Contracting.* Worthington, Ohio: Charles J. Jones, 1972.

Medley, D. M., and Mitzel, H. E. "Measuring Classroom Behavior by Systematic Observation." In N. L. Gage (Ed.), *Handbook of Research on Teaching.* Chicago. Rand McNally, 1963.

Mehrens, W. A., and Lehmann, I. J. *Measurement and Evaluation in Education and Psychology.* New York: Holt, 1973.

Meredith, J. C. *The CAI Author/Instructor.* Englewood Cliffs, N.J.: Educational Technology Publications, 1971.

Merwin, J. C. "Historical Review of Changing Concepts of Evaluation." In R. W. Tyler (Ed.), *Educational Evaluation: New Roles, New Means. The Sixty-Eighth Yearbook of the National Society for the Study of Education, Part II.* Chicago: University of Chicago Press, 1969.

Messick, S. "Personality Measurement and College Performance." In D. N. Jackson and S. Messick (Eds.), *Problems in Human Assessment.* New York: McGraw-Hill, 1967.

Messick, S. "Response Sets." In D. L. Sills (Ed.), *International Encyclopedia of the Social Sciences.* Vol. 5. New York: Macmillan and Free Press, 1968.

Messick, S. "The Criterion Problem in the Evaluation of Instruction: Assessing Possible, Not Just Intended, Outcomes." In M. C. Wittrock and D. E. Wiley (Eds.), *The Evaluation of Instruction: Issues and Problems.* New York: Holt, 1970.

Messick, S. "Evaluation of Educational Programs as Research on the Educational Process." In F. F. Korten, S. W. Cook, and J. I. Lacey (Eds.), *Psychology and the Problems of Society.* Washington, D.C.: American Psychological Association, 1970.

Messick, S. "Research Methodology for Educational Change." In *Educational Change: Implications for Measurement. Proceedings of the 1971 Invitational Conference on Testing Problems.* Princeton, N.J.: Educational Testing Service, 1972.

Messick, S., and Anderson, S. B. "Educational Testing, Individual Development, and Social Responsibility." *Counseling Psychologist*, 1970, *2*, 80-88.

Messick, S., and Barrows, T. S. "Strategies for Research and Evaluation in Early Childhood Education." In I. J. Gordon (Ed.), *Early Childhood Education. The Seventy-First Yearbook of the National Society for the Study of Education.* Chicago: University of Chicago Press, 1972.

Miller, D. C. *Handbook of Research Design and Social Measurement.* New York: McKay, 1964.

Miller, R. "Task Description and Analysis." In R. Gagné (Ed.), *Psychological Principles in System Development.* New York: Holt, 1962.

Millman, J., Bishop, C. H., and Ebel, R. "An Analysis of Test-Wiseness." *Educational and Psychological Measurement,* 1965, *25*, 707-726.

Millman, J., and Pauk, W. *How to Take Tests.* New York: McGraw-Hill, 1969.

Mood, A. M. "Macro-Analysis of the American Education System." *Operations Research,* 1969, *17*, 770-784.

Mood, A. M. "Partitioning Variance in Multiple Regression Analyses as a Tool for Developing Learning Models." *American Educational Research Journal,* 1971, *8*, 191-202.

Morrison, D. F. *Multivariate Statistical Methods.* New York: McGraw-Hill, 1967.

Moses, L. E. "Nonparametric Statistics for Psychological Research." *Psychological Bulletin,* 1952, *49*, 122-143.

Mosteller, F., and Moynihan, D. P. *On Equality of Educational Opportunity.* New York: Random House, 1972.

Mouly, G. J. *The Science of Educational Research.* (2nd Ed.) New York: Van Nostrand Reinhold, 1970.

Mulaik, S. A. *The Foundations of Factor Analysis.* New York: McGraw-Hill, 1972.

Nadiri, M. "Some Approaches to the Theory and Measurement of Total Factor Productivity: A Survey." *Journal of Economic Literature,* 1970, *8*, 1137-1177.

Nagel, E. *The Structure of Science.* New York: Harcourt, Brace, 1961.

National Association of Secondary School Principals Bulletin, October 1972, *56*.

National School Public Relations Association. "PPBS and the School." In *Education U.S.A.* Washington, D.C., 1972.

National Study of Secondary School Evaluation. *Evaluative Criteria.* (4th Ed.) Washington, D.C., 1969.

Newton, R. G., and Spurrell, D. J. "A Development of Multiple Regression for the Analysis of Routine Data." *Applied Statistics,* 1967, *16*, 51-64.

Newton, R. G., and Spurrell, D. J. "Examples of the Use of Elements for Clarifying Regression Analyses." *Applied Statistics,* 1967, *16*, 165-176.

Novick, D. (Ed.) *Program Budgeting.* Cambridge, Mass.: Harvard University Press, 1965.

Office of Strategic Services (OSS) Assessment Staff. *Assessment of Men.* New York: Holt, 1948.

Ohlsen, M. M., and Schultz, R. E. "Projective Test Response Patterns for Best and Poorest Student-Teachers." *Educational and Psychological Measurement,* 1955, *15*, 18-27.

Page, E. S. "Quality Control, Statistical: Process Control." In D. L. Sills

(Ed.), *International Encyclopedia of the Social Sciences.* Vol. 13. New York: Crowell-Collier and Macmillan, 1968.

Pap, A. *An Introduction to the Philosophy of Science.* New York: Free Press, 1962.

Parden, R. J. "Planning, Programming, and Budgeting Systems." In W. W. Jellema (Ed.), *Efficient College Management.* San Francisco: Jossey-Bass, 1972.

Parker, C. A. "Questions Concerning the Interview as a Research Technique." *Journal of Educational Research,* 1957, *51,* 215-221.

Parsons, H. M. *Man-Machine System Experiments.* Baltimore: Johns Hopkins University Press, 1972.

Phi Delta Kappan, 1974, *55* (5).

Phillips, B. N., and Weathers, G. "Analysis of Errors Made in Scoring Standardized Tests." In D. N. Jackson and S. Messick (Eds.), *Problems in Human Assessment.* New York: McGraw-Hill, 1967.

Phillips, B. S. *Social Research: Strategy and Tactics.* New York: Macmillan, 1966.

Plumlee, L. B. "Estimating Means and Standard Deviations from Partial Data —an Empirical Check on Lord's Item Sampling Technique." *Educational and Psychological Measurement,* 1964, *24,* 623-630.

Popham, W. J. (Ed.) *Criterion-Referenced Measurement.* Englewood Cliffs, N.J.: Educational Technology Publishers, 1971.

Popham, W. J., and Baker, E. L. *Establishing Instructional Goals.* Englewood Cliffs, N J.: Prentice-Hall, 1970.

Potthoff, R. F. "On the Johnson-Neyman Technique and Some Extensions Thereof." *Psychometrika,* 1963, *29,* 241-256.

"Proceedings of the Symposium on Operations Analysis of Education." *Socio-Economic Planning Sciences,* 1969, *2,* 105-520.

"Protection of Human Subjects." In *Grants Administration Manual.* Washington, D.C.: Department of Health, Education, and Welfare, 1971.

"Protection of Human Subjects." *Educational Researcher,* 1973, *2,* 10-19. (Reprinted from *Federal Register,* Oct. 9, 1973.)

Provus, M. *Discrepancy Evaluation.* Berkeley, Calif.: McCutchan, 1971.

Quirk, T. J. "Some Measurement Issues in Competency-Based Teacher Education." *Phi Delta Kappan,* 1974, *55,* 316-319.

Radcliffe, J. A. "Some Properties of Ipsative Score Matrices and Their Relevance for Some Current Interest Tests." *Australian Journal of Psychology,* 1963, *15,* 1-11.

Raths, L. E., Harmin, M., and Simon, S. B. *Values and Teaching.* Columbus, Ohio: Merrill, 1966.

Reeves, B. F. *The First Year of "Sesame Street": The Formative Research.* New York: Children's Television Workshop, 1970.

Reichenbach, H. *The Theory of Probability.* Berkeley: University of California Press, 1949.

Riley, M. W. *Sociological Research II: Exercises and Manual.* New York: Harcourt, Brace, 1963.

Rippey, R. M. (Ed.) *Studies in Transactional Evaluation.* Berkeley, Calif.: McCutchan, 1973.

Rivlin, A. M. *Systematic Thinking for Social Action.* Washington, D.C.: Brookings Institution, 1971.

Roethlisberger, F. J., and Dickson, W. J. *Management and the Worker.* Cambridge, Mass.: Harvard University Press, 1941.

Rokeach, M. *The Nature of Human Values.* New York: Free Press, 1973.

Rosenshine, B. *Teaching Behaviors and Student Achievement.* Windsor, Berkshire, England: National Foundation for Educational Research in England and Wales, 1971.

Rosenshine, B., and Furst, N. "The Use of Direct Observation to Study Teaching." In R. M. Travers (Ed.), *Second Handbook of Research on Teaching.* Chicago: Rand McNally, 1973.

Rosenthal, R. R., and Jacobsen, L. *Pygmalion in the Classroom.* New York: Holt, 1968.

Rosenthal, R. R., and Rubin, D. B. "Pygmalion Reassessed." In J. D. Elashoff and R. E. Snow, *Pygmalion Reconsidered.* Worthington, Ohio: Charles A. Jones, 1971.

Rosner, B. *The Power of Competency-Based Teacher Education: A Report.* Boston: Allyn and Bacon, 1972.

Rossi, P., and Williams, W. (Eds.) *Evaluating Social Action Programs: Theory, Practice, and Politics.* New York: Seminar Press, 1972.

Rossi, P. H. "Practice, Method and Theory in Evaluating Social Action Programs." In J. L. Sundquist (Ed.), *On Fighting Poverty: Perspectives from Experience.* New York: Basic Books, 1969.

Rothney, J. W. M. *Evaluating and Reporting Pupil Progress.* What Research Says to the Teacher, No. 7. Washington, D.C.: National Education Association, 1955.

Roueche, J. E., and Kirk, R. W. *Catching Up: Remedial Education.* San Francisco: Jossey-Bass, 1973.

Rubin, D. *Estimating Causal Effects of Treatments in Experimental and Observational Studies.* Princeton, N.J.: Educational Testing Service, 1972.

Rubin, S., and Asher, W. "Comment on 'Intellectual Differences in Five-Year-Old Underprivileged Girls and Boys with and Without Pre-Kindergarten Experience.'" *Psychological Reports,* 1969, *25,* 297-298.

Runyon, R. P., and Haber, A. *Fundamentals of Behavioral Statistics.* Reading, Mass.: Addison-Wesley, 1967.

Sanford, N. (Ed.) *The American College: A Psychological and Social Interpretation of the Higher Learning.* New York: Wiley, 1962.

Sarason, S. B., Davidson, K. S., Lighthall, F. F., Waite, R. R., and Ruebush, B. K. *Anxiety in Elementary School Children.* New York: Wiley, 1960.

Saretsky, G. "The OEO P.C. Experiment and the John Henry Effect." *Phi Delta Kappan,* 1972, *53,* 579-581.

Saunders, D. R. "Moderator Variables in Prediction." In D. N. Jackson and S. Messick (Eds.), *Problems in Human Assessment.* New York: McGraw-Hill, 1967.

Scannell, D. P., and Marshall, J. C. "The Effect of Selected Composition Errors on Grades Assigned to Essay Examinations." *American Educational Research Journal,* 1966, *3,* 125-130.

Schaie, K. W. "Cross-Sectional Methods in the Study of Psychological Aspects of Aging." *Journal of Gerontology,* 1959, *14,* 208-215.

Schaie, K. W. "A General Model for the Study of Developmental Problems." *Psychological Bulletin,* 1965, *64,* 92-107.

Schmieder, A. A. *Competency-Based Teacher Education: The State of the Scene.* Washington, D.C.: American Association of Colleges for Teacher Education, 1973.

Schrader, W. B. "Norms." In C. W. Harris (Ed.), *Encyclopedia of Educational Research*. (3rd Ed.) New York: Macmillan, 1960.

Schrader, W. B. "A Taxonomy of Expectancy Tables." *Journal of Educational Measurement*, 1965, *2*, 29-35.

Scott, W. A. "Comparative Validities of Forced-Choice and Single-Stimulus Tests." *Psychological Bulletin*, 1968, *70*, 231-244.

Scriven, M. "Student Values as Educational Objectives." In *Proceedings of the 1965 Invitational Conference on Testing Problems*. Princeton, N.J.: Educational Testing Service, 1966.

Scriven, M. "The Methodology of Evaluation." In *Perspectives of Curriculum Evaluation*. AERA Monograph Series on Curriculum Evaluation No. 1. Chicago: Rand McNally, 1967.

Scriven, M. *Evaluation Skills* (tape 6B). An instructional cassette recording produced by W. J. Popham. Washington, D.C.: American Educational Research Association, 1971.

Scriven, M. "Prose and Cons about Goal-Free Evaluation." *Evaluation Comment*, 1972, *3* (4), 1-4.

Seashore, R. H. "Work and Motor Performance." In S. S. Stevens (Ed.), *Handbook of Experimental Psychology*. New York: Wiley, 1951.

Selden, W. K. *Accreditation: A Struggle over Standards in Higher Education*. New York: Harper, 1960.

Selltiz, C., Jahoda, M., Deutsch, M., and Cook, S. W. *Research Methods in Social Relations*. New York: Holt, 1959.

Shaver, J. P., and Larkins, A. G. "Research on Teaching Social Studies." In M. M. W. Travers (Ed.), *Second Handbook of Research on Teaching*. Chicago: Rand McNally, 1973.

Shaw, M. E. *Scales for the Measurement of Attitudes*. New York: McGraw-Hill, 1967.

Sheldon, E. B., and Moore, W. E. (Eds.) *Indicators of Social Change: Concepts and Measurements*. New York: Russell Sage Foundation, 1968.

Shimberg, B., Esser, B., and Kruger, D. H. *Occupational Licensing: Practices and Policies*. Washington, D.C.: Public Affairs Press, 1973.

Shimberg, B., and Thornton, R. F. *Development of Improved Examination Procedures for the Promotion of Police Officers in New York City*. Princeton, N.J.: Educational Testing Service, 1972.

Shoemaker, D. M. *Principles and Procedures of Multiple Matrix Samples*. Technical Report No. 34. Inglewood, Calif.: Southwest Regional Laboratory for Educational Research and Development, 1971.

Sidman, M. *Tactics of Scientific Research: Evaluating Experimental Data in Psychology*. New York: Basic Books, 1960.

Siegel, A. I., Bergman, B. A., and Federman, P. *Some Techniques for the Evaluation of Technical Training Courses and Students*. Lowry Air Force Base, Colo.: Technical Training Division, 1972.

Siegel, S. *Nonparametric Statistics for the Behavioral Sciences*. New York: McGraw-Hill, 1956.

Sigel, E., and Sobel, M. *Accountability and the Controversial Role of the Performance Contractors: A Critical Look at the Performance Contracting Phenomenon*. White Plains, N.Y.: Knowledge Industry Publications, 1971.

Sills, D. L. (Ed.) "Evaluation Research." *International Encyclopedia of the Social Sciences*. Vol. 5. New York: Macmillan and Free Press, 1968.

Simon, A., and Boyer, E. G. (Eds.) *Mirrors for Behavior: An Anthology of*

Classroom Observation Instruments. Philadelphia: Research for Better Schools, 1967-1970.

Singer, J. E. "The Use of Manipulative Strategies: Machiavellianism and Attractiveness." *Sociometry,* 1964, *27,* 128-150.

Sjoberg, G., and Nett, R. *A Methodology for Social Research.* New York: Harper, 1968.

Smith, E. R., and Tyler, R. W. *Appraising and Recording Student Progress.* New York: Harper, 1942.

Snedecor, G. W. *Statistical Methods.* (4th Ed.) Ames: Iowa State College Press, 1946.

Snider, J. G., and Osgood, C. E. *Semantic Differential Technique: A Sourcebook.* Chicago: Aldine, 1969.

Snow, C. E. "Research on Industrial Illumination." *Tech Engineering News,* 1926, *8,* 257-282.

Special Projects Office, Department of the Navy. *PERT Summary Report, Phase I.* Washington, D.C.: U.S. Government Printing Office, 1962.

Spiegel, M. R. *Theory and Problems of Statistics.* New York: Schaum, 1961.

Spielberg, H. *Phenomenology in Psychology and Psychiatry.* Evanston, Ill.: Northwestern University Press, 1972.

Stacey, C. L., and DeMartino, M. F. *Understanding Human Motivation.* New York: World, 1965.

Stake, R., and Gjerde, C. *An Evaluation of T City: The Twin City Institute for Talented Youth.* Urbana: Center for Instructional Research and Curriculum Evaluation, University of Illinois, 1971.

Stake, R. E. "The Countenance of Educational Evaluation." *Teachers College Record,* 1967, *68,* 523-540.

Stake, R. E. "Objectives, Priorities, and Other Judgment Data." *Review of Educational Research,* 1970, *40,* 181-213.

Stalnaker, J. M. "The Essay Type of Examination." In E. F. Lindquist (Ed.), *Educational Measurement.* Washington, D.C.: American Council on Education, 1951.

Stanley, J. C. "Insight into One's Own Values." *Journal of Educational Psychology,* 1951, *42,* 399-408.

Stanley, J. C. "Controlled Experimentation: Why Seldom Used in Evaluation?" In *Toward a Theory of Achievement Measurement. Proceedings of the 1969 Invitational Conference on Testing Problems.* Princeton, N.J.: Educational Testing Service, 1970.

Stanley, J. C. (Ed.) *Compensatory Education for Children, Ages 2 to 8.* Baltimore: Johns Hopkins University Press, 1973.

Stanley, J. C., and Hopkins, K. D. *Educational and Psychological Measurement and Evaluation.* (5th Ed.) Englewood Cliffs, N.J.: Prentice-Hall, 1972.

Stephan, F. F., and McCarthy, P. J. *Sampling Opinions.* New York: Wiley, 1958.

Stevens, S. S. *Handbook of Experimental Psychology.* New York: Wiley, 1951.

Stoker, H. W. "Automated Data Processing in Testing." In S. C. Stone and B. Shertzer (Eds.), *Guidance Monograph Series.* III: *Testing.* Boston: Houghton Mifflin, 1968.

Stone, J. C. *Breakthrough in Teacher Education.* San Francisco: Jossey-Bass, 1968.

Stones, E., and Anderson, D. *Educational Objectives and the Teaching of Educational Psychology.* London: Methuen, 1972.

Stouffer, S. *Social Research to Test Ideas.* New York: Macmillan, 1962.

Stouffer, S. A., Guttman, L., Suchman, E. A., Lazarsfeld, P. F., Star, S. A., and Clausen, J. A. *Measurement and Prediction: Studies in Social Psychology—World War II.* Vol. 4. Princeton, N.J.: Princeton University Press, 1950.

Straus, M. A. *Family Measurement Techniques: Abstracts of Published Instruments, 1935-1964.* Minneapolis: University of Minnesota Press, 1969.

Stufflebeam, D. L., Foley, W. J., Gephart, W. J., Guba, E. G., Hammond, R. L., Merriman, H. O., and Provus, M. M. *Educational Evaluation and Decision-Making.* Bloomington, Ind.: Phi Delta Kappan National Study Committee on Education, 1971.

Suchman, E. A. *Evaluative Research: Principles and Practice in Public Service and Social Action Programs.* New York: Russell Sage Foundation, 1967.

Suczek, R. F. *The Best Laid Plans.* San Francisco: Jossey-Bass, 1972.

Suppes, P. *Facts and Fantasies of Education.* Technical Report No. 193, Psychological and Education Series. Stanford, Calif.: Institute for Mathematical Studies in the Social Sciences, Stanford University, 1972.

Suppes, P., and Morningstar, M. *Computer-Assisted Instruction at Stanford, 1966-68: Models, Data, and Evaluation of the Arithmetic Programs.* New York: Academic Press, 1972.

Svalastoga, K. *Social Differentiation.* New York: McKay, 1965.

Taylor, J. A. "A Personality Scale of Manifest Anxiety." *Journal of Abnormal and Social Psychology,* 1953, *48,* 285-290.

Test Bias: A Bibliography. Princeton, N.J.: Educational Testing Service, 1971.

Thistlethwaite, D. L. "Accentuation of Differences in Values and Exposures to Major Fields of Study." *Journal of Educational Psychology,* 1973, *65,* 279-293.

Thomas, W. L. *The Differential Value Profile.* Grand Rapids, Mich.: Educational Service Company, 1967.

Thorndike, R. L. "Marks and Marking Systems." In R. L. Ebel (Ed.), *Encyclopedia of Educational Research.* (4th Ed.) New York: Macmillan, 1967.

Thorndike, R. L. "Reliability." In D. N. Jackson and S. Messick (Eds.), *Problems in Human Assessment.* New York: McGraw-Hill, 1967.

Thorndike, R. L. "Concepts of Culture Fairness." *Journal of Educational Measurement,* 1971, *8,* 63-70.

Thorndike, R. L. *Educational Measurement.* (2nd Ed.) Washington, D.C.: American Council on Education, 1971.

Thorndike, R. L., and Hagen, E. *Measurement and Evaluation in Psychology and Education.* (3rd Ed.) New York: Wiley, 1969.

Thornton, R. F., and Wasdyke, R. G. *A Taxonomy for the Development of Multidimensional Test Specifications.* Princeton, N.J.: Educational Testing Service, 1973.

Thurstone, L. L. *The Vectors of the Mind.* Chicago: University of Chicago Press, 1935.

Thurstone, L. L. *Multiple Factor Analysis.* Chicago: University of Chicago Press, 1947.

Thurstone, L. L. "The Measurement of Values." In *The Measurement of Values.* Chicago: University of Chicago Press, 1959.

Tiffin, J., and McCormick, E. J. *Industrial Psychology.* (5th Ed.) Englewood Cliffs, N.J.: Prentice-Hall, 1965.

Timmer, C. P. "On Measuring Technical Efficiency." *Food Research Institute Studies in Agricultural Economics, Trade, and Development,* 1970, *9,* 99-171.

Tobias, S., and Hedl, J. J., Jr. *Test Anxiety: Situationally Specific or General?* Tech. Memo No. 49, Project NR 154-280. Tallahassee: Computer Assisted Instruction Center, Florida State University, 1972.

Toward a Social Report. Washington, D.C.: U.S. Department of Health, Education, and Welfare, 1969.

Trow, M. "Survey Research and Education." In C. Glock (Ed.), *Survey Research in the Social Sciences.* New York: Russell Sage Foundation, 1967.

Trow, M. "Methodological Problems in the Evaluation of Innovation." In F. G. Caro (Ed.), *Readings in Evaluation.* Rensselaer, N.Y.: Russell Sage, 1971.

Tucker, L. R. "Experiments in Multi-Mode Factor Analysis." In *Proceedings of the 1964 Invitational Conference on Testing Problems.* Princeton, N.J.: Educational Testing Service, 1965.

Tucker, L. R. "Some Mathematical Notes on Three-Mode Factor Analysis." *Psychometrika,* 1966, *31,* 279-311.

Tucker, L. R., Damarin, F., and Messick, S. J. "A Base-Free Measure of Change." *Psychometrika,* 1966, *31,* 457-473.

Tumin, M. M. "Evaluation of the Effectiveness of Education: Some Problems and Prospects." *Interchange,* 1970, *1* (3), 96-109.

Turner, C. P. (Ed.) *A Guide to the Evaluation of Educational Experiences in the Armed Services.* Washington, D.C.: American Council on Education, 1968.

Tyler, L. E. *The Psychology of Human Differences.* New York: Appleton-Century-Crofts, 1965.

Tyler, L. E. *Tests and Measurements.* (2nd Ed.) Englewood Cliffs, N.J.: Prentice-Hall, 1971.

Tyler, R. W. "The Function of Measurement in Improving Instruction." In E. F. Lindquist (Ed.), *Educational Measurement.* Washington, D.C.: American Council on Education, 1951.

Tyler, R. W. (Ed.) *Educational Evaluation: New Roles, New Means. The Sixty-Eighth Yearbook of the National Society for the Study of Education, Part II.* Chicago: University of Chicago Press, 1969.

Tyler, R. W., Gagné, R. M., and Scriven, M. *Perspectives of Curriculum Evaluation.* AERA Monograph Series on Curriculum Evaluation No. 1. Chicago: Rand McNally, 1967.

Uhl, N. P. *Encouraging Convergence of Opinion, Through the Use of the Delphi Technique, in the Process of Identifying an Institution's Goals.* Princeton, N.J.: Educational Testing Service, 1971.

United States Employment Service (Bureau of Employment Security). *Training and Reference Manual for Job Analysis.* Washington, D.C.: U.S. Government Printing Office, 1965.

Urban Institute. "Signals Devised to Reveal School Performance." *Search,* January-February 1973, 5-8.

Urgo, L. A. *A Manual for Obtaining Government Grants.* Boston: Robert J. Corcoran Co., 1972.

Van Dalen, D. B., and Meyer, W. J. *Understanding Educational Research: An Introduction.* New York: McGraw-Hill, 1962.

Vernon, P. E. *Personality Assessment: A Critical Survey.* London: Methuen, 1963.

Walker, H. M., and Lev, J. *Statistical Inference.* New York: Holt, 1953.

Waller, W. *The Sociology of Teaching.* New York: Wiley, 1965.

Walsh, J. E. *Handbook of Nonparametric Statistics.* New York: Van Nostrand, 1962. 3 vols.

Walton, W. W., Epstein, M. G., Margosches, E. H., and Schrader, W. B. *Selection of Products for Focused Dissemination.* Princeton, N.J.: Educational Testing Service, 1971.

Warner, W. L., Meeker, M., and Eells, K. *Social Class in America.* Chicago: Science Research Associates, 1949.

Weaver, W. T. "The Delphi Forecasting Method." *Phi Delta Kappan,* 1971, *52,* 267-272.

Webb, E. J. "Unconventionality, Triangulation, and Inference." In *Proceedings of the 1966 Invitational Conference on Testing Problems.* Princeton, N.J.: Educational Testing Service, 1967.

Webb, E. J., Campbell, D. T., Schwartz, R. D., and Sechrest, L. *Unobtrusive Measures: Nonreactive Research in the Social Sciences.* Chicago: Rand McNally, 1966.

Weber, M. "Class, Status, Party." In H. H. Gerth and C. W. Mills (Eds.), *From Max Weber: Essays in Sociology.* New York: Oxford University Press, 1946.

Weinberg, E. *Community Surveys with Local Talent: A Handbook.* Chicago: National Opinion Research Center, 1971.

Weislogel, R. L., and Schwartz, P. A. "Some Practical and Theoretical Problems in Situational Testing." *Educational and Psychological Measurement,* 1955, *15,* 39-46.

Weiss, C. H. "The Politicization of Evaluative Research." *Journal of Social Issues,* 1970, *26* (4), 57-68.

Weiss, C. H. (Ed.) *Evaluating Action Programs.* Boston: Allyn and Bacon, 1972.

Weiss, R. A. *The Effects of Practicing a Test: A Review of the Literature.* Princeton, N.J.: Educational Testing Service, 1961.

Werts, C. E., and Linn, R. L. "A General Linear Model for Studying Growth." *Psychological Bulletin,* 1970, *73,* 17-22.

Westinghouse Learning Corporation and Ohio University. *The Impact of Head Start: An Evaluation of the Effects of Head Start Experience on Children's Cognitive and Affective Development.* Contract OEO B89-4536. Washington, D.C.: Office of Economic Opportunity, 1969.

Wilcox, L. D., Brooks, R. M., Beal, G. M., and Klonglan, G. E. (Eds.) *Social Indicators and Societal Monitoring: An Annotated Bibliography.* San Francisco: Jossey-Bass, 1972.

Wilcoxon, F. "Individual Comparisons by Ranking Methods." *Biometrics Bulletin,* 1945, *1,* 80-82.

Wine, J. "Test Anxiety and Direction of Attention." *Psychological Bulletin,* 1971, *76,* 92-104.

Winer, B. J. *Statistical Principles in Experimental Design.* (2nd Ed.) New York: McGraw-Hill, 1971.

Witkin, H. A., Dyk, R. B., Faterson, H. F., Goodenough, D. R., and Karp, S. A. *Psychological Differentiation.* New York: Wiley, 1962.

Wittrock, M. C., and Wiley, D. E. (Eds.) *The Evaluation of Instruction: Issues and Problems.* New York: Holt, 1970.

Witty, P. "A Study of Children's Interests: Grades 9, 10, 11, 12." *Education,* 1961, *82,* 39-45, 100-110, 169-174.

Woellner, E. H. *Requirements for Certification for Elementary Schools, Secondary Schools, Junior Colleges.* (38th Ed.) Chicago: University of Chicago Press, 1973.

Wright, S. "Path Coefficients and Path Regressions, Alternative or Complementary Concepts?" *Biometrics,* 1960, *16,* 189-202.

Wylie, R. C. *The Self-Concept: A Critical Survey of Pertinent Research Literature.* Lincoln: University of Nebraska Press, 1961.

Zamoff, R. B. *Guide to the Assessment of Day Care Services and Needs at the Community Level.* Washington, D.C.: Urban Institute, 1971.

Zdep, S. M., and Irvine, S. H. "Reverse Hawthorne Effect." *Journal of School Psychology,* 1970, *8* (2), 89-95.

INDEXES

NAME INDEX

Abelson, R. P., 229
Acland, H., 272
Airasian, P. W., 103, 237
Alkin, M., 140
Allport, G. W., 464
Alpert, R., 424
Alter, M., 169
Ammons, C. H., 298
Ammons, R. B., 298
Anastasi, A., 52, 108, 109, 169, 208
Anastasiow, N., 433
Anderson, D., 421, 422
Anderson, J. G., 271
Anderson, R. C., 19
Anderson, S. B., 4, 19, 46, 70, 105, 106, 174, 385, 386, 427, 435, 457
Anderson, T. W., 253
Angoff, W. H., 135, 266, 347, 362, 385
Appley, M. H., 250
Argyris, C., 174
Arnold, W., 92
Arrow, K., 94, 97
Asher, W., 161
Astin, A. W., 139, 204, 205
Auclair, G., 154
Ayres, L., 142

Baker, E. L., 389
Baker, F. B., 114
Baker, J. P., 320
Ball, S., 66, 84, 86, 169, 191, 195, 198, 217
Bancroft, T. A., 240
Bane, M. J., 272
Barcikowski, R. S., 221
Barro, S. M., 40, 41
Barrows, T. S., 310, 468
Bauer, R. A., 376
Beal, G. M., 377
Beaton, A. E., Jr., 67, 74, 76, 364, 373
Beatty, W., 433
Bechtoldt, H. F., 462
Becker, H. S., 47
Bennett, G. K., 435
Berdie, F. S., 14, 20
Berelson, B., 84
Berg, I. A., 338
Berger, B., 433
Bergman, B. A., 20, 55, 139, 317, 468
Berliner, D. C., 449
Binet, A., 206, 296
Bingham, W. V., 154
Bishop, C. H., 436
Blalock, A. B., 53

Blalock, H. M., Jr., 48, 50, 53, 271, 272
Block, J. H., 237
Bloom, B. S., 26, 64, 65, 82, 83, 139, 140, 177, 237, 238, 408, 418, 419, 422
Bock, R. D., 439
Bogatz, G. A., 66, 86, 169, 191, 195
Bolda, R. A., 154
Bommarito, J. W., 433
Bonjean, C. M., 433
Borgatta, E. F., 286
Borich, G. D., 4
Boring, E. G., 145
Bowles, D., 97
Boyer, E. G., 269, 433
Bracht, G. H., 126, 449
Bray, D. W., 28, 441
Brickell, H. M., 243, 244
Brodbeck, M., 353
Brooks, R. M., 377
Browder, L. H., 4
Brown, J. A., 20
Brown, R., 250
Brune, R. L., 154
Buros, O. K., 213, 295, 433
Butcher, H. J., 208

Cahen, L. S., 190, 221, 229, 449
Cain, G. G., 132
Callahan, R. E., 142, 145
Campbell, D. T., 71, 125, 126, 155, 157, 158, 160, 168, 169, 210, 232, 235, 236, 240, 286, 306, 310, 321, 324, 427, 439, 457
Campbell, E. Q., 50, 74, 76, 106, 471
Campbell, J. T., 289
Campbell, R. J., 441
Campeau, P. L., 132
Carey, A. A., 198
Carnap, R., 353
Caro, F. G., 174, 198
Carpenter, P., 276
Carroll, J. B., 237
Carter, L. F., 369, 416
Carver, R. P., 59
Case, C. M., 293
Cattell, R. B., 166, 167, 220, 433
Chapin, F. S., 159, 160
Charters, W. W., Jr., 129, 454
Churchman, C. W., 22, 416

Cicirelli, V. G., 71, 236
Clausen, J. A., 39
Cleary, T. A., 45
Clemans, W. V., 220
Cochran, W. G., 210, 240, 344
Cofer, C. N., 250
Coffman, W. E., 20, 45, 190
Cohen, D., 272
Cohen, D. K., 70, 139
Cohen, W. M., 67, 74, 76, 364
Coleman, J. S., 50, 68, 74, 76, 105, 106, 471, 472
Cook, D. L., 197, 198, 280, 293
Cook, S. W., 47, 246, 314, 457
Cooley, W. W., 253
Cooper, J., 72
Cox, D. R., 210
Cox, R. C., 383, 421, 422
Crawford, M. P., 139
Creager, J. A., 67
Cremin, L. A., 143, 145
Crissy, W. J. E., 190
Crist, J. L., 320
Cronbach, L. J., 58, 59, 110, 111, 139, 141, 143, 146, 208, 237, 238, 329, 338, 388, 389, 427, 432, 449, 462
Crooks, L. A., 45
Cyphert, F. R., 122

Dalkey, N. C., 122
Damarin, F., 59
Damrin, D. E., 373
Das Gupta, S., 253
Davidson, K. S., 424
Davis, A., 108, 109
Davis, F. B., 238
Davitz, J. R., 84, 217
Deighten, L., 269
DeMartino, M. F., 250
Dempster, A. P., 253
Denny, T., 139
Deutsch, M., 47, 314, 457
Diaz-Guerrero, R., 191, 195
Dick, W., 329, 462
Dickson, W. J., 197, 198
Diederich, P., 53
Doppelt, J. E., 435
Downie, N. M., 362
Dressel, P. L., 205
Duncan, O. D., 272, 378, 380

Dunn, T. F., 14, 19
Dyer, H. S., 3, 4, 47, 49, 50, 106, 151,
    328, 329
Dyk, R. B., 63

Ebel, R. L., 9, 10, 19, 39, 103, 141,
    146, 188, 266, 298, 362, 389,
    435, 436
Edwards, A. L., 200, 210, 390, 394,
    397, 398, 399, 405
Eells, K., 108, 109, 380
Eisner, E. W., 238
Ekstrom, R. B., 64, 65
Elam, S., 72
Elashoff, J. D., 320, 364
Ennis, R. H., 50
Epstein, M. G., 244
Erlebacher, A., 71, 235, 236, 321, 324
Esser, B., 55
Evans, F. B., 271
Evans, J. W., 71
Eysenck, H. J., 92, 295

Farr, M. J., 79
Farr, R., 499
Faterson, H. F., 63
Fattu, N. A., 144, 146
Fay, L., 229
Fear, R. A., 214, 216
Federman, P., 20, 468
Feigl, H., 353
Feldman, K. A., 26, 205
Feldmesser, R. A., 257, 276
Feller, W., 353
Ferguson, G. A., 394
Festinger, L., 198, 317
Finley, C. J., 14, 20
Finn, J. D., 320
Fishbein, M., 39
Fisher, R. A., 86, 92, 200, 238, 240,
    394, 397, 399
Fitzpatrick, R., 20, 432
Fleishman, E. A., 297, 298
Foley, W. J., 120
Forehand, G. A., 471
Fowler, H., 250
Fox, D. J., 468
Frederiksen, N., 144, 146, 373
French, J. R. P., Jr., 197, 198
French, J. W., 64, 65
Frey, P. W., 169

Frieder, B., 4
Furby, L., 59
Furst, N. J., 269

Gadway, C. J., 29
Gage, N. L., 158, 160, 190, 210, 240,
    269, 310, 383, 439
Gagné, R. M., 140, 184, 226, 422
Gallagher, J. J., 454
Galton, F., 87, 322
Gant, W. L., 122
Gardner, R. W., 63
Gephart, W. J., 120
Gerth, H. H., 380
Gessner, P. K., 317
Getzels, J. W., 213
Gilmer, B. von H., 382
Gintis, H., 272
Gjerde, C., 22
Gladney, M. B., 186, 188
Glaser, R., 43, 103, 139, 140, 146,
    184, 298, 382, 442, 449
Glass, G. V., 4, 126, 439
Glennan, T. K., Jr., 232
Gleser, L. J., 220
Glock, C. Y., 174, 411
Goldfried, M. V., 295
Goldstein, L. G., 14, 19
Goodenough, D. R., 63
Goodenough, F. L., 107, 109
Goodlad, J. I., 111, 129
Gordon, I. J., 310, 468
Gossett, W. S., 391
Gottman, J. M., 439
Grant, D. L., 28, 441
Green, J. L., 214, 217
Greenwood, E. R., Jr., 262
Gronlund, N. E., 213, 362
Gross, B. M., 376
Guba, E. G., 117, 120, 129, 139
Guetzkow, H., 373
Guilford, J. P., 64, 65, 219
Guion, R. M., 100, 432
Gulliksen, H., 15, 29, 32, 329
Guttman, L., 39

Haber, A., 200, 397, 399
Haber, R. N., 424
Hagen, E., 328, 329
Hagerty, N., 329, 462
Haggart, S. A., 276

Hahn, F., 94, 97
Hall, G. R., 276
Hall, G. S., 143
Hall, M., 334
Hamaker, H. C., 301
Hammond, R. L., 120
Hand, H. H., 232
Hansen, W. L., 97
Haran, E. M., 193
Harless, J. H., 257, 440, 442
Harman, H. H., 74, 162, 163, 167, 369
Harmin, M., 464
Harris, C. W., 7, 32, 59, 146, 266, 298, 439
Harris, D. B., 107, 109
Harrocks, J. E., 26
Hartley, H. J., 280
Hastings, J. T., 139, 177, 408
Hatt, P. K., 380
Havighurst, R. J., 109
Hawkridge, D. G., 132
Hays, W. L., 88, 92, 200, 324, 397, 399
Hedl, J. J., Jr., 424
Hellmuth, J., 71, 169, 174, 236, 324
Helmer, O., 122
Helmstadter, G. C., 314
Hempel, C. G., 353
Henrysson, S., 20
Herrick, V. E., 109
Heynes, B., 272
Hill, R. J., 433
Hills, J. R., 186, 188, 389
Hilton, T. L., 106, 289
Hitch, C. J., 279, 281, 417
Hobson, C. J., 50, 74, 76, 106, 471
Hoepfner, R., 433
Hollingshead, A. B., 378, 380
Hollister, R. G., 132
Holt, J., 187, 188
Holtzman, W. H., 191, 195
Holzman, P. S., 63
Hopkins, K. D., 39, 289, 295, 314
Housam, R. B., 382
Houston, W. R., 382
Humphreys, L. G., 45
Huntsberger, D. V., 397
Husek, T. R., 221

Irvine, S. H., 227
Isaac, S., 158, 310

Jackson, D. N., 26, 29, 100, 266, 301, 329, 338, 427, 462, 468
Jacob, P. E., 204, 205
Jacobs, P. I., 454
Jacobsen, L., 364
Jacquette, B. L., 334
Jacquette, F. L., 334
Jahoda, M., 47, 314, 457
Jamison, D., 97
Jellema, W. W., 97, 281
Jencks, C., 272
Jensen, A. R., 169
Jensen, O., 373
Johnson, B. L., 298
Johnson, G. H., 139
Johnson, N. L., 344
Johnson, O., 433
Johnson, P. O., 229
Jones, J. E., 129, 454
Jones, L. V., 347

Kagan, J., 63
Kaplan, A., 468
Karp, S. A., 63
Katz, D., 198, 317
Katz, J., 81
Katz, M., 432, 435
Kaya, E., 433
Kelman, H. C., 82
Kendall, M. G., 91
Kennedy, C., 97
Kerlinger, F. N., 449
Kersh, B. Y., 287
Kershaw, D. N., 174
Kessen, W., 66
King, R. G., 328, 329
Kirk, R. W., 71
Kish, L. A., 344, 406
Klein, G. S., 63
Klein, S. P., 103
Klonglan, G. E., 377
Knapp, R. R., 289
Kneller, G. P., 184
Kogan, N., 63
Komoski, P. K., 241, 244
Korten, F. F., 246
Kosecoff, J., 103
Kourilsky, M., 21, 22
Krathwohl, D. R., 24, 26, 184, 334, 418, 419, 422
Kruger, D. H., 55
Kruger, W. S., 42

Lacey, J. I., 246
Lansing, J. C., 411
Larkins, A. G., 331
Larrabee, E., 457
Lau, L., 98
Lawley, D. N., 161, 167
Lawshe, C. H., 154
Lazarsfeld, P. F., 39
Lehmann, I. J., 14, 20, 238
Lennon, R. T., 4
Lessinger, L. M., 4, 42
Lev, J., 390, 394
Levin, H., 98
Levine, D. M., 276
Levine, M., 21, 22
Levine, R. S., 135
Lieberman, M., 40, 42
Light, R. J., 240
Lighthall, F. F., 424
Lindquist, E. F., 20, 112, 200, 238, 394
Lindvall, C. M., 184
Lindzey, G., 84, 295, 464
Linn, R. L., 45, 59, 106, 229
Linton, H. B., 63
Livingstone, S. A., 328, 329
Llewellyn, K. N., 47
Loevinger, J., 462
Lohnes, P. R., 253
Lopez, F. M., 316, 317
Lord, F. M., 31, 32, 57, 59, 74, 76, 92, 135, 221, 233, 236
Lorge, I., 266
Lortie, D., 140
Lubin, A., 445, 449
Lumsdaine, A. A., 139
Lykken, D. T., 330, 331
Lyman, H. B., 427

McCarthy, P. J., 344
McClelland, D., 250
McCormick, E. J., 224, 225, 226, 383
McDill, E. L., 71
McDill, M. S., 71
McDonald, F. J., 381, 382, 471
McGehee, W., 226
MacGinitie, W. H., 84, 198
McGuire, C. H., 373
MacKinney, A. C., 100
McLean, L. D., 215, 217
McLemore, S. D., 433
McMorris, R. F., 14, 20, 386

McNemar, Q., 92, 406
McPartland, J., 50, 74, 76, 106, 471
McReynolds, P., 29
Madaus, G. F., 103, 139, 154, 177, 408
Mager, R. F., 184
Maier, M. H., 105, 106, 454
Mann, J., 174
Marco, G. L., 471
Margolin, J. B., 79
Margosches, E. H., 244
Marshall, J. C., 190
Masia, B. B., 26, 422
Maxwell, A. E., 92, 161, 167
Maxwell, G., 353
Mayeske, G. W., 67, 74, 76, 364, 471
Mayor, J. R., 7
Mecklenburger, J. A., 276
Medley, D. M., 189, 190, 269, 381, 383
Meeker, M., 380
Mehrens, W. A., 14, 20, 238
Meili, R., 92
Melmed, A., 97
Melville, S. D., 19
Meredith, J. C., 79
Meringoff, L., 193
Merriman, H. O., 120
Merwin, J. C., 140, 146
Messick, S. J., 26, 29, 46, 59, 61, 63, 100, 140, 160, 246, 266, 301, 310, 329, 338, 366, 386, 427, 462, 468
Meyer, W. J., 126
Michael, W. B., 158, 310
Michelson, S., 272
Miller, D. C., 411
Miller, R., 226
Millman, J., 436
Mills, C. W., 380
Misch, M. R., 79
Mitzel, H. E., 190, 269, 381, 383
Mood, A. M., 50, 68, 74, 76, 106, 471, 472
Moore, W. E., 376
Morgan, J. N., 411
Morningstar, M., 79
Morris, R. F., 53
Morrison, D. F., 254
Morrison, E. J., 20
Moses, L. E., 262
Mosteller, F., 240, 364, 472

Mouly, G. J., 217, 314
Moynihan, D. P., 364, 472
Mulaik, S. A., 162, 163, 166, 167
Murphy, R. T., 471
Mussen, P. H., 63, 66

Nadiri, M., 98
Nagel, E., 353
Nelson, J. K., 298
Nett, R., 412
Newcomb, T. M., 26, 205
Newton, R. G., 68
Neyman, J., 229
Nitko, A. J., 43, 103
North, C. C., 380
Novick, D., 281
Novick, M. R., 32, 74, 76, 92
Nummendal, S. G., 433

Ohlsen, M. M., 84
Okada, T., 67, 74, 76, 364
Oppenheim, P., 353
Osgood, C. E., 39

Pace, C. R., 204
Page, E. S., 301
Panos, R. J., 139
Pap, A., 353
Parden, R. J., 281
Parker, C. A., 217
Parsons, H. M., 369
Patrick, C., 106
Patton, M. J., 106
Pauk, W., 436
Payne, D. A., 53, 184, 386
Pearson, K., 88
Phillips, B. N., 301
Phillips, B. S., 412
Pick, A. D., 66
Pitcher, B., 289
Plumlee, L. B., 221
Popham, W. J., 104, 184, 244, 389
Potthoff, R. F., 229
Price, L. A., 64, 65
Proshek, J. M., 67, 74, 76, 364
Provus, M. M., 120, 129
Pruzek, R. M., 20

Quirk, T. J., 383, 472

Radcliffe, J. A., 220
Rapp, M. L., 276
Raths, L. E., 464

Reeves, B. F., 177
Regan, J. J., 190
Reichenbach, H., 353
Reiss, A. J., Jr., 380
Reynolds, J. H., 184
Rice, J. M., 142
Riley, M. W., 314
Rippey, R. M., 452
Rivlin, A. M., 281, 417
Roethlisberger, F. J., 197, 198
Rokeach, M., 464
Romberg, T. A., 221
Rosenshine, B., 269
Rosenthal, R. R., 364
Rosner, B., 72
Rossi, P. H., 71, 174, 177, 232, 286, 408
Rothney, J. W. M., 188
Roueche, J. E., 71
Rubin, D. B., 240, 241, 364
Rubin, S., 161
Ruebush, B. K., 424
Runyon, R. P., 200, 397, 399

Sanford, N., 205
Sarason, S. B., 424
Saretsky, G., 227
Saunders, D. R., 468
Scannell, D. P., 190
Schaie, K. W., 66, 106, 232
Schiller, J., 71
Schmieder, A. A., 72
Schrader, W. B., 154, 244, 266
Schultz, R. E., 84
Schwartz, P. A., 373
Schwartz, R. D., 321, 457
Scott, W. A., 220
Scriven, M., 110, 111, 140, 178, 179, 244, 247, 353, 367, 408
Seashore, R. H., 296, 298
Sechrest, L., 321, 457
Selden, W. K., 8
Seligman, E. R. A., 47
Selltiz, C., 47, 314, 457
Shaver, J. P., 331
Shaw, M. E., 433
Sheldon, E. B., 376
Shertzer, B., 114, 362, 427
Shimberg, B., 55, 435
Shoemaker, D. M., 221
Short, J., 382
Sidman, M., 330, 331
Siegel, A. I., 20, 55, 139, 317, 468

Siegel, S., 258, 262
Sigel, E., 276
Sills, D. L., 47, 210, 301, 338, 442
Simon, A., 269, 433
Simon, S. B., 464
Simon, T., 206
Singer, J. E., 188
Sirotnik, L., 221
Sisson, R. L., 369
Sjoberg, G., 412
Slocum, J. W., 232
Smith, E. R., 143, 146
Smith, H., Jr., 344
Smith, M., 272
Snedecor, G. W., 240, 394
Snider, J. G., 39
Snow, C. E., 196, 198
Snow, R. E., 320, 364
Snyder, G. W., 20
Sobel, M., 276
Spearman, C., 88, 162
Spence, D. P., 63
Spiegel, M. R., 439
Spielberg, H., 195
Sprehe, J. T., 71
Spurrell, D. J., 68
Stacey, C. L., 250
Stake, R. E., 22, 110, 111, 112, 129, 139
Stalnaker, J. M., 16, 20
Stanley, J. C., 4, 39, 70, 125, 126, 155, 157, 158, 160, 168, 169, 210, 232, 240, 289, 295, 306, 310, 314, 439, 464
Star, S. A., 39
Stephan, F. F., 344
Stern, C., 433
Stevens, C., 272
Stevens, S. S., 298, 347
Stoker, H. W., 114
Stolurow, L. M., 454
Stone, J. C., 191, 205, 214, 217
Stone, S. C., 114, 362, 427
Stones, E., 421, 422
Stouffer, S. A., 39, 49, 50
Straus, M. A., 434
Stricker, G., 295
Stufflebeam, D. L., 117, 120, 129, 139
Styan, G. P. H., 253
Suchman, E. A., 39, 86, 140, 146, 158, 232, 286, 320, 367, 408, 468

Suczek, R. F., 47
Summer, G. C., 276
Sundquist, J. L., 177, 408
Suppes, P., 79, 125, 126, 141, 143, 146
Svalastoga, K., 380

Tabler, K. A., 67, 74, 76, 364
Taylor, J. A., 424
Thayer, P. W., 226
Thirwall, A. P., 97
Thistlethwaite, D. L., 26
Thomas, W. L., 464
Thorndike, E. L., 142
Thorndike, R. L., 20, 43, 103, 109, 114, 135, 139, 184, 190, 266, 328, 329, 347, 362, 389, 428, 462
Thornton, R. F., 26, 55, 65, 298, 422
Thurstone, L. L., 36, 37, 162, 167, 465
Tiffin, J., 224, 225, 226, 383
Timmer, C. P., 98
Tinkelman, S. N., 20
Tobias, S., 424
Travers, M. M. W., 331
Travers, R. M., 269
Trickett, P. K., 132
Trow, M., 140, 174, 198, 320
Tucker, L. R., 59, 166, 167
Tukey, J., 320
Tumin, M. M., 100, 286
Turner, C. P., 106
Turner, M., 272
Tyler, L. E., 213, 347
Tyler, R. W., 109, 110, 112, 129, 140, 143, 146, 184

Uhl, N. P., 122
Unks, N. J., 421, 422
Urgo, L. A., 334
Uttal, B., 276

Valentine, L. D., Jr., 67
Van Dalen, D. B., 126
Vernon, P. E., 295, 464

Waite, R. R., 424
Walker, H. M., 390, 394
Waller, W., 151
Walsh, J. E., 258, 263
Walton, W. W., 244
Warburton, F., 433

Warner, W. L., 378, 380
Wasdyke, R. G., 26, 55, 65, 298, 422
Weathers, G., 301
Weaver, W. T., 122
Webb, E. J., 310, 320, 321, 457
Weber, M., 377, 380
Wechsler, D., 206
Weinberg, E., 174
Weiner, I. B., 295
Weinfeld, F. D., 50, 67, 74, 76, 106, 364, 471
Weislogel, R. L., 373
Weiss, C. H., 126, 158, 178, 286, 310
Weiss, R. A., 289
Werts, C. E., 45, 59
Wesman, A. G., 9, 20
White, B. F., 323
Wilcox, L. D., 377
Wilcoxon, F., 263
Wiley, D. E., 63, 140, 246, 320, 367
Williams, W., 71, 174, 232

Willson, V. L., 439
Wine, J., 424
Winer, B. J., 254, 406
Winokur, H. S., 240
Wisler, C. E., 67, 74, 76, 364
Witkin, H. A., 63
Wittrock, M. C., 63, 140, 246, 287, 320, 367
Witty, P., 213
Woellner, E. H., 55
Wright, S., 272
Wylie, R. C., 434

York, R. L, 50, 74, 76, 106, 471
Yotopoulos, P., 98

Zamoff, R. B., 217
Zdep, S. M., 227
Zimiles, H., 71
Zwirner, W., 221

─────────── SUBJECT INDEX ───────────

Abilities, 63-65, 296-297
Acceptance of programs, 441
Acceptance sampling, 299, 342
Accountability, 1-4, 119-120, 290-293; and cost considerations, 92-98; defined, 1-2; and performance contracting, 272-273; and responsibility, 3; and student performance, 2. *See also* Accreditation, Audit of evaluation
Accreditation, 4-8, 46-47, 71-72, 191; and certification, 54-55; defined, 4-5; evaluative criteria for, 6-7; goals of, 5-6
Achievement anxiety scale, 424
Achievement test construction, 8-20, 371-374; and essay tests, 15; and goals, 8; and guessing, 13; items for, 15-17; matching items for, 15; multiple-choice items for, 10-15; recognition items for, 9-15; reliability and, 19; short-answer items for, 16; technical characteristics of, 17-19; true-false items for, 9-10; validity and, 19. *See also* Test wiseness, Tests

Adoptability of materials, 243
Adversary model, 21-22
Advertising Research Foundation, 250
Affective variables, 23-26, 444-449; dependent, 23-25; independent and moderator, 25-26; and long-term effects, 24-25; measurement of, 26. *See also* Attitudes, Variables
Age equivalent score, 361-362
Allport-Vernon-Lindzey study of values, 218, 463
American Institutes for Research (AIR), 138
Analysis of covariance, 393-394. *See also* Covariance
Analysis of variance, 252-253, 391-392. *See also* Variance
Anova. *See* Analysis of variance
Aptitude-treatment interaction (ATI), 444-449
Archival measures, 455-456
Assessment, 26-29; of attitudes, 33-39; defined, 26-27; and experimental design, 28; grades as, 184-188; national, 27; of needs, 128, 254-258; and response set,

334-338. *See also* Interviews, Questionnaires, Ratings, Tests, Unobtrusive measures

Attenuation, 29-32; and partial correlation, 30-31. *See also* Reliability

Attitudes, 32-39; assessment of, 33-39; defined, 32-33; and self-report, 35-37; and semantic differential, 37-38; and teacher ratings, 33-35; unobtrusive measurement of, 38

Audit of evaluation, 4, 40-42, 362-364; evaluator's role in, 147-148. *See also* Accountability

Baseline measures, 42-43. *See also* Pretest

Behavioral objectives, 179-183. *See also* Goals and objectives

Bias: in interviewing, 216; nonresponse, 411; in testing, 43-46, 107-109, 423-424. *See also* Validity

Blocking in experimental design, 238

Canonical correlation, 251-252

Case-study method, 46-47, 191. *See also* Accreditation

Category systems in observation, 267-269

Causality, 48-50, 198-200, 258, 348-353; versus correlation, 48-49; ex post facto, 159-160; and path analysis, 270-271

CEEB. *See* College Entrance Examination Board

Ceiling effect, 51-53

Census, 338

Center for the Study of Evaluation (CSE), 257

Central tendency, 402-403

Certification, 53-55, 71-72; and accreditation, 54-55; institutional, 7

Chance. *See* Probability, Statistical significance

Change measurement, 56-59; and attenuation, 31-32; difference scores and, 56-58; and equivalent scores, 133-135; need for, 58-59; and performance contracting, 274-275; reliability of 327

Chi square, 259, 345

Children's Manifest Anxiety Scale, 424

Cluster sampling, 341-342

Cognitive styles, 60-63, 444-449; and abilities, 61-62; examples of, 60-61

Cognitive variables, 63-65; taxonomies of, 64. *See also* Variables

Cohort, 65-66

College Characteristics Index, 204

College Entrance Examination Board (CEEB), 200, 301, 346, 357; as source of typical standard score, 358

Commonality analysis, 67-68

Compensatory education, 68-71; control group in, 86; evaluation problems in, 69-70; design problems and, 123; fade-out in, 168; and Lord's paradox, 235-236; measuring change in, 57-58; and quasi-experimental designs, 307

Competency-based education/training, 71-72

Complex Coordination Test, 297

Component and composite variables, 73-76, 400-406. *See also* Factor analysis, Scores

Comprehension: as cognitive variable, 64; and intelligence, 205-208; tested by multiple choice items, 10-11

Computer-assisted instruction (CAI), 77-79

Confidentiality of data, 79-82, 131

Construct-referenced measurement, 103

Construct validity, 459-460

Content analysis, 82-84; in formative evaluation, 82; in job analysis, 83; in questionnaire construction, 83-84; of self-reports, 35; and techniques of observation, 267-268

Content-referenced measurement, 101-102

Content validity, 460-461

Context evaluation, 117-118, 127-129, 254-258

Continuous variable, 465
Control group, 85-86, 122-126, 155-158, 196, 301-310; and causal inferences, 48; and John Henry effect, 226-227; in longitudinal study, 230; and pretest differences, 232-236
Correlation, 87-92; canonical, 251-252; versus causation, 48-49; and expectancy tables, 153; and factor analysis, 161-162; formulas for, 88; kinds of, 88-91; multiple, 91; partial, 30-31, 91; product-moment, 88; rank order, 88-89, 262; and reliability, 326; significance of, 399
Cost, 2, 92-98, 119, 412-417; of materials, 243-244; and performance contracting, 274-275
Cost benefit analysis, 369, 413-416. See also Cost
Cost effectiveness, 119, 416. See also Cost
Council on Postsecondary Accreditation (COPA), 7
Covariance, 233-236; analysis of, 393-394; and Lord's paradox, 233-236; in multivariate analysis, 215-254
Criterion measurement, 98-100. See also Criterion-referenced measurement
Criterion-referenced measurement, 98-104; and ceiling effect, 51; in certification, 54; and competency-based education/training, 72; versus construct-referenced, 103; versus content-referenced, 101-102; with performance contracting, 275; and reliability, 327-328; validity of, 101. See also Norms
Criterion-related validity, 461
Critical incident technique, 224-225
Cronbach alpha, 327
Cross-sectional study, 104-106, 155-158, 229-232
Culture-fair tests, 43-46, 107-109
Cumulative frequencies, 153, 402
Curriculum evaluation, 109-112, 127-129, 178-179, 450-452; history of, 141-145. See also

Formative evaluation, Materials evaluation, Side effects
Curriculum reform, 110

Data preparation, 112-114. See also Field operations, Quality control
Data sources, 114-117. See also Test selection
Decision-making typology, 117-120, 136-140
Delayed posttest. See Posttest
Delphi technique, 119, 121-122
Dependent variables: affective, 23-25; and criterion measurement, 98-100; outcome, 466-467
Descriptive statistics, 400-406
Design of evaluation, 122-126; experimental, 155-158; ex post facto, 159-161; quasi-experimental, 301-310
Deviation IQ, 207
Diaries. See Logs
Difference scores. See Change measurement
Diffusion effects, 86
Discrepancy evaluation, 127-129
Discrete variables, 465-466
Discriminant analysis, 253
Discrimination of test items, 18
Disordinal interaction, 445-448
Dissemination of results, 79-82, 130-132
Distracters, 14

Economic analysis. See Cost
Educational Products Information Exchange (EPIE), 244
Edwards Personal Preference Schedule (EPPS), 218-219
Efficiency, economic, 95-97. See also Accountability
Eight-year Study, 143
Elementary and Secondary Education Act (ESEA), 40, 69, 145
Engineering model of evaluation, 245
Equality of opportunity. See Accountability
Equivalent scores, 133-135; in change measurement, 56; and practice effect, 287-289; and test wiseness, 434-435

Errors of measurement: and attenuation, 29-30; in covariance, 236; and grades, 184-185; Type I, 199-200

Essay tests, 15-17

Evaluation: and accountability, 1-4; adversary model of, 21-22; and audits, 40-42; by case study, 46-47; and certification, 53-55; of compensatory education, 68-71; concepts of, 136-140; context, 117-118; and decision-making, 117-120; design of, 122-126; discrepancy, 127-129; dissemination of results of, 130-132; engineering model of, 245; and evaluator, 147-151; evidence in, 191-195; and field operations, 166-175; goal-free, 178-179; hard and soft, 191-195; history of, 140-146; in institutions, 202-205; of materials, 241-244; medical model of, 245-247; phenomenological, 191-192; planning of, 277-279; process, 119-120; product, 120; quality control in, 299-301; secondary, 362-364; side effects of, 137; of staff, 380-383; summative, 406-408; theory in, 348; training, 439-442; transactional, 450-452. See also Curriculum evaluation, Formative evaluation, Model, Politics of evaluation

Evaluator role, 21-22, 129, 136-140, 147-151; in curriculum evaluation, 111. See also Training of evaluators

Evidence, 191-195

Expectancy tables, 152-154

Experimental and ex post facto design, 65-66, 122-126, 155-161, 301-310

Experimental independence, 201-202

Ex post facto design. See Experimental and ex post facto design

F test, 252-253, 390-394

Face validity, 373

Factor analysis, 161-167; applications of, 165-167; example of, 162-165; historical background of, 162; and need for independence, 201; three-mode, 166. See also Component and composite variables

Factor-referenced measurement, 103

Factor scores, 165

Fade-out, 167-169

Federation of Regional Accrediting Commissions of Higher Education (FRACHE), 60

Feedback loops: in simulation, 368; in systems analysis, 413

Field dependence-independence, 60

Field operations, 79-82, 131, 169-175; and interviews, 215-216. See also Politics of evaluation

Floor effect, 52

Follow-up study, 229-232, 246

Formative evaluation, 175-178; in computer-aided instruction, 78; content analysis in, 82-83; delphi technique in, 121-122; and evaluator's role, 148; historical antecedent of, 143; by longitudinal study, 229-230; and testing materials, 175, 241-244

Frequency distribution, 152-153; and norms, 264; table of, 400-401

Frequency histogram, 257, 401

Frequency polygon, 401

General Anxiety Scale, 424

Goal-free evaluation, 178-179. See also Goals and objectives, Side effects

Goals and objectives, 2, 128, 137, 179-184; in achievement test construction, 8-9; for certification, 54; and criterion measurement, 98-100; in context evaluation, 117; defined, 179-181; and delphi technique, 121; and formative evaluation, 176; history of, 143; and mastery learning, 236-237. See also Taxonomies of objectives

Grade equivalent score, 359-361

Grades, 184-188; in individual assessment, 184-187; in program evaluation, 187-188

Group test, 206

Guessing, 13; as response set, 335-336
Guttman scalogram, 38

Halo effect, 189-190, 315; in attitude assessment, 34-35; and independence, 201
Hard and soft evaluation, 155-158, 191-195. *See also* Evaluator role
Hawthorne effect, 195-198, 318-321; and evaluation design, 125; in performance contracting, 275; and time series design, 303. *See also* John Henry effect
History of evaluation, 140-146; of institutions, 202-203
Homogeneity of test items, 18
Hotelling T^2, 252
Hypothesis, 198-200, 258, 348-353
Hypothesis testing, 198-200, 258, 348-353. *See also* Causality
Hypothetical construct, 162

Impact study, 406-408
Impulsivity-reflectivity, 61
In-basket test, 371-372
Independence, 200-202
Independent variables, 118-119, 466; affective, 25-26. *See also* Variables
Individualized instruction, 77-79, 273
Individually administered test, 206
Inferential statistics, 395-397. *See also* Statistical analysis, Statistical significance
Input evaluation, 118-119
Institutional evaluation, 202-205. *See also* Accreditation
Institutions, accreditation of, 4-8
Intelligence measurement, 43-46, 107-109, 205-208. *See also* Scores, Variables
Intended and unintended outcomes, 245-247, 365-366. *See also* Goals and objectives, Side effects
Interaction, 208-210; disordinal, 445-448; ordinal, 445-448; trait-treatment, 444-449
Interest measurement, 211-213
Internal consistency and reliability, 327
Interval scale, 346

Intervening variable, 466
Interviews, 214-217; as data source, 114-117; in job analysis, 222-223; structured, 214-215; unstructured, 214-215
Ipsative measures, 217-220
IQ, 206-207, 356-358
Item difficulty, 18; with ceiling effect, 51-52
Item sampling, 16, 220-221

Job analysis, 222-226; for certification, 54-55; content analysis in, 83-84; and criterion-referenced measures, 102
John Henry effect, 226-227, 318-321; and evaluation design, 125; and performance contracting, 275. *See also* Hawthorne effect
Johnson-Neyman technique, 198-200, 228-229, 258

Kuder Interest Inventory, 211
Kuder-Richardson formula, 327

Latent structure analysis, 38
Leveling-sharpening, 60
Levels of significance. *See* Statistical significance, Probability
Licensure, 7. *See also* Certification
Likert scale, 36-37
Logistics, 174
Logs: content analysis of, 82-84; in job analysis, 223
Longitudinal study, 65-66, 104-106, 122-126, 155-158, 229-232, 301-310
Lord's paradox, 232-236, 306

Management, 4, 119-120, 277-279, 290-293. *See also* Cost, Politics of evaluation
Mann-Whitney U test, 258, 260-261
Manocov, 252-253
Manova, 252-253
Mastery learning, 18, 236-238; ceiling effect and, 51. *See also* Certification, Criterion-referenced measurement, Job analysis
Matched sampling, 155-158, 160, 238-241; and culture-fair tests, 108; and quasi-experimental de-

sign, 306; and sign test, 259-260; and validity, 240
Matching. *See* Matched sampling
Matching items, 15
Materials evaluation, 241-244; history of, 142-143
Materials pretesting, 175, 241. *See also* Materials evaluation
Matrix sampling, 16, 220-221
Mean, 402-403; in computing correlation, 88; of IQ, 357-358; in norms tables, 264; of raw scores, 354; standard error of, 395; and t and F tests, 390-394
Measurement: of achievement, 8-20; and assessment, 26-27; of attitudes, 33-39; and ceiling effect, 51-53; of criteria, 98-100; criterion-referenced, 100-104; data sources for, 114-117; factor-referenced, 103; of intelligence, 205-208; of interest, 211-213; by interviews, 214-217; of motivation, 247-248; by situational tests, 371-374; of treatment, 452-454; unobtrusive, 454-457; of values, 462-465. *See also* Achievement test construction, Attitudes, Bias, Change measurement, Errors of measurement, Test selection, Tests
Median, 402-403
Medical model of evaluation, 245-247. *See also* Side effects
Mental age, 207
Minimum competency, 237
Mode, 402-403
Model: adversary, 21-22; engineering, 245; medical, 245-247; in scientific inquiry, 349-350
Moderator variables, 467; affective, 25-26
Motivation, 247-250, 423-424, 462-465; as side effect, 248-249; and test performance, 44
Multiple-choice items, 10-15
Multiple regression, 324
Multitrait-multimethod, 27
Multivariate analysis, 250-254
Multivariate analysis of covariance, 252-253

Multivariate analysis of variance, 252-253

National assessment, 27
National Commission on Accrediting (NCA), 6
National Council for Accreditation of Teacher Education (N-CATE), 54-55
National Merit Scholarship, 204
National Teacher Examination, 55
Needs assessment, 128, 254-258
Nominal scale, 345
Nonequivalent group design, 303-306
Nonparametric statistics, 257-263, 400-406; with ceiling effect, 51
Nonrandomized studies. *See* Matched sampling, Quasi-experimental design
Nonresponse bias, 411
Normal distribution, 405
Norms, 263-266; and ipsative measures, 217-218; and item sampling, 220-221; and score types, 357-358. *See also* Scores, Standardized tests
Norms-referenced. *See* Norms, Criterion-referenced measurement
Null hypothesis, 258, 398

Objective data, 191-195
Objectives. *See* Goals and objectives
Observation techniques, 266-269; as data source, 114-117; history of, 144; in interest measurement, 212; in job analysis, 223. *See also* Unobtrusive measures
Operational definition, 467-468
Ordinal interaction, 445-448
Ordinal scale, 345-346
Outcomes. *See* Intended and unintended outcomes

Paper-and-pencil tests, 206; in interest measurement, 211-212. *See also* Measurement
Parameters, 395
Parametric tests, 257
Partial correlation, 30-31, 91
Path analysis, 270-272. *See also* Correlation, Regression
Percentile rank, 263-264, 357-358

Performance contracting, 4, 227, 272-276
Performance tests, 17
Persistence, 248-249
Personality: and grades, 186; projective tests and, 293-296; and response set, 338; and test anxiety, 423-424; and trait-treatment interaction, 444. *See also* Motivation
PERT. *See* Program evaluation and review technique
Phenomenological evaluation, 191-192
Physical trace measures, 455-456
Pilot test. *See* Pretest
Placebo, 85, 196
Planning, 4, 119, 121-122, 277-281. *See also* Cost, Field operations, Politics of evaluation
Planning-Programming-Budgeting system (PPBS), 2, 4, 119, 277-281, 412-417. *See also* Cost, Politics of evaluation
Politics of evaluation, 277-279, 281-286; negative impact of, 283-284. *See also* Cost, Field operations
Population and sampling, 339
Population sampling unit (PSU), 341
Posttest, 286-287; and ceiling effect, 51-52; and change measurement, 56-59; and longitudinal study, 229-232; and practice effect, 287-289
Posttest-only design, 157
Power in statistics, 262
PPBS. *See* Planning-Programming-Budgeting system
Practice effect, 287-289; and posttest scores, 287. *See also* Test wiseness
Prediction: and criterion measurement, 98-100; and culture fairness, 108-109; and expectancy tables, 153-154; regression techniques for, 322-324
Predictive validity, 461-462
Pretest, 42-43, 289-290; and change measurement, 56-59; differences in, 232-236; and floor effect, 52; of materials, 175, 241; types of, 289-290

Priorities, 255-256, 277-279
Probability, 152-154, 352-353; in nonparametric tests, 258-263; and sampling, 338-344
Process evaluation, 119-120. *See also* Formative evaluation
Product effectiveness. *See* Materials evaluation
Product evaluation, 120, 406-408. *See also* Materials evaluation, Quality control
Product-moment correlation, 88
Productivity, 94-97; and Hawthorne effect, 196-197
Program evaluation and review technique (PERT), 4, 119-120, 290-293
Projective tests, 293-296
PSU, 341
Psychomotor variables, 296-298
Pygmalion effect, 318

Q sort, 38, 218
Quality control, 112-114, 299-301, 408-412; and observation systems, 268-269. *See also* Field operations
Quasi-experimental design, 155-158, 301-310
Questionnaires, 311-314; and bias, 45; as data source, 114-117; early use of, 143; and interviews, 214-217; and job analysis, 222-223. *See also* Interviews

Random samples, 340-342
Range, 400
Rank order correlation, 88-89, 262
Ranking, percentile, 263-264, 357-358. *See also* Scores
Ratings, 315-317; in attitude measurement, 33-38; and bias, 45; as data source, 114-117; and halo effect, 189; and independence, 201; in needs assessment, 255; in observation techniques, 266-267; by teachers, 33-35
Raw data, 400
Raw score, 354-356, 400-406
Reactive effect, 318-321. *See also* Hawthorne effect, John Henry effect
Readability, 82

Rectangular distribution, 257
Regression, 321-324; and commonality analysis, 67; in Lord's paradox, 233-236; in matched sampling, 240; multiple, 324
Regression-discontinuity design, 307-310
Regression effect, 57-58, 321; and performance contracting, 275
Reliability, 2, 19, 325-329; and accountability, 2; of achievement tests, 19; of affective variables, 24; and attenuation, 30-32; with ceiling effect, 51; of change measurement, 56-57; of criterion measures, 99-100; of intelligence measures, 207; of interviews, 215-216; measurement of, 326-329; of observations, 268; of projective tests, 295; split-half, 327; test-retest, 326
Repeated measures, 268
Replication, 330-331
Request for proposal (RFP), 331-334
Residual gain, 58
Response rate, 312
Response set, 315, 334-338; and ipsative measures, 219; as reactive effect, 319-320; types of, 335-336
RFP. See Request for proposal
Rights of subject, 79-82, 131
Rorschach, 294
Rotary Pursuit Test, 297

Sampling, 338-344; acceptance, 299, 342; item, 16, 220-221; and population, 339, 341; random, 340-342; and site selection, 370-371; subjective, 339. See also Field operations, Matched sampling
Scales, 345-347; achievement anxiety, 424; in attitude measurement, 34-38; and change measurement, 56; and factor analysis, 161-165; interval, 346; Likert, 36-37; nominal, 345; ordinal, 345-346; Thurstone-type, 36-37
Scatter diagram, 152, 234-235

Scientific inquiry, 198-200, 258, 348-353. See also Causality
Scores, 354-362; age equivalent, 361-362; equivalent, 133-135; factor, 165; grade equivalent, 359-361; of intelligence, 205-208; on ipsative measures, 217-220; raw, 354-356; standard, 356-359; Z, 354, 356, 358
Secondary data, 224-225, 362-364
Secondary evaluation, 362-364. See also Audit of evaluation
Selection: and criterion measurement, 98-99; and equivalent scores, 133-135; interviews for, 214; of site, 370-371
Self-report, 35-37
Self-study, 5-6, 203-205
Semantic differential, 37-38
Side effects, 137, 178-179, 245-247; interests as, 212-213
Sign systems in observation, 267-269
Significance. See Statistical significance
Simulation, 367-369; and certification, 53; in cost benefit analysis, 369; ratings during, 35. See also Situational tests
Site selection, 370-371. See also Field operations, Sampling
Situational tests, 17, 371-374; in certification, 53; history of, 144; in interest measurement, 212; and simulation, 368
Skewness, 402
Social desirability, 219; and situational tests, 372. See also Response set
Social indicators, 374-377; as data source, 115-116. See also Unobtrusive measures
Socioeconomic status (SES), 377-380
Soft evaluation. See Hard and soft evaluation
Solomon four-group design, 156-157
Spearman-Brown formula, 327
Spearman correlation, 88-89, 262
Special Projects Office (Navy), 293
Speededness, 18, 427; and item sampling, 220
Split-half reliability, 327
Staff: evaluation of, 380-383; training

of, 442-443. *See also* Field operations, Job analysis

Standard deviation, 403-404; in correlation coefficient, 88; of means, 395; in norms distributions, 264; of raw scores, 354; of score types, 357-358

Standard score, 356-359

Standardized tests, 383-386; and situational tests, 371. *See also* Norms

Standards, 128, 254-258, 386-389; and mastery learning, 236-237. *See also* Goals and objectives

Statistical analysis, 198-200, 258, 389-397, 400-406; and Lord's paradox, 233-236. *See also* Statistical significance

Statistical independence, 200-202. *See also* Statistical analysis

Statistical inference, 198-200, 258, 395-397. *See also* Statistical significance

Statistical significance, 198-200, 258, 395-399; and Johnson-Neyman technique, 228; in nonparametric tests, 262

Statistics, 400-406; power in, 262. *See also* Statistical analysis

Strong Vocational Interest Blank, 211

Structured interview, 214-215

Student's distribution, 390-394, 398-399

Study of values, 218

Subjective data, 191-195

Subjective sample, 339

Summative evaluation, 128, 178-179, 191-195, 245-247, 406-408, 450-452. *See also* Formative evaluation, Side effects

Survey methods, 408-412. *See also* Field operations

Systems analysis, 2, 119, 369, 412-417. *See also* Accountability, Cost

t test, 390-394, 398-399

Target group, 175-176

TAT. *See* Thematic Apperception Test

Taxonomies of objectives, 4, 417-422; in cognition, 64; in content analysis, 82-83; examples of, 419-421. *See also* Affective variables, Goals and objectives

Teacher ratings, 33-35

Teachers: and accountability, 2-3; competency testing of, 71-72; and grades, 185-187; and materials, 241-244; roles of, 147

Test anxiety, 423-424. *See also* Motivation

Test-retest reliability, 326

Test selection, 428-434; and criterion measurement, 98-100. *See also* Measurement, Standardized tests, Tests

Test wiseness, 434-436; and bias in testing, 44; and true-false items, 9-10. *See also* Equivalent scores, Practice effect

Tests, 2, 425-428; bias in, 43-46; culture-fair, 107-109; essay, 15-17; F, 390-394; group, 206; in-basket, 371-372; individually administered, 206; parametric, 257; performance, 17; projective, 293-296; *t*, 390-394, 398-399. *See also* Achievement test construction, Paper-and-pencil tests, Situational tests, Standardized tests, Test selection, Test wiseness

Thematic Apperception Test (TAT), 294

Theory in evaluation, 348

Three-mode factor analysis, 166

Thurstone-type scale, 36-37

Time-series analysis, 301-310, 436-439

Time-series design, 302-303, 436-439

Training evaluation, 439-442

Training of evaluators, 191-195, 442-443. *See also* Evaluator role

Training of interviewers, 215-216. *See also* Field operations

Training programs, 144; job analysis and, 222; and new materials, 244

Trait-treatment interaction (TTI), 444-449. *See also* Cognitive styles, Interaction

Transactional evaluation, 128, 450-452

Treatment measurement, 452-454. *See also* Content analysis, Observation techniques

True experiment, 155-158. *See also* Design of evaluation

True-false items, 9-10; in attitude assessment, 35-36

Type I error, 199-200

Unintended outcomes. *See* Intended and unintended outcomes

Unobtrusive measures, 454-457; in attitude assessment, 38; as data source, 115-117; and interest measurement, 212; versus reactive effects, 320. *See also* Situational tests

Unstructured interview, 214-215

Urban Institute, 324

Validity, 2, 19, 458-462; and accountability, 2; of achievement tests, 19; of affective variables, 24; with ceiling effect, 52; construct, 459-460; content, 460-461; of criterion measures, 98-100; of criterion-referenced tests, 101; criterion-related, 461; and design, 124; face, 373; and halo effect, 189-190; of intelligence measures, 206; of ip-

sative scores, 219; of observations, 311-312; predictive, 461-462; of ratings, 35; reactive effects on, 319-320; and reliability, 325; as seen by replication, 330; types of, 458-462

Values measurement, 211-213, 462-465. *See also* Attitudes

Variables, 2, 23-26, 114-117, 465-468; component, 73-74; composite, 74-76; continuous, 465; costs as, 92-96; and criteria, 98-100; discrete, 465-466; in interaction, 208-210; intervening, 466; and multivariate analysis, 250-254; psychomotor, 296-298; SES as, 379; types of, 465-467. *See also* Affective variables, Cognitive variables, Dependent variables, Independent variables, Moderator variables

Variance, 228-229, 400-406, 469-472; analysis of, 252-253, 391-392; and F test, 392-394. *See also* Statistical analysis

Verification, 198 200, 258, 351

Wilcoxon test, 258, 260

Z score, 354, 356, 358